U. S. buys more from Latin America
than from any other part of the
world. 1/3 of our imports.
Canada 2 nd.
Western Europe + Britain follow.

Historical
Evolution
of Hispanic
America

Historical
Evolution
of Hispanic
America

by

J. FRED RIPPY

Professor of History
The University of Chicago

THIRD EDITION

APPLETON-CENTURY-CROFTS, INC.
New York

BOLÍVAR

To My Three Sons
FRAZIER, ROBERT, AND FRED

PREFACE TO THE FIRST EDITION

In writing this survey of the history of Hispanic America I have kept the following objectives constantly in mind: (1) To strike a proper balance between solid facts, synthesis, and interpretation; (2) to treat the colonial era in such manner as to give a correct impression of the movement of the stream of history through a period of three centuries, and especially to convey an adequate impression of change and progress between the years 1600 and 1750; (3) to avoid the handbook method in dealing with the national period and give the student the benefit of suggestions regarding the similarities and contrasts in the historical development of the twenty republics of Hispanic America; (4) to emphasize the important changes which have taken place in the region since the beginning of the second decade of the twentieth century; and (5) to present an adequate survey of the foreign relations of these nations. In treating this last phase of the subject I have reproduced large sections of my recent book entitled *Latin America in World Politics*.

Although I have devoted comparatively small space to scientific, literary, artistic, and educational achievements, I have not failed to point out that important developments have taken place in these fields. I have deemed it advisable, however, to leave the fuller treatment of such matters to more competent hands: to *literati*, scientists, critics of art, painting, and architecture, and educational experts. In the reading lists I have called attention to a few of the best historical works of Hispanic-American authors. I have not presented more numerous citations because of the well known linguistic limitations of the students and readers of the United States.

In the preparation of the present volume I have received helpful suggestions from Professor L. F. Hill of Ohio State University and Professors John Tate Lanning and Alan K. Manchester of Duke University. I acknowledge with gratitude the assistance of these scholars, but I must assume entire responsibility for errors in fact or interpretation. To Professor Herbert E. Bolton I am deeply indebted for assistance in the preparation of the maps. In this task I also have received aid from others who are cited at the proper place. Harold F. Peterson has rendered valuable service in preparing the index.

J. FRED RIPPY

Duke University,
August 1, 1932

PREFACE TO THE SECOND EDITION

In this second edition I have brought the story of Hispanic America down to date, again assuming that the foreign relations of the region are as important as its internal history—at least to readers and students of the United States for whom the text is primarily intended. Responding to the objection that social phases were not sufficiently stressed in the first edition, I have given somewhat more attention to that subject. An examination of the present edition will reveal that some fifty-five pages—a tenth of the volume—are devoted to social and cultural matters. While one section of the work, the two chapters entitled "The Age of the Dictators," may appear to be misnamed in view of the continuance of dictatorships in Latin America, I have preferred to retain the heading. The reader may call the section "The First Age of the Dictators" if he chooses. The Reading Lists have been thoroughly revised.

J. FRED RIPPY

University of Chicago,
July 16, 1940

PREFACE TO THE THIRD EDITION

Another edition of this text has given me the opportunity to bring the bibliography up to date, to make minor changes throughout, and to add brief sections on World War II. I wish to thank those who have kindly made suggestions for such revision.

J. FRED RIPPY

University of Chicago,
September, 1945

TABLE OF CONTENTS

THE COLONIAL PERIOD

THE NATIONAL PERIOD

TABLE OF MAPS

TABLE OF ILLUSTRATIONS

Historical
Evolution
of Hispanic
America

THE COLONIAL PERIOD

CHAPTER I

THE PHYSICAL ENVIRONMENT

THE present work is concerned primarily with the history of the people who inhabit that portion of the New World which lies south of the United States. This area is commonly referred to as Latin America or Hispanic America; sometimes it is also called Indo-Hispanic America and Ibero-America. The terms "Hispanic" and "Ibero" will be most appropriate if one desires to emphasize the Spanish and Portuguese influences in the culture of the area; the word "Latin," if one wishes to recognize that Latin nations other than Spain and Portugal have influenced its development; and the term "Indo-Hispanic," if it seems desirable to stress the large Indian element in its population.

For the sake of variety in expression each of these terms will be employed in the present text. The region under consideration, whatever the expression we may use to designate it, is that part of the New World which is now occupied by the twenty republics extending from Cuba, Haiti, and Mexico to Chile, Argentina, and Brazil. Its size has varied from time to time: near the close of the eighteenth century it was much larger than at present, for it then included the vast borderland regions of New Mexico, Texas, the Floridas, Louisiana, and Upper California, and these regions were considerably larger then than their present boundaries indicate. Reduced as it now is, the area which is the subject of our study is three times as large as continental United States and embraces more than half of the New World.

GENERAL CHARACTERISTICS

Hispanic America is so vast that it is difficult to make general statements regarding its physiography and natural resources. One of the

3

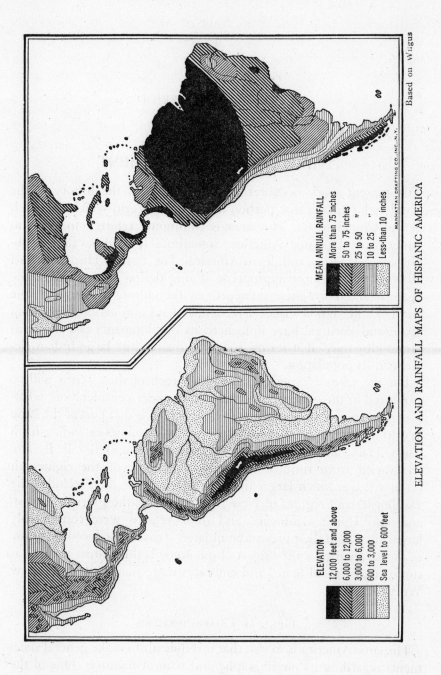

MEAN ANNUAL RAINFALL
More than 75 inches
50 to 75 inches
25 to 50 "
10 to 25 "
Less than 10 inches

ELEVATION
12,000 feet and above
6,000 to 12,000
3,000 to 6,000
600 to 3,000
Sea level to 600 feet

Based on Wigus

MANHATTAN DRAFTING CO. INC. N.Y.

ELEVATION AND RAINFALL MAPS OF HISPANIC AMERICA

4

most obvious facts is that the bulk of the region lies within the tropics. Therefore, tropical problems and tropical products are prominent. Yet there are three countries and a part of a fourth which lie south of the tropics, and many of the others have important areas which are in high altitudes, above tropical heat. The average of soil fertility is high, much of the soil being limestone or a mixture of limestone and lava or the alluvial deposits of rivers and vanished lakes. The region has been, and is, characterized by a very large area of magnificent forests, no other equal area of the earth's surface being so richly endowed. It is likewise a region of rich minerals, the West Indies, most of Central America, and the Plata basin being the only exceptions. Counterbalancing these advantages of soil and other natural resources, is the uneven distribution of rainfall which makes irrigation necessary in many of the areas best adapted to agriculture. There are also fewer good natural harbors and waterfalls, less coal, higher mountains, and greater exposure to earthquakes, than in the United States.

With reference to the native fauna of Hispanic America several general statements may be made. In the first place, many important Old World animals were totally lacking when the Europeans came. For instance, there was no elephant, camel, gorilla, or chimpanzee; and, perhaps of greater importance to man, there were no horses, asses, oxen, sheep, or goats prior to the advent of the Europeans. The llama, the vicuña, and the guanaco could furnish only very inadequate substitutes for these useful domestic animals. Secondly, while a few fur-bearing animals were found to the south of southern Mexico, they were far less important than the fur animals of North America. The fur trade accordingly has played by no means as significant a rôle as in the history of Anglo-Saxon America. Thirdly, although there were many edible fish in the streams of Hispanic America and in the waters which bathe its shores, salmon and mackerel, black bass and cod—important foods of Anglo-Saxon America—have been largely or totally lacking. Fourthly, there were more venomous reptiles and pestiferous insects than in other portions of the New World. In many regions of Latin America these poisonous and pestiferous creatures have inflicted great suffering upon both man and beast. There were and are "Gila monsters," deadly spiders, snakes, and vipers; alligators, crocodiles, caymans, boa constrictors, and anacondas; electric eels, whose electric organ produces a shock which disables horses and cattle; bloodsucking (vampire) bats, which attack both man and his favorite domestic animals; gnats, fleas, mosquitoes, flies, stinging ants, locusts, grasshoppers, jiggers, ticks, and scores of other insects, which attack in relays in many sections and give their victims rest neither by day nor by night; and, more harmful still, the malaria and yellow fever mosquitoes which until recently infested the entire Atlantic Coast of Latin America as far south as the fortieth parallel as well as the Pacific Coast from Guayaquil to Valparaiso.

MEXICO

Mexico is endowed by nature with a luxurious variety of climate and scenery, rich soil, superb timbers, an abundance of minerals, and an isthmus of great potential value in world trade and strategy. The country is somewhat handicapped by insufficient rainfall in important areas, certain almost impenetrable mountains, inadequate harbors, and a scarcity of coal, rivers, and waterfalls.

The Central Plateau.—The heart of Mexico is the great Central Plateau, a fish-shaped area extending from northwest to southeast and lying roughly athwart the twentieth parallel. Although the region is about six hundred miles from northwest to southeast, nowhere is it wider than two hundred miles. Thus the area of this central plateau is only about one-sixth that of present-day Mexico. Yet its natural resources are so rich and its climate so attractive that it has always been the most densely populated section of the country. It consists of a number of fertile lacustrine plains bordered by volcanic ranges and peaks. The altitude of the plateau runs from 6,500 to 8,000 feet, and some of the peaks rise 10,000 feet higher. Gold and silver are its most important mineral resources, but other minerals also appear. With an average temperature of from fifty-five to sixty-five degrees Fahrenheit for every season of the year, with warm days and cool nights during which frost sometimes occurs, the region is more temperate than the temperate zone itself. The rainfall comes mostly from April to October and is sufficient in most of the region to render irrigation unnecessary.

The Northern Basins.—The plateau area of Mexico really extends northward to the international boundary, but the nature of the country becomes considerably different as one approaches the twenty-second parallel. The surface slopes gradually downward toward the north, and the rainfall decreases until semidesert conditions prevail in the region of modern Chihuahua. Thus the northern boundary of the Central Plateau is the northern limit where crops will grow without irrigation. Here begin the Northern Basins enclosed by rugged and barren desert ranges and receiving a scanty rainfall which comes mainly in summer. It is distinctly a grazing and mining area, with a climate decidedly warmer than that of the Central Plateau to the south. A few rivers like the Nazas, the Nieves, and the Conchos, flow through the vast area, but they are inadequate for irrigation purposes. Nor is it certain that mountain reservoirs and subterranean streams can be made to supply the deficiency. The only important coal deposits yet discovered in Mexico, the Sabinas deposits of Coahuila, are found in this region.

The Sierras.—There are three mountain ranges in Mexico, the Western, the Eastern, and the Southern Sierras. The Sierra Madre Occidental constitutes the western boundary of the Northern Basins. With a mean altitude of 10,000 to 12,000 feet, it is characterized by valuable mines along both flanks, by coniferous forests above and green pastures below; and from its summits come streams which carry water for irrigation into the basins region on the east and the coastal plains on the west. Since, however, the valleys of these streams are, for the most part, narrow gorges, they furnish little or no land for agriculture. Lastly, the Western Sierra has thus far proved an almost impenetrable barrier, no railway having as yet been constructed through its narrow cañons or across its precipitous summits. The Sierra Madre Oriental forms the eastern boundary both of the Northern Basins and of the Central Plateau. An escarpment rather than a mountain range, its mean altitude is about 6,000 feet and there are numerous passes leading to the lowlands bordering the Gulf of Mexico. There are many fertile valleys adapted to the production of cereals, and on the mountain slopes are forests of pine and deciduous hardwoods, chiefly oak. The climate of the middle slopes of the Eastern Sierra is agreeable, but as one descends toward the east through areas adapted to coffee, tobacco, and sugar cane, the rainfall becomes heavier and the temperature unpleasantly warm. In the southern portion of the range there are numerous falls where hydroelectric power and manufacturing may be developed. South of the Central Plateau is the third mountain range of Mexico, the Sierra del Sur. Cut through by a complicated system of valleys tributary to the Balsas, whose deep gorge constitutes a large portion of the boundary separating the region from the Central Plateau, the Southern Sierra is the most dissected area of Mexico. As yet (1940) no railways have penetrated it, and the navigation of the Balsas is interrupted by numerous rapids. It is therefore an isolated section composed of a series of isolated districts—a splendid rendezvous for rebels and bandits. The deep valleys are covered by tropical vegetation, mainly thorn forest, and the flanks and summits of the ranges sustain conifers interspersed with hardwoods. Minerals of considerable value are not wanting.

The Sonoran Desert.—The arid region between the Sierra Madre Occidental and the Gulf of California is sometimes called the Sonoran Desert. With this region should also be classed the peninsula of Lower California. The Sonoran Desert is a land of ragged, dry grass dotted with cacti, with areas here and there covered by a prickly jungle or a growth of chaparral. Across it flow several small rivers which supply water for irrigation. Near the United States border extreme desert conditions prevailed until the early years of the twentieth century, when the Colorado delta irrigation project brought relief. The whole region is adapted to cotton, sugar cane, fruit, and truck farming. Lower California is, for the most part, barren and torrid, the troughs of its valleys sheltering a few strips of scattered chaparral, and its tidal marshes tolerating short fringes of mangrove bushes. Fish are plentiful in the waters which bathe its shores and there are a few minerals, orchilla in certain sections, and some areas which may be irrigated. Toward the southern point of the peninsula the irregular monsoons and the granite soil make possible the production of tropical fruits and encourage the growth of oaks and pines. The peninsula appears not to be capable of sustaining more than a sparse population.

The Coastal Plains.—The coastal plains of Mexico are confined mainly to those bordering on the Gulf. Except for the western portion of the Sonoran Desert, which might in a sense be considered as such a plain, the coastal plain on the Pacific is confined to the narrow strip of hot land (*tierra caliente*) extending from Central

America along the southern coast of Mexico to the ninety-seventh meridian. Here the surf of the Pacific beats upon a white sandy beach, mile after mile. Behind the beach is often a fringe of cocoanut trees and a lagoon, and behind this a flat bushy plain, sometimes swampy and almost always malarious. Still further inland is a belt of grassland, often with clumps of trees and thickets of thorn forest. The area has a rainy season and a dry season. Agricultural land is confined to narrow isolated valleys. Some of the drier sections might be made to produce sisal.

The Gulf coastal plain falls into two distinct divisions separated by the near approach of the Eastern Sierra Madres to the sea near the twentieth parallel (between Vera Cruz and Tampico). The northern section, though it lies outside of the belt receiving tropical rains, has ample but irregularly distributed rainfall. It is therefore a region of agricultural possibilities. It is also one of the greatest oil-producing regions of the world, the fields of Tampico and Tuxpam being located here. The southern section of the Gulf coastal plain has been called by modern geographers the Eastern Tierra Caliente. It spreads out toward the south and east from the vicinity of Vera Cruz, thus embracing most of the isthmus of Tehuantepec and the peninsula of Yucatán. In all of this area the climate is hot throughout the year, but the rainfall differs in different localities. The peninsula of Yucatán receives some thirty or forty inches per year, while the precipitation in Tehuantepec and in certain other sections reaches two hundred inches. The limestone plains of Yucatán will grow a little corn and beans, but in modern times sisal hemp has constituted the main crop. Elsewhere the *tierra caliente* is characterized by vast stretches of sandy lands and swamps, of scrubby jungle in the dry places and luxuriant rain forests in the moist sections, valuable trees often being widely scattered among those of a more or less worthless nature. In more recent times the region has become noted for chicle, rubber, and tropical fruits. Except in Yucatán, mosquitoes and malaria have been constant pests.

THE WEST INDIES AND CENTRAL AMERICA

Considered from the standpoint of physiography and climate, Central America and the West Indies are in some respects similar.

Both areas are trade-wind lands—the one a string of islands, the other a long, narrow mainland—set in warm seas. In each case easterly winds bring moisture and rain, and therefore luxurious vegetation, to the eastern slopes and highlands and render the western slopes and plains somewhat arid. Both areas are fertile, but relatively poor in minerals, and both are handicapped by tropical pests and diseases. Strategically, both are of great value.

The West Indies.—The West Indies probably represent the remnant of a much larger land mass which at one time connected Florida and the north coast of South America. The islands of the region are reckoned by the hundreds, but only a few of them offer an agreeable habitat for man. Their combined area is about 90,000 square miles, and they are commonly divided into three groups, the Greater and Lesser Antilles and the Bahamas. Only the Greater Antilles—Cuba, Española,[1] Jamaica, and Puerto Rico—need concern us here. A mountain chain, which in historic times has been partially submerged, extends from Cuba to Puerto Rico, rising to a height of more than 8,000 feet in the former island, culminating with peaks some 12,000 feet high in Española, and falling to an elevation of less than 4,000 feet in Puerto Rico. Española is the most mountainous of the group, having in fact three parallel ridges running from east to west, with fertile valleys between. The minerals of the islands, though varied, have not been of great importance commercially. The Greater Antilles are characterized by a fertile soil adapted to the growth of tropical fruits and supporting dense tropical forests interrupted by occasional patches of grassland. All alike receive a heavy rainfall except on the leeward side—it is usually adequate even there—and all bear the brunt of terrific cyclones. The climate in Cuba and Jamaica is usually pleasant, though monotonous, but it is often unpleasantly hot in Española and Puerto Rico. The islands constitute the key both to the Gulf of Mexico and to the Caribbean and a base whence the southern coast of North America, all of "Middle America," and the northern coast of South America may be dominated. They were the scene of the American colonial beginnings of all the great European powers.

Central America.—With an area of some 220,000 square miles,

---

[1] This is the name which the Spaniards applied to the island that the English and the Americans usually call Haiti.

Central America is two and one-half times as large as the West Indies and hardly one-third the size of Mexico. Its chief assets are its position between two great oceans; its forests of superb timber, which formerly covered ninety per cent of its surface and which still cover about seventy-five per cent; and the capacity of its soil and climate to grow coffee, cacao, tropical fruits and vegetables, and other tropical products demanded by modern society. Topographically the region is made up of many isolated districts, which have been likened to islands separated by deep gorges or insect-infested, fever-ridden jungle. It has been a barrier separating two oceans rather than a link connecting two continents. A backbone of highlands runs the full length of the Isthmus and even extends to the Isthmus of Tehuantepec, in southern Mexico. The portion of the highlands which stands nearest the Pacific is of young volcanic origin, the highest peaks being volcanic cones, of which some are still active. Above three thousand feet the climate of this mountainous region is pleasant, the temperature averaging some seventy degrees Fahrenheit and the annual rainfall averaging about seventy to eighty inches. The upper altitudes are clothed with forests of oak and pine, sometimes interrupted by savannas; the lower flanks are bordered by tropical hardwoods. The Pacific slope, where the forest is inclined to be somewhat thorny and scrubby, is admirably adapted to the production of coffee. The Caribbean Lowlands are hot all the year, and the humidity is almost unbearable. In many places the rainfall is much in excess of 100 inches and there is no dry season. Until recently the region was covered by tropical rain forests and mangrove swamps. During the first decades of the twentieth century these were cleared away and the lowlands were becoming the world's greatest banana center. The Pacific Lowland of Central America is much narrower than those of the Caribbean and is deeply indented by gulfs and bays, with lakes farther inland. There is less rain here, the heat is less oppressive, and the forests are more scrubby and thorny. Both of the lowland sections are unhealthful.

SOUTH AMERICA

South America is a continent of great rivers and lofty mountains, of vast plains, extensive forests, and rich minerals. The Amazon basin is the largest in the world; the basin of the Río de la Plata is almost as extensive as that of the Mississippi; the Orinoco and the Magdalena rank among the large rivers of the world. It is important to note, however, that none of the big rivers of South America flows into the Pacific. The most important feature of the continent is the lofty Andean range which runs almost within sight of this ocean for a distance of more than four thousand miles. Of scarcely less significance is the fact that sixty-five per cent of the surface of South America is below one thousand feet in altitude. Until recently half of the continent was covered by forests. Few other areas of the globe have been so richly endowed with minerals. The precious metals have played no small rôle in its history, and a recent survey of its mineral deposits lists some thirty which are known to exist in large quantities.

Between North America and South America there are several similarities: Both are triangular in form; a huge mountain chain traverses each from north to south, running nearer the Pacific than the Atlantic coast; older and less lofty mountain masses lie along the eastern side of each; both contain vast central plains bordering extensive rivers; both have active and extinct volcanoes; and deserts appear in both. But the differences are more striking than the similarities. "The northern continent is broadest in cool latitudes that are most favorable for human activity. The southern expands most widely in latitudes whose debilitating monotony of heat and moisture is the worst of handicaps to human progress." [2] The great river basins of North America lie mainly in the temperate zone; those of South America, mainly in the tropics. Lastly, North America is less subject to earthquakes and has better natural harbors, greater quantities of coal, vaster coastal plains, more numerous fur-bearing animals, and perhaps more water power.

Having made a few generalizations regarding South America as a whole, we may now pass to a more detailed consideration of the physiography of the continent. Perhaps it will be sufficient to consider its coastal plains, its mountains and plateaus, its rivers and river basins, and its interior plains.

Coastal Plains.—As already noted, the area of the coastal plains of South America is comparatively small. On the northern and eastern

[2] Huntington, *The Red Man's Continent*, pp. 48–49.

side a narrow plain extends along the Caribbean, merges in the Orinoco and the Amazon deltas, extends in disconnected strips to the pampas, appears again south of the fortieth parallel, and skirts the upland plains of Patagonia. Most of this long, narrow strip receives heavy rainfall; but its easternmost portion is subject to severe droughts, and the section just east of Panama is somewhat drier than the rest. Much of this plain is forested and some of it is swampy. It is intersected by inlets and bays which form South America's best harbors. The western coastal plain is even narrower than the eastern. It stretches from Panama to the forty-first parallel, where it is broken off by a series of islands. It really consists of three sections. The region between Panama and the southern shores of the Gulf of Guayaquil is characterized by a hot, rainy climate and dense evergreen forests containing much valuable timber, nuts, and dyewoods. Here, moreover, living conditions are very unhealthful. To the south, extending to the parallel of thirty degrees, is a coastal desert. The northern portion of this middle area is traversed by a few streams which make irrigation possible and, supplemented by occasional fogs, produce a few grassy areas. The southern portion is extremely arid but is rich in nitrates and contains considerable iodine, borax, salt, copper, gold, silver, iron, and manganese. On the adjacent Pacific islands are perennially renewed guano deposits. South of the desert, the coastal plain forms the heart of Chile, one of the garden spots of the continent. Between the thirtieth and the thirty-sixth parallels the rain is not sufficient to render irrigation unnecessary, but the water supply is amply supplemented by the streams which descend from the near-by Andes. The area south of thirty-six degrees receives more rain and is considerably cooler. The whole of this third section of the coastal plain is essentially an agricultural area, but important minerals are not lacking.

Mountains and Plateaus.—There are three mountain areas in South America; namely, the Brazilian Highlands, the Guiana Highlands, and the Andes. The Brazilian Highlands—with a mean elevation of three to four thousand feet and a few peaks reaching ten thousand— run parallel with the eastern coast of South America from about the eighth to the thirtieth parallel and extend far into the interior of the continent. They comprise about one-fourth the area of modern Brazil and contain very important mineral deposits. The rainfall is ample, except in a small area in the northeast, and several rivers cut across large sections of the region, furnishing valuable waterfalls. The summer days are hot, but the nights are usually comfortable. The winter climate is delightful, particularly in the south, where frosts occasionally occur. There are large areas adapted to the growth of coffee and cotton. There are also great stretches of grassland interspersed by open woods and sometimes by heavy forests.

The Guiana Highlands lie between the Amazon and the Orinoco basins, in the very heart of the tropics. In the main a deeply dissected plateau, the area has some peaks which rise to eleven thousand feet. To the northern slopes the northeast trade winds bring heavy rainfall, but the southern slopes of the highlands are semiarid. Dense tropical forests which flank the uplands, and falls and rapids in the rivers which penetrate the interior render the region almost inaccessible. Yet it is known that minerals and medicinal plants abound; that rubber, balsam, and balata are plentiful; and that there are probably important areas of grassland.

In the long chain of the Andes are four regions which differ from one another in important respects. South of thirty-nine degrees the area receives heavy precipitation and there are large lakes, glaciers, and snow fields. In the extreme south the western gales discourage fishermen and sailors.

Lying between the twenty-eighth and thirty-ninth degrees of southern latitude is an arid and barren stretch characterized by great daily and seasonal extremes of temperature and offering little inducement for human occupation. Here the Andes constitute a single lofty range with summits from eighteen to twenty-three thousand feet in height and with very few passes. There are known deposits of copper, gold, and silver, but the region has hitherto remained almost impenetrable for Indians and whites alike.

North of the twenty-eighth parallel the Andes break into an inner and an outer cordillera with enclosed plateaus, usually called *punas,* which range in height from eleven to sixteen thousand feet. There are passes across the mountain chains, but few of them are lower than twelve thousand feet. The nights in this region are cold the year round, the summer temperatures are so cool as to preclude the growth of any save the hardiest crops and grasses, and the little rain which falls comes in thunderstorms between the seasons. Most of the region is therefore characterized by growths of scrub, moss, cacti, grass, or alpine plants. There are also many snow-capped heights, inaccessible and uninhabited, as well as great salt plains and lakes, Titicaca, thirteen thousand feet above the sea, being the most important of the latter. Important deposits of such minerals as silver, tin, gold, copper, and bismuth exist in the region.

North of the fifth parallel the inner and outer cordilleras merge once more into a single lofty range which, crowned by an avenue of active or extinct volcanoes and flanked by temperate plateaus, runs northeastward for almost five hundred miles and then breaks again, forming three distinct cordilleras. These latter are separated by the chasm of the Cauca and the great valley of the Magdalena, the fourth largest river of South America. The easternmost of these northern ranges slopes gradually downward toward the banks of the Magdalena so as to form the delightful plateau of Cundinamarca, with its temperate climate, its mean annual rainfall of about forty inches, and its enchanted Lake Guatavitá. Still farther north, in the vicinity of the seventh parallel of north latitude, the eastern cordillera sends a branch across northern Venezuela. The northern Andes are characterized in general by an increased rainfall and a warmer temperature, which insure a rich vegetation. High forests alternate with tall jungle and temperate valleys with plateau grasslands. There are also cold, bleak, misty, semibarren *páramos;* and crowning the whole landscape are majestic peaks rising into eternal winter. The Venezuelan portion of the Andes is more arid, and hence characterized by lighter tropical forests frequently interrupted by barren cacti and grassy savannas.

Rivers, River Basins, and Inland Plains.—South America has four great river systems and as many great plains. Some forty per cent of its area is less than six hundred feet in elevation, and about sixty-five per cent is less than one thousand feet above sea level. In great interior grasslands the continent is almost as richly endowed as North America.

The largest of South American rivers and river basins is the Amazon. The main stream of the Amazon is about four thousand miles in length, and has fourteen large tributaries. The entire system offers a means of inland transportation for about twenty thousand miles and drains a basin of some two million square miles, or more than one-fourth of the continent. The basin supports a huge equatorial forest which is one of the marvels of the world. The vegetation extends in broad belts away from the banks of the rivers —first the flood forest, then the selva, and then the lighter forest or woodland which is occasionally interrupted by a grassy park. "From the slimy, hardly solid mud" along the banks of the great streams "has sprung a rank and dense growth of tall trees overgrown with a continuous drapery of lianas, . . . forming an unbroken dark canopy, a green wall impenetrable from the outside"—"a gloomy, stifling, musty, shady, damp vault, supported by innumerable pillars, and choked with a perfect tangle of climbers inside." The typical selva is taller than the flood forest, the trees reaching a larger size and having a more solid structure. The Amazon forest is at once the crowning glory of the vegetable world and a baffling obstacle to human progress. The very rankness of the vegetation renders it a potent enemy to agriculture, and few men are able to withstand the ravages of malaria and other tropical diseases which infest the area. Aside from cacao and nuts, the basin produces building timbers, rubber, balsam, sarsaparilla, and various dyewoods.

The lack of great open plains in the Amazon basin is partially compensated for by the vast campos which lie between the middle basin and the highlands of Brazil. They are a succession of "wonderful rolling plains, here stretching as far as the eye can reach without other vegetation than tall tufts of . . . grass, perhaps interspersed now and then with large brakes and stemless palms, arboreal cacti, or mimosas; here sparsely covered with scattering, scrubby, gnarled trees . . . ; or again, having a parklike appearance, with isolated clumps of trees dotted over the grassy plains." The campos have a dry summer season and a wet winter season, but there is no great variation of temperature, the annual average being about seventy-five degrees Fahrenheit and the mercury rarely falling below freezing. Some parts of the area occasionally suffer from prolonged droughts.

The Orinoco and its tributaries drain an area of almost four hundred thousand square miles and furnish more than four thousand miles of navigable waters. In fact, it is connected through the Casiquiare with the great Amazon system itself. The Orinoco basin is characterized by vast grassy plains, dotted here and there by stately palms and traversed by narrow ribbons of dense forest which grow along the banks of the main river and its important tributaries. The famous llanos (plains) lie for the most part to the north and west of the main stream. Here, "as far as the gaze can reach, the undulating grassy plain appears like a shoreless ocean petrified by a storm." The temperature of the basin is warm to hot throughout the year, and the mean annual rainfall is about seventy-six inches, the region being subjected to periodic droughts and floods.

The Magdalena and its tributaries drain an area of some two hundred thousand square miles. The main river is more than a thousand miles in length and is navigable, in three sections, for more than nine hundred miles. The only extensive plains in the Magdalena basin are those which stretch away toward the east from the lower three hundred miles of the main stream. The valley of the Cauca, the main tributary of the Magdalena, is rather narrow but exceedingly fertile. The climate of the area is tropical and semitropical.

First in importance, though second in size, among the river basins of South America is that of the Río de la Plata.[3] This great system drains more than a million square miles lying mainly in the temperate zone. The Plata estuary and its tributaries—the Paraná, the Paraguay, and the Uruguay are the most important—are navigable for hundreds of miles into the heart of the continent. The basin is characterized by a variety of vegetation. Stretching away from the banks of the Plata and the lower Uruguay and Paraná, are the vast pampas, comparable to the grassy prairies of the United States. To the north, subtropical forests grow along the valleys of the streams, while, farther inland, grassy parks alternate with jungle and swamp or cacti and stunted trees. The immense northwestern section of the basin is known as the Gran Chaco. It is characterized by swamps, grassy expanses, forest patches of small and scrubby trees, the quebracho prominent among them, and, occasionally, by a dense tropical growth not unlike that found in portions of the Amazon basin. The temperature and rainfall of the vast basin vary with different sections. In the pampas area precipitation decreases from forty inches in the east to less than sixteen in the west, and nearly all of the rain comes between October and March. Here, likewise, the winters are mild and the heat of the summers seldom extreme. Elsewhere in the basin

[3] Strictly speaking, however, the Plata proper is only an estuary.

there is more abundant rainfall along with greater heat. Few areas are better adapted to agricultural and pastoral pursuits. There are also valuable timbers and forest products, but the region is comparatively poor in minerals.

Not all of the pampas lie within the Plata basin. A large pampa area stretches away toward the southwest from the broad mouth of the Plata and eventually merges into the plains of Patagonia, a rolling, grassy expanse, semiarid and temperate in the north and west, but moister and much colder in the far south. Patagonia is adapted to stock raising; it also shows some indications of mineral wealth and has considerable water power.

The Approaches to America.—Prior to the invention of steam-propelled vessels there were at least six possible approaches to America, three from the Atlantic and three from the Pacific. On the Pacific side there is the shortest of all routes, that across Bering Strait, some fifty-six miles in length and with two small islands in the center, but full of ice—a cold, bleak route between cold, bleak portions of Asia and America. On this side also is the Kurile Islands–Kamchatka–Aleutian Islands route, milder but having intervening waters one hundred and even two hundred miles wide between the land masses; and the north-central Pacific route, favored by the westerly winds but broad and stormy. In the northern Atlantic is the Norway to Lofoten Islands to Iceland to Greenland route. Here the islands are farther apart than in the northern Pacific and the climate is equally forbidding. Farther toward the south is the central route, but the westerly winds serve as a barrier. Still farther south the trade winds make it fairly easy for boats to make their way from Africa or southern Europe. Along this route came Columbus and many of his successors, returning northward, beyond the thirtieth parallel, in the zone of the westerlies. Once approached, America is more accessible on the Atlantic than on the Pacific side, where good ports are comparatively scarce.

CHAPTER II

PRIMITIVE PEOPLES OF AMERICA

ORIGIN AND CULTURAL AREAS

ALTHOUGH scholars have long discussed the origin of man in America, they have not yet solved the problem to their satisfaction. A few years ago the Argentine scientist Florentino Ameghino advanced the theory that the human race originated in the pampas of Argentina, migrating from there by a convenient land mass to Africa and Oceania, spreading out over the Americas, and eventually finding its way to Asia and Europe; but his hypothesis was warmly combated and gained few adherents. Others have expressed the view that the American Race came from China, Africa, Australia, and Polynesia, or northern Asia. It seems very probable that the majority of the indigenes who peopled the New World came from Asia, although a small number may have migrated from Australia and Polynesia.

Those who accept this latter view suppose that between 10,000 and 15,000 years ago a detachment of early Mongoloid peoples, or probably several successive detachments, left northeastern Asia and came over the Bering Strait route to America. Subsequently, climatic and other changes occurred, cutting off communication with the motherland and driving the American Mongoloids southward across the New World. They probably brought to their new home such primitive culture traits as the fire drill, the bow, the throwing stick, and the harpoon; stone chipping and polishing, string twisting, simple basketry and nets, and hunting complexes; cooking by means of heated stones placed in vessels of wood, bark, or skin; body painting and perhaps tattooing, and the domestication of the dog. Although they had passed out of the old stone age, none of them were acquainted with agriculture. They were still in the nomadic stage, living on the results of the chase and on such wild fruits and roots as they could secure.

For these people, whom the Europeans later called Indians, to

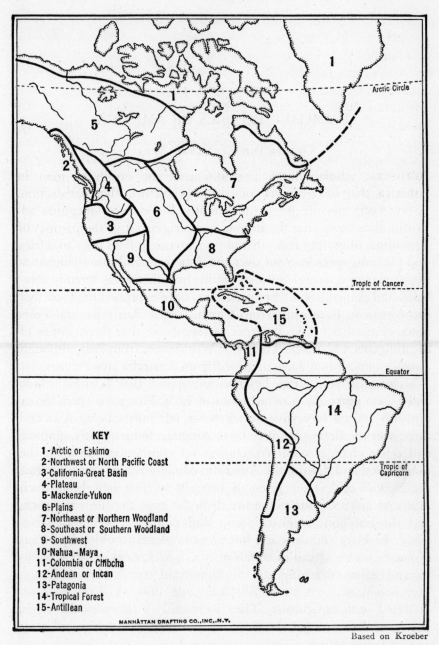

KEY

1 - Arctic or Eskimo
2 - Northwest or North Pacific Coast
3 - California-Great Basin
4 - Plateau
5 - Mackenzie-Yukon
6 - Plains
7 - Northeast or Northern Woodland
8 - Southeast or Southern Woodland
9 - Southwest
10 - Nahua – Maya ,
11 - Colombia or Chibcha
12 - Andean or Incan
13 - Patagonia
14 - Tropical Forest
15 - Antillean

MANHATTAN DRAFTING CO., INC., N.Y.

Based on Kroeber

THE PRINCIPAL CULTURAL AREAS OF PRIMITIVE AMERICA

spread out over the Americas, many centuries were required. They probably reached the great valley of Mexico about 8000 or 9000 B.C. and began their trek into South America a thousand years later.

Their progress upward was likewise slow, and few records have been found to serve the historian who would narrate their early advance. About 4000 B.C. they developed agriculture, pottery, and loom weaving, probably somewhere in central Mexico. Shortly before the opening of the Christian era they made the beginnings of a higher stage of culture in Central America and Yucatán, and before 500 A.D. they achieved similar beginnings in Peru (Nasca and Chimú), central Mexico (Totonac), and in New Mexico (Pueblo). Everywhere the cultures which followed the early nomadic and neolithic—namely, the Archaic, the Maya, the Inca, the Pueblo, the Chibcha and the Aztec—are believed to have developed in plateau areas. By the time the Europeans reached America they found the most advanced groups in a stage of progress which scholars have called "semicivilized." The earliest of these advanced cultures was that of the Mayas, and some authorities believe that the other higher cultures of America borrowed from them.

In the course of their wanderings the first inhabitants of America developed various languages. Viewed linguistically, they constituted a veritable Babel after the first millennium of the Christian era in Europe. No Alexander, no conquering Rome, gave them unity. There may have been as many as eighty-six linguistic stocks in Central and North America and eighty-four in South America. Differences in speech among the branches of the same stock added to the confusion, to say nothing of the hundreds of tribal names which the Europeans gave to the many groups which they encountered. Scholars have therefore found it more convenient to classify the Indians according to culture areas, and they have divided them into some fifteen such areas. The Spaniards and Portuguese came into contact with nine of these cultures. The scope of this work makes it necessary, however, to confine our discussion mainly to the five semicivilized areas.

The Southeastern Area.—On the northern frontier of the vast region ultimately occupied by Spain was the Southeastern, or Southern Woodland, Culture Area, embracing all south and east of a line drawn from the mouth of the James River in Virginia to central

Missouri and thence to San Antonio, Texas. In this extensive territory the Muskhogean and the Iroquoian linguistic stocks predominated and gave the region its typical culture. Among the many tribes, too numerous to list here, the most important were the Creeks, Chickasaws, Choctaws, Cherokees, Seminoles, and Apalachees. On the west, among the Indians of southern Texas, there was a deflection towards the Plains Area. On the east, the Biloxi of Mississippi and Alabama and the Timucua and Calusa of Florida were probably variants. Among the Timucua the Spaniards were to establish their most successful Florida missions.

The following are the important traits of the prevailing stocks of the area: They engaged in agriculture, growing maize, millet, pumpkins, melons, tobacco, and, after the coming of the Spaniards, quickly took up the cultivation of European fruits. Although they ate a great deal of vegetable food, they also consumed a considerable quantity of game, such as turkey, bear, bison, and deer. They also ate fish and dogs, the latter being the only animal they had domesticated. They lived in rectangular houses having curved roofs covered with thatch or bark and dwelt in towns fortified by means of palisades. They used weapons of bone, cane, and stone, but they were not sculptors and had little skill in metal work. They did considerable weaving and were good potters. In their small temples, constructed for sun worship, they kept perpetual fires burning. They had elaborate planting and harvest rituals and medicine men held a prominent place among them. A clan system prevailed and their social order was composed of chiefs and four grades of subjects. Their government reached a fairly high degree of development in strong confederacies. The Europeans accordingly found them no mean foes when they were once aroused.

The Southwestern Area.—Arizona, New Mexico, and that portion of old Mexico lying north of a line drawn westward from the mouth of the Rio Grande constituted what Wissler calls the Southwestern Culture Area. Here the culture of the semicivilized Pueblos, who reached the highest peak of development in the region, prevailed. They engaged in irrigated agriculture; ate mainly vegetables, using the grinding stone for preparing their maize; developed the art of masonry, inventing a new type of building—a rectangular, terraced, apartmentlike structure made of adobe or stone, which served as a dwelling place for the entire village; employed the spindle and the true loom, cultivating cotton for textile material; domesticated the turkey; and practiced an intense ritualism. Each of the seventy villages in existence when the Spaniards arrived appeared to be independent, with an elective governor and war chief, the final sanction resting with a religious officer. The total population in the middle of the sixteenth century was about 70,000. Their prevailing spirit of localism rendered their conquest by the Spaniards much easier, but the strong influence of their religious leaders was to make them restive under the sway of the Catholic priests.

The less advanced tribes of the area possessed traits analogous to those of the Pueblos. The Pimas, for instance, raised cotton and wove cloth, made excellent baskets, and once lived in adobe huts. The Papagos were similar but less advanced, and the Mohave, Yuma, Cócopa, Maricopa, and Yavapai still more backward; but they nevertheless had traits connecting them with Pueblo culture. The same is true of the Indians of the northern plateau of Mexico, of the Sonoran Desert, and of the northern and central portions of Lower California. The Athapascan-speaking tribes—the Jicarilla, Mescalero, etc.—to the east, however, assimilated the plains culture.

The Plains Area.—Wedged in between the Southeastern and the Southwestern areas was the Plains Culture Area, a region never successfully occupied by the Spaniards. For this reason, and because the general character of the Indians is well known, they need not be discussed at length here. Aside from the Jicarilla and the Mescalero, already mentioned as intermediate between the Southwestern and the Plains Area, the Comanches, the Kiowas, and the Kiowa-Apaches gave the Spaniards most concern, particularly after the horse and modern arms had been introduced among them. Organized in roving bands, clothed in buffalo and deer skins, subsisting mainly on buffalo meat, mounted on Spanish ponies and armed with bows, arrows, and shields, or with guns, they were for decades the terror of Europeans and neighboring tribes alike. It required the Anglo-Saxon frontiersmen to tame them, and this was done at great cost and not until near the end of last century.

The California Culture Area.—On the extreme northwestern frontier of what was destined to be Spain's colonial empire in America was the California Culture Area. Here dwelt those Indians of a

very low type who were to be converted to Christianity and reduced
to a settled existence near the close of the third century of Spanish
effort in the New World. In general, the some 130,000 Indians inhabiting California were in the stage of culture known as upper
savagery when the Spaniards arrived. They lived upon acorns,
berries, and roots, occasionally supplemented by fish and small game.
They wore very scanty clothing, developed skill in no arts save
basketry, and constructed simple dwellings of tule, brush, or poles
in lean-to fashion. Their religion was characterized by restrictions
connected with birth, death, and sexual matters, as well as by mourn-
ing and initiation ceremonies. Shamanism—healing by means of
tricks of medicine men—was conspicuous. They had a simple, loose
social organization and were quite unwarlike.

The Mexico, or Nahua, Area.—In central Mexico, Yucatán, and
northern Central America lived the Mayas and the Nahuas, peoples
who had reached a relatively high plane of civilization. Although
there are differences in the cultures of these two important groups,
as well as between their mode of life and that of the Terascans,
Zapotecs, Mixtecs, and so-called Toltecs, anthropologists prefer to
apply the term Mexico, or Nahua, Culture Area to the entire region.
The Aztecs, comparative newcomers (twelfth or thirteenth century)
who borrowed most of their culture traits from the Mayas and
others, represented the prevailing culture in 1500.

The Aztecs (one of the Nahua tribes) had a highly organized
government, headed by an elective chief who maintained large
armies, and a gentile social order (namely, one in which children
born of a mother acquired outside of the group took the name of
the father) with gens land rights. They were skilled in agriculture,
growing maize, beans, peppers, gourds, cotton, and fruits and con-
cocting an intoxicating drink (*pulque*) from the maguey (century)
plant. They were not only skillful builders, but made ornaments of
gold, silver, and copper, as well as tools of copper and tin. They had
perfected a gold wire technique from which filigree work was derived, and they wrought fine feather mosaics for which large aviaries
were maintained. Their work in jadeite and obsidian was highly
developed, and they wove cloth of cotton and agave, coloring it with
excellent dyes. They were also fair potters, and they made books
(mainly pictographic) of parchment and maguey paper. They had

an organized priesthood which was entrusted with religious ceremonies, education, and higher knowledge. In their elaborate religious system sacrifices were prominent. Rituals were recited in the temples for regular parts of each day and night, and there was almost constant sacrificing of quails, rabbits, and flowers. Moreover, human sacrifices were numerous and frequent, and at certain of these the flesh of the victim was ceremoniously eaten. The Aztecs also cultivated literature, maintained separate schools for boys and girls, and possessed a calendar derived from that of the Mayas, although not as accurate.

Such in brief was the culture of the Aztecs. It may be added that their social order was composed of nobility, freemen, and slaves; that polygamy was practiced by the upper class; that the nobles lived in large dwellings several stories high built of polished stone and adorned with sculpture and paintings, while the houses of the common people were made of adobe and covered with maguey leaves; that their government was a sort of triple alliance composed of three leading cities—Tenochtitlán, Tezcuco, and Tlacopán—which dominated the restless surrounding tribes and exacted heavy tribute both in produce and in human beings for sacrifice; and that they and their Nahua predecessors constructed many magnificent pyramidal temples to their numerous gods—the sun, moon, wind, war, productivity, and so on. Among these deities was Quetzalcoatl (the Fair God), destined to a fatal rôle in the relations of the Aztecs with the Spaniards. He was their cultural hero, who had once instructed them in arts and agriculture, and who was expected some day to return and perfect their wisdom and skill in these matters. The population of the Aztec Confederacy perhaps numbered about eight million, Tenochtitlán alone containing between one hundred thousand and three hundred thousand.

Southeastern Mexico and the northern part of Central America were once the scene of what archæologists believe to have been the highest point of development attained by aboriginal Americans. Within this region have been found some of the most impressive ruins (temple and palaces) of the New World. The people of this area, the Mayas, excelled in architecture, sculpture, mathematics, and astronomical knowledge, as is shown by scores of their ruined cities, such as Copán, Quiriguá, Tikal, Palenque, Uxmal, and Chichén

Itza. Starting their great cultural advance about 100 B.C. and suffering two severe reversals, the Mayas reached the first zenith of their civilization before 700 A.D. and the second before the opening of the thirteenth century. When the Spaniards came, this civilization had fallen into decay, and the Mayas were no longer dwelling in "pretentious cities." They were then in a stage of culture lower than that of the Aztecs, to whom many of their gods and cultural traits had passed. They were agriculturists, raising maize, peppers, beans, cacao, etc.; they domesticated bees for their honey and wax; and they wove cotton so fine that the Spaniards mistook it for silk. Formerly they had written books, employing a combination of the hieroglyphic and phonetic systems still for the most part undeciphered, recorded important dates in their history on stone shafts (*steles*), and made canoes large enough to engage in trade with Cuba. In astronomy they had coördinated the lunar month with the solar calendar, and in mathematics they had learned the use of the zero. Essentially a stone-age people, they used copper and gold mainly for ornament. In the early part of the sixteenth century the Spaniards found them living in wooden huts covered with straw, and organized in some eighteen independent tribal groups, which division was fortunate for the intruders, for otherwise they would have confronted very dangerous foes.

The semicivilized Nahuas and Mayas were surrounded on all sides by wild and often fierce tribes. The total population of the Nahua-Maya Area is left only to conjecture. Perhaps there were as many as ten million, about half the total of the present population of the region.

The Colombia, or Chibcha, Area.—In southern Central America begins the area of Chibcha culture, which had its center in the distant plateau of Cundinamarca, Colombia. It was an island of comparatively advanced culture surrounded by a sea of wild tribes, and streams of lowly folk even appeared among the more highly organized groups themselves. Of this vast area the Chibcha culture may be taken as typical.

The Chibchas engaged in agriculture, developing systems of irrigation and raising maize, potatoes, manioc, beans, and squashes. They also cultivated cotton and were experts in dyeing and weaving. They were skilled in gold work, but had no copper. They built roads and suspension bridges and had a commercial system with markets and a kind of currency. Salt, which the Chibchas produced in large quantities and sold to the bordering tribes, was an important commodity. They chewed coca and made much use of a drink called *chicha*. They had a fairly well developed calendar, but, although they used pictographs, they had no books. Along with frequent sacrifices of all kinds, they sometimes offered human beings to the sun. They had numerous sacred places, among which were five lakes, Guatavitá being the most important. A mythical white man was their cultural hero, and they had a deluge myth and an Atlas idea of the world. The Chibchas were clearly a rising people at the opening of the fifteenth century. When the Spaniards came they found them living in houses of wood, cane, or thatch, with walls of wattling, plastered with clay. At that time they had a fairly compact political organization embracing 1,200,000 people, but there were two *caciques* (chiefs) —a Zipa at Bacatá and a Zaque at Tunja—whose desperate rivalries the Iraca, or religious chief, was not always able to prevent from breaking out in bloody combat. Their arms consisted of bows and arrows, slings, darts, lances, and clubs. The population of the entire Chibcha Cultural Area was about 3,000,000.[1]

The Peruvian, or Inca, Area.—The Peruvian, or Inca, Culture Area, the most famous of the New World, extended from the vicinity of the equator (in the highlands of Ecuador) to the Atacama Desert or beyond, embracing the mountains and plateaus of this extensive region and including also the narrow Pacific coastal belt. The population of the Inca empire in 1500 was eight or ten millions, perhaps even more; the chief languages spoken were the Quichua and the Aymará.

The main characteristics of their culture, which arose upon the ruins of much earlier civilizations—the Chimú, Nasca, and Tiahuanaco—have been summed up as follows:

"An organized government based upon gentile groups [the Ayllu], the supreme authority resting in a council who appointed from a hereditary group a war chief, or Inca; agriculture advanced, maize, manioc, peppers, potatoes, fertilization with guanaco and other manures, elaborate irrigation systems; domestication of the llama,

---

[1] López de Velasco estimated the Indian population of what is now Colombia and Panama at 2,500,000 in 1574.

with the dog, guinea pig, birds, and monkeys as pets; some fishing on the coast and hunting in the interior; spinning and weaving highly developed, cotton cultivated, vicuña wool, elaborate designs and rich dyes; pottery carried to a high state of development . . .; gold, silver, and copper mined, smelted, and skillfully worked; true bronze was made by use of tin; tools and mechanical appliances simple, digging stick and spade for farming, no hoe; no saws, drilling by rolling in hands; architecture massive, but plain and severe [stones weighing many tons being used]; a system of roads; stone, and suspension bridges; some water travel by balsa; an organized army [equipped with weapons made of bronze and copper as well as stone] and fortifications; no writing, but the quipu as a counting device; sun worship, an organized priesthood; a mythical white man founder called Viracocha; a deluge myth; human sacrifices rare, but offerings of animals common; a series of gens gods, or *huacas;* religious orders of virgins; a sacred shrine on Lake Titicaca; conventional confessions of sins to a priest; two important ceremonies, the new-fire with the banishment of disease and the sun festival." [2]

Worthy of special notice is the organization of the Inca empire. The Aztecs, who approached nearest to them in political capacity, exacted only tribute and warriors from their subject peoples. The Incas, on the contrary, took pains to consolidate their dominions. Their empire was held together by a hierarchy of officials, a large army, and a series of fortresses located at strategic points and connected by military roads. Quichua-speaking colonies were planted as police and spies among the conquered tribes. Despite this fact, however, these subject peoples did not often learn the Quichua language. Possibly no more than one million inhabitants of the Inca empire spoke the language of this dominant stock. The empire has been characterized as a "communistic despotism" or a "military system applied to industrial purposes," but it should be noted that the despotism was decidedly religious in nature, the Inca being religiously a god as well as politically an emperor, and having around him a powerful priesthood no less than a civil nobility and a military oligarchy. A supreme state in association with a state church regulated every activity of the people; there was little personal liberty in ancient

[2] Wissler, *The American Indian,* p. 248.

Peru. When the Spaniards arrived, they found the empire divided and two half-brothers struggling with each other for supreme power.

The Guanaco, or Patagonia, Area.—The Indians of southern Chile, Uruguay, and most of the Argentine have been grouped into a single cultural area which has been called the Guanaco, or Patagonia, Culture Area. The most important linguistic stocks were the Araucanian, the Guaycuran (Abipones, etc.), the Puelchean, the Calchaquian (Diaguites), the Charruan, and the Tsonecan (Tehuelche). The culture of the typical group was somewhat similar to that of the Plains Indians of North America. They lived upon meats and wild plants, following agriculture to a limited extent. They wove some cloth, but used skins much more extensively. Their most important weapons were the lance and the bolas; their principal occupations, warfare and the hunting of the guanaco and the rhea. They used skin boats for fording rivers. Very soon after the Spaniards came, these Indians managed to acquire horses, and the cattle of the Europeans soon took the place of the guanaco. To the lance and the bolas they then added the lasso and became formidable enemies despite the fact that they often rode naked into battle. Perhaps the Araucanians were the best warriors. They were organized into a kind of confederacy based upon the family group, and the bow and arrow, wooden clubs, lances, and lassos were their weapons. Some of their warriors developed a strategy which filled the Spaniards with awe. Their prowess has been immortalized in Ercilla's ambitious epic, *La Araucana*.

The Tropical Forest, or Amazon, Area.—The remainder of South America, except northern Venezuela, has been called the Tropical Forest, or Amazon, Culture Area. The dominating linguistic stocks are the Tupi and the Tapuya in the southeast and the Carib and Arawaks in the center and north. The Tupi (Guaraní) and the Arawaks are lowland peoples, while the other two appear to have preferred the higher elevations. The tribes were legion, and there were of course considerable variations in culture, but there was nevertheless a fundamental unity. They were characterized by a certain amount of agriculture, with manioc as the chief staple; by a very loose political organization; by canoes, hammocks, pottery, blowguns, thatched houses, scanty clothing and absence of footwear, calabash rattles, cannibalism, shamanism, flutes made of human bone, sword clubs, the use of honey and wax, and ceremonial whippings of boys. All were in a comparatively low stage of development. Many of the tribes ate all animal life indiscriminately, monkey being the most nearly staple.

Antillean Area.—The culture of the Antillean Area was very similar to that of the tropical forest and the Amazon. The area included the West Indies and northern Venezuela. The islands of the region were overrun in pre-Columbian times by two races of canoe men, the Arawaks and the Caribs. The former came first and were occupying the Greater Antilles and the smaller islands to the north when the Spaniards arrived. The Caribs were occupying the Lesser Antilles and northern South America. They were fierce and warlike and inclined toward cannibalism. Distinctive traits of the region are "manioc culture, raising of cotton, use of the hammock, tobacco taken as snuff and inhalation, ceremonial emetics, fish poison, cigars instead of pipes." The population of the area is left largely to conjecture, for the exaggerated figures of the early Spaniards must be discounted. Perhaps there were as many as two million.

Conclusion

The most advanced of these American peoples were considerably behind their Mongoloid kinsmen in Asia as well as their European contemporaries. Their knowledge of astronomy was admirable, but hardly equal to that of the Old World at that time. In mathematics the Mayas had discovered the use of the zero; and the system of writing of the Aztecs and the Mayas was clever, but they had not progressed far in the use of phonetics. In ceramics the American Race had developed a rather advanced technique, but they had not discovered the potter's wheel. If their metallurgy had produced pretty objects of gold, silver, and bronze, they had not learned the use of iron—a serious handicap in their cultural progress. In agriculture, architecture, and road-building they had made much progress without having discovered the plow or the arch. In connection with their religion there were much oppression, cruelty, and superstition, and the government of the Aztecs and the Incas left little or no place for human liberty and individual initiative. Private property in lands was rare if not indeed nonexistent. Cereals, domesticated cows and horses, the plow and wheel, the arch, printing, gunpowder, the compass—all of these culture traits so typical of Europe, and many of them, strangely enough, the inventions of the Mongoloids of Asia, were unknown to the American Race.

Yet it must not be concluded that the aborigines of the New World had nothing to give to the Europeans. From them they received some thirty or thirty-five useful domesticated plants, among which are maize, cacao, beans, the potato, the squash, the tomato, and to- bacco, to say nothing of medicinal herbs and barks, useful gums and dyes, decorative designs, paintings, and sculpture, and the do- mestication of the turkey, the llama, and the alpaca. To the Spaniards and the Portuguese, as will presently be seen, they also yielded up themselves—their very bodies and blood—to form a new society and a new race. That they had not advanced more rapidly before the Spaniards and Portuguese came may possibly be explained by the absence in the New World of animals adapted to domestication, by lack of contact with different forms of culture, and by a certain stolidity resulting from the elimination of the higher types during the bleak journey across the cold regions of northeastern Asia and northwestern America. What they might have done in a few thou- sand years more, if left to themselves, we can only speculate. "A militant civilization from without, fired by a zeal not only to plunder the material treasures of mankind, but to seize the very souls of men in the name of its God, fell upon the . . . great centers of aboriginal culture like a thunderbolt from a clear sky." [3] The blow was fatal and their manner of life was violently transformed. Nor do we know how many aborigines lived in the New World in 1500, al- though it does not seem unreasonable to suppose that there were at least twenty-five million in the vast regions later occupied by Spain and Portugal.[4]

[3] Wissler, *The American Indian,* p. 400.
[4] The eminent French scholar, Paul Rivet, estimates that there were 40,000,000 in the Americas. North America, north of the twenty-fourth parallel, was sparsely inhabited.

CHAPTER III

OLD WORLD BACKGROUND

Influences Leading to the Age of Discovery

WHILE aboriginal Americans were struggling upward through the successive stages of barbarism, the people of Western Europe were passing through a great intellectual awakening. Each group was probably ignorant [1] of the other's existence, but the quickened curiosity of the Europeans, their religious zeal, their fondness for luxuries, were finally to bring them into contact with the American Race. And Western Europe's renaissance was in a measure the product of the activities of the Asiatic kinsmen of the American Mongoloids!

In the year 1073 the Seljukian Turks, with Mongolian blood in their veins, destroyed the Holy Sepulcher in Jerusalem. By this wanton act they lighted up more than a century of crusading zeal, which broke the fetters of Europe's provincialism, banished many of the terrors of the unknown, and stimulated among Europeans a taste for the learning and luxuries of the East. Those "half military, half migratory movements," "Crusades," as the historians have called them—movements "strangely compounded of religious enthusiasm and political ambition, of the . . . spirit of the knight-errant and the cool calculation of the commercial bandit"—marked the "beginning of that return of the West upon the East which is so persistent a factor in all modern history. Christendom, so long isolated, now first broke the barriers that had closed it in, and once more extended its frontier into western Asia. . . ." [2]

At the opening of the thirteenth century the Mongols under their leader Genghis Khan rode out from their original home in central Asia upon one of the most remarkable careers of conquest in all history. In less than a half-century they had conquered most of China and swept across western Asia to the Black Sea. In 1240 they

[1] The Norsemen are an exception.
[2] Carl Becker, *Beginnings of the American People*, p. 4.

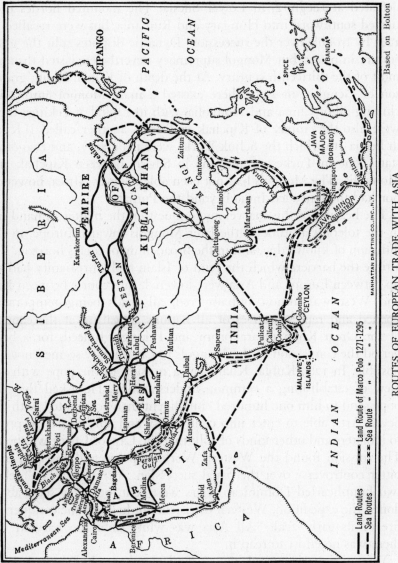

ROUTES OF EUROPEAN TRADE WITH ASIA

Based on Bolton

Land Routes
Sea Routes

Land Route of Marco Polo 1271-1295
Sea Route

MANHATTAN DRAFTING CO., INC., N.Y.

destroyed Kiev and made nearly all Russia tributary to them. A
year later Poland was overrun and an army of Poles and Germans
defeated at Liegnitz, in Lower Silesia. The mounted hordes then
turned southward into Hungary and Rumania, but were recalled in
1242 by trouble over the succession. Dynastic disputes split the great
empire in pieces, but Mongol supremacy nevertheless lasted through
most of the thirteenth century. At the death of Kublai Khan, grand-
son of Genghis, in 1294, there existed a main Mongol empire including all of China and Mongolia, with its capital at Peking; there
were also the empire of Kipchak in Russia, another called Il-Khan
in Persia (to which the Seljuk Turks were tributary), and two other
states, one in Turkestan and one in Siberia between Kipchak and
Mongolia. The Mongols had not been able to enter Africa, however;
nor had they invaded India beyond the Punjab.

The bearing of this marvelous conquest on the matter in hand lies
in the tolerant attitude of the later Mongols toward Europe, in the
diffusion of knowledge, and in the broadening of men's horizon. For
a time the barriers which the feud of Islam and Christianity had set
up between Europe and Asia were lowered. Intercourse between East
and West was almost unhampered, all roads being temporarily
opened and representatives of all nations appearing at the capitals
of the Great Khan (Karakorum and Peking). Indeed, for a brief
period the conversion of the Mongols to Christianity seemed not impossible. In 1269 Kublai Khan sent a mission to the pope with the
view of establishing a common understanding. He asked that the
pope send to him one hundred "intelligent men acquainted with the
Seven Arts, able to enter into controversy and able clearly to prove
to idolaters and other kinds of folk that the Law of Christ was best."
The mission found the Western World popeless and engaged in a
bitter controversy over the papal succession. After two years' delay,
two faint-hearted Dominican friars were sent, but they soon abandoned the expedition. Western Christendom had lost the conquering
fire of its early zeal. "All Asia was white unto the harvest, but
there was no effort to reap it."

Yet, missionaries, royal envoys, and merchants had preceded the
Dominicans; and missionaries, royal and papal envoys, and merchants were to follow them, advancing far beyond the point where

the Dominicans had turned back. From 1245 to 1253 John de Plano de Carpini, Neapolitan Franciscan and legate of Innocent III, and William of Rubruquis, agent of Saint Louis of France, penetrated central Asia to Karakorum. Between 1255 and 1265 Nicolo and Matteo Polo, two Venetians, traded in Mongolian Russia and eventually made their way to the court of Kublai Khan. Seven years later they again visited the Far East, accompanied by the young Marco Polo, whose account of his travels was to render the Polos immortal. From 1275 to 1353 John of Monte Corvino, Odoric of Perdenone, and John of Marignolli, as friars and papal legates, visited Il-Khan (Persia), Mongol China, Tibet, and the Malay Archipelago. These are only a few whom chance has rescued from oblivion.

Marvelous tales were brought back from the East by these travelers—tales of Cathay (northern China) "with ports thronged with ships and wharves glutted with costly wares"; of the "city of Kinsay ('stretched like Paradise through the breadth of Heaven') with lake, canals, bridges, pleasure barges, baths and lights-o'-love"; of imperial Cambulac (Peking) "with its Palace of the Great Kaan, its multitude of crowned barons in silken robes, its magic golden flagons, its troops of splendid white mares, its astrologers, leechers, conjurers," and "sweet singing" chorus girls with "cheeks full as the moon"; of India with its rubies and sapphires and diamonds; of the Moluccas "drowsy with perfumes and rich with drugs and spices" and abounding in "golden temples and uncouth gods," eunuchs, ivory, beasts, serpents, and brilliant birds.[3]

Perhaps Western Europe would have heard little of all this had not the Mongols tolerated and even invited intercourse. Nor would the response to the invitation have been so eager had not the Crusades emancipated Europeans from their provincialism and created a desire for the wisdom and wares of the East. Once curiosity had been thoroughly aroused and the appetite for luxuries created, they became almost irresistible. Men's credulous imaginations filled the unknown seas with islands and the islands with weird animals, rich commodities, strange men, or kingdoms of exiled Christians. Men's bold curiosity sent them in search of these "new lands," a search which was greatly facilitated by such opportune new inventions as the

[3] I. B. Richman, *The Spanish Conquerors*, p. 5.

compass, the astrolabe, and mariner's charts. It was mainly this eagerness to learn more of the world and to acquire more of its luxuries that led to the discovery of America.

The influence of the Ottoman Turks upon the Portuguese explorations along the African coast and the first voyage of Christopher Columbus has been too much emphasized. Perhaps the Portuguese, led by Prince Henry and his school of navigators, were mainly in search of African commodities, such as gold, ivory, and slaves, or under the influence of a crusading spirit which compelled them to seek the Christian Kingdom of "Prester John" and dream of expelling the Moors from the African continent. A new route to India may have come as an afterthought. In like manner, it may be that Columbus was not trying to reach the Far East by sailing west in 1492, but was merely in search of "islands and lands," or, as a recent French author contends, the island of the Seven Portuguese Bishops once expelled by the Moors. Of course he carried a letter from his sovereigns to the "Most Serene Prince," who may have been the Great Khan of Mongolia, but this could have been for the purpose of placing him on the safe side in case chance brought him that far. He also called the new lands he discovered the "Indies" and the natives of the West "Indians," but this may have been due to a resemblance of these lands to certain portions of the East as represented on the maps with which he was familiar. Prior to 1500 the desire to find a new route to India was perhaps not an important influence upon the voyages of discovery.

The voyages of Vasco da Gama (1497-1498) and his successors around Africa to India, however, soon revealed the economic advantage of an all-water route to the Far East; and the Turkish conquests of Damascus (1516) and Egypt (1517), followed by their policy of laying heavy tribute upon the trade passing through their dominions, placed the overland routes at far greater disadvantage. Soon after the opening of the sixteenth century, therefore, mariners did begin to search for a western route to the East; but this factor hardly figures before that time. To assign this motive to the earlier explorers is to be guilty of the historical anachronism of attributing to men of one decade the motives of the men of another.

Moreover, it is interesting to note—without any purpose of disparaging the great Italian who sailed under the Spanish flag—that

Columbus might have perished in mid-ocean in 1492 without long delaying the discovery of the New World. For less than eight years after his historic voyage the Portuguese sailor Pedrálvarez Cabral, who was on his way to India, sighted the coast of Brazil (April 21, 1500).[4]

Soon after Columbus's return to Spain, the lands newly discovered and still to be discovered throughout the major portion of the earth were divided between the two Hispanic Powers. The division was effected by Papal Bulls (1493) and the Treaty of Tordesillas (1494). Spain and Portugal forthwith set up monopolistic claims and launched upon a career of colonization which has profoundly influenced the entire course of modern history.

SPAIN'S EQUIPMENT

What was the equipment of these powers for the retention and development of their claims? An answer to this question will involve a survey of Iberian history with the view of discovering the factors that have influenced the colonial careers and policies of Spain and Portugal.

It should be noted at the outset that the Spanish people were a compound of many elements—Oriental and north African, as well as European—which had come to the peninsula in successive waves during prehistoric and historic times; but for present purposes it is hardly necessary to go back into Spanish history beyond the reign of Ferdinand of Aragon and Isabella of Castile (1479–1516). It was in this era that territorial unity was achieved and modern institutions crystallized into definite and durable form. It was during this time, likewise, that Spanish nationalism came into being and Spanish character cast itself in a mold which three subsequent centuries did not greatly modify.

Ferdinand and Isabella, *Los Reyes Católicos,* as they are called in Spain, were sovereigns of extraordinary ability, recognized as such even by their foreign contemporaries. Ferdinand drew forth the admiration of Machiavelli, who praised him in his *Prince.* Another

---

[4] Vicente Yáñez Pinzón explored the coast of eastern and northern South America a few weeks earlier, but he was influenced by the successful voyage of Columbus. John Cabot, who saw the coast of North America in 1497, was likewise influenced by Columbus's voyage.

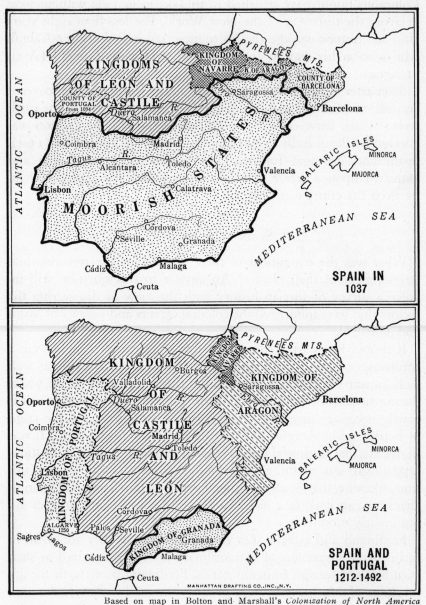

Based on map in Bolton and Marshall's *Colonization of North America*

THE RECONQUEST AND UNIFICATION OF SPAIN AND PORTUGAL

Italian (Guicciardini) who knew the king personally describes him at greater length:

"The feats that Ferdinand has accomplished, his words, his ways, and his general reputation prove that he is an extremely sagacious man. He is very secret, and unless obliged to, does not communicate important matters; he could not be more patient. He leads a very regular life, assigning times for this and that. He likes to know about all the affairs of the kingdom, great and little, and has them go through his hands; and though he exhibits a willingness to hear everybody's opinion, he makes up his own mind, and directs everything himself. . . . He is good at knightly exercises, and keeps them up; he makes a show of great piety, speaks of holy things with great reverence, and ascribes everything to God. He also makes a great parade of worship and attendance at church. . . . He gives audience freely and answers petitions with great dignity, and there are few who are not satisfied with what he says. . . . My opinion is that he can dissimulate better than any other man. . . . In short, he is a very notable king and has many talents; and the only criticisms upon him are that he is not generous and that he does not keep his promise." [5]

The same observer remarked that Isabella was even superior to her husband. "It is said," he wrote, "that she was a great lover of justice, and a lady of the best breeding, and made herself greatly beloved and feared by her subjects. She was generous, of a high spirit, and very ambitious of renown, as much so as any woman of the time, no matter who." Out of deference to her imperious will or excellent judgment, the king often followed her advice. A German visitor once observed that "the Queen is king, and the King is her servant." [6] Her very strenuous life is supposed to have had a fatal effect upon her children: several of them died in infancy; one became insane.

Ferdinand and Isabella founded an absolutism which continued until the opening of the nineteenth century. Turbulent nobles were either attracted to the court or ruthlessly suppressed; the local brotherhoods for defense against highwaymen (the *Hermandades*) were organized into royal police; the grand masterships of the great

[5] H. D. Sedgwick, *A Short History of Spain*, p. 126.
[6] *Ibid.*, pp. 127–129.

military orders, orders which had been organized during the long struggle against the Mohammedans in the peninsula and which not only numbered a million vassals and members but also enjoyed an annual revenue only slightly less than two and one-half million dollars, were taken over by the crown; royal councils were set up; royal courts—*audiencias* and *chancillerías*—were established; and the old Cortes (Parliaments) of Castile, Aragon, Valencia, and Catalonia were often defied or ignored. *Visitadores* traveled through the kingdom and examined the administration of justice and finance, and officials of the crown began to be subjected to the *residencia*— a judicial investigation of their conduct while in office. The captains-general, who in medieval times had exercised both military and civil authority in extensive Castilian territory, had been superseded by the *adelantados,* the most important of whom was probably the adelantado of the Canaries; but the former office could be resurrected if need should arise. Viceroys (vice-kings) were in charge of Sardinia, Sicily, and Naples. Even the ancient privileges and immunities of the municipalities began to be infringed, for the crown acquired a measure of control over the *ayuntamientos* (town councils) and sent out *corregidores* to inspect the town governments. Lastly, the Catholic Kings reorganized the Inquisition, conquered Granada, recovered Naples (1504), and began those negotiations with the papacy which culminated in the acquisition of royal patronage over the church in Spanish dominions. For two hundred years surprisingly few additions were made to the institutional structure which they had set up. Subsequent monarchs modified, perfected, or abused it, but they originated little save in the realm of taxation. The Catholic Kings were truly able monarchs.

In connection with social and economic conditions under Ferdinand and Isabella, several important facts may be noted. Agriculture was only fairly prosperous; industries, such as the manufacture of swords, silks, and woolens, flourished in nearly all the cities; commerce was encouraged by the crown; a respectable navy and merchant marine developed and consulates were set up. The population of Spain in 1500 was approximately seven million. It was divided into three classes, the higher nobility and the clergy composing the upper class. The clergy were wealthy. Spain's forty bishoprics and seven archbishoprics received an income of seven

million dollars, and the total annual rents of the secular clergy
amounted to about sixty million. The regular clergy—there were
about nine thousand religious houses in the country—were equally
rich and perhaps more numerous. At the head of the nobility were
the grandees, who either held office or lived upon the vast estates
which they or their ancestors had seized from the retreating Mos-
lems. The lower nobility—*hidalgos* and *caballeros*—were neither so
wealthy nor so fortunate, but higher and lower alike enjoyed many
privileges and exemptions, despised manual labor, and were supported largely by the toil of peasants in a semiservile condition. The
bottom class was composed of these agricultural laborers and tenants,
who, after the virtual abolition of serfdom in 1480 and 1486, were
gradually transformed into a free peasantry. In this class also were
the personal servants and industrial laborers of the towns, as well as
most of the beggars. Although serfdom was on its way to extinction,
the semifeudal institution called *encomienda* still persisted in some
quarters, free peasants or smaller landowners "commending" themselves to a powerful noble in the community and rendering him
certain services in return for protection. We shall hear of the institution again. The middle class was not numerous, being composed of
emancipated peasantry and of such members of the lesser nobility as
were attracted into business and industry.

Of conditions in 1513 Guicciardini gives a vivid, if somewhat unfriendly, description:

"The kingdom is thinly populated; there are some fine cities,
Barcelona, Saragossa, Valencia, Granada, and Seville, but they are
few for so large a country, and the other towns for the most part are
of little account. The southern regions are far the most fertile, but
only the land in the neighborhood of the cities is cultivated. Wool,
silk, wine, and oil are exported in large quantities. There is sufficient
wheat for the home market, and, if the nation were only industrious
and given to trade, their iron, steel, copper, hides, and other products
would make them rich. But as it is, the country is very poor, not
from natural resources but from the laziness of the people. They are
proud, and think that no other nation compares with theirs. . . .
They dislike foreigners, and are discourteous toward them. They
are more warlike, perhaps, than any other Christian nation; agile,
quick, and good at the manage[ment] of arms; they make a great

point of honor, and prefer to die rather than submit to shame. Their light cavalry is excellent, their horses very good; and the Castilian infantry enjoys a great reputation. . . .

"Spaniards are thought to be shrewd and intelligent, but they are not good in liberal and mechanical arts; all the artisans at the king's court are French, or foreigners of some sort. All Spaniards look down on trade and put on airs as hidalgos and prefer to be soldiers or (before Ferdinand's time) highwaymen than to engage in trade or any other such occupation. It is true that in some parts of Spain they weave and make rich stuffs, as in Valencia, Toledo, and Seville; but the nation as a whole is opposed to industrial life. The country people . . . till the ground much less than they might. Spaniards are fond of show; wear fine clothes abroad; ride a stylish horse; but at home, in the house, they live in a beggarly fashion hard to believe. They do not care for literature. . . . In outward appearance they are very religious, but not so really. They are very ceremonious, full of fine words and hand-kissings, and everybody is their 'lord' and they are 'at his disposition'; but their fair words are not to be taken literally. They are avaricious and great dissemblers." [7]

In brief, Spain had in 1500 "much of the reality as well as the appearance of greatness"; but it already contained also some elements of decline and decay. Political, racial, and religious unity had been achieved, considerable prosperity prevailed, and an elaborate political organization had been perfected. Moreover, the conclusion of the Moorish wars had produced a soldiery all aglow with crusading zeal, admirably fitted by training and temperament to carve out new dominions across the sea; and, despite the testimony of Guicciardini, intellectually and artistically Spain was at the threshold of a Golden Age. Yet, the very power of the monarchy would become a menace when turned toward unwise policies or when the character of the royal family declined. The intolerance which had deprived the country of the financial genius of the Jews was not to be satisfied until it caused Spain to lose the agricultural and industrial talent of the Moors (1501) and the Moriscos (converted Moors, expelled in 1609) and set up barriers against immigration in the future. Disdain for manual labor would result in stagnation when there were no more dominions to subdue. Then an idle nobility would become a

[7] Sedgwick, op. cit., pp. 153-154.

pest, fomenting political disorders, living upon administrative graft, and infesting the streets and highways as robbers and beggars. Huge landed estates, held together by mortmain and primogeniture, would retard the progress of the middle class and contribute to a general economic decline. The very wealth of the church would attract a too numerous clergy, who would succumb to luxury, idleness, and corruption, losing their former zeal and becoming a fearful social liability.

Before many decades these fateful elements began their work. In a single century Spain passed through her Golden Age into a long period of moral and material decrepitude. Of the many possible causes which might be assigned—exhaustive wars, vast colonies, false pride, neglect of science, industry, and public health, idle churchmen and nobility, religious absorption and superstition, political folly, economic ignorance—two need to be emphasized: bad government, and the attempt to play an imperialistic rôle in Europe.

For both of these the Spanish monarchy was to blame. Four of the nine kings who ruled over Spain between 1517 and 1808 were corrupt weaklings. Only four can be said to have been at all able or energetic—Charles I, Philip II, Ferdinand VI, and Charles III—and these were stanch exponents of an intolerant absolutism or the devotees of an exhausting imperialism which looked to Europe and the strength of armies and not to America and the efficacy of sea power. All of them expended Spanish blood and treasure upon European wars or lavished wealth and favors upon an idle and often corrupt nobility. The consequences are seen in the burdensome taxes and restrictions which contributed to the ruin of commerce and industry, to decline in population, to the general material backwardness and poverty of the Spanish nation.

The population of Spain was almost three million less in 1723 than in 1594. In 1723 one Spaniard out of every three was an ecclesiastic, a noble, or a servant; and this takes no account of the rogues and beggars, who at any time between these dates numbered 150,000 to 200,000. Thanks to the attempted reforms of Ferdinand VI (1746–1759) and Charles III (1759–1788), conditions had somewhat improved near the close of the eighteenth century, but they were still sufficiently bad. The population had increased to a little more than 10,000,000, but there were still more nobles and ecclesiastics than manufacturers, artisans, and merchants; and there were fewer than 1,700,000 farmers and farm laborers. More than fifty per cent of the lands were concentrated in the hands of the clergy and nobility; only one Spaniard in forty was a landed proprietor. Moreover, there were still some 140,000 vagabonds and beggars, and the government employees and army numbered 181,000.

We are now prepared to answer, with reference to Spain, the question propounded at the beginning of this section. The following, in brief, are the main factors in Spanish character and history which are to influence Spain's colonial policy and achievements:

(1) An absolute monarchy will consider its American dominions as the personal possessions of the crown and not of the nation. These dominions will therefore be used for the benefit of the monarchs and their favorites.

(2) A certain group of officials and institutions: the viceroyalty, the audiencia, the captaincy-general, the visitador, the adelantado, the corregidor, the residencia, may be expected to appear in the colonies. In the presence of an inferior race even the passing encomienda will be revived in a somewhat different form.

(3) To the religious orders will be intrusted in the main the task of converting the Indians of the New World colonies.

(4) The system of *latifundia* (large landed estates) will be transferred to America.

(5) Intolerance and dislike of foreigners will close the colonies to heretics and non-Spaniards, destroy priceless relics of aboriginal culture, and retard intellectual progress.

(6) A tendency toward municipal autonomy, struggling against monarchical centralization, may be expected to reappear.

(7) Certain traits of Spanish character, impetuosity, dislike of manual toil, love of display, fondness for official position and military adventure, will profoundly influence the nature of the colonies.

(8) Spain's ideal of economic monopoly in reference to her colonies and of a leading position in Europe will not only retard the progress of Spanish America but make her the center of attack by the other nations of Europe, and her colonies will often be considered the prize in the contest.

(9) The colonies will feel the heavy hand of taxation and administrative graft and suffer because of the material decline of the

mother country, at the same time that they receive some of the benfits of Spanish higher culture, which was in 1500 at the dawn of its *Siglo de Oro* (Century of Gold).

PORTUGUESE BACKGROUND

The character and history of the people of Portugal are strikingly similar to the character and history of the Spaniards. Both peoples are compounded of virtually the same racial stocks, the Portuguese receiving after the beginning of the sixteenth century an infiltration of Negro blood, which never entered Spain to any appreciable extent. The two kingdoms are not separated by effective barriers, and their languages are not radically different. Prior to the close of the eleventh century their histories merge; politically the two kingdoms were again united from 1580 to 1640; and even subsequently Spanish monarchs often influenced Portuguese affairs. Both peoples went through centuries of war, both racial and religious, on native soil against the Moors. This long struggle engendered in Portugal, as in Spain, a martial spirit, a national unity, and a religious zeal characterized by fanaticism and intolerance and leading to the establishment of the Inquisition and the persecution and expulsion of aliens and nonconformers. Each nation developed a strong monarchy at a comparatively early period. Each was characterized by a system of land tenure based upon large estates cultivated during a portion of the colonizing period by a semiservile peasantry. The upper classes of each country usually held manual labor in contempt. The commodities of each were similar, wool, silk, olives, and wine being important among them. The church in both countries was wealthy and powerful, the Jesuits being particularly strong in Portugal. In Spain, however, the church was usually the subordinate agent of the state, while in Portugal it not infrequently dominated the state. The vigorous municipal life which characterized each nation at the beginning of the colonizing era was gradually subordinated to the central government. Lastly, each had its golden age, its royal weaklings and corrupt court, its period of decline, and its reformer kings of the eighteenth century.

Accordingly, we may expect the colonial policies and achievements of the two countries to be somewhat similar. It must be noted, however, that Portugal is a much smaller nation than Spain. In 1500 its population was only about 1,800,000; by 1586 it had dropped to 1,080,000; and it was only a little over 3,000,000 in 1800. It may have been for this reason, in part, that Portuguese monarchs did not attempt to play an important rôle in Europe. Yet, the very position of their kingdom made involvement in European affairs unavoidable, and they were often forced to ally themselves with England or France. After 1642 English influence usually predominated, a fact significant for Brazil, for England induced the mother country to relax the rigor of its political and economic control. It should also be noted that long absorption in Africa and the East resulted in an attitude of indifference on Portugal's part toward her American colony. Brazil, like the thirteen English settlements in North America, experienced something of that salutary neglect which Edmund Burke so decidedly approved.

Founding of the Catholic Religious Orders

Already incidental reference has been made to the regular clergy of Spain and Portugal. Since their rôle in Hispanic colonization in America was to be very significant, a brief reference to their foundation and ideals seems appropriate.

The most important were the four great mendicant orders—the Franciscans, the Dominicans, the Carmelites, and the Augustinians —the Mercedarians (Order of the Blessed Virgin Mary of Mercy), and the Jesuits. The mendicants and the Mercedarians were organized, all of them, before the middle of the thirteenth century in response to the moral and religious needs of the times and the spirit of the new age. The Mercedarians were originally founded for the purpose of rescuing Christian captives from the Moors and their membership included knights as well as ecclesiastics; but the knights were later dropped, and this order also became mendicant in ideals. The mendicants inveighed against the wealth of the clergy, preaching and practicing austere poverty and a return to the simple life of Christ and the apostles. They increased in numbers very rapidly, the Iberian peninsula becoming one of their great centers. Many of them eventually departed from their early ideals, but many others retained the zeal and austerity of their founders. Before the New World was discovered, they began the great era of modern missions by their labor and sacrifices in the Far East. They came to America with the first explorers and conquerors and were soon bearing the brunt of frontier defense and expansion.

The Society of Jesus was founded in 1540 by Ignatius Loyola and other Spaniards. The Jesuits, like the mendicant orders, were pledged to poverty, chastity, and obedience. Their purpose was to reform the Catholic Church and counteract Protestantism, which had recently become an important religious factor in Western Europe. They entered Brazil in 1549 and all the main jurisdictions of Spanish America before the end of the sixteenth century. During the next century and a half their efforts in connection with the Christianization and civilization of the Indians were very effective. Moreover, their attempt to counteract the Lutheran Reformation in Europe tended to embitter the religious sentiments of the time and to call down upon Spain and Portugal, the principal champions of Catholicism, the ire of the Protestants, who often sought revenge, along with plunder, in attacks upon the Hispanic colonies overseas.

THE RISE OF THE COMPETITORS OF SPAIN AND PORTUGAL

The leading rivals of Spain and Portugal, Catholic as well as Protestant, were France, England, and the Dutch Netherlands. Detailed consideration of the rise of these three Powers would transcend the scope of this work. As already suggested, they profoundly influenced the history and colonial career of the Iberian nations. Achieving national unity and strength and coming upon the American scene somewhat later than Spain and Portugal, they not only raided Hispanic commerce but founded colonies in unoccupied areas and at times even attempted—occasionally with success—to conquer some of the Iberian settlements themselves. France first became a menace during the sixteenth century (particularly after the rise of the Huguenots); England, during the Age of Elizabeth; and the Dutch, during the first half of the seventeenth century. Owing to political decline, the Dutch soon ceased to constitute a serious threat; but the English and the French continued to be a grave danger, to the Spanish colonies, at least, until the end of the colonial period. The menace consisted mainly in the commercial enterprise and the sea power of these three nations, and in the ability of the English and the Dutch to play upon the religious motive.

CHAPTER IV

A CENTURY OF MARVELOUS ACHIEVEMENTS

DURING the century which followed the voyages of Columbus and Cabral, the Spaniards and Portuguese explored most of the coast lines of the two Americas and all of the important river basins from the Plata to the Colorado and the lower Mississippi. They also conquered all the semicivilized Indian societies and many of the wilder tribes, established numerous towns, and transferred Hispanic institutions and culture to more than half of the New World.

EXPLORATION OF THE COAST LINES

The running of the coast lines of the Americas from the northern border of modern Maine on the Atlantic to Cape Mendocino on the Pacific—a distance almost equal to the circumference of the earth—was the work of not more than thirty intrepid leaders. Although Italian, Spanish, and Portuguese experts participated in the exploration, nearly all of the pioneering was done under the Spanish flag.[1]

The examination of more than four thousand miles of the Atlantic coast [2] was the work of Columbus and the companions of his early voyages: Alonso de Ojeda, Vicente Yáñez Pinzón, Diego de Lepe, and Rodrigo de Bastidas. The Atlantic coast of South America from the eleventh to the thirty-second degree south latitude was explored first by the Florentine Amerigo Vespucci (1501) in company with a Portuguese captain. The southern portion of the same continent was first coasted by Ferdinand Magellan on his voyage around the world. The examination of the coast line bordering upon the Gulf of Mexico was first achieved by the combined efforts of Ponce de León (1513), Hernández de Córdoba (1517), and Alonso de Pineda

---

[1] Cabral (Portuguese) ran a small portion of the South American coast line (1500) in the vicinity of the 18° parallel, south; and a Portuguese captain, in company with Vespucci, sailed through twenty-one degrees along the coast of South America.

[2] Namely, from the easternmost point of Brazil to Honduras, and from near 32° to 40° south latitude.

(1519). The running of the eastern coast of what later became the United States was the achievement of four Spanish voyages: those of Ponce de León, Francisco Gordillo, Quexos,[3] and Estevan Gómez. The entire Atlantic coast line of the Americas from the Strait of Magellan to the northern boundary of what is now the United States had been explored by 1525. The search for slaves, pearls, and a strait had been the main motives.

Within thirty years of the discovery of the Pacific Ocean by Vasco Núñez de Balboa (1513) the entire western coast line of the Americas was run by intrepid Spanish pioneers. South of Panama the coastal exploration appears to have been the work of two men: Pascual de Andagoya and Alfonso de Camargo. North of Panama the achievement was the result of the combined efforts of some eight or ten leaders, but the most extensive explorations were those of Gaspar de Espinosa, Gil González Dávila, Hurtado de Mendoza, Francisco de Ulloa, Juan R. Cabrillo, and his pilot Ferrello. Meanwhile, two explorers, aside from Magellan, had crossed the Pacific to the Far East —Álvaro de Saavedra and López de Villalobos—and in 1565 two other leaders, López de Legazpi and Fray Andrés de Urdaneta, found their way to the Philippines, the latter making the return voyage by a convenient route destined to be followed often in the future. It was truly a marvelous achievement, this running of the extensive coast lines of the two Americas—and much of the effort was privately financed.

The poverty of resources with which it was undertaken makes the achievement all the more striking. "Vessels that had been used only in coastwise trade were fitted out to hazard the depths of the 'Ocean Sea'; and many a lusty mariner set off without charts, instruments, or sufficient supplies, to follow the fortunes of those more favored ones who had a little knowledge and enjoyed the royal favor." [4] The equipment of those who started from the American base was seldom any better and sometimes even worse. The vessels of the most fortunate were tiny enough. Columbus's *Santa María* had a capacity of about one hundred and thirty tons, while the *Niña* had only forty. The displacement of Pinzón's caravel was forty-seven tons and that of the first vessel to circumnavigate the globe was but eighty-seven.

[3] Gordillo and Quexos were financed and directed by Lucas Vásquez de Ayllón.
[4] Priestley, *The Coming of the White Man*, p. 5.

Their speed varied from eight to fifteen miles an hour. For the officers and chance passengers conditions aboard were bad: tiny cabins, swarms of cockroaches, droves of rats, stale food, unpalatable water, filthy decks. For the common sailors they were much worse.

CONQUEST OF THE SEMICIVILIZED INDIANS

A large part of the Arawaks of the Greater Antilles—Española, Cuba, and Jamaica—had been subdued and the occupation of southern Central America begun before news of the existence of the more advanced groups of Indians was received. Once their location was learned, however, their conquest proceeded with great rapidity. The Nahuas and Mayas, the Incas, and the Chibchas were conquered before the middle of the sixteenth century; the Pueblos of the distant northern frontier were at the point of conquest when it closed.

Aztecs.—The subjugation of the Aztecs was the work of Hernando Cortés and his lieutenants. They left the shores of Cuba in February, 1519; reached the Island of Cozumel and the coast of Mexico, where they picked up two interpreters and lingered for several months; set out for the interior in August, after having sunk their ships; entered the great Aztec city of Tenochtitlán without striking a blow, and by the middle of November persuaded the chief Montezuma to reside at the Spanish headquarters. The conquest might have been achieved without serious difficulty had not Cortés been forced to leave the city in the hands of Pedro de Alvarado until he could reckon with an envoy of the Governor of Cuba. The latter official had repented of his choice of Cortés for the subjugation of the rich land of the Nahuas, had tried in vain to intercept his voyage, and had now sent Narváez to subdue the defiant conqueror. While Cortés was winning over the followers of his foe, his lieutenant in the Aztec city provoked the natives to the point of revolt. The great conqueror reentered Tenochtitlán late in June, 1520, just in time to make preparation for a desperate flight. The Aztecs were not to be conquered without a bloody struggle. Thanks, however, to the efforts of his doughty soldiers and lieutenants and the loyal support of Indian allies who had no love for the Aztec Confederacy, the proud capital of the Aztecs was taken by assault on August 13, 1521. The agents of Cortés were then sent out in every direction to demand and enforce

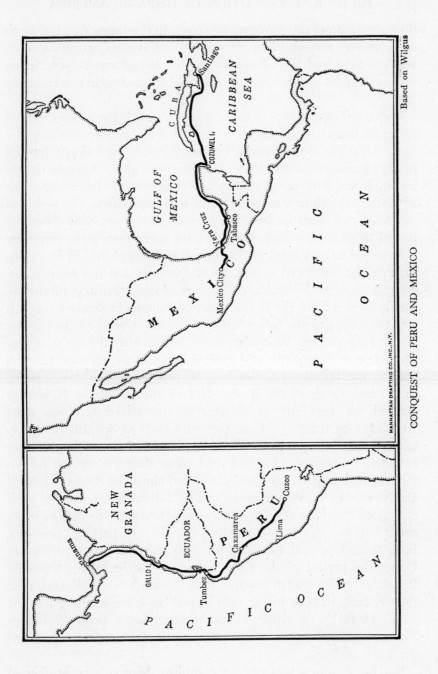

MANHATTAN DRAFTING CO.,INC.,N.Y.

CONQUEST OF PERU AND MEXICO

CUBA

Santiago

CARIBBEAN SEA

COZUMEL I.

GULF OF MEXICO

Vera Cruz

Tabasco

M E X I C O

Mexico City

P A C I F I C   O C E A N

NEW GRANADA

Panamá

GALLO I.

ECUADOR

P E R U

Tumbez

Caxamarca

Lima

Cuzco

P A C I F I C   O C E A N

the submission of the surrounding tribes. In the course of a few years the task was accomplished. Several million dollars' worth of booty was collected and the foundation of the Kingdom of New Spain, with its capital at Mexico City (the old Tenochtitlán), was firmly laid.

Mayas.—The conquest of the Mayas was mainly the achievement of either the lieutenants of Cortés or the men who had seen service under him: Alvarado in Guatemala, Cristóbal de Olid and Cortés himself in Honduras, Francisco Montejo in the peninsula of Yucatán. It was accomplished with much cruelty and difficulty, the latter being due as much to the climate as to the prowess of the Indians. The power of the Mayas of Yucatán was not broken until 1545, and they continued to be restless and dangerous for more than three centuries.

Incas.—The overthrow of the Incas was accomplished by Francisco Pizarro, the untutored swineherd of Estremadura, and his supporters and dauntless followers. After years of unsuccessful planning, he finally set sail from the Pacific coast of Panama in January, 1531. It was the spring of the following year before he reached the borders of the Inca empire. Soon afterwards he founded the town of San Miguel, near the equator and some distance in the interior. Leaving here in the following September, he proceeded southeast, crossed the eastern range of the Andes, and by the middle of November entered the Inca city of Cajamarca and seized the war chief Atahualpa by treachery. Here the main body of Spanish troops remained for almost a year collecting plunder. Late in August they executed Atahualpa, who had paid more than $15,000,000 for his ransom, and prepared to move southward along the Andes to Cuzco. On November 15, 1533, Pizarro and his followers entered this great capital of the Inca empire, where they managed to collect booty about half as valuable as that which they had secured at Cajamarca. Both Atahualpa and Huascar, his rival war chief, were dead, but Quito, the capital of the former, had yet to be taken. Sebastián Benalcázar, who was dispatched thither with a few followers, took the city early in 1534, just in time to prevent it from falling into the hands of Pedro de Alvarado, of Mexican fame. Soon afterwards Pizarro returned to the coast and, early in January, 1535, founded the town of Lima.

But the conquest was not yet complete. Manco Inca, brother of the murdered Huascar, rallied his Indians while Francisco Pizarro was away in Lima. A desperate struggle for the control of Cuzco followed, during which the remnant of the Spaniards was led by Hernando Pizarro, brother of the conqueror. Almost four months of war ensued, but the Spaniards eventually won. The Spanish leaders then fell to fighting over the spoils and the country was not pacified until near the middle of the century. By that time nearly all of the early leaders were dead.

Chibchas.—The Chibchas were subdued by Gonzalo Jiménez de Quesada, a talented lawyer of southern Spain. He set forth from Santa Marta, a town recently founded on the Caribbean coast of what later became the Viceroyalty of New Granada, on April 6, 1536. The journey up the steaming Magdalena valley and over the mountains to the plateau of Bogotá required almost nine months, during which time the adventurers encountered hardships that baffle description. The Zipa, the Zaque, and the Iraca were soon overthrown, with considerable slaughter, and some two million dollars' worth of plunder was collected. Quesada fixed his headquarters at Bacatá (Muequeta), tortured to death or killed in other ways most of the Indian leaders, and on August 6, 1538, founded the town of Santa Fé de Bogotá.

Pueblos.—Of all the semicivilized Indians of America, the Pueblos were the last to be conquered. Although their villages had previously been visited several times, their final subjugation was the work of Juan de Oñate and Pedro de Peralta (1598–1614).[5] These leaders succeeded without difficulty in pacifying the Pueblos, founding both the temporary town of San Juan and the permanent Spanish settlement of Santa Fé (1610) and introducing Catholic missionaries among the natives.

The conquest of the more cultured natives had been no less remarkable than the exploration of the extensive coast lines. And this, too, had been accomplished with scanty equipment. Cortés left Cuba with fewer than 700 men, entered Tenochtitlán with about 600, and never had more than 1,300 Spaniards at any time prior to his final seizure of the Aztec capital. Alvarado started to Guatemala with 420 soldiers; Quesada overthrew the Chibchas with 166; Pizarro confronted Atahualpa at Cajamarca with only 168 and overthrew the

---

[5] Most of the pacification must be attributed to Oñate, who was in charge from 1598 to 1608.

Incas with fewer than 400; Oñate entered the Pueblo country with only 130 soldiers!

The secret of the superior prowess of the Spaniards lay but in part in their firearms and horses, for only a small portion of their troops were equipped with these and the firearms were not of the best quality to be had at the time. It was due rather to their excellent strategy, to their amazing gift for intrigue which brought to their side many Indian allies, to the bitter rivalries and enfeebling superstition of the natives, and also, in the case of the Aztecs, and perhaps the Mayas, to a desire to take the Spaniards alive in order to have victims for sacrifice to their gods.

The Subjugation of the Backward Peoples and the Exploration of the Interior

Compared with the overthrow of the semicivilized natives, the conquest of the less advanced tribes holds little of interest. Yet the pacification of the Araucanians of southern Chile proved exceedingly difficult, and that of the Charruas of the Plata basin only a little less so; and the conquest of the Zenús of the interior of northern New Granada by Pedro de Heredia, founder of the city of Cartagena (1533), yielded more treasure than the subjugation of the Chibchas.

The establishment of Spanish rule in southern Central America was largely the work of Balboa and Pedrarias Dávila and his lieutenants. In Chile, it was the achievement of Diego Almagro, erstwhile associate of the Pizarros in Peru, Pedro de Valdivia, and Hurtado de Mendoza; in the great basin of the Río de la Plata, it was the difficult task of Pedro de Mendoza, Domingo Martínez Irala, Juan de Ayolas, Juan de Garay, and others; in northern and eastern Venezuela, it was the work of such men as Juan de Ampués, the agents of the Welzers (German bankers of Augsburg),[6] Juan de Villegas, and Diego Losada; in northern New Granada, it was mainly the accomplishment of Rodrigo Bastidas and Pedro de Heredia, while in the Cauca River valley it was due to the efforts of Sebastián Benalcázar and Jorge Robledo, a companion of Quesada. Far away to the north, Spanish rule was definitely established in Florida, after

---

[6] The main interest of the Welzers was in gold and plunder.

Hernando Cortés

Francisco Pizarro

Gonzalo Jiménez de Quesada

Pedro de Valdivia

Pedro de Alvarado

Sebastián Benalcázar

THE SPANISH CONQUERORS

many costly failures, by Menéndez de Avilés and Jesuit missionaries, and New Spain's frontier was advanced by a dozen bold leaders.[7]

Meantime, the Spaniards had explored the majority of the vast interior of the two Americas. Belief in the fabulous, induced by the extraordinary treasures of Mexico and Peru, was an important cause of this rapid exploration. In 1536, Cabeza de Vaca, who had been shipwrecked on the coast of Texas, reached Culiacán, a Spanish settlement on the northwestern frontier of New Spain. He had tramped all the way across the continent, and he brought stories of wealthy kingdoms to the north.[8] This soon set men to searching for the Seven Cities, Grand Quivira, and the Northern Mystery. By 1603 the Spaniards had gone beyond the plains of central Kansas to the South Platte River. In 1539, Hernando de Soto, brother-in-law to Balboa, former lieutenant of Pedrarias in Nicaragua, and companion of Pizarro in the land of the Incas, set sail for the coast of Florida. He was in search of another Peru, and the quest led him to most of the Indians of the southeastern portion of North America, and eventually to the discovery of the Mississippi River and its Arkansas tributary.

In South America even more amazing feats were accomplished. Here the Spaniards were dazzled by stories of the Gilded Man, the rich kingdoms of Meta and Omagua, and the wonder-city Manoa. The stories indicated that these would be found in the valley of the Orinoco or the Amazon or somewhere in the vast interior of the continent, and daring leaders set forth through tropical heat, flood, pest, and jungle. The suffering was terrific, and the cost was great both in men and in money; but the explorers gave to the world much knowledge regarding the interior of South America. At least a score of long expeditions were made by the close of the century, the majority of them from the northern coast of Venezuela. There were others, however, which set forth from Peru and Bogotá. Some of the leaders made their way from the Venezuelan town of Coro southward across the plains and jungles to the main tributaries of the Orinoco and even to the plateau of Cundinamarca. Others entered one of the mouths of the Orinoco and followed that river and

[7] San Augustín was founded in 1565.
[8] Vaca lived to explore a route across Brazil to Paraguay.

its tributaries into the forests to the east of Bogotá. Still others proceeded southeast from Bogotá until they reached the junction of the Guaviare and the Orinoco, or farther south until they explored some of the northern tributaries of the Amazon. Important among the Venezuelan group were Nicholas Federmann and George Speyer, agents of the Welzers, and the Spaniards Diego Ordaz and Jerónimo de Ortal. From Bogotá the most significant expeditions were made by Jiménez de Quesada, the conqueror, and his brother Hernán Pérez de Quesada.

The most extensive of all these expeditions into the interior of northern South America proceeded from the land of the Incas. In 1540 Francisco Orellana, companion of the Pizarros, embarked with a small group of companions upon one of the upper tributaries of the Amazon and followed that great river across the continent to the sea. In 1560–1561, Lope de Aguirre, a desperate character who had seized the command of a Peruvian expedition after having murdered its leader, proceeded down the Amazon to the vicinity of the Orinoco tributaries and thence by the latter to the Orinoco and the Atlantic.

While these bold adventurers were searching for fabled kingdoms, important explorations were made farther to the south. Ayolas ascended (1535) the Paraná and the Paraguay as far as twenty degrees south latitude, and then crossed the plains to Peru; Irala went up the Paraguay three degrees farther north than Ayolas had gone and opened a permanent line of communication between Peru and the Río de la Plata; Cabeza de Vaca, who already had walked across the North American Continent, explored a route from the southeastern coast of Brazil to the town of Asunción in Paraguay (1542); and the daring navigator Juan de Ladrillero proceeded from the Chilean frontier to the Strait of Magellan and through the main channel to the Atlantic Ocean (1557).

ESTABLISHMENT OF INSTITUTIONS AND TRANSFER OF CULTURE

It was likewise during the sixteenth century that Spanish colonial institutions were thoroughly developed. Intelligent consideration of the evolution of these institutions must begin with emphasis upon the relationship of the New World to the Spanish crown. The fundamental conception back of Spanish colonial enterprise was that this new region belonged to the Spanish monarchs. They possessed not only the sovereign rights but the property rights, and every privilege and position, whether economic, political, or religious, must come from them. It was on this basis that the conquest, occupation, and government of the New World were achieved. The undertaking was "by and for the crown, not the Spanish nation," and it was placed "immediately and thoroughly under the care of officers appointed by the crown and responsible directly to it."

"When a leader went forth to add new domains to the crown he sought first the royal license. To obtain it, he had to show sufficient financial backing to insure probable success. His profits were to be taken from the area subdued. He was to have the right to exact labor from the Indians, to appoint municipal officers for the first year, to possess a tract of land in his own right, and to bestow lands upon his followers according to their merits or services. He might recruit companies of soldiers or settlers, offering them inducements from the conquest and taking from them such pledges of loyalty as he himself gave the king or his representative. Sometimes royal funds were invested if the venture were of strategic importance. There were judiciously chosen missionaries, in large number usually, to effect a spiritual conquest. And there were never lacking royal officials, or treasury representatives, who kept account of all treasure-trove, gold mines discovered, or any visible sources of wealth, of which the king and the leader were each to have one-fifth. Never varying greatly in plan, all the expeditions of discovery and conquest closely followed this system."

It was an excellent system—for the monarch. "Financial responsibility was shifted by enlisting private capital; thus, losses from shipwreck, uncompleted voyages, and unsuccessful establishments were largely borne by the unhappy victims of the misadventure," not only the leaders but the humble participants as well.

According to his contract, a leader might become an adelantado, a lieutenant, a simple governor, or even a captain-general. "Always he had to be a man of daring and resource, for he possessed potential enemies within the expedition in the missionaries, who sought the temporal as well as the spiritual advantage of the church, in the royal officials, who were intended as checks upon profits on behalf of the crown, and in his captains, who were all likely to have delusions of grandeur and watch eagerly for mistakes or missteps in his management." [9]

As the monarch's overseas dominions grew, he set up in the homeland two institutions to assist him in governing them. As early as 1503 he established in Seville the *Casa de Contratación,* or House of Trade, whose duties were the supervision of trade, navigation, and emigration. By 1524 he had set up a permanent Council of the Indies, to which was entrusted supreme legislative and judicial control, under the king, of all the colonies in the New World, as well as advisory and nominating functions in regard to all colonial civil and ecclesiastical officials.

In the Indies themselves, the principal executive officials have already been noted. The adelantado soon disappeared, his functions being connected exclusively with frontier regions. To the governor and the captain-general was soon added the viceroy,[10] the most dignified and powerful of all colonial functionaries. Within the area under his control he was not only civil governor but also commander-in-chief of the army, vice-patron of the church, presiding officer of the supreme court which met in his capital city, and superintendent of finances. During the sixteenth century two viceroyalties were established, one in New Spain, or Mexico (1535), and the other in Peru (1544). Only two captaincies-general were set up during the sixteenth century: Gautemala (1527) and Chile (near the end of the century). The former embraced Central America north of Panama and included a small portion of southern Mexico. Within his less important jurisdiction, the captain-general had about the same functions as the viceroy. There were about twenty-eight *gobernaciones,* or provincial administrative jurisdictions, by 1574.

The Spanish monarchy, always eager for profits and jealous of its prerogatives, not only sent to America its treasury officials (*oficiales reales*) but also extended to the Indies its system of investigators and investigations (*pesquisidores, visitadores,* and *residencias*). Executive officials were carefully watched, often judicially investigated in the midst of their term, and nearly always subjected

[9] Priestley, *The Coming of the White Man,* pp. 11–12.

[10] In fact, Columbus was granted the title of viceroy and governor as well as admiral; but the Columbus family soon lost the title of viceroy, and it did not appear again until 1535.

to the residencia at its end. Perhaps the most effective check upon these officials, however, and one of the most important institutions in the colonies, was the audiencia. Seven of them were established by the middle of the sixteenth century, and nine by 1600. These bodies had many functions, judicial, advisory, and administrative. They constituted the supreme court within the boundaries of their jurisdiction and also served as an advisory council to the chief executive, often sitting in judgment upon his acts and communicating with the Council of the Indies over his head. In the absence of the executive, on account of death or for any other reason, the *audiencia* served as an *ad interim* administrative body.

A conspicuous feature of Spanish colonization was the founding of towns and the establishment of municipal institutions. There were some two hundred Spanish towns in America by 1574 and perhaps two hundred and fifty by 1600. Among them were fourteen [11] destined to be the capitals of as many independent nations of a later period. Not a score of the important towns of the twentieth century were unfounded at the end of the sixteenth.[12] Many others were founded during this early period and later abandoned.

"The Spanish towns, which must be distinguished from the Indian towns, were legally established by groups of settlers numbering from ten to one hundred heads of families. . . . The grants to the towns were almost uniformly four square leagues (about eighteen thousand acres). . . . As in the New England towns, the land was divided among the colonists in proportion to their merits, capacity or number of family dependents. The small husbandman received, inside the building area of the town, which was laid out foursquare about a public plaza, a house lot measuring fifty by one hundred feet. Outside the building area he received enough land to sow one hundred quintals (10,000 pounds) of wheat or barley and ten of corn. He was also given a measured plot of ground for a garden and an orchard, besides pasture ground for ten sows, five mares, one hundred sheep and twenty goats, in return for which he must provide the beginning of

[11] They were: Habana, Santo Domingo, Mexico City, San Salvador, Guatemala City, Panama, Caracas, Bogotá, Quito, Lima, La Plata (later called Chuquisaca and Sucre), Santiago, Asunción, and Buenos Aires.

[12] Among those not yet founded were: Port au Prince, Barranquilla, Medellín, Rosario, and Montevideo.

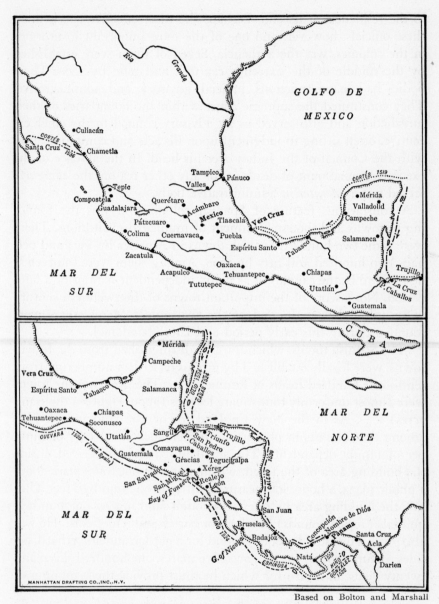

Based on Bolton and Marshall

PRINCIPAL COLONIAL SETTLEMENTS IN CENTRAL AMERICA AND SOUTHERN MEXICO

these herds. . . . A pioneer who had the status of a mounted soldier might receive . . . a house lot one hundred by two hundred feet and cultivable [and] pasture lands five times as extensive" as those given to a small husbandman. "The town was established by a leader, or by the group acting as a unit; the officers were generally elected, though when a leader had taken the initiative he was permitted to appoint them for the first year. From this type of grant sprang the Spanish pueblo or town. . . . All the cities of Spanish America . . . had such an origin." [13]

The essential officers of the municipalities were the *regidores* (town councilmen), ranging in number from four to twelve. From their number were chosen two *alcaldes ordinarios* (municipal judges) and an *alférez* (herald or ensign). During the sixteenth century two or three treasury officials of the crown resided in each of the towns and sat in their councils (*cabildos* or *ayuntamientos*) with voice and vote. At first the towns were centers of local self-government, but before the end of the century their autonomy was reduced by the sale of offices and the encroachments of the *gobernadores* (provincial governors), the corregidores, and the *alcaldes mayores,* who were agents of the central authority.

These towns were units of Spanish culture set down in the New World. Each of them had its plaza and beautiful parks, its imposing churches and its monasteries and often its schools,[14] and its substantial municipal buildings. In them dwelt, in 1574, about 160,000 people of pure Spanish descent, besides many Negroes, mulattoes, and *mestizos* (people of mixed Spanish and Indian blood).

Toward the end of the sixteenth century, the subdued Indians were, for the most part, under the rule of the *encomenderos* (Spaniards who had charge of their labor and their education but who still often employed the chiefs as agents of social control), the corregidores or alcaldes mayores (crown officials who supervised the Indian villages usually with the help of the native chiefs), and the clergy, both regular and secular. The Indians, however, had the right of appeal to the *protectores* (protectors), the audiencias, and even to the Council of the Indies itself.

[13] Priestley, *op. cit.*, pp. 96–97.
[14] The religious orders had scores of *colegios*, and before 1600 universities were established at Mexico, Lima, Santo Domingo, and possibly at Mérida (New Spain).

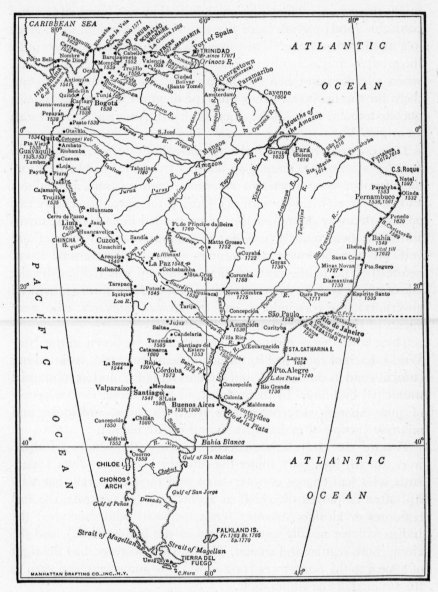

PRINCIPAL SETTLEMENTS IN COLONIAL SOUTH AMERICA

The conquest and subsequent readjustments had been very destructive to the native races. The Indians of the West Indies and northern Venezuela—namely, those of the Antillean Culture Area —had been almost exterminated long before 1600. Father Las Casas alleged that twelve or fifteen million natives had been exterminated by 1541, but many writers contend that his estimates were the preposterous guesses of an advocate. He may indeed have misinterpreted the motives of some of the conquerors and exaggerated their cruelties, but his figures appear to have been essentially correct. The later estimates of López de Velasco (1574) seem to indicate that there were only about seven or eight million Indians living in subjection to Spanish rule at the end of the third quarter of the century. Perhaps there were at that time no more than two or three million still unsubdued by the Spaniards. If these figures be approximately correct, it would appear that some thirteen or fourteen million had been exterminated by war, disease, grief, hard labor, and starvation.

Formerly hundreds of thousands of Indians had been reduced to slavery; but of the some eight million under Spanish rule in 1600, comparatively few were slaves any longer, although their status was not far above that of slavery, since their labor was often forced and their wages frequently withheld, and all able-bodied, male, adult Indians were compelled to pay tribute to the encomenderos or the crown.

In many respects, perhaps, their condition was much better than before their white masters came. Their tribal feuds and their religious oppressions and cruelties had been suppressed, and some of their gross superstitions had vanished. They had been taught, in part, at least, the principles and comforts of a higher form of religion. The Spaniards had also brought them better tools and implements for agriculture and industry, as well as the superior food plants, the meat-producing animals, and the beasts of burden [15] of Western Europe, although the Indians were not allowed to possess firearms or ride horseback.[16] All these things must have brought about an improvement over their ancient position, despite the fact that they

---

[15] It seems that Spaniards had transferred to America before 1600 specimens of all the cereals, fruits, vegetables, and domestic animals which they had been accustomed to grow in the mother country.

[16] The motive here was order and the security of the dominant Spaniards.

were offset in part by labor in the mines, in the pearl-fisheries, and on some of the haciendas (country estates), labor more strenuous than many of them had known hitherto.

By the close of the century their place in society had been fixed, and there was little change during the remainder of the colonial period.[17] Of the two or three million still in their primitive state in 1574, some were subsequently reclaimed by the missionaries and reduced to a settled mode of living. Of the millions under encomenderos, many were gradually transferred to the supervision of royal officials, but this had little influence upon their status. Village life, Christianization, civilization, racial fusion with the Spanards— these were the main objectives of Spain's Indian policy; and notwithstanding much attendant cruelty and exploitation—which occurred in violation of many humane laws—the fate of the aborigines of Spanish America was probably more fortunate than that of the backward races subdued by any other modern colonizing power.

There was no more important institution in the colonies than the Roman Catholic Church. To it early Spanish-American society owed much that was good as well as some things that were harmful. The clergy, both regular and secular, came over with the first explorers and settlers and continued to arrive in ever increasing numbers until by the closing decades of the century the civil officials complained of a superabundance. By 1574 the church was organized in four archbishoprics and twenty-four bishoprics. Besides these, there were two Tribunals of Inquisition, one at Lima and the other at Mexico City. By 1600 the archbishoprics had increased to five [18] and the bishoprics to twenty-seven, and there were scores of other ecclesiastical dignitaries and retainers as well as hundreds of priests. At that time there were also more than four hundred monasteries with probably two thousand Jesuits and padres of the mendicant orders. The clergy had played an important part in sixteenth century achievement. If the intolerant zeal of a few had sometimes supported the cruelties of the *conquistadores,* the tender human sympathy of others had often restrained ruthless leaders and softened the hard lot of the

[17] According to the estimates of Humboldt, there were 7,530,000 Indians in Spanish America in 1800. This would mean that the Indian population was about stationary for two centuries.

[18] They were, in the order of their establishment: Santo Domingo, New Spain, Peru, New Granada, and Charcas.

natives. If many of the padres and priests exploited the Indians, many others undertook the task of Christianizing and civilizing them with a devotion seldom equaled in modern history. If there was just ground for complaint at their accumulation of wealth, it must be admitted that the colonists owed to them nearly all that they had of learning and charity. The earnest preaching of such men as Padre Las Casas aroused the Spanish monarchs to the oppressed condition of their native wards and led to humane, if ineffective, legislation. The failure of the laws of 1542—designed to abolish the encomiendas in a generation or two—was due far more to the opposition of the laity than to that of the clergy, and those laws would probably never have been issued had it not been for Las Casas.[19] The Spanish monarchy deliberately used the carefully controlled state church as an agency of colonial enterprise.

Another characteristic of Spanish culture transferred to America or displayed in connection with this century of marvelous achievement was the strong tendency toward literary expression. Prior to 1800, few periods were so completely revealed by their literature as was the sixteenth century in colonial Spanish America.

The conquerors and explorers were often men of literary attainments. Cortés, Bernal Díaz, and Quesada are conspicuous examples. Balboa, Cabeza de Vaca, Andagoya, and, in fact, most of the leaders sent back *cartas de relación* to Spain.

The friars who accompanied the explorers and conquerors or followed closely upon their heels presented valuable first-hand accounts of events. The Spanish monarch employed his geographers, chroniclers, and historians to write of the New World. And even some of the men with Aztec or Inca blood in their veins, like Garcilaso de la Vega, produced valuable narratives of Indian life or of the conquest.

The numerous works of the period were concerned mainly with war, natural phenomena, religion, and language. At least one able writer, Juan Matienzo, dealt with government and commerce. Most of these productions were written in prose, but many writers expressed themselves in poetry. In 1585 some three hundred poets are said to have participated in a contest held in Mexico. The most famous of

[19] They provided, among other things, for the abolition of Indian slavery and the suppression of certain *encomiendas*.

these poems are *La Araucana,* written by Alonso de Ercilla y Zúñiga (1533–1594), and Bernardo de Balbuena's (1568–1627) *Grandeza Mexicana.* The first dealt with the author's personal adventures during the Spanish attempt to conquer the Araucanian Indians of Chile. The second gave a vivid portrait of New Spain, its riches, beauties, wonders, and native inhabitants. Of less note is Martín del Barco Centenera's poetic account of the conquest of the Río de la Plata. Shortly before 1600 Juan de Castellanos of New Granada finished his *Elegías de Varones ilustres* (*Elegies of Illustrious Men*), the longest poem of its kind in any language.

The sixteenth century was also marked in Spanish America by considerable achievement in architecture, sculpture, and painting. Much of the painting and sculpture, which were devoted mainly to religion, has perished. A few examples of architecture still survive.

The sixteenth century was characterized, of course, by important mining developments. The first three decades witnessed the despoiling of the semicivilized areas rich in gold. Cortés, Pizarro, Quesada, and Heredia were the most fortunate of the gold-mad conquerors; but all of the conquistadores sent the natives in search of this precious metal and even tortured them in the hope of compelling them to bring it in. The explorers of the interior continued to seek other Perus and other Mexicos, but the widespread contagion passed before the middle of the century and men turned their attention to the more prosaic business of working the mines. The mines of Tasco, some eighty miles south of Mexico City, began to be worked about 1535; and those of Zacatecas, Guanajuato, Fresnillo, Sombrerete, San Martín, Santa Barbara, and San Luis Potosí, to the north, long before the close of the century. In Peru, the rich silver mines of Potosí were discovered in 1545, and the quicksilver mines of Huancavélica began to be developed soon afterwards (1564). New Granada, Venezuela, and Central America were by no means as rich in minerals, but gold and silver were found and worked there also. Between 1503 and 1530 the annual imports of these two metals into Spain from America had ranged from about 134,000 to 1,000,000 pesos. From 1546 to 1550 the annual average rose above 5,500,000 pesos, and between 1591 and 1600 it reached thirty-five million.[20] Be-

[20] For these figures I am indebted to my friend and colleague, Earl J. Hamilton, of Duke University.

tween 1541 and 1575 North America, mainly Mexico, furnished the bulk; thereafter South America, mainly Peru, supplied about two-thirds of the treasure.

It would be a mistake, however, to assume that Spain's economic interest in America centered exclusively in the precious metals at any time during the sixteenth century. An important phase of the early colonial policy of Spain was the successful introduction into the New World of all the plants and animals and agricultural implements of the metropolis. The process began with the early colonization projects of Columbus and was continued as a conscious policy. The testimony of contemporary writers [21] supports the conclusion that by the close of the century virtually all of the fruits, vegetables, and useful animals of the mother country were thriving in many parts of the colonies. Moreover, the cultivation of native plants and fruits was persistently encouraged. Products of farm, ranch, and forest furnished an important share of the total exports of Spain's American empire. Hides, sugar, and dyewoods were prominent during the early period and cochineal became important after 1573.

CORSAIRS, TRADE REGULATIONS, TAXES

Actuated by motives compounded of national animosity and greed, French corsairs began to attack Spanish colonial trade at a very early date. At first they hovered along the coasts of Europe or hid in the harbors of the Canaries, Azores, and Madeiras. They met Columbus on his return voyage in 1493 and forced him to change his return route in 1496. In 1521 they seized two treasure-laden caravels and in 1522–1523 captured nearly all the plunder sent home by Cortés. By 1537 they were busy in the Caribbean, seizing treasure-ships and capturing and pillaging towns—Havana, Chagres, and Cartagena among them. When peace between France and Spain interrupted their raids (1559), Elizabethan sea dogs, such as Drake, Hawkins, and Cavendish (1563 ff.), took their place, seizing treasure fleets and bullion trains and plundering not only the towns of the Caribbean but those of the Pacific coast as well. The losses ran into millions of pesos, and these corsair and sea-dog raids, supplemented by the monopolistic ideal, led to the confinement of colonial trade to

[21] López de Velasco (1574), José Acosta (1590), and Vargas Machuca (1609).

convoyed merchant fleets sailing at stipulated dates from the Spanish port of Seville (and its subsidiary, Cádiz) to the American ports of Havana, Cartagena, Vera Cruz, and Porto Bello.[22] This system, in turn, led to the concentration of the American trade in the hands of a few merchants at Seville, who also sought to control the importing business of the colonies by establishing agents at Vera Cruz, Mexico City, Panama, and Lima. Moreover, it proved cumbersome and expensive, raised the price of colonial imports by limiting their quantity, and predisposed the colonists to welcome smugglers. Its successful operation depended upon thriving industries in the Peninsula and superior sea power, neither of which Spain possessed during the closing decades of the century.[23]

After the conquest of the Philippines by Spain (1565–1572), trade tended to spring up between those islands and the Pacific coast of Spanish America; but this, too, was rigidly controlled. In 1593 Mexican commerce with the Philippines was restricted to two vessels with a total capacity of six hundred tons, with Acapulco as the sole port of entry. No other jurisdiction bordering on the Pacific was permitted to enjoy a direct trade with them, nor could Peru, which was permitted to carry on a limited traffic with the Captaincy-general of Guatemala, bring home any goods from the Far East.[24]

The effect of this rigid system did not become fully evident for many years. Until near the close of the century large mercantile fleets left Seville for the Indies almost annually, bringing out a supply of goods which would appear to have been fairly adequate to meet colonial needs. Forty-two vessels sailed with the fleet in 1537; eighty-nine in 1548; sixty-five in 1555; seventy-one in 1585; seventy-two in 1592; but only thirty-two in 1601. The number of vessels returning was usually less than the number going out, although the pirates were never able to seize more than a few detached merchantmen.

The taxes levied by Spain upon the colonies and colonial trade do not appear to have been burdensome during the period now under review. They were certainly not heavy during the first forty years of the sixteenth century. Prior to 1543 no taxes were levied in Spain on the trade to the Indies. From the outset a duty of seven and one-

[22] A few vessels were allowed to stop in the ports of Venezuela and Guatemala, but the port of Buenos Aires was closed except to an occasional "register" ship.

[23] The destruction of the Spanish Armada by England in 1588 will be recalled.

[24] Nor was Central America allowed to engage in direct trade with the Philippines.

half per cent was collected on goods entering the American ports, but the proceeds were devoted to the expense of governing the colonies. The vast amount of precious metals and stones brought from the Indies would appear to have made burdensome taxes unnecessary. Of these the crown usually took only a fifth—a share far less than had been customary in the case of the mines of the mother country. Even this relatively small portion brought large returns. The remissions to the crown of gold and silver from the Indies amounted to an annual average of 313,000 pesos between 1511 and 1515. Between 1531 and 1535 the annual average was 432,000; between 1551 and 1555 it amounted to a total of four millions; and by the period 1591 to 1600 it had passed the ten million mark. After 1543, however, the customs duties were raised gradually until all goods going to the colonies paid fifteen per cent *ad valorem* and those coming from the colonies to Spain seventeen and one-half per cent. In addition, this commerce had to pay a convoy tax which varied from one to seven per cent during the century. The *alcabala,* or sales tax, long customary in Spain, was not introduced into the colonies until the last quarter of the century. This tax amounted to about two per cent *ad valorem* and was resented from the outset. Aside from these sources of income, the crown shared a portion of the tithes and other ecclesiastical revenues, enjoyed a monopoly of the sale of such necessary commodities as salt and quicksilver, and collected a small tribute from all male adult Indians not under the control of private encomenderos.

Prominent Viceroys of the Century

It is not possible nor desirable to note in this brief survey the numerous acts and decisions nor even the names of the many administrative and judicial officials of the Spanish colonies. The judges of the audiencias and the captains-general must be omitted entirely. Of the eighteen viceroys of the sixteenth century—nine in Mexico (1535-1603) and nine in Peru (1544-1604)—only seven will be discussed here.

Antonio de Mendoza.—Antonio de Mendoza, the first viceroy of New Spain (1535-1550), was an outstanding administrator. In a day when executive clemency was rare, he usually managed to refrain from acts of brutality. He calmed bickering strifes, quelled several rebellions, brought the petulant conquerors under control, promoted the building of churches and hospitals and schools, expanded the frontiers of the viceroyalty, began the codification of the colonial laws, and collected the revenues with a fair degree of honesty and efficiency. He failed, however, to enforce the "New Laws" of 1542 and to improve the pitiable condition of the Indians. Royal recognition of his talents was expressed by transferring him to Peru, which was then in a turbulent condition, and there, during the brief period of nine months before death ended his career (1552), he revealed equal administrative ability.

Martín Enríquez.—Another successful administrator was Martín Enríquez, the fourth viceroy of New Spain (1568–1580). He repelled an attack by the Englishman John Hawkins on Vera Cruz, strengthened the coast defenses, protected the northern frontier with great skill and ingenuity, made some modifications in the system of local government, and gave much attention to the church. Since he found many of his subordinates untrustworthy, it was necessary for him to attend to most of the duties of his office in person. His tasks were so exacting and complaints against his decisions so numerous that he came to consider public office in Mexico only a misfortune for an honest man. One of his unusual policies was that of employing creoles in positions of governmental responsibility. Convinced of their integrity and efficiency, he recommended that his policy be continued; but his advice was not consistently followed. Like Mendoza, he was transferred to Peru. By this time, however, he was an old man. He died two years later without having accomplished anything of significance in his new post.

The Velascos.—Perhaps the greatest colonial administrators of the century were the Velascos, father and son. Luis de Velasco served as viceroy of New Spain for fourteen years (1551–1564) and died a poor man at the end of the period. A relative of the royal family, he was industrious, patient, affable, and efficient. Because he carried out a royal order freeing thousands of Indian slaves, he has become known as "The Emancipator." Because he checked and even tried to eliminate other abuses of the Indians by the Spaniards, the native races and certain other inhabitants of the viceroyalty have often called him the Father of his Country. In addition, he was founder of the royal and pontifical university of Mexico, the initiator of a project to protect the capital from floods, and a zealous promoter of expansion. The son, whose name was also Luis de Velasco, was the eighth viceroy of New Spain (1590-1595). Since he had already spent much time in Mexico, he knew his kingdom thoroughly. Able, intelligent, industrious, and honest, he added luster to a name already famous by reopening woolen and cotton mills which Mendoza had initiated, beautifying the capital, strengthening the defenses of Vera Cruz, and successfully defending the northern frontiers. Rewarded by a transfer to Peru, he became one of the noted viceroys of that kingdom (1596-1604), protecting its coasts against foreign attack, ameliorating the condition of the Indians and Negroes, putting down revolts of the native races on the frontiers, repairing damages done by the earthquake of 1600, reducing corruption in administrative circles, and giving some attention to education. Moreover, he lived to serve another term (1607-1611) as viceroy of New Spain —a term noted mainly for the drainage of the lake district of the plateau, the suppression of a Negro revolt near Orizaba, explorations in the Pacific Ocean, and the sending of an embassy to Japan.

The Mendozas.—Hardly less famous than the Velascos, were Andrés Hurtado de Mendoza and his son García Hurtado de Mendoza. The former governed Peru from 1556 to 1561 and was noted for his effective and reasonably honest, though severe, rule. He put an end to the lawlessness which had afflicted the country for many years and set up an efficient and economical government. He failed, however, to win merited appreciation from Philip II and died of grief shortly before the expiration of his six-year term. His son García was somewhat more fortunate. After governing Peru for six years (1590-1596) he was permitted honorably to return to Spain for his health. His administration was noted for financial reforms, the promotion of higher education and internal improvements, and attempts to protect the natives from exploitation by the Spaniards.

Francisco de Toledo.—Perhaps the most outstanding of all the Peruvian viceroys of this century was Francisco de Toledo (1569-1581), sometimes called the Solon of Peru. With the view of Christianizing and civilizing the Indians, he compelled them to live in towns under the theoretical protection of corregidores. He also inaugurated other measures designed to improve the native races, but all his efforts in this sphere were largely frustrated. Institutions set up with benevolent intentions usually became means of oppression. In addition, he thoroughly organized the local governments, attempted to improve the administration of justice, put down Indian revolts, set up the Inquisition at Lima, encouraged the use of mercury in the silver mines, supported explorations in the southern portion of South America, developed the University of San Marcos, established peace, and promoted the prosperity of the viceroyalty. Although he was sometimes cruel, as when he executed one of the Incas, few of the viceroys of the entire colonial period surpassed him in prudence and zeal.

Such were the outstanding viceroys of the century. Of the eight [25] others who cannot be discussed here, it may be said that all were more or less inefficient and some were corrupt. Taking the group as a whole, however, and giving due consideration to the many difficulties they confronted—earthquakes, pestilence, floods, foreign enemies, bewildered and stupid Indians, greedy and ambitious conquerors and their sons, the backward state of communications, exacting monarchs demanding revenues, untrustworthy subordinates, obstreperous judges, inquisitorial visitors, querulous ecclesiastics, and the new and strange environment—one must admit that they deserve a rank equal, if not superior, to that of the colonial administrators of other nations. The Spanish colonies were not to see their like again until the middle of the eighteenth century, if even then.

The Founding of Brazil

During the sixteenth century Portugal's achievement in the New World by no means equaled that of Spain. Vessels under the Portuguese flag did only about 1,500 miles of pioneering along the southeastern coast of South America. Cabral had seen a small portion of the coast in the vicinity of the eighteenth parallel of south latitude and Gonçalo Coelho sailed with Vespucci (1501 or 1503) through twenty-one degrees of the same coast. Elsewhere, including the interior along the Plata and its tributaries, Portuguese vessels were

[25] Although, as has been noted, there were nine viceregal administrations in New Spain and nine in Peru during the century, three men served in both countries, so that only fifteen individuals were involved. Their salaries varied from seventy thousand to two hundred thousand dollars.

preceded by those of Spain. If Portugal was the pioneer along the African coast and in the Far East, Spain decidedly took the lead in America.

In fact, it was mainly because Portugal was facing east that the occupation of her portion of the New World was delayed. At first Brazil was used officially merely as a dumping ground for criminals and other undesirable subjects or as a way station to the East Indies. A few private expeditions were sent out by the nobility, but they came to grief, leaving, however, some of their shipwrecked victims to raise up a numerous progeny of *mamelucos* (mixed breeds) and facilitate later colonization.

Even at this late date the Portuguese monarch (John III, 1521–1557) showed a disposition to shift the financial responsibility of defending so vast an area. With this end in view, he divided the country between the parallel of twenty-eight twenty in the south and the Bay of São Marcos in the north into twelve or thirteen captaincies or hereditary fiefs.[26] Each of them extended along the coast an average distance of about fifty leagues and into the interior, theoretically, to the line of demarcation designated by the Treaty of Tordesillas (1494). To the *donatarios,* or grantees of these captaincies, were given almost sovereign rights. They had judicial, military, and civil jurisdiction over their fiefs, including the right to found towns and settlements, to raise armies, to distribute lands, enslave the Indians, and collect taxes. The Portuguese crown reserved to itself only the right to levy export duties, the monopoly of Brazil-wood, and a fifth of the precious stones and metals which might be discovered.

Long before there were thirteen English colonies in North America, there was thus at least a possibility of the establishment of twelve or thirteen Portuguese colonies in South America. But the *capitanias* did not prosper. Indian hostilities, difficulties of communication, indisposition to coöperate, and lack of resources soon proved fatal. Only ten of them were occupied by the owners or their agents, and only two of these—São Vicente and Pernambuco, with the towns of São Vicente, Santos, and Pernambuco—revealed any signs of prosperity at the end of fifteen years. Perhaps their chief

[26] See map on p. 74. Some changes were soon made in the original names of the captaincies. There were ultimately thirteen as shown on the map. See also map on p. 62.

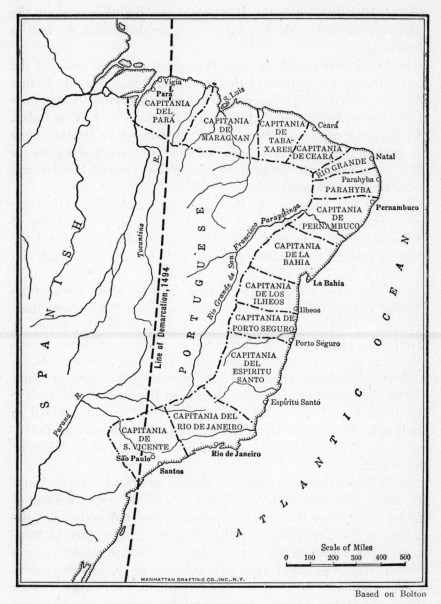

Based on Bolton

THE CAPITANIAS IN BRAZIL (SIXTEENTH CENTURY)

74

importance lies in the fact that ten of them furnished the geographical background of as many states on the coast of modern Brazil and seven of their names actually appear in the units of the present Brazilian federation.

Private enterprise having thus failed, and along with it the Portuguese monarch's attempt to evade the financial responsibility of defending his American possessions, John III decided to bring Brazil under the direct control of the crown. A governor-general, Thomé de Souza, clothed with full administrative and judicial powers, was sent out in 1549 with six Jesuits, among them Father Manoel Nobrega, to convert the Indians. The town of Bahia was founded immediately and made the capital; the French, who attempted to seize the region, were definitely expelled from the bay of Rio de Janeiro by the third governor-general, Mem de Sá; and several new towns sprang up: São Paulo (1554–1560), Rio de Janeiro (1567), Parahyba (1583), Natal (1597). Meanwhile, the Jesuits, who came to the colony in considerable numbers (there were one hundred and twenty before the close of the century), achieved some success in their work among the Indians within reach of the coastal settlements, although they were handicapped by the disposition of the Portuguese and mixed breeds to make slaves of the Indians.

Toward the end of the century Brazil began to reveal signs of prosperity. By 1574 nine of the captaincies had been occupied and some 17,000 Portuguese were living in sixteen villages. About a decade later the number of Portuguese was estimated at 25,000, and it may have reached 40,000 by the end of the century. Despite the heroic efforts of the Jesuits, the number of Christianized and settled Indians was probably not so large, but several thousand Negro slaves had been imported. The Portuguese had by this time introduced cows, oxen, hogs, goats, and a few sheep and horses, together with all the useful plants of the mother country that were found to be adapted to the soil and climate. The chief industry was sugar, although some cotton and olives were grown and the colonists continued to collect Brazil-wood and balsam. Gold and silver in quantity had yet to be discovered.

The government of Brazil was somewhat similar to that of the Spanish colonies, and strikingly so after 1580, when Portugal was taken over by Spain. At first, finances and revenues were under the supervision of an inspector of finances, whose powers were limited by a sort of ecclesiastical body (*Mesa da Consciencia e Ordens*) created in 1532. In 1591 the inspector of finances was abolished and a Council of Finance (*Conselho da Fazenda*) created to take over its functions. In 1604 a Council of the Indies (*Conselho da India*) was set up and given most of the prerogatives of the Spanish model. Over all the colony presided a governor-general residing at Bahia. The captaincies, which were now gradually reverting to the crown, were placed under royal officials called captains-general, captains, or governors, who were nominally, at least, subordinate to the governor-general, but they had the privilege of corresponding directly with the king. After the captains-donatary were deprived of their political functions in 1549 ordinary justice was administered by local judges appointed by the administrative heads of the captaincies. More important cases were decided by judges sent out from Lisbon. Municipalities, which were to fall more and more under the domination of the creole landed aristocracy, were governed by councils (*cameras* and *senados da camera*) which corresponded roughly to the cabildos or ayuntamientos of the Spanish régime. Thus a striking similarity will be observed, but it should be noted that indifference or neglect on the part of the home government often permitted a larger amount of real autonomy. "Portuguese colonization in America," writes a French scholar, "differs much from Spanish colonization and approaches rather the English system." [27]

[27] Leroy-Beaulieu, *Colonisation chez les peuples modernes* (1902), I, 52.

CHAPTER V

SPANISH AMERICA UNDER THE LATER HAPSBURGS
(1598-1700)

IN Spanish America, the seventeenth century saw far less achievement than the sixteenth had witnessed. Comparatively few towns were founded, trade and the output of the mines diminished, and the Indian population remained stationary or even decreased. Yet considerable progress was made. Thousands of roving Indians were Christianized and induced to settle in villages; Spanish immigrants came in at the rate of five to ten thousand a year; numerous Negro slaves were imported; agriculture and stock raising made some advance; new schools and universities were founded; and important new areas were occupied on the northern frontier of Mexico. If progress was comparatively slow, this fact may be explained by the numerous handicaps which were confronted.

HANDICAPS

No Constructive Colonial Policy.—Many of the impediments to progress may be traced to the mother country. The seventeenth century was an epoch of decline and poverty in Spain. Feeble and corrupt monarchs wasted state revenues on court favorites and European wars. Heavy taxes unwisely imposed upon a people already lacking a strong urge toward trade and industry prevented the expansion of Spanish manufactures and even ruined those already in existence. The rising prices caused by the influx of gold and silver from America were not sufficient to induce industrial development in Spain, and the mercantile theory tended to prevent industries from growing up in the colonies. Economic juntas and members of the Cortes demanded a reduction in the exportation of manufactured commodities to the Indies, but they said little about the encouragement of increased production at home. To the colonists was left the choice of paying extortionate prices for the limited supply

77

sent from Spain, purchasing from smugglers, setting up industries of their own, which they generally did, or going naked.

Moreover, the monarchs failed to formulate a constructive colonial policy and neglected sea power while emphasizing large armies and a dominant rôle in Europe. The frightful damage done the navy by the British in 1588 was never fully repaired. The control of the seas passed to the English, the French, and the Dutch; and these rivals established colonies and naval bases not only in the Caribbean but also on the northeastern coast of South America. The effect on the colonies was profound. Their scanty supply of much needed articles from the mother country was rendered uncertain;[1] their coasts were laid bare to the enemy; and the increased quantity of cheaper smuggled goods could hardly compensate for the corruption of political life which smuggling produced.

Increase of Taxation.—The colonists felt keenly the increase of taxation demanded by European wars, coastal and commercial defense, and royal extravagance. If it may be contended that taxes were not burdensome to the colonists during the sixteenth century, the same is not true of the subsequent period. Old rates were increased, new contributions were levied, and an increasing number of revenue officials swarmed into the colonies. Indian tributes were doubled and then multiplied by three before 1650; the alcabala (sales tax) was raised to four per cent in 1632 and to six in 1635; the convoy tax rose to twelve per cent or more; the royal monopoly was applied to an increasing number of commodities; nearly all offices were sold to the highest bidder; stamped paper for all legal transactions was forced into general use by 1640; half annates (namely, a contribution of half of the first year's salary) began to be collected from virtually all colonial officials in 1632; and a royal license was required for nearly every business enterprise. In addition to all these contributions, profligate kings confiscated gold and silver and demanded gifts in times of misfortune. The American colonies had given Philip III 432,342 pesos in 1624 and New Spain finished paying another donation of 1,100,000 in 1629; but 2,000,000 pesos were demanded in 1634 as that viceroyalty's share of three times as

---

[1] Between 1580 and 1700 there were forty-seven different years when no fleet cleared for the American colonies.

much which was needed for the erection of a new palace, and in 1661 Peru gave another 97,000 pesos despite the fact that the country had just been afflicted by a dreadful earthquake. Such were some of the handicaps thrust upon the colonies by the mother country.

Geographical Handicaps.—There were others of a geographical nature or arising from a combination of trade restrictions and physical environment. In this connection, the salient facts set forth in the first chapter of this work should be recalled. Fully a fourth of the vast area claimed by Spain consisted of tropical lowlands covered with jungle and infested by disease and various pests. Two large regions—one in northern Mexico and one on the borderland of Peru and Chile—had most of the characteristics of a desert. In addition, there were vast Andean mountain stretches too high and cold for comfortable human habitation. The bulk of the native population had long resided on the plateaus and in the upland plains of the interior. Attracted by the climate and the semicivilized Indians, the sixteenth-century Spaniards had settled down in these areas and established their rule. Few of them remained in the Greater Antilles or on the mainland coasts. In New Spain, in Central America, in New Granada, in Venezuela,[2] in Peru, in the Audiencia of Quito, in Chile, the Spaniards had spread out over the interior plateaus and valleys. Since there were few navigable rivers [3] furnishing a continuous line of communication to the sea, they found themselves confronted by transportation problems far more difficult than any known to subsequent English and French colonists in North America. Moreover, the peculiarities of physical environment meant that there would be few pleasant new areas for the seventeenth century Spaniards to occupy; swarms of pirates which followed the breakdown of Spanish sea power rendered the tropical coasts still more unpleasant for habitation; and rigid limitation of ports of entry im-

[2] In Venezuela there was a range of mountains not far from the coast.

[3] The basins of the Amazon, the Orinoco, and the Magdalena did not attract settlers from the mountain areas thickly populated by the native races. The settlers in the plateau regions of Venezuela and Colombia were far away from the sweltering banks of the Orinoco. It was almost three thousand miles from the centers of Spanish settlement in Peru to the mouth of the Amazon, and the Spaniards of the plateau of Cundinamarca (New Granada) had nearly a hundred miles between them and the Magdalena—which was not really well adapted to navigation—and yet another five hundred miles of this river before they emerged at Cartagena or Barranquilla.

peded the development of the Plata basin. Add to all this occasional volcanic eruptions and frequent earthquakes [4] which destroyed life and property and ruined fertile upland valleys, and you will begin to see the magnitude of the handicap of physical environment. Owing to the restriction of emigration to orthodox Spaniards, the number of new settlers which annually arrived was small, but it may be doubted whether a larger influx would have brought great prosperity; for available land was somewhat limited, not only by geographical decree and by hostile Indians on the frontier—another handicap to be reckoned with—but also by a land policy which permitted the gradual accumulation of large estates in the hands of the clergy and the descendants of the early settlers.

Activities of Spain's Rivals.—Spain had been vexed by pirates and smugglers during much of the sixteenth century, but they became a far greater pest, from the Spanish viewpoint, during the next hundred years. The pirates shifted their base to the islands of the Caribbean, and the smugglers plied their trade both in the Peninsula and in the colonial ports.

The seventeenth century was a time of almost universal contraband traffic with the Spanish colonies in America. It has already been noted that Spain held to the monopolistic ideal in the matter of colonial trade. In order to traffic with South America, a merchant had to be a native of Spain or the son of a Catholic foreigner who had maintained his domicile in that country for twenty years. All others were forbidden to trade with the colonies through Spain or directly, on their own account or through the agency of a Spaniard or a Spanish company; and there were heavy penalties for the infraction of the rule. Yet it was often violated at both ends of the line. Foreigners loaded goods from their vessels into the *flotas* (fleets) at Cádiz or San Lúcar without registration at the Casa and received their value in gold and silver at the same points upon the return of the fleets. They also eluded the law by trading under the name of Seville merchants who were hardly more than factors of a foreign commercial house. As the difficulty of enforcing the law became more patent, the Spanish government sought compensation by the imposition of fines upon the interlopers. These sometimes amounted

---

[4] Most of the important towns of Spanish America were disturbed by earthquakes, many of them several times, during the colonial period.

to as much as 200,000 pesos in a single year. "Under the later Hapsburgs, with the increasing demands of the colonies on the one hand,
and the utter ruin of Spanish industry on the other, the dependence
of the Seville export commerce upon foreign manufactures was
complete. They supplied five-sixths of the cargoes of the outbound
fleet."

"The most serious and widespread development of contraband
trade, however, was in merchandise introduced into the colonies
directly from foreign markets. Portuguese, French, Dutch, and other
interlopers smuggled their cargoes into the West Indies, through the
closed port of Buenos Aires, or even to the Pacific shores of Spanish
America. The illicit trader was eagerly welcomed by the colonists,
for he supplied their needs at reasonable prices, gave them an opportunity of enriching themselves and of adding to the comforts and
luxuries of living. Two circumstances combined to make this commerce easy. One was the great length of sparsely settled coast on
both the Atlantic and the Pacific side of the continent, effective surveillance over which was beyond the resources of any nation in that
era. The other was the venality of the Spanish governors in the ports
themselves. Apparently they often tolerated or encouraged the
traffic, on the plea that the necessities of the colonists demanded it.
They not only accepted bribes, but engaged in the buying and selling of contraband articles." [5]

Direct smuggling had begun early. Sixteenth century corsairs and
sea dogs had engaged in it as well as in piracy. In the seventeenth
century, however, it greatly increased. The Portuguese, taking advantage of their annexation to the Spanish empire, took up their
residence in the Spanish colonies and became receivers of smuggled
goods. Near the beginning of the seventeenth century they are said
to have sent out from Portugal about 200 vessels annually laden with
cargoes intended largely for the Pacific provinces of Spanish America. The commodities were introduced by way of the Río de la Plata or
turned over to Spanish or Portuguese agents in Brazil. In 1636 Portuguese Jews controlled the retail trade of Lima. English, French, and
Dutch, having occupied strongholds in the American tropics, sent

[5] This and the previous quotation are from Haring, *Trade and Navigation between Spain
and the Indies,* pp. 113, 115.

out goods to most of the ports of the Caribbean.[6] The feeble Spanish government tried in vain to drive out the settlers and suppress the traffic. Colonial officials were removed for connivance, and yet the trade continued. The captain of the interloping vessel, standing off near a port, sent the Spanish governor a polite note and an attractive gift, and informed him that he had sprung a leak or lost a mast. The ship was allowed to come in with its most conspicuous ports sealed. Others were found unsealed, however, and the goods were taken out at night, products of the country being substituted for them. In a day or two the ship sailed away with its new cargo. Smaller vessels pushed up the jungle rivers and creeks and notified the inhabitants of their location by firing a cannon. At nightfall the Spanish Americans swarmed down to the vessel in canoes laden with native commodities. In a few days men and their wives were seen with some of the luxuries of northern Europe. The galleons which came out in the fleet of 1662, after an interruption of two years, found the American markets so glutted with contraband wares that they could dispose of only a part of their cargoes.

A multitude of restrictions, a jealous monopoly, a flood of contraband goods—such is the history of Spanish colonial commerce in the seventeenth century. The crown lost most of its treasures, the Seville merchants lost their monopoly, and the precious metals and trade of Spanish America passed largely into the hands of the subjects of rival powers.

The colonies profited economically, though perhaps not morally, from the trend of the times in matters of commerce, but this cannot be said of another development which took place. Some of these smugglers were buccaneers when occasion presented. Many other adventurers of the Caribbean specialized in buccaneering, and they were sometimes supported by the fleets of their mother countries. Three times during the century the Spanish mercantile flota on its way from the Indies was seized and destroyed; many detached vessels were taken; and the galleons sailed at irregular intervals. But this is not the worst of the story. So far as the colonies were concerned, indeed, it was comparatively of minor importance. The economic and naval decline of Spain had a more injurious repercus-

---

[6] Richard Pares has observed that Spain's enemies never gave her a "fair chance to show how she could have settled and organized the whole continent of America."

sion. During the seventeenth century the colonies were left in a state "of military and naval defenselessness, forts without artillery, nominal companies of infantry without soldiers, and the inhabitants more ready to take to the hills and woods than to oppose any resistance to the invader." [7] It was about 1650 that the raids of the buccaneers became most destructive. Hardly a town in the Caribbean and the Gulf regions escaped, and both before and after this date piratical or semipiratical expeditions harried the coasts of the Pacific. Between 1655 and 1671 they plundered eighteen cities, four towns, and some thirty-five villages of the Caribbean and the Gulf. Between 1665 and 1685 the Spaniards and Spanish Americans suffered losses at the hands of the buccaneers estimated at 60,000,000 crowns, not counting damages from the destruction of ships. Near the end of the century the pirates lost their power to distinguish between Spanish towns and treasure and the towns and treasure of other nations. This proved to be a fatal error. The navies of all the European powers joined in their suppression, and they soon passed from the scene.

COLONIAL EXPANSION; CONQUISTADORES OF THE CROSS

The seventeenth century can hardy be called an era of expansion in Spanish America. The bulk of the Spanish population, about 200,000 at the beginning of the century and probably still considerably less than a million at its close, preferred to remain in the old centers, as did also the mestizos, the only other element capable of constructive enterprise. The mother country, too feeble and bankrupt to support any vigorous advances, could not be aroused to effective effort even by the threat of European encroachments. Only the mendicant and Jesuit missionaries, who busied themselves on every frontier and bore the brunt of nearly every colonization enterprise, revealed something of the old energy. The tribes encountered everywhere after the semicivilized Indians of New Spain, Guatemala, Peru, and New Granada had been reduced to virtual serfdom, were "hostile, had few crops, were unused to labor, had no fixed villages, would not stand still to be exploited, and were hardly worth

[7] So writes Haring; but the point should not be pressed too far. The colonists often resisted the invaders and thus developed a spirit of unity which contributed to the independence impulse of a later era.

the candle. Colonists were no longer so eager for encomiendas, and were willing to escape the obligation to protect and civilize the wild tribes, which were as uncomfortable burdens, sometimes, as cub tigers in a sack. Moreover, the sovereigns, with increasing emphasis, forbade the old-time abuses of exploitation, but as strongly as before adhered to the ideal of conversion and civilization. Here, then, was a larger opening for the missionary, and to him was entrusted, or upon him was thrust, consciously or unconsciously, not only the old work of conversion, but a larger and larger element of responsibility and control." [8] In fact, before 1600 the mission was rapidly becoming Spain's most important frontier institution.

More than a century ago Alexander Humboldt made the following penetrating remarks regarding frontier advance in Spanish America:

"The whites advance slowly. The religious orders have founded their establishments between the domain of the colonists and the territory of the free Indians. The Missions may be considered as intermediary states. . . . As the missionaries advance toward the forests, and gain on the natives, the white colonists in their turn seek to invade . . . the territory of the Missions. In this protracted struggle, the secular arm continually tends to withdraw the reduced Indian from the monastic hierarchy, and the missionaries are gradually superseded by vicars [secular priests]. The whites, and the castes of mixed blood . . . establish themselves among the Indians. The Missions become Spanish villages, and the natives lose even the remembrance of their natural language. Such is the progress of civilization . . . ; a slow progress, retarded by the passions of man, but nevertheless sure and steady." [9]

The Spanish monarch consciously employed the missionary as an agent of expansion and frontier defense. He usually not only bore the expense of the padre's initial equipment and transportation to his field of service, but also paid him a meager annual stipend, shared the cost of erecting mission buildings, and furnished a small squad of soldiers for protection against hostile uprisings. Hundreds of missionaries were on the royal pay roll during the century, and they

[8] Bolton, "The Mission as a Frontier Institution . . ." in American Historical Review, XXIII (Oct., 1917), 45.
[9] Travels (Bohn ed.), I, 297.

rendered valiant service in more than a dozen important areas, besides continuing work already begun in New Mexico and Florida. According to the letter of the law they were the front column of two advancing lines of Spanish civilization, each of which was supposed to move forward every ten years. But the plan did not work out. A decade proved insufficient to prepare the way for the second line; the new environment often did not allure the Spaniards and mestizos, and the missionaries were loath to part with their wards. Comparatively few Spanish settlements followed the padres during the century and, even today, in some sections, the civilian column has not yet reached the frontier blazed by their heroic efforts.

In New Spain the missionaries were the main agency in carrying Spanish culture forward in Sinaloa, Sonora, Chihuahua, and Coahuila; but attempts to occupy Lower California and Texas failed. In the Captaincy-general of Guatemala the friars descended from the pleasant uplands and labored among the wilder tribes of the littoral, where they suffered martyrdom almost as often as they achieved success. It was, to use the words of one of their number, as if they had entered the "gates of hell from within which there was no redemption." In the Audiencia of Panama the story was virtually the same, while on the frontiers of New Granada their efforts were almost as futile. They advanced into the sweltering valley of the Atrato, where they made a number of reductions; and, descending eastward from Bogotá, they pursued their work among the Indians of the plains of Casanare and the jungle valleys of the Meta and the Orinoco, only to fall back near the end of the century, defeated by the terrific raids of the Caribs. From Peru and the Presidency of Quito the padres crossed over the Andes and entered the tropical plains and forests of the vast region of Mainas (an area lying between the fourth and fifth parallels in the basin of the upper Amazon) or turned far toward the south and ministered to the Moxos, the Chiquitos, and the tribes of the Gran Chaco. In the former region they made very considerable progress; among the latter, however, their efforts were less availing. The Araucanians, despite the heroic labors and sacrifices of the missionaries, remained beyond the reach of their redemptive powers. From Cumaná, Caracas, and Barcelona (all in Venezuela) the padres proceeded slowly southward toward the vast interior llanos or entered the steaming valley of the lower Orinoco, in order to hold Spanish Guiana against the intrusions of the Dutch, French, and English. In central Venezuela and the plains they made many converts, but success in the lower Orinoco region awaited a coming epoch. In the area of La Plata, near the beginning of the century, they entered the fertile Paraná-Uruguay mesopotamian basin, where the Jesuits were destined to win undying renown.

Such was the work of the far-flung line of the Conquistadores of the Cross. Almost everywhere they confronted appalling obstacles—depressing heat, drought, famine, flood, insect and reptile pests, treacherous, ignorant, or hostile Indians, roving encomenderos looking for natives to exploit, Portuguese raiders in search of slaves. The mission frontier advanced, receded, advanced, and sometimes receded again. The number of reductions which the missionaries established and of neophytes which they won probably no one save the recording angel will ever know; but by dint of almost superhuman patience and energy, and by a zeal which ran to meet martyrdom, they made a good beginning. For America they ushered in the great missionary age.

From the viewpoint of the Spanish monarchy, however, their work, when completed, was but half of the process. They might, and did—for this was their duty—partially Christianize the natives, teaching them to say prayers, repeat psalms, produce sacred music on instruments of their own make, march in religious processions, enact religious dramas, keep faith with one wife, and observe the Ten Commandments. They might, and did—this was their persistent policy—partially civilize the Indians as well, instructing them in rudimentary letters, industry, art—particularly sacred art—agriculture, stock raising, and the application of simple medicinal remedies. But this, after all, was only in preparation for the advancing civilian phalanx. The royal plan embraced the absorption of the natives into the body politic and the creation of a new race. In this respect Spain was the most original of all colonizing powers.

During the seventeenth century the second phase of the process, as already noted, lagged behind. In many areas the Spanish and mestizo elements approached the missions, if at all, not to settle down, but to raid, plunder, and capture the neophytes for plantations, mines, and industries back home. They established several

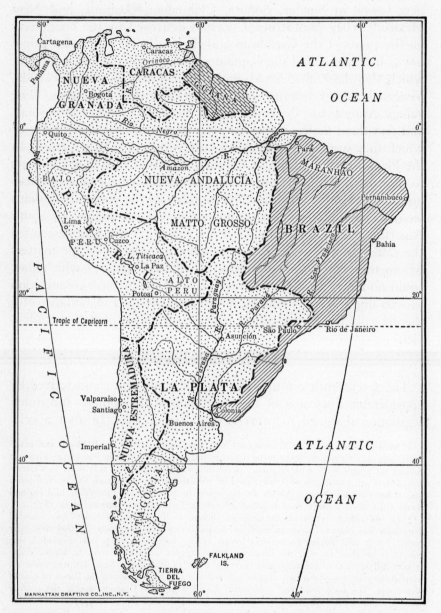

POLITICAL DIVISIONS OF SOUTH AMERICA IN THE SEVENTEENTH CENTURY

87

new towns in Sinaloa, Sonora, Chihuahua, Coahuila, and New Mexico.[10] They reconstructed pueblos destroyed by the buccaneers on the coasts of the Caribbean and the Gulf. They founded a few towns in Panama and the Captaincy-general of Guatemala, most of which they later abandoned, and several towns in New Granada, Venezuela,[11] and eastern Peru.[12] But in Chile they lost ground. The valiant Araucanians destroyed five of their settlements in the south and sent them fleeing across the river Biobio, on the north bank of which they were able to establish only two to take their place.[13] In the Plata area the pueblo of Catamarca (founded in 1680) appears to have been about the only new Spanish settlement of any consequence. Moreover, a considerable number of the sedentary Indians seem to have escaped to the mountains and the jungle. In South America, at least, many natives fled across the Andes and descended the eastern slopes to the forests beyond, in order to escape masters whom they hated and oppressive "civilizing" agencies which they could no longer bear. The second phase of the Spanish colonization process might have developed more rapidly if the functionaries of a theoretically benevolent policy had softened its exploitative tendencies.

Labor and Politics

The seventeenth century, like the sixteenth, was characterized by considerable discussion of the oppression of the Indians and much legislation designed to prevent their exploitation. In 1601 a cele-

[10] By 1700 there were in Sinaloa only 600 families of pure Spanish blood, but many more half-caste Christians, there being 1,200 Spaniards and mestizos in San Felipe alone. In Sonora the people of Spanish or mixed blood numbered about 500 at that time. In Chihuahua, Parral was founded in 1631–1632, and by 1680 the civilian population had reached Janos and Casas Grandes. After a bloody Pueblo revolt in New Mexico (1680 ff.), El Paso and Santa Cruz de la Cañada were founded. Monclova, Coahuila, was refounded in 1674.

[11] In 1637, after conquering the bellicose Indians of the region, Juan de Urpín founded Barcelona and Nueva Tarragona near the northeast coast of Venezuela. In the same year Santo Tomé, after having been burnt by Sir Walter Raleigh in 1619 and refounded, was moved to another site near the junction of the Orinoco and the Caroni. In Bolívar's day it was still farther up the river and bore the name of Angostura. Several towns grew up around the missions established along the friars' line of advance toward the llanos of central Venezuela. The most important settlements founded in New Granada during the century were Quibdó, in the Atrato valley, Barranquilla (1629) and Medellín (1675), which became a thriving mining center, and Socorro (1681).

[12] The mining town of Oruro, northeast of Potosí, was erected in 1604; and the celebrated silver mines of Cerro de Pasco began to be worked about 1630.

[13] The new settlements were Rere and Talca, both founded in 1695.

brated *cédula* (decree) dealing with personal service was promulgated. Among other things, it provided that the natives should no
longer be distributed for forced labor in the fields, stock ranches,
and textile factories, or in the sugar mills, building trades, and pearl-
fisheries, or in the olive and grape orchards, or among those engaged in collecting anil and coca leaves, or in domestic service, or
in the work of draining the mines, or even in the new mines themselves. The cédula also attempted to prevent the merchants from
forcing the natives to carry burdens along the trade routes and to
substitute voluntary or Negro slave labor for the forced service of
the Indians in the old mines; and it likewise sought to force the
encomenderos to accept a fixed tribute in money or commodities in
lieu of the personal service which they had so long demanded of
their Indians.

This cédula, like the famous New Laws of 1542, would have developed in Spanish America a system of free labor if its provisions
had been carried out. But, as in the former case, this proved to be
impossible. Distance and powerful vested interests defeated the
whole program. The regulations either were not put into operation
or were evaded. Another cédula of 1609 met a similar fate. Yet the
interest of the monarchy in the status of the Indians continued to
manifest itself in numerous benevolent laws. The heavy volumes of
Solórzano Pereira give much space to the legal position of the Indian and more than a fourth of the famous compilation of 1680—
Recopilación de las Leyes de las Indias—is devoted to the laws which
attempt to ameliorate the condition of the native race.

It is impossible to determine how much the condition of the Indians improved, if at all, during the century. It is certain that the
number of encomiendas decreased, but this reform was probably
largely nullified by the growing exploitation of the clergy and the
royal officials (corregidores and alcaldes mayores) and the increase
in the rate of the royal tribute. The impressed labor of the natives
seems to have been indispensable to the development of Spain's
colonies in the New World. The lower class of Spaniards would not
turn their hands to manual labor, and the Indians were probably
too lazy to apply themselves voluntarily to the steady performance
of tasks necessary to the progress and prosperity of the Spanish
establishments. In most cases the Indians who were forced to work

had wages and hours provided by law. The wages varied from ten to twenty cents per day, and the hours usually lasted from sun to sun, with several holidays and a minimum of clothing and food. Doubtless these regulations were often violated, but competent scholars have contended that the condition of the Indians of Spanish America was probably not much worse than that of the contempory lower classes of Europe.

The political life of the century was characterized by much friction and quarreling and occasional revolts. Not only were there conflicts of jurisdiction between the executive officials—viceroys and captains-general—and the audiencias, but there were conflicts between the civil and ecclesiastical functionaries, between the secular and the regular clergy, and even between the various orders of the regulars themselves. Several Indian revolts and Negro uprisings occurred, all of which were ruthlessly suppressed; twice during the century turbulent mobs burned the royal palace of the viceroy in Mexico City; and criminals sometimes ran riot in the leading towns and cities of all the colonies.

Owing to the venality of the judges and the distance from the tribunals of last resort, the administration of justice was defective and slow. Decisions upon important cases, which had to be submitted to the Council of the Indies, required months and even years. The jurisdictions of the audiencias were very extensive, and those in pursuit of justice were often required to make long and expensive journeys. For southern South America a partial remedy was provided by the establishment of an audiencia in Santiago in 1609 and another in Buenos Aires in 1661, although the latter was later discontinued.

During the century there were some fourteen viceregal administrations in Peru and more than twenty in New Spain. The viceroys were hardly as distinguished as their predecessors of the sixteenth century. Some were honest and reasonably efficient; many were not notoriously corrupt or incompetent; at least five, including Luis Velasco II (already mentioned), were chief executives both of New Spain and of Peru. Without oppressing their subjects, none of them, no matter how able, could have governed to the satisfaction of monarchs so clamorous for revenues, for, in addition to most of the difficulties confronted by their predecessors, the viceroys of the seventeenth century suffered the further handicap of having to serve extravagant and unworthy sovereigns. On the whole, it must be admitted that the colonies were badly governed.

INTELLECTUAL LIFE

The seventeenth century was marked in England and northern Europe by the beginning of the age of science; but little of the scientific spirit reached distant Spanish America. As Humboldt has remarked, contact with the magnificent natural phenomena and the strange native races of a new world might have resulted in a great advance of knowledge, had not the free range of the intellect been stifled by superstition and fanaticism. During the sixteenth century, as has been noted, Spaniards who had been ruthless in the destruction of native culture nevertheless produced many unsystematic works on geography, biology, zoölogy, anthropology, and Indian languages, but their value for the historian and the scientist was greatly diminished by the interjection of many gross superstitions. Since Spaniards of the seventeenth century, whether in Spain or in America, were far less literary, equally fanatic, and perhaps more superstitious, their writings on the New World were no better and sometimes even worse than those of their predecessors. It is impossible to determine how many of the works were Spanish and how many Spanish-American, for most of the writers spent about as much time in the mother country as in the colonies. Whatever their prevailing residence, however, their preoccupations continued to be war, natural phenomena, theology, language, and government, with a strong tendency, often, to express themselves in dull and tedious Gongoresque poetry. Difficulties of printing limited the number of their productions, while a strict censorship and the Inquisition confined their contents to the tenets of a rigid dogma. Five new universities were founded during the century, but they, as well as their predecessors, continued to devote themselves largely to canon law, scholastic philosophy, theology, and letters. Little attention was given to mathematics or medicine.

Few minds of Spanish America were able to rise above the dark clouds of superstition. Comets and eclipses portended calamities soon to be visited upon the people by an enraged deity. Thunderstorms, volcanoes, and earthquakes sent the people fleeing in terror to the churches in order to ask forgiveness for their sins while the massive walls tumbled down upon them and their abandoned homes crumbled in upon unremoved furnishings. If they escaped with their lives, it was only through the intervention of some saint or the Virgin. For them life was filled with miracles and the punishments of an angry God. Yet many of them, and not a few churchmen among the number, persisted in a course of morality low even for the age in which they lived.

But a narrow provincialism should not be permitted to lend asperity to the student's judgment. During the same century Massachusetts divines consumed much ink on theology, attributed toothache to sins of the teeth, saw in calamities the vengeance of an offended God, gave the Indian little or no place in the Divine Plan, filled their histories with almost as many miracles as facts, and hanged witches or burned them at the stake.

Moreover, the drab depressiveness of Spanish-American life was relieved by magnificent homes, churches, public buildings, plazas, and patios, which displayed a highly developed artistic taste along with considerable architectural skill. It was also modified by the charming hospitality of the upper classes, the warm sympathy of some writers for the oppressed Indians, the wit and banter of poets, and the gorgeous display of festival and drama. Occasionally there appears a scientist who discovers the medicinal properties of a new herb or bark,[14] or, with telescope and quadrant, stands observing an eclipse of the sun which had caused the superstitious populace to flee in dread and terror; and who, even while dying, wills his body to physicians in the hope that its dissection may throw new light upon the ills that afflict his fellow men.[15]

A restricted "literary activity . . . cultivated by an infinitesimally small and select group of intellectuals, standing like a tiny edifice upon a vast foundation composed of an ignorant and hopeless native population" [16]—such was the situation in seventeenth century Mex-

[14] The properties of quinine, which is made from chinchona bark, were discovered by the Spaniards about 1638, although the Indians had long known some of its virtues.

[15] Don Carlos Sigüenza y Góngora.

[16] Irving A. Leonard, *Góngora,* p. 183. At the opening of this century the greatest poet of colonial Chile wrote some works of real merit and before its end a real poetic genius saw the light in Mexico. The name of the Chilean was Pedro de Oña; the genius of New

ico. It was no better in Peru and New Granada, and probably worse elsewhere. Upon such a scene dawned the eighteenth century, which was destined to witness important reforms and bring new currents of dynamic thought.

Spain was Juana Inés de Santa Cruz, a woman whose collected works fill three volumes. One of the best poems of the century was written by Father Matías de Bocanegra. A few histories which possessed some merit also appeared, and Juan de Solórzano Pereira's valuable work on law and government in the Spanish Colonies (*Política indiana*) was published shortly before the middle of the century.

CHAPTER VI

SPANISH AMERICA UNDER THE BOURBONS

In 1701 Philip V, a French Bourbon prince, ascended the throne of Spain. It was a very significant event. For the European states it constituted a serious threat to the balance of power. For Spain it meant new ideas, new methods of government, new stimuli for agriculture, industry, and learning—in a word, new life. For Spanish America it was the prelude to important readjustments and reforms.

At the death of Charles II (1700), the last of the Hapsburgs, Spain was only a "little less cadaverous than its defunct master." Without army, navy, or funds, with disordered administration and respect for authority gone, without prestige or power, the weak and exanimate kingdom "lay before Europe . . . awaiting partition as another Poland of another day." Into this crisis came the Bourbons and a "new exposure to European civilization." Little wonder that pious Spanish writers, unwilling to be Gallicized though they were, saw in the event something akin to the interposition of Providence.

Yet, from a viewpoint strictly Spanish, the coming of the Bourbons was not an unmixed blessing. Their dynasty produced a Charles IV and a Ferdinand VII as well as a Charles III and a Ferdinand VI; their inevitable involvement in European wars drained away the wealth and energy of a reviving nation; and through open doors from France eventually came to metropolis and empire more than the Bourbons were willing to admit: new convictions of the rights and dignity of common men, new notions regarding the basis of political power, and a radicalism that dealt old systems a shocking blow. When, after more than a century, Ferdinand VII passed from the scene, he left a Spain bleeding and almost empireless—and decadent once more.

Commercial Reforms

Spanish America felt the reforming spirit of the Bourbons first in

the field of commerce. In 1701 the French were conceded the privilege of introducing annually a number of slaves and of putting in
at the colonial ports in order to purchase supplies. In 1713 this concession, in somewhat expanded form, was transferred to England.
At the same time, the growing industries of Spain were furnishing
a more bountiful supply of commodities, and the Seville merchants
were deprived of their monopoly. In 1718 the Casa de Contratación
was removed to Cádiz. In 1728 the Guipúzcoa Company was organized for the purpose of engaging in American trade. The establishment of other companies soon followed: that of Galicia in 1734 and
that of Barcelona in 1755. The fleet system was abolished in 1748.
In 1765 nine different Spanish ports were allowed to trade with
Cuba, Santo Domingo, Porto Rico, Margarita, and Trinidad, a privilege soon afterwards extended to Campeche, Yucatán, and Louisiana (ceded to Spain by France in 1763). About the same time, direct
exchange of produce was permitted between several American colonies. In 1778 thirteen other ports of Spain and its adjacent islands
were granted the privilege of trading with twenty-four additional
ports—including Buenos Aires, Montevideo, Valparaiso, and Guayaquil—in Spanish America. In 1797, while Spain was involved in the
Napoleonic wars, neutral vessels were permitted to engage in the
carrying trade with the colonies. Already, in 1764, monthly and bi-
monthly mail packets had been established between Spain and the
oversea possessions. In all these ways the colonies were stimulated
to new enterprise and brought in to contact with European thought.

If the mercantile ideas of the Bourbons had permitted the encouragement of manufacturing, if their financial necessities had allowed
a reduction of taxes, a permanent economic revival might have
resulted. As it was, the output of the mines, stimulated by a decrease
in the percentage demanded by the king, increased enormously,
agriculture improved, and trade grew by leaps and bounds. Shortly
before 1800 the annual production of the mines appears to have
been about thirty-nine million pesos. Carlos Calvo estimates that the
total trade between colonies and mother country increased from
171,900,000 francs in 1753 to 430,100,000 in 1784 and 638,500,000 in
1800.[1]

[1] Apparently Calvo made some allowance for contraband in the figures for importations
into the colonies.

The chief exports of the colonies to the mother country may be ascertained by a statement for the year 1747. They were, in pesos: gold, 4,000,000; silver, 30,000,000; precious stones, 600,000; cochineal, 1,200,000; hides, 340,000; wood, 60,000; vicuña wool, 50,000; quinine, 40,000; sugar, indigo, tobacco, and other products, 2,000,000; total, 38,290,000 pesos. Among the commodities imported by the colonies were: gold and silver ware, stockings and gloves, textiles and linens, thread, hats and all kinds of articles of felt, furs, drugs, paints, perfumes, candles, haberdashery, toys and trinkets, playing cards, articles of copper, bronze, and iron, furniture, harness, paper, bottles and other glassware, rope and twine, canvas, tar, pitch, tackle, rigging, domestic utensils, and certain kinds of food. Many of these articles had come through Spain from northern Europe, but Spanish industries were furnishing an increasing proportion.

ADMINISTRATIVE REFORMS; EXPULSION OF THE JESUITS

The Bourbon era was also characterized by important administrative readjustments and reforms. Among them, the most important were the widespread enlistment of colonial militia for colonial defense, the final abolition of the encomiendas, the introduction of the intendant system, and the expulsion of the Jesuits.

The need for reform was imperative. Not only did the direct smuggling of the previous century persist, aided by the privileges granted France and England, but rival powers threatened to conquer some of the mainland colonies. Not only did higher officials engage in graft and peculation, but they also revealed a tendency to defeat the royal will by their formula of *"obedezco pero no cumplo"* ("I obey but do not execute"). At the same time, alcaldes mayores, corregidores, and priests exploited and oppressed the native races until numerous uprisings occurred; creoles and mestizos, seeking to avoid odious taxes, or to gain control of the mission Indians, or to secure a larger participation in the local government, defied the royal authorities; and the Jesuits of Paraguay (1754) led their Indians in revolt against an unjust treaty. Moreover, the whole situation was rendered more acute by constant rivalry between the civil authorities and the religious leaders, between the regular and the secular clergy, and even among the civil authorities themselves.

Crying injustices were perpetrated upon the native races. From numerous reports of conscientious observers came many complaints which leave no doubt of the existence of shameful exploitation. It was perhaps worst in Peru, where corregidores and priests combined to terrorize the Indians and deprive them of lands, wages, women and children, personal freedom—everything which men are supposed to esteem. But the evil also existed in Mexico, where the alcaldes mayores and sometimes the priests victimized the Indians, as well as in all of the important areas where the natives still survived. It would be an error to assume that such evils were universal, for this would be analogous to generalizing too broadly upon the abuses portrayed in *Uncle Tom's Cabin*. There were many conscientious Spaniards, else we should not have had all these reports. Yet there is no doubt that the evils were widespread.

Such were the conditions which demanded reform. The Bourbons began by creating new administrative and judicial jurisdictions. The Viceroyalty of New Granada was established in 1717, abolished in 1723, and reëstablished in 1739. The Viceroyalty of Río de la Plata was created in 1776, largely for the purpose of holding the frontier against the Portuguese. In 1731 the provinces of Venezuela were erected into a captaincy-general, which in 1777 was freed from dependence upon New Granada. Cuba became a captaincy-general during the same year; and soon afterwards the Captaincy-general of Guatemala was made more independent of the Viceroyalty of New Spain. The Audiencia of Panama, no longer so necessary now that the major portion of South American commerce had ceased to pass across the Isthmus, was abolished in 1751, and this area was made to depend upon the tribunal at Bogotá. In 1783 the Audiencia of Buenos Aires, which had been discontinued in 1671, was reëstablished. Three years later Caracas became the seat of another; and in 1789 one was created at Cuzco. Thus Spanish America was now divided into four viceroyalties: New Spain, New Granada, Peru, and Río de la Plata; four captaincies-general: Cuba, Guatemala, Chile, and Venezuela; and twelve audiencias: Santo Domingo, Mexico, Guadalajara, Guatemala, New Granada, Caracas, Cuzco, Quito, Peru, Charcas, Chile, and Buenos Aires. Already, in these major administrative units, one may observe the geographical setting of nineteenth century republics.

But this reorganization was by no means the most important of the Bourbon administrative reforms. Charles III, the ablest of the Bourbons, sent out visitadores to America in order to check up on the whole colonial system, and their visitations proved to be the preliminary step in the establishment of a new group of officials with numerous and weighty functions. These new officials, the intendants, were the most significant of all Bourbon innovations in the colonies. One of them was introduced into Cuba in 1765, and in less than twenty-five years they were established in all Spanish America save New Granada. There were twelve in Mexico, eight in Río de la Plata, eight in Peru, four in Guatemala, two in Chile, and one in Venezuela. Their salaries were comparatively high, varying from 6,000 to 12,000 pesos; and although they were sometimes appointed by the chief executive officials of the colonies, more often they were chosen by the king, with whom they had always the privilege of corresponding directly.

The functions of the intendants varied somewhat in different areas. In general they were classified under four heads corresponding to the four phases or departments of government of the Spanish colonial system, namely, justice, general administration (*policía*), finance, and war; but in considering their manifold duties it is necessary to bear in mind the confusion of powers which characterized Spanish government. Without going into tedious detail, it may be stated that they were directed to watch over local administrations, particularly in matters of justice, protecting the Indians from their oppressors and serving as judges of first instance in cases involving the assessment of taxes and the collection of revenue; to guard against graft and smuggling; to promote internal improvements of all kinds, rural and urban; to encourage agriculture and other industries not competing with those in Spain; to look after the supply and equipment of the army in their jurisdiction; and to make detailed reports upon the population and wealth of the areas under their charge. In fact their numerous powers constituted a limitation upon all authorities from the viceroy to the town councils and from the bishop to the parish priests. With their installment, governors, alcaldes mayores, and corregidores were for the most part eliminated, and the intendants also exercised the right of royal patronage in the regions entrusted to them. With reference to their qualifications, an order of 1800 remarked: "The capable fulfillment of these . . . very important duties . . . demands that they show certain elevated talents, and exquisite instruction, a consummate prudence, and inflexible probity; it demands, moreover, that, imbued with the spirit which cannot fail to inculcate love of king and country, they find nothing delightful if not sobriety and work at all hours and on all occasions; it asks that they be economical of their time, which they must regard as precious, since at almost every instant there may be furnished them an opportunity to do some good; it asks that they never indulge themselves in frivolous occupations nor know other hours of distraction than those of sleep; and it asks that they show a will just, firm, and constant in order not to be deterred by any difficulties, in order to resist all . . . artful tricks. . . ." [2]

It is difficult to measure the results of the Bourbon administrative reforms. The abuses and avarice of the Guipúzcoa Company provoked a revolt in Venezuela (1749). An agent of the royal treasury who attempted to control the production of alcohol in Quito caused an uprising in that city (1765), which was only quelled by the mediation of the Jesuits; and Chilean insurgents prevented the collection of certain odious taxes in that region (1776). Visitor José Antonio Areche was partially responsible for the formidable uprising of the Peruvian Indians under Tupac Amarú, descendant of the Incas (1780–1781). The attempts of Visitor Francisco Gutiérrez Piñeres to increase the revenues from New Granada led to the widespread revolt of the *Comuneros* there (1781). It was the old story of important reforms hindered by the exactions made by a needy treasury drained in supporting European wars. The inauguration of the sweeping intendant system would have proved difficult under any circumstances, for it not only demanded a variety of talents which few men possessed, but naturally aroused the opposition of many whose offices, graft, or powers it limited or eliminated. Given its persistent emphasis upon revenues, there is small wonder that it was doomed to only partial success. The operations of peculators were considerably restricted, the oppression of the Indians temporarily ameliorated in some quarters, and the whole tone of colonial administration energized and somewhat improved. Yet the very

[2] Pierson, *"Intendencia* of Cuba," p. 89.

thoroughness of the change which the *intendencias* involved tended
to unsettle colonial life; and just as some of its best results began to appear, Charles IV, a weak and unworthy sovereign, ascended the Spanish throne and the French Revolution transformed
the mental attitude of the Western World. The intendant system
was the last effort of a rigid old order doomed to ultimate defeat
because of inability to adapt itself to the changing conditions and
demands of a new age.

The Bourbons probably numbered the expulsion of the Jesuits
(1767) among their reforms; but whatever the virtues of this drastic
measure from other points of view, it was, so far as the colonies were
concerned, perhaps an erroneous readjustment. The expulsion of
hundreds of these padres from all parts of Spanish America may
have pleased many of their rivals and enemies, but it could not fail
to grieve thousands of Indians whom they had protected and served.
It must also have aroused the resentment of their numerous creole
and mestizo pupils or relatives. Many doubtless found it difficult to
believe in the justice of a monarch guilty of such a ruthless act. Nor
could the Jesuits conveniently be spared on the frontiers, where they
had always been a potent agency of expansion and defense. In expelling the Jesuits, Charles III had acted in the interest of a regal-
istic control which resented what appeared to be an empire within
an empire, but it may be that his apprehension was exaggerated. At
any rate, it was a costly act which deprived the colonies of their best
teachers and missionaries and perhaps left many of them in a dis-
loyal mood.[3]

The rule of the eighteenth century Bourbons was also signalized
by notable improvement in the character of the viceroys sent out to
America. To span the century, twenty-two viceregal administrations
were required in Mexico, fourteen in Peru, thirteen in New Granada
(after 1717), and six in Río de la Plata (after 1776). Although occasionally corrupt and inefficient and frequently stern, not to say cruel,
on the whole the viceroys were men of considerable integrity, zeal,

[3] From Brabo, *Expulsión de los Jesuitas,* I take the following figures: Number of Jesuits
in America at the time of their expulsion, 2,260; number of Indians in their different missions, 717,000; number of colleges, residences, and missions, 191; incomplete estimate of
the value of Jesuit property seized in Spain and America, 71,483,917 pesos *duros.* Except
in Paraguay, where the enumeration appears to be incomplete, Brabo's list contains *only
the mission centers, not each separate mission.* If these had been included, the number of
establishments would have approached three hundred.

enlightenment, and administrative talent. Such viceroys as Bucareli (1771-1779) and the second count of Revilla Gigedo (1789-1794) of Mexico, Manso de Velasco (1745-1761) and Ambrosio O'Higgins (1796-1801) of Peru, Caballero y Góngora (1779-1788) of New Granada, Vértiz (1778-1784) of Río de la Plata, and Guirior (1773-1780) and Gil y Lemos (1789-1796) of both New Granada and Peru—not to mention a few less notable rulers of earlier decades—deserve to rank among great colonial administrators of any nation or age. They devoted themselves with energy and loyalty to the economic, political, and social problems of their kingdoms and not a few of them were real patrons of learning and art.

Unfortunately, Charles IV and Ferdinand VII, the last of the Spanish Bourbons, were weak and inefficient monarchs whose character was reflected in their colonial agents. The viceroys of the first two decades of the nineteenth century, like their royal masters, were for the most part impotent and undesirable administrators. Most of them were unfit to cope with the new spirit and the new aspirations which were so rapidly developing in the colonies.

The Missions and the Expansion of the Frontiers

The period from 1700 to 1767 witnessed the golden age of frontier missionary enterprise in much of Spanish America; and, as in the previous century, the missions continued to constitute important agencies of frontier defense and expansion. At the time of their expulsion the Jesuits alone are said to have had 717,000 neophytes in their establishments. All the other orders combined probably did not have so many; but there must have been at least a million Indians in the missions of Spanish America in 1767. Comparatively few new centers were occupied during the century, but most of the old centers were expanded and worked with greater success. Increased progress was probably due largely to the more consistent backing of the first three Bourbons, who, with all the numerous demands upon their treasury, never ceased to support missionary effort in their American colonies.

Northern Frontier.—On the northern frontier the padres made progress. In Florida, because of the hostility of the wild Indians and of English and French neighbors in Georgia and Louisiana,

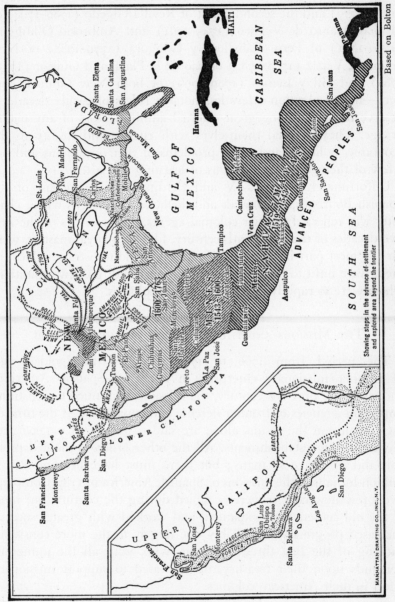

EXPANSION OF NEW SPAIN (to 1800)

Showing steps in the advance of settlement
and explored area beyond the frontier

Based on Bolton

MANHATTAN DRAFTING CO., INC., N.Y.

the missions declined. In New Mexico, after the Indian revolt and the Spanish reconquest near the end of the seventeenth century, missionary progress was slow. In 1744 there were twenty-five missions, scattered for the most part up and down the Rio Grande, with about 12,000 neophytes. Thirty years later there were probably not many more. In 1716 successful missionary work was begun among the Indians of Texas, and during the next three decades some twenty missions were founded; but few of them were permanent. In 1762 there were fewer than 2,000 neophytes, most of them in the vicinity of the present San Antonio and Goliad. In 1746 successful missionary enterprise began in Nuevo Santander—lying between the Pánuco and the San Antonio rivers—and by 1756 some twenty-four flourishing missions had been established there. In 1697 the Jesuits advanced from Sinaloa and Sonora to Lower California, where they founded, prior to their final expulsion, twenty-three missions. By 1767 there were in fourteen of these—the only ones which were successful—about 10,000 Indians.

Central America.—In Central America the missionaries made only a little more progress than during the previous century. The work was carried on mainly by the Franciscans and Dominicans. There appear to have been only eleven Jesuits in the entire captaincy in 1767. By 1697, after almost a century of effort, the Itzas of the northern frontier of Guatemala had been subdued and induced to receive missionaries. By 1769 they had been gathered into seven villages. Their neighbors on the southwest were also partially Christianized, as were the natives of the mountains of southern Honduras, those of the eastern section of Nicaragua, those of Talamanca in the province of Costa Rica, and, in fact, a considerable number of Indians in all the provinces.

South America.—In South America only two important new fields were occupied: the lower Orinoco, or Guiana, and southern Chile. The pacification of the first was mainly due to the work of the Capuchins, who established their first successful mission in the area in 1724. By 1766 they had gathered more than 5,000 Indians into eighteen villages. In Chile, after the bloody combats of the previous century, the Jesuits at last succeeded in establishing themselves among the Araucanians, where they founded eight villages before their expulsion.

With the exception of Mainas, most of the old fields of endeavor continued to prosper. Among the Guaranís of the Paraná-Uruguay basin the Jesuits had in 1767 thirty missions, with over 100,000 converts, in spite of the disturbances of 1754–1755. At the time of their expulsion they also had fifteen reductions among the Chiquitos, fifteen in the Gran Chaco, and sixteen in the plains of the Casanare, Meta, and Orinoco. Moreover, in 1752 they were administering to 31,345 neophytes of the Moxos region. In the Mainas area, however, the Jesuits had lost ground; for they could claim in 1767 only 15,000 souls, whereas in 1653 there were as many families. Disease and Portuguese raids explain the diminution. The main centers of Franciscan missionary effort in South America were southern Mainas and east-central Venezuela. In Mainas they continued to have great difficulties with the natives and the climate. They frequently ended "their days by being murdered by the very savages whom they had come to humanize," and one of the Peruvian viceroys called the area a "vegetable hell which holds its own against heaven." In Venezuela they continued to achieve the successes of a previous era, probably having no fewer than 50,000 Indians under their care in the vast areas south of Cumaná, Caracas, and Barcelona.

In these numerous missions, scattered from Lower California and New Mexico to Chile, and from Texas to Guiana and Paraguay, were hundreds of well cultivated farms, orchards, and gardens, and thousands of horses, cattle, sheep, and goats. Usually there were also weaving rooms, blacksmith shops, tanneries, and warehouses. In fact, the neophytes, under the direction of the padres, engaged in most of the economic activities which characterized the civilian communities.

Such was the state of the missions during their most flourishing period. The closing decades of the century witnessed a decided decline in most areas, due to the transfer of the wards of the Jesuits to less tactful ministers and to the general cooling of missionary zeal. In 1769, owing to fear of Russian intrusion, the Franciscans, supported by soldiers and settlers, went forward into Upper California, where, by 1806, they gathered more than 20,000 Indians into nineteen missions. In the basin of the lower Orinoco (Guiana) the missions progressed until in 1799 there were twenty-eight establishments with only a little fewer than 16,000 Indians. Almost everywhere else, however, there appears to have been retrogression. A recent survey of the period, based upon authentic sources, gives a depressing picture: buildings dilapidated; scarcity of missionaries, and those in the field lazy, indifferent, and inadequately trained; neophytes reverting to their old roving habits or falling under the corrupt and oppressive influence of the worst elements of Spanish and mestizo society. A few years more, and only abandoned architectural ruins in forests, jungles, deserts, or grasslands would be left to remind the chance visitor of a former heroic epoch.[4]

New Settlements.—In the eighteenth century, as earlier, the missionaries were usually supported by small groups of soldiers stationed in frontier *presidios* (forts). Sometimes, as in Texas, Nuevo Santander, and Upper California, they were accompanied by Spanish and mestizo settlers who founded towns at the very outset. Sometimes, moreover, military conquest preceded the successful introduction of missionaries; and occasionally the Indians were driven farther out upon the frontier in order to give place to ranchmen and miners, who brought with them a labor supply from the old settlements. The secularization of the missions also went on, although the large number of Indians under the missionaries at the middle of the century shows that the process did not occur with the rapidity contemplated by the law.

The epoch was, in fact, characterized by considerable expansion on the part of the civilian and military phalanx. In the founding of towns and the discovery of new mines the eighteenth century was surpassed only by the sixteenth. Among the scores of new towns founded, the following may be mentioned as illustrative of increased vigor: San Francisco, Albuquerque, San Antonio, Pensacola, Montevideo, Bucaramanga and Cúcuta (New Granada), Copiapó and Rancagua (Chile). In addition to these new towns, several old ones had to be rebuilt or refounded on account of the devastation of earthquakes or the destructive raids of European enemies. It was necessary, also, to spend millions of pesos on walls, coast defenses, war vessels, and armies; for this was the era of bitter colonial wars, and Spain's rivals tried to seize some of the mainland colonies.

Spain and the loyal elements within the colonies were able, however, to hold their own against all enemies. Cartagena and Santiago

---

[4] In California the mission buildings have been restored.

warded off formidable attacks in 1741; Río de la Plata drove out the British in 1807; and other assailants were sometimes severely punished. The English succeeded in seizing Cuba in 1762, only to exchange it a year later for Florida; and Florida itself was finally returned in 1783. Española and Trinidad were definitely lost, but these losses were more than compensated by the acquisition of Louisiana (1763). At the end of the century Spanish America reached its maximum extent. There were then in the New World more than three million people of Spanish descent and a fraction of Spanish blood ran through the veins of still another five million. At the same time the population of the mother country was well over ten million. It was indeed a tribute to the virility and prowess of the Spanish race.

Colonial Society and Culture at the End of the Century

Although Bourbon officials gave some attention to population statistics, apparently no accurate tables covering the whole of the Spanish colonies were ever compiled. According to the best estimates the population was as follows:

Colony	1788	1810	1823
New Spain	5,900,000	7,000,000	6,800,000
Guatemala	1,200,000	(^{a})	1,600,000
Cuba and Puerto Rico	600,000	(^{b})	800,000
Venezuela	900,000	950,000	785,000
New Granada	1,800,000	2,000,000	2,000,000
Peru	1,700,000	2,050,000	1,400,000
Chile	(^{c})	(^{c})	1,100,000
Río de la Plata	1,100,000	2,350,000	2,300,000

a Included in New Spain.   b Not given.   cIncluded in Peru.

Perhaps it will do no harm to accept these figures as reasonably accurate and assume that the total population of Spanish America was 13,200,000 in 1788, some 15,000,000 in 1810, and 16,785,000 in 1823. The racial components of this population—as given by Alexander Humboldt, from whom we have taken the estimates for 1823 —were as follows:

Colony	Indians	Whites	Negroes	Mestizos
New Spain	3,700,000	1,230,000		1,860,000
Guatemala	880,000	280,000		420,000
Colombia and Vene-zuela	720,000	642,000		1,256,000
Peru and Chile	1,030,000	465,000		853,000
Río de la Plata	1,200,000	320,000	387,000[a]	742,000
Cuba and Puerto Rico	[b]	339,000	389,000	197,000
Total	7,530,000	3,276,000	776,000	5,328,000[c]

[a] Total, all colonies except Cuba and Porto Rico.   [b] Few, if any, Indians.

[c] The total population resulting from the addition of these figures differs slightly from that given by Humboldt in the preceding table.

These racial groups, whatever the number in each, furnished the basis for sharply drawn class distinctions. In addition, there was a definite cleavage between the Peninsular Spaniards and the creoles, as those born of Spanish blood in the colonies were called; and it appears that Spain actually fostered all these distinctions on the theory of divide and rule.

Peninsular Spaniards.—At the apex of the social hierarchy were the Peninsular-born Spaniards, numbering under three hundred thousand in 1800 but regarded as the bulwark of Spanish rule in America. They monopolized, and had always monopolized, the highest offices in church and state. They controlled the army and the universities; they were the viceroys, the captains-general, the governors, the intendants, the judges in the audiencias; they were the archbishops and bishops, and the important officials of the cathedrals. They were also the leading merchants of the colonies. Not all of them were wealthy. Some, in fact, were poor and little better than vagabonds. But rich and poor alike looked with a certain amount of contempt upon the colonial-born Spaniard. "The most miserable European, without education or intellectual cultivation, thinks himself superior to all other white men in the new continent." Such was the view of Humboldt; and his testimony is corroborated by others.

Creoles.—Below the Spaniards in the social scale were the creoles, nearly three million in 1800. They owned most of the haciendas and mines, as well as much urban property. They were among the best physicians, lawyers, and notaries. They rushed eagerly into all the minor positions open to them in church and state. They virtually dominated the town councils and frequently became judges or attorneys in the audiencias; but they were seldom permitted to become viceroys, captains-general, intendants, or bishops. The wealthy among them often purchased titles of nobility and made a great display of their riches. Yet the vast majority were not wealthy. All were equally disdainful of manual labor; and, since there were comparatively few honorable and lucrative positions for them in the universities, the church hierarchy, the regular orders, the army, and the civil service, they spent much time in litigation, dances, and festivals, as well as in drinking, gambling, and other forms of dissipation and vice.

They came more and more to resent the discriminations set up against them by the mother country. Soon after the opening of the century, Don Melchor Macanaz, an able minister of Philip V, called attention to this resentment and advised a change of policy. "As the natives of those . . . dominions are equally deserving of filling the principal offices of their own country," he remarked, "it appears reasonable that they should not be divested of all management in their own homes. I am fully persuaded, that in those countries there are many discontented persons, not because they are under the control of Spain; but because they are cast down, and tyrannized by the very persons who are sent over to exercise the duties of judicature. Let your Majesty give these offices to subjects of that country, and by this means disturbances will be avoided." The advice was not heeded, and by 1800 the creoles were regarding "as an injustice every employment bestowed on any others than themselves."

Mestizos.—Beneath the creoles were the mestizos, more than five million at the end of the century. Set off from the whites above and the Indians and Negroes below, some of them filled the humbler positions in the parishes, convents, and missions or became small proprietors, but the vast majority were to be found among the artisans and vagabonds of the towns and cities. Still others were employed as *mayordomos* (overseers) in the mines and on the vast estates. The Spanish crown had deliberately fostered the production of this hybrid race; yet there is much evidence indicating that the monarchs feared the growing class which they had produced. They were careful to deprive them of their natural leaders. Social and civil position was made to depend largely upon one's complexion, and the conviction that "every white man was a cavalier" (*"todo blanco es caballero"*) was almost universal. The crown had therefore only to give to enterprising and aggressive mestizos patents declaring them white in order to cause them to cast their lot with the classes above them.

Indians.—Next in order were the Indians, still almost as numerous as all other classes combined. A few of them continued to reside in the missions; some dwelt detached in mountain fastnesses or roamed the forests and jungles, and hence could hardly be considered a part of colonial society; others were personal servants, common laborers, or humble artisans in the cities and towns; a considerable number spent their lives trudging behind mule trains through tropical jungle and along mountain trails, or poling rafts up and down the rivers, or as servants in the country inns; but the majority were still under their chiefs in villages located near the rural mining areas or scattered over the vast estates of the creoles and Peninsular-born Spaniards. The encomiendas had been abolished, as well as most of the *mitas* (allotments of Indians for forced labor), but the vast majority were still driven to work by masters who evaded the law or to whom they were indebted; nor can it be said that the mission Indians were free, always, from forced labor and oppression. The wages of the natives were low; sometimes they were paid nothing at all. Many of them had some spare time for work on their little community farms and gardens or in household industries carried on mainly by the women. Poor, ignorant, exploited by a more sagacious race, superstitious, much given to strong drink, they lived in their floorless, vermin-infested huts promiscuously with their pigs, chickens, and dogs. Almost unanimous testimony declares that they had failed to grasp the significant truths and lessons of the religion forced upon them, and from the Catholic and native cults had compounded a religion of their own (the cross and the sun). Rankling hatred and a spirit of insurgency sometimes appeared. Now and then leaders arose among them and reminded them of far-off happy days before the white men came; but such leaders were ostentatiously and ruthlessly slain or bought off by patents of whiteness or titles of nobility. Truly the position of the Indians was not envi-

able, but that of the lower classes of Europe was not much better—
and the Indians of Spanish America were still alive. Their exploitation was the huge sacrifice exacted in the interest of the ruling
classes of the Old World and for the development of the New.

Negroes.—The burden fell heavier upon the Indians because Negro
slavery never took deep root in the Spanish colonies. Introduced at the
opening of the sixteenth century in order to relieve the Indians from
work in the mines, the Negroes were brought in steadily under
private license and asiento contract. Yet there were fewer than 800,-
000 in the colonies at the close of the eighteenth century. More than
half of these were in Cuba and Puerto Rico, areas where there was
comparatively little mining. There were only a few in Mexico and
Río de la Plata. Most of those not in the West Indies were the personal servants or slaves of the wealthy families of Lima, Quito,
Caracas, Panama, and Cartagena. Of the remainder, probably very
few were working in the mines.

The Spanish slave code was comparatively humane, and there was
a strong tendency toward emancipation. More than half the Negroes
of Spanish America were free at the close of the colonial period. They
had obtained their freedom mainly by purchase money earned during holidays and at other spare times. If their suffering was ever great,
it was from neglect rather than severity.

The Church.—Such were the social classes in Spanish America in
1800. The most important social institution was, as always, the
church. At the end of the century it was organized into six archbishoprics (Santo Domingo, Mexico, Guatemala, Lima, Bogotá, and
Charcas) and some thirty-four bishoprics. To the mendicant orders
were added, during the course of the seventeenth and eighteenth
centuries, several other orders. The clergy was never so numerous,
however, as in Spain. It appears indeed that their number declined
after 1750 to a degree not accounted for by the expulsion of more
than two thousand Jesuits. According to Humboldt there were only
14,000 regulars and seculars in New Spain in 1803; and Altamira
thinks there were no more than 35,000 or 40,000 in all Spanish
America at that time. Spain, with a population less than its American colonies, had almost four times as many.

Nevertheless, the Spanish-American church was very wealthy. Not
only did it receive large sums from gifts, tithes, and other ecclesias-

tical revenues; it is said to have owned between one-third and one-half of all the property in the colonies. Besides many large temples of worship elegantly and sometimes gaudily furnished and decorated, it had many urban and rural properties and an extensive money-lending business. Moreover, the tribunals of the Inquisition in Lima and Mexico City enjoyed large incomes and, toward the last decade of the century, had two or three million pesos in their coffers.

Much of the income of the church was expended on charity, religious festivals, and schools. In fact, nearly every educational institution in the colonies owed its initiation and support largely to the church, which also controlled curricula and educational policy and furnished almost all the teachers. Yet many ecclesiastics of every order and degree are said to have spent their lives in luxury and dissipation little becoming the followers of the lowly Nazarene. Moreover, tithes and other dues, as already noted, were often oppressive to the lower classes, while ecclesiastical administration of real estate was not such as to bring forth the best returns. "On the economic affairs of Spanish America, as on those of Spain, the church cast the blight of its dead hand."

The influence of the church in the field of learning was not an unmixed good. If it must be admitted that at least a dozen universities, scores of seminaries, and hundreds of elementary and secondary [5] schools owed their existence to the clergy, it must be pointed out that ecclesiastical method was somewhat inefficient and much of the content of ecclesiastical education of doubtful value. The children were taught to memorize but not to think. Formalities and indoctrination were emphasized rather than the training of the character and the mind. Frequently the clergy stood with flaming swords at the gates of knowledge. This was true in particular of the officials of the Inquisition, who undertook a rigid censorship of all reading matter and placed thousands of books upon the list of forbidden literature.

Yet, in spite of all these limitations, learning made some progress in the colonies during the eighteenth century. The Bourbons themselves, and their viceroys, were its patrons until the extravagances

[5] There was a *colegio* in every important town and city, but it seldom amounted to more than a sort of grammar school.

of the French Revolution drove them to a reversal of their policy. A new university was founded in Caracas in 1725, and another in Santiago de Chile in 1738. Several printing presses were added to the few previously set up. During the century presses were introduced into Vera Cruz, Guadalajara, Quito, Ambato, Santa Fé de Bogotá, Santiago de Chile, Córdoba, and Buenos Aires. By 1801, moreover, periodicals had appeared in Mexico City, Lima, Quito, Bogotá, and Buenos Aires. While the old types of colonial literature —poetry, history, treatises on Indian languages, books on dogma, speculative philosophy, and theology—continued to appear, gradually more emphasis was placed upon medicine and other sciences, as well as upon politics and social criticism. The stream of new thought now flowing so strongly in Western Europe, and even to a considerable extent in Spain itself, could not entirely be shut out. Spanish-American students returning from their European studies broke the dikes; traders from France, England, and the United States lent a hand; some of the universities felt its influence and became centers of new learning (namely, medicine, jurisprudence, and mathematics); and even a few of the churchmen themselves were swept into the current. Although it cannot be said that education was very widespread even among the whites and mestizos at the end of the century, the group of intelligentsia had greatly expanded, and the long intellectual isolation of the colonies had broken down. Baron Humboldt, who visited the region only a few years later, was often surprised at the scientific progress which had been made.

Scientists.—Among the scientists of the century several deserve to be mentioned. Besides writing numerous poems, Pedro de Peralta Barnuevo of Peru produced many works on navigation, astronomy, metallurgy, engineering, and history. Antonio Alzate of New Spain published a number of articles on a wide range of philosophical and scientific subjects and gave his name to a scientific society of modern Mexico. Francisco José de Caldas, a pupil of the able Spanish scientist José Celestino Mutis, won fame by a botanical survey of New Granada and by astronomical observations in Santa Fé de Bogotá. Santiago de Cárdenas even wrote a book near the middle of the century on a "new system of navigating by air." Because of this work he became known as *El Volador* (The Flyer).

The Arts.—During this century there appeared also at least a score of historical and descriptive works of great value to students. The writers of greatest merit in this class were Alonso de Zamora, Francisco de Medrano, Juan Rivero, and José Gumillo of New Granada; José de Oviedo y Baños and José Luis Cisneros of Venezuela; Dionisio and Antonio de Alcedo (father and son) of Peru; Miguel de Olivares, Pedro C. Figueroa, and Juan Ignacio Molina of Chile; Pedro Lozano, José Guevara, and Juan P. Fernández of the Río de la Plata area; and Francisco J. Alegre, Eusebio Francisco Kino (late seventeenth and early eighteenth century), Francisco Clavijero, Andrés Cavo, and Francisco Palóu of New Spain.

The period was also noted for the production of pure literature of some merit. Among the literati of the century Antonio Valdés (author of the drama *Ollantá*), Manuel de Navarette, and Manuel José Labardén (writer of the ode *Al Paraná* and the play *Siripio* deserve mention.

Lastly, in art, music, and architecture there occurred considerable progress. Groups of artists existed in most of the leading cities of the colonies and a School of Fine Arts was established in Mexico City near the end of the century.

THE WORK OF SPAIN IN AMERICA

The close of the eighteenth century virtually brought to an end the constructive work of Spain in America. The next twenty-five years were almost entirely occupied by the struggle which ended in independence. A critical estimate of Spain's work will go far toward removing the black legend created by her colonial enemies aided by certain partisan agitators of Spain and Spanish America. Yet the record is not as lily-white as some Hispanophiles would have it appear.

Millions of natives had been preserved, but their preservation had been due in part to their usefulness at the bottom of the economic order. The language of the mother country had been introduced and given a permanently predominant place. Yet numerous Indians could not write or even speak Spanish, and many others who knew the language preferred to employ their native tongues.

The establishment of mail systems had brought increasing contacts between colonial minds; but communications were still very slow and uncertain, and private correspondence was difficult and unsafe. There were few roads adapted to carriages, wagons, or even oxcarts, and the ports and rivers were very scantily improved. Unlike Rome, Spain was not a builder of roads.

The land system had encouraged or permitted the concentration of large agrarian holdings in the hands of the church and the nobility, who cultivated them in very indifferent fashion. Many Indian villages continued to retain the community lands which Spanish authorities had carefully assigned them; but others had lost their *ejidos* (lands held in common by Indian villages), and the great mass of the people were landless. An aristocracy of wealth and privilege had been thoroughly established.

The some twenty [6] universities were probably sufficient in number to accommodate such of the sons of the upper classes as were able to attend them, even if the course of study was limited and defective. But comparatively little had been done to educate the masses.

Legal, judicial, and administrative systems had been set up, but political and geographical boundaries had been carelessly defined—a carelessness replete with difficulties for the future. Moreover, a multiplicity of officials and traditions of graft constituted a heavy inheritance for the new nations soon to appear.

Roman Catholic Christianity had been instilled, often to the point of fanaticism, into all the white and mestizo groups as well as into great masses of the natives; but numerous Indians had been very imperfectly Christianized, if at all. Moreover, both the church and the state had combined to restrict thought and prevent scientific development, and the church, because of its wealth, its control over intellectual life, and its habit of participating in politics, was destined to an important and somewhat reactionary rôle in the future.

On the whole it was a rather depressing heritage, but it contained certain factors, either in its theory or in its practice, which pointed the way to a new régime. "In spite of the difference in inspiration and the apparent contradiction in attendant circumstances, there is

---

[6] Professor John Tate Lanning, who has made a special study of institutions of higher learning in Colonial Spanish America, informs me that there were at least twenty universities. The three best were in Mexico, Lima, and Chuquisaca.

a certain connection between the highest human ideals of the revolution [namely, the Wars of Independence, 1810–1825] and the deep and silent moral forces of colonial society. To political and civil equality corresponds, evidently, the moral equality of all the races which was proclaimed by various intellectual leaders in Spain since the time of the conquest and was the underlying principle of the best legislation of the Indies. To the idea of popular sovereignty . . . corresponds, in essence, the idea of kingdoms, practically national groups, that existed not only in the mind but also in the vocabulary during the colonial period. To the principle of division of powers . . . correspond the system of checks and balances and the greatly developed idea of responsibility of the earlier period." [7]

Attention is directed once more also to the Spanish emphasis on the artistic. In all of the leading towns were impressive public buildings, political and ecclesiastic, as well as beautiful parks and patios filled with flowers, shrubs, and trees. Some of the countryside, moreover, was made impressive by the dignified homes of the *hacendados,* approached by stately avenues of palms, poplars, ceibas, or other arboreal species. This emphasis was to be continued in the national period until many parts of Spanish America were as beautiful as any other region in the world. Even the poorest frequently possessed a keen appreciation of art so that the most miserable dwelling was often surrounded by flowers and shrubbery.

[7] Victor Belaunde, in *The Hispanic American Historical Review,* IX, 145. The viceroyalties and captaincies-general were referred to as "Kingdoms."

CHAPTER VII

TWO CENTURIES OF PORTUGUESE RULE IN BRAZIL

In Portugal, the seventeenth and eighteenth centuries were a period of storm and stress. United with Spain in 1580, it soon witnessed attacks upon its colonies by the enemies of the Iberian nations. Always restive under Spanish domination, the Portuguese began in 1640 a twenty-eight years' war for freedom from their "Babylonian captivity." The effort was successful, but during the course of the struggle important commercial concessions were made to Holland and France, and Portugal virtually became the vassal of England. During these two centuries, moreover, the country was handicapped by several weak and disreputable monarchs and by a too numerous and wealthy clergy.

All these factors naturally influenced the development of Brazil. Intermittently for more than a century it suffered from the attacks of the French and the Dutch. Having repelled these largely by its own efforts, the colony then profited by trade concessions wrung from the mother country by the European powers, by the neglect of feeble monarchs, and to some extent through the policies of an able minister or two. Between 1600 and 1800, Brazil first became a flourishing agricultural colony; later many of its inhabitants abandoned the plantations for the mines; but having largely exhausted the mines after a half-century, they returned to the plantations to revive the agricultural prosperity of a previous epoch.

Foreign Attacks and the Breakdown of the Trade Monopoly

The French and the Dutch were the chief menace to Portugal's hold upon Brazil. It is true that near the end of the sixteenth century such English sea dogs as Fenton, Witherington, and Cavendish had attacked Santos and Bahia and harassed the coasts in general; but permanent conquest and settlement were not intended by the English, and they ceased to give trouble during the period now under consideration.

As early as 1594 the famous French corsair Jacques Riffault landed on the coast of Maranhão, an act which was followed by a regular trade between that captaincy and Dieppe. Soon afterwards Henry IV began to dream of an Equinoctial France in northern Brazil, but he was assassinated in 1610 before definite steps had been taken to realize the project. The French queen-regent renewed the concession to Daniel de la Touche, whom Henry had chosen for the conquest and settlement of fifty leagues of the coast-line of Maranhão, but gave him no material aid. He managed to equip an expedition by private enterprise, however, and in 1612 established a fort and colony named Saint Louis. The Frenchmen then began to explore the region with the view of occupying the mouths of the Amazon, but the colonists of Brazil, aided by reinforcements from the mother country, drove them back to Guiana in 1615. The French did not make another important attack upon Brazil until ninety-five years later.

Meantime, the Dutch had been more successful. Although they were able to retain Bahia, which they seized in 1624, for less than a year, they captured Recife and Olinda in 1630 and soon afterwards extended their sway over northern Brazil. These attacks had been made under the auspices of the Dutch West India Company, and the rule of this company under the governorship of Prince Maurice of Nassau was enlightened, tolerant, and considerate of the interests of the colonial inhabitants; but the oppressive greed of the manager of the company after 1644 and Portugal's war for liberation from Spain deeply stirred the people of Brazil. In 1642 the Portuguese settlers of Maranhão rose in revolt against the Dutch invaders and succeeded in expelling them from that area after a two years' war. Encouraged by this initial success, all classes of the colonists—Portuguese, mixed breeds, Indians, and Negroes—in the Captaincy of Pernambuco started an uprising in June, 1645. The struggle continued for nine years and ended in the final expulsion of the Dutch. The war has been called the "Brazilian Iliad." The destiny of northern Brazil still wavered in the balance, however, until the Dutch Netherlands through the mediation of England signed the treaty of 1661, in which they acknowledged the elimination of the Dutch from the colony.

A half-century later the French renewed their attack. During the

War of Spanish Succession Louis XIV struck at Portugal by authorizing and supporting a filibustering raid upon Brazil. The first onslaught, against Rio de Janeiro, failed (1710), but during the following year the town was seized, sacked, and held for ransom. The Frenchmen carried away an enormous booty, but it was their last attack against Brazil.

Portugal's territorial claim to Brazil had thus been preserved, but the trade pretensions of the mother country met a different fate. Portuguese rulers, like those of the other colonizing powers of the age, were committed to the mercantile theory. They attempted to confine the trade of Brazil to the mother country. They also adopted the fleet system, although the fleets were comparatively large, no single port of the mother country was permitted to monopolize the trade, and all of the leading ports of the colony were thrown open to commerce. Until near the middle of the seventeenth century, therefore, the system was more liberal than that of Spain; and even subsequently, when a more exclusive tendency showed itself, the colonists by strenuously opposing the new régime usually managed to have their way.

The General Commercial Company of Brazil, organized as early as 1649, was forced out of existence by the colonists in 1720. The Commercial Company of Maranhão, established in 1682 and given a monopoly of that region, soon provoked a revolt which led to its suppression. Two other companies, one for northern Brazil and another for north-central Brazil, set up by Pombal in 1755 and 1759 respectively, were likewise disbanded in 1777. Compared to the narrow Spanish system which concentrated the commerce of Spanish America in the hands of the Seville merchants until the reforms of Charles III, the Portuguese system was rather liberal.

There was one respect, however, in which Portugal clung tenaciously to the mercantilist policy. Brazil was never permitted to enjoy a direct trade with any European power save the mother country. But this restrictive system proved to be less burdensome than the analogous one of Spain. Double taxation—namely, in the ports of the mother country and in those of Brazil—and high freight rates, which resulted from the Portuguese monopoly of the colonial carrying trade, raised the prices of commodities imported into Brazil. The operation of the same causes probably also reduced the prices of Brazilian products. Otherwise, however, the application of the system was without important effects; for, after the middle of the seventeenth century, the leading European powers were permitted to traffic with the colony through the mother country and, after 1661, English and later French mercantile houses were allowed to maintain resident merchants in Pernambuco, Rio de Janeiro, and Bahia. This development was caused by scarcity of manufactures in Portugal and its inevitable involvement in European politics. It really meant the breakdown of the Portuguese monopoly of Brazilian trade.

In fact, Brazil's commerce fell largely under the control of the merchants of the British Isles. According to an estimate of about the year 1700, "half of the Brazil trade" was in "English hands, the remainder being carried on [through the mother country] by France and Holland." This may have exaggerated the rôle of the foreign merchants, but its importance cannot be doubted. Allowing for certain variations caused by occasional economic and political changes, the British advantage increased during the next century. Despite attempts to destroy this predominance by the organization of commercial companies and other devices, Portugal and its American colony became the economic vassals of England. As in the case of Spain, the trade and treasures of a vast empire flowed out to alien merchants and into the coffers of another power. For Brazil it was probably a distinct advantage.[1]

The development of Brazil was retarded, however, by a somewhat burdensome fiscal policy and limitations upon colonial industry. The mother country exercised a monopoly with reference to such important commodities as salt, Brazil-wood, timber for shipbuilding, and whale fisheries. Portugal also monopolized the sale of certain drinks and made vigorous attempts to exercise a monopoly of the gold and diamond mines, although these efforts were never quite successful.

Portuguese taxes were similar to those of Spain, but hardly so numerous or burdensome. Important among them were the royal fifth levied upon mines worked by private enterprise, tithes, sales taxes, duties upon imports and exports, and a tax upon Negro slaves.

[1] Smuggling was not so extensive as in Spanish America, but a considerable amount went on, particularly in the eighteenth century.

In accordance with the mercantile theory, colonial industries were not allowed to compete with those of the mother country. Although the prohibitions varied from time to time, tending to grow more numerous near the end of the colonial period, it may be said in general that the Brazilians were not permitted to make wine, or to manufacture articles out of gold, silver, silk, flax, and cotton, or to refine sugar. A considerable portion of the tobacco of the country had likewise to be reserved for the factories of Portugal. The restrictions relative to tobacco, salt, diamonds, gold, silver, and cotton were most keenly felt. The high price of salt was a great burden upon the stock raisers, who needed this important article for their animals and the preservation of their meat.

Yet, in spite of all these taxes and restrictions, Brazil was for two centuries a fairly prosperous colony. Between 1693 and 1821 some five hundred tons of pure gold were extracted from the mines, and between 1721 and the close of the colonial epoch about twenty million dollars' worth of diamonds was found. In 1800 Brazilian foreign trade was valued at more than $21,000,000. By this time the output of the mines had greatly diminished, and the important commodities of Brazil were once more the products of the forests and the farms: cotton, tobacco, hides, indigo, cacao, rice, coffee, balsam, cinnamon, pepper, ginger, dyewoods, ipecac and other drugs, sugar, perfumes, and many other commodities. In return, Brazil received manufactured products of all kinds and many foods and drinks, which the colony itself ought to have produced.

EXPANSION

"The story of Xenophon's Ten Thousand is but a child's tale compared with the fearless adventure of our colonial brothers." [2] The westward movement of seventeenth- and eighteenth-century Brazil was really an epic. It recalls that great migration which took place in the United States between 1763 and 1860. There were the same search for virgin soil adapted to slave labor and plantation economy, the same rush to the mines, the same eagerness for pasture lands, and something of the same ruthless destruction of the natives. In some respects, however, the movement differed from

2 Ronald de Carvalho, *Pequena Historia da Literatura Brasileira*, p. 127. See map on p. 62.

that of the United States. It confronted greater climatic, if not topographic, obstacles. The westward-moving emigrants were less numerous and, hence, the frontier was less compactly settled. Missionaries of the great orders, particularly the Jesuits, often went in advance, serving as a buffer between frontiersmen and Indians and thus preserving some of the natives. The interior migration began before the littoral was fully occupied, and the movement was often toward the southwest, the north, and the northwest as well as toward the west.

In the south, the Paulistas, as the inhabitants of São Paulo—mainly mixed-breeds or mamelucos—were called, played the leading rôle. With the object of capturing Indians for the slave markets of Rio and São Paulo, or of discovering mines, they organized expeditions known as *entradas* or *bandeiras*—bands consisting of entire families and all their worldly possessions—which proceeded several hundred miles westward to the missions of Paraguay, the Gran Chaco, and even southern Mainas, or, turning to the northeast, eventually discovered gold and diamonds in Minas Geraes. The entradas resulted in the death or captivity and enslavement of many thousand Indians. The discovery of gold and diamonds caused wild excitement followed by a general rush of miners and pitched battles between the Paulistas and the immigrants from Portugal and other parts of Brazil. From the General Mines the pioneers advanced into Goyaz, Cuyabá, and to some extent into far-away Matto Grosso. In 1742 Manuel Felix de Lima made a long voyage of more than two thousand miles by way of the Guaporé, the Mamoré, the Madeira, and the Amazon to the town of Pará. Ten years later Villa Bella (or Matto Grosso) was established on the upper reaches of the Guaporé; and soon afterwards a fort (Beira) was erected at the junction of the Guaporé and the San Miguel, fully eighteen hundred miles northwest of São Paulo. Meanwhile, other frontiersmen were moving southwest into Santa Catharina and Rio Grande do Sul, where they met kinsmen on their way northward from Colonia (founded in 1680) and other settlements in Banda Oriental.

Brazilian missionaries had little to do with this vigorous advance, for the whites and mixed breeds of southern Brazil would permit no humanitarian interference in behalf of the natives. The padres were lucky if they were allowed to remain in the region at all.

In the north, however, they contributed a large share. The frontier of settlement moved rapidly for twelve hundred miles along the north coast to Ceará (1615), to San Luis de Maranhão (1616), to Pará (Belem, 1616), and to the island of Marajó. It then proceeded up the Amazon to Gurupá (1623), to Barra do Rio Negro (Manaos, 1674), and to the junction of the Amazon with the Javary (Tabatinga, 1780), almost two thousand miles from Pará. In the meantime, Pedro Teixeira had led an expedition up the Amazon to the head of navigation and then over the mountains to Quito (1637–1638).

In 1653, when the Jesuits, after their recent expulsion, were being readmitted to the captaincy of São Paulo on condition that they cease to protest against the enslavement of the Indians, some of their brothers were on the point of having their way with the natives in the vast region of Maranhão. In 1655 they were granted spiritual and temporal authority over the Indians not yet subdued. At the same time, an executive friendly to Antonio Vieira, the great Jesuit leader in this part of Brazil, took charge of the government of Maranhão. The courageous Jesuits set out at once into the wilderness in search of souls. "In the island of Marajó, in the basin of the Tocantins, the Xingú, and the Amazon, wherever the 'black robes' appeared, the Indians by the thousands exchanged their liberty for the gentle sway of the Jesuits and established themselves in villages under the direction of the Fathers. Even the redoubtable cannibals of Ceará and Piauhy began to assemble . . . and submit to work in the fields." [3] The raids of the Indians upon the frontier settlements ceased, and the land route between San Luis and Pernambuco became as safe as the passage by sea.

But the Brazilians of the north, still longing for their slaves, soon renewed the attack upon the Jesuits, and turbulent days followed. In 1685 a compromise was reached, which represented a partial defeat of the order. They were to have neither an independent Jesuit state nor a monopoly of the field. The Capuchins, Mercedarians, and Carmelites were to share the labor and the spoils. As in other portions of Brazil, the whites were not to enter the neophyte villages. Yet they were allowed to settle near the Indian establishments.

Nevertheless, in spite of every handicap, the efforts of the missionaries of all orders achieved considerable success. A contemporary

[3] Boehmer, *Les Jésuites*, pp. 181–182.

map of the Spanish-Portuguese frontier represents the Portuguese Jesuits as having, about 1749, numerous establishments upon the upper right banks of the Madeira and all along the south banks of the Amazon between the mouths of the Madeira and the Tapajos, while the Carmelites are shown to occupy the western bank of the Negro as well as the southern basin of the Amazon from the junction of the Purus to that of the Javary. In 1755 the Jesuits had twenty-eight missions, the Capuchins fifteen, the Carmelites twelve, and the Mercedarians five: a total of sixty mission establishments, located mostly in the steaming tropical jungle and in the grasslands.

West of the captaincies of Bahia and Pernambuco are the hills and rolling plains (campos) of central Brazil. The occupation of this great *sertão,* or hinterland, proceeded more slowly than in the mining and missionary areas, but more rapidly than in the plantation regions. During the last century and a half of the colonial era many ranchers and a few planters came in. Here they were so cut off from the world and so impressed by drought, heat, flood, and other characteristics of their environment, that, like the mountaineers of Tennessee and Kentucky, they developed peculiar traits which set them apart from the Brazilians of the north and south. The *"sertanejo"* of this region, notes a recent writer of Brazil, "is somber, thin, mistrustful, and superstitious, rarely aggressive, rash in his impulses, as silent as the vast plains that surround him, calm in gesture, laconic in speech, and, above all, sunk in an inexpressive melancholy. . . ." [4]

Thus Brazilian frontiersmen and missionaries had carried the boundaries of the colony far beyond the imaginary line of the Treaty of Tordesillas (1494). In many places, however, they had confronted the somewhat more feeble Spanish advance. This had been particularly true in the Banda Oriental and along the reaches of the upper Amazon. The time had come, therefore, for the negotiation of boundary agreements with Spain. Such agreements were ratified in 1750, 1777, and 1801. They represented a triumph of Portuguese diplomacy. In the main, actual occupation was taken as the basis of settlement, and Portugal, profiting by the superior vigor of its expansive forces, obtained more than twice the area assigned in the

[4] Carvalho, *op. cit.,* pp. 13–14.

ancient Tordesillas pact. Moreover, in 1713, thanks to the pressure of England, France gave up its old pretensions to the northern basin of the lower Amazon, as well as the right to navigate that great stream, and agreed to the river Oyapock as the dividing line between French Guiana and Brazil. Thus the definitive boundaries of Portuguese America had been agreed upon; but, owing to the failure to survey and actually mark them on the earth's surface, much negotiation and even some fighting remained to be done.

POLITICAL ORGANIZATION AND DEVELOPMENT

The outstanding feature of the political organization of Brazil was its lack of unity. If Spanish-American viceroyalties, captaincies-general, and audiencias pointed to a multiplicity of states in that region, the capitanias of Portuguese America, and the existence for more than a century of two major jurisdictions in Brazil, predicted at least a federation as the destiny of that colony.

Divided at first into some twelve or thirteen captaincies, the colony numbered seventeen at the close of the eighteenth century. The unified control set up by Governor-General Thomé de Souza at Bahia in 1549 was rent in twain by the establishment of two chief executives in 1572, one at Bahia and the other at Rio de Janeiro, with Porto Seguro as the limit between their respective jurisdictions. Five years later the former unity was restored by eliminating the governor of the south and concentrating authority in the hands of the executive at Bahia. But the schism was virtually renewed in 1607 by the appointment of a superintendent of the mines for the southern region.[5] This situation continued for a little more than eight years, when the former administrative integrity was restored. In 1624 the large state of Maranhão (stretching from Pará to Ceará and extending westward to the Spanish frontier) was erected into a separate jurisdiction directly responsible to the government at Lisbon. During this and the following century, however, it was gradually reincorporated into Brazil, and eventually split up into four captaincies: Pará, Maranhão, Piauhy, and Ceará. During all of

[5] Some minerals had been discovered during this early period, but the great mining era began in 1693.

this period it appears that the authority of the governors-general did not extend far beyond the captaincy of Bahia, the capital city. After 1640 Brazil became technically a viceroyalty, but the title of viceroy was not often employed until after 1763 (there were eight viceroys before 1763 and seven afterwards). In that year the capital was transferred from Bahia to Rio. "Theoretically, the viceroy and captain-general residing at the capital exercised supervisory authority over" the chief executives of the other captaincies; "in reality his power outside his own captaincy was largely nominal," [6] except in the southern captaincies in the later eighteenth century.

Justice continued to be administered in minor cases by judges appointed by the captains and in more important matters by those sent out by the crown. In 1608 a higher tribunal was set up at Bahia; in 1751 another was established at Rio. The rights of all of the *capitanias-donatarios* of the ancient régime were finally extinguished during the ministry of the Marquis of Pombal (latter part of the eighteenth century).

It cannot be asserted that colonial Brazil was well governed. The governors-general and viceroys were often reactionary, sometimes merely conservative, only rarely liberal, always likely to confuse authority with despotism. Mediocre statesmen, almost all of them, some were distinguished by considerable courage and military talent. The subordinate officials often made themselves odious by "the venality and corruption of the processes by which they governed the people." [7] Brazilian historians contend—and the viceroys even admitted—that the administration of justice was often corrupt and unfair.

During the ascendancy of the able Marquis Pombal (1750–1777) something of the spirit and practice of enlightened despotism was infused into the colonial administration. He corrected many long-standing abuses, extinguished the remaining feudal captaincies, unified the administrative system, removed the capital to Rio de Janeiro, employed native Brazilians in important civil and military posts, and stimulated agriculture as well as certain industries which did not compete with those of the mother country. Yet Brazil lost

[6] James and Martin, *Republics of Latin America*, p. 75.
[7] Ribeiro, *Historia do Brazil*, pp. 195–204.

something of its former "salutary neglect," for everywhere the reins of government were tightened.

The motives and practices of the period are set forth in the counsel given by one of the viceroys, Marquis de Lavradio, to his successor. Lavradio had governed Brazil for nearly eleven years, retiring in 1779. His report to the executive who succeeded him reveals a lieutenant-general outstretching his authority, acting with "asperity towards the troops and his officers" and despising the colonial militia. It also reveals a system of universal military service so organized as to keep the men of the colony in proper "subordination"; attorneys serving as judges in cases in which they had already acquired an interest as advocates; judges accepting bribes, thinking mainly of accumulating riches, and refusing to promote harmony by discouraging litigation. These and other evils the viceroy had tried to remedy in his own haughty manner, while attempting to give the impression that popular "murmurs" were beneath his notice. He had also endeavored in a high-handed way to promote the cultivation of rice, indigo, hemp, mulberry trees, and fiber for rope; and he had given much attention to timbers, oils, balsams, gums, and shrubs.

Lavradio was evidently eager to promote the best interests of the colonists by methods which statesmen of his school approved. "As the good of the people has ever been my chief object," he avowed, "I endeavoured by all the means possible to avoid all prejudice to them, and at the same time to benefit their credit and reputation." "My self-love," he went on to declare, "does not bind me to the point of inducing me to defend all of my resolutions as judicious; I did what I could and what my limited talents permitted me, and I never omitted any labours which appeared likely to prevent my falling into error. Your Excellency will act with more discretion, and, by correcting my imperfections and mistakes, will bring about that felicity of the people which I have ever desired, and still desire." [8] It was not a high purpose which was lacking in this statesman of the old régime. It was perhaps not ability either. It was rather the haughty spirit and the method which were at fault. Much was done *for* the people, but they were not permitted to do enough by and for themselves.

[8] Armitage, *The History of Brazil*, II, 161 ff.

COLONIAL SOCIETY AND CULTURE

For colonial Brazil, as for colonial Spanish America, there are no thoroughly reliable statistics of population. The following estimates are given as the most accurate which we have:

1,900,000 in 1776
3,300,000 in 1800
3,617,900 in 1818
4,000,000 in 1823 (Humboldt)

In the estimate for 1818 the racial elements were fixed as follows:

Whites   843,000
Negroes 1,887,500
Mixed   628,000
Indians   259,400 (civilized only?)

A contemporary estimate for the year 1819 places the number of Indians, both "catechized" and wild, at 800,000. If these figures are approximately accurate, there were more than 500,000 natives still in the tribal state in 1818. Doubtless there were fully this many; and there were probably more than 259,400 civilized Indians.

Class and race distinctions were not so apparent in Brazil as in Spanish America. Nevertheless, castes did exist in custom as well as in law.

The Whites.—At the top were the whites, who ruled the colony and owned most of its wealth. Those born in Portugal held the majority of the offices in church and state, although since the reforms of Pombal there was no serious discrimination against the creoles, who in any case dominated the town councils (camaras). Ownership of lands and of mines not in possession of the crown was fairly widely distributed among the creoles. Yet extensive holdings were the rule, and the church owned a large amount of real estate. The whites were fond of displaying their riches in fine town and country homes, numerous servants, and expensive garments; but they really lacked many conveniences then enjoyed by the upper classes of Western Europe.

The Mestiços.—Next to the whites were the *mestiços* (or mamelu-cos), the descendants of the Portuguese and the Indians. Many of them possessed considerable property; others were skilled mechan-ics or overseers on the plantations and ranches or in the mines. They possessed full civil rights, including the right to hold office in church and state.

Ex-slaves.—Just below this group were the ex-slaves—Negroes and mulattoes. There were said to be 159,500 free Negroes in Brazil in 1818. The number of mulattoes is not known; but they, like the Africans, were either ex-slaves or the sons of freedmen. Both the free Negroes and the free mulattoes were excluded from the priesthood and all civil employment and forbidden to hold a commission in the army save in their own battalions. In other respects, however, they were supposed to enjoy the rights of citizenship.

Slaves.—At the bottom of the social order were the slaves, esti-mated at 1,930,000 in 1818. Since the mulatto child of a Negro woman inherited the status of its mother, there were numerous mulatto slaves, some 202,000 in 1818. Except for the inhumanities of the slave traffic, the slave system of Brazil was fairly mild. Custom ceded the slaves two days of each week for work of their own, and often also a small plot of ground. Since 1700 the law had recognized their right to possess private property, to exchange a cruel master for one more humane, and even to purchase their liberty. Yet the small number of free Negroes and free mulattoes indicates that emancipation was proceeding very slowly.

The Indians.—Somewhere above the slaves, perhaps, were the Indians of Brazil. Portugal showed far less concern for the natives than did Spain. Yet it can hardly be said that the Portuguese were entirely indifferent to their fate. The labor and agitation of the missionaries has already been noted. The monarchs of the mother country also promulgated several humanitarian laws and decrees. As early as 1570 King Sebastian had forbidden the enslavement of any Indians save those captured in a just war or redeemed from captivity among other tribes. A decree of 1595 had confirmed the order of the previous date and limited the period of enslavement to ten years. Other measures of similar import were issued in 1605, 1609, and 1611, the latter providing heavy penalties for the infringe-ment of the law. Yet the enslavement of the Indians continued to take place on a large scale. Slave traders from São Paulo and Pará seized and sold not only the adjacent tribes, but even those of the Spanish and Portuguese missions on the frontier.

Little further action was taken in behalf of the Indians in the south, where the Paulistas had their way. In the "State of Maranhão" (as already noted), an attempt was made to protect the Indians by placing them in villages under the Jesuits and other missionaries. This scheme was only partially successful. A considerable number of Indians continued to be held in slavery, and the missionaries in charge of the villages were compelled to furnish the planters native labor at the average customary wage.

Finally, in 1755, the energetic Pombal declared all the Indians of Brazil free citizens of the colony, with all the privileges that such a status implied. This step probably marked the end of Indian slavery in Brazil, but in most other respects it was little more than an empty gesture. Few of the Indians were prepared for such complete incorporation into the body politic. Followed four years later by the expulsion of the Jesuits, the declaration meant the rapid decline of the missions, but it really provided nothing which could adequately take their place. Most of the frontier Indians went back to the forests and their old life. A few of those in the more populated areas, having made peace with their civilized neighbors, continued to live largely in their tribal state. Most of them, however, were living in towns and villages more or less separated from the mestiços and the whites. Some of these settlements were allowed to govern themselves under officials of their own selection. The majority, however, were placed in charge of a European "director."

Most accounts agree that this superior officer did little to raise the status of his wards. The bishop of Pernambuco said that the director was not of the smallest service to the Indians; "for instead of there being chosen a truly wise, discreet, and penetrating philosopher to educate them, this choice usually fell upon some ignorant person . . . of no use among civilized [people] . . . , who only sought to reap his sole individual advantage from the labours of the unhappy Indians, whom he treated as slaves, and made them toil like beasts of burthen." [9] A contemporary English writer adds a few

[9] Da Cunha de Azeredo Coutinho, *An Essay on the Brazils* (English ed., London, 1807), pp. 43–44.

more details. He said that this European official was "invested with
the power of directing all their concerns, and of punishing or re-
warding them according to their deserts. He superintends the sale
of all commodities in behalf of the community, delivers to the government agents a tenth of the . . . products, and appoints the portion
of labour to be performed by those who have fallen into a state of
vassalage; and these agents act under the direction of a chief to
whom is delegated still more extensive authority." [10]

Perhaps these are rather severe criticisms from prejudiced wit-
nesses who failed to consider the benevolent motive back of
Pombal's reform; but, after due allowance is made for exaggeration,
they suggest the extent of the gulf between the ideal of citizenship
and the reality of exploitation and semiserfdom. The Portuguese
government had never created a group of encomenderos, but it had
now established what really amounted to a set of corregidores. In
all of the more populated areas of Brazil the natives were a vanish-
ing race.

The Church.—In Brazil, as in Spanish America, the Catholic
Church was an important social institution. The clergy were perhaps not too numerous and hardly as wealthy as in Peru and New
Spain; but they owned considerable real estate as well as personal
property, and there were several imposing temples of worship in
the leading towns—many of them elaborately furnished and decorated—besides many monasteries and a few convents. At the end
of the century the secular organization was composed of an archbishop and nine bishops, those of Pará and Maranhão being subject
to the archbishop of Lisbon. Although tribunals of the Inquisition
were never established in Brazil, the bishops had inquisitorial powers. Those accused of heresy were sent to Portugal for trial.

To the church the colonists owed virtually all the educational
advantages they enjoyed. The primary and secondary schools as
well as the seminaries had been established, in the main, by the
religious orders which continued to support and control them. During the eighteenth century there existed two military academies,
but an attempt (about 1776) to found a university at Rio failed.
Nor were the efforts to set up colonial printing presses more suc-

[10] Grant, *History of Brazil* (London, 1809), p. 116.

cessful until 1808. Outside of the few missions and the leading towns there were hardly any educational opportunities at all.

The Arts.—The people of Brazil, even the whites and mestiços, were for the most part ignorant and superstitious; their minds were occupied in the contemplation of miracles, calamities, disease, and the ecstasies or horrors of heaven or hell, and much of their time was consumed in funerals and religious parades or in love-making. Viceroy Lavradio remarked that his subjects were "devoid of education, licentious in character," and British travelers at the close of the century were shocked at the total absence of scientific appreciation.

Nevertheless, there were signs of an awakening, and Brazilians had already produced literature worthy of notice. Some of the colonials had graduated from the university of Coimbra and made their contribution to the intellectual life even of the mother country. Others had written chronicles or histories of Brazil; and still others had produced fairly good poetry inspired by Brazilian life, history, or scenery. An outstanding characteristic of this literature was the love of the colonial writers for their native land. The historian Rocha Pitta, writes:

"In no other region is the sky more serene, nor does dawn glow more beautifully; in no other hemisphere does the sun flaunt such golden rays . . . ; the stars are more benign and ever joyful; the horizons where the sun is born or where it sinks to rest are always unclouded; the water, whether it be drunk from the springs in the fields or from the town aqueduct, is of the purest; Brazil, in short, is the Terrestial Paradise discovered at last, wherein the vastest rivers arise and take their course." [11]

Moreover, the new political ideas which were stirring Europe had begun to attract attention by the opening of the nineteenth century. A contemporary British traveler makes the following interesting note: "Many of the more opulent inhabitants both" at Bahia "and at Rio have their apartments decorated with sets of French engravings, illustrative of the exploits of their victorious generals, which they regard with feelings of the warmest enthusiasm. Even their scanty libraries are furnished with the writings of d'Alembert, Buffon, Adam Smith, Thomas Paine, etc., etc." The writer might also have added to the list the state papers of the United States, for some

[11] As translated by Goldberg, *Brazilian Literature*, p. 49.

Brazilians had already been inspired by the example of the famous Thirteen. As early as 1789, Joaquin José de Silva Xavier (*"Tiradentes,"* or "The Toothpuller") and other idealists had vainly tried to set up a republic in which there should be no slaves, no monopolies, no restrictions upon thought and industry. Brazil, like Spanish America, was at the dawn of a new epoch, although discontent with the rule of the mother country was evidently less pronounced than in the Spanish colonies.

CHAPTER VIII

THE ACHIEVEMENT OF INDEPENDENCE

WITH the opening of the nineteenth century Spanish America entered the second epic period of its history. After the two centuries of repose which followed the epoch of conquest, the heroic energy of the race exerted itself anew in a successful struggle for independence. Portuguese America, however, effected its separation from the mother country by the aid of a happy accident which made possible an almost bloodless transition. The emancipation of these vast colonies was an event of major importance in modern history. It not only opened a vast new region to the trade and intercourse of Europe and the United States, but carried the Western World forward toward the goal of liberty and republicanism.

CAUSES AND NATURE OF THE INDEPENDENCE MOVEMENT IN SPANISH AMERICA

If ever a movement illustrated the potency of new ideas, that movement was the Wars of Independence in Spanish America. They were a part of the great struggle of Liberty against Traditionalism which had begun in seventeenth-century England, found exemplification in the revolt of the Thirteen English colonies, and experienced a tragic *dénouement* in the French Revolution. The political ideals of liberty, natural rights, equality before the law, and popular sovereignty, which were developed in England, given irresistible literary expression in France, and first put into practice in the United States, found their way into intolerant and decadent Spain, and even into the jealously isolated colonies, where they constituted the great spiritual force back of the heroic struggle of Spanish America for emancipation.

The existence of other causes does not diminish the significance of this idealism. There were much oppression and many injustices in Spanish colonial policy and practice. The application of mercantilism continued to hamper the development of the colonies, even though its rigidity had already somewhat relaxed. The judicial administration was manifestly corrupt and unfair, and taxes were burdensome. Civil and inquisitorial restrictions upon human thought were stifling, and discriminations against creoles and mestizos extremely irritating. The oppression of the Indians, despite many partially successful attempts at reform, was still little short of outrageous. The violent expulsion of the Jesuits and the confiscation of their property had not been forgotten by the padres in exile or their friends in the colonies. But, after all, the inspiring and sustaining force which carried the movement of independence to its successful issue was this group of new political ideals that had already begun to change the face of the modern world. If these had not been present, it may be doubted whether the insurgents would have begun their struggle at a time when they were in reality less oppressed than ever before.

There were other factors which set the time for the outbreak or facilitated its progress to a successful conclusion. Among these were the promise of assistance by British statesmen; the prospect of aid from the United States; the contribution of foreign soldiers of fortune; the commercial policies of Washington and London; the French invasion of the Spanish Peninsula and resultant chaos in the mother country; the stubbornness of Ferdinand VII; and the defiance of the Neo-Holy Alliance by Britain and the United States. "From 1808 to 1825," as García-Calderón has so aptly written, "all things conspired to help the cause of American liberty; the revolutions in Europe, ministers in England, the independence of the United States, the excesses of Spanish absolutism, the constitutional doctrines of Cádiz, the romantic faith of the Liberators, the political ambitions of the oligarchies, the ideas of Rousseau and the Encyclopædists, the decadence of Spain, and the hatred which all the classes and castes in America entertained for the Inquisitors and the viceroys." [1]

Perhaps the nature of the struggle will be understood better if

[1] *Latin America*, pp. 84–85.

it be compared to the Spanish Conquest and the revolution which preceded the birth of the United States.

To the first of these movements it was in many ways similar. The conquest, as Victor Belaunde has noted, was "due to individual initiative and to individual efforts" rather than to the "organized plans or work of the state." It was also characterized by a mystical faith which inspired the Conquerors with the desire to seize a new world for the Catholic religion; and it was the achievement of daring men who displayed heroic will and ambition in the face of tremendous obstacles.

The same traits characterized the great leaders of the movement for independence. San Martín conceived a plan of his own; raised an army largely by his own initiative; disobeyed the orders of the Buenos Aires government; and not only liberated Chile, but turned northward to proclaim the independence of Peru. Bolívar defied civil authorities, devised his own military plans, violated accepted rules of military strategy, and pressed victoriously toward his goal. They and other leaders were inspired by the nationality and destiny of America even as the conquerors had been inspired by patriotism and the Catholic faith. Bolívar, convinced of his providential rôle, fought under the auspices of the god of Great Colombia, and had prophetic visions of America's future. San Martín explained his disobedience by saying, "My destiny called me to Lima." Nor were the Liberators inferior to the Conquerors in heroic will. "They had the same audacity, the same courage, the same constancy. When all seemed lost, they retained the same faith, and started to work again. They fought against primitive forces, against nature, and against primitive men." [2] Corresponding to Pizarro, Cortés, Quesada, Balboa, Alvarado, Benalcázar, and Valdivia, were Bolívar, San Martín, Sucre, Páez, Hidalgo, Morelos, and Guerrero. Most of the liberators were creole Spaniards, and their activities showed that the energy of the race was not extinguished.

Compared with the revolution of the Thirteen English colonies, the Spanish-American Wars of Independence reveal more points of contrast than of similarity. Both were inspired by the same political ideals and owed their success in large measure to a group of remark-

[2] Belaunde, "The Centennial of South American Independence," in *The Rice Institute Pamphlets*, X (1923), 239–241.

able leaders. Both were likewise civil wars; for if one-third of the people in the English colonies were loyalists, fully as many in Spanish America supported the cause of the mother country; and in both instances the loyal elements were composed in part of the official classes in church and state and the satellites of these classes. (In some of the Spanish colonies there were large Indian and mestizo contingents who remained for a time faithful to the monarch.) Here, however, the similarity ceases. In Spain the insurgent colonials had comparatively few sympathizers, but in England the Thirteen colonies found many. The war in Spanish America extended over a much greater area, and military operations were rendered far more difficult by topography and climate. It also lasted almost three times as long, was characterized by more bloodshed and greater cruelty, received no direct official aid from the rivals of the mother country, and was neither accompanied nor followed by a political unity; nor were victories upon the field of battle acknowledged by immediate recognition of independence by the metropolis.

THE PRECURSORS

Although many of the Spanish-American leaders were undoubtedly inspired by the example of the United States, it would be an error to deny originality of conception to the colonials of the South, for some of them dreamed of independence long before the idea occurred to their Anglo-Saxon neighbors of the North. The earliest of the projects for independence date back, indeed, to the sixteenth century and connect themselves with Gonzalo Pizarro of Peru and a son of Cortés in Mexico. Later, about 1659, Guillermo Lombardo de Guzmán and other conspirators formed a plan for the emancipation of New Spain. There were still others during the first two centuries of Spanish rule, but they were so completely suppressed that little trace was left for the historian.

It was not until the third and fourth decades of the eighteenth century, however, that the aspiration assumed an ominous aspect. By that time a widespread spirit of insurgency forecast general reforms or eventual independence. In Paraguay (1725 ff.) Antequera and his *Comuneros* spoke of the "sovereignty of the people." In 1740–1741 town juntas in Peru prepared to proclaim the Inca Felipe

"King of the Seas of the North and the South," and the conspiracy was so widespread that it had centers in New Granada, Venezuela, Chile, and Buenos Aires. In New Spain (1742) dissatisfied subjects sent a deputation to a British military officer in New England in order to offer a monopoly of commerce for arms and men. They were dreaming of founding an independent kingdom under a prince of the House of Austria. Their plan is said to have reached London, where it received the favorable consideration of Sir Robert Walpole. In 1750 the conspirators of South America were still working in the interest of the Inca Felipe, for in that year a commissioner from Lima was in London offering in the name of the Inca Prince the commercial monopoly of the proposed new kingdom in return for artillery, rifles, and munitions of war.

And so the conspiracies continued. In 1765 the insurgents of Quito talked of expelling the Peninsular Spaniards and placing a crown upon the head of Count Vega Florida. In 1780 three emancipatory movements were under way in Spanish America. The first was in Chile and centered around a certain noble Spaniard by the name of Don Juan. It was supported by both creoles and *chapetones* (Spaniards) who favored a constitutional monarchy like that of England. The kingdom was to extend from the equator to Patagonia, and once more British support was solicited. A vast commercial monopoly and large sums of money were to be granted, provided the London government would furnish 6,000 men for the occupation of Buenos Aires and the coasts of Chile. The second was none other than that of Tupac Amarú, which had connections in the whole of South America. The third had its centers in Caracas and Bogotá and was in correspondence with Francisco Miranda, who was then an officer in the Spanish army stationed at Havana. In 1781 Antonio Rojas and two Frenchmen were discovered in an attempt to effect the emancipation of Chile, and a Comunero revolt occurred in New Granada. In 1783 Francisco Miranda (1750–1816) talked with prominent leaders in the United States about the prospects of revolutionizing Spanish America. A year later three agents of the suppressed Comuneros of New Granada were in London making another appeal for British support. They argued that if Spain had aided the emancipation of the British colonies, Great Britain ought not to have any scruples in favoring the "independence of South America."

They assured the British government that, if it would furnish the succor which they needed, they were in a position to offer freedom of commerce and freedom of worship, and that the insurgents would, "if it were necessary, proclaim themselves British subjects." At the same time other members of the South American aristocracy put themselves in touch with the restless elements of Mexico and sent an emissary to London to solicit arms and munitions in exchange for an advantageous treaty of commerce. In 1790 Miranda, now a familiar figure in most of the courts of Europe, presented to William Pitt his first plan for emancipating the Spanish colonies. Soon afterwards Antonio Nariño (1765–1824) and his compatriots began their conspiracies in New Granada and two uprisings occurred in Venezuela. By this time many colonial patriots were bound together in secret lodges both in Spain and in Spanish America.

No wonder that Spanish statesmen began to be alarmed! As early as 1783 Count Aranda had advised Charles III to establish Spanish princes upon thrones in Mexico, Peru, and Costa Firme (northern South America), reserving for himself Cuba, Porto Rico, and certain trading stations, as well as the title of Emperor. Aranda advised that Spain and the three new kingdoms be bound together by family compacts, treaties of alliance, and commercial reciprocity. If such a project had been adopted and the American monarchs had been willing to promulgate constitutions and set up parliaments, as Godoy appears to have suggested later (1804), the history of Spanish America might have been far different. But the stubborn Bourbons were committed to doctrines of popular repression; and conspiracies and propaganda continued to go on.

By 1806 Miranda thought the time had come to begin the revolt in Venezuela. But the "Immortals" who sailed with him from New York soon made the tragic discovery that their effort was premature. In the pestilential dungeons of Venezuela they paid dearly for their rashness. The majority of the Venezuelans were still loyal.

The same appears to have been true of the inhabitants of the Río de la Plata in 1806–1807. At any rate, they refused to submit to British conquest. Yet the very act and manner of expelling the British stimulated a national spirit, while the cheap goods introduced during the English occupation created a longing for a freer commercial régime.

Meantime, the first successful revolt in Latin America had occurred in Española (called Saint-Domingue by the French, who had gained possession of the western portion of the island by 1697 and of the entire island in 1795). The Negroes and mulattoes of the western region, exasperated by racial discrimination, oppression, and injustice, and inspired by the radical ideas of the French Revolution, began their insurgent career in 1790. Taking advantage of disorders and wars in France and Europe, the colored leaders— Toussaint l'Ouverture and later Jean Jacques Dessalines—succeeded in driving the French authorities from the whole island by the end of 1803. On January 1, 1804, the independence of the new state was proclaimed and it assumed the name of Haiti. The people of the eastern part of the island, inhabitants of the area which years later became the Dominican Republic, were restive, however, under Negro rule.

POLITICAL CONDITIONS IN SPAIN

Political disturbances in Spain, disorders which began in 1808 and lasted for several years, profoundly influenced the destiny of the colonies. The Franco-Spanish Treaty of Basel (1795) provided for the cession to France of the remainder of the island of Española and indicated that, despite the overthrow of the French Bourbons, Spain's destiny was still to be linked with that of France. The Franco-Spanish alliance of 1796 and subsequent agreements led to the loss of the Spanish navy and the territorial possessions of Trinidad (to England, 1797) and Louisiana (to France, 1800). Early in 1808 Napoleon, resorting to treachery, invaded the Spanish Peninsula, forced the Bourbons to sign their abdication, placed his brother Joseph upon the Spanish throne, and dispatched agents to the colonies.

These drastic measures led to an outburst of Spanish nationalism. Provincial juntas, or committees, sprang up on every hand, and in September, 1808, a Supreme Central Junta was organized in Madrid. Soon afterwards, however, it was forced to flee to Seville and then to the isle of León, where it called into existence a Council of Regency and then dissolved. The Regency, in turn, called together a Cortes, which first assembled at León and later in Cádiz. Meanwhile, the British government, which already had resolved that the "Little Corsican" should not seize Spanish America along with Spain, decided that he must not seize either and sent to the Peninsula troops which had been assembled for the colonies.

Miranda, who had returned to London after the fiasco of 1806, was deeply disappointed; but the cause in which he was interested was really not so desperate as it seemed. The events of the period aroused many of his compatriots to full political consciousness and a sense of their importance in world affairs. Thrilled by the struggle of the Spaniards against the Corsican tyrant, they prepared to defend themselves against French conquest. They were further stimulated by the attitude of the Spanish provisional governments, although many of them were hardly in a mood to submit to their dictation. The very doctrine of residuary sovereignty upon which these provisional governments based their action constituted an argument that the colonists could use to justify their temporary autonomy; and the promulgations of the Central Junta and the Regency promised a new régime.

The Central Junta declared (1809) that the Americans had the same rights as Spaniards, including the right to send deputies to the Junta and the Cortes. In calling for the assembly of the Cortes at Cádiz (1810), the Regency went even further, employing the following stirring words: "You are elevated to the dignity of free men. You are no longer in the same condition as you were before: bent under the yoke of tyranny more oppressive because you are farther from the center of power; looked upon with indifference, harassed by greed, and ruined by ignorance. . . . Your destinies now no longer depend either upon ministers, or viceroys and governors. They are in your own hands." Nobody in the colonies had uttered more revolutionary language; but the Regency was then in desperate straits for funds and probably meant something of what it said. Soon afterwards its attitude changed.

The sessions of the Cortes of Cádiz were notably liberal, and in them twenty-six colonial deputies took part, just as they had taken part previously in the meetings of the Central Junta. Freedom of the press was declared, Indian tributes were abolished, freedom of

(From a Painting by Kronstrand)

GENERAL SAN MARTIN

agriculture and industry was proclaimed, the colonists were admitted to public employment on terms of equality with the Spaniards, and the alcabalas were abolished. Moreover, the constitution which the Cortes promulgated for Spain in March, 1812, embodied all these liberal principles, and in 1813 the Inquisition was abolished. The ideals of the philosophers had invaded Spain.

But the colonies had not been given adequate representation in the Junta and Cortes, the obstinate Council of Regency finally insisted upon the absolute rights of Spain in America, and as the European Allies rolled back Napoleon's legions, the forces of conservatism came once more into their own in Spain. Early in 1814 the Corsican was sent into exile and Ferdinand returned to his throne. He fell into the hands of the reactionaries, and on May 4 declared null and void both the Constitution of 1812 and the decrees of the Cortes. It was 1820 before the Spanish Liberals regained power and placed their favorite organic law again in operation. Even then their hold was only temporary, for early in 1823 French troops invaded the Peninsula in support of Ferdinand VII and the old régime. The reaction which followed the triumph of the absolutists was even more violent than that of 1814; and the situation was soon further complicated by intrigues for the succession which eventually resulted in the Carlist wars. Such, in brief, was the history of Spain during the period when the oversea colonies were fighting for independence and recognition as independent powers.

EARLY FAILURES

The Wars of Liberation in Spanish America fall into two periods separated by the year 1816. The first was characterized by failure everywhere except in Río de la Plata and the second by slowly rising success until complete separation from the mother country was finally effected (1825).

Although the invasion of Spain by Napoleon in 1808 caused a general ferment in the colonies, the colonial leaders were at first hesitant regarding the exact course which they should take. At the outset, the creoles and even some of the Spaniards met in their town cabildos and general juntas, protested against the imposition of Joseph Bonaparte as king of Spain, refused to receive his agents, and while preparing to set up their own provisional governments sent funds to Spanish nationalists and declared their loyalty to Ferdinand VII. In view of the many activities of the "Precursors" (already described), it is difficult to believe that all their protestations were sincere. Yet their very avowals of loyalty reveal the strength of loyal sentiment which the leaders assumed to exist, and it seems only natural that Hispanic nationalism should have been fomented by events in the Peninsula. A little later, when it appeared that Spain was completely subjugated by Napoleon, large groups in some of the colonies proceeded to declare independence, alleging that they did so in order to escape French domination. Others deferred action until the restored Ferdinand VII left them no hope of securing larger liberties under Spain. In Peru little could be done because of the strength of the viceroy.

Audiencia of Charcas.—This Audiencia (Presidency), since 1776 a part of the Viceroyalty of Río de la Plata, was the first to reveal insurgent tendencies during this period. On May 25, 1809, the inhabitants of Chuquisaca deposed President Pizarro and set up a governmental junta composed of creoles. In the following July the people of La Paz overthrew the intendant, created a "protective junta," and proclaimed their loyalty to Ferdinand, although it is probable that they intended to strike for independence. Under their leader, Pedro Murillo, they waged a brief but unsuccessful war against royal troops sent from Buenos Aires and Lima. At the time of his execution Murillo is said to have exclaimed: "I die; but the torch which I have lighted no one will be able to extinguish." Subsequently, until 1824, this area followed the Viceroyalty of Río de la Plata in its convulsions.

Audiencia of Quito.—In the Audiencia of Quito, President Ruiz de Castilla was deposed by a group of colonists and thrown into prison (August, 1809). A "supreme junta" was then set up, with Marquis de Selva Alegre as its presiding officer. The members of the junta were given the title of "Excellency," and Selva Alegre, that of "Most Serene Highness." The powers of the audiencia were taken away and conferred upon a senate; secretaries of foreign relations, war, and grace and justice were established; but the junta proposed to exercise its authority in the name of Ferdinand VII. Royal forces from the Viceroyalty of New Granada assisted in overthrowing the

VICEROYALTY OF NEW SPAIN

Calderon × ⊙Mexico

Havana

Captaincy General of Cuba

Captaincy General of Guatemala

Guatemala ⊙

VICEROYALTY OF NEW GRANADA

Carabobo ×
⊙ Caracas

Captaincy General of Caracas

GUIANA

Audencia
Bogotá ⊙ × Boyacá
of Santa Fé

Quito ⊙ Presidency
of Quito
Pichincha

VICEROYALTY

BRAZIL
(Portuguese)

Junín ⊙
Lima ⊙ ×
Ayacucho

Presidency
of
Charcas

Chuquisaca ⊙

VICEROYALTY OF BUENOS AIRES ORI LA PLATA

OF

PERU

Rio de Janeiro

Chacabuco ×
Santiago ⊙ San
Lorenzo
× ×
Maipú

Captaincy
General
and
Presidency
of Chile

Buenos
Aires

Audiencia of
Buenos
Aires

SPANISH AMERICA
DURING THE WAR FOR INDEPENDENCE
1810–1825

Showing approximately the
Political Divisions in 1808
⊙ Capitals   × Battlefields

MANHATTAN DRAFTING CO., INC., N.Y.

SPANISH AMERICA DURING THE WAR FOR INDEPENDENCE

new government, and the leaders of the insurrection were ruthlessly executed in August, 1810. Another movement begun late in September was likewise suppressed. The region then remained quiet until shortly before the arrival of General José Antonio de Sucre in 1822.

Peru.—In Peru, stronghold of royal authority in South America, the patriots made little headway prior to 1816. In Lima, under such leaders as José de la Riva Agüero and José Baquíjano reforms were discussed, secret societies organized, and seditious propaganda distributed. An abortive movement also occurred in Cuzco (1813); but liberation awaited the arrival of San Martín (1821) and Bolívar (1823).

Plata Basin.—In the Plata basin the new era dimly forecast by the expulsion of the British had its dawn in 1810. During the English invasion the viceroy had revealed a craven inefficiency. The colonists had accordingly chosen for that position Jacques Liniers, a Frenchman who had led them to victory over the invading foe. In 1809, however, a royalist uprising had gained the upper hand and demanded his resignation. He was soon replaced by a new viceroy sent out by the Central Junta of Spain. In May, 1810, when news of Napoleonic successes in the mother country reached Buenos Aires, this viceroy was in turn deposed and a "Provisional Junta of the Provinces of the Plata River" set up. Spanish authority was never reëstablished in the region.

Nevertheless, conditions in the Plata area continued to be turbulent. The patriots were disturbed by divided councils and the outlying provinces were difficult to subject to the central authorities at Buenos Aires. Expeditions sent to Paraguay failed to win over that section; its inhabitants set up their own "governmental junta" at Asunción in 1811 and declared their independence of Spain. Two years later they issued a similar proclamation with reference to the Buenos Aires government. The inhabitants of Banda Oriental, under the redoubtable José Gervasio Artigas, at first remained loyal to the authorities of the provincial junta, but later became disaffected and were routed by the rebel armies of Río de la Plata and Brazil (1817), Artigas himself finding refuge in Paraguay (1820). Among the delegates who assembled in a general congress at Tucumán in 1816 and declared the independence of the "United Provinces" of southern South America, were none from Paraguay or Banda Oriental and few from Charcas. Moreover, the government of the Plata region continued to be menaced by invasions from Charcas and Peru. Until the royalists had been driven from that viceroyalty there could be no permanent security.

Fortunately, this was realized by José de San Martín, an able soldier who had cast his lot with the Argentine insurgents in 1812, as well as by the "Supreme Director" Martín de Pueyrredón. In 1814 the former had been appointed governor-intendant of the interior province of Cuyo, where he was permitted to train an army for the invasion of Peru by way of Chile. The growing consolidation of the government of the United Provinces and the work of San Martín were the most hopeful aspects of patriotic effort in south-eastern South America as the year 1816 drew to a close.

Captaincy-general of Venezuela.—In the Captaincy-general of Venezuela the colonials became active within two years after Miranda's unsuccessful expedition of 1806. They were inspired largely by events in the mother country. In July, 1808, the cabildo of Caracas proclaimed Ferdinand VII king of Spain and the Indies, but proposed the establishment of a governmental junta in the capital. Near the end of the following year a number of conspirators were thought to be planning a revolution. Then, on April 19, 1810, an extraordinary cabildo in Caracas deposed the captain-general and created a governmental junta, but the leaders still professed that they were acting in behalf of Ferdinand. Soon afterwards the junta deported the captain-general and other Spanish officials, established administrative bureaus, undertook certain political reforms, and issued a manifesto disavowing the Spanish regency. It also directed to other Spanish Americans a proclamation asserting that Venezuela claimed a place in the rank of free nations, and issued an address to the municipal governments of the Spanish-American capitals urging them to join the insurrectionary movement.

In December, 1810, Miranda, encouraged by the activities of his compatriots, returned to his native land. At about the same time Simón Bolívar, who had been sent by the junta to London as a member of a diplomatic mission, again made his appearance in Caracas. The champions of drastic action had arrived. A general congress was installed in March, 1811, and on July 5 the independence of the "United Provinces of Venezuela" was proclaimed. The next step was the framing of a constitution modeled after that of the United States and also showing the influence of the French Declaration of the Rights of Man. Soon afterwards the insurgents had to face the Spanish troops under General Monteverde. Miranda was forthwith proclaimed dictator and placed in charge of the revolutionary forces. Bolívar was one of his lieutenants. A desperate struggle ensued; but an ill-timed earthquake broke the resistance of the patriots. The cities in control of the rebels were virtually annihilated, while those remaining faithful to the king escaped unharmed. The clergy declared that the earthquake was an unmistakable intervention of Providence. The superstitious elements withdrew from the ranks of the rebels, and Miranda was forced to agree to a humiliating capitulation (July 25, 1812). Disgruntled patriots, Bolívar among them, later arrested him and allowed him to fall into the hands of the Spaniards, who carried him away as a prisoner to Cádiz.

It was not until August, 1813, that the patriots under the command of Bolívar were able to enter Venezuela from New Granada and regain their lost capital. Bolívar was then given the title of "Liberator" by an extraordinary cabildo of that city. But the war to the death proclaimed by this energetic leader in the previous June had scarcely begun. Creoles, mestizos, and Indians led by Bolívar fought Spaniards, *llanero* Indians, and a few creoles and mestizos under royalist commanders and loyal lieutenants of Venezuela. Neither side gave quarter nor showed any mercy. By the end of the year 1814, however, the rebellion once more had been suppressed everywhere save in the island of Margarita. In September, Bolívar himself had fled to Cartagena, and he did not return to his native land until the end of 1816.

Viceroyalty of New Granada.—The Viceroyalty of New Granada was likewise stirred by events in Spain. The uprisings at Quito already have been noted. At Santa Fé de Bogotá, in the summer of 1808, Ferdinand was proclaimed king. During the following year the viceroy was forced to call an advisory junta in the capital for the purpose of considering what steps should be taken with reference to the insurgents at Quito. The junta evinced dissatisfaction with Spanish rule and delegated Camilo Torres to frame a memorial of grievances to be transmitted to the Central Junta of Spain.

The document which Torres drew up contained a threat of separation from the mother country. On July 20, 1810, an extraordinary cabildo created a junta for the entire viceroyalty, naming as president of the governing body the viceroy himself. But the cabildo declared its loyalty to Ferdinand, as did the junta a few weeks later when it broke with the Spanish Regency and expelled the viceroy.

Most of the leading towns of New Granada followed an analogous course. The cabildos, professing loyalty to the captive king, overthrew the Spanish authorities and created provincial juntas. Cartagena was the first, however, to declare its independence from Spain (November 11, 1811). The province of Cundinamarca appears to have been the next, taking this step on July 16, 1813. By this time several other provinces had set up their own governments and framed constitutions.

Unfortunately, however, the various provinces revealed violent particularist tendencies. Few of them were willing to submit themselves to the rule of the central government of Bogotá. With the hope of remedying the situation, a congress had framed an "Act of Federation of the United Provinces of New Granada" in November, 1811. Although this was ratified by several of the provinces, the government set up under it was quite ineffective and sectionalism continued to run riot. The time which the various regional governments should have used in preparing for defense against the Spaniards and the loyalists, was wasted in quarrels and fights among themselves. Bolívar, who had fought under the banner of Cartagena in 1812–1813, was employed late in 1814 by the congress of the United Provinces to help subdue the recalcitrant governments of Cundinamarca, Cartagena, and Santa Marta. He soon conquered the first, thus enabling the general government to move its seat from Tunja to Bogotá; but while he was engaged in laying siege to Cartagena in order to secure arms and supplies for the campaign against Santa Marta, General Pablo Morillo landed in Venezuela with a Spanish army of 10,000 men. Realizing that the situation was hopeless, Bolívar abandoned the *"Patria Boba"* ("Foolish Fatherland") of New Granada and sailed for Jamaica. By the middle of 1816 Morillo, who had left half of his forces in Venezuela, had completely reconquered northern South America.

Captaincy-general of Chile.—In the Captaincy-general of Chile the patriots, largely because of violent disagreements among themselves, likewise had their rise and fall. In September, 1810, the colonists deposed Captain-General García Carrasco, set up a governmental junta, and proclaimed their fidelity to the captive king. In the following July a general congress was held at Santiago. The first important act of the delegates was to take an oath of fidelity to Ferdinand and pledge themselves to support the constitution and any laws which the congress might promulgate. The delegates soon discovered that they were hopelessly divided. There were moderates who opposed drastic reforms and a definitive rupture with the metropolis; radicals who desired independence and a republic; and royalists who favored the restoration of the fallen régime. The radicals eventually withdrew, and the remaining deputies constituted themselves into an "Executive Power." In September, 1811, this government was overthrown by José Miguel Carrera (1785–1821), a military officer recently returned from Spain, where he had been fighting against the French. In 1812 he took the somewhat ambiguous step of sanctioning a republican constitution while recognizing the sovereignty of Ferdinand VII. Since he found his followers among the radicals, there is little doubt that he desired complete independence. The constitution vested supreme authority in a junta of three members controlled by Carrera. He and his two gifted brothers proceeded to rule the country with a stern hand. Their action provoked Bernardo O'Higgins (1778–1842)—himself a radical and the talented, though impetuous, son of an Irishman with a distinguished record in the Spanish colonial service—into open opposition. Subsequent dissensions furnished Carrasco, the able Peruvian viceroy, a favorable opportunity. Although the forces of O'Higgins and Carrera eventually united, the revolutionary army was defeated, Santiago was captured, and the colonial government reestablished in October, 1814. Frightful reprisals were visited upon some of the insurgents; others fled over the Andes to Argentina.

Captaincy-general of Guatemala.—Although some of the people of the Captaincy-general of Guatemala were stirred by the events of 1808–1810 in Spain, it appears to have required the additional stimulus of news from insurgent centers of Spanish America to arouse them to action. The first armed uprising occurred in November, 1811, in the city of San Salvador. The intendant of El Salvador was overthrown, a thousand new rifles were seized, and some two hundred thousand pesos taken from the royal treasury. Among the leaders were the priest José Matías Delgado, the friar Nicolás Aguilar, and Manuel José de Arce, who was to become prominent in the later history of the country. Other influential members of the clergy and the aristocracy opposed the movement, however, and it was easily suppressed. In December, 1811, a more important insurrection broke out in Nicaragua. Organizing in the city of León, the insurgents overthrew the intendant, seized Granada, and enlisted partisans until a thousand men were under arms. After an encounter with the troops of the captain-general, the patriots surrendered on condition that a general pardon be granted. But the captain-general refused to accept the terms promised by his military commander and the insurgents were thrown into prison.

The Spanish Constitution of 1812 was received in the captaincy-general with great solemnity and acclaim, but in 1813 there occurred an alleged conspiracy in the Convent of Bethlehem (Belén) in Guatemala City. It involved several men of diverse races and professions, some of the regular clergy among them. Informed of the plot, the captain-general sent troops who took the building and seized the conspirators. Although nearly all of them swore that they had assembled to "raffle off certain objects and play cards," it appeared that they were planning to strike for independence. They were accordingly cast into prison, where they lingered for several years. In 1814 another uprising, led by Arce and Juan Manuel Rodríguez, occurred in San Salvador, but it was no more successful than the one of 1811. Apparently the people were not ready for independence.

The Antilles.—In the Antilles, where by 1804 L'Ouverture and Dessalines had freed the colonists of Española from French rule, certain reverses were suffered. Although the Negroes of Haiti managed to preserve their independence, the creole and African elements of the other portion of the island were reconquered by Spanish soldiers between 1806 and 1814. Cuba and Porto Rico served as bases for the dispatch of royal troops and supplies to the insurgent areas of the mainland and therefore had little opportunity to revolt. The achievement of their separation from Spain had to await a more opportune occasion.

New Spain.—New Spain was the scene, during this early period, of bloody combats. News of the Napoleonic invasion of the mother country, the organization of Peninsular juntas, and the Spanish war of liberation induced the creole elements of the viceroyalty to aspire to a larger participation in its government. The viceroy, José de Iturrigaray—hoping to profit by catering to the creoles and even dreaming of becoming Mexico's first king, in case, as now seemed certain, Napoleon should completely subjugate Spain—favored the calling of a general junta elected by the municipal cabildos of the entire kingdom. The audiencia, filled with Spaniards, feared and distrusted the native elements; and although it was not able to prevent the assembling of the general junta in August, 1808, only a month later it instigated a group of Spaniards to seize the viceroy and expel him from the country. Four viceroys now followed each other in rapid succession (1808–1813). Amid the confusion secret societies were formed, revolutionary propaganda was carried on, Valladolid became the scene of an uprising (December, 1809), the aspiration for independence rapidly spread, and a few bold leaders struck out for a new régime.

One of these, Miguel Hidalgo y Costilla (1753–1811), a learned creole priest with a decided fondness for French philosophy and a deep interest in the Indian masses, seemed to have struck somewhat blindly. He appears to have had few notions of statecraft and even to have been uncertain at times whether he was fighting for Ferdinand VII or independence. In general, it may be said, however, that he fought for liberty and social reform. He was able to attract to his standard, emblazoned with a portrait of the Virgin of Guadalupe, not only a large group of Indians but a considerable number of mestizos and creoles as well. They had little concern about ultimate goals; what they desired was freedom from oppression and new opportunities. Starting (September 16) from the village of Dolores in the intendancy of Guanajuato with four thousand untrained followers, he began a zigzag advance upon the viceregal capital. One town after another—San Miguel, Celaya, Guanajuato, Guadalajara, Valladolid—fell before his ever-increasing hordes, who slew and pillaged with little restraint. Near the end of October he encamped with an undisciplined multitude of some eighty thousand within eighteen miles of Mexico City. Up to that time he had had only one severe encounter with the viceregal troops, and in that encounter his forces had managed to retain the field. By a sudden movement he might now have taken the capital, but he hesitated because royal troops were both in front and in the rear, and then decided to retire to Guadalajara, apparently with the view of training his army and organizing a government.

The delay gave General Félix Calleja, commander of the viceregal troops, time to collect his forces and assume the offensive. On January 17, 1811, the patriots to the number of about 80,000 and the royalists—only 6,000 strong, although many of them were soldiers seasoned by experience in the Peninsular War—confronted each other on the banks of the river Lerma near the bridge of Calderón, some forty miles from Guadalajara. A desperate fight ensued and the royalists were all but defeated when an explosion set fire to the grass field which constituted Hidalgo's position. Stampeded by the smoke and flames, the patriots fled precipitately, pursued by the enemy, who perpetrated a horrible butchery.

Hidalgo and his lieutenants, collecting a small remnant of their forces, continued the flight northward but were soon betrayed and turned over to the Spanish government of New Spain. They were tried and speedily executed, and the heads of four of the leaders—Hidalgo, Ignacio Allende, Mariano Jiménez, and Juan Aldama—were hung in cages at the corners of the public granary which they had recently taken by storm in Guanajuato.

Thus a formidable insurrection had virtually been suppressed after four short months, but the priest had lighted a persistent flame. "The spirit of Mexican nationality may be said to date from the rebellion of Hidalgo. . . . In the lurid background of Mexican national history, there may be discerned standing beside the sacred banner of Guadalupe the figure of the curate of Dolores,—the daring but unfortunate leader of a bloody revolt of the lower classes in Mexico against the dominant aristocracy." [3]

The mantle of Hidalgo fell upon José María Morelos (1765–1815), a humble mestizo (or was he a mulatto?) priest who was so completely inspired by his predecessor that the fatal error of his

[3] Robertson, *Rise of the Spanish-American Republics*, p. 106.

career was due to an attempt to follow Hidalgo's advice. Morelos was the most brilliant leader produced by the Mexican revolution, something of a statesman as well as a great soldier.

In October, 1810, he had been commissioned by Hidalgo to capture the strongly fortified port of Acapulco on the Pacific coast. At the end of three brilliant campaigns, in which his poorly equipped army had never numbered more than five thousand men, he was still not in possession of this stronghold; but he had gained control of the vastly more important region between Acapulco and the Valley of Mexico. On one occasion, early in 1812, he was within striking distance of Mexico City itself. Instead of advancing immediately, however, he established his headquarters at Cuautla, two hundred miles to the south. Forced eventually to abandon this place, he moved northeastward to Tehuacán, from which base he could menace Orizaba, Oaxaca, Puebla, Vera Cruz, and even Mexico City. At Tehuacán he probably should have set up his permanent headquarters, for early in 1813 he was in control of a good part of southern Mexico, including portions of both coasts. After taking Oaxaca, however, he recalled the commission of Hidalgo. Abandoning the center of the viceroyalty, where the ultimate issue of his revolt would certainly have to be decided, he set out to conquer to relatively unimportant port of Acapulco. This he accomplished after serious losses in April, 1813.

He then turned his attention to the political organization of the country—a process which he and other political leaders had already begun. A congress was installed in Chilpancingo, not far away. Here on November 6, 1813, a Declaration of Independence was issued and certain reform decrees of Morelos were adopted as fundamental law; but the work of the organizers had by no means been finished when Morelos decided to conquer a more appropriate seat for his government. He accordingly advanced upon Valladolid, the scene of his childhood; but his attempt to seize this town failed miserably. The congress later opened its sessions at Apatzingán, about ninety miles to the west, where on October 22, 1814, it promulgated Mexico's first constitution. But Morelos's star was already on the decline. The government soon became a migratory body. While conducting it toward the old center of Tehuacán, Morelos was captured (November, 1815). He was sent to the viceregal capital and soon

Miguel Hidalgo (1753–1811)

José María Morelos
(1763–1815)

Agustín de Iturbide
(1783–1824)

THE LIBERATORS OF MEXICO

afterwards shot. With his death Hidalgo's flame was almost extinguished. Only a few *guerrillas,* among them Vicente Guerrero, held on in the mountains to the south.

Such were the early tragic failures of the emancipation movement in Spanish America. Everywhere save in Río de la Plata Spanish arms were triumphant. Looking through history's perspective, however, one may discover lights as well as shadows. Napoleon in St. Helena, absolutism enthroned in Spain and Europe, trained Spanish soldiers free for the fight in America; but the treasury of Spain empty, British warriors looking for employment in patriot armies, English and North American merchants eager for markets, nationalism and republicanism rampant in the United States, Bolívar in Margarita, San Martín in Cuyo, Guerrero in the Mexican Sierra del Sur, and Iturbide, formally an implacable foe of Mexican insurgents, now sulking like Achilles in his tent—all these elements were in the balances of fate at the end of the year 1816. Time would soon tip the beam in favor of the Spanish colonies.

FINAL SUCCESS

It was not long before success began to crown the efforts of the insurgents in both northern and southern South America. In the north, Bolívar, ably seconded by José Antonio Páez (1790–1873) and Antonio José Sucre (1793–1830), was the conquering hero; in the south, it was San Martín—assisted by the half Spanish, half Irish patriot O'Higgins and the impetuous Scotchman Thomas Cochrane —who led the insurgents to victory. In Mexico, where Augustín de Iturbide (1783–1824) was the fortunate leader, emancipation awaited the turn of events in Spain and then swept down into Central America. Bolívar and San Martín were both men of extraordinary ability who deserve to rank with the great of all time. Iturbide mounted to success on a compromise which involved the sacrifice of virtually every ideal of the emancipation movement save one—independence—and was therefore a liberator only in this limited sense.

The Liberator of the South.—San Martín was "a concrete genius with more calculation than inspiration," as Bartolomé Mitre has said. Born of Spanish parents out on the Argentine frontier (1778), he lived in Spain from his eighth to his thirty-fourth year, serving the mother country in Africa, against the French Republicans, against England, against Portugal, and finally against the eagles of Napoleon himself. Through Miranda he was placed in contact with the American patriots who dreamed of independence from Spain. Returning to Buenos Aires in 1812, he organized the Lautaro Lodge, a secret society designed to spread revolutionary propaganda. His military prestige soon won him preëminent rank. In the province of Cuyo, in 1814, as already noted, he began to train an army for the liberation of Chile and Peru.

It was not until toward the end of January, 1817, that he was ready to advance. For nearly three weeks he led his heroic little army of fewer than 4,000 men over the lofty, bleak Andes, as Napoleon had crossed the Alps seventeen years before. On February 12 he and his soldiers sallied forth from the mountains into Chile and defeated a surprised Spanish army at Chacabuco. Soon afterwards San Martín entered Santiago in triumph, the Spanish government having fled from the capital. Offered the supreme government of Chile, he declined to accept it, and O'Higgins was chosen instead. An exile at Mendoza for nearly three years, O'Higgins had been a general in the Army of the Andes and had done valiant service at Chacabuco. Early in January, 1818, the independence of Chile was declared and on April 5, following, San Martín routed the royalists on the plains of Maipú.

Preparations then went forward for the emancipation of Peru. Two trips made by San Martín to Buenos Aires brought aid from that quarter; O'Higgins loyally supported the project in Chile; and a small navy was collected under the command of Lord Cochrane. In August, 1820, the expedition left Valparaiso. There were eight war vessels, sixteen transports, 1,600 seamen and marines, and something over 4,000 soldiers—Chileans, Argentines, and a few Europeans, mainly Englishmen. In the following September the army of liberation began to land in Peru, but San Martín was in no hurry. It was not to be "a war of conquest and glory," he said, but one "entirely of opinion." He accordingly sent out his propagandists and began to negotiate with the viceroy. Negotiations failed; propaganda succeeded. On July 6, 1821, the viceroy, considering his position unsafe, marched out from Lima and retired toward the mountains. The people of the capital then invited San Martín to enter.

ANTONIO JOSÉ SUCRE, Mariscal de Ayacucho

Having satisfied himself that the invitation was sincere, the hero of Chacabuco entered the "City of the Kings" and on July 28, 1821, formally proclaimed the viceroyalty to be independent of Spain. A few days later he assumed supreme authority under the title of "Protector."

The war for the liberation of South America had not yet terminated, however; for, although Bolívar had emancipated Venezuela, New Granada, and Quito, the royalists still controlled the Peruvian highlands and the Audiencia of Charcas. Anticipating a desperate struggle and desiring to join forces with Bolívar, San Martín went to Guayaquil for an interview with the Liberator of the North. It was the month of July in the year 1822. Sensing the towering ambition of Bolívar, disagreeing with him in regard to political institutions, and perceiving that the great Venezuelan was called by destiny to conclude the task of emancipation, the Liberator of the South decided to withdraw. With the loftiness of a hero of Plutarch, he wrote: "It would have been greater glory for me to serve under the orders of Your Excellency." Soon afterwards he embarked for Europe, where he spent nearly thirty years in exile, dying in 1850. He never saw his native land again.

San Martín was a solid character, a Stoic, as he himself said. To the men whom he commanded he appeared as a rock, solitary and unyielding. For this reason he was little loved by those who surrounded him. His soldiers felt the distance which separated them from him; San Martín did not draw men to him. Sometimes they conspired against their chief.

His political ideas were clear, firm, and few. "I am," he said, "an American, republican by principles and inclination, but willing to sacrifice this for the good of the people." He thought that "it was not necessary to give to the new nations the best laws [theoretically], but those best adapted to their character, grade of instruction, habits, and manner of life." It was not yet "in season to give them too many liberties. . . . Only a purely military control [was] capable of rescuing them from the Morass." He remarked that either Bolívar would have to employ a "strong arm" in Peru or everything would go to the Devil. Thus he was a monarchist, and monarchism permeated all his words and 'acts. The people noted this and drank toasts to "King Joseph."

The Liberator of the North.—But what were the achievements of Bolívar after 1816? They were so brilliant that they eventually made him one of the heroes of the whole Spanish race.

In fact, his entire career possesses the irresistible attraction of a romance. He was born (1783) rich and he died (1830) poor, having spent his fortune in the struggle for South American independence. He was of pure Spanish blood and noble descent. At the age of three he was left an orphan in care of his uncle. His early teachers were an errant philosopher, Simón Rodríguez, and a poet, Andrés Bello. He was not yet sixteen when sent abroad to complete his education in Europe. He visited Mexico, Cuba, France, and Spain. In Madrid he associated with the nobility and saw the corruption of the court of Charles IV. Before the end of 1802 he had fallen deeply in love and married. He returned to his vast estates to settle down. In less than a year an epidemic carried away his wife, and he returned to the Continent in order to avoid losing his mind. In Paris he witnessed in 1804 the brilliant coronation of Napoleon. He met his old, austere teacher, Simón Rodríguez, and confessed to him his patriotic yearnings. A new Hannibal, on the Sacred Mountain in Rome he took an oath to redeem oppressed America. He returned to Venezuela in 1807, stopping *en route* long enough to visit the battle fields of the United States. His connection with the early emancipation movement in northern South America has already been mentioned.

Early in 1817 Bolívar left Margarita for the valley of the lower Orinoco. Aided by Páez and a few guerrillas, he soon conquered this region and established his headquarters at Angostura (formerly Santo Tomé). Early in 1819 he called together a congress and, as a "tribute of submission," presented a constitution. Meantime, in spite of wretched climate and sanitary conditions, he proceeded to collect recruits—several hundred British officers and soldiers among them. His plan was to invade New Granada by way of the steaming, flooded plains of the Orinoco and its tributaries and the ice-capped mountains immediately to the southeast of Bogotá. Leaving Páez to keep Morillo busy, he set out toward the west near the end of May, 1819. Within eighty days he had crossed the plains and the Andes, seized Tunja, fought the decisive battle of Boyacá, and entered the viceregal capital. His army numbered about 3,400 at the outset; he lost nearly a thousand on the way; and he met on the plains of Cundinamarca a superior number of fresh royal troops. Yet he had swept all before him. It was his first brilliant achievement.

In December, 1819, the congress at Angostura, enlarged by the admission of a few delegates from New Granada, inscribed upon paper the new nation of Great Colombia, which was declared to consist of Venezuela, Quito, and New Granada. Bolívar set about the task of making the dream a reality. While a new congress assembled at Cúcuta, he dispatched Sucre with a small force by sea to Guayaquil. He then proceeded with the remainder of his army to join forces with Páez in Venezuela. On June 24, 1821, the united insurgent army, some 6,500 strong, met and routed a slightly inferior number of royalists on the plains of Carabobo. The emancipation of Venezuela was thus assured. But news had arrived of Sucre's initial reverses near Guayaquil, and Bolívar hurried to the far south. Before the Liberator arrived, Sucre won the decisive engagement of Pichincha (May 24, 1822). On June 16, 1822, Bolívar entered the city of Quito, and a few weeks later proceeded to Guayaquil, where he had his interview with San Martín. Great Colombia was now a reality, except for the stubborn loyalist region around Pasto.

Bolívar and Sucre soon directed their forces towards Peru, Sucre proceeding in advance of the Liberator, who did not reach Lima until September, 1823. They found the Peruvian insurgents divided, quarreling among themselves and on the point of civil war. The Spanish forces were in the upland valleys to the northeast. It was the summer of 1824 before Bolívar and Sucre were ready to advance with their patriot army. After weeks of marching through the high mountains, on August 6, 1824, they confronted the royalist army under José de Canterac at Junín, on the borders of Lake Reyes near lofty Cerro de Pasco. The patriots numbered 8,080; the royalists, 8,300. It was, however, strictly a cavalry engagement, fought with saber and lance while the others looked on. Not a shot was fired, but in forty-five minutes the insurgent cavalry numbering 1,100 put to flight the royalists, who outnumbered them by some two hundred. Shortly afterwards Bolívar returned to Lima to look after the civil government, while Sucre continued his march to the southeast. On December 8, 1824, with a force of 5,780 fighting men, he met and routed an army of 9,310 royalists at Ayacucho in the Andes,

11,600 feet above the sea. The viceroy was compelled to agree to withdraw all the Spanish forces from Peru. A few insubordinates continued to hold on in Charcas, but Sucre soon dislodged them and set up the republic of Bolivia. In January, 1826, the Spanish troops evacuated the port of Callao. The war was over. The success of the rebellion had been due to several factors: to Spain's inability to prosecute the war vigorously; to the anticlericalism of 1820–1821 in Spain (which drove the higher clergy of Spanish America into the insurgent camp); to the aid of foreign officers and soldiers (mainly British); to funds lent by English bankers or paid as revenues into patriot coffers by British and North American merchants. But in the main it had been the result of the military genius of Bolívar, San Martín, O'Higgins, Sucre, and Páez.

In northern South America Bolívar stands out supreme, the most versatile man of his time. He possessed an ardent and soaring imagination and was both an industrious reader and a profound thinker. He knew the Greek and Latin classics, Bacon and Holbach, Montesquieu and the Encyclopedists. He discussed with José Olmedo the *Ode to Junín*. He penetrated the hidden mysteries of his epoch and gave out permanent political formulas. A prophet, in a sense, he predicted the future of Spanish America so accurately that its future appears to have obeyed his incantation. Most of his ideas were expressed while in motion or in the midst of anarchy or in exile. He passed with marvelous rapidity across tropical jungles and snow-clad mountains, thrilling men by his eloquence, organizing military campaigns and governments, dictating plans and constitutions, creating nations. Difficulties exalted his will: defeat rendered him more terrible than victory. "What can we do?" asked his destitute and discouraged lieutenants while crossing the bleak Andes on the way to meet the enemy. He replied in a word "Triunfar!"—"Triumph!" "He alone is war," said Morillo. His captains feared and loved him. "At times," confessed Santander, "I approach him full of rancor, and the very sight of him disarms me, and I go away filled with admiration." Always the grand cavalier, he freed a thousand of his slaves by the stroke of his pen, renounced pensions, thought of committing suicide because of his poverty, thrice refused a crown.

When the struggle for independence terminated, his power rap-

idly declined. The waning genius of his later years could not organize the great state of his dreams—Charcas, Quito, Peru, New
Granada, and Venezuela welded into unity under a strong government which would permit an untrained populace only very limited
participation in political affairs. Much less could he bring into existence a Latin-American league of nations. His feverish imagination had
carried him far beyond his strength and his epoch. He accordingly
spent his last years in profound disappointment. Anarchy threatened to devour everything. The Liberator himself was in danger
from his ambitious captains, to whom his power and his glory were
insufferable. They revolted, they tried to assassinate him. Bolivia,
Peru, Venezuela, Ecuador, and finally Colombia passed beyond his
control. As the end of the third decade of the new century approached, chaos was triumphant in Spanish America. "There is no
faith in America," he said, "either between men or nations. Treaties
are papers, constitutions books, elections combats, liberty anarchy,
and life a torment." Although he was broken, infirm, poor, and
childless, men still denounced him for his ambitions. In December,
1830, he lay slowly dying in an hacienda near Santa Marta. An attendant, a Spaniard, placed in his trembling hands a book. It was
Don Quixote. Reading the old classic again, he was reminded of
Christ—and of himself. In one respect, he thought, they were all
three alike: they were deluded persons who had plowed the sea.

New Spain and Guatemala.—The final achievement of independence in New Spain and Guatemala was a sort of anticlimax. The
revolution of 1820 in Spain restored the Constitution of 1812 and
threatened the wealth and power of the clergy and nobility. The
conservative elements of Mexico then decided that they had more
to fear from the rule of the mother country than from the insurgents whom they had tried to destroy. In the obscure hamlet of
Iguala, in southwestern Mexico, Augustín de Iturbide began negotiations with Vicente Guerrero. An agreement was soon reached.
The Roman Catholic religion, with all the possessions and privileges
of the church, was to be preserved; Spaniards, creoles, mestizos, and
Indians were to unite; independence was to be effected under the
rule of Ferdinand VII or some other Bourbon prince. All this really
meant that little save independence was to be gained. The church
and the privileged classes were to rule in Mexico, and the oppres-

sions of the Indians and other humble folk were to persist. The army of the "three guaranties" was organized; the viceroy was deposed; the Bourbon prince refused to come; and the creole Iturbide was crowned emperor. The Captaincy-general of Guatemala, without bloodshed except in El Salvador, was then annexed to the Mexican Empire. But the liberal elements soon became restless both in Central America and in Mexico.

The Antilles.—In the Antilles, Cuba and Porto Rico remained under Spanish control and Haiti continued independent. But the eastern half of Española, shortly after declaring its independence in 1821, was absorbed by its island neighbor. It did not regain its autonomy until 1844.

THE INDEPENDENCE OF BRAZIL

The Brazilian nation was born in a maze of intrigue, but its movement toward independence was in many ways similar to the movement in Spanish America. For instance, it was a part of the struggle of Liberty against Traditionalism; the occasion for it was furnished by Napoleon's temporary conquest of Portugal and the policy of the Portuguese governments during and following that conquest; and it was characterized by the organization of colonial juntas. It differed in that it was delayed for a time by the arrival of the royal family in Brazil, was accomplished more speedily and with less bloodshed, and was followed by the achievement of unity under a constitutional monarchy.

Napoleon's soldiers invaded Portugal late in 1807. The royal family—Prince Regent Dom John, his wife Carlota Joaquina, his son Dom Pedro and the rest of the children, and the courtiers—avoided captivity by embarking for Brazil under the convoy of a portion of the British fleet. Dom John was received with much rejoicing at Rio, and immediately decreed certain reforms. The trade of Brazil was thrown open to all nations, a printing press was set up, other institutions for the dissemination of learning were established, a supreme court and important financial tribunals were created, and foreign settlers and scientists were invited to come in. In 1815 Brazil was declared to be a coördinate part of the Portuguese empire; henceforth Portuguese and Brazilians were to be equal before the law. In 1816 John's demented mother died and he became John VI of the "United Kingdom of Portugal, Brazil, and Algarves." The next year a republican uprising in Pernambuco was suppressed, but for a time thereafter political affairs remained quiet.

Then, in 1820, there occurred a liberal revolution in the mother country. It demanded the calling of the Cortes, which had not met for a century, as well as the adoption of a constitution. The liberal elements of Brazil were deeply stirred. Juntas were set up in the leading towns, and in Rio the vacillating, pusillanimous Dom John was forced on two occasions to take an oath to support a constitution. He was frightened by visions of Louis XVI's head! In the meantime, the Portuguese provisional government urged John to return. In April, 1821, he responded to the call, against the wishes of the reactionaries of Brazil but to the delight of the liberals and perhaps also of his son Pedro, who was left as regent and lieutenant of the colony.

When John reached Lisbon he found already in existence a Constituent Cortes which was demanding the reduction of Brazil to its former colonial status. In Brazil itself some Portuguese merchants and other reactionaries were likewise in favor of the ancient régime. The Cortes abolished the higher tribunals and most of the other institutions recently established in Brazil. It also planned to restore the old commercial policy; and it actually placed in charge of the ancient captaincies governors who were to overthrow the juntas and receive their instructions from Lisbon instead of from Rio de Janeiro, sent out detachments of soldiers to support the reactionaries, and attempted to transfer Brazilian troops to Portugal. Finally, late in 1821, it ordered Dom Pedro to return home for "the completion of his education."

Although rather conservative at heart, the young prince was forced to cast his lot with the liberals under the able leadership of the Andrada brothers—José Bonifacio and Martínez Francisco—in order to preserve his position, resist the actions of the Cortes, and save the colony from chaos. By the beginning of 1822 Brazil was clearly on its way to independence, although probably against the wishes of Dom Pedro. On January 9, he announced his intention to defy the Cortes and his father and remain in Rio. In May he accepted the title of "Perpetual Protector and Defender of Brazil." In June he agreed to convoke a legislative and constitutional assembly. On September

7, near São Paulo, he uttered the famous *Grito de Ypiranga:* "Comrades, the Cortes of Portugal wishes to reduce Brazil to slavery; we must declare forthwith her independence. . . . Independence or death!" On October 12, he became constitutional emperor of Brazil.

It was then necessary to expel the Portuguese soldiers from the garrisons and to control the malcontents—the reactionaries and the republicans. Thanks to the support of the liberal monarchists and the able assistance of Lord Cochrane, who had left Chile for employment in Brazil, these tasks were soon accomplished. There was much turbulence but comparatively little bloodshed.

It was not a very difficult matter to suppress the reactionaries, expel the Portuguese troops, or even to put down the republicans of Pernambuco and the north, but it proved impossible to evade the demands of the liberals for a constitution. Dom Pedro dissolved the constituent assembly by use of bayonets (late in 1823), but he found it wise to grant a fairly liberal constitution of his own making (1824). Soon afterwards the independence of Brazil was recognized by the United States, the mother country, and England.

Thus a new nation was admitted into the comity of the powers. During the next decades, however, it was destined to a somewhat stormy career. It was not altogether satisfied with its emperor, and its emperor was not entirely pleased with the new entity which he had helped to create.

THE END OF SPANISH RULE IN CUBA

After a long period of conspiracies, insurrections, and wars in behalf of freedom, the Cubans, unlike the inhabitants of the rest of Spanish America, finally received the aid of a foreign power in effecting their liberation from the mother country. Cuba's independence from Spain was achieved in 1898.

The main causes of Cuban discontent during the nineteenth century were the Spanish system of taxation, trade restrictions, and the virtual exclusion of the natives from high positions in the colonial government. It is probable, however, that, even if oppression and injustice had been far less, the leaders of the island would have developed an aspiration for independence.

Although the burdensome nature of Spanish taxes in Cuba has

Francisco de Paula Santander
(1792–1840)

Juan A. Lavalleja
(1786–1853)

Bernardo O'Higgins
(1778–1842)

José Gervasio Artigas
(1764–1850)

José Antonio Páez
(1790–1875)

José Miguel Carrera
(1785–1821)

OTHER LEADERS OF THE INDEPENDENCE MOVEMENT

perhaps been exaggerated, it can hardly be doubted that they were numerous, varied, and vexatious, nor is there any doubt that the operation of the revenue laws was too often subject to favoritism and bribery. It is likely, however, that the "fundamental dissatisfaction of the Cubans" in this matter arose from the fact that they "objected to paying any taxes at all that were imposed by Spaniards and not by themselves." [4]

Cuba, along with the rest of Spanish America, received concessions in the direction of greater freedom of trade during the reign of Charles III. Moreover, during the frequently recurring wars of the period from 1756 to 1815, the island often engaged in trade in spite of the laws which confined its commerce to the mother country. Indeed, in 1801 Spain opened Cuba to world commerce; and trade with other countries continued in defiance of Spanish regulations after this freedom was withdrawn in 1809. At last (1818) the Spanish government, seeking to turn to its advantage a difficult situation, adopted the policy of permitting the Cubans to engage in foreign trade subject to heavy import and export duties and to certain discriminations in favor of the mother country. Although this new policy benefited the island to some extent, it did not satisfy the natives, who were growing more and more insistent upon trading with the United States without being embarrassed by harsh and inconvenient regulations. A reciprocity treaty with the United States was finally granted in 1891, but it was withdrawn three years later.

The discrimination against creoles, which had long caused complaint in the Spanish colonies of America, was continued in Cuba. In general, the Cubans were not permitted to hold public office except in a subordinate capacity. The captains-genereal and (later) the governors-general sent out from Spain dominated the political life of the island; and resentment was increased by the fact that the post was often a lucrative one. By serving a brief term most of these high officials were able to accumulate fortunes.

There was comparatively little insurgency in Cuba during the period when the other colonies were fighting for independence. This was owing to the fact that Cuba was fairly prosperous, and that such disaffection as existed had little opportunity to express itself while the island was used as a base of operations against the revolu-

---

[4] Chapman, *A History of the Cuban Republic*, p. 28.

tionists of the mainland. Indeed, the Spanish authorities of this era often referred to Cuba as "the ever faithful isle." Nevertheless, it was a time of considerable disaffection and sympathy for patriots of other parts of Spanish America, and Spanish officials were kept busy suppressing secret societies in the island and keeping watch over the plans of Colombia and Mexico.

Later, 1848–1851, discontent expressed itself in a desire for annexation to the United States, and in the Narciso López conspiracies, which were designed to effect such a change. After these had been suppressed by Spain, the island was fairly quiet for a time, only to be more seriously disturbed than ever during the period from 1868 to 1878 by what has become known as the Ten Years' War for independence, which cost about two hundred thousand lives and caused the destruction of seven hundred millions dollars' worth of property.

This widespread uprising was likewise suppressed, but economic discontent and the desire for independence eventually led to another serious outbreak in 1895. On this occasion Spain found it very difficult to quell the rebellion or reconcile the inhabitants by any measures short of home rule or perhaps even of independence. After the revolt had dragged on for three years, the United States, motivated by economic and strategic considerations and humanitarian sentiment, intervened and assisted Cuba to throw off the Spanish yoke. Spain's dominion in the Americas [5] officially ended in the spring of 1899, and the former colony was granted self-government on May 20, 1902. In the last phases of the struggle Cuba developed tireless and courageous propagandists and generals: José Martí and Tomás Estrada Palma, Antonio Maceo and Máximo Gómez.

[5] Puerto Rico continued its somewhat restive colonial status until 1898, when it was annexed by the United States as a war indemnity. Since this island did not become an independent nation, a discussion of its history during the period subsequent to 1820 does not fall within the scope of this text.

CHAPTER IX

POLITICAL APPRENTICESHIP

THE achievement of independence, unity, and stability by the people of the Thirteen colonies which later became the United States is one of the important developments of recent history. The break-up of the Indo-Spanish peoples of the Western Hemisphere into numerous turbulent and discordant elements is perhaps one of its tragedies. The leaders of the former molded thirteen units and a vast hinterland into a single strong nation. Those of the latter eventually formed nineteen states out of the eight major administrative jurisdictions of the late colonial era. Even Brazil itself was to be only comparatively free from disruptive tendencies and internecine strife.

Largely because of topographic, climatic, and ethnic variations, the tendency toward differentiation of interests and aspirations had revealed itself even in colonial Spanish America. The administrative reorganization of the eighteenth century had been in part a recognition of this tendency. But after eight large administrative entities had been created it would seem that the process of division had gone far enough.

The movement for independence was characterized in certain areas, as has already been pointed out, by an impulse toward coöperation and unity. The Viceroyalty of Río de la Plata assisted the Captaincy-general of Chile; the Viceroyalty of New Granada and the Captaincy-general of Venezuela gave each other mutual aid; the insurgent forces of northern and southern South America coöperated in the liberation of Peru; a Mexican army was largely responsible for the emancipation of Central America; Mexico and Colombia talked of freeing Cuba and Puerto Rico from the Spanish yoke, and perhaps were only deterred by the interference of the great powers, particularly the United States. Moreover, Spanish-American unity was prominent among the ideals of Bolívar and some of his contemporaries. The Liberator not only dreamed of welding Vene-

zuela, New Granada, Ecuador, Peru, and Bolivia into one great entity, but is said to have considered granting aid to the Plata region
in its contest with the Brazilians for the control of Banda Oriental;
and at Panama his agents sought an even wider unity.

Yet the particularist urge which showed itself in Río de la Plata
and New Granada during the struggle for independence rapidly
gained strength after separation from the mother country. The long
contest with Spain developed a large number of military leaders,
each eager to dominate his own and even adjacent provinces. When
the war ended, and particularly after the death of Bolívar, these
leaders—*caudillos,* as they have been called—profited by and stimulated the provincial sentiment. Accordingly, by 1831, the five
major administrative divisions of Spanish colonial South America
had split up into nine independent states. Mexico, the United Provinces of Central America, and Haiti, the eastern portion of which
was threatening to secede, raised the number of Spanish-American
states to twelve. Before 1850 it had increased to seventeen, and it
reached its maximum of nineteen late in 1903. The result was a series
of disputes and wars between kindred states which weakened and
retarded the development of the Spanish-American peoples.

Nor is this the complete story of the influence of the provincialism
and the caudillos. Some of these so-called nations were dissolved
during much of the time into from three or four to more than a
dozen virtually independent units, each dominated by its military
chief, or caudillo, who seriously interfered with the development of
a constitutional régime. There resulted numerous revolutions which
cost many thousands of lives and millions of dollars.

This period of riotous militarism and particularism has been
termed the Age of the Dictators. Its length varied in the different
states of Spanish America. The reign of the caudillos virtually ceased
in Chile by 1833 and in the Argentine by 1862. Elsewhere a longer
time was required to achieve civil stability. "Caudilloism" in fact
continued to cast its somber shadow over some of the states even
down to the end of the third decade of the twentieth century. A
nation may be said to have passed beyond this stage when it develops
the capacity to make the transition from one administration to another of opposing political views without resort to arms.

HISPANIC AMERICA, 1925

▨ SPANISH-AMERICAN REPUBLICS

▨ SPANISH-AMERICAN REPUBLICS-
FORMED SINCE 1828

▨ UNITED STATES OF BRAZIL

CAUSES OF POLITICAL DISORDERS IN SPANISH AMERICA

The causes of this age of political chaos vary slightly in the different countries, and for this reason each nation must be subjected to special scrutiny. It is possible, however, to discover a few factors which appear to have been general in their operation. These may be summed up in two broad divisions: (1) the colonial heritage, and (2) the aftermath of the Wars of Independence.

Any one who gives careful consideration to the Spanish colonial régime will not be surprised at the turbulence of the national period in Spanish America. "Freedom from previous restraint . . . accomplishes nothing by itself. The released energies of man may not be beneficent. . . . The acquisition of freedom permits change," but does not insure "advancement." Indeed, when despotism is destroyed by revolution, the immediate reaction may be violent and even retrogressive. Moreover, a sweeping political change is not likely to be effective if the people concerned have not served an apprenticeship in preparation for it. "Political growth is subject to the same slow-acting formula as all other growth." In order to be successful in their experiment, the democratic republics established by the peoples of Spanish America required intellectual leaders to formulate programs and plans of action. And, what is more important, they required men skilled in administration to direct the common action and carry out their plans and policies.

The Colonial Heritage.—From the political viewpoint, what was the heritage left to these new states by Spain? In the first place, there was the negative condition of political inexperience. The creoles, and perhaps occasionally the mestizos, had participated in the sessions of the town cabildos and, after 1809–1810, in the meetings of the provisional juntas, but these were deliberative rather than administrative bodies. Until great leaders like Bolívar and San Martín sprang up and acted more or less independently of these organizations, the revolution had been a failure. In the second place, administration was made more difficult by the wide separation of the centers of population which characterized Spanish colonization—by mountain, desert, and jungle—and the absence of any system of good roads, and of any adequate system of river or coastal transportation. In the third place, the population which the mother country left behind lacked homogeneity in race, culture, and ideals. Forty-five per cent of the people were Indian, thirty-one per cent mestizo, four per cent Negro, one per cent mulatto, and nineteen per cent white. Racial animosities had been permitted and even encouraged to develop. The ethnic groups did not understand one another; there was no community of ideals or interests. In a heterogeneous empire held together mechanically no organic unity had developed. In the fourth place, the population was for the most part untutored and lacking in initiative and capacity for invention. Comparatively few of the whites even were educated, hardly any of the other groups; and those who were educated had seldom been trained to think for themselves or allowed to do so. A tedious paternalism had not permitted men to plan and direct their own lives. Fifthly, the limitation of colonial participation in politics to the town councils tended to develop strong local loyalties.

More important perhaps than any of these inheritances in explaining the caudillo era were the caciques and the landlords of the colonial period. Both contributed to a régime of personalism and delayed the formation of an adequate conception of the state. The Spanish system of government, benevolently and perhaps unavoidably, retained many of the Indian chiefs (caciques), who controlled the natives through customary law aided by religious beliefs. This meant that many people were "habituated to a form of personal control" and to the concentration of their "loyalties into support of personal leadership." In like manner the landlords and mine owners were accustomed to dominate thousands of Indians on their large holdings. This dominating tendency was more emphatic after the restraint of the metropolis was removed. By means of compulsion and prestige both landlords and caciques controlled the lowly folk who surrounded them through leadership of a purely personal type. Thus there occurred a reign of personalism which is the antithesis of an impersonal state. To simple men long used to the personalistic régime the state appeared to be a conquerable trophy which might be captured and employed for the benefit of the personal leader and his group. It was not an instrument to be wielded in the interest of the whole nation.

Lord Bryce speculates in an interesting manner with reference to certain lines of development which might have been followed in

Spanish America "if things had been left to take their natural course." In this connection he says:

"One of these lines would have been the growth of small local, loosely connected or practically independent, communities, some with an urban centre, some semi-tribal, each ruled by a chief (native or mestizo) or by a group of the wealthier and more capable Spanish colonial landholding families. Such families represented the civilizing forces, and would have been obeyed by the Indians, some of whom were their tenants, some otherwise dependent upon them. The rule of the chiefs or oligarchic groups would have been harsh and not very progressive, but there would have been some sort of order, with the chance of a peaceful aggregation of the communities into larger wholes as the country began to be developed and opened up to commerce." In other words, Spanish America would have been permitted to have its long Middle Age.

Another possible line of "natural" development which Bryce mentions would have been the formation in each major division of the liberated colonies of an oligarchy composed of the leading families of the division. "This came to pass," he writes, "and has worked with comparatively little friction, in Chile, where no doubt the conditions were exceptionally favourable. It would have been difficult in Peru and Bolivia and Venezuela, owing (among other things) to the wide empty spaces between the small centres of population, and impossible in such a country as Haiti, where there were no families superior in knowledge and vigour to the ignorant and semi-savage masses. But in most of the countries it would have corresponded better to the elements of strength which the actual conditions presented . . . than did a sham Republic. . . . Such an oligarchy would have been likely to pass naturally, in the fulness of time . . . , into a more popular form of government." [1]

These speculations reveal only in part the author's usual powers of observation. He has pointed out two important social factors which had to be reckoned with in the history of these countries. What he failed fully to realize is the fact that, republics or no republics, constitutions or no constitutions, these local chiefs and family oligarchies would have their day. Certain forces unleashed by the revolution interfered somewhat with their course, but they were nevertheless a

[1] *Modern Democracies*, I, 205–206.

potent factor not only in Chile but also in Mexico, Peru, Central America, Colombia, Argentina, and almost everywhere else.

Influence of the Struggle for Independence.—Such was the colonial heritage. What of the influence of the long struggle for independence? At the outset it may be observed that fifteen years of war had done much to fasten the shackles of militarism upon the people. The military leaders of Spanish America, as those of all countries, were not easily reconciled to the obscurity of a civil order. The common soldiers, accustomed to the adventure and excitement of military combat, were loath to exchange the camp for the field and the shop. For the civilian, moreover, the man in uniform and on horseback had come to have a mighty appeal. With common men ready to follow and military chiefs ready to lead, what wonder that an era of militarism resulted?

Moreover, the close of the war and the expulsion of the Peninsular Spaniards left the new nations impoverished financially and administratively. The new governments lacked means and agents to carry on their difficult work. The reduction of racial animosities brought about by the common struggle for liberty could not atone for other losses. The Spanish yoke had been thrown off, but few constructive elements remained. Liberalism and radicalism arrived in a windy chaos, and there were not at hand adequate funds or sufficient administrative ability to control the storm and create order. Dr. Belaunde[2] has stated the case admirably:

"The struggle for independence explains in itself[3] the condition of many South [Spanish] American countries during the nineteenth century. The war that destroyed the economic basis of society, developed, in compensation, original personalities, and the nineteenth century is characterized by the lack of economic progress and a dangerous increase of individualism.

"After the [Spanish] conquest, [which was] due chiefly to the individual initiative of the great captains, the Spanish government succeeded in checking the development of individualism. It suppressed the rebellions and built the whole organization of the most powerful colonial empire. The aggressive work of Pizarro, Cortés, Alvarado, and Valdivia was followed by the organizing work of

---

[2] *Rice Institute Pamphlet*, X (1923), 242.
[3] This puts the matter a little too strongly.

Mendoza, Velasco, Gasca, Toledo. After the individuals came the action of the state. The War of Independence, in contrast, left the new nations to their own resources. And this is the difference between the colonial period and the nineteenth century. The organization of the new states demanded men of great administrative ability, strongly supported, to suppress anarchy and dissensions. The War of Independence developed military qualities and military leaders—not all men of constructive qualities. But even when *great* administrators *did* appear, they lacked the solid support [and the finances] enjoyed by the colonial organizers, and were bound to fail in a struggle determined by personal rivalries and amid constant anarchy."

IDEALS, CONSTITUTIONS, AND ISSUES

Strong governments and able administrators were the great need of the time. San Martín and many other thinkers throughout Spanish America realized this and advocated monarchies. Our own Martin Van Buren, ardent champion of a democratic republic, revealed a growing comprehension when he wrote: "Public opinion will not require from the Liberator . . . more than the actual condition of his country will allow. It is well known that circumstances, which are the results of centuries, cannot be overcome in an hour. The world will, therefore, give him [Bolívar] full credit for advising . . . the establishment of institutions as liberal as circumstances will permit." Bolívar understood the situation, but, more penetrating than the Spanish-American monarchists, he realized that the establishment of monarchies would prove impossible. Some may have urged monarchical or semimonarchical forms of government because of selfish motives or reactionary impulses, but it is hard to believe that Bolívar and San Martín were insincere. Both were republican and liberal by preference, but their convictions led them to advocate strong and undemocratic governments.

Bolívar's plans and utterances, in particular, deserve serious consideration. He was a man of his epoch, impregnated with ideas fabricated in the forge of the French Revolution. He cited Rousseau continually and always carried with him a copy of the *Social Contract*. He also read Montesquieu diligently. But he believed that usurpers and tyrants were the fatal termination of all demagogies.

Bolívar never betrayed his liberal ideals, but neither did he turn his back upon reality. The anarchic reality which he steadfastly opposed but could not dominate taught him the necessity of strong, solid, centralized governments; and so likewise did his natural inclinations and his habits of absolute command. From the conflict of his political philosophy and stubborn reality was born a moderate liberalism. The Letter from Jamaica, the Discourse at Angostura, and the Constitution of Bolivia contain most of his political doctrines.

Theoretically, he admitted that even a monarchy might be considered a good form of government for his people. But the Spanish-American revolution had been a rejection of monarchy, and an American throne was not a prize calculated to attract ambitious princes. "No foreign prince would desire to mount a royal scaffold," he remarked. The tragic failure of Iturbide rose up before him. "Who could be king in Colombia?" "No one, in my opinion," he wrote to Daniel F. O'Leary, "because no foreign prince would accept a throne surrounded by dangers and miseries. The generals would be least inclined to submit themselves to a [royal] colleague and renounce forever the supreme authority. The people would be terrified by this innovation and would consider themselves lost because of a series of consequences which they would deduce from the structure of this government." Agitators would arouse them to violent opposition. "The poverty of the country would not permit the creation of an ostentatious government which would consecrate every abuse of luxury and dissipation. The new nobility, indispensable in a monarchy, would have to come up from the mass of the people. . . . No one would suffer without impatience this miserable aristocracy enveloped in poverty and ignorance and animated by ridiculous pretensions." Moreover, the United States would oppose a monarch of any sort, England would not favor a French prince, and the people of Spanish America would object bitterly to a Spanish Bourbon. "Do not talk to me about this chimera!"

What, then, a democratic republic? It cannot be denied that Bolívar had strong democratic inclinations. "Only democracy, in my concept, is susceptible of an absolute liberty," he had remarked at Angostura. And, besides, he noted that America was a country inherently democratic. "Legal equality," he wrote on one occasion, "is indispensable where there is physical inequality, in order to correct in a certain mode the injustice of nature." All this tended to support a republic; but Montesquieu had taught him that republics must be founded in virtue. Was it possessed by the Spanish Americans who had "advanced suddenly, without previous training and . . . without practice in public affairs, to represent on the world's stage the lofty dignities of legislators, magistrates, fiscal administrators, diplomats, generals, and all the other supreme and subordinate authorities which form the hierarchy of a regularly organized state?" The Liberator was always extremely doubtful of their capacity. While in Jamaica (1815) he had remarked that they were "neither Indians nor Europeans," but a "species that lies midway. . . . Is it conceivable that a people recently freed from its chains can launch itself into the sphere of liberty without shattering its wings . . . and plunging into the abyss?" More than a decade later he wrote: "The majority are mestizos, mulattoes, Indians, and Negroes. An ignorant people is a blunt instrument for its own destruction. To it liberty means license, patriotism means disloyalty, and justice means vengeance." And again: "These countries will fall into the hands of the unbridled multitude and pass afterwards under the sway of little tyrants, . . . of all colors and races, devoured by every crime and extinguished by ferocity. . . . A thousand revolutions will make necessary a thousand usurpations."

Bolívar considered the federal republic the worst type of republic. It was too perfect. It was the work of the United States, which appeared "destined to plague America with a thousand miseries in the name of liberty," a régime only for saints, contrary to the traditions of his America, unadapted to his people, and calculated to nurture their most dangerous tendencies. It would be better to adopt the Koran!

Such was the dramatic conflict, the profound contradiction, which permeated all the political ideology of Bolívar. He was a liberal, a democrat, a republican, a humanitarian at heart, but he was confronted by what appeared to be a stern reality. He did not trust his people; he thought he knew them. "Let us seek a middle course between the two extremes" of republicanism and monarchy, he said. Let the statesmen be modest and seek a government appropriate to the character and nature of the people. Let them aspire to the British Constitution without imitating it in a servile manner. In his own constitutional projects he provided for life presidents, long-term or even life senators, and censors to look after the morals and education of the people and preserve the political equilibrium.[4] He would grant the people a certain amount of civil liberty but very little direct participation in government, and he would subject them to a sort of intellectual and moral tutelage. In this manner he proposed to deal with the eternal problem of restraint in a turbulent democracy.

The Liberator's views regarding the capacity of the Spanish-American people for liberty and self-government were probably sound. Subsequent disorders under the republican régime would appear to prove it. From the Latin-American experiment during almost a century of independence a great student of modern democracies draws the following moral: "Do not give to a people institutions for which it is unripe in the simple faith that the tool will give skill to the workman's hand. Respect Facts. Man is in each country not what we may wish him to be, but what Nature and History have made him." [5]

Whether Bolívar's actual plans of government were practical, it is impossible to say. They were never given a serious trial. If a constitutional monarchy worked fairly well in Brazil where conditions were in many ways similar, it appears probable that a "monarchy in disguise," as Bolívar once termed his Bolivia project, might have been successful in Spanish America, provided it had been accepted willingly and applied in good faith. In this latter respect, however, all plans for monarchy were impractical; it was impossible to secure their hearty acceptance. The majority of the Spanish-American intellectuals were doctrinaire republicans, and the republic, as García Calderón has said, was "obscurely linked with the destinies of the continent." Except in Mexico, monarchy virtually ceased to be an issue in Spanish America after 1830, although the House of Braganza continued to rule for almost sixty years in Brazil.

The general adoption of the republican system gave free rein to constitution-making. In fact, the Spanish-Americans developed a mania for this line of endeavor. Once freed from the rigid intellectual restrictions of the colonial period, their minds not only soared but

---

[4] The Angostura plan and the Bolivia constitution were somewhat different, but this is a composite statement of their substance, with emphasis on the latter.

[5] Bryce, *Modern Democracies,* I, 206.

became politicocentric. Indeed, it was an epoch of decided emphasis upon political affairs throughout the Western World. Each nation of Spanish America [6] drew up by the close of the century from five to seventeen constitutions or organic bases of government. Deluded idealists, the leaders endeavored to create utopias by the mere promulgation of laws. The oratory of the period reveals their lofty optimism in all of its absurdity. Here are two examples from Mexico, where the federal constitution of 1824 had just been framed:

"Opinions of respectable men sustained with heat; enormous difficulties which confronted you—nothing, nothing could terrify you; and the valor of your spirit never gave way to discouragement. You, emulating the Creator of heaven and earth, said: Let there be a Federation! and the Federation was made. In six days appeared the elements of this celestial system. O Franklin! O Washington! illustrious regenerators of the Federal Republics of the North, come to the Capitol of Mexico and contemplate with amazement the little group of men who, by following your footsteps, have had to overcome horrible obstacles, . . . but who have placed the Fatherland in the enviable position of advancing unfettered to the peak of its felicity!"

Such were the ridiculous utterances of the President of a Constituent Congress of Mexico. The following is a sentence taken from a speech made by the President of the Mexican Chamber of Deputies in 1826: "It is not a paradox, but a truth which the history of all nations have consecrated, that the vices of men, their valor, their effeminacy, their talents, illumination, ignorance, power, and riches, are not the effect of climate or the attributes of a privileged ancestry, but the exclusive work of laws." [7]

This impractical idealism was not the only reason, however, for the multiplicity of constitutions. There were numerous conflicting groups, numerous political issues, and champions of certain ideas and causes insisted upon incorporating these into fundamental law. There were centralists and unitarists who believed in subordinating the local units to the national government, and federalists who advocated a system like that which prevailed in the United States. There were liberals and radicals who demanded universal manhood

[6] Uruguay was an exception.

[7] As quoted in Carrancá y Trujillo, La Evolución Política de Iberoamérica, p. 173, note.

suffrage, the abolition of the death penalty, unrestrained freedom of the press, the disestablishment of the Roman Catholic Church and the reduction of its wealth and power, and the free admission of immigrants. There were conservatives and clericals who favored a limited suffrage, an established religion, a privileged and wealthy clergy, an official aristocracy, numerous limitations upon popular liberty, and the exclusion of foreigners of alien faith. There were militarists who favored a large, well paid, and highly privileged army, and civilians who held opposite convictions.

The Old Régime versus the New Age

Taking a broader view of the subject, one may contend that the fundamental issue of the national period of Latin-American history has been the old régime versus the new age of democracy, capitalism, and secularization. It must be admitted, however, that the issue was not always clearly defined or understood by the contestants.

During the latter part of the eighteenth century and all of the nineteenth an intellectual and social revolution was taking place. Another new world was being discovered, not across the ocean, but everywhere, a new world of the resources of the earth and of man. It was the dawn of the age of science, democracy, capitalism, and material progress.

The political philosopher, the scientist, and the business man were the creators of the new era. The political philosophers brought forth new ideas regarding the rights of man and his capacity to improve himself while on this earth. The scientists unfolded the secrets of physical nature. Business men seized upon these secrets and turned them into practical use and profits. Scientists discovered steam, electricity, and the laws of metals, gases, and oils; business men financed the practical applications of the discoveries and inventions, employed them to manufacture goods in quantity, and sold the goods in the world market. Under their combined pressure, the old régime dominated by the landed aristocracy, the established churches, and the small traders and artisans tended to disappear. The new régime spread rapidly over much of the world, from England to France, the United States, and nearly all of continental Europe, and more slowly to the Near and Far East and Latin America.

In Latin America there were many obstacles which retarded the movement toward the new age. Liquid capital, experienced leaders, scientists, and technologists were lacking. Appalling geographical handicaps were present. A landholding and a mining aristocracy opposed the merchant class and the rise of the plebeians. There were primitive and mixed races with deep-rooted superstitions, with comparatively little knowledge of politics or skill for industrial labor, and with low living standards and purchasing power. Numerous Indian villages continued to hold lands in common, and many Indians were still exploited by a system of forced labor. There was an established church holding vast estates in mortmain, often hostile to science, and generally conservative. And there was scarcely any democratizing frontier with its cheap and inviting lands, as in the United States.

Nevertheless, the new world era beckoned to Latin America, and in nearly all of the countries there arose leaders on fire to usher it in. The people, as already noted, had become acquainted with the traders of the United States and England during the struggle for independence. The political and material progress of the United States, which was rapidly becoming democratic, capitalistic, and industrial, was looked upon as a worthy example to follow. The philosophers of France in the late eighteenth century, the exploits of the French revolutions of 1789 and 1848—revolutions in the spirit of the new age—were well known and widely praised. The Masonic orders of the Continent spread throughout Latin America and became the heralds of the new era. Moreover, new demands for the products of Latin America were coming from the capitalistic, industrial states of the north, and Latin Americans looked to trade and business as sources of revenue for their treasuries or their own private purses.

Accordingly, Latin America soon tended in a measure to go "Liberal." "New Men" strove for political power, demanded a position among the landed aristocrats, and sought to bring about conditions which would make possible land speculation and industrial development. They also championed republican forms of government. In fact, they achieved them, at least on paper, at the outset in Spanish America and, in 1889, with the aid of disgruntled landlords and others, they succeeded in overthrowing the monarchy of Brazil. They desired to set up trading nations, with tariffs, much buying and selling of land, houses, and commodities, and much borrowing and lending of money. They championed individualism, secularization, material progress, and even the rule of the people, although their system was headed ultimately toward a plutocracy.

Because great obstacles confronted the new régime, it proved necessary to wade through blood in order to reach it. The winning of independence from Spain was merely the beginning of the struggle against traditionalism. The successful revolt against the rule of the mother country did not result in the overthrow of the old order. The churchmen and the landholding aristocracy—the conservatives —bitterly opposed the "reformers." The beneficiaries of the old régime now that Spain had been expelled, churchmen and landlords at once became its supporters. They were prepared to fight and not infrequently to win.

When the leaders of the Liberals managed to get into power, they often quarreled among themselves over ideals or spoils. Once in control of the government, they usually proclaimed the omnipotence of the state. In assuming this attitude they were in part traditionalists, for the Spanish monarchy was omnipotent. In another respect, however, they were innovators: they refused to delegate to any other institution functions which they conceived to belong to the state. They had the state assume nearly all of the ancient functions of the church—its control over property, education, burial, marriage ceremonies, vital statistics, and charity. They wished to employ to the limit the organizing and borrowing power of the state; they would lift themselves by their political boot straps into the new era.

The status of the Roman Catholic Church became the most bitter and persistent of all issues. Allying itself with the politicians of the old régime, it became the political enemy of the reformers. Moreover, it was wealthy, and the reformers needed money. It was using its property to support in luxury an episcopacy and a numerous priesthood as well as to finance schools, asylums, and monasteries. The reformers resented the wealth of the clergy and desired the state to take over the institutions for education and benevolence. Without these institutions the church would have less need for its properties. Moreover, there were still other inducements for expropriation: church lands were held in mortmain and hence were not subject to traffic, and churchmen were often opposed to freedom of thought, which was necessary to the development of scientists and scholars, and particularly to religious toleration, which was essential in order to encourage immigrants required for the development of the new prosperity. For all these reasons, the Liberals declared war on the Catholic Church.

Perhaps it was inevitable that the church should become a leading political issue. Owing to its great services during the colonial era, owing to its central position and its vast wealth, it became a sort of magnet attracting all men of conservative tendencies, and therefore an object of attack by the reformers. Every measure which tended to deprive the church of its wealth and power—the civil patronage, lay education, freedom of religion, speech, and the press, the abolition of mortmain, the secularization of marriage ceremonies, and state administration of the graveyards—had to be effected at the expense of a terrific struggle.

Already it has been pointed out that at the initiation of the movement for independence the lower clergy brought to the American cause its directing influence. Although most of the higher clergy at first cast their lot with the traditional régime, the liberal revolution of 1820 in Spain, which attacked the wealth, privileges, and censorship of the church, drove this group in the colonies into the revolutionary camp. Thereafter bishops and priests edited plans and *reglamentos* and participated in constituent juntas and congresses. Ferdinand VII hastened to secure from Leo XII an encyclical letter recommending that the American church support the cause of the metropolis. But it was already too late. Higher and lower clergy were alike deaf to the appeal. In taking this stand, churchmen were motivated mainly by a desire to serve their own interests.

Since the time of Ferdinand and Isabella the Spanish state had succeeded in asserting its right to intervene in ecclesiastical affairs. It was different, however, in the case of most of the infant states of Spanish America. Living precariously in the midst of anarchy, without any real internal strength save the church itself, they not only were unable to seize the right of patronage, but often were actually subjected to the ecclesiastical power. Churchmen, exercising their universal moral influence, frequently mediated political conflicts. "Against the encroachments of the liberals the church zealously defended, inch by inch, ever-enlarging powers which it had never possessed during the colonial régime. It contended that, since the Spanish patronage had disappeared in America, the American states absolutely could not intervene in ecclesiastical affairs without a concession from Rome. This was never granted, for although Brazil, Chile, Ecuador, New Granada, Venezuela, and Central America had agents accredited to the Holy See, they obtained from it only partial settlements, never general bases for the arrangement of the affairs of the church. An aggressive ultramontanism opposed itself to a nascent regalism [i.e., a growing secular or national spirit]. The liberal caudillos were stigmatized as heretics, antipatriotic, while other caudillos docilely submitted themselves in return for being supported in power. Meanwhile, the people, among whom the abuse of ecclesiastical power had led gradually to the loss of clerical prestige, upon perceiving the clearly defined opposition between church and nation, allied themselves more and more with liberalism, which meant independence [from papal control]. Facing imminent defeat, the church still refused to proceed with moderation; it came forward openly in the conflict as a champion ready for the fight. It was now a vast political organization." [8] Frequently there could be no compromise; war inevitably resulted in many of the nations of Latin America.

These clashes with the church as an institution did not indicate hostility to the Catholic religion itself, however. A century of Protestant missionary effort succeeded in making only a few thousand converts in each nation.

Such were the conditions, motivating influences, issues, and struggles of Spanish America's apprenticeship: militarism which was the product of the colonial heritage, the physical environment, and the long struggle for independence; an old régime, ecclesiastical and partially feudal, in conflict with men striving toward the age of secularization, capitalism, industrialism, and democracy; constitutions which were at once the embodiment of lofty aspirations and the effort of an inexperienced, confused people to bridle the wild, clashing forces in their midst—documents whose very perfection necessitated their violation and thus called for new struggles and new

[8] Carrancá y Trujillo, *La Evolución Política de Iberoamérica*, pp. 110–111.

documents, for aspiring reformers took up arms in an effort to bridge the chasm between the utopias described and the exasperating realities which they saw about them.

Magnificent expressions of the idealism of idealistic peoples, these constitutions remained for the most part ideals and nothing more. As suggested at the beginning of this chapter, administrative ability, material resources, even an appropriate constituency were lacking. *Alas y plomo*—wings and lead; constitutions, caudillos, and chaos. It was a tragic apprenticeship, as we shall see.

Brazil itself, as previously intimated, did not pass smoothly from the colonial status to the national era. Here, too, there was a struggle between traditionalism and the new age, between church and state, between sectionalism and nationalism, between militarism and the civil régime, between obscurantism and freedom of thought, between slaveholders and humanitarians. Despite the fact that the monarchy was retained for nearly seventy years and the politicians proceeded with greater moderation, several revolutions occurred.

CHAPTER X

THE AGE OF THE DICTATORS (I)

In the previous chapter the ideals and clashing forces of Spanish America's apprenticeship have been stressed, but there has been no intention of overlooking its more sordid aspects. There were ideals and forces difficult to reconcile, but there were also selfishness, corruption, and brutality. A survey of the first Age of the Dictators will reveal both sides.

The States of the River Plate

The Argentine.—The difficulties which prevented unity and delayed stability in the Plata area were due in part to the conflict between liberalism and conservatism, but more largely to disrupting forces which first split the former viceroyalty into four states and then temporarily divided the largest of these into several semi-independent provinces. The destiny of the new states was also influenced to some extent by rivalries for the control of the great Río de la Plata system.

The achievement of unity and political stability in the Argentine required more than a half-century. The most fundamental and disturbing factor in this region was the spirit of local autonomy struggling against the domination of the city and province of Buenos Aires. To this ardent sentiment of localism at least five forces made their contribution: (1) the caudillos; (2) the origin of the leading settlements; (3) the colonial policy of Spain; (4) the character of the settlers; (5) the ambitious policy of the province of Buenos Aires.

The first of these forces needs no further comment than the statement that the military chiefs were ambitious to rule in their respective provinces. The second requires that the reader be reminded of the diverse bases whence the colonists came. The Plata basin had been "settled by three distinct streams of immigration—one from Chile, which established its settlements in the district of Cuyo, another from Peru, which settled the district of Tucumán, and a third, which entered by way of the River Plate, settling in Paraguay and in the district of Buenos Aires. Although speaking a common language and of essentially the same race, there was little feeling of unity between the peoples inhabiting the new viceroyalty." [1]

The significance of the third factor may be summarized by the statement that more than two centuries of virtual neglect on the part of Spain led to the formation in this region of a sort of Greek system of city-states. Largely because of the failure to find important deposits of precious metals in the area which now constitutes the Argentine Republic, the control of the Spanish crown and its agents was never very rigid. The towns assumed and were permitted to exercise a large amount of freedom of action.

In the fourth place, the leading settlers were individualistic and decidedly provincial in their outlook and habits. "The majority of the Spanish settlers in the Argentine Republic came from Navarre, Aragon, and the Basque provinces, with the spirit of local independence and the adherence to local privileges strongly developed." [2]

Lastly, during much of the colonial period Buenos Aires was not an important center of settlement. There was no port of entry in the region and some of the other centers outranked it in prestige, population, and culture. In the time of Charles III, however, Buenos Aires was made not only the capital of the newly created viceroyalty, but the sole port of entry as well. It soon became an important center of politics and trade, and after independence was achieved it attempted to dominate the late viceroyalty both commercially and politically. The ultimate domination of the city and province of Buenos Aires was apparently inevitable, but the outlying provinces were not disposed to accept a subordinate position without a desperate struggle.

The declaration of independence (1816) and the elimination of the European Spaniards from participation in the management of the public affairs of the region were followed by twenty years of virtual anarchy. During this period the caudillos, profiting by the strong sentiment of localism, seized political control in the provinces and defied the central authorities at Buenos Aires. This led to hos-

---

[1] Rowe, *The Federal System of the Argentine Republic*, p. 28.
[2] *Ibid.*, pp. 23–24.

tilities between the military chiefs and the national government. But the disorders did not end there. The caudillos found excuses for contention with their neighbors or aspired to a larger rôle than that of ruling merely a district. The outcome was the division of the country into fourteen semi-independent provinces—to say nothing of the loss of Paraguay, Bolivia, and Uruguay—and a long orgy of violence which exhausted the country and prepared it in a measure for the bloody dictatorship of Manuel Rosas.

While armies fought each other, administrators debated the questions of centralism and federalism or undertook reforms. The first national government framed for Argentina, that of 1813, was federal. It was followed in 1816 and 1826 by unitary, or centralized, constitutions. The first president under the latter was Bernardino Rivadavia, who, although a centralist, was a liberal reformer, as revealed by his previous connection with the government of Buenos Aires province as well as by his career as national chief executive. He closed convents, refused to recognize ecclesiastical privileges, secularized the cemeteries, nationalized the property of the church, and even attempted to found a national church which would permit freedom of thought and expression. He also inaugurated certain educational, agrarian, and financial reforms.

These centralizing and reforming tendencies furnished the provincial chiefs the issues for which they were looking, and they flew to arms again. At least one important leader, Facundo Quiroga, raised the cry of *"Religión y fueros!"* ("Religion and legal privileges!")

Perhaps only a people bled and exhausted by militarism would have permitted such a tyrant as Manuel Rosas to dominate their country for almost twenty years. He came to power, however, as the champion of the "sacred cause of federalism," a cause supported not only by the five factors already mentioned but by a social force which mingled with them. The movement for a centralized national government was, as Dr. Rowe has remarked, "essentially an urban movement sustained in the main by the city of Buenos Aires. . . . The propertied classes, who represented an incipient aristocracy of wealth, were convinced that a strong centralized government was the only means of securing order, protecting property, and developing a healthy political life. The conflicts between local leaders in the provinces strengthened this belief. The large landed proprietors, who lived for the most part in Buenos Aires, and who had suffered greatly from internal strife, joined hands with the commercial element in supporting the movement for a centralized national government. Inasmuch as the establishment of a unified political system inevitably meant the predominance of the province of Buenos Aires, the movement also found considerable support in this province among other elements of the population." Federalism, on the other hand, was championed by the rural masses, who, under the direction of their local leaders, fought not only for local autonomy but also for the protection of their interests against what they considered to be the tyranny and oppression of the aristocracy seated in Buenos Aires. It was this clash of social forces, this struggle "between the democratic aspirations of the mass of the people of the provinces and the conservative oligarchic tendencies of the well-to-do urban population," [3] which, when combined with the particularistic sentiment, offered Rosas his opportunity. He first rode into power at the head of an army of *gauchos* (cowboys) and Indians, but he gained control of the nation by virtue of the support of nearly all of the rural elements. Once thoroughly established, he was astute and ruthless enough to maintain himself in spite of the defection of many of his former adherents. His position was further strengthened by the menaces of England and France, who had disagreements with him over commercial matters, and he appears also to have courted the favor of the church. On the whole, his rule favored Buenos Aires Conservatives.

A descendant of an influential family of Buenos Aires, he was apparently destined to prominence in the unitarian aristocracy; but the experiences of his youth and early manhood admirably fitted him for leadership of the rural democracy. As a boy—he was born in 1793—he spent his summers on his father's ranch in the southern part of the province of Buenos Aires, where his reckless audacity won him the friendship and admiration of Indian and cowboy alike. At the age of nineteen he appears to have broken with his parents and begun an independent career as drover. He soon earned sufficient money to purchase a ranch of his own about one hundred and fifty miles south of Buenos Aires, near the Indian frontier. At the age of thirty-six (1829) he became governor of his native province. In 1835 he was chosen by an alleged plebiscite for a second term.

[3] Rowe, *op. cit.*, pp. 20–21.

Already his partisans were in control in many parts of the country, and before the end of the year twelve provinces delegated to him the attributes of chief executive, thus creating the "Argentine Confederation."

His rule of seventeen years has become known chiefly for its drastic and brutal despotism. It has been said that more than twenty thousand excellent and intelligent men were either killed or sent into exile merely for differing with him in political and administrative matters. A society of cutthroats, the *Mazorcas,* hunted down the "Unitarians" like wild beasts. Such conduct made him "the most bitterly hated man in Argentine history." But recent writers have observed another aspect of his work. He was surrounded by wild and dangerous elements. He slew some men who scarcely deserved a better fate. He served his nation a good turn when he executed the provincial caudillos or played them against each other. He stirred the rural masses to self-consciousness and progressive activity. He aroused a spirit of nationalism by resistance to European dictation in Argentine affairs. And the method of his rise to power taught the "Unitarian" statesmen that provincial autonomy could not be ignored. "Before him was the anarchy of 1820 and the unitarian bankruptcy of 1826; after him the powerful unity of 1853 and 1860, and the triumphal progress of the Argentine democracy." [4]

Opposition to Rosas increased with the increasing length and violence of his rule, but long domestic strife had so weakened the country that it was difficult to find strength to accomplish his overthrow. At length, however, General Justo José de Urquiza, governor of the province of Entre Ríos and formerly a stanch supporter of the Rosas régime, succeeded, with the aid of Uruguay and Brazil, in driving the tyrant from power. On February 3, 1852, Urquiza met and routed the army of the dictator at Caseros; and Rosas, escaping to a British war vessel, proceeded to Southampton, where he spent the remainder of his long life in poverty. He died in 1877.

For the next decade Urquiza was virtually supreme, and he made wise use of his power. In the summer of 1852 thirteen of the provinces, Buenos Aires not included, gave him the title of "Provisional Director of the Argentine Confederation." A constitutional convention was assembled before the end of the year. The result of

[4] García Calderón, *Latin America,* p. 145.

its work was the fundamental law of 1853, which, with several subsequent amendments, has continued in force. In many ways similar to the constitution of the United States, it was fairly successful in harmonizing the federalistic and centralistic tendencies. It also contained most of the guaranties embodied in the liberal constitutions of other parts of the world, including religious toleration but requiring the president and vice president to be Roman Catholics. It asserted the state's right of patronage over the church at the same time that it bound the state to subsidize the church.

With the violent force of caudilloism destroyed, statesmen taught the lesson of wholesome respect for local autonomy, and a moderate liberalism written into the constitution, affairs now moved along more smoothly. The province of Buenos Aires refused for a time to come into the Confederation, but Urquiza made no immediate attempt at coercion. At length (1861) increasing friction culminated in armed conflict and Urquiza was overthrown by General Bartolomé Mitre, who had command of the provincial forces of Buenos Aires. This province then proposed certain amendments to the constitution, which were accepted by the other provinces, and the capital of the nation was moved from Paraná—where it had been established by Urquiza—to Buenos Aires. At last the fourteen provinces were united, with General Mitre as the first chief executive of the whole of the Argentine (1862–1868).

Mitre was a man of sincere patriotism, great moderation, and much political sagacity. Few Latin Americans have shown greater ability to conciliate factions and promote national unity and prosperity. He encouraged immigration and the construction of railways; he promoted postal and telegraph service; he founded national colleges and encouraged congress to subsidize national education; he reformed the customs service and laid plans for the conquest of Patagonia. More important still, he prepared the way for the free election of his successor and left to the Republic the political testament of a president's not using his influence to elect a favorite to succeed him. President D. F. Sarmiento was actually chosen president while he was serving as minister in the United States and Mitre relinquished the government without the slightest protest. Argentina had thus met the acid test of political stability. An election had been determined by ballots and not by bullets, and the reign of caudilloism had passed, although the bitterness against the province of Buenos Aires did not subside until 1880, when the city of Buenos Aires was detached and made a federal district. The town of La Plata then became the capital of the province. ➤

Republic of Uruguay.—The little republic of Uruguay owes its existence to a spirit of localism, Spanish-Portuguese rivalry in the Plata basin, and the interference of the British government, which was determined to erect a buffer state between Argentina and Brazil. The provincial tendency revealed itself in Banda Oriental as early as 1808 when the cabildo of Montevideo appointed a junta which was declared to be dependent directly upon the legitimate king of Spain and in no way upon the provisional government at Buenos Aires. This tendency was stimulated by José Artigas, the chief and hero of the Gauchos of Uruguay, during the years when he domi-nated the country. Although it may be doubted whether Artigas represented any more than a violent hostility to Brazilian domina-tion and the desire to incorporate Banda Oriental as an autonomous state into an independent Argentine confederation, he nevertheless profoundly stirred the national feeling of the people of Uruguay and won for himself the title of the Founder of the Uruguayan nation. The annexation of Banda Oriental to Brazil in 1821 could not extinguish autonomous aspirations, as was revealed by the spon-taneous uprising which greeted Juan Lavalleja and his famous "Thirty-three" in 1825.

The beginning of the Uruguayan nation dates from August 28, 1828, when Argentina and Brazil, in response to British mediation, concluded a treaty by which they abandoned their claims to Uruguay, recognized the state as independent, and agreed to guarantee its inde-pendence for five years. At that time its population was no more than sixty thousand; nor did the ratification of this treaty mean that the little nation was to be free from external influence. Both Brazil and Argentina continued to look with covetous eyes upon the region; and intolerant caudillos, such as Lavalleja, Fructuoso Rivera, Manuel Oribe, and Venancio Flores, did not hesitate to call upon their Argen-tine and Brazilian neighbors for support against rival compatriots. For at least forty years subsequent to 1828 foreign soldiers and money were a constant influence in Uruguayan politics, and between 1830 and 1911 some thirty administrations ruled the country, although according to the constitution there should have been only twenty.

Military factions and ambitious caudillos were the main factors which contributed to the disorders of the Republic. Indeed, parties —*Colorados* (Reds) and *Blancos* (Whites)—took their names from the colors of the banners of rival commanders. Yet certain opposing social forces were not without influence. The Colorados represented the democracy; the Blancos the aristocracy. Around Oribe (1836 ff.) gathered the big landlords, the merchants, the higher clergy, and the small group composing the learned professions. Rivera, his rival, was the leader of the more intelligent and energetic contingent of the common people—artisans of the towns, cowboys of the ranches, and a few men of moderate wealth. Oribe was authoritarian, loving order and discipline, intolerant of all cults save the Roman Catholic. Rivera was generous and somewhat anarchistic, a theoretical champion of all the liberties, whether of conscience, industry, or the press. Colorado policies eventually prevailed—the aristocracy was never numerous—but not without a hard struggle and many reverses as well as divisions among themselves. As late as 1883, and even as late as 1900, presidents and legislators are seen endeavoring to establish civil marriage and otherwise to limit the powers and prerogatives of the church.

Perhaps only the word "chaos" is adequate to describe political conditions in Uruguay at almost any time between 1811 and 1868. Patriots fought loyalists, Argentines fought Brazilians, Uruguayans fought Argentines or Brazilians, and factions of Uruguay allied with factions of Argentina or Brazil fought each other.

After 1868 conditions improved somewhat, but revolutions still frequently occurred. It was not until 1894 that a president was able to complete his term without suppressing a rebellion. By the time the plague of foreign meddling had run its course, partisan hatred had become so deeply embedded that almost half a century was required to obliterate it. As already intimated, party names date from 1836, when the forces of the government backed by the tyrant Rosas carried white pennants and their antagonists carried red pennants. Thereafter the children of Uruguay were born either into the Colorado or the Blanco party. "Uruguayans," says Akers, "profess to be one or the other because their parents were so before them." They remind one of the feuds of the Scotch Highlanders or of the Kentucky mountaineers. Unfortunately, the contents of the treasury, the emoluments of office, often comprised the main objective. But political intolerance was probably the major besetting sin. After 1868 all the revolutions, with possibly two exceptions, represented attempts of the Blancos, the weaker party, to secure political recognition. The exceptions were revolts within the Colorado party itself. Not until 1900 [5] did the more powerful Colorados evince a disposition to conciliate their rivals and tolerate their participation in public affairs. A revolution of considerable magnitude took place in 1904, and a Blanco uprising occurred as late as 1910. After the former date, however, there was considerable improvement, and Uruguay soon became one of the progressive nations of Latin America. Thousands of immigrants, mainly from Italy and Spain, contributed to the prosperity of the country.

Uruguay's political apprenticeship was characterized by the absence of a mania for constitutions. During all of the long disorderly period of its history the nation lived under the moderate organic law of 1829, framed before the reformer Rivera came to power. It provided for a centralized republic with nine local jurisdictions called Departments, each to be governed by a *jefe político* appointed by the national chief executive. The president was to be elected by a bicameral legislature for a term of four years and was not permitted to serve for a second term until the expiration of another four years. The election of the senators was to be indirect; the members of the lower chamber direct. Property qualifications were required as follows: ten thousand pesos for the president and the senators; four thousand for the members of the popular chamber and the *jefes políticos*. The Roman Catholic religion was declared to be the religion of the state, but other forms of worship were not expressly prohibited; and officials of the church were forbidden to hold office in the national government. Most of the usual guaranties of persons and property were embodied in the constitution, including jury trial.

The Paraguayan Nation.—The Paraguayan nation owes its independent status in part to physical environment and racial factors and in part to the caudillos who dominated its national life during the first half of the nineteenth century. A somewhat isolated position, a sub-

---

[5] President Tomás Gomensoro (1872 ff.) and President Juan Cuestas (1897–1903) had shown a rather conciliatory spirit.

tropical climate, and a population in which the Indian and mestizo elements predominated, sharply differentiated it from the province of Buenos Aires as well as from the other important regions of the Río de la Plata. The area had enjoyed a considerable amount of autonomy prior to 1776, when it became a part of the Plata viceroyalty; and the autonomous spirit reasserted itself in 1811. In January of that year, as we have seen, a military force sent out by the revolutionary junta of Buenos Aires for the purpose of winning Paraguay's allegiance, was met and defeated. A few months later a provisional government of the province drove out the Spanish governor and declared Paraguay independent of Spain. In 1813 independence from the insurgent government at Buenos Aires was likewise declared. The declaration was but the statement of an accomplished fact, although the destiny of the new nation was profoundly affected by Argentina, Uruguay, and Brazil until 1870. The moving spirit of this early period was Dr. Francia, who based his action upon Roman history, the *Social Contract,* and his own political aspirations.

For the first twenty-seven years of its independent existence, in fact, Paraguay was under the control of the dictator José Rodríguez de Francia (1766–1840), just as it was dominated during the next thirty by the elder and the younger López. All three rose to absolute power largely as the result of the docility of the Indians and mestizos and the menaces of the other states of the Plata basin.

Francia was a solitary, mysterious figure whose real character and motives are not fully known and whose work is difficult to evaluate. Honest, methodical, industrious, and able, but capricious, vain, austere, and often cruel, he appears to have been a benevolent despot in dealing with the Indians and mestizos and a bloody tyrant in his relations with the creoles and especially the clergy whom he found in charge of the religious life of the country when he assumed dictatorial powers in 1813.

He resented ecclesiastical power and scorned the superstitions which the clergy tolerated and even inculcated. Discussing with a Swiss scientist the charms and spells in general use in Paraguay, he said: "You see what priests and religion are good for; they make us believe more in the Devil than in God." When a commandant asked for the image of a saint in order to place a new frontier fortress under its protection, the dictator shouted: "O people of

Paraguay, how long will you remain idiots? When I was still a Catholic, I believed as you do, but now I know that bullets are the best saints you can have on the frontiers." "Profess the religion that pleases you best, be Christians, Jews, or Mussulmans,—anything but Atheists," he remarked to a foreign visitor.[6] He evidently believed in religious toleration.

Even before the close of the colonial régime he acquired a remarkable ascendancy over the common people by his fearlessness in defending their interests before the courts and corrupt officials, and he continued to act as their champion after he became the supreme ruler of the Paraguayan nation. He seemed to be convinced that their cause could be served best by the imprisonment and extermination of the aristocratic creoles or their absorption through intermarriage with the Indians. The members of the leading families were confined, executed, or forbidden to marry within their own group.

Francia annihilated hierarchy and privilege. He struck down the power of the church by confiscating its property, abolishing religious orders, reducing the number of religious holidays and festivals, and placing his own tools in ecclesiastical positions. He curtailed the power of the creoles by suppressing the municipal councils in which they exercised their authority. For the upper classes his rule became a reign of terror.

He sought to promote the prosperity of his country in many ways: for instance, he encouraged the manufacture of leather goods, furniture, and coarse cotton cloth. But he was opposed to communication with foreign nations—largely because of the fear of Argentine anarchy and intrigue—and hence forced these industries to rely upon the home market. In agriculture he inaugurated a kind of state socialism, taking under his control and supervision some two-thirds of the arable land of the nation and introducing new crops and methods. He established several state stock farms for developing the best breeds of horses and cattle. He rebuilt Asunción and constructed numerous public works. But he kept a comparatively large army for the maintenance of his power and the defense of his country against possible attacks and did little or nothing to stimulate education. When his "reign" came to an end there were numerous signs of stagnation and backwardness, but the country was probably

[6] Rengger and Longchamps, *The Reign of Francia* (London, 1827), p. 204.

better off than it would have been under a succession of temporary dictators. A long era of peace had been maintained, the material progress of the country had been advanced to some extent, the population, a little more than 100,000 when he came to power, had increased to 220,000, and an intense nationalism had been fostered among the masses.

After the death of Francia in September, 1840, the cycle of the early independence period was repeated. A junta, which was immediately organized, gave way to a provisional government, followed by a consulate and then a dictatorship. A year had hardly passed when Carlos Antonio López (1790–1862), a well-to-do creole ranchman trained for the law, emerged as the dominating figure. First Consul in 1841, he became President in 1844 under a fundamental law which gave him extraordinary powers and said nothing about the liberty and sovereignty of the people. Elected again in 1854, he became after 1857 chief of state for ten years with power to dictate his successor. Thus he succeeded to all the absolute power and prerogatives of Francia, despite a law of 1842, which had declared that the Republic of Paraguay should never become the "patrimony of any person or family."

His government was milder, however, than that of his predecessor. In many ways he resembled the benevolent despots of a previous century in Europe. Although he exercised patriarchal supervision over the people, they enjoyed substantial liberty of movement and, during a part of the time, considerable freedom of expression. Justice was administered regularly and with reasonable impartiality, and life and property were safe. The gradual emancipation of slaves was also decreed. Unlike Francia, he believed that national prosperity would be promoted by immigration and contact with the outside world. He accordingly sought and obtained recognition from several powers, negotiated boundary agreements with his neighbors, and encouraged foreign settlers and investors to enter the country. His relations with English subjects and citizens from the United States involved him, however, in humiliating difficulties with these two governments. His rule was characterized by a marked increase in the prosperity of Paraguay, and at his death in 1862 the population of the country had passed the million mark.

He was succeeded by his eldest son, Francisco Solano López, who proved to be a despot with few redeeming features. In his youth he had been petted and pampered by a too indulgent father, and wicked propensities had been allowed to develop. Vain and arrogant, reckless and unscrupulous, corrupt and cruel, he executed, imprisoned, or banished several thousand of the creoles and leading mestizos while wielding a masterful influence over the Indian and mestizo masses.

Born in 1826, at an early age he evinced a taste for military affairs. His father, exasperated by international complications during the latter part of his reign, made Francisco secretary of war and encouraged his efforts to organize a large army. In this manner, and by study and observation in Europe, the natural military taste of the son was cultivated until it became a veritable obsession. He imagined that he was a Napoleon. Hardly three years of his rule had passed when he involved himself in a desperate struggle with the combined armies of Brazil, Argentina, and Uruguay. The Paraguayan masses, who looked upon him as the greatest ruler in the world, and whom he inspired with a "loathing and contempt for their enemies," fought until almost the last man of them had been killed or incapacitated. In 1862 the population of Paraguay was said to be more than a million; in 1871, several months after the six years' war had ceased, it was only a little more than two hundred thousand, of whom only some 28,000 were men. Routed by his enemies early in 1870, the second López committed suicide in order to escape from the Brazilians. Aside from the tragic loss and degradation of its citizens, Paraguay also suffered the reduction of its territorial limits by the cession of two large strips to Argentina and still another to Brazil. The sins of López required a double expiation.

Reflecting upon the reign of Paraguay's three tyrants, a native remarked recently: "This country . . . was oppressed in the stifling air of despotism. We repeat constantly this truth: liberty is the ideal end of our existence upon earth. There is no moral grandeur, nor real culture without liberty. Only liberty impresses a moral character upon human actions. . . . Tyranny, on the contrary, being the negation of liberty, degrades and debases. It stifles in the heart of

man the sentiments of honor and duty, of righteousness and justice . . . The Paraguayan people have paid dearly for the crime of
tyranny." [7]

Since 1870 Paraguay has been theoretically under a constitutional
régime. The constitution promulgated in November of that year
long continued to be the fundamental law of the land, although
slight amendments were added. It provided for a centralized republic with a president, a vice president, a bicameral legislature,
and national courts. The usual guaranties were stipulated, including
those of trial by jury, freedom of expression, and religious toleration. The Roman Catholic religion was declared to be the religion
of the state, but civil patronage over the church was asserted.

Actually, however, the constitution was frequently violated. The
political life of the country was characterized by a rapid succession
of chief executives who, for the most part, secured office through
the support of the army and resigned or lost their lives before the
expiration of the constitutional four years. In fact, only four or five
presidents served out full terms and hardly any won their office
by means of an election free from military interference. After 1912
conditions improved somewhat, but it would have been hazardous
at that time to predict that Paraguay had passed beyond the Age of
the Dictators.

CHILE, BOLIVIA, AND PERU

Chile.—In spite of the fact that it was the first of the Spanish-
American nations to achieve political stability, Chile began its national life amid disorders which fell just short of chaos. Freed from
Spanish control largely through the efforts of San Martín and
O'Higgins, its independent career was inaugurated under the dictatorship of the latter. Although O'Higgins did not believe that the
Chileans were prepared for a democracy and, hence, concentrated
nearly all power in his own hands, there was a good deal of moderate liberalism in his reforms. A firm believer in public education,
he revived the Instituto Nacional, which his revolutionary predecessors had set up at Santiago, established a public library in the
capital city, and founded a number of Lancasterian schools which he

[7] Cecilio Báez, *Le Paraguay*, p. 60.

placed under the direction of the distinguished Englishman, James Thompson. Other reforms inaugurated by him included the abolition of titles of nobility, the suppression of brigandage through effective police and courts, the abolition of bullfights and cockfights, and the prohibition of the sale of public offices. The wealthy and influential classes were antagonized by some of these measures. They particularly disapproved his financial policy and his proposal to abolish entailed estates. At the same time, many men of liberal tendencies became disaffected and denounced O'Higgins for his tyranny, and ambitious military chiefs were eager for power and the spoils of office. Early in 1823 a revolution led by General Ramón Freire forced the dictator to resign. Then followed a seven-year period of ruinous disorder, during which there were no fewer than ten governments and three different constitutions. Presidents— "ephemeral figures which a turbulent democracy set up and destroyed"—succeeded one another with bewildering rapidity. Between 1827 and 1829 alone there were five revolutions. National life reached a very bad state: "vandalism in the country, commerce paralyzed, industry at a standstill, finance in disorder, credit vanished, and politics revolutionary." The Chilean people passed "from liberty to license, and from license to barbarism."

This decade of internecine strife had its hopeful phase, however. It was not entirely a struggle between military leaders for dominance and the spoils of office. Ideas sometimes played their part. By 1828 the issues were pretty clearly defined. Two parties, the Conservatives (called "Pelucones," or "Bigwigs") and the Liberals ("Pipiolos," or "Novices"), had come into existence. The latter stood for federalism, the curtailment of the power of the church, and certain reforms in the system of landholding. The former, composed largely of the clergy and the owners of large landed estates, were determined to protect the interests of these groups. Since the beginning of Chile's movement for independence, men of liberal or radical tendencies had been in charge of the government. The leaders of this group had often allowed lust for power to outweigh other considerations, thereby contributing to the defeat of their own party. In the end they proved to be dogmatists rather than statesmen; they could not create a strong government and maintain order. In 1830 they were overwhelmingly defeated at the battle of Lircai and the Conservatives took charge of the destiny of Chile. The defeat and virtual destruction of the Liberal party and the thorough organization of their antagonists meant the dawn of a stable, if somewhat reactionary, régime. A war against Peru and Bolivia contributed to the consolidation of their power.

The most conspicuous figure in the new government was Diego Portales (1793–1837), a shrewd business man with a gift for practical politics. He did not aspire to the presidency. He preferred instead to play the rôle which Bismarck and Cavour were later to play upon different stages. Taking charge of the important portfolios in the president's cabinet, he became a sort of minister-dictator. He has been called the founder of the Chilean nation, a title which rests upon the following achievements: the organization of a strong civilian party; the destruction of caudillos and bandits; the reorganization of Chilean finances; the founding of a national militia; the support of primary and normal schools; the sponsoring of a civil code; and, most of all, upon the calling of a national convention which drafted the Constitution of 1833, the organic law under which Chile was governed until 1925.

This constitution was such as might have been expected from a sane conservatism. It provided for a highly centralized republic under a president with absolute veto power and indirectly elected for a term of five years, a bicameral legislature with a conservative senate, and a highly dignified national judiciary. The Roman Catholic religion was declared to be the religion of the state, public worship by any other cult was forbidden, and church property was guaranteed, although the right of the state to exercise ecclesiastical patronage was proclaimed and clergymen were excluded from the higher offices of the nation. Property qualifications were required for the presidency and for membership in the legislative body. Except for the failure to guarantee liberty of worship, which was not a real handicap where nearly everybody was Catholic, the personal and property guaranties were definite and ample. Thus the constitution was moderate rather than reactionary. With considerable liberty there was to be no real democracy; but reactionary tendencies were in the dominant party rather than in the constitution.

Although Portales was killed by mutineers in 1837, his work had been too thoroughly done for his death to affect it. Chile had emerged from the caudillo period. Two insurrections occurred during the ten-year term of Manuel Montt (1851–1861), but they represented a fight between the reorganized Liberals and the Conservatives over such issues as the limitation of the power of the executive, the extension of the franchise, freedom of the press, the relation of church and state. They did not constitute a tendency to return to the era of militarism. Nor did the revolution of 1891 represent such a tendency. To all appearances a civilian order had come to stay.

Bolivia.—A colonial audiencia and a provincial spirit were largely responsible for the creation of the nation of Bolivia. Its territory does not constitute a unity, for there are three geographical divisions: the lofty plateau between two chains of the high Andes, the area drained by the tributaries of the Amazon, and the region drained by the Plata system. The centers of population are widely separated and difficult of access. Prior to 1776 the area had formed a part of the Viceroyalty of Peru, but it had been under a separate audiencia (Charcas) since 1559. In 1776 it was incorporated into the Viceroyalty of Río de la Plata. Coöperating during the Wars of Independence with first one and then the other of these major jurisdictions, it was the theater of constant and destructive warfare. When the last Spanish army was expelled, the leaders of the region objected to annexation either to Peru or to Argentina. In this attitude they were encouraged by Bolívar, who did not wish to see the area absorbed by the Río de la Plata confederation. His influence was thus the third factor which contributed to an independent Bolivia. On August 10, 1825, the chief inhabitants of the ancient Audiencia of Charcas proclaimed the new republic of Bolivia, giving it this name in honor of the Liberator. In 1826 they ratified a constitution which he had framed.

This document embodied the moderately conservative ideas of the great man who produced it. The government was highly centralized, Bolivia being divided into five departments and these departments subdivided into provinces and cantons. The president was to serve for life and exercise his many functions without responsibility to the national congress. Presumably the vice president was also to enjoy a life term. The legislature consisted of three chambers; namely, tribunes, senators, and censors. The last were to serve for life, the

tribunes for four years with the privilege of reëlection, the senators
for eight years with a similar privilege. The tribunes and senators
were to make the laws. The censors were to watch over the conduct
and morals of the authorities and the people. The members of the
national judiciary served during good behavior. The constitution
contained no stipulation regarding religious faith, but presumably
there was to be religious liberty, unless it should be limited by the
censors. There were ample guaranties of personal liberty and property. Popular participation in government was limited by infre-
quent and indirect elections and a literacy test for voting. Thus there
was to be considerable liberty but little democracy.

The constituent congress of Bolivia accepted Bolívar's constitution
after adding a clause which provided for the establishment of the
Roman Catholic Church. At the same time, it dissolved the religious
orders and disposed of ecclesiastical property.

For seventy-two years after the adoption of the first constitution
Bolivia passed through a dreadful period of revolution and anarchy.
In the course of seven decades (1826-1898) sixty military uprisings
occurred, ten constitutions were promulgated, and six presidents
were struck down by assassins. Here was caudilloism in its worst
phase! In deference to the wishes of Bolívar, General Sucre had
been chosen as president in 1826, but a local uprising and a Peruvian
army forced him to retire in 1828. Between 1829 and 1839 Marshal
Andrés Santa Cruz (1792-1865), a mestizo caudillo produced by
the Wars of Independence, dominated the country. For some time
he gave Bolivia order and moderate prosperity. But he dreamed of
founding an empire—was it due to Inca blood in his veins?—and
the attempt to realize this dream had fatal consequences. In 1836
he succeeded in forming the Peru-Bolivian Confederation; but Chile
opposed the project, and many Peruvians objected. In 1839 he was
overthrown by an army of Chileans and Peruvians. The military
leaders of Bolivia then began to fight each other for the privilege
of ruling and exploiting the country, for little else was at stake.

Writing in 1865, a Chilean scholar remarked that "Bolivia has not
had liberal or conservative parties," nor parties of any other kind.
"At times the people, tired of the corruption of military despotisms,
have risen up and deposed them," but other military leaders immediately took their place. In the presence of the militarists men of

ideas were impotent. They confined their efforts for the most part
to a shackled press and the teaching of the younger generations.[8]
In 1910 a Bolivian writer made a similar assertion for the entire
national history of the country.[9] Yet the powers and functions of the
church and the broadening of the suffrage were sometimes issues.
The constitution of 1880 required property and literacy tests for
voting, denied religious toleration, and guaranteed the property and
privileges of the church. Toward the end of this turbulent period
signs of the approach of a better era appeared.

By 1898 the Liberals found certain definite issues and began a revolution which soon resulted in the seizure of the government. Taking
charge of the nation in 1899, they began to carry out their policies.
Among these were the encouragement of public schools and internal
improvements, financial reforms, the abolition of military and ecclesiastical courts (1906), religious toleration (1906), and a more
vigorous development of the natural resources of the country. They
also negotiated boundary agreements with Chile and Brazil, agreements which not only brought in much needed funds but also led
ultimately to the construction of railways that gave Bolivia commercial outlets to the Pacific and the Amazon. Finally, they moved
the capital to La Paz, where it has since remained. The outstanding
Liberal presidents of the period were José Manuel Pando (1899-
1904) and Ismael Montes (1904-1909).

Peru.—Almost the entire national history of Peru has been characterized by frequent revolutions and caudillo presidents. In less
than fifty years from the time of San Martín's entrance into Lima
(1821) the country suffered from more than forty revolts and
adopted fifteen constitutions. In the single year 1834 it witnessed the
rise and fall of eight chief executives. After 1895 political conditions improved, but several military uprisings occurred after 1900.

Genuine political issues had comparatively little to do with the
disorders. A civilian party sprang up, but some of its leaders were
militarists. The Democratic party was organized, but its founder
and many of its members were aristocrats. A prominent leader posed
as the "protector of the native race" and levied a salt tax particularly
burdensome to the poverty-stricken Indians. The Roman Catholic

[8] Lastarria, *La América*, pp. 142-143.
[9] Arguedas, *Pueblo enfermo*, Chap. IX.

Church maintained a strong position and was never violently opposed. Complete religious toleration was not granted until the adoption of the constitution of 1919, which still declared the Roman Catholic Religion to be the religion of the nation. A centralized republic was generally accepted as the proper form of government for Peru. Literacy and property qualifications for the suffrage usually prevailed without confronting serious opposition. Dawson has noted, however, that between 1862 and 1904 "successful revolutions" were "few and . . . always undertaken for the maintenance of the regular constitutional order—not its overthrow—or [were] inspired by national feeling when the fatherland was in danger." [10] In addition to the general factors which contributed to the Age of the Dictators throughout Spanish America, Peru's militarism was promoted by wars with Ecuador, Bolivia, Spain, and Chile as well as by rich deposits of ore, nitrates, and guano which made the emoluments of office peculiarly attractive.

"The gestation of the Republic of Peru was a lengthy process. The vice-kingdom defended itself against Colombian, Peruvian, and Argentine troops: against the armies of Bolívar and San Martín . . . It was not until 1824, when [most of] America was already independent, that the victory of Ayacucho liberated Peru from . . . Spanish rule.

"Bolívar wished to give Peru the same constitution as Bolivia; to force the institution of the irremovable president on the anarchy of these republics . . . The Peruvians exalted the Liberator; 'hero' and 'demigod' the poets called him; his praises were sung in the churches; the Congress granted him riches and honours." [11] But some Peruvians objected to the Bolivian fundamental law; the generals of "Great Colombia" grew menacingly restive; and Bolívar returned to Bogotá. Then came chaos and, in 1845, Don Ramón Castilla, an extraordinary mestizo. Unlike Bolivia, Peru was to be a land of great caudillos.

Born in 1797 on the borders of the desert of southern Peru, Castilla became a sort of nomad with all the skill of an Arab on horseback. He fought against the patriot army at Chacabuco and was made prisoner, but he was by the side of Sucre at Ayacucho. After

[10] Dawson, *The South American Republics*, II, 132.
[11] García Calderón, *Latin America*, 113.

spending five years in modest retirement, in 1830 he began to take part in the civil wars of his native land, usually supporting the side which promised stability and respect for the constitution. In 1839 he participated in the struggle which freed Peru from Bolivian control. In 1845 he was elected president for a six-year term, after which he retired. In 1854 he took up arms against a corrupt dictator and in 1855 was again elected president, retaining his position until 1862. Small, quiet, honest, stern, he possessed "virile features and a penetrating glance." "Without much culture, he was astute enough to seem learned. He intuitively knew the value of men and the manner in which to govern them." During the thirteen years of his rule he promoted education and internal improvements, reorganized the finances, effected numerous economies in administration, freed the slaves, abolished Indian tributes, reduced ecclesiastical privileges, maintained order, and promulgated two constitutions. The second of these, that of 1860, was the fundamental law of Peru for more than fifty years.

The country then passed through a decade of disorder, corruption, and extravagance, interrupted in 1872 by the election of its first civilian president, Manuel Pardo. Born in Lima in 1834, he was the son of a poet, but he preferred action to dreams. Banker, minister of finance, and fiscal agent in London, he represented the reaction of lawyers and merchants to militarism and waste. He was the founder of the "Civilist" party, which became his chief title to fame, but he made many other notable contributions to his country. He cleansed the public service, stimulated public education in many ways, re-established the national guard, and preferred practical statesmen to poets and philosophers. Yet he was unable to prevent financial disaster; and by a monopoly of saltpeter and an alliance with Bolivia he helped to bring on a war with Chile (1879–1883). In many respects his "efforts were fruitless, both at home and abroad. He was succeeded by a military president. The alliance of Peru and Bolivia was powerless against the might of Chile, and Pardo himself was assassinated during a supreme reaction of the demagogy which he hoped to rule." Nevertheless, "death made his influence lasting." [12] He is often referred to as Peru's best chief executive.

The war with Chile was largely responsible for the emergence of

[12] García Calderón, *op. cit.*, p. 118.

Nicolás Piérola, a restless and romantic caudillo who was "always ready to seize the reins of power by the violent aid of revolution." Born in 1839, he became minister of finance at the age of thirty. In 1874 he tried in vain to overthrow Pardo; in 1878 he led another unsuccessful insurrection. Taking advantage of the crisis of 1879, he made himself military dictator for a little more than a year. Overthrown because of defeat in the Chilean war, he became president for a four-year term in 1895. Like his rival Pardo, he became the founder of a party—the Democratic party, which was also, ostensibly, opposed to militarism. From his administration García Calderón dates the "Peruvian renaissance." "Without loans he transformed an exhausted country into a stable republic. Like all the great American caudillos, he was an excellent administrator of the fiscal wealth of the country; he established a gold standard as the basis of the new monetary system, promulgated a military code and an electoral law, and by means of a French mission endeavored to change an army which was the docile servant of ambitious factions into a force capable of preserving domestic peace. His organizing talent, his patriotism, his extraordinary ability, surprised those who had known only the revolutionary leader." [13]

He was succeeded by Eduardo Romaña (1899–1904), who continued to carry out the policies of the new party, and, after the brief period of Manuel Candamo (late 1904), by José Pardo, son of the former *"Civilista"* president. Pardo proved to be another outstanding Peruvian executive, noted mainly for his promotion of sanitation, internal improvements, and education.

It must be admitted, however, that neither party was strongly devoted either to democratic reforms or to a civilian régime. The country continued to be ruled, no matter which was the successful party, by an aristocracy of army officers, clergy, landlords, and merchants. After 1895 professional and business interests became influential. Two decades later there began to emerge an assertive proletariat profoundly dissatisfied with its political and social heritage.

ECUADOR, COLOMBIA, AND VENEZUELA

Ecuador.—Still another state whose separate existence was promoted

---

[13] *Ibid.*, p. 120. Other Peruvian writers are less enthusiastic. One charges that Piérola was guilty of graft.

by the caudillos was Ecuador. At the close of the colonial period certain equatorial provinces of the Viceroyalty of New Granada were known as the Presidency and Audiencia of Quito. Freed from Spanish control by General Sucre in May, 1822, it was soon incorporated by Bolívar into Great Colombia. This aroused dissent among some of the leaders, who preferred either independence or annexation to Peru. For some years the Liberator and his supporters managed to hold the secession tendencies in check, but in 1830 General Juan José Flores (1800–1864), a Venezuelan, proclaimed the independence of the ancient presidency. The new state, which was unable to assert its authority over the northern portion of the former audiencia, was named Ecuador.

For more than eighty years after 1830 the political life of the new nation alternated between anarchy and military dictatorships. Twelve changes in the fundamental law occurred, and most of the chief executives—there were twenty-three by 1916—were overthrown before the expiration of their constitutional terms. Four of them—Flores, Gabriel García Morena, Flavio Eloy Alfaro, and Leonidas Plaza—managed to retain power for two terms or more. Virtually every "president" got into the national palace by force of arms and attempted to dictate his successor, provided he was not overthrown too quickly and did not see any prospects of longer enjoying the position himself.

The disorders and tyranny of which Ecuador was the victim resulted in part from the overweening ambition of selfish leaders. Such men could have achieved a measure of success only in a society composed largely of uneducated Indians and mestizos to whom personalities counted for more than political ideals. Yet it must not be inferred that such ideals were unimportant in the political life of the country. If any nation ever suffered from conflicting ideas, that nation was Ecuador. There were Liberal leaders who sought to improve the condition of the lower classes, to secularize education by establishing a state system of elementary schools, to achieve religious liberty, and to limit the wealth and power of the church; and there were Conservatives who maintained that the welfare of the nation could best be promoted by strengthening the influence of the church even to the point of setting up a theocracy. In fact, a conflict between these opposing views was present in nearly all of the struggles through which Ecuador passed during this long period. The record would have been more to the credit of the country, however, if factions of the same political group had never fought each other and leaders had not changed their faith in order to promote their political fortunes. The outstanding chief executives were the four already mentioned.

Flores (1830–1834, 1839–1845) governed in accordance with conservative ideals and under the constitutions of 1830 and 1843, which concentrated large powers in the hands of the executives, provided for a national legislature composed of men of wealth, a limited suffrage, a centralized state, and Roman Catholicism as the exclusive religion of the nation. Succeeded (1834–1839) by the Liberal caudillo Vicente Rocafuerte (1783–1847), who sought to protect the Indians against priests and corregidores, promote a state of system of education, guarantee religious liberty, and even, it was said, to introduce Protestantism, Flores regained his position in 1839 and continued to dominate the country for another six years. This gave him time to nullify most of Rocafuerte's reforms and restore the church to its former state. Finally deposed in 1845, he was pensioned and sent into exile. The following year he and some of his partisans attempted to obtain Spanish aid in order to restore the colonial régime. Such was the length to which the reactionaries were willing to go.

The next fifteen years were unusually turbulent, with Liberals and Conservatives rapidly alternating in power and disturbing political life by frequent changes of policy. The Jesuits were recalled and then expelled; privileges and wealth were taken from the church and then returned. The only permanent reform was the emancipation of Negro slaves, of whom there were probably about 60,000. Affairs were further complicated by disputes with factions in Peru and New Granada.

Out of the chaos came García Moreno, who dominated the country for fifteen years, although he was actually chief executive for only ten (1861–1865, 1869–1875). With the possible exception of Núñez of Colombia, he stood alone among South American caudillos.

Born of Castilian parents at Guayaquil in 1821, he was given his early education by a pious mother and a priest. At the age of fifteen he entered the University of Quito, where he was known for his industry, mental equipment, and dominating personality. His favorite studies were mathematics and philosophy. Before he reached thirty-five, he was a well known journalist. When Spain threatened a reconquest in 1846, he aroused Latin America by his writings and pacified his native city, where partisans of Flores attempted an insurrection. As a young man he passed through a moral crisis which ended by deepening his religious faith and arousing conservative tendencies. These were reinforced by a visit to Europe, where he witnessed the disorders of the Revolution of 1848. He returned to his native land in time to be shocked by the expulsion of the Jesuits both from Ecuador and from New Granada. He published a pamphlet in their defense, in which he declared that the padres were "creators of peace and order" and candidly stated that he was proud to confess he was a Catholic. Exasperated by the brutality of José María Urbina, dictator of Ecuador from 1852 until the latter part of 1856, he founded an opposition newspaper and was exiled for his pains. He went to Europe a second time and further indulged his taste in science and politics. He returned late in 1856 with his conservative convictions intensified. He was now an anachronism: he no longer believed in the supremacy of the state over the church; he was a mystic whom the Conservatives, particularly the bishops and the priests, proclaimed as their Moses. He immediately became alcalde (mayor) of Quito and rector of his *Alma Mater*. A senator in 1860, he ascended to the presidency a year later. Tall, with severe aspect, broad forehead, and forceful eyes, he was a man to be reckoned with.

During his long tenure of office he promulgated two conservative constitutions (1861, 1869) and signed (1862) a renunciatory Concordat with the pope. These were the basic laws of the theocratic government which he introduced. Catholicism became the religion of the state to the exclusion of all other cults; education was placed entirely in charge of the bishops and the religious congregations. The civil power became the guarantor and the executor of the absolute independence of the church, insuring the exclusive exercise of the Catholic faith. All bulls, briefs, and rescripts were circulated without the necessity of the sanction of the state. None of the schools, colleges, or universities were permitted to use books condemned by the church. No society disapproved by Rome was allowed to exist in Ecuador. Ecclesiastical courts had exclusive jurisdiction over all

members of the clergy. Thus García Moreno renounced the patronage and set up the Inquisition.

All these measures were apparently based upon sincere convictions. García Moreno believed "in respect and protection for the
Catholic church, unshakable attachment for the Holy See, education based upon faith and morality. . . ." He maintained that civilization itself was the fruit of Catholicism: it "degenerates and becomes impure in proportion as it departs from Catholic principles.
. . . Religion is the sole bond which is left to us in this country,
divided as it is by the interests of parties, races, and beliefs. . . . Religion is the only national tradition in these democracies at the mercy
of anarchy—the creative agent, the instrument of political unity."
In 1873 he consecrated the Republic to the Sacred Heart of Jesus.

He was therefore essentially a religious reformer, "a Christian
Hercules, a disciple of Charlemagne and Saint Louis," as one Catholic partisan has called him; "a hero of Jesus Christ and not of
Plutarch," another has said. Yet Moreno did not neglect the material development of his country. He increased revenues by sys-
tematizing taxation and suppressing frauds and contraband. He
made regular payments on the public debt, founded a mint and a
hospital at Quito, and constructed a great road from that city to
Guayaquil. He executed the little caudillos and suppressed bandits.
He gave his nation order and prosperity at the expense of liberty.

One of Ecuador's able journalists, Juan Montalvo, took up his pen
against Moreno and gained a hearing among the Liberals of the
entire Latin world. He called Moreno a terrible monster who "ought
to be killed as one kills a tiger or a snake." These denunciations had
their effect. In August, 1875, young Faustino Rayo assassinated the
theocrat in front of the Palace near the Cathedral. "It was not Rayo
who killed the tyrant," exulted Montalvo, "it was my pen."

The overthrow of García Moreno was followed by twenty years
of ruinous disorder, with Conservatives and Liberals again alternating in power. In the end the Liberals gained the ascendancy. Eloy
Alfaro (1895-1901, 1906-1911) and Leonidas Plaza (1901-1905,
1912-1916) undid most of Moreno's religious reforms and greatly
curbed the power of the church. They dissolved religious orders and
seized their property, legalized religious toleration and civil marriage, secularized education, and abolished ecclesiastical privileges

of all kinds. They also devoted considerable attention to material development, promoting the construction of the railway between Guayaquil and Quito as well as other internal improvements, reorganizing finances, and encouraging the exploitation of the material resources of the country.

Republic of Colombia.—Brought into existence in 1830 after the dissolution of Bolívar's Great Colombia, the Republic of New Granada—later known as the Republic of Colombia—passed through a bloody apprenticeship. Up to 1903 the country had been governed under seven constitutions and ravaged by seventy civil wars. In one of them (1879) 80,000 men were lost; in another (1899–1903) almost 100,000. These disorders resulted, however, not so much from the jealousies and conflicting ambitions of aspiring leaders as from almost irreconcilable differences in ideals and group interests. Powerful colonial traditions promoted reactionary tendencies; the church was strong and often uncompromising. The topography of the country also made the achievement of unity difficult. Three ranges of high mountains separated by tropical river valleys rendered speedy communication impossible. Finally, there were rivalries between the coastal towns of Cartagena and Barranquilla and the capital city far in the interior; between the extremely conservative leaders of Pasto and Popayán and the more progressive chiefs of other sections; between the thrifty, industrious inhabitants of Medellín and the dreamy, literary politicians of Bogotá.

Soon after the beginning of Colombia's national existence two deeply antagonistic parties came into existence. On the one side were the Conservatives, the exponents of administrative centralization, church and class privileges, religious intolerance, and a limited suffrage; on the other were the Liberals, who favored federalism, disestablishment, religious toleration, secularization, universal suffrage, and other ideals of the French revolutions of 1789 and 1848. For a long time these groups were nearly even in strength; hence the fierceness of the struggle. The Conservatives ran the national government most of the time until 1849; from that date until 1880 it was in the hands of the Liberals. Although Rafael Núñez, who became president in 1880, was the choice of the Liberals, he actually followed out the policies of the opposing party, which retained power until 1930 with the exception of the administration of Carlos

E. Restrepo (1910–1914) who ascended to power by means of a coalition. In 1903 Colombia, partly because of the shock occasioned by the loss of Panama, appears to have emerged from the caudillo era, although Rafael Reyes ruled as dictator from 1904 to 1909. Thereafter no important uprising occurred, and two presidents actually resigned rather than plunge their country into internecine strife. Political intolerance, however, continued until recently to be much in evidence.

Between 1830 and 1914 the country was governed by forty-six national chief executives. The disturbing issues and the character of these chiefs find illustration in the personality and policies of Tomás de Mosquera (1798–1878) and Rafael Núñez (1825–1894). Mosquera was a Conservative who turned Liberal, and Núñez was a Liberal who turned Conservative; but both, and Núñez in particular, may have been soundly converted.

A military hero, Mosquera ruled by means of the army and imposed his policy by terror. During his first administration (1845–1849) he encouraged the construction of railways and initiated steam navigation on the Magdalena River, reformed teaching methods in the institutions of higher learning, promoted popular education, and tried to improve the country's finances. During his second and third terms (1861–1864, 1866–1867) he declared a *Kulturkampf,* expelled the Jesuits, who had been called back to Colombia by the Conservatives, seized church property, suppressed convents and other religious houses, separated church and state, and promulgated a federal constitution which abolished the death penalty and guaranteed all liberties, including that of religious worship.

Núñez depended largely upon logic, eloquence, and political manipulation to carry out his program, although he sometimes resorted to the sword. He was chief executive for twelve years and actually dominated the country for fourteen (1880–1894). During this time he promulgated a centralized constitution (1886), signed a Concordat with the pope (1887), reformed the public service, and promoted internal improvements. Like García Moreno, he was a religious philosopher and a mystic, but he did not totally renounce the national patronage. Roman Catholicism was made the state religion; the church was allowed to acquire, possess, and manage property; properties which it had lost through the action of the Liberals were restored or purchased; the reëstablishment of religious orders was permitted; all education was to be conducted in accordance with Catholic dogma; and the church was in many respects made independent of the civil power, although partial toleration of non-Catholic worship was provided.

Venezuela.—Venezuela, like most other Spanish-American nations, has suffered much from the destructive sway of militarism. Beginning its independent existence in 1830, when it broke away from Great Colombia, the country experienced during the next seventy years fifty-two revolutions, twelve of which were successful, and changed its fundamental law eleven times.

These disorders sometimes represented more than the contest between leaders for the control of the government and its revenues. They were in part a clash between local sentiment, based upon traditional organization,[14] and administrative centralization. To some extent also they were the result of divergent views with respect to the position and privileges of the church as well as of clashes between the creole aristocracy and the mixed races. Nevertheless it would appear that the revolutions frequently were merely the expression of violent dispositions and greed for power and spoils. Nor did they lead anywhere, viewed from the standpoint of liberty and democracy. Until 1935 Venezuela was under the domination of militarism. There is, however, one streak of light on the dark picture: long-term dictators with something of enlightenment frequently emerged from the pandemonium and furnished a régime of order and material progress. Among these rulers, José Antonio Páez and Antonio Guzmán Blanco (1829–1899) may be mentioned as most conspicuous until the second decade of the twentieth century.

Páez, who has been called the Founder of the Venezuelan Nation, served as chief executive from 1830 to 1835, from 1839 to 1843, and from 1861 to 1863; and during much of the intervening time his influence was in reality dominant. A creole with little education and a native of the broad plains of Apure (born in 1790), he became a refractory and violent, although dashing and brilliant, cavalry officer of Bolívar. The logical champion of the humble classes, the unlettered proletariat, he soon allowed himself to be taken in by the landlords and wealthy inhabitants of the towns and by the literary

---

[14] It was not until near the end of the colonial epoch that Caracas became the political and ecclesiastical center of all Venezuela.

ideologues whom he once detested. In the end he became the leader —or perhaps the tool—of a group who in Venezuela may be characterized as Conservatives, but who, if they had been found in Chile or Colombia, might have been called Moderates. The constitution which they drew up in 1830 was a compromise between the federal and the centralistic types; and they later abolished tithes, suppressed monasteries, granted a measure of liberty to the press, declared themselves in favor of religious freedom, and encouraged immigration. Such measures may certainly be characterized as moderate, perhaps liberal. Páez also encouraged road building, supported higher education, and inaugurated important financial reforms. Indeed, under the rule of Páez and the "presidents" largely controlled by him Venezuela experienced considerable prosperity. Foreign trade increased and the national debt was reduced from nine million to two million pesos.

Although some of these reforms must have pleased the Liberals who were slowly consolidating into a party, there were still other measures which an ardent Liberal might demand: for instance, the liberation of the slaves, further limitation of the power and privileges of the church, public schools for the masses, larger local autonomy, and the broadening of the suffrage from a property to a manhood basis. The radicals might even demand, as certain of them did, the redistribution of the land. Moreover, in 1862, Páez had negotiated a somewhat objectionable Concordat with the pope.

Between 1846 and 1868, but mainly under the Monagas brothers, who were Conservatives with liberal tendencies (1846–1858), and the Liberal Juan Falcón (1863–1868), several of these Liberal demands were granted. The slaves were freed (1854), universal suffrage was proclaimed, the provinces became legally and in fact virtually independent states, and provision was made for larger freedom of expression. Such reforms came, however, very haltingly and with frequent interruptions in the form of revolutions and counter-revolutions which left the country bankrupt. Things had almost reached a state of chaos when Antonio Guzmán Blanco took possession of the government in 1870.

Guzmán Blanco was master of Venezuela from 1870 until 1889, although not actually chief executive during all of this period. The son of Antonio Leocadio Guzmán, a distinguished journalist and candidate of the Liberals for the presidency in 1846, Guzmán Blanco came to power as a Liberal; but he made a vain bid for the support of the church and proceeded to ignore the principles of free discussion and local autonomy, quelling all opposition with vigor and ruthlessness. Such action he justified as necessary to order and prosperity. At the same time, he inaugurated certain measures which proved that he had not wholly departed from the Liberal faith. He issued decrees making primary education free and compulsory, legalizing civil marriage, secularizing the cemeteries, and suppressing religious orders. He likewise sponsored the codification of the national laws, reorganized the finances, restored credit, and undertook internal improvements on a large scale. Although venal and arbitrary, augmenting his private fortune at public expense and committing acts of unjustifiable cruelty, he was able and sometimes patriotic, his rule being on the whole better than anything which Venezuela had experienced. It was a period of peace, prosperity, and, in a way, of social betterment. The foreign debt decreased fully seventy-five per cent, in spite of large loans floated in Europe; and the dictator completed, began construction upon, or projected nearly all of the railroads which Venezuela had prior to 1913. Moreover, his educational work alone has been considered ample compensation for his faults.

After the overthrow of Guzmán, Venezuela passed through a turbulent decade into another period of long-term dictators. The first of these, Cipriano Castro (1899–1908), was a cruel and somewhat crude mountaineer whose rule became notorious because of many difficulties with foreign nations. The second, Juan Vicente Gómez (1908–1935), revealed considerable administrative ability and achieved the distinction of having ruled for a longer period than any other Latin-American dictator except Porfirio Díaz of Mexico.

CHAPTER XI

THE AGE OF THE DICTATORS (II)

IN the previous chapter a brief summary was given of the history of the nine states of Spanish South America during the Age of the Dictators. It is now necessary to examine the island "republics," Central America, and Mexico, for they also experienced an epoch of caudilloism.

HAITI AND THE DOMINICAN REPUBLIC

Haiti.—After the achievement of its independence in 1804 Haiti suffered severely from military uprisings and political corruption. During the first ·eleven decades it was theoretically governed under ten different constitutions and by twenty-seven chief executives—emperors, kings, and presidents. Sixteen of them were driven into exile, or fled, frequently with the contents of the treasury. Three were assassinated, one committed suicide, three others died from unknown causes. Only two retired alive after completing the regular constitutional term of office. Between 1908 and 1915 there were eight "presidents," but during the early national period some of the executives enjoyed a longer lease of power, a few of them ruling for periods varying from seven to twenty-five years. Alexandre Pétion ruled southern Haiti from 1806 to 1818; Henri Christophe governed in the north from 1806 to 1820; Jean Boyer ruled from 1818 to 1843; Soulouque, from 1847 to 1859; Geffrard, from 1859 to 1867; Salomon, from 1879 to 1888; and Hyppolite, from 1889 to 1896.

Indeed, it would not be difficult to exaggerate the extent of Haitian disorders. Not only has Haiti, like most of the states of Spanish America, had its long-term dictators, but many of its rebellions were not accompanied by widespread fighting and some of its executives were patriotic and respectable. Many of the uprisings were in the nature of palace revolutions. Foreigners did not often suffer violence, and up to 1914 Haiti usually met its foreign obligations. Unfortunately, however, political and fiscal conditions grew worse instead of better, and from 1915 to 1934 the United States tried to make a contribution to a more orderly régime.

Perhaps the people of Haiti merit sympathy rather than scornful criticism. At any rate, certain factors in their national life deserve to be understood. Their movement for independence, in so far as it was motivated by ideas at all, was based upon the radical doctrines and violence of the French Revolution. After the French planters had been driven out or executed no one was left with experience in government. The population was made up entirely of mulattoes and Negro ex-slaves, many of the latter having arrived only recently from Africa. The war for independence destroyed both the wealth of the country and its roads, so that there were lacking the material means for the achievement of unity. Even the ideal of national unity hardly existed in illiterate minds accustomed to violence and embittered by racial animosity. The mulatto minority, most of whom had been slave owners, were hated and distrusted by the blacks, nor would the mulattoes tamely submit to ex-slaves or the sons of ex-slaves. Negroes and mulattoes accordingly fought each other for the privilege of ruling the country, and light men and dark men alternated in power.

The Dominican Republic.—The Dominican Republic has the unenviable distinction of being politically one of the most turbulent of the countries of Latin America. During the first seventy-two years following its release from Haitian domination (1844) the country had some forty-three "presidents," four captains-general (under the Spanish reoccupation, 1861–1865), thirty-nine military uprisings—the majority of which overthrew the executive authority—and twenty changes of constitution. One of its caudillos was in charge of the government on five different occasions amounting to a total of fifteen years; another served four periods totaling nine years; a third was dictator for almost seventeen years; and the remainder averaged a little less than twelve months each. Only some two or three were assassinated; the remainder, however, without exception, were driven from power by military force.

The most tenacious of all the caudillos were Pedro Santana ("president," 1844–1848, 1853–1856, 1859–1861; captain-general under Spanish rule, 1861–1862); Buenaventura Báez (1849–1853, 1856–

1858, 1865–1866, 1868–1874, 1876–1878); and Ulises Heureux (dominant from 1882 to 1899). The first was a creole, the last two mulattoes. Santana and Báez were corrupt, particularly the latter, and favored the annexation of their country to some foreign power. Heureux was a venal and cruel despot with hardly a redeeming quality.

For these political disorders it would seem that there have been sufficient causes: the Spanish heritage of political inexperience, intolerance, administrative graft, and caciquism; the more than two decades of suffocating oppression under Haiti; the long struggle for independence which developed many ambitious military chiefs; the Spanish reoccupation; the large mulatto and ex-slave Negro elements in the population; the almost constant menace of interference by Haiti. In 1905 the United States began its attempt to help the Dominicans maintain political and fiscal order, pursuing between 1916 and 1924, indeed, a somewhat drastic policy.

The Five Republics of Central America

Union vs. Disunion.—The "Five Republics of Central America" launched upon a turbulent career immediately after the separation from Spain (1821) and the Mexican Empire of Iturbide (1823). But the group should not be described indiscriminately as lands of revolutions, bankruptcy, and absconding presidents. Some of them have been far more disorderly than others. Only Chile and Argentina, of all the Spanish-American countries, have enjoyed greater stability than Costa Rica; El Salvador was fairly orderly for a period extending over a quarter of a century; and even Nicaragua, the most turbulent of them all, had its thirty years of peace (1863–1893). Moreover, constitutions were not bewilderingly numerous, and many of the military uprisings involved directly only a small number of the people.

A student of these little states has explained their disorders as follows: "first, the attempt to impose political institutions copied from one of the world's most advanced democracies upon a country where elections were absolutely impossible; second, what may be called the habit of revolution among the ruling class and the people of many of the towns,—a habit formed during the turbulent years

that followed the breakdown of the federal constitution, and per-
petuated by the bitterness of personal feuds and sectional jealousy,
the pursuit of politics as a money-making occupation, and the mutual persecutions of rival factions; and third, the backwardness of
the masses of the people, which has not only made the republican
constitutions unworkable, but has also prevented those who in the
long run suffer most from civil war from exerting any effective
influence for peace." [1]

This list of causes requires, however, some elaboration. The political institutions described in the organic laws were largely the
result of political inexperience and lofty idealism, and sometimes the
revolutions were attempts to bridge the chasm between intellectual
utopias and actual facts. Moreover, uprisings were facilitated by the
colonial inheritance of *personalismo* (personalism) inculcated in
mixed races by priests, Indian caciques, and big landlords; and lack of
adequate means of communication and the meagerness of financial
resources at the government's command made defiance of the central authorities easy. Lastly, the following factors exerted a strong influence: the ideal of Central American unity that certain leaders sought
to achieve either by common consent or by "blood and iron"; the
conflict between federalists and centralists; monarchist machinations and foreign intrigues; and the religious issue, which arose during the confederation period (1824–1838), continued to transcend
national boundaries, and aroused animosities between men who na-
tionally were brothers. In other words, the list comprises a convenient
summary of all the forces which tended to produce political disorders
in other parts of Spanish America. There was only one important exception: the struggle for separation from Spain was brief and almost
bloodless.

For the first fifteen years of their independent existence the people
of the former Captaincy-general of Guatemala—with the exception
of the inhabitants of Chiapas and Socunusco, which continued to
be a part of Mexico—were theoretically united under a federal republic. There were five provinces (really states): Guatemala, Honduras, Nicaragua, Costa Rica, and El Salvador. The Constitution of
1824, in many ways modeled after that of the United States and the
Spanish Constitution of 1812, contained most of the usual guaranties

[1] Munro. *The Five Republics of Central America*, p. 186.

of persons and property, although it proclaimed Roman Catholicism to be the exclusive religion of the nation. It was the expression of the triumph of the progressives over the reactionary group who had annexed the country to Mexico in 1822. The first elections represented a further victory and the new federation started out under Liberal auspices. The president, Manuel José Arce, and the majority of the national Congress were men of liberal tendencies. Liberal leaders also gained control for a brief period of most of the state (provincial) governments.

The Conservatives, or "Serviles," soon became active, however. This group was largely under the domination of the landed aristocracy and the ultramontane clergy. Most of its members opposed the federal system; a few favored a monarchy or a return to the rule of the mother country. President Arce alienated the Liberals by trying to conciliate the Conservatives and ended by abandoning his own party. Largely under ecclesiastical domination, he violated the national constitution by frequent interference with the provincial governments. The other members of the Federation also resented the predominant position of Guatemala. Near the close of 1826 the Liberals took up arms.

It was the beginning of a politico-religious war which lasted intermittently for several decades and ended in greatly reducing the wealth and power of the church. Nuns and priests pretended to observe palm trees floating in the heavens portending Conservative victories, and interpreted opportune earthquakes and volcanoes as punishments sent against the Liberals by an angry God.

In April, 1829, Arce was overthrown by the Liberal General Francisco Morazán (1792–1842), and in September, 1830, Morazán became president of the Federation. Meantime, the Liberals had recovered or retained control of nearly all the state governments. The ascendancy of this group was the signal for a series of "reforms," both state and federal. The Spaniards, apparently discovered plotting to restore the colonial régime, were driven from the country. The archbishop of Guatemala was expelled along with many members of the religious orders, and numerous church properties were taken over by the governments. Religious liberty was proclaimed, the nation asserted the right of patronage, the priests were encouraged to marry, marriage was declared to be a civil contract, and theaters and schools of science were opened; but an attempt to secure the ratification of a new constitution in 1835 failed.

This failure probably indicated that the power of Morazán had begun to decline. Already, in 1833, it had become necessary to remove the capital from Guatemala City to San Salvador. The province of El Salvador was resentful of the influence of its neighbor, and Guatemala was becoming a stronghold of Conservative reaction. In 1837 an epidemic of cholera broke out in the latter country. The priests declared that the Liberals had poisoned the wells in order to rid themselves of their enemies. Fanatical Indians and mestizos, under the leadership of a young man of mixed blood (or perhaps entirely Indian) named Rafael Carrera (1814–1865), rose in revolt. Carrera proved to be an able, though an exceedingly cruel, warrior. He was hailed by the clergy and a part of the aristocracy as an agent of Providence for wreaking vengeance upon the "profane" Liberals and restoring the holy religion to its former position. By the spring of 1839 he had seized the government of Guatemala, driven Morazán into exile, and dissolved the Federation.

The former provinces became independent states and the union was never again restored, although unity continued to be a potent ideal. Six subsequent attempts were made to renew the federation by means of negotiation: in 1842, 1849, 1895, 1898, 1907, and 1921. Two ambitious presidents, Barrios of Guatemala and Zelaya of Nicaragua, sought in vain to achieve the same end by the employment of force.

For much of this time the five republics continued to experience a turbulent political existence, tempering dictatorships by assassination or overthrowing them by revolutions which merely prepared the way for other dictators. The disorders were occasioned, as formerly, by ambitious military chiefs and oligarchies, recalcitrant churchmen, intrigues of foreign agents, local and state rivalries, and boundary disputes. Partisanship proved to be a stronger bond of unity than patriotism. Conservatives who suffered defeat in one state were offered refuge and assistance by the Conservative governments of other states until they returned and overthrew their enemies; and the Liberals, with an organization likewise extending across state boundaries, pursued a similar policy. The inhabitants of the towns of León and Granada fought for the domination of Nicaragua, even going so far on one occasion (1855–1858) as to call in the Yankee filibuster Walker and the Yankee financier Vanderbilt. In fact, foreign residents not infrequently made contributions to the caudillos, either under compulsion or in the hope of securing profitable concessions. Numerous constitutions were promulgated in order to crystallize ideals or legalize abuses of power: by 1913 Guatemala had had three, El Salvador six, Honduras five, Nicaragua seven, Costa Rica five.

Between 1839 and 1865 the Conservatives usually had their way, calling home the proscribed clergy and restoring their property, negotiating Concordats with the pope, and adopting a policy of religious intolerance. During the next thirty years, however, the Liberals frequently had the upper hand, except in Nicaragua (to 1893), and used their power to resubjugate the church, to proclaim freedom of conscience, and, in all the states except Costa Rica, to disestablish the church. Before the close of the century religion had almost ceased to be a political issue. By that time, also, Costa Rica and El Salvador had virtually achieved political stability. In fact, by 1889 Costa Rica escaped from the constant scourge of revolutions and military dictators. Afterwards there occurred in that nation only a few military uprisings of any importance. The successive presidents usually devoted themselves "with enlightened patriotism to promoting the welfare of the country, and great advances [were] made in reorganizing the finances, in safeguarding the public health, and in providing for the education of the masses of the people." [2] In El Salvador General Tomás Regalado, after serving his full term of four years (1894–1898), "passed on the chief magistracy in an orderly manner to" his successor. Afterwards there occurred few revolutions in the country. The other three republics continued to be dominated by militarism, however—a militarism which, moreover, often threatened the peace of the entire region. After 1906 the United States took an active interest in the political affairs of the Central American countries, perhaps making some contribution to a more orderly life.

Dictators of Central America.—In general, it may be said that Central America has not been a land of *long-term* dictators. Honduras has not had any, nor has El Salvador.[3] Costa Rica has been

[2] Munro, *The Five Republics of Central America*, p. 148.
[3] Two or three of Salvador's dictators were in power from five to eight years.

dominated by two: Juan Rafael Mora (1849–1859), and Tomás Guardia (1870–1882). Nicaragua has been ruled by only one, José Santos Zelaya (1893–1909). Guatemala, however, has had three: Rafael Carrera, already mentioned (dominant from 1839 to 1865), Justo Rufino Barrios (1873–1885), and Manuel Estrada Cabrera (1898–1920).

Mora (1814–1860) was an able conservative whose rule was noted for internal peace, the subordination of the army to the civil authority, the recognition of Costa Rica by Spain, the negotiation of treaties with the United States and several of the Latin-American countries, a Concordat with the pope, and a vigorous fight against William Walker, who was trying to conquer Nicaragua. Guardia was an army officer who, with a mere handful of men, boldly entered the artillery barracks of San José concealed in an oxcart under a load of fodder, overpowered the guard, and proceeded to seize the chief executive of the nation, call a convention, and have himself elected president. From a material standpoint his rule might easily have been worse. Although he allowed finances to fall into disorder near the end of his administration, he succeeded in the promotion of railroads, telegraphs, and schools. He also published a military code and promulgated the constitution of 1871, which (with certain modifications) was for many years the organic law of Costa Rica. "However, his government was a repressive military dictatorship, in which his own personal followers held all the principal offices. The great families, whose leaders were exiled and deprived of their property, were reduced almost to insignificance as a political factor, and have never entirely regained their former influence." [4]

Although Zelaya, who for sixteen years was dictator of Nicaragua, belonged to the Liberals of that country, he displayed great skill in playing faction against faction and managed to avail himself of the support of strong groups in each party. During his long rule he extended and improved the railway system and the steamer service on the lakes, developed the coffee districts by generous subsidies, transformed the capital (Managua) into a progressive city, opened many new schools, and sent several bright young men abroad to study. In 1905 he promulgated a new constitution which disestablished the

[4] Munro, *The Five Republics of Central America,* p. 146.

church, guaranteed religious liberty, prohibited religious orders, and forbade entails and the holding of property in "dead hands" (namely, by religious corporations). In dealing with his political opponents he was "a brutal and unscrupulous tyrant." He tortured and imprisoned his enemies, executed them, or sent them into exile after confiscating their property. Yet "friends of the government prospered, and the people as a whole suffered comparatively little." "He and his ministers established monopolies of all sorts, and sold valuable concessions to foreigners or acquired them themselves." They also enriched themselves by debasing the currency. In foreign relations he showed little regard for international obligations, meddling in the domestic affairs not only of the states of the Isthmus but even of Ecuador and Colombia, arbitrarily interfering with foreign trade, and giving little heed to the payment of contracted debts. He also dreamed of restoring Central American unity by armed force and opposed the interference of the United States in Isthmian affairs. His hostility toward Washington was largely responsible for his overthrow. After his exile in 1909 the Conservatives, who had controlled the country from 1863 to 1893, once more took charge of the government.

Rafael Carrera, who dominated not only Guatemala but a good portion of Central America for more than a quarter of a century (1839–1865), was a despot of the worst type. He was uneducated, superstitious, fanatical, arbitrary, ambitious, cruel, and yet he undoubtedly possessed great sagacity and bravery; the best that can be said of him is that he gave Guatemala an era of comparative peace under the scourge of a dictatorship which debased all who suffered it and destroyed virtually every manifestation of progress. Few public works of any kind were undertaken, commerce almost ceased to exist, public instruction was neglected, and liberty was proscribed. In 1852 he signed a Concordat with the pope. Only during the latter part of his prolonged control did he reveal any disposition to rescue the country from the benighted condition to which he had been mainly responsible for bringing it.

Eight years after Carrera's death the government of Guatemala was seized by Justo Rufino Barrios (1835–1885), one of Central America's outstanding Liberals. Following in the footsteps of Morazán, Barrios expelled the powerful religious orders and confiscated their property, brought the church hierarchy under subjection, promoted internal improvements, encouraged agriculture, and established schools in almost every village and hamlet. Under his auspices was framed a constitution which provided for religious liberty and lay education and prohibited entails and the retention of property in "dead hands." Subsequently modified in several particulars, it has continued to be the fundamental law of the land. Responding to the stimulation of his enlightened despotism, Guatemala experienced a material and intellectual revival. Barrios also revealed an ambition to unify Central America and lost his life in the attempt.

The long dictatorship of Manuel Estrada Cabrera in Guatemala has been denominated a "reign of terror." It was described as follows by an eyewitness (Munro): "The administration firmly maintains its authority by means of a large standing army and police force, and promptly and mercilessly checks the slightest manifestation of popular dissatisfaction. An elaborate secret service attempts, with a large measure of success, to inform itself fully of everything which occurs in the Republic. . . . It is dangerous to express an opinion on political matters even in private conversation. Much of the mail, and especially that coming from abroad, is opened and read in the post office. The formation of social clubs is discouraged because of possible political results, and it is impossible for a man prominent in political circles to have many friends without arousing distrust. Persons who fall under suspicion are imprisoned or restricted in their liberty, or even mysteriously disappear. The ruthless execution of large numbers of persons, many of whom were probably innocent, have followed attempts to revolt or to assassinate the President." Yet the same witness goes on to remark upon the many public improvements constructed by the dictator: parks, monuments, buildings for schools, hospitals, and other public institutions. Although Estrada Cabrera was undoubtedly a cruel exploiter of his country, it is nevertheless true that he promoted education, agriculture, and industry and encouraged the construction of roads, railways, and telegraph lines. His rule was approved by many influential natives and most foreign investors. It furnished another illustration of the choice between order and a considerable degree of prosperity on the one hand and instability with perhaps somewhat more of liberty and justice on the other.

CUBA AND PANAMA

Cuba and Panama, the youngest nations of Spanish America, revealed soon after winning their independence characteristics similar to those displayed by their kindred. As a part of Colombia until 1903, Panama had shared in that nation's seventy years of storm and stress; and Cuba, which continued, as we have seen, to be a part of Spain's American empire until 1898, had been restive and often revolutionary under Spanish rule. Neither Cuba nor Panama received training tending to inculcate a capacity for orderly government under democratic institutions. Both were introduced into the family of nations under the patronage and protection of the United States, but its guardianship did not entirely suppress the turbulent and dictatorial tendencies of certain elements of their population.

Panama.—Under the treaty of 1903 the United States was granted the right to intervene in Panama for the purpose of suppressing disorder. It was not long before the authorities at Washington found it necessary to exercise this right. In 1904 a prompt warning and the prospect of intervention by marines of the Canal Zone prevented a *coup d'état.* In 1906, when the first popular elections were held in Panama for the purpose of choosing certain members of Congress, it was alleged that President Amador Guerrero (1904–1908) was attempting to control the ballot boxes and force the choice of his partisans. The United States was accordingly asked by the opposition to intervene in order to insure fair play. The White House refused to grant the request on this occasion, but marines were sent to the Isthmus to supervise the national elections of 1908. The United States also supervised the national elections of 1912 and 1918, but afterwards, although repeatedly urged to do so, it refused to take such action. Meantime, the dominant party rendered suffrage ineffective and party spirit developed to a tenseness which was sooner or later to break out in a revolution or a *coup d'état.* Strictly speaking, however, Panama has never had a military dictator.

Cuba.—In Cuba political affairs took a similar direction. Under the Platt Amendment (1901) the United States might intervene to restore order. The first Cuban election was held on December 31, 1901, while General Leonard Wood was still head of the military government of the island. The partisans of one of the candidates for the presidency, Bartolomé Masó, refused to go to the polls because they objected to the constitution of the national electoral board, and Tomás Estrada Palma won the election for the four-year term beginning in 1902. Late in 1905 he accepted the nomination of the Moderates for a second term. This party proceeded to make up a registry of 432,313 voters, of whom more than a third represented fraudulent names. As a consequence of this procedure the Liberals abstained from voting, declaring at the same time that they declined to "be responsible for the future." This meant that they were determined to seek their rights through revolution. Within a few months they staged an uprising, and by the end of the first week in September, 1906, they were threatening the capital. Unable to put down the rebellion, Estrada Palma appealed to the United States. President Roosevelt sent William Howard Taft and Robert L. Bacon to Havana in the hope of solving the problem without formal intervention, but their efforts failed; and on September 29, Taft assumed the rôle of governor. Soon afterwards he was replaced by Charles Edward Magoon.

One of the main tasks of Magoon was the preparation of effective laws governing electoral procedure. This and other legal work was undertaken by an Advisory Law Commission consisting of nine Cubans and three citizens of the United States, with Colonel Enoch Herbert Crowder as chairman. In the fall of 1908 General Mario García Menocal was the presidential candidate of the newly formed Conservative party (the successor of the Moderates), and José Miguel Gómez was the standard bearer of the Liberals. In an honest, well managed election, Gómez obtained the victory. On January 28, 1909, Magoon turned over the government to him and the first intervention of the United States after 1901 ceased.

In spite of the irregular procedure which characterized the election of 1905, for which the Moderate party was more responsible than the president, Estrada Palma ranks with Spanish America's greatest chief executives. A patriot of long standing and an agent of the Cuban insurgents in New York for many years, he devoted himself whole-heartedly to the welfare of the new nation. His rule was characterized by mildness, justice, honesty, economy, a scrupulous regard for the law, and an effort to promote the material and intellectual progress of the country.

Although Gómez (1909–1913) was a popular president, he was a man of very different type from Estrada Palma. He built up a strong military establishment in order to insure himself against the fate which overtook his predecessor in 1906. He allowed some roads to go to ruin, but built others, and he revived the Spanish tradition of handing out political plums. During his administration, moreover, the municipal alcaldes were deprived of their proper and legitimate functions, cockfighting was restored, a notorious amnesty bill was passed, and an even more notorious lottery system was put in operation.

Gómez was eager for the Liberal nomination for the presidency in 1912, in spite of his single-term preëlection promise. When Alfredo Zayas won this nomination, however, Gómez threw his influence to García Menocal, the Conservative candidate, who came off victorious. Cuban presidents were thus forming the habit of dictating their successors. The evils which would develop from the tendency did not fully reveal themselves, however, during the Gómez administration. The "Veteranists" (soldiers of the recent war for independence) planned a revolt, but the threat of United States intervention deterred them; a Negro political party staged an uprising, which led to the landing of American marines, but this was a sort of race war. Nevertheless, in later years the dangers which lurked in electoral frauds and presidential interference with the suffrage would stand revealed. Such procedure was eventually to lead to interference from Washington, to dictatorships, and perhaps to even greater evils.

MEXICO

It would be rash to contend that none of the revolutions which Mexico experienced after the achievement of its independence represented a struggle between caudillos for authority and spoils, for Ignacio Comonfort changed from a Liberal to a Conservative and Antonio López de Santa Anna fought on both sides of nearly every issue which arose during his long career. And yet it is true that Mexico was more disturbed by the violent clash between ideas and group interests than most of the countries of Spanish America. None of these nations produced more conspicuous leaders or suffered from revolutions of greater magnitude and destructiveness. Between 1828 and 1867 civil war was almost continuous: the form of government changed eight times and the country was ruled by thirty-seven different administrations. The next ten years witnessed only a few minor outbreaks, and the revolution which brought Porfirio Díaz into power. Then came the "Porfirist Peace" which lasted more than three decades, but proved to be only a long calm preceding a most violent storm. In 1932 Mexico had probably not yet passed beyond the age of dictators supported by the army, but after 1911 principles and ideas usually furnished the basis for the struggle.

Few of the elements of discord which appeared elsewhere in Spanish America were absent from Mexico. The country was perturbed by a combination of them all. Monarchists opposed Republicans; Centralists fought Federalists; Conservative clericals, landlords, and militarists were pitted against Liberals who stood for secularization and a civil régime; agrarian reformers struggled against the landed aristocracy; creoles fought men of color; military heroes moved back and forth through these jarring elements; and above all hovered the shadow of foreign intervention.

The important influences in Mexican national history were democratic idealism, ambitious military chieftains, untutored masses, a small group of big landowners, and the Roman Catholic Church. The ideals of political and civil democracy, drawn largely from France and the United States and kept fresh by currents of thought which continued to flow in from these two countries, never lacked champions among the intelligentsia and the political leaders of Mexico. Militarism scarcely ever ceased to be a dangerous factor, revealing itself even as late as March, 1929. The Indian and mestizo masses were ignorant and superstitious in 1821, and their intellectual condition did not greatly improve during the next ninety years. A country of large haciendas at the beginning of its national life, Mexico saw no reform in this respect during the first century of its independence. Comparatively few small farmers developed, the holdings of the land barons increased, and many of the Indian groups lost the community lands of their ancestors.

The Church.—The influence of the Roman Catholic Church in Mexican political contests was so pervasive and constant that much of the national history of the Aztec Republic clusters around this central theme. The church was so strongly intrenched at the opening of the second decade of the nineteenth century that few of the leaders of the independence movement dared speak or even think of religious toleration, lay education, the separation of church and state, the secularization of cemeteries, the abolition of tithes, the adoption of civil marriage, or the suppression of religious orders. Yet its immense material resources soon furnished a strong temptation for greedy or financially desperate dictators, and its uncompromising attitude, supported by foreign priests and often by the pope himself, stirred men to bitter hostility. The first attempts to limit its wealth, privileges, and functions (1833–1834, 1838, 1842, 1847) confronted a coalition of clergymen, militarists, and land barons, and hence achieved little success; but the "Laws of Reform" and the Three Years' War (1856–1859) so completely shattered its power that it could not be restored by Conservatives and Monarchists even by calling in a French army and Maximilian (1861–1867). Indeed, one of Emperor Maximilian's many difficulties arose from the fact that he was too liberal for the churchmen. The "Reforms" were embodied in the Constitution of 1857 and subsequent amendments, and the church never fully recovered from these vigorous blows. Its properties were gone, its orders disbanded; and religious liberty, lay education, and civil marriage came to stay. Yet it continued to exert a strong influence over the masses, and during the long conservative reign of the "Liberal" Díaz it rose again to a position of wealth and strength which enabled it to threaten the program of an even more radical group of "Reformers" who expressed their goals in the Constitution of 1917 and advanced upon a path of practical achievements a few years later.

Between 1824 and 1911 Mexico was ruled by three long-term dictators. Two of them, Juárez and Díaz, were men of great ability who possessed many admirable qualities. The third, Santa Anna, was an amazingly successful charlatan. Juárez was a pure Zapotec Indian; Díaz had some Indian blood in his veins; Santa Anna was a creole. Juárez died in office at the age of sixty-six, while the other two lived to be octogenarians, one of them dying in disgrace and the other in exile.

Santa Anna.—Born of wealthy Spanish parents at Jalapa, near Vera Cruz, in 1795, Antonio López de Santa Anna served for a decade in the Spanish army, hunting down the rebels and rising to the rank of captain. In 1821 he supported Iturbide and the Plan of Iguala; in 1823 he helped to overthrow him. He fought in 1828 to place Vicente Guerrero in power, but soon afterwards took up arms with the view of deposing him. In 1829 he fought against the Spanish attempt to reconquer Mexico and became the "Hero of Tampico." He ascended to the presidency in 1833 as a Federalist and opponent of the church and in a short time was found interrupting all Liberal reforms and erecting a centralized government. He maintained his power either in Mexico City or on leave at his hacienda until 1836, when he marched northward into Texas to be routed and captured by Sam Houston. Instead of being shot for his cruel treachery toward the Texans in the early part of his campaign, he was sent to Washington for an interview with President Jackson, who was so much impressed by the distinguished visitor that he returned him to Vera Cruz in a war vessel. But Santa Anna's failure in Texas had destroyed his prestige and he was forced into a brief period of retirement.

Late in 1838 an opportunity to win popularity and return to power presented itself. The French navy seized Vera Cruz and forced the Mexican government to pay an unreasonable indemnity for injuries to French citizens and their property. When Santa Anna learned that the French marines were beginning to embark he rushed down with a small band of soldiers and fired on them as they departed. He came too close to the French guns and received a wound in the leg which compelled its amputation. Although he had no idea of dying, he issued an emotional and bombastic farewell address. The incident was sufficient to restore him to favor. He was now the hero of both Tampico and Vera Cruz. For nearly five months (March to July, 1839) he was dictator, while the "president" was away putting down a revolution. When the chief executive returned, Santa Anna reluctantly surrendered the National Palace to him.

Two years later he led a Conservative revolution and once more seized the government, retaining power in person or through a substitute until he was driven into exile in 1845. As the war with the United States approached, he got in touch with President Polk, who sent a man-of-war to Havana in order to take him back to Mexico, where he was expected, apparently, to seize the government and bring hostilities to a speedy close. He reached Vera Cruz in September and took charge of the Mexican government before the close of the year. By this time, however, peace was far from his mind. He placed himself at the head of a fairly large army and was eventually utterly routed by the Yankees. Disgraced and fearing capture, he retired in 1847 to Jamaica and later to New Granada, where he remained until the Conservatives called him back in 1853.

For more than two years thereafter he was Dictator and "Most Serene Highness" only to be driven once more into exile by Mexico's first really popular revolt. He later offered his sword in vain to Maximilian and then to Juárez. It was not until 1874 that he was allowed to return to his native land. Poor, broken, and blind, he died two years later, after having written his memoirs. Impetuous, dissipated, corrupt, unscrupulous, without any fixed political principles, he was nevertheless a consummate actor, a moving orator, with superficial brilliance and great personal magnetism—Mexico's representative genius of dissolution, defeat, and political buffoonery and one of the most individual of Latin America's caudillos.

Benito Juárez.—Born of Indian parents in the mountains near the city of Oaxaca in 1806, Benito Juárez was educated for the church by a charitable merchant, but later turned aside to study law in Oaxaca's Institute of Arts and Sciences, where he taught for a time and received his degree of bachelor of law in 1832. Two years later he became for a brief period an advocate of the Supreme Court of the republic. But just as he had evinced more interest in law than in the priesthood, so now he became more devoted to politics than to law. Beginning as a member of the cabildo of Oaxaca (1831), he occupied nearly every office within the gift of his native state, including the governorship (1847-1852) and a term in the National Congress.

Always an ardent and consistent Liberal, he was imprisoned in 1853 by his "Most Serene Highness" Santa Anna, who was at that time the agent of the Conservatives. He soon managed, however, to escape to New Orleans, where he is said to have made his living by working in a cigar factory. He returned to his native land in 1855 and joined the revolt of Juan Álvarez and Ignacio Comonfort against the chameleon dictator. He became minister of justice late in 1855 and constitutional president in 1858, maintaining himself in this latter position, despite French intervention and domestic uprisings, until his death in 1872.

As minister of justice and chief executive, he faithfully supported the "reform" program of the Liberals. Most of their measures struck at the wealth and power of the church. They originally intended to compel the sale at reasonable prices of its vast holdings of real estate, but were provoked by opposition into a policy of frank confiscation. Moreover, church and state were separated, religious liberty proclaimed, civil marriage instituted, and education and cemeteries secularized. All of these measures the Liberals promulgated by laws later incorporated in the Constitution of 1857 and in subsequent amendments.

The success of their policies was limited by domestic revolts and French intervention, which brought on fiscal emergencies that prevented a wise sale of church properties and a real decentralization of land ownership. Juárez and his party also made the mistake of including the Indian communities among the corporations which were forbidden to hold real estate, thus preparing the way for the division of the community lands among individual Indians who did not really possess the astuteness to retain them as private property. Although Juárez saw the evil and interrupted the process, it was allowed to continue after his death, much to the injury of the natives.

During Juárez's long rule Mexico never enjoyed complete peace, but from 1868 to 1872 conditions were comparatively quiet and the country revealed everywhere signs of increasing prosperity and enlightenment. His greatest contribution, aside from his own lofty character, consisted in his tenacious defense of democratic ideals and policies and the independence of his country against Conservatives so bent upon the retention of their privileges that they sought a French protectorate and a foreign monarch in the hope of achieving their purpose. Honest, astute, brave, simple in his manner of life, never admitting defeat, he was truly a great man. The nation which produced him and later almost unanimously accepted him as an ideal statesman cannot be totally lacking in political virtue.

Porfirio Díaz.—Porfirio Díaz, an able soldier and Spanish America's most widely known statesman, was born of poor parents in Oaxaca in 1830. His mother was a mestizo and physically he possessed decided Indian traits. At first educated for the church, but later persuaded by Juárez to study law, he received his degree from the Oaxaca Institute of Arts and Sciences in 1853. Already he had seen military service in the war with the United States, and in 1855 he participated in the revolt against Santa Anna. In the years following he supported the Laws of Reform and the Juárez government against the Conservatives and the French. In 1871 he permitted his ambition to drive him into an unsuccessful revolt against his old friend and teacher, who thought far more of the military than of the political talents of Díaz. Fleeing to the United States, he returned from exile soon after Juárez's death and in 1877 seized control of the government. From that date until 1911 he dominated the political life of his country, although he was not actually chief executive from 1880 to 1884.

Díaz emphasized upper-class prosperity and the material development of the country to the neglect of liberty and enlightenment for the Mexican masses. He built railroads and telegraph lines, opened post offices, reformed finances, abolished vexatious restrictions on internal trade, scrupulously met international obligations, and encouraged in every way the exploitation of the rich natural resources of Mexico; but he neglected the native races, allowing them to be deprived of their lands, gave too little attention to public education, ruthlessly repressed discontent, alienated the young intellectuals by denying them participation in public affairs and showing too much favor to foreign concessionaires, and allowed himself to be surrounded by a small coterie of administrators, many of whom were notoriously corrupt.

In an age quick to applaud order and material advancement he won for himself and his native land a position of international respect and esteem seldom equaled by any of the Spanish-American statesmen or countries. Mexican foreign trade grew by leaps and bounds, increasing from $63,000,000 in 1885 to $239,000,000 in 1907; and national revenues augmented in proportion. But the dictator was growing old. He had failed to raise up a successor or prepare the people for the democratic system described by its constitution. Many were smarting under a sense of injustice and neglect, and Díaz was unable to stem the tide of economic and social discontent which rapidly developed as the new century opened. When the crisis came he found his army not only "honeycombed with padded muster rolls and petty larceny," but of questionable loyalty. In May, 1911, he was forced to abdicate and leave the country. He died in Paris in 1915 after Mexico had entered once more into a long era of revolution.

PROFIT AND LOSS

It is impossible to calculate the total material losses occasioned by the numerous revolutions of Spanish America. One writer [5] has estimated at 418 million pounds sterling the wealth consumed in all the revolts which occurred in these states down to 1924. The losses of life and the cases of permanent disability must have run far up into the hundreds of thousands. The constant disturbances had the further effect of discouraging economic effort and diverting human energies from constructive pursuits. And yet the influence of these numerous military uprisings may easily be exaggerated. In preceding pages it has frequently been pointed out that many of them were little more than "palace revolutions." The implements of destruction were often rudimentary, and the opposing armies nearly always quite small. When everything is taken into account, it must be observed that the total cost has been rather insignificant compared to the immense expense and destructiveness of the World War. It is doubtful, indeed, whether the cost of Spanish-American revolts equaled the material and human losses of the Civil War and Reconstruction in the United States.

The growth of population and foreign trade in the turbulent states would seem to indicate that the importance of these revolutions has been overestimated. Figures bearing upon these points are by no means accurate, being in many instances mere estimates, but they are perhaps sufficiently trustworthy to show the main trend. The foreign trade of continental Spanish America appears to have increased fourfold between 1800 and 1860. The population of the same area was approximately 15,000,000 in 1810 and 24,600,000 in 1861. Since Chile and Argentina achieved stability about 1833 and 1862 respectively, a fairer representation of the later growth of the disorderly states will result if these two republics are excluded. The total population of the continental states, not including Argentina

[5] Sanín Cano in *Boletín de la Unión Ibero-Americana*, June, 1924.

and Chile, was approximately 21,450,000 in 1861 and some 38,500,000 in 1913. The increase was almost entirely a natural one, for there was very little immigration except in the case of Uruguay. The trade of these continental states, again eliminating Argentina and Chile, increased fivefold between 1860 and 1913, amounting to $1,095,400,000 in the latter year. Between 1844 and 1913 the population of Haiti and the Dominican Republic quadrupled, and between 1896 and 1913 their foreign trade increased in value from less than eighteen to more than thirty-seven million dollars.

It should also be noted that these disturbances gave a sort of fluidity to the social order and thus furnished many an individual of the lower classes an opportunity to rise to a new level in society. An orderly régime in independent Spanish America would have meant a hierarchy of churchmen, landlords, mine owners, and wealthy merchants, with a following of creole lawyers, physicians, army officers, and the like. It would have made impossible the rise of such men, for instance, as Juárez, Díaz, Páez, Santa Cruz, Sarmiento, and Castilla. In the midst of revolution there flourished a sort of anarchistic equalitarianism, since all were equal before the dictators with their extensive powers. The comparatively easy achievement of military rank was a democratizing influence which placed on the same level men of all races and all strata. On the battle field the idea of equality, with the abolition of all special privileges as its corollary, gradually penetrated the soul of even the common mass. Revolutions have been the process by which the aristocratic society and the caste system of the colonial period have been propelled toward more liberal commonwealths. Such uprisings correspond to the Reform Bills of England and the pacific political revolutions of 1800 and 1828 in the United States. There were many setbacks and much wandering in the wilderness, but the trend was clearly toward a more liberal and democratic order, toward greater social unity and an ardent nationalism.

It would be a mistake to consider the legal and constitutional provisions in the retarded states as indicative of actual conditions, for in many cases they expressed little more than ideals of personal liberty, democracy, and governmental structure. Yet it is a fact that by 1913 such states as Uruguay, El Salvador, Costa Rica, and Colombia had achieved a fair amount of stability and administrative regularity. It is also a fact that religious toleration, proclaimed almost everywhere by the constitutional or statutory law, was a political reality, although the Roman Catholic Church was still the state church in several of the republics and personal and social intolerance persisted in some quarters. Moreover, slavery had been abolished, freedom of education prevailed in most of the republics, freedom of speech and the press were not entirely unknown, the ancient colonial fetters had been removed from commerce, there were no titles of nobility or special courts for the privileged classes, art and literature had begun to flourish, impressive public buildings and monuments had been erected in many of the cities, railways and telegraph lines had been inaugurated, financial conditions slowly improved, and the clergy had lost their exclusive control over education, marriage ceremonies, cemeteries, and registration of births and deaths.

In general, it was the native races who profited least by the changes of the century. It is true that the odious tribute and the encomienda system of colonial times were suppressed, but debt peonage had developed, and that vast body of benevolent and protective legislation which characterized the colonial period had disappeared. With the achievement of independence the Indians were assumed in law and in practice to be no longer wards but the equals of other citizens. As a matter of fact, however, they were not equal in intelligence or political and military power to the whites and the mestizos; hence, they became the prey of the exploiting groups above them—groups no longer restrained by law or special political functionaries.

The ease with which the destructive factors of the Age of the Dictators may be exaggerated will be clearly demonstrated by a consideration of the progress which occurred during the period in music, art, and literature. García Calderón made the following sagacious remark in 1911: "He who knows [Spanish] America only by its imperfect social framework, its civil wars, and its persistent barbarism sees only the outer tumult; there is a strange divorce between its turbulent politics and its refined art. If ever Taine's theory of the inevitable correspondence between art and its environment was at fault, it is in respect of these turbulent democracies

which produce writers whose literary style is so precious, such refined poets and analysts." [6]

In every capital and in almost every important city, even in many
of the most turbulent countries, centers of music, sculpture, and
painting sprang up. Members of the upper classes revealed their
superiority both in the production and in the appreciation of art.
Their progress in these fields of culture, however, was based largely
upon the tragic exploitation of the lower classes, whose innate artistic
capacities were suppressed.

There was much greater progress in all forms of literature. The
aristocrats, who had little interest in active business and industrial
pursuits, were intensely devoted to poetry, journalism, law (both
domestic and international), and history as well as to politics and military affairs. Many of the generals and dictators were writers of no
mean ability.

Literature was not often divorced from action. It reflected political
strife and unrest, preparing for or justifying political change. The
Argentine thinker, Juan Alberdi, wrote: "Philosophy is meant for
politics, morality, industry, and history, and if it does not serve them
it is a puerile and trifling science." The ablest journalists usually
championed liberalism and opposed tyrants. Francisco Bilbao and
José Lastarria were the champions of liberalism during the first half
of the nineteenth century in Chile; Juan Montalvo attacked cleri-
calism and the dictatorship in Ecuador; Francisco Vijil represented
the struggle of liberalism against the church in Peru; Antonio L.
Guzmán was the champion of liberalism in Venezuela, and so likewise was José Batlle y Ordóñez of Uruguay, while Sarmiento and
others violently attacked the tyranny of Rosas in Argentina. Some
able journalists, however, undertook to defend conservatism, and
Núñez of Colombia first championed one side and then the other.
Students of jurisprudence busied themselves with legal codes and
legal reforms. International lawyers whetted their wits on the Monroe Doctrine, sought to define the rights of aliens living in their
midst, or attempted to limit the employment of armed force in the
collection of claims. Historians occupied themselves with reminis-
cences and national history or sought to draw moral lessons from
biography, ecclesiastical lore, or universal history. Much of the his-

[6] *Latin America*, pp. 270–271.

torical literature was marred by prejudice, although several reliable works appeared in Mexico, Cuba, Peru, Colombia, Uruguay, and Venezuela. Poetry often tended to become rhymed oratory or lyrical declamations execrating tyrants and evoking liberties. A few writers turned to botany and medicine, in which there was considerable progress, while others occasionally dealt with political science or sociology.

Perhaps the greatest achievements occurred in the realm of pure literature. Some have contended that Spanish America had too many poets as well as too many generals and politicians. During most of the nineteenth century the poets imitated Spanish classicism or French romanticism, but their themes were often national. In the earlier period they devoted their talents to the composition of national anthems or the praise of the liberators. Later they turned to colonial history and traditions, to the Indians, or to the luxuriant nature which surrounded them. Near the end of the century a reaction took place. A new poetic movement began, and soon Europe began to go to school to America.

The precursors of this movement were all from the more turbulent nations of Spanish America: Manuel Gutiérrez Nájera of Mexico, José Asunción Silva of Colombia, and José Martí and Julián Casal of Cuba. And the "recognized master of the new school and one of the greatest lyric writers of all time in the Spanish language" was Rubén Darío of chaotic Nicaragua! Moreover, none of the other outstanding poets of the group were from the more stable nations; they were Rufino Blanco-Fombona of Venezuela, José Enrique Rodó of Uruguay, and José Santos Chocano and José María Eguren of Peru.

Much of the poetry of the turbulent states was characterized by melancholy and pessimism: poetic martyrdom, unrequited love, lovers killed by the villain or dying by suicide in the belief that their sweethearts had proven false. In part this sadness was a pose, but in much greater measure it was genuine; it was the result of depressing climate, poverty, the strain of aboriginal blood, and political disorders and persecutions.

The poetry of the "Modernist Renovation" was distinguished (in addition to the characteristics of sadness and pessimism) by a richness of form and vocabulary, pronounced individualism, ardent love of beauty, deep devotion to the Spanish-American *patria,* and often by a defiant anti-Yankeeism. The writers aimed at a native art, free from stereotyped rhetoric, "innocent of imitation, declamation, or affected sensibility." It was a sharp, a revolutionary, change in the direction of greater freedom and naturalness. No such literature could have been produced under a monarchical-clerical régime like that which prevailed in the previous century. Freed at last from the shackles of the old order, the self-conscious individual set out upon a new mission of conquest in the realm of the mind and the spirit.

Practically all the writers, whatever the form of literature they produced, were members of the wealthier classes, but some of them portrayed the miserable life of the exploited Indians and mestizos. The educational system, too, was aristocratic, emphasizing secondary schools and institutions of higher learning which were rarely attended by the sons and daughters of the people and giving too little emphasis to state-supported schools for the masses. Yet a number of rulers, some of the dictators prominent among them, were champions of compulsory and gratuitous public education for all the children of the land, and there is not the slightest doubt that ability to read and write was far more widely spread in most countries in 1925 than in 1825.

CHAPTER XII

THE RISE OF THE A B C STATES

In previous chapters it has been noted that the history of all the states of Spanish America was characterized by an epoch of militarism and disorder, that some of the states, such as Chile and Argentina, emerged from the period sooner than others, and that several of them were still under the sway of military chiefs at the beginning of the twentieth century. It was also pointed out that Brazil, the Portuguese nation of America, virtually escaped the age of military dictators. The present chapter will deal with one of the outstanding phenomena of Latin-American history, the rise of the A B C powers in southern South America.

CAUSES OF THE UNEQUAL DEVELOPMENT OF THE LATIN-AMERICAN STATES

The unequal development of the Latin-American nations has been due to a variety of causes. Among these, perhaps climate, racial elements, foreign immigrants, enterprise, and capital, and opportune leadership were the most important.

Although the exact relation between civilization and climate is most difficult to determine, it is safe to assert that there is some connection between climate and human energy, temperament, and industry. The more orderly, vigorous, and progressive civilizations have developed in the temperate zones, and the advanced peoples of Western Europe appear to prefer these zones. There is probably some significance in the fact that Argentina, Uruguay,[1] Chile, and southern Brazil—really the most progressive part of Brazil—are situated in a temperate climate.

Innate racial capacity, like the relation between civilization and climate is still undetermined. Yet, whatever their ultimate capacities

[1] Much of what is said in this section will apply with equal force to Uruguay, which, for special reasons set forth in Chapter X, lingered in the caudillo era until 1904.

may be, it is a fact that hitherto certain races have achieved greater development than others and shown superior adaptability to changing environments. It is also true that racial and cultural homogeneity have an important bearing upon both the political stability and the economic and social progress of a nation. In Argentina the Western European peoples have long constituted almost the entire population, Indian and Negro elements being almost totally absent. Western European elements are also in the ascendancy in Chile and southern Brazil. In Chile, to be sure, there is a large Indian and mestizo contingent, but it is of an unusually virile and intelligent type. In Brazil the Indian element is unimportant, for it really does not form any considerable portion of the body politic. Although the Negroes and mulattoes constitute the majority of the population in certain portions of central and northern Brazil, they have not often occasioned serious discord or disturbance, and the nation is ruled largely by the whites. Whether Brazil will some day break up into two nations largely on the basis of race and climate remains to be seen.

It is not a reflection upon the nations situated in southern South America to set down what appears to be the established fact that they are deeply indebted to European immigration and capital for their stability and progress. The same may be said, although perhaps not to an equal degree, of the United States. The channels along which European immigrants and capital have flowed run toward the temperate-zone nations of South America, and the current began to move toward them at the dawn of their independence. Yankee capital and enterprise likewise have contributed to the development of these countries, and this contribution appears destined to become larger in the future.

Whatever the ultimate capacity of backward peoples for development, the Indian, Negro, mulatto, and mestizo elements of Latin America have lingered behind the peoples of Western Europe and the whites of the United States. It appears only natural, therefore (other factors being the same), that those countries of Latin America which have received the largest increment of white immigrants should be found in the lead; and these countries are Argentina, Brazil, Uruguay and—to a lesser extent from the standpoint of immigrants, but in excess of most of the other states of Latin America —Chile.

Some 3,200,000 immigrants landed in Brazil between 1820 and 1912. Italians were at the head of the list with 1,300,000, followed by the Portuguese with 900,000, the Spaniards with 400,000, and the Germans with 116,000. More than 136,000 immigrants came to Brazil in the single year of 1911, the Portuguese leading with 47,000 and the Spaniards and Italians following with 27,000 and 22,000 respectively. The immigrants flourished in their new home, so that in numbers and wealth they constituted an important element in the population of the country.

Although its immigrant tide started somewhat later, Argentina received an even greater influx. Between 1857 and 1917 some 4,550,000 aliens entered the republic. Among them were 2,247,000 Italians, 1,420,000 Spaniards, 211,000 Frenchmen, 155,000 Russians, 130,000 Syrians, 85,000 Austrians, 59,000 Germans, 53,000 Britons, and 6,000 North Americans. More than 300,000 immigrants arrived in 1913. By 1895 the foreigners in Argentina comprised more than one-fourth of the population and in 1914 they numbered 2,378,217 in a total population of 7,905,502.

Chile by no means received so many immigrants during the last century, the total varying from only one thousand to eight thousand annually. They came mainly from Great Britain, Germany, and Spain. Like Brazil, Chile has a "Little Germany" in the southern portion of its national domain.

With such a stream of aliens, there is no wonder that the population of Brazil almost doubled between 1890 and 1910, or that the inhabitants of Argentina more than doubled during the same period. The growth of Chile's population was much slower, however. Starting at 600,000 in 1800, it reached only 3,500,000 in 1913.

In like manner, these nations have been the fields for large investments of foreign capital, the influx being in part the cause and in part the result of political stability. The flow of investments began to reach them soon after the winning of independence, but the most rapid movement prior to the outbreak of the World War occurred between 1870 and 1913. Although the exact amount of foreign capital invested in the nations under consideration is not known, the following estimate of the value of these investments in 1913 is believed to be approximately correct: Argentina, three billion dollars; Brazil, two and one-half billion; Chile, one billion two hundred million. The principal European nationals represented were, in the order of their importance on a numerical basis, the British, the French, and the Germans. Prior to the outbreak of the World War, citizens of the United States had not invested more than 120 million dollars in these countries.

This capital brought with it the skill, ingenuity, and energy of the foreigners. A large part of it was invested in railways, steamships for coasting trade, urban public utilities, port and harbor improvements, mining and manufacturing enterprises (including the nitrate industry of Chile), live-stock and meat-packing industries, and agricultural projects. Europeans and citizens of the United States came in to initiate and operate most of these industries for the simple reason that the nationals of Argentina, Brazil, and Chile were not qualified for such work. Without foreign talent many of these improvements and enterprises would not have been perfected nor even initiated.

The foreign capitalists and their alien employees were primarily interested in salaries and dividends, and for this reason their operations were not an unmixed benefit. The governments of these countries usually managed, however, to exercise a salutary control; and more satisfactory conditions may be expected eventually to result from the employment of the practical talents of the descendants of the immigrants, who tend to become enthusiastic and loyal citizens of these countries, as well as from the gradual equipment of the Latin Americans themselves for these fields of endeavor.

Meantime, much has depended and will continue to depend upon the leadership of the Latin Americans in politics, law, journalism, education, and literature. Through these instrumentalities national ideals and integrity have been and must be preserved. Fortunately, it has been mainly into these pursuits that the leaders of these countries have directed their talents and energy, and their achievements often have been notable. If Europeans and North Americans have made important contributions even in these fields, such contributions have been more than counterbalanced by the accomplishments of certain Chileans, Brazilians, and Argentinians in business, natural science, and technology. In the main, the people of Argentina, Brazil, and Chile have not had to look beyond their borders for leadership in politics, law, education, and letters.

The Development of Chile (1833–1913)

The history of Chile [2] between the years 1833 and 1913 was characterized by a steady economic development and a vigorous struggle between intrenched privilege and democratic progress, with the forces championing the latter gradually winning their desires. That the contest was waged without frequent bloodshed is a tribute to the orderly disposition of the Chilean people. One of Chile's historians, Luis Galdames, has divided the history of the country since 1831 into three periods: the Autocratic Republic (1831–1861), the Liberal Republic (1861–1891), and the Democratic Republic (1891 ff.). The criterion is mainly political, and the terms have meanings which vary with the setting. Nevertheless, it seems desirable to employ them in this narrative.

The rule of the autocrats, as already noted, lasted from 1831 to 1861. They were a small group who represented the landed aristocracy. The constitution of 1833, essentially their handiwork, was designed to insure the perpetuation of their power.

During the autocratic period three able administrators ruled the country, each retaining power for two terms. The first two were chosen mainly because of their military reputations; the third was a distinguished civilian and scholar. They gave Chile strong and vigorous governments which maintained peace and tended to promote upper-class prosperity; but their policies also resulted in the growth of a bourgeoisie whose wealth was accumulated in mining and commercial enterprises and who eventually formed the backbone of a new Liberal party.

Joaquín Prieto.—Joaquín Prieto's (1831–1841) administration was noted for the constitution of 1833; a victory over the Peru-Bolivian Confederation resulting in the break-up of that combination; the supression of a revolt led by ex-President Freire; and the reforms of Manuel Renjifo, Prieto's able minister of finance. It was also signalized by the work of Portales, whose character and achievements have been discussed in another connection. In fact, the president was somewhat overshadowed by his ministers, but he displayed one characteristic which deserves mention because of its rarity in Latin

[2] Area, some three hundred thousand square miles, or seventy per cent of the combined areas of France and Germany.

America. In 1839, after the victory over Peru and Bolivia, he divested himself of his extraordinary powers and pursued toward his political opponents the policy of "conciliation and forgetfulness."

Manuel Bulnes.—Manuel Bulnes (1841–1851), the hero of the war against the Peru-Bolivian Confederation, followed a similar course and even attempted to govern with the aid of a cabinet composed of the representatives of the different political groups. His administration was also characterized by striking economic and educational progress. Foreign trade was stimulated by the establishment of steam navigation on the Pacific (William Wheelwright, 1840); coal mines were opened near Talcahuana; and foreign credit was improved through the consolidation of the British debt. In education, also, several important advances were made. A national university and a normal school were founded; the military academy was reëstablished; and a school of arts and crafts as well as a school of agriculture was created in Santiago. Moreover, several secondary schools were opened, and the course of study for these institutions reorganized. The Bulnes administration was also signalized by the establishment of prosperous German colonies in southern Chile and the extension of Chilean sovereignty over the Strait of Magellan.

Near the close of Bulnes's second term the Liberals, largely under the influence of the Revolution of 1848 in France, revealed signs of increasing strength; and perhaps it was because of their growing influence that Bulnes undertook a few liberal reforms. These related mainly to the church: certain religious practices were suppressed; dissenters were exempted from the obligation of performing wedding ceremonies in accordance with the rites of the Catholic faith; and agents of the executive were given authority to supervise the parish priests. Such reforms, however, were not sufficient to conciliate the Liberals; and, besides, they were more than counterbalanced by the suppression of Liberal journals and the expulsion of the more ardent members of this party. In the end, the interference of President Bulnes in the national elections of 1851 furnished the signal for a revolutionary outbreak which shook the whole country. Although Manuel Montt, the administration candidate, was chosen to succeed Bulnes, the insurgents were still under arms on September 18, 1851, when the new executive took charge of the government, and it was not until near the close of the year that the revolution was finally suppressed.

Manuel Montt.—In the main, President Montt (1851–1861) continued the policies of his predecessors, encouraging the construction of railways and telegraph lines, establishing schools and other institutions of learning, and making certain concessions to the Liberals. Perhaps the most noteworthy measures under the last category were the abolition of primogeniture, the encouragement of primary schools, the opening of public libraries in some of the provincial towns, the replacement of the tithe by a tax, and the occasional challenging of the power and prestige of the church in other ways. Montt's administration was also noted for the promulgation of a civil code which became a model for other states of Latin America and the enactment of a law making insurgents personally responsible for damages occasioned by their uprisings.

As Montt's last term drew to a close, the Liberal elements once more became active. In fact, a reorganization of parties took place in 1857. Moderate Conservatives and moderate Liberals combined in a National party—the Montt-Varista party, as it was usually called —and the reactionary Conservatives, who had been offended by restrictions placed on the church and the abolition of primogeniture, evinced a willingness to coöperate with the Liberals, whose policies for the most part were anathema to them. Violent opposition to Montt was the cohesive force which brought together such obviously incompatible groups, and when the president prepared to dictate his successor, sporadic outbreaks warned him that such a policy would result in the reënactment of the bloody scenes of 1851. He accordingly made a concession to the opposition. He turned aside from Antonio Varas, the candidate of his preference, and gave his support to José Joaquín Pérez, a statesman more acceptable to the Liberals. Pérez was elected, and his inauguration (September 18, 1861) in many ways marked the beginning of a new régime in Chile. For one thing, it indicated that the balance of power was shifting from the landed aristocracy to the merchants and miners of the cities. The control of the government was passing into the hands of the Liberals—that is, liberals after the order of the Whigs of eighteenth century England.

During the next three decades five able executives wielded the national scepter, each maintaining power for a five-year term, with the exception of the first of the group, who served two terms, and the last, who was overthrown by a revolution. Although their domestic programs were interrupted by a war with Spain (1866) and with Peru and Bolivia (War of the Pacific, 1879–1883) as well as by uprisings of the Araucanian Indians in southern Chile, numerous important Liberal measures were enacted.

José Joaquín Pérez.—Despite a period of financial stringency at the beginning of his first term and the brief war with Spain, Pérez (1861–1871) was able to give considerable encouragement to internal improvements and education. His administration was also characterized by the repeal of the law against the instigators of popular revolt (passed during the Montt administration); by an act which not only permitted non-Catholics to practice their faith within their own buildings, but also allowed them to found and support special schools for the education of their children in conformity with their creeds; and by a constitutional amendment prohibiting the president from serving two consecutive terms.

Federico Errázuriz.—The single term of Federico Errázuriz (1871–1876) was rendered notable by the encouragement of public works, by the modernization of education through emphasis upon the natural sciences, and by important political and constitutional reforms. The press was granted almost unlimited freedom; the clergy were deprived of their special courts; burial rights were granted to Protestants within certain portions of Catholic cemeteries; the "Comisión Conservadora," which the Constitution had endowed with the power to exercise legislative functions during the recesses of Congress, was placed under the control of the more popular branch of the national legislature; and the Council of State was made more directly responsible to Congress.

Aníbal Pinto.—Although the administration of Aníbal Pinto (1876–1881), who holds the distinction of being the first Chilean president nominated by a convention, was occupied largely with vexing financial problems and the "War of the Pacific," he found opportunity to inaugurate certain judicial reforms, suppress the tobacco monopoly, and reorganize secondary and higher education. The election of 1881 took place during the critical weeks of the war; and the Conservatives, eager to return to power, supported the candidacy of the popular war hero, General Manuel Baquedano. Pinto vigorously opposed him both on account of his political affiliations and because his election would appear to be a return to the Age of the Caudillos. For its candidate the administration selected Domingo Santa María, an experienced and energetic statesman. In order to avoid provoking a domestic crisis at a time when Chile confronted grave foreign complications, General Baquedano patriotically withdrew from the race. Santa María was accordingly elected, entering upon the duties of his office on September 18, 1881.

Domingo Santa María.—Much of the new President's time was consumed by the international struggle, but after its close (1883) Santa María and Congress turned once more to the Liberal program. They stimulated agriculture and mining, opened new roads, constructed bridges, and encouraged the establishment of schools of technology, although it might have been better if they had expended the money devoted to these purposes in the redemption of the paper money which had been issued to finance the late war. More noteworthy were the religious measures adopted by Santa María's administration: the law of civil marriage, the law of civil registration of births and deaths, and the removal of practically all restrictions upon the use of cemeteries. Lastly, during this administration the constitution was amended so as to permit a two-thirds majority of the chambers to pass a law over the executive's veto; all property qualifications for voting were removed, and the local intendants and governors were shorn of many of their attributes.

Chile appeared to be entering an era of real political liberty. Unfortunately, however, the president did not refrain from electoral interference. Not only did he resort to official intervention in almost every conceivable form in order to control the congressional elections of 1885, but he also prepared to dictate his successor in 1886. His conduct provoked an unfavorable reaction even among some of the congressional groups who supported him, but Santa María had his way. His candidate, José Manuel Balmaceda, was elected.

José Manuel Balmaceda.—Balmaceda was one of Chile's most sincere and picturesque presidents. In his early days—he was born in 1838—he had shown an inclination for the priesthood, but his faith had been shaken by wide reading in literature and science. In the silence of the fields where he devoted some time to agricultural pursuits, the tendency to revolt against the religious spirit became more pronounced; and he entered politics, having become a liberal, a reformer, a laical and almost an atheistic thinker. In the Chamber of Deputies at Santiago he was an eloquent and towering figure before he entered the cabinet of Santa María as minister of interior and cult. In this latter capacity he is supposed to have been the leading spirit in bringing about the clerical and constitutional reforms which characterized Santa María's administration.

Balmaceda's first task upon assuming office as chief executive was to harmonize the various Liberal groups which had appeared during the last years of his predecessor's rule. After having effected a measure of solidarity, he embarked upon an ambitious program of public works and of educational promotion and reform. He also put through legislation reducing the voting age from twenty-five to twenty-one years and equalizing representation. But graft unfortunately appeared in the execution of the contracts for public works, and the clerical and oligarchical groups were tireless in their machinations against him. By 1890 the opposition had secured the balance of power in Congress and a spirited struggle ensued between the national legislature and the national executive. When Congress refused to vote the budget for 1891, Balmaceda declared that the budget for the previous year would be considered as in effect. He also refused to dismiss his cabinet, which was out of harmony with the congressional majority, and planned to dictate his successor by electoral interference. Congress thereupon attempted to depose him, and in January, 1891, a civil war broke out. It proved to be a very sanguinary struggle, but in the following August the forces of Balmaceda were finally routed and the president abdicated, leaving General Baquedano, who had remained neutral during the war, in charge of the government. Balmaceda remained in hiding in the Argentine legation until September 19, when he committed suicide in order to avoid prosecution by his political enemies, who had come to power on the previous day. In the contest there was something of historical irony. The overthrow of Balmaceda had been occasioned mainly by the Conservatives in the name of the Liberal principle of Parliamentary Responsibility!

Thereafter, for several years at least, the power of the Chilean presidents declined and Congress played a rôle of increasing importance. In fact, the presidential system made way for the parliamentary system. Most of the immediate successors of Balmaceda, although men of ability and distinction, failed to exert any great influence upon the march of events.[3] By a law of 1891 executive interference in elections was forbidden and the right of electoral supervision, local as well as national, was conferred upon the municipalities. Moreover, the lower middle class and the proletariat were already beginning to make their voices heard in national affairs. An indication of the trend of the times may be seen in the occurrence of the first labor strikes during the administration of Balmaceda and the organization of the Democratic party in 1887. According to the view of Galdames, the era of the Democratic Republic had dawned.

Yet it can hardly be contended that the Chilean masses wielded any very great influence between 1891 and 1913. There was universal manhood suffrage with only a literary test not rigidly applied; there were also a large amount of political liberty and a measure of freedom from electoral interference by the use of force, but the democracy failed to develop its potentialities by making use of the devices placed in its hands. It was too ready to sell its votes for a week's wages; it was somewhat handicapped by the property qualifications still required of senators and deputies; and it was unable to organize a strong party based upon a program of genuine democratic reform. Hence the Chilean people were unable to push through important measures of social legislation. Aside from laws designed to prevent epidemics and improve the health of the masses—laws which would naturally benefit all classes—aside from the beginnings of labor legislation and the establishment of certain benevolent institutions supported in part by the state, the most signal triumph was along the line of primary education. The number of primary schools was doubled between 1890 and 1910, and by 1913 the revenues devoted to this purpose bulked large in the national and local budgets. And yet the primary schools were sufficient at the latter date to take care of only about one-half of the children of school age, the curriculum of these institutions did not furnish a basis for entrance into the

[3] The following were the successors of Balmaceda to 1915: Jorge Montt (1891–1896); Federico Errázuriz (1896–1901); Germán Riesco (1901–1906); Pedro Montt (1906–1911); Ramón Barros Luco (1911–1915).

secondary schools, and illiteracy among the masses stood at an appalling height.

Nevertheless, Chile deserved to be classed among the progressive
states of Latin America. During the century since the beginning
of its independence movement many important changes had occurred. In 1800 its population was about 600,000, of whom 100,000
were unsubdued Indians, 350,000 were mestizos, and the remainder
Spaniards. By 1913, as noted elsewhere, Chile's population reached
3,500,000 and was molded into a racial, if not a social, unity. The
foreign commerce of the country in 1800 was some six million
dollars, but by 1913 it was valued at 265 million. Chile had no newspapers at the beginning of its national life, nor any primary schools
of a secular nature. Indeed, there were few schools of any sort, and
probably ninety per cent of the people could neither read nor write.
In 1913 the country had more than 3,000 free primary schools, several schools of mining, commerce, and technology, numerous establishments for the training of teachers, a great national university,
public libraries in every city and almost every town, some of the
best journals to be found anywhere in the world, and a group of
intellectuals who would have been a credit to any nation. Moreover,
Chile had made important progress toward the establishment of great
railway, telephone, and telegraph systems and was entering upon
the era of hard-surfaced highways and automobiles, to say nothing
of its beautiful parks and its magnificent public buildings. Although
the condition of the masses still left much to be desired, public health
had greatly improved, wages had trebled during the century, and
not more than sixty per cent of the people were illiterate. Survey-
ing their past, the Chileans of 1913 could be optimistic regarding
the future. They had made progress, and they were enjoying political and a large measure of religious liberty.

The Evolution of Argentina (1868–1913)

The history of Argentina [4] since the close of the era of military
dictators presents in many ways a marked contrast to that of Chile.
In Argentina there occurred no vigorous clash between clerical and
aristocratic privileges on the one hand and the forces of liberalism

4 Area, more than a million square miles.

and democracy on the other. Although the established church still existed in 1913 and the national constitution required that the president be a Catholic, the temporal power of the church had long ago been shattered. The establishment of the principles of secular schools and cemeteries, civil marriage, and state registry of births and deaths, as well as the abolition of tithes and the suppression of certain religious institutions, took place during the caudillo period. Nor did Argentina have a conservative party corresponding to the Conservatives who dominated Chilean politics between 1831 and 1861 and are still a group to be reckoned with in that country. Rosas and his gaucho hordes all but overwhelmed the urban oligarchy of merchants and absentee landlords; agricultural labor threw off the feudal trammels which bound it to the soil; universal manhood suffrage was established; and the constitution of 1853 not only recognized the principle of local autonomy but contained a long list of individual rights and immunities.

This did not mean, however, that democracy had permanently triumphed in Argentina during this early period. As in Chile at a later date, the people did not appreciate their liberty or set the proper value upon the instruments placed in their hands. Nor did they understand how to obtain their desires. Under the constitution their influence was not limited; but actually they were too ignorant and perhaps too poor to defend and promote their interests. At least seventy-eight per cent of the people of Argentina were illiterate in 1869 and more than fifty-four per cent in 1895; and the last figure was exceeded in certain rural sections as late as 1913. Constitutional guaranties and political devices could not prevent wealth and intelligence from ruling poverty and ignorance, and unfortunately the rule of the former was not always benevolent toward the latter.

Nevertheless, it remains true that the history of Argentina since 1868 has not been characterized by that dramatic contest between the forces of reaction and progress so interestingly featured in the national development of Chile. In the political evolution of the Argentine during the period there was but one important issue: that of centralism versus local autonomy, and it would appear that the autonomists engaged in a losing contest after 1868. Parties formed not so much around issues as around personalities. With the rapid increase of wealth—due in large measure to the rising value of land—and the growing industrialization of the country, however, a struggle between democracy and plutocracy began shortly before 1913. Moreover, Argentina holds the unflattering distinction of having had more political corruption than has Chile.

Between 1868 and 1913 Argentina was governed by eleven administrations, able for the most part, but unfortunately not always impeccable. As in the case of Chile between 1831 and 1891, the presidents were the predominating figures in the national government. Only four of the eleven served full constitutional terms of six years. Two were forced by political opposition to resign, one died in office, and one resigned on account of ill health. Most of them dictated their successors by means of electoral interference. They were noted or notorious for the presence or absence of political corruption during their official tenure; for their disposition or indisposition to intervene in the provinces; for the ability which they revealed in suppressing armed revolts or dealing with financial problems; and for their policies toward education, internal improvements, immigration, frontier expansion, and the distribution of the public domain.

Domingo Faustino Sarmiento.—Doctor D. F. Sarmiento (1868–1874), a distinguished educator, publicist, diplomat, and statesman, is known as the Schoolmaster-President of Argentina. Born in poverty in the province of San Juan, he was distinctly a self-made man. Forced into exile during the reign of the tyrant Rosas, he taught school in Chile and found opportunity to study the educational systems of Europe and the United States. As president, he founded normal schools, introduced teachers and methods from the United States, and reorganized the course of study in the secondary schools. He was likewise an ardent promoter of railways, telegraph lines, and immigration, but he followed the ominous precedent of federal intervention (in the province of Entre Ríos), although he did so in order to depose an assassin who had made himself governor. He was also accused—and perhaps there was some truth in the charge—of using his official influence, or allowing it to be used, in order to dictate his presidential successor. Nicolás Avellaneda, the official candidate, was successful in the election of 1874.

Nicolás Avellaneda.—Avellaneda (1874–1880), who had been Sarmiento's secretary of justice and public instruction, was a noted journalist, orator, and statesman and thoroughly fitted for the presidency. During his administration he not only succeeded in suppressing several armed revolts—one of them led by ex-President Mitre as a protest against the employment of official influence in the national election of 1874—but also conducted with sagacity delicate frontier negotiations with Chile and Paraguay, dealt with a financial crisis occasioned by land speculation, continued Sarmiento's educational work (founding numerous primary and secondary schools), promoted internal improvements, encouraged immigration, and made an important contribution to two crucial problems which had long agitated the life of the nation: the Indian problem and the capital question. The expedition which in 1879 he sent under General Julio A. Roca against the Patagonian Indians succeeded in advancing the southern frontier of the nation to the Río Negro. During the following year, after a bloody battle, he succeeded in expelling the provincial government from the city of Buenos Aires, detaching that city from the province of the same name, and permanently erecting it into the federal capital. This step marked the beginning of the decline of the animosity and jealousy between the national government and that of the province of Buenos Aires. It was the end of a political epoch.

The outbreak which furnished the opportunity for the "federalization" of Buenos Aires was occasioned by the presidential campaign of 1880. The politicians of Buenos Aires—*porteños,* as they were called—were supporting one of their number, Carlos Tejedor; and when they realized that both the Córdoba League (of twelve provinces) and President Avellaneda were backing General Julio A. Roca, they resolved upon war. Of course Roca was elected after the collapse of the revolt.

Julio A. Roca.—"Roca's Presidency (1880–1886) was a time of unprecedented peace and also of unprecedented growth in national wealth. The railways doubled their length; and the railway, wherever it went, multiplied the value of land, sometimes tenfold or more. The 'Conquest of the Desert' was rounded off by subjecting the few remaining savages; and wider tracts of the southern plains were thus opened . . . first to pasture and later to tillage. British capital poured into the country. Improved steam navigation brought Europe nearer. Year by year export of grain increased, and the first essays were made towards export of meat, to become later a great industry." [5] Immigrants also came in in ever-increasing numbers, although large landed estates were beginning to constitute a real problem, making it difficult for the newcomers to obtain land. Unfortunately, Roca's successful interference in behalf of his vain and inefficient relative, Miguel Juárez Celman, during the presidential election of 1886 prepared the way for a financial and political crisis from which the country did not fully recover for several years.

Miguel Juárez Celman.—Celman (1886–1890) proved to be Argentina's worst ruler since the days of Rosas. Under him an alliance was formed between the government and corrupt business interests and the growing prosperity of the country was seriously checked by reckless inflation of the paper currency and excessive borrowing, by extravagance and scandal in public finance, and by favoritism in the granting of public lands, monopolies, and concessions. The debauchery in the capital was also reflected in the provinces, where the local politicians caught the infection of wasteful borrowing, speculation, and graft. This financial orgy, together with Celman's despotic tendencies and his interference in the provinces, "provoked widespread indignation." In 1890 a "Civic Union" was organized which issued a manifesto denouncing not only the economic abuses of the government but certain more fundamental faults as well: its suppression of the suffrage and its exercise of arbitrary authority both in the provinces and in the national government. In short, the régime was denominated "an ominous and intrusive oligarchy." Moreover, a far more radical group, headed by the vehement democrat Leandro Alem, sprang into being, a party which demanded the overthrow of the president by armed revolt and the establishment of a provisional government by a fair and "uncontrolled" election. In the summer of 1890 Alem actually started an uprising in Buenos Aires, but it was suppressed after two days of bloody fighting. Although the revolution "was beaten, . . . the Government was killed," for public opinion forced Celman to turn over his authority to Vice President Carlos Pellegrini, who served out the remainder of the term.

[5] F. A. Kirkpatrick, *The Argentine Republic*, p. 198.

Pellegrini, Peña, Uriburu, Roca.—Pellegrini (1890–1892) and his three successors [6] were occupied with financial troubles, provincial interventions, boundary disputes with Brazil and Chile, and the activities of the radical party, the "Radical Civic Union." Pellegrini did much to "retrieve the disaster" which had fallen upon the nation. He stopped the construction of public works, dismissed superfluous public officials, recovered much public land which had been improperly alienated, suspended the amortization of the public debt, and founded a National Bank. But he caused considerable resentment by casting into prison and afterwards exiling Alem and his friends and imposing Luis Sáenz Peña upon the country as president in 1892. Most of Sáenz Peña's efforts were devoted to the maintenance of his position. He did not have the support of Congress and was compelled to dismiss his cabinet on several occasions. In 1893 he had to suppress a revolt led by Alem, whom the Radicals had proclaimed president. Soon afterwards he took one of the leading members of this party into his ministry, but the death of this minister compelled other changes and in January, 1895, the president resigned in favor of Vice President Uriburu. The latter settled the boundary dispute with Brazil (1895), resumed full service (1897) on the foreign debt, and added to the cabinet two new ministers, those of agriculture and of public works. His successor, General Roca, signed a law in 1899 providing for the redemption of paper currency—at the rate of forty-four centavos in gold for each paper peso—and reached a settlement of the boundary dispute with Chile (1902), a dispute which more than once had threatened war between the two countries. With the beginning of the redemption of the paper money by the *caja de conversión,* which was established for that purpose, Argentina may be said to have fully recovered from the crisis occasioned by the misgovernment of Celman.

Quintana-Alcorta Administration.—The Quintana-Alcorta administration (1904–1910) [7] was marked by labor troubles and a revolt of the Radicals led by Hipólito Irigoyen, who had become the leader of that party after the suicide of his uncle, Leandro Alem. The revolt, which was a protest against the violation of the liberty of the suffrage,

---

[6] These were: Luis Sáenz Peña (1892–1895); José E. Uriburu (1895–1898); and Julio A. Roca (1898–1904).

[7] Manuel Quintana died in office (1906) and was succeeded by the Vice President, Figueroa Alcorta.

was not difficult to put down, for public opinion now condemned such outbreaks. Alcorta closed the Chamber of Deputies because it refused to vote the budget, and prepared the way for a more democratic régime by intervening and overthrowing the landowning oligarchies in the provinces.

Roque Sáenz Peña.—Although the next president, Roque Sáenz Peña (1910–1913), owed his election to the old régime, he "had the courage and self-abnegation to introduce a measure which meant the abdication of the powerful caste to which he himself belonged. . . . In 1911 he recommended to Congress the law of the secret, compulsory, and universal [male] vote: the ballot was to secure freedom of voting, and in addition every citizen was to perform the public duty of voting under penalty of a fine." [8] The law was passed in 1912, and the election of that year brought a number of Radicals to the Chamber of Deputies. But ill health obliged the author of the great democratic reform to turn over his duties (1913) to Vice President Victoriano de la Plaza, and he did not live to see the full results of the new law.

Argentina was by this time one of the most powerful and progressive nations of Latin America. Since 1868 its foreign trade had increased in value from 69 million dollars to more than a billion dollars and its population, now predominantly white, had grown from considerably less than two million to almost eight million. Its railway mileage had reached twenty thousand, and it had excellent telegraph, telephone, and postal systems. Its public buildings were stately and beautiful, its parks delightful and impressive, and its educational system probably the best in Latin America. There were five universities with an enrollment of some eight thousand, numerous normal schools, and a secondary and primary educational system almost, if not quite, adequate for the children of the nation. Although some forty-four per cent of the people were still illiterate, this percentage was being rapidly reduced. Moreover, increasing attention was being given to public health and welfare; newspapers, periodicals, and public libraries were numerous; and there had developed a group of scholars and *literati* who were known for their works throughout Western civilization. Finally, the Argentine people were now in possession of a potentially effective ballot which could

[8] Kirkpatrick, *op. cit.,* p. 215.

be employed to inaugurate further democratic reforms as soon as they learned to employ the instrument that Roque Sáenz Peña and the Radicals had placed in their grasp.

BRAZIL (1822–1913)

Although several revolutions occurred in Brazil [9] during the first ninety years of its independent existence, the development of that country during this period was considerably more tranquil than was that of even the most orderly states of Spanish America. This comparative stability may be explained in large measure by the following considerations: In Brazil there was no prolonged and bloody struggle for independence to exhaust the resources of the country and produce a group of ambitious generals and turbulent soldiers, no powerful and reactionary clergy to oppose the rising tide of secularization, and no sudden change from absolutism to the republican system. It was probably due also in part to the superior ability of Dom Pedro II and some of the statesmen who surrounded him and succeeded him in the government of Brazil.

The main political issues during these ninety years were: nativism versus the Portuguese inhabitants; absolutism versus a limited monarchy; monarchy versus republicanism; slavery; centralism versus local autonomy; militarism versus civilian control; and jealousies among some of the states. During the early days of the republican period (1889 ff.) personalities usually counted for more than issues. Only a small minority of the people interested themselves in politics. The monarchy gave way to a republic dominated by wealthy landlords and army officers and poverty and ignorance excluded the vast majority of the masses from holding office or voting. Between 1822 and 1914 Brazil was governed by two emperors, four regencies, and eight presidents. Both of the emperors and one of the presidents were overthrown by armed force.

Dom Pedro I.—The rule of Dom Pedro I (1822–1831) was a period of discontent and disorder. The best that can be said of the young emperor is that he was not devoid of intelligence, that he was sometimes capable of firmness, and that he usually desired to do what was right. Ambitious, impulsive, energetic, fond of popularity, deficient

[9] Area, 3,286,170 square miles; larger than continental United States plus another Texas.

in education and political experience, often lacking in dignity and tact, he was not equal to the task which fortune had thrust upon him.

The constitution which he gave Brazil—the fundamental law under which the country was to be ruled for sixty-five years—conformed in many respects with the traditions and desires of the nation. Freedom of speech and the press, religious toleration—although the exercise of non-Catholic religions was confined to private homes and edifices which were not to have the external forms of churches—and equality of all citizens before the law were guaranteed. The legislative power was vested in a general assembly composed of two houses. The deputies of the lower house, selected by provincial electors chosen by popular vote, served for a term of four years. The senators served for life and were selected by the emperor from a triple list submitted to him by the provincial electors. The executive power was vested in the "constitutional emperor and perpetual defender of Brazil," who was to rule through ministers and a council of state named by himself. The emperor was given the power to convoke the general assembly, dissolve the Chamber of Deputies, and exercise a suspensory veto over the acts of the legislature. The judicial power was declared to be independent of the other branches of government.

The constitution, however, did not make adequate provisions for local government. The existing captaincies were now declared provinces and the spirit of local independence developed during the colonial period was virtually ignored. Although the constitution provided for provincial and municipal councils, to be chosen by direct election, these were little more than debating societies. The emperor had the right to approve and temporarily to suspend the acts of the provincial councils, and presidents appointed and removed by the emperor dominated the provinces directly and the municipalities indirectly.

Signs of dissatisfaction with the emperor soon revealed themselves. In order to secure the recognition of the mother country and remove the danger of reconquest, Pedro agreed to assume $10,000,000 of the Portuguese debt. Since a part of this debt had been incurred by Portugal in fighting the colony during the brief struggle for independence, resentment was naturally aroused in some quarters.

At the same time Brazil was threatened with disorder and disintegration. Uprisings due largely to republican sentiment occurred in Parahyba, Rio Grande do Norte, and Ceará, anarchy threatened in Maranhão, and in Pernambuco Manoel de Carvalho and his followers not only denounced the emperor as a traitor who intended to turn the country over to the Portuguese, but called upon the northern provinces to throw off the imperial yoke and set up the republican "Confederation of the Equator."

No sooner had these revolts been crushed by the able assistance of Lord Cochrane, who once more came to the aid of Pedro, than an uprising occurred in the Cisplatine province. After a bloody war of three years with Argentina over this province, and the intervention of Great Britain, the inhabitants of the extreme southern portion of the empire set up the independent republic of Uruguay. The outcome of the struggle caused further resentment toward Pedro.

And while the war was in progress other factors roused feeling against the emperor: his easy familiarity with the masses of his subjects; his favoritism in creating peers and conferring other distinctions; his scandalous attachment for the marchioness of Santos— known as "Madame Pompadour"; alleged mistreatment of the popular Empress Leopoldina; expenses incurred in defending the claims of his daughter to the Portuguese throne; and his tendency to prefer ministers from the "Portuguese party." Moreover, the press, taking advantage of its new freedom, did much to foment and crystallize the feeling against the emperor.

News of the French revolution of 1830 furnished an incentive for further resentment and restlessness. Conditions became so threatening that certain sections were placed under martial law and Dom Pedro visited the province of Minas Geraes in the hope of recovering his lost popularity in that region. His reception was disappointing. When he returned to the capital the Portuguese and other friends celebrated the event with illuminations and bonfires, but his opponents refused to do so. Conflicting attitudes toward the monarch led to collisions between the Portuguese and the Brazilians, in which the latter were worsted. This gave rise to a demand that the emperor punish the Portuguese offenders and dismiss the Portuguese members of his cabinet. The monarch refused to comply, but when he learned that his army had deserted him, he abdicated in favor of his

infant son, Pedro de Alcántara. The political leaders of Rio de
Janeiro and a number of deputies who were present in the capital—
the national assembly was not then in session—had been responsible
for his overthrow (April 7, 1831).

The Regency.—Since the ex-emperor's son was only five years of
age, it was necessary to set up a regency. This step was taken immediately by a special session of the Brazilian Congress. During the
next nine years there were four regencies; a provisional regency, a
regular regency consisting of three men, and two regencies each consisting of a single individual. It was a stormy era both in the national assembly and in the provinces, and the insubordination of the
army increased the disorders of the time. An effort was made to
maintain the parliamentary principle and keep the ministry in harmony with the Chamber of Deputies. The Liberal Monarchists, who
governed during much of the period, were opposed by the Federalists, who were Republicans for the most part. In 1837 the Conservatives won the parliamentary elections, and a member of their party
became regent. However, neither the Liberal Monarchists nor the
Conservatives, neither the triple regency nor the one-man regency,
was able to restore complete order in the provinces or curb the lawlessness of the army. The Federalists forced through an amendment
to the constitution which conceded to the provinces much greater
autonomy: the futile councils were replaced by elected legislatures,
whose authority could be limited in only a few cases by the central
government. But the provincial presidents were still to be the agents
of the national executive, and dissatisfaction continued to prevail
in some regions, particularly in Rio Grande do Sul, where the war of
secession which began in 1835 continued for ten years. In 1840 the
Liberals began an agitation for the declaration of the majority of
young Dom Pedro, and on July 23, 1840, he took charge of the national government, becoming Pedro II.

Thus the first eighteen years of Brazil's national history were years
of disorder and trouble. It would be a mistake, however, to regard
them as a fallow period in the development of Brazilian nationality.
The people enjoyed a degree of personal liberty scarcely to be found
in contemporary Spanish America, for freedom of speech and the
press were seldom restricted and religious tolerance became firmly
established with the approval of many of the clergy who had been

deeply influenced by French philosophy. The general assembly of the country, although usually characterized by lack of efficiency, served as a school for the training of political leaders. During the regency, in particular, many of the future statesmen of the empire gained their political education and at the same time revealed in their character something of the Puritan stamp. Moreover, newspapers sprang up in every important center of population, libraries were founded here and there, something was done to encourage education, mining, and agriculture (particularly coffee growing), and plans were made to attract immigrants from Europe. Finally, notwithstanding the disorders of the period, population increased rapidly and foreign commerce augmented in value from some 35 million dollars in 1823 to 52 million in 1834 and 61 million in 1840.

Dom Pedro II.—Brazil was exceedingly fortunate in its second monarch, for he soon developed into an able statesman. Tall and commanding in appearance, dignified and reserved, simple and refined in tastes, democratic in manners and dress, fond of intellectual pursuits, noted for his breadth of learning and progressive thinking, anxious to rule with justice and wisdom, a model of domestic virtues, Dom Pedro II loved his subjects and was loved and respected by them. His long reign (1840–1889) was a most happy epoch in the history of the nation, and few monarchs have left a more lasting impression upon the country over which they ruled.

Not only was the second Pedro a more able and attractive ruler than Pedro I, but it must also be admitted that he confronted a far less difficult task than did his father. Since he was a Brazilian, he was not embarrassed by the anti-Portuguese prejudice. Since the strong Liberal party which had harassed Pedro I had been largely responsible for the accession of Pedro II, this group was inclined to support the new ruler. Moreover, many Brazilians had lost their enthusiasm for republicanism because they felt that the Republicans had been largely responsible for the provincial turmoil which had characterized the previous epoch. Lastly, the leaders of the country, as already noted, had acquired valuable political experience.

Yet Pedro II had to deal with several serious problems during his long reign. The first of these was the pacification of the country. Uprisings occurred in São Paulo and Minas Geraes soon after his accession; desultory revolts continued in Rio Grande do Sul; and

in 1847 and 1848 disturbances—those of the latter year largely a re-
percussion of the 1848 revolutions in Europe—took place in Pernambuco. By 1849, however, the whole country had been pacified and for
the next forty years it enjoyed almost complete internal peace, although in 1852–1853 a war was fought with Rosas and Argentina
and in 1864–1870 a long and expensive conflict was carried on with
Paraguay.

With the achievement of domestic peace, Brazil entered an era
of progress and prosperity. Railway construction under government
encouragement, which began in 1853, proceeded with considerable
rapidity, and by 1888 more than six thousand miles were in operation. Telegraphic communications were likewise fostered after 1851
and in 1888 there were twelve thousand miles of wire in operation.
Responding to Pedro's encouragement, immigrants arrived in increasing numbers, a flood of 131,000 coming in through the ports of
Rio de Janeiro and Santos in 1888. Between 1841 and 1889 foreign
trade grew from 62 million dollars to more than 285 million, and
the value of the products of the empire increased nearly tenfold.
During the same period, moreover, population doubled, in spite of
unfavorable sanitary conditions, and important progress was made
in education, although illiteracy still stood at the enormous percentage of ninety. In brief, under Dom Pedro II Brazil took its place
among the liberal and progressive countries of the Western World.
If its masses were still poor and ignorant, its upper classes were
prosperous, highly educated, and gifted in politics, diplomacy, and
literature.

Toward the end of his reign the monarch had serious difficulties
with the slave-holding aristocracy, the church, the Republicans (who
once more began to thrive), and the army. Although England had
committed the Brazilian government to the abolition of the slave
trade long before Pedro II came to power, the disgraceful traffic
continued until 1853. At that time there were nearly three million
slaves in the country. In the sixties, however, thanks largely to the
attitude of the emperor, the emancipation movement began to make
headway and by 1870 the number of Negro slaves had decreased to
less than two million. In the following year a law [10] for the gradual
emancipation of these unfortunate people was passed—a law which

[10] Known as the "Rio Branco Law" because Viscount Rio Branco was its chief supporter.

provided that henceforth all children born of slave mothers should be free. By 1880 an Antislavery Society had been launched, and in 1888 there were only 720,000 slaves. It is possible that in the course of a few decades these might have been set free by a gradual process which would have avoided the alienation of their owners from the monarchy; but in 1888, while the emperor was in Europe in search of health, his daughter, Princess Isabella, pushed through a measure for immediate and uncompensated emancipation (May 13, 1888). In view of the other difficulties which the monarchy faced, the law was most inopportune; for already (1874) the emperor had offended the church by opposing the expulsion of the Masons from the religious brotherhoods and by his latitudinarianism in religious matters, and the Republican party, launched with new vigor in 1871, was rapidly gaining recruits among the professional classes. Moreover, Dom Pedro had gradually alienated the army by his pacifist leanings and his refusal to accord it a privileged position in the state. By 1889, when he returned from Europe, ecclesiastics, army officers, Republicans, and disgruntled landlords were ready to take action. The movement might have been delayed until the death of the great emperor if it had not been for dislike of the French husband of Isabella, who had assumed an attitude of haughty aloofness toward the Brazilians. In view of the succession prospects it was decided to act at once. On November 15, 1889, a revolt led by General Deodoro da Fonseca and Benjamin Constant—professor of mathematics in the military school of the capital—took place in Rio de Janeiro. On the following day Dom Pedro was formally deposed and banished with his family from the country. Two years later the ex-emperor, who had departed with the hope of soon being recalled, died in Paris. Immediately after Pedro's overthrow a provisional government was set up, headed by Fonseca and with Constant as minister of war, and Brazil was proclaimed a federal republic.

The Republic.—The republican constitution proclaimed on February 24, 1891, was in many respects similar to that of the United States. It provided for the three customary departments of government, each separate and distinct from the others. The national Congress was to be composed of two houses, the senators representing the twenty "states" and the federal district and the deputies representing the people. The senators, sixty-three in number, were to be elected by direct vote for nine years, one-third going out of office every three years. Members of the Chamber of Deputies were to be elected by popular vote for three years on the basis of population, but each state was to have at least four representatives. In general, the powers of Congress were to be the same as those of the national legislative body of the United States, and national suffrage was conferred upon all male citizens twenty-one years of age who were able to read and write, with the exception of beggars, common soldiers on pay, and members of religious orders or organizations whose rules or vows implied the surrender of liberty. The powers of the president were likewise to be very similar to those of the chief executive of the United States, but his power with respect to executive ordinance was somewhat broader: he could issue decrees, instructions, and regulations for the faithful execution of the laws and ordinances of Congress. Both the president and the vice president were to be elected for a term of four years, and the former was not to be eligible for immediate reëlection. The judicial power was conferred upon the supreme court and such inferior courts as Congress might create. All federal judges were to be appointed by the president and to hold office for life unless removed by judicial procedure. The jurisdiction of the federal courts was in most respects similar to the jurisdiction of analogous courts in the United States, including the power to pass upon the relative spheres of the state and national governments.

The Constitution of 1891 also contained a somewhat elaborate bill of rights. Among its provisions were: freedom of worship, speech, and the press; trial by jury; and abolition of the death penalty. Church and state were to be separate and independent, marriage was declared to be a civil institution, and cemeteries and public instruction were secularized.

The constitution forbade the interference of the federal government in matters pertaining peculiarly to the states, except (1) to repel foreign invasion or the invasion of another state; (2) to maintain a republican form of government; (3) to reëstablish order at the request of any state government; and (4) to secure the execution of federal laws and judgments. This power of federal intervention in the affairs of the states was destined to be used frequently and to give rise to most delicate problems.

Deodoro da Fonseca.—The first four years of the republic were far from tranquil. In February, 1891, the constituent assembly chose General Fonseca, who had been chief executive of the provisional government, president and Floriano Peixoto, a high officer of the navy, vice president. Fonseca proved to be selfish, tactless, and dictatorial, dissolving Congress, suggesting a revision of the constitution, interfering in the affairs of the states, and making himself generally obnoxious. He had been in office only a short time when a group of prominent Brazilians protested against his corrupt and arbitrary rule. Although opposition to him was widespread, it was strongest in São Paulo and Rio Grande do Sul. Before many months the army and a portion of the navy abandoned him, Admiral José de Mello being among the naval insurgents. Finally, on November 23, 1891, the warships stationed in the harbor of Rio de Janeiro threatened to bombard the city and forced Fonseca to resign in favor of Vice President Peixoto.

The Peixoto Administration.—The latter proved even more unsatisfactory than his predecessor, however. Not only did he depose several state presidents and place the capital under martial law; he also permitted his administration to indulge in extravagance, bribery, and corruption and forced Ruy Barbosa, the distinguished editor of *Jornal do Brasil,* to flee the country in order to avoid arrest. In 1892 a famous *gaúcho* chieftain named Gumercindo Saraïva began an uprising in Rio Grande do Sul, and early the following year Admiral de Mello resigned as minister of marine in order to begin a naval revolt. After eight months of fighting and the loss of thousands of lives the insurgents were finally suppressed. While the conflict was going on, the presidential campaign of the spring of 1894 took place and Prudente de Moraes Barros, a distinguished lawyer of São Paulo, was elected. It was freely predicted that Peixoto would refuse to surrender his authority at the expiration of his legal term (November 15, 1894), but the prediction was not fulfilled. Brazil had narrowly escaped an era of caudilloism: henceforth the country was to be governed in the main by civilian presidents. The military element continued, however, to be a menacing factor.

Moraes Barros.—The restoration of order and the elimination of militarism from the government were the most substantial achievements of the Moraes Barros administration (1894–1898). He granted amnesty to the participants in the recent rebellion, but he expelled numerous military men from civilian offices to which they had been appointed by his predecessor, gradually discarded prætorian methods of government, and put down uprisings in several of the states, the most formidable of these revolts being that of the Brazilian mystic Antonio Maciel [11] on the frontier of Bahia. Moraes's administration was also noted for an attack upon political corruption and the settlement of the boundary dispute with Argentina (1895). He found himself unable, however, to solve the financial problems which confronted the nation.

Manoel de Campos Salles.—Partly by the aid of Moraes, Manoel de Campos Salles (1898–1902), another Paulista, won the presidency against the candidate of the militarists in 1898. The campaign took place in the midst of a financial crisis, and the president-elect immediately visited Europe, where he negotiated with the Rothchilds a loan of ten million pounds sterling. The terms were somewhat onerous, but the loan aided the country in surmounting its most urgent financial difficulties. Returning to assume his duties, Campos Salles began at once a policy of retrenchment and a search for new revenues, securing the latter in the main by levying a stamp tax and increasing import duties. He was strongly opposed to federal interference in state affairs; and during his administration boundary disputes were settled with Bolivia (1903, the Acre territory) and with France (1900, French Guiana).

Rodrigues Alves.—The presidency of Rodrigues Alves (1902–1906), likewise a Paulista, was signalized by the modernization and beautification of Rio de Janeiro and the final adjustment of two other boundary disputes—one with England (1904, British Guiana) and the other with Holland (1906, Dutch Guiana). In 1905 boundary negotiations were also begun with Venezuela, but delays occurred and it was not until 1929 that a definite settlement was reached. Ably assisted by Pereira Passos, the prefect of the city, and Dr. Oswaldo Cruz, Rio was transformed from a backward colonial town into one of the most beautiful and healthful capitals in the world.

Penna, Peçanha, and Hermes da Fonseca.—During the electoral campaign of 1906 the political leaders of the other states, by joining

[11] The rebellion of Maciel, known to his followers as "The Counselor," was attributed in part to the influence of the monarchists.

forces, succeeded in breaking the São Paulo monopoly of the presidency. The successful candidate was Affonso Penna, an old and distinguished statesman from Minas Geraes, whose administration (1906–1909) was noted mainly for financial reform. With the view of gradually calling in the inconvertible paper money and stabilizing the currency, he established a national bank, called the *caixa de conversão*. Much of this paper was soon redeemed, with marked improvement in the stability of the other media of exchange, and if it had not been for the disturbing effects of the World War Brazilian finances might have been placed on a gold basis. Penna died in 1909 and was succeeded by Vice President Nilo Peçanha.

The presidential campaign of 1910 was one of the most interesting in Brazilian history. The Conservatives, joined by the military element, who displayed a new aggressiveness, presented as their candidate Marshal Hermes da Fonseca, nephew of Deodoro da Fonseca. Those who favored the continuation of civilian rule supported the Liberal Ruy Barbosa of the state of Bahia. The eloquent candidate of the Liberals campaigned vigorously throughout São Paulo and Minas Geraes, pleading for a more strict adherence to the constitution and the elimination of the influence of the army from civil affairs. But President Peçanha, perhaps in part because of his jealousy of the north, supported Hermes, and the latter won the election. His opponent charged that the victory had been due to fraud and military intimidation, and soon after the inauguration of the new president the navy again revolted. The rebellion was sternly suppressed by Hermes (1910–1914): some of the insurgent leaders were shot and Bahia, the city where Ruy Barbosa was born, was bombarded. If it had not been for the economic depression which resulted mainly from the drop in the prices of coffee and rubber, serious trouble might have ensued, for the Liberals, with Barbosa as candidate, planned a vigorous antimilitarist campaign in 1914. By the end of 1913, however, the crisis had become so grave that Barbosa withdrew in the interest of Wenceslau Braz, former governor of Minas Geraes.

During the first twenty-five years of the republican régime Brazil had made remarkable progress. Foreign trade had augmented in value from 285 million dollars to 640 million dollars; railway mileage had increased from six thousand to fifteen thousand; and by

1913 there were 38,000 miles of telegraph line and 110,000 miles of telephone wire. Moreover, in spite of numerous revolts and financial depressions, the country had made some advance socially, politically, and culturally. Population had increased from approximately fourteen million to twenty-four million; sanitation and public health had improved somewhat; and considerable progress had been made in literature, art, architecture, and education, although fully eighty per cent of the people were still illiterate. The more retarded areas were found, however, in the north and on the frontiers where the Negro, Indian, and mulatto elements constituted the bulk of the population. In politics, militarism had been held in check and many of the popular liberties preserved, but graft had not been entirely eliminated and scarcely a beginning had been made in those various forms of social legislation which characterize all progressive modern states. Nevertheless, from the history of their past Brazilians might justly draw hope and inspiration for the future.

Artistic and Literary Achievements in the A B C Countries

Preoccupation with political and economic matters in Argentina, Brazil, and Chile did not prevent important achievements in art and literature. French influence was strong in all three of these countries; Italian immigrants affected the milieu in Argentina and Brazil; and the African element was a factor in the latter. Among the upper classes everywhere there was a decided taste for music, painting, sculpture, and literature, and even the lower classes possessed a decidedly artistic temperament.

In Brazil an academy of fine arts was founded shortly before the winning of independence and a national school of music in 1847, both institutions being established in the capital. A school of fine arts was opened in Santiago in 1843, a school of sculpture in 1854, and a school of painting a few years later. An international exhibit of fine arts was held in the Chilean capital in 1910 in a beautiful building which afterwards became the home of the National Museum of Fine Arts. The Argentine capital had its school of painting before the close of the Caudillo era, an establishment which was transformed into the National Academy of Fine Arts shortly after 1900. Almost every town of any size in each of these countries had its orchestra and its small group of artists before the close of the century. In painting and sculpture Chile made greater progress than the other two countries. In 1887 the Chilean Virginio Arias received a prize for his sculptured representation of "The Descent from the Cross," being the first South American to win laurels in art at the great cultural center of Paris.

Perhaps the best historical writing of Hispanic America during this period was produced by the authors of the A B C nations. Miguel L. Amunátegui, Diego Barros Arana, Benjamín Vicuña Mackenna, and José Toribio Medina were the outstanding historians of Chile. The best writers on historical subjects in Brazil were Francisco A. Varnhagen, Pereira da Silva, Manoel de Oliveira Lima, and Rocha Pombo. Among the many historians prominent in Argentina during the last half of the nineteenth century, Bartolomé Mitre, Martín García Mérou, Vicente Fidel López, Antonio Zinny, and Luis V. Varela deserve special mention. The period was also marked by numerous valuable works on diplomacy, international law, and science (particularly medicine).

In the field of pure literature there were produced several poems and novels of real merit. As in the rest of Spanish America, Spanish classicism and French romanticism were influential in Chile and Argentina. Early Brazilian writers drew their inspiration largely from the motherland, but were later decidedly influenced by the French romanticists. Many of the themes, however, were strictly national.

The Argentine *literati* of the period under consideration dealt mainly with the pampas, the gauchos, Italian immigrants, life in the capital, and patriotic or Pan-Latin sentiments. The most famous poets were Estanislao del Campo, José Hernández, Francisco y Calvo, and Victor Andrade, who is regarded by Argentine critics as their greatest poet "because he reflects in his beautiful songs the aspirations of that young and lively democracy which frets itself in supreme longings for liberty, progress, and civilization, while it is the melting pot for the diverse elements of the Latin races from which will spring a new American type, destined to preside over an important evolution of the human species in the new world." An important Argentine novelist of the period was Carlos María Ocantos.

"A review of verse writing in Chile shows that . . . it has closely followed the currents of European literature without producing more than a very few poets of first rank among its numerous versifiers." [12] Its upper class is composed largely of somber and practical Spaniards of Basque origin. Chile's greatest writer in the field of *belles-lettres* was an adopted son, Andrés Bello, born in Venzeuela. Perhaps the best Chilean poets of the nineteenth century were Guillermo Matta, José Antonio Soffia, Eduardo de la Barra, and Diego de Urrutia. In prose writing the natives of this republic revealed greater genius. In Alberto Blest Gana, Chile presented to the world one of Latin America's greatest writers of fiction. Other Chilean novelists of note during the century were Martín Palma and Diego Barros Grez. The poets frequently revealed a practical attitude, praising science, adoring justice, and expressing respect for industry. Intensely patriotic, they often indulged in heroic verse as well, and some of them dwelt upon the splendor of the Chilean landscape. The novelists, likewise with an intensely practical disposition, employed historical themes or engaged in social criticism. Palma, a follower of Blest Gana, frankly admitted: "We have in mind the improvement of the people. Our customs are examined attempting to improve them, our vices to correct them, our virtues to enhance them, at the same time tilting full against our prejudices, against our social and political errors, against our bad habits. . . ."

Writing in 1902, Sylvio Romero, the leading historian of Brazilian literature, remarked: "Intellectual labour in Brazil is torture. Wherefore we produce little; we quickly weary, age and soon die. . . . The Brazilian is . . . made rather to complain than to invent, contemplative rather than thoughtful; more lyrical and fond of dreams and resounding rhetoric than of scientific, demonstrable facts." Not only is the climate of most of the country depressing, but the reading public has been small. "Just as the nation, ethnologically, represents the fusion of three races, with the whites at the head, so, intellectually, does it represent a fusion of Portuguese tradition, native spontaneity, and European culture, with France still predominant." [13] Strangely enough, nearly all of Brazil's outstanding literary men were natives of the tropics rather than of the more temperate portions of the country. Several of them had African blood in their veins.

---

[12] Coester, *The Literary History of Spanish America*, p. 224.
[13] Goldberg, *Brazilian Literature*, p. 25.

Among the poets were Gonçalves de Magalhães, Gonçalves Dias, Cruz e Sousa, Castro Alves, Machado de Assis, and Olavo Bilac. The greatest Brazilian novelists of the period were José de Alencar, Escragnolle de Taunay, Euclydes de Cunha, and Graça Aranha. Despite the somewhat pessimistic statement of Romero, these writers entitle Brazil to a place in the front rank of the literary nations of Hispanic America.

CHAPTER XIII

A BRIEF EPOCH OF PROSPERITY AND REFORM

BETWEEN 1913 and 1929 the history of Latin America was characterized by important political and social changes and notable material progress. In several countries the middle and lower classes became more assertive and exercised no little influence over governmental policy. In others strong executives revealed greater interest in the masses and inaugurated systems of social welfare under state control. Of the seven new constitutions framed in as many countries, at least five were significant because of their provisions with reference to labor; and everywhere the period was marked by unprecedented social legislation. Almost everywhere, moreover, the period was signalized by unusual prosperity, although some countries suffered from depressions in certain industries, such as coffee-growing and the production of nitrates. The World War stimulated enterprise by creating an enormous demand for the commodities of the region. It was also mainly responsible for a large influx of capital from the United States, where it had accumulated during the catastrophe. And although French and German investments decreased because of the war, the investments of the British, after diminishing or remaining stationary for a time, increased by a considerable sum by 1929. The period was also marked in most countries by growing political stability. Owing, however, to the rising price of commodities and occasional unemployment as well as to the increasing assertiveness of the workers, there were considerable labor unrest and numerous strikes in many of the nations. There were also occasional revolts, but these were by no means as frequent as before. Finally, the period witnessed the removal of the last of the legal restraints upon freedom of worship.

ECONOMIC AND SOCIAL PROGRESS

Between 1913 and 1929 British and North American investments, particularly the latter, served as a great stimulus to economic activity in Latin America. Unprecedented prices also stirred the inhabitants of the region to unwonted effort. The major portion of the investments of citizens of the United States was located in Mexico and the Caribbean; the greater part of British investments, in southern South America. This capital, whether English or Yankee, was employed mainly in public utilities, in transportation enterprises, and in the development of natural resources. Besides bringing profits to the investors, it tended to promote the prosperity of Latin America itself. It not only made possible important internal improvements and a rise in living standards; it also contributed to a vast increase in the foreign trade of the region.

Between 1913 and 1929 the value of the foreign commerce of the Latin-American nations increased from less than three billion dollars to more than five billion, and at its peak in 1920 it was valued at more than six billion. The largest growth during these years occurred in the foreign trade of Colombia, Honduras, Venezuela, the Dominican Republic, Peru, Guatemala, Cuba, and El Salvador (in the order named), but there were important increases in all the countries save Ecuador. The average increase in terms of market value for the whole of Latin America was seventy-one per cent, as compared to an increase of fifty-five per cent for the rest of the world. In some of the countries of Latin America the growth was enormous: in Colombia, nearly 310 per cent; in Honduras, more than 239 per cent; and in Venezuela, more than 213. Much of this trade represented the transactions of foreign individuals and corporations— that is, a large part of the profits went to foreigners—but even in such cases the national wealth was often increased by wages and revenues derived from this business.

In 1929 the countries of Latin America supplied the outside world with commodities valued at more than two billion dollars. Argentina and Uruguay furnished mainly hides and skins, wool, meat, linseed, and wheat. Brazil exported coffee, cacao, hides and skins, rubber, and certain minerals. In addition to sheepskins and wool, Chile supplied mainly copper, nitrates, and iodine. Bolivia furnished copper, tin, gold, and silver. Peru supplied copper, cotton, rubber, sugar, tungsten, wool, and petroleum. Colombia exported mainly petroleum, bananas, coffee, and sugar; Venezuela, mainly petroleum, hides, coffee, and cacao. Mexico exported copper, gold, silver, petroleum, hides and skins, coffee, sisal, and mahogany. The rest of the countries exported such well known tropical products as sugar, bananas, cacao, coconuts, indigo, ivory nuts, coffee, balata, and balsam. During the same year Latin Americans or foreigners engaged in business in the region purchased from abroad an approximately equal amount of manufactured products such as locomotives, steel rails, automobiles and other machinery, clothing, building materials, hardware, drugs, and cosmetics.

Material evidences of the new prosperity appeared almost everywhere. Between 1913 and 1929 the mileage of railways and telephone wire doubled, the number of telephone instruments trebled, great highways were built, automobiles rapidly multiplied, airplane lines were established along all the important trade routes, numerous impressive public buildings were constructed, streets were paved and lighted, municipalities were provided with modern public utilities, attractive new residential sections were added to the towns and cities, vast irrigation projects were undertaken, and in some sections new industries sprang up.

The period was also marked by social and cultural progress and change. There was decided improvement in sanitation and public health, for veritable campaigns against disease were the order of the day; sums larger than ever before were devoted to education and enrollment in the institutions of learning decidedly increased; temperance movements were initiated in several states, and athletic sports became popular; newspapers, periodicals, books, and historical documents were published in unprecedented number and much attention was given to art and music; penal reforms occurred in many states; labor legislation was placed upon the statute books everywhere; and in some places there was revealed a growing disposition to give the exploited Indians a better deal. The changed attitude toward the native race was most evident in Peru (where protective laws were passed and a society was organized to look after its welfare), in some of the states of Central America, in Ecuador, and in Mexico (where restoration of land to the natives and the revival of Indian culture became the keynote of a vast social revolution).

Of all the indications of social progress during the period, none is more impressive than the labor legislation enacted almost everywhere. Such legislation was due in part to the insistence of the workers, who had learned the potency of organization and strikes; in part to influences coming from Versailles and Geneva and perhaps even from Moscow; and in part to political leaders prompted by genuine humanitarianism, idealism, or a desire to appear well before the "progressive" nations of the Western World. A recent compilation [1] of Latin-American constitutional and statutory provisions regarding labor reveals that these countries have taken their place in the vanguard. In the legislation of most of the countries— legislation passed for the most part since 1913—few provisions found in the most advanced labor codes of the world are lacking. The right to organize and to strike, the eight-hour day, the minimum wage, the weekly day of rest with pay, limitations on the labor of women and children, sanitary working and living quarters, workmen's insurance, employers' liability, and, in some instances, arbitration boards are all provided for. In the modern utopias of Latin America labor has its place! It is probable that in many countries the laws were not enforced. Moreover, they were in most instances primarily concerned with industrial rather than agricultural labor. Why not? In other parts of the world such legislation was designed mainly for the workers in industry; and, besides, most of the landlords of Latin America were natives and citizens, while industry was largely under the management of alien capitalists.

There appeared also during the sixteen years under consideration certain indications of reform in political habits. In no other period of equal length since the region achieved its independence from Spain were there so few revolutions or so many instances of the peaceful transfer of the reins of government from one administrator to another. As already suggested, however, the Latin-American nations were not entirely free from military uprisings between 1913 and 1929. Paraguay had several revolts, but none very serious except those of 1920–1924, which occasioned the overthrow of three chief executives. In Ecuador occurred a few minor outbreaks, and the government was seized by a dictator in July, 1925. In Bolivia there were occasional disturbances, including Indian uprisings, but only one chief executive was overthrown there (1920). In Peru two presidents were forced out by armed uprisings (1914, 1919); several chief executives were compelled to resign in ordinarily stable Chile; four

[1] Oficina Internacional de Trabajo, *Legislación Social de América Latina* (Geneva, 1928).

or five military uprisings occurred in Brazil; Mexico was torn by revolt during much of the period; Honduras experienced one minor uprising (1919) and one serious revolt (1923–1924); and even in orderly Costa Rica one president was deposed by a military coup (1917) and another was forced to resign (1919); but nothing occurred to disturb the tranquillity of El Salvador or Nicaragua (until 1925), and, thanks in part to the influence of the United States, there were comparatively few revolts in Cuba, Haiti, and the Dominican Republic and none in Panama. Finally, Colombia, Uruguay, Argentina, and Venezuela (except for slight disturbances in 1928 and 1929) enjoyed domestic peace throughout the period.

Thus Latin America continued to suffer from military disorders, but as a whole, in comparison with the earlier national period, the region gave the observer of 1913–1929 the impression of orderliness. The fact that six of the twenty republics remained quiet for a period of sixteen years and most of the rest suffered from military disorders for only a part of the period, tended to inspire optimism regarding their political future.

The A B C States

Chile.—In Chile after 1891 the common man gradually became more aggressive. Individuals of moderate wealth slowly increased in numbers, and rising wages brought new living standards to many of the laboring classes. Shortly after the outbreak of the World War, however, mounting costs of living made it difficult for wage earners to satisfy their new wants. After 1915 strikes became more numerous and alarming and the influence of the I.W.W. began to be felt within the ranks of Chilean labor. But agitation brought scanty results—among other things, employers' liability and one day of rest in seven—and restlessness and some unemployment continued. Moreover, after the close of the World War, an economic depression and a rather serious financial situation resulted from a decrease in the demand for nitrates.

Men looked in vain to the government for a remedy. The president was impotent under the parliamentary system adopted after the fall of Balmaceda (1891), and parliament did little or nothing because its members placed factional and personal interests above the national welfare and leadership and party cohesion were lacking. As a result, many began to recall with a sigh the days of strong presidents.

The time was evidently ripe for a reformer, and his appearance was not long delayed. In the presidential campaign of the summer of 1920, Arturo Alessandri, an eloquent lawyer of humble origin with a strain of Italian blood in his veins, offered himself as a candidate of the labor and middle-class interests represented by a party known as the Liberal Alliance. This group also embraced a considerable number of the Radicals and Liberals of the landed aristocracy, who joined the Alliance either because of their long opposition to the Conservatives or because they favored the policies advocated by the new leader. Alessandri proposed an elaborate program of social and political reform: the abolition of the parliamentary system, greater autonomy for the provinces, election of the president by direct popular vote, religious toleration, separation of church and state, improvement of the legal status of women, labor legislation, extension of the free public school system, either an income tax or a higher land tax, and national control of banks and insurance companies.

The campaign was bitter and close. The three Conservative factions combined as the Union party and supported Luis Barros Borgoño. According to the returns of the election officials Alessandri won by five electoral votes, but the Constitution required that both houses of Congress meet in joint session to pass upon the election, and the Conservatives still hoped that some device might be found to defeat Alessandri. The situation was most tense, however, and Congress realized that the employment of questionable means might plunge the country into civil war. Accordingly, a special board, called the "court of honor," was appointed to scrutinize the ballots. The board decided that Alessandri had received a majority of one electoral vote, and in December, 1920, he was inaugurated. He was the first president of the Chilean *people*.

Alessandri's task was by no means easy. The economic depression continued; tremendous losses were suffered on account of the earthquake of 1922; the cost of government increased as it did in most other countries during the period, but there were not sufficient revenues to pay the public officials and the military establishment; and

Alessandri's agreement to permit the United States to mediate in the Tacna-Arica dispute caused dissatisfaction in some quarters. At the same time, the parliamentary system stood in the way of reform, for the Conservative groups continued to dominate the senate, and in the lower house the members of the Liberal Alliance, who were in control, soon had disagreements among themselves. Hence, Alessandri, like many of his predecessors since 1891, found himself powerless.

In one important respect, however, the situation was different. The forces demanding reform were so strong and insistent that they would not accept defeat. Reform must come even if by unconstitutional methods.

The outcome was a series of bloodless revolutions (September, 1924 to February, 1927) which deposed Alessandri and two succeeding presidents, recalled him from Europe only to have him resign a second time, coerced or overreached the national legislature, and eventually placed the country in the hands of General Carlos Ibáñez (February, 1927), a dictator—who ruled, however, with the consent of the people (as revealed in the elections of May, 1927) and was careful to fill the public offices with civilians. The revolutions were none the less popular because their instrument was the army. By July, 1929, virtually all of the reforms advocated by Alessandri had been achieved. Finances were reorganized; an income tax was adopted; the country was given a new constitution which substituted the presidential for the parliamentary system, granted larger autonomy to the provinces, reduced qualifications for the suffrage, permitted religious freedom, and separated church and state; progressive labor legislation was passed; many measures providing for the welfare of the masses were placed upon the statute books; and sweeping reforms were introduced in the educational system, reforms which emphasized primary instruction and the elimination of illiteracy. Personally Alessandri had been defeated, but his program of reform was adopted. The ineffective agent had been discarded, but the social forces once back of him moved forward toward their goal despite all opposition. Progress had been made, however, at the expense of personal liberty and political persecution, for freedom of expression had been denied and several political leaders sent into exile. Such procedure was an ill omen for the future.

Argentina.—Owing to recent electoral reforms (the law of 1912), a notable election occurred in Argentina in 1916. Perhaps for the first time in history, the citizens of the nation *freely chose in every province electors* who were to select the president. Hipólito Irigoyen, who for many years had been the leader of the Radicals, was elected by a narrow margin. His victory was in a way analogous to that of Andrew Jackson in the United States in 1828. An ex-rancher of humble Basque origin, Irigoyen was the first man of the people to be elevated to the presidency. Like "Old Hickory," he was defiantly independent and possessed of unlimited courage; but, unlike Jackson, he was well educated.

On assuming his duties, he faced a most difficult task. He was committed to radical reforms because of his party connections; but he was confronted by the crisis occasioned by the World War, there was much unrest and labor agitation, and he had to administer the government and overcome the opposition by the aid of a new party composed of men untried in public life and lacking a tradition of public service. Probably in defiance of the sentiment of the majority of the intelligent leaders of the country, he kept Argentina out of the war. He contributed little, however, to effective and maturely considered legislation, for he was seriously handicapped by parliamentary opposition and the post-war industrial slump, and he spent much of his time and energy in securing control, often by dubious methods, of various provincial governments. Moreover, he justified only in part his reputation as a friend of the workingman. He put through legislation affecting hours of labor, minimum wages, sanitation, protection of children, arbitration of industrial disputes, and penalties for strikes; but he sternly suppressed a strike of stevedores in Buenos Aires.

Since the constitution of Argentina prohibits two successive terms, Irigoyen was not a candidate in 1922. In that year, however, a moderate Radical named Marcelo T. Alvear was elected to the presidency. Near the beginning of his administration the Radicals split into two factions, the supporters of the president and the followers of Irigoyen. The result was virtual legislative paralysis. However, some aid was granted to the farmers, and the railways were brought to an agreement to colonize the lands adjacent to their lines by the settlement of farmers on small holdings with fixed tenure and ultimate ownership. Moreover, a workmen's pension act was passed, although it proved unsatisfactory to the laborers and was later repealed.

In 1928 Irigoyen was reëlected by an overwhelming majority. His victory was due in part to an effectively organized political machine and in part to personal popularity.

Despite labor disturbances and the brief post-war economic slump, the sixteen-year period was one of great material prosperity in Argentina. The telegraph mileage doubled, telephone instruments quadrupled in number, postal service increased in efficiency and in the quantity of mail handled, extensive highways were constructed, railway lines were extended, new industries sprang up and old industries were expanded, increasingly large sums were devoted to education, many thousand automobiles were purchased, the population augmented by fifty per cent, and the value of foreign trade increased by thirty-five per cent between 1913 and 1929.

Brazil.—Although it suffered from two brief economic depressions (1914–1915, 1920–1922), Brazil was no exception to the general rule of material prosperity during the period. Railway mileage increased some thirty per cent, the mileage of telephone and telegraph wire trebled; mining, industry, and agriculture prospered; foreign trade more than doubled; and the population increased from twenty-four million to nearly forty million. On the political horizon, however, clouds slowly gathered.

The administration of Wenceslau Braz (1914–1919) was occupied for the most part by financial difficulties and problems arising from the World War. The latter part of his term, however, was an era of prosperity marked by the beginning of important manufacturing industries. In March, 1918, ex-President Alves was again elected as chief executive of the nation, but since he was too ill to take charge of the office, the vice president assumed control for a few months, until July, 1919, when Epitacio da Silva Pessôa of Parahyba became chief magistrate. During his term Brazil passed through the post-war depression. New issues of paper currency failed to remedy the ills of the time, but in spite of the scarcity of revenues, the president aided the arid states of Rio Grande do Norte, Ceará, and Parahyba by building storage dams at government expense, a step for which he was criticized. Nor did the popular mind fail to blame him for the rising cost of living. Moreover, notwithstanding the hard times, the centennial of Brazilian independence was celebrated by a grand international exhibition and much rejoicing.. It was also during this administration that the decree of banishment issued against the royal family in 1889 was repealed—a gesture which indicated that Brazil no longer feared the possibility of the reëstablishment of a monarchy.

Thus, for more than a decade the nation enjoyed internal peace. With the approach of the election of 1922, however, the political atmosphere was again disturbed. The victory of the official candidate, Arturo Bernardes of Minas Geraes, aroused bitter resentment both among the military faction and in opposition circles. The Military Club, made up of army officers who interested themselves in politics, considered Bernardes to be the bitter enemy of the militarists and worked hard for his defeat. When he was elected in spite of their opposition, they alleged that there had been violence and fraud. This was also the opinion of many of the civilian followers of the unsuccessful candidate, Nilo Peçanha. Soon after the election, Hermes da Fonseca, the leader of the military faction, was arrested, and in July, 1922, his son, Euclydes da Fonseca, staged a twenty-four-hour revolt during which he shelled the city of Rio. It was afterwards learned that the rebellion was a premature plan to make the father of this young naval officer the dictator of Brazil and prevent the accession of Bernardes. Although President Pessoa speedily suppressed the revolt, discontent continued in the military ranks, and the president increased the number of his enemies by his vindictiveness and autocratic tendencies. In July, 1924, the garrison of São Paulo seized the city and held it until expelled by the federal troops three weeks later. Some of the military leaders were inspired by purely personal motives, but there were many young officers involved in the uprising who believed that they were fighting for the overthrow of a corrupt oligarchy and the establishment of a more honest and democratic régime. In 1923 and 1924 military uprisings also occurred in Rio Grande do Sul, where an attempt was made to overthrow a corrupt president who had dominated the state for almost a quarter of a century; and in 1925 there were plots and rumors of plots in various sections of the country. As a result, a state of siege was maintained in the greater part of the republic during most of Bernardes's term, and the president was able to devote only a portion of his energies to urgent economic and social reforms. Among the latter were several measures designed to improve the status of the working class. A National Council of Labor was created, a housing program launched, work in the bakeries of the Federal District regulated, and a law passed providing for an annual vacation of fifteen days for laborers in mercantile establishments, industries, and banks.

His successor, Washington Luis Pereira de Sousa (1926–1930), was a Paulista whom long years of public service had proved to be a man of unusual gifts as an organizer and administrator. At the beginning of his term he was compelled to suppress uprisings in the west and south, a task which he performed with efficiency and speed, bringing the reign of martial law to an end early in 1927. He then set to work on the coffee market and financial problems. He also began an extensive program of road building, but this was interrupted by the world depression, which started late in 1929.

Progress in Uruguay and Colombia

Uruguay.—During the period under consideration Uruguay experienced the most remarkable progress of any nation in Latin America and became a democracy in fact as well as in name. Elections, which formerly had been a farce, now became orderly and reasonably fair; revolutions entirely ceased; presidents quietly surrendered their power at the end of their constitutional terms; and the people, under the encouragement of progressive governments, advanced in culture and education while increasing in numbers and material prosperity.

From beginnings made during the late caudillo period, Uruguay developed one of the best educational systems in Latin America. In 1929 it not only possessed primary schools almost adequate for all pupils of school age, but had good normal schools, trade and commercial schools, night schools for adults, and an excellent university attended by more than ten thousand students annually. As a result, its illiteracy was the lowest in the New World with the exception of the United States and Canada.

Since 1908, its population, which consists almost entirely of whites of European stock, had doubled, the number of inhabitants being approximately two million in 1929. And this increase had not been entirely due to immigration, for modern sanitation had greatly reduced the death rate. In per capita purchasing power this population ranked fourth in Latin America, and nowhere else in this region was wealth so evenly distributed.

Like Chile, Argentina, and Brazil, Uruguay had long been an important field for foreign investments, the capital coming principally from England and the United States and entering the country in spite of social welfare legislation which some considered radical. Facilities for transportation and communication were not entirely adequate in 1929, but many improvements had occurred during the past sixteen years. During this period, also, Uruguay's foreign trade had increased in value from 124 million dollars to approximately 200 million.

Such was the progress of Uruguay during the second and third decades of the twentieth century. It seems reasonable to assume that it was due in considerable measure to the quality of the nation's statesmen.

Among Uruguayan statesmen of the modern period, the most outstanding was José Batlle y Ordóñez, twice president of the Republic (1903–1907 and 1911–1915), twice president of the National Council of Administration, and for forty years the head and guiding spirit of the Colorado party. The son of General Lorenzo Batlle—a former president of Uruguay (1862–1872)—he was born in 1865 and was educated in his fatherland and in Europe. Although he had studied law, he devoted himself to the field of journalism. He became for a time the editor of *La Nación,* but soon founded a paper of his own, *El Día* (1885). Gradually he became almost completely absorbed in politics.

His first task was the renovation of the Colorado party. Observing that its prestige had greatly suffered under unworthy leaders and that it was in danger of losing the support of men of intellect and character, he set about giving the party ideals, rendering it more truly democratic, and endowing it with cohesion and strength to carry out reforms. By 1903 he had so far succeeded that he was the victorious candidate of the Colorados for the presidency.

As chief executive, he was confronted with an intolerable situation which had developed in the government of the departments. By virtue of a revolt in 1897, the Blancos, who had not been able to capture the presidency a single time since 1865, had extorted the privilege of appointing the jefes políticos of six of the eighteen departments into which the republic was then divided. These six departments, or "fiefs," had fallen under the domination of a Blanco "boss" named Aparicio Saravia, a wealthy *estanciero* (rancher) of "little culture" and less political education. In order to break the hold of this dictator over the departments a civil war of two years was necessary; and the remaining two years of the administration had to be devoted to repairing its damages.

Batlle was followed by the enlightened and progressive Colorado, Claudio Williman, who carried out several judicial, educational, financial, and administrative reforms and left a surplus of nine million pesos in the treasury. Then, on March 1, 1911, Batlle became president for a second time. He now had an opportunity to carry out a program which he had long cherished. During the next four years he laid the foundation for social legislation which placed Uruguay in the vanguard of the progressive nations of the world—legislation which many have criticized, indeed, as radical and even unwise. Under him the government began a serious study of the social welfare of its citizens, establishing a national labor office, calling in foreign experts, and collecting statistics regarding wages, living costs, and the demand for and supply of labor. He also made plans for encouraging agriculture, beautifying towns and cities, and revising the constitution. Lastly, he caused political persecutions to cease and strictly observed the policy of freedom of the press.

Under able successors, whom he continued to support, Batlle's reform program was fully carried out. Feliciano Viera (1915–1919), Baltasar Brum (1919–1923), and José Serrato (1923–1927) devoted themselves to the continuation of his policies. Among the reforms written upon the statute books during this period were the eight-hour law, old age pensions, indemnity for accidents, factory inspection, a minimum wage for agricultural laborers, the suppression of the death penalty, the creation of a state mortgage bank, the nationalization of electric energy, the beginning of a system of national railways, the erection of a national refrigeration plant, the foundation of a state insurance bank, the control of telegraph and telephone lines, national inheritance and income taxes, several measures designed to broaden the curricula and improve the educational system, and a modern electoral law which virtually eliminated fraud.

Among the changes for which Batlle y Ordoñez is mainly responsible, none is more interesting than Uruguay's new constitution (adopted in 1917, effective on March 1, 1919). In many ways it is a unique document.

The General Assembly of the nation, according to the provisions of this constitution, has the usual functions of legislation and control over finance. In addition to these, however, it has the following powers: to declare war, ratify all treaties, confer amnesties or pardons in extraordinary cases, to create and regulate banks, to nominate in joint session of the two houses the members of the High Court of Justice, to amend and interpret the constitution, and to settle conflicts of jurisdiction between the president and the National Council.

These provisions, which limited the power of the executive, were the expression of Batlle's conviction that political disorders in Spanish America, and especially in Uruguay, were caused largely by the tyranny and electoral abuses of strong executives. The powers of the president were further restricted by the National Council of Administration. This body was to be composed of nine members chosen by direct popular vote on the date of the presidential election. Their term of office was six years, but one-third must retire every two years. It was to have jurisdiction over all matters relating to public instruction, public works, labor, industries, agriculture, charities, sanitation, and finances. It was also to have charge of national elections and look after the observance of electoral laws.

The functions of the president, who was to be elected for a term of four years by direct popular vote and deprived of reëligibility until eight years after the expiration of his term, were therefore much reduced. Nevertheless he retained important functions. He was to represent the state both externally and internally, convoke the legislature in special sessions, propose legislation, approve and disapprove bills passed by the national assembly (although measures might be adopted over his veto), negotiate treaties, and serve as commander-in-chief of the military forces. He was also to appoint and remove ministers of foreign affairs, war, navy, and interior; fill the civil and military offices under his direction; appoint diplomatic and consular representatves, as well as the police chiefs of the departments; and he had much to do with budgets and fiscal policy.

Although the government was to be centralized in form, the eighteen departments were to exercise considerable autonomy through an administrative board and a representative assembly. The chief of police in each department was to be the agent of the central government.

The constitution also abolished titles of nobility, hereditary honors, primogeniture, and entails; separated church and state; provided ample personal guaranties; and fixed qualifications for suffrage. Among personal guaranties were equality before the law, habeas corpus and speedy trial by jury, the suppression of the death penalty, and freedom of speech, press, and worship. None of these guaranties was to be suspended except in extraordinary cases of treason or conspiracy. No property qualifications were required for voting and holding office, and suffrage was to be enjoyed by all male citizens above eighteen years of age, provided their names were inscribed in the civil register. The constitution also stipulated that suffrage might be extended to women when two-thirds of all members of each chamber of the General Assembly should agree to do so.

Colombia.—As already suggested, none of the South American republics which had been doomed to a long era of militarism and chaos made such remarkable economic, political, and social progress during the period under consideration as did Uruguay. Colombia, however, was a close second.

This country, after a long era of disorder and poverty, experienced unprecedented material prosperity and considerable social and political progress. Large sums of foreign capital flowed in—mainly from the United States and Great Britain—reaching a total of more than 300 million dollars in 1929. Foreign trade grew from 61 million to 227 million dollars; oil was developed in large quantities; a large growth took place in agricultural products, particularly coffee, tropical fruits, tobacco, and sugar cane; and the new prosperity was reflected in increased support of public schools and in extensive programs of public works and sanitation. The period also witnessed the passage of important legislation relative to labor and temperance.

It will be recalled that the political outlook began to improve in

Colombia after 1903. Rafael Reyes (1904–1909) was one of the most efficient presidents the republic ever had. He stressed internal improvements and the beautification of the capital, reorganized the territorial divisions of the country, reformed the army and established a military school, supported public education (especially schools for laborers), and permitted minorities to have representation in the legislative bodies. Having represented Colombia in the Pan American Congress which met in Mexico City (1901–1902), he was greatly impressed by Porfirio Díaz, whom he seems to have tried to imitate. The Colombians were offended, however, by such dictatorial policies; and when Reyes attempted, by employing a hand-picked Convention, to secure the ratification of a treaty with the United States regarding Panama, the nation rose up in protest. Confronted by the dilemma of revolution or retirement from power, Reyes had the patriotism to choose the latter course and avoid bloodshed.

He was succeeded after a brief interval by Carlos Restrepo, elected by a coalition group known as the Republican Union party. Restrepo (1910–1914) was an honest and able administrator. During his term much attention was given to sanitation, education, penal reform, the codification of laws, the amendment of the constitution, and the development of the natural resources of the country. He was also noted for his tolerance and justice.

By the end of his administration, however, the strength of the coalition party had declined and the Conservatives, who had dominated the country since 1880, returned to power. There followed a succession of fairly able conservative presidents and, except for a brief interval (1919–1921), a period of unprecedented material progress. At the beginning of 1929 modernization was proceeding at a rapid pace, but the Liberals were restive under the unfair electoral procedure which prevented them from exercising the political power which their numbers seemed to warrant.

OTHER STATES OF SOUTH AMERICA

Peru.—In Peru the outstanding man of the period was Augusto B. Leguía. His reputation for financial ability and sympathy for the "under dog" had caused him to be elected president of the country in 1908. With his four-year term began what was known as the "modernization" of Peru. He was considerably handicapped, however, by attempted revolution and financial difficulties.

He was succeeded by Guillermo Billinghurst, a man of English descent and a former mayor of Lima, whose administration was noted mainly for his arbitrary conduct and his effort—due largely to pressure from the United States and England—to improve the condition of the exploited Indians in the eastern rubber region of Putumayo. Billinghurst suppressed opposition newspapers, quarreled with the national Congress, and arrested several prominent politicians. The disaffection aroused by these measures was further increased by the suspicion that he was too favorable to Chile in his attitude toward the Tacna-Arica [2] dispute. On February 4, 1914, he was boldly seized by Colonel Oscar Benavides and other military leaders, who forced him to resign and depart for Chile. In spite of the opposition of the vice president, Benavides then organized a provisional government and ruled the country for a year.

In 1915, however, General José Pardo, who had served as chief executive from 1904 to 1908, was again elected president. Like Leguía, Pardo was a member of the *Civilista* party, an organization composed largely of landed proprietors. During his second administration much of Pardo's time was occupied by problems arising from the World War: financial difficulties, restive Indians, and protesting laborers in the mines and other industries. Because of the increased demand for copper and cotton, however, Peru enjoyed relative prosperity during his term.

Leguía's political fortunes had been eclipsed by Pardo's election in 1915. In fact, he had been sent into exile and had resided in London. In 1919, however, he again became a candidate for the presidency, supported this time by the Constitutionalists and the Democratic Reform party. It was generally admitted that he received a majority of votes, but he feared that his enemies were planning to rob him of his victory. He accordingly led a revolt against Pardo, deposed him (July, 1919), dissolved Congress, and called a national assembly to amend the constitution. He was proclaimed president in October, 1919, a month before his constitutional term was supposed to have begun. His elevation to power was in a measure a vic-

[2] See *post,* pp. 484–486.

tory for the middle class and the labor interests. In this respect there was a similarity between his career and that of Alessandri of Chile, for both represented analogous groups and were comparatively humble in origin.

Moreover, the programs of the two men were similar, although that of Leguía was somewhat more elaborate. He proposed a new constitution under which religious toleration and freedom of speech and the press were to be guaranteed, the municipalities given greater autonomy, and the executive held in check by a responsible ministry, a stronger legislature, and ineligibility for reëlection. He also promised that labor should be more effectively protected, education brought to the masses, the land redistributed, and the lot of the Indians improved. Finally, he proposed to endow the country with railways, roads, reclamation works, and modern ports and cities.

It was an ambitious program and Leguía seems to have made vigorous efforts to carry out at least its economic and social phases. He borrowed more than 117 million dollars from the United States and some fifteen million dollars from the British. He raised other funds by means of taxes, which were increased both in rate and in number. He also called in from the United States technical experts as advisers in education, agriculture, engineering, finance, and commerce. Largely as the result of his policy, hundreds of new primary schools were opened and enrollment in these schools more than doubled; provisions for the welfare of labor were written into the constitution and the statute books; and a bureau of Indian affairs and later a society for the protection of the native races were organized. At the same time, the port of Callao was improved; public buildings were erected in Lima; nearly three hundred miles of railway were built; almost seven thousand miles of highway were constructed; several cities were given improved streets and drainage systems; and thousands of acres were reclaimed for agriculture. On all these internal improvements the national government spent more than 65 million dollars, but they constituted a genuine stimulus to the enterprise of the country. The national wealth considerably increased, and Peru's foreign trade grew from only 72 million dollars in 1913 to 210 million in 1929.

Leguía was guilty, however, of oppression and cruelty toward his enemies, many of whom he killed, threw into jail, or sent into exile.

He was also accused of misappropriation of funds. His rule of more than a decade was a despotism tempered only by eagerness for national progress, mainly material.

Paraguay.—Paraguay, whose previous history had been marked by so much tyranny and chaos, revealed during the period some signs of greater political stability and economic progress. Eduardo Schaerer, a Paraguayan of German descent who became president in 1912, succeeded in serving out his four-year term, a feat which no president of the country since 1870 had accomplished; and although Manuel Franco (1916–1919) died shortly before the end of his term, he was followed in an orderly manner by Vice President José P. Montero. Manuel A. Gondra, who was inaugurated on August 15, 1920, was overthrown, however, by ex-President Schaerer in October of the following year, and after a brief period Eusebio Ayala took charge of the government. In April, 1923, the latter resigned and was succeeded by Eligio Ayala, who was elected by Congress as provisional president to serve during the remainder of Gondra's term. In spite of revolution, Eligio not only succeeded in doing so, but managed to be elected for a second period, which came to a successful termination on August 14, 1928. On the following day José P. Guggiari was inaugurated.

During these years of relative tranquillity evidence of progress began to appear. Between 1913 and 1929 the foreign trade of the country doubled; capital flowed in from abroad, especially from Argentina, England, and the United States; railway and fluvial transportation improved; several highways were built; telephone systems were installed in Asuncíon and several other towns; agriculture and stock raising progressed; and there was considerable expansion in industry. In addition, a comprehensive system of public schools was inaugurated, some effort was made to improve the condition of the laborers, and population increased by about twenty per cent. In 1927 plans were initiated to bring in one hundred thousand colonists from the United States and Canada.

Ecuador.—During the years between 1913 and 1929 the political atmosphere of Ecuador was far less stormy than during much of the previous national period. Between 1912 and 1924 three presidents —Leonidas Plaza Gutiérrez, Alfredo Baquerizo Moreno, and José L. Tamayo—completed their constitutional terms and quietly gave up their power. Only the first of these was confronted by revolt of a serious nature. The successor of Tamayo, Gonzalo S. Córdova, was less fortunate. On July 9, hardly a year after his inauguration, he was deposed by a bloodless *coup d'état*. A military junta then ruled the country until January 13, 1926, when a civil junta was constituted. On April 2, 1926, the latter finally surrendered its authority to Isidro Ayora, who governed the nation as acting president until April 17, 1929, when he became constitutional president under a new fundamental law—the thirteenth for Ecuador—promulgated on March 25 of that year.

This period of comparative political calm was marked by social reform and a measure of economic progress. The church was kept under strict surveillance; foreign priests were expelled; the secular authorities expanded their functions at the expense of the ecclesiastical organization; state educational facilities increased; labor laws were passed; some attention was given to the protection of the Indians; and yellow fever and the bubonic plague were exterminated at Guayaquil. Improvements also occurred in communications and transportation, the value of foreign trade augmented between 1913 and 1929 by ten million dollars (a comparatively small expansion), the output of the mines increased, petroleum began to be exploited in large quantities, and significant developments took place in the field of foreign finance, for experts were called in from the United States and the monetary and tax systems were revised.

Although the sanitation of Guayaquil was effected under Moreno, most of Ecuador's contemporary reforms were sponsored by Tamayo and Ayora. Córdova was overthrown largely because of his inefficiency and indifference toward reforms, and Ayora, who came to power as a result of Córdova's downfall, was an able and enlightened, although a somewhat despotic, ruler.

On the whole, it may be said that Ecuador never experienced a happier epoch. Between 1910 and 1929 the population increased by about sixty-five per cent.

Bolivia.—In Bolivia during the period under consideration politics continued largely under the domination of a numerically small, white, landowning aristocracy interested mainly in the spoils of office and maintaining power by virtue of its control of the army. Little or no middle class developed, and the proletariat of Indians

and mestizos had almost no share in the government save the doubtful privilege of furnishing "cannon fodder."

On August 3, 1913, Ismael Montes, a distinguished lawyer, publicist, and soldier, became president for the second time. A member
of the Liberal party which had dominated Bolivian politics since
1899, he came to power by means of a popular election, and his term
of four years was characterized by political order and upper-class
prosperity. He was succeeded in 1917 by another Liberal, José Gutiérrez Guerra, who, like most Bolivian presidents, owed his victory
to executive interference in the elections. This fact, and supposed
unpatriotic negotiations regarding the perennial Tacna-Arica question, furnished his ambitious opponents—members for the most part
of the so-called Republican party—an excuse for overthrowing him
in the summer of 1920. Early in 1921, General Bautista Saavedra, a
member of this party, became chief executive of the nation.

Saavedra's term was characterized by the passage of three important labor laws, the negotiation of a loan of twenty-nine million
dollars in the United States, considerable industrial development
(particularly mining), and public improvements—such as paved
streets, water systems, boulevards, and public buildings—in La Paz
and Cochabamba. He was accused, however, of being a dictator, resorting to strong-arm methods, and corrupting the public service
in the interest of his partisans. "In 1925 he secured the election of
J. C. Villanueva, but when the president-elect showed signs of independence, had Congress quash the elections. He then made a deal
with a former Liberal, Dr. Hernando Siles, whose choice as president he procured in the following year." [3]

Like Saavedra, Siles revealed some interest in "modernization."
Under his rule internal improvements were supported, mining and
agriculture given considerable attention, a national department of
labor provided (1926), and large loans contracted in the United
States. He likewise revealed the intention of becoming his own
master, recalling Villanueva from abroad, inviting Liberals and
Legitimists (friends of Villanueva) into his cabinet, and sending
Saavedra "into honorable exile as minister to Paris"; and he displayed
decidedly despotic tendencies. Employing the critical dispute with

[3] C. H. Haring, in *Foreign Affairs*, Jan., 1931, p. 285.

Paraguay over the Chaco boundary [4] as a means of bolstering up his régime, posing as the champion of the nation's sovereignty over the region and stirring up the latent jingoism of the Bolivian people, he deported the vice president and other opponents and forced Montes to seek asylum in the Chilean legation.

Venezuela.—During this period Venezuela's political life was dominated by Juan Vicente Gómez. He was vice president of the republic late in 1908 when President Cipriano Castro departed for Europe, ostensibly for surgical attention. Shortly after Castro's departure Congress suspended him from office and permitted Gómez to assume authority. The protests of the deposed president were vain: Congress accused him of official misconduct and, in December, 1909, proclaimed Gómez provisional president. In August of the following year, after Venezuela's twelfth constitution had been proclaimed, Gómez was elected president for a term of four years. According to the provisions of the constitution, however, he was not to succeed himself. In the summer of 1913 ex-President Castro made a desperate effort to regain his power, but Gómez, turning over the civil authority to José Gil Fortoul (president of the Council of Government), took the field and routed the insurgents. Returning to Caracas in January, 1914, he resumed his presidential functions. He then convoked a congress of deputies who framed a new fundamental law for the nation. Before promulgating this constitution, however, the deputies elected Victoriano Márquez Bustillos provisional president and Gómez commander-in-chief of the national army.

In view of this action, the most significant provisions of the new fundamental law were those which declared that the provisional president and the generalissimo of the army should continue to exercise their functions until the constitutional president should assume his office. Among the other features of the constitution, the following may be noted: the republic was to be federal in form; the president was to be elected by Congress in secret session for a term of seven years, with no provision against immediate reëlection as was the case in the constitution of 1909. The powers of the president were numerous and extreme, including the right to name his

[4] *Post*, pp. 527–528.

own substitute; there was to be no vice president; the senators were to be chosen by the state legislatures; and religious liberty was guaranteed—subject to the supervision of the federal executive!

The first congress which assembled under the constitution of 1914 unanimously elected (May 3, 1915) Gómez president for a term of seven years. But the president-elect did not choose to assume his duties. He preferred to remain commander-in-chief of the military forces while Bustillos acted as chief executive! Under the special terms of the constitution this was legal, for the provisional president was permitted to exercise his functions until the constitutional president took the oath of office, and until this oath was taken by the constitutional president, the generalissimo of the army could, by the terms of the fundamental law, continue at the head of the military forces of the nation. The significance of these special provisions of the constitution was thus revealed. It was not until several weeks after Congress reëlected him for another term of seven years in May, 1922, that Gómez took charge of that high office! On June 19 of that year Venezuela's fourteenth constitution was promulgated. Most of its provisions were identical with those of the previous document; but there were to be two vice presidents, the special provisions regarding the provisional president and the commander-in-chief of the army—now no longer considered necessary—were omitted, and the president was granted leave to change the location of the capital.—He preferred to reside in Maracay! It was on June 24, 1922, that he relieved Márquez Bustillos of the duties which the latter had exercised since 1914.

On May 3, 1929, Congress elected Gómez for another term of seven years, but he declined the honor. Like the famous old Roman, he retired to his farm. Serious revolts of students and others in 1928 appeared to indicate, however, that the country was becoming tired of his rule. In his place Congress selected Juan Bautista Pérez, but it chose Gómez commander-in-chief of the army, which suggested that his retirement from political control was a farce.

To his enemies, Gómez, "constitutional dictator" of Venezuela, was a ruthless tyrant, who had been responsible for the imprisonment, exile, or death of numerous opponents. In the eyes of his supporters he was the champion of "national rehabilitation," the man who had given Venezuela a strong financial standing, eliminated her foreign debt, and placed her on the road to order and prosperity.

There is much truth in both contentions, for while enriching himself, Gómez made a significant contribution to the economic development of his country, and while suppressing liberty and democracy, he did not entirely neglect the cultural aspects of Venezuelan life. Like Porfirio Díaz he exemplified the military and administrative ability of the Indian element in Latin America. Although lacking the polish of Don Porfirio—he had little or no formal education—he was not contemptuous of culture, for he surrounded himself with men of learning and placed in the hands of the aristocratic minority unprecedented opportunities for intellectual pursuits. At the same time, he built numerous public schools for the masses. It was along material lines, however, that he rendered the greatest service. Between 1913 and 1929 the foreign trade of Venezuela increased in value from 46 million to 237 million dollars and its mileage of railways and telephone wire trebled. During the same time, the number of pieces of mail handled by the post offices increased nearly threefold, a great oil boom occurred, and many hundred miles of improved highway were constructed. Although sanitation and public health were not sufficiently emphasized, there was some improvement. The population increased more than fifty per cent during this period.

MEXICO

After the fall of Porfirio Díaz, Mexico underwent the most momentous changes which it had experienced since the days of the Spanish conquest. For a decade revolution followed revolution in rapid succession; but after May, 1920, there were fewer outbreaks, and none succeeded in overthrowing the national government. During this long turbulent period, which was marked by almost incredible loss of life and property, the Mexican people managed to move forward gradually toward the goal of democracy. In spite of great calamities, they achieved not only social change but economic progress; for while the common man was slowly rising, and the white aristocracy was giving way to the dominant mestizo and Indian masses, the population recuperated from its losses and increased by a million, the foreign trade of the nation almost doubled, the country experienced a great oil boom, and between 1913 and 1929 there was considerable increase in the production of wheat, corn, rice, cotton, sugar, henequen, and other agricultural commodities. The same period also witnessed an increase in the production of silver, copper, lead, and zinc as well as an important growth in the coffee and banana industries. Lastly, the mileage of telegraph and telephone wire more than doubled, almost fifteen hundred miles were added to the railways, several automobile highways were constructed, important irrigation projects were undertaken, much attention was given to public health and sanitation, the power of the Catholic Church was greatly reduced, and nothing less than an educational renaissance occurred.

The fundamental causes of the revolution which began late in 1910 were: (1) the rapid growth of capitalism, largely under foreign control, which resulted in increasing concentration of land, monopolistic developments in trade, and rising prices for food; (2) the slow rise of a Mexican middle class; and (3) a dictatorship which encouraged foreign investments and enterprises, fostered the church and the remnants of the creole aristocracy, denied the middle class political expression and limited its economic opportunities, and permitted the masses to be exploited while denying them the hope of political freedom which the revolution of 1855–1857 had promised them. The immediate causes of the uprising were: (1) the financial depression of 1907; (2) the virtual failure of crops in 1907 and 1908; (3) the bloody suppression of strikes in the Cananea Copper Company of Sonora (1906) and in the Orizaba cotton mills (1907); (4) political agitation; (5) increasing fear of Yankee imperialism; and (6), possibly, the competition of foreigners for the oil lands of Mexico.

That this very significant revolution should have extended over a longer period than the war for Mexican independence is not surprising if the various factors which entered into the situation are taken into account. It was difficult for the middle and lower classes to draw up a program and find sympathetic leaders of administrative ability; the old tendency toward militarism reappeared; and the forces, foreign as well as domestic, opposing the new movement, were powerful. After the overthrow of Díaz, the leaders of the revolt faced a situation similar to that which the patriots confronted immediately after the separation from Spain. It is true that a small middle class had begun to develop, literacy was more widely distributed, and the masses were somewhat more assertive; but there were the same paucity of resources, the same lack of political experience on the part of the leaders, the same tendency toward riotous militarism, and the same reactionary privileged groups—the church and the creole landed aristocracy—to be dealt with. If the growing intelligence of the people enabled them better to appreciate their interests and, as a consequence, brought them to the support of the revolution, the influence of the vested interests of the foreigners (an influence which hardly existed in the earlier period) was usually exerted in behalf of the old régime, and the increased assertiveness of the middle and lower classes made them more difficult to manage.

Shortly before 1910 the nature of the revolution was forecast. In the state of Morelos such labor and agrarian agitators as Soto y Gama, Villareal, and the Magón brothers began their work, even attempting a revolt as early as 1906. Expelled from the country, they joined a Mexican revolutionary committee with headquarters in St. Louis, Missouri. At about the same time, Felipe Carrillo and other leaders began similar agitation in Yucatán. In 1908 James Creelman published the substance of his now famous interview with Díaz, in which the dictator stated that since his country was then ready for democracy, he would allow political opposition and retire in favor of any opponent legally elected. General Rodolfo Reyes at once gave new emphasis to his covert campaign, carried on through Masonic lodges and Reyes clubs to supplant Díaz, and a few months later Francisco Madero published a mild criticism of the Díaz régime under the title of *The Presidential Succession in 1910.* It then became evident, however, that the dictator did not mean what he had said. He adroitly sent Reyes on a diplomatic mission to Europe and imprisoned Madero during the electoral campaign of 1910. As a matter of course, Díaz was elected for another term.

Released shortly after the election, Madero now became frankly revolutionary. In October he issued a call to revolt and a program of reform which demanded "effective suffrage and no reëlection," the abolition of the jefes políticos (local bosses and agents of the central government), and (vaguely) the redistribution of lands. For the moment Madero received the support of all dissatisfied factions from the conservative supporters of Reyes to the radical agrarian and labor reformers. In May, 1911, he captured Ciudad Juárez on the northern border; in June he entered Mexico City; and before the end of the year he became chief executive of the nation. On May 25, 1911, Díaz had resigned and set out for Paris. All attempts to turn Madero aside had proved futile, but he had risen to power not so much because of the genuineness of his program as because he had dared take the leadership in overthrowing a dictator whose rule had become intolerable to both the middle class and the masses.

Impractical, weak-willed, and handicapped by a large following of greedy relatives of the old landholding aristocracy, who blocked all attempts at land reform, Madero was clearly not the leader that the revolution demanded. The reactionaries, backed by foreign and domestic vested interests, revolted in the center and north; the agrarians, led by Zapata, began a formidable uprising in the south; Henry Lane Wilson, the ambassador of the United States, assumed an antagonistic attitude; and Victoriano Huerta, commander of Madero's army, proved a traitor. Late in February, 1913, Madero was deposed and shot, and Huerta took charge of the government.

Temporarily, at least, the revolution had been defeated. But President Woodrow Wilson opposed Huerta from Washington and other ambitious military leaders revolted against him in Mexico. As a result, he was forced to resign in July, 1914. For the next few months militarism ran riot, but—thanks largely to the assistance of Wilson —Venustiano Carranza finally emerged as the dominant figure in October, 1915. Like Madero, Carranza proved not to be the leader for whom the middle class and the masses were looking. A member of the landed aristocracy, he had taken charge of the movement against Huerta less on account of interest in the common people than because of a burning ambition for power. Somewhat reluctantly, it appears, he issued (January 6, 1915) a decree which provided for the restoration or granting of lands to the Indian villages, but many of the provisions of the constitution of 1917 were placed in that document in defiance of his wishes. After its promulgation he made little attempt to put in force any of its stipulations save those which related to the nationalization of the deposits of the subsoil. It soon became evident not only that he was indifferent to the demands of the masses for reform, but that he was tyrannical, stubborn, and in-

efficient, not to say corrupt. In May, 1920, he was overthrown by a
group of military leaders who took the reform movement seriously.
Among these were Alvaro Obregón, Plutarco Elias Calles, and the
brilliant educator José Vasconcelos. At last the revolution had found
its champions.

The most noteworthy achievement of the Carranza period was
the framing of the Constitution of May 1, 1917, by the Constituent
Congress of Querétaro. This document contains many advanced—
even radical—conceptions regarding labor legislation, such as the
the eight-hour day, the protection of women and children in industry,
a minimum wage, profit sharing, workmen's compensation, housing,
social insurance, protection of health and morals, safety of the workers, the right to strike, and arbitration and conciliation boards. It
also contains detailed provisions with reference to agrarian reforms,
the nationalization of petroleum and other subsoil treasures, the
curbing of foreign acquisition of property, particularly agricultural
property, and religious and educational matters. In brief, it was the
most elaborate social program ever issued in Mexico.

The task of carrying out this program was undertaken with great
zeal and sincerity by Obregón, Calles, and Portes Gil, aided by an
industrious group of ministers in the federal government and an enthusiastic band of leaders in the states and municipalities. Mexico
soon became the scene of a mighty crusade of social uplift and transformation. A veritable war was waged on poverty, disease, and ignorance, mankind's worst enemies. Writing in 1927, a careful observer and eyewitness said: "Probably there is not in the world so
elaborate a system of social welfare under state control. . . . The
tremendous campaign of the Federal Sanitary Department against
smallpox and other infectious diseases, vaccination of hundreds of
thousands of individuals monthly, the inspection of foods and bev-
erages, go hand in hand with an educational program that adds a
thousand schools annually, develops teachers, provides material
equipment and mental pabulum for added thousands of the lower
classes. Agricultural credits, banks, loans of seeds and tools and animals, seek to fill the gap in the agricultural situation. Colonization
laws seek to introduce new farmers. Macadam roads for the automobile thread the desert reaches. Irrigation reservoirs prepare for
their irrigation. Most of this work is being done effectively and

economically, and under expert advice where necessary. Given political peace, it is bound to produce beneficent results before long." [5]
Millions of acres of land were placed in the hands of hundreds of
villages and thousands of heads of families. A vigorous effort was
made to recover for the nation the water, timber, lands, and subsoil resources of the country. And the Roman Catholic Church, because its leaders were considered as enemies of the reform movement, was subjected to rigid supervision and even persecution. It was
indeed a new and momentous epoch for old Mexico. Neither foreign remonstrance nor the opposition of landlords and ecclesiastics
could check the progress of social revolution. The republic was in
the hands of the Indians and the mestizos.

THE FIVE REPUBLICS OF CENTRAL AMERICA

In general, the period following 1913 was a comparatively prosperous epoch in Central America. Foreign capital flowed in; improvements were made in transportation, communications, education, and public health; the output of the mines augmented; new
areas were placed under cultivation; labor legislation was improved
and wages increased somewhat; foreign trade more than doubled;
and the population, under improved health conditions, grew from
approximately five million to some six and one-half million.

In the achievement of political stability less progress was made.
Although El Salvador remained tranquil and conditions were less
turbulent than formerly in Guatemala, Honduras, and Nicaragua,
Costa Rica, which had achieved stability in an earlier period, suffered from political disorders. The United States made earnest efforts to contribute to peace and order in the region, but with doubtful success.

El Salvador.—Between 1913 and 1927 El Salvador was ruled by
the Meléndez dynasty, Carlos Meléndez, Jorge Meléndez (his
brother), and Alfonso Quiñones Molino (a brother-in-law). These
executives were followed by Pío Romero Bosque (March 21, 1927).
The period from 1913 to 1929 was one of economic and social progress. Population increased to the extent of a half-million; the value

---

[5] Herbert I. Priestley, in *Proceedings of the Pacific Coast Branch of the American Historical Association, 1927,* p. 110.

of foreign trade grew from fifteen million to thirty-six million; improvements occurred in transportation and communication, as well
as in sanitation, agriculture, and industry; and illiteracy was reduced
to fifty-five per cent by 1926.

Guatemala.—In Guatemala, which had been ruled by the iron
hand of Estrada Cabrera since 1898, several revolutions occurred.
The first of any importance took place in April, 1920, and resulted
in the overthrow of the dictator. Carlos Herrera y Luna then took
charge of the government, but was later deposed by a revolt led
by General José María Orellana, who served as chief executive from
December 6, 1921, until his mysterious death on September 26,
1926. After a brief interregnum, General Lázaro Chacón became
president (December 5, 1926). These disturbances did not seriously
retard the economic development of the country, however. Large
investments of foreign capital flowed in during the period; finances
were placed on a firmer basis; some progress was made in the
production of coffee, bananas, and minerals; and foreign trade more
than doubled.

Costa Rica.—Costa Rica's revolutions were due to unfortunate influences of a peculiar nature which are not likely to be repeated.
Early in 1914, largely on account of the adoption of direct suffrage,
an indecisive presidential contest occurred. None of the three candidates received an absolute majority, and under the constitution it
became the duty of Congress to choose one of them for president.
Because of political combinations in this body a deadlock arose,
which was finally broken by passing over all three of the candidates
and selecting Alfredo González Flores as chief executive. Although
this procedure caused dissatisfaction in some quarters, González was
inaugurated on May 8, 1914, for a four-year term.

The new president was a man of high principles and unques-
tioned honesty, but he lacked administrative ability and did not
belong to the ruling aristocracy. He not only aroused the opposition
of Costa Rican and foreign property owners by the enactment of
land and income tax measures, but made the mistake of appointing
Federico Tinoco, an ambitious and unscrupulous man, as minister
of war. He also became involved in a contest between the British
and the Yankees for oil concessions, which made it possible for
Tinoco to obtain followers (and probably funds from the Sinclair

petroleum interests) to effect his overthrow. At any rate, on January 25, 1917, he was deposed by an almost bloodless *coup d'état* executed by Federico Tinoco, who took charge of the government and maintained himself in power (despite the refusal of the United States to recognize him) until he was forced to resign more than two years later (August 12, 1919). He was followed by two chief executives who ruled the country for a few months until popular elections could be held. With the inauguration of Julio Acosta García on May 8, 1920, the republic returned to an era of normalcy. After a regular term of four years Acosta was followed by Ricardo Jiménez Oreamundo, who was succeeded four years later by Cleto G. Víquez.

Although these disturbances interrupted the even tenor of progress which had characterized the history of Costa Rica for several decades, the period between 1913 and 1929 was marked by important economic and cultural development. In spite of political disorders, Costa Rica managed to retain its rank among the progressive states of Latin America.

Honduras.—Of all the countries of Central America, perhaps Honduras suffered most from political disorders during the period under consideration. From 1913 to 1919 the republic was under the despotic rule of Francisco Bertrand, who had been prominent in Honduran politics for many years. Alleging that Bertrand was planning to control the elections of October, 1919, with the view of having Nazaro Serrano, a brother-in-law, elected president, General López Gutiérrez started a revolt in the previous August. On September 8 the minister of the United States sent a note to Bertrand expressing the "gravest concern" at the revolution in progress. He advised that a peaceful agreement be reached between Bertrand and his opponents and free elections guaranteed. He also said that the Washington government hoped Bertrand would seek its good offices, and in case the president of Honduras was not willing to do so, the United States would be "obliged to consider actively assisting in the reëstablishment of order and in the overseeing of the coming Presidential elections." Bertrand immediately resigned, placing his authority in the hands of a Council of Ministers, and left the country. In the name of the diplomatic corps, the minister of the United States sent out several notes to the revolutionary leaders urging them to stop fighting and sustain the provisional government, which had given guaranties of a fair election in the following October. This election was held in due time and López Gutiérrez, the leader of the revolution, was chosen president for a term of four years. Soon after his inauguration on February 1, 1920, he was recognized by the United States.

Months before the date for the presidential elections of 1923 it became evident that trouble would again occur. The Liberal party, to which López Gutiérrez belonged, split into three factions. The Conservatives ran a single candidate; but the administration threw its influence against him, and he failed to receive the absolute majority demanded by the constitution. It then became necessary for Congress to decide the matter, but Congress could not reach an agreement. On December 27 López Gutiérrez declared martial law, and on January 31, 1924, the last day of his legal administration, established a dictatorship. He pointed out, in connection with his action, that Congress had failed to elect a chief executive and there was no one to occupy the presidential office. Accordingly, he proposed to assume supreme power until a constitutional assembly could meet to establish a new régime. The Conservatives, led by General Tiburcio Carías (one of the recent candidates), Gregorio Ferrara, and others, at once organized a revolt; the United States suspended relations with López Gutiérrez on the ground that his retention of authority was illegal; and on March 10, 1924, he was killed.

A Council of Ministers then took charge of the government and continued to hold out against the revolutionists, who had secured control of a good part of the country and were threatening the capital. Their advance upon Tegucigalpa was delayed by the calling in of American Marines and the attempt of the United States to mediate between the factions. While diplomatic agents of Washington and some of the Central American republics and representatives of the revolutionary factions were engaged in a peace conference, the insurgents finally took the capital on April 28. Shortly afterwards the conference brought the rival parties to an agreement and "one of the most disastrous civil wars in Honduran history, destroying $20,000,000 worth of property, came to an end." [6]

According to this agreement, the terms of which were subse-

[6] R. L. Buell, in Foreign Policy Association, *Foreign Policy Reports*, July 22, 1931, p. 196.

quently carried out, the Council of Ministers was to give way to General Vicente Tosta, who was to become provisional president, call a constitutional convention, and remain in power until a new president had been chosen under the new fundametal law. The United States prevented Carías or any of the leaders of the revolution from becoming candidates in the forthcoming elections, and Miguel Paz Barahona, a moderate Conservative, was the successful contestant. Following the approval of the election by the national assembly, the United States announced that it would recognize Paz Barahona after his inauguration on February 1, 1925. After Paz Barahona completed his term, Vicente Mejía Colindres became president (February 1, 1929). The elections of 1924 and 1928 were orderly and reasonably fair, except for the elimination of the candidacy of Carías by the United States in the first of them. General Gregorio Ferrara, however, continued to cause trouble. In August, 1924, he led a revolution against Provisional President Tosta. The United States landed a hundred Marines and supported Tosta, and the revolt was suppressed in October. In February, 1925, Ferrara again took up arms, but the United States once more came to the aid of the established authorities, selling Paz Barahona arms and munitions from the national arsenals. With this aid, it was possible to suppress Ferrara a second time.

These numerous political disturbances did not prevent a considerable amount of progress, especially material progress. Foreign investments, mainly British and American, increased rapidly; finances were reorganized; there was an enormous growth in the banana industry and a slight increase in other agricultural products; postal, telegraph, railway, and post-office facilities were expanded; and the school system was improved until nearly half of the children of school age were enrolled in 1929. Moreover, foreign trade increased nearly 240 per cent between 1913 and 1929, and the population grew between 1910 and 1929 from 553,000 to approximately 800,000.

Nicaragua.—After thirteen years of comparative peace imposed largely by the United States, Nicaragua entered once more upon a period of disorder late in 1925. Adolfo Díaz, who became president in May, 1911, confronted a revolution led by General Luis Mena during the summer of the next year; but Díaz, aided by eight warships from the United States, suppressed the revolt. He then manipulated the electoral machinery so as to effect his reëlection for the four-year term beginning January 1, 1913. This self-succession was unconstitutional, but the United States made no objection—the state department was in pursuit of a canal concession. In April, 1915, a small revolution led by Salvador Castrillo was crushed. In October, 1916, the Conservative General Emiliano Chamorro, the man who had served as minister at Washington and had negotiated the treaty which gave the United States the Nicaragua Canal concession, was elected president by virtue of the support of the United States minister and the Marines. The Liberals desired the withdrawal of the military forces of the United States so that they would have a chance to win the election, but the "security" of American interests demanded that the Marines stay and maintain the Conservatives in power. When the Liberals nominated Julián Irías, an ex-minister of Zelaya, they were warned by the United States that no one who had been connected with the Zelaya régime would be recognized by the Washington government. Chamorro was inaugurated on January 1, 1917, and was succeeded four years later by his uncle, Diego Chamorro, who died in office on October 12, 1923. Vice President Bartolomé Martínez then took charge of the government with hopes of succeeding himself in January, 1925; but these hopes were dashed by the state department, which informed him that self-succession was unconstitutional. In the election which occurred late in 1924 Carlos Solórzano, a Conservative, was chosen president and the Liberal Juan B. Sacasa vice president. Solórzano was inaugurated on January 1, 1925, and early in the following August the Marines were withdrawn. In October a revolution was started, not by the Liberals, but by ex-Presidents Emiliano Chamorro and Adolfo Díaz. It was the beginning of serious trouble.

Forcing Solórzano to resign and Sacasa to flee the country, Chamorro had himself elected president by Congress—some of the members of which he had expelled and replaced by his friends—on January 17, 1926. Because he had come to power by a *coup d'état,* the United States refused to recognize him. This gave the exiled Sacasa and the Liberals what appeared to be a favorable opportunity to fight their way to power, and early in May Sacasa's partisans began a revolt. They made the mistake, however, of accepting aid from

Mexico, and the Washington government, in order to safeguard both its interests and its prestige, was compelled to intervene. It could not do so in behalf of Chamorro, since it had already refused to recognize him, but after considerable maneuvering it managed, with the aid of the Conservatives in the Nicaraguan Congress, to restore Díaz to power. He was inaugurated on November 15, 1926, and recognized despite the fact that he had been connected with the Chamorro *coup d'état* directly by his own action and indirectly through his kinsman Humberto Pasos Díaz. The United States was in desperate need of a government which it could back, and the friendship of Adolfo Díaz could be relied upon! In order to prevent the Liberals, aided by Mexico, from overthrowing Díaz, it was necessary for the United States to employ more than five thousand marines and agree to supervise the elections of 1928. The supervised voting of November 4, 1928, resulted in the election of José María Moncada, a prominent Liberal general who had been connected with the uprising against Díaz. He was inaugurated on January 1, 1929.

During the recent period progress in Nicaragua has probably been slower than in any other Central American country. Between 1913 and 1929 foreign trade increased in value only from 13 million to 21 million dollars. There was a slight increase in the mileage of railway and of telephone wire, but a decrease in the length of telegraph line. Population increased by about 150,000, but only a small percentage of the children of school age was in school, and over seventy-two per cent of the total population was illiterate in 1920.

PANAMA AND THE ISLAND REPUBLICS

During the period now under consideration the political and economic life of Panama, Cuba, Haiti, and the Dominican Republic was greatly influenced by the United States, which maintained protectorates over them. Its influence was exerted in behalf of sanitation, education, transportation, exploitation of economic resources, and political stability, with varying degrees of success in the different republics. In the case of Cuba and Panama, the protectoral relationship was defined by treaties ratified—reluctantly by the Cubans and more willingly by the Panamanians—during a previous period. In Haiti the Washington authorities dominated after 1915 by armed intervention and with a large detachment of Marines; in the Dominican Republic the United States exercised a similar influence between 1916 and 1924.

In all of the countries political disturbances occurred. In Haiti and the Dominican Republic insurrectionary movements, which were partially responsible for the intervention of the United States, did not entirely cease. Revolts or threats of revolt in Cuba led to interventions of the United States (1917, 1919–1923) to establish order and effect political reforms. Although no uprisings of any importance occurred in Panama, there was considerable dissatisfaction regarding electoral practices. The United States was requested by certain groups to supervise every presidential election during the period, but it acceded to the request only in 1918. More serious disturbances might have occurred if it had not been certain that the United States would intervene against the insurgents.

Despite political tension, occasional political disorders, and a few economic difficulties, most of these republics enjoyed unprecedented prosperity until the beginning of the world depression. The foreign trade of Cuba increased in value from 304 million dollars in 1913 to 486 in 1929 and stood at nearly a billion and a half at its peak in 1920. Foreign commerce more than doubled in Haiti and the Dominican Republic, and there was considerable increase in Panama. Foreign capital poured into all four of the countries; transportation and communication facilities expanded; population increased; and there was some advance in education, although this continued backward, especially in Haiti and the Dominican Republic.

CHAPTER XIV

LATIN-AMERICAN CIVILIZATION AFTER A CENTURY OF INDEPENDENCE

NOTWITHSTANDING the progress achieved by most of the states during the century following their independence, the majority of the nations of Latin America were still backward in many respects. From an ideal viewpoint, even Argentina, Uruguay, Chile, Brazil, and Costa Rica—the most progressive of the republics—still had much to accomplish. Let us take a broad view of conditions in 1929.

Few, if any, of the countries had adequate facilities for transportation and communication in 1929. The United States had nearly 195 miles of highway per 1,000 inhabitants; Argentina and Uruguay, which were most progressive in this respect, had 25 and 20 respectively; all the rest ranged from Cuba, with less than 13, to Bolivia, Ecuador, Haiti, Honduras, and Nicaragua, all of which had less than one mile of highway per thousand inhabitants. With the exception of Argentina, none of the republics had adequate railway facilities. The average was about one-third as many miles in proportion to the population as were in operation in the United States. The United States had 148 telephones for each thousand of its inhabitants, while Argentina led Latin America with 19 per thousand. Cuba had 17, Uruguay and Panama 15 each, and the rest ranged from nine to less than one telephone for each thousand of their population. With the exception of Argentina, which had more mileage of telegraph wire per thousand inhabitants than the United States, the Latin-American countries were considerably handicapped in this respect, the average being about four miles of wire per thousand of population against seventeen in the United States and nineteen in Argentina. The United States had 21,723 automobiles per 100,000 inhabitants. Argentina led Latin America with 3,259; Uruguay followed with 2,485; none of the rest had as many as a thousand for each 100,000 of population, Ecuador bringing up the rear with only 69 per 100,000 of its people. The post offices of the United States handled six times as many pieces of mail as did all the post offices of Latin America combined! In many of the countries of Latin America pack animals prodded by barefoot peons still trudged over the mountain trails with burdens which should be borne by trucks or railways, while antiquated canoes, sailing vessels, and steamboats plied along the coasts or up and down the rivers.

Public Health and Sanitation.—Public health and sanitation were very inadequately looked after in most of the nations of the region. Statistics bearing on these subjects are usually incomplete and inaccurate. Indeed, statistics could not possibly give an adequate impression of the unsanitary conditions and the diseases which afflicted these people, particularly in the tropical lowlands: polluted water and milk, hookworm, malaria, dysentery, leprosy, typhus, venereal diseases, pestiferous and poisonous insects working in relays day and night, continuous sweltering and debilitating heat. One could see comparatively few old people in the tropics. Owing largely to the climate and defective sanitation the inhabitants usually died young. In Argentina, Uruguay, and Cuba, however, health conditions were good.

Briefly, the Latin Americans in general were still greatly handicapped by lack of scientific knowledge and technological skill. In many places they had not yet substituted machinery for human beings in handling heavy commodities or even in transportation. The traveler might still observe human drudges loading and unloading boats in tropical heat until the sight became almost unbearable. One might see even women and children plod along under the burden of an ox. Nor was machinery sufficiently employed in exploiting the natural resources of most of these countries.

Political and Financial Disorder.—Another difficulty which confronted the Latin Americans was that of political and financial instability. Historically of all the countries, and during the first part of the twentieth century in many of them, it may be said that political cliques spent borrowed capital with great extravagance, often squandering it upon themselves with little regard for the mortgages and financial burdens which they shifted to the backs of the masses of their own day and the generations of the future. There were many "bureaucratic cannibals" in Latin America, many "budget devourers" who consumed capital which should have been spent for the uplift of the people. Too few of the leaders felt a social responsibility for those who toiled, lived in filth and rags, and died young. It is true that some of these countries had developed social programs; some of the leaders were, in fact, keenly aware of their duty to the masses. In recent years this had been particularly true of many of the statesmen of Argentina, Uruguay, Mexico, Chile, and Colombia. But the evil was still far too prevalent in Latin America as a whole. Eagerness for spoils, and dire poverty among the lower classes, often led to revolution, pillage, and bankruptcy.

Need of Better Living Standards.—The masses of Latin America were in desperate need of better living standards, standards which could be attained only by the application of modern science to the environment, by a more equitable distribution of wealth and opportunity, and by arousing latent desires and ambitions. In many of these countries most of the available wealth was in the hands of foreigners or of a small group of natives.[1] If the purchasing power index of the average citizen of the United States in 1929 be placed at one hundred, the comparative purchasing power of the average inhabitant of Argentina, where it was highest, was less than thirty-two, while the average for the poorer countries fell below five.[2] The masses were for the most part without land or comfortable living quarters, and without most of the essentials of high-grade living.

Illiteracy.—It is hardly necessary to note, after what already has been said, that the rate of illiteracy was rather high in Hispanic America at the end of the third decade of the twentieth century. The percentage of people able to read and write was about seventy-five in Uruguay, Argentina, and Costa Rica; somewhere between sixty-five and seventy-three in Cuba; sixty in Chile; and forty-five in El Salvador. In the other republics it ran from thirty to thirty-five per cent in Colombia and the Dominican Republic to ten or fifteen per cent in Guatemala and Haiti. Of Latin America as a whole, it may be said that not half of the people above eight years of age were able to read and write. Hardly anywhere were the schools sufficient to accommodate the children; in many places they were poorly equipped, some of them being conducted in rented buildings not

[1] Wealth was probably best distributed in Uruguay.
[2] George J. Eder, *Commerce Reports*, Feb. 18, 1929, p. 387.

constructed for educational purposes at all. Almost everywhere the teachers were much underpaid, and in many countries they were poorly trained, a large number being mere political appointees.

Political Intolerance.—Another serious problem was political intolerance. After a long and arduous struggle, most of these nations had won religious toleration so far as the law was concerned, and apparently there had never existed any decided racial intolerance. But politics was different: opposition newspapers were still frequently suppressed; members of opposing parties were persecuted and banished; and the transfer of the government from one political group to another was usually accomplished with great difficulty. Often there was no way to effect a change in administration except by revolution.

There were still other problems of a purely moral nature, such as alcoholism, gambling, and illegitimacy. But these were present in most civilizations of the time and need only be mentioned in this connection.

Such was the somewhat somber picture of Latin-American civilization after a century of independence. It is well to note, however, that the emphasis has been placed mainly on its material phases. On the intellectual and spiritual side many Latin Americans of all classes possessed numerous excellent qualities and had made considerable achievements. They were artistic, imaginative, idealistic, self-effacing, long-suffering; and, in most of their moods, they were kind, gentle, generous, polite, loyal, and affectionate. Citizens of the United States who knew the Latin Americans usually spoke with appreciation and pride of their Latin-American friends or personal servants. The upper classes possessed a high grade of culture and were able to move with ease in the best social circles of any nation. Latin America's art, music, parks and patios, public buildings, and temples were beautiful and inspiring; much of its pure literature, journalism, and historical writings possessed considerable merit; and several of its universities had good equipment and high standards. In a phrase, the civilization of Hispanic America was aristocratic, artistic, and literary, rather than scientific and democratic, but even the untutored lower classes were not lacking in certain traits and talents (particularly artistic) which deserved high praise.

RECAPITULATION OF HANDICAPS

The observer of Latin America near the end of the first third of the twentieth century would have been unfair in his judgments if he had failed to recall the handicaps under which the people of the region had lived. The "backwardness" of the area could be explained in large measure, as already suggested, by four factors which had profoundly influenced its development. These were: (1) physical environment, (2) primitive and mixed races, (3) the Spanish and Portuguese colonial heritage, and (4) the prolonged and bloody struggle for independence.

Physical Environment.—It should be recalled once more that most of these countries are in the tropics or near the tropics; which means tropical insects, reptiles, and diseases, the reduction of human energy by constant debilitating heat, and an almost impenetrable jungle difficult to conquer for agriculture and transportation. In addition, there are the lofty dissected mountains and the terrific destructiveness of tropical floods and hurricanes. To be sure, many elevated portions of the tropics enjoy a delightful climate the year round; but this is not true of the major part of Latin America. Padre Gumilla, who worked for many years as a missionary on the Orinoco, argued, for instance, that the plagues of this region were more numerous than those of Egypt in biblical times.

Moreover, much of Latin America is in the zone of volcanoes and earthquakes, which wrought great destruction, nurtured superstition, and contributed to an improvident and listless fatalism. Many of the leading cities of the region had been destroyed not once, but several times by physical catastrophe.

It is also important to note that the areas best adapted to progress are usually located in the highlands of the interior, areas cut off from the coast by swamp and jungle and steaming heat. Among the continental republics, only Chile, Argentina, Uruguay, and southern Brazil, which are in the temperate zone, are exceptions. Accordingly, there had not been in Latin America, as in the United States, a progressive movement from the coast to the interior. In general, there had been no frontier in the sense in which Turner had used the word—no great area of free land to be occupied by the small farmers moving west in perpetual waves, giving fluidity, creative activity, and increasing energy to American life. Hence, much of the freshness and vigor which our frontier brought was lacking. Instead, there were motionless cities with stagnant populations, and a slow-changing society almost in a state of crystallization. In areas where such a frontier might have been found, scarcity of water or a land policy permitting concentration into a few hands usually made impossible a development analogous to that which occurred in the United States.

Such physical handicaps, hardly offset by rich soils, minerals, forests, and a great variety of tropical products, were most difficult to surmount.

Primitive and Mixed Races.—Primitive and mixed races were another important factor. The Anglo-Saxons of America came in contact with few, if any, sedentary groups of semicivilized Indians. In what is now the United States there were probably only six or seven hundred thousand roving natives, and these were rolled back with the advancing frontier. There was little of social amalgamation or incorporation into the body politic until the whites reached sixty or seventy million and the Indians were reduced to a mere three hundred thousand. In Latin America—particularly the Spanish portion—the situation was vastly different. It contained in 1500, as should be recalled, some twenty million semicivilized Indians, and four or five million of the migratory type known in the United States. Millions of both types were exterminated—they were killed in war or else died of disease, overwork, and worry—during the colonial period; but most of the rest were absorbed into the body politic and social. We have seen that in 1823 there were over five million mestizos (namely, people of mixed Spanish or Portuguese and Indian blood) in Latin America. At that time there were also about seven million Indians who had become an integral part of Latin-American society, and perhaps another two million still roaming their native haunts. In 1929 there were probably twenty million pure Indians in the region and more than thirty million mestizos.

To these fifty million with Indian blood in their veins must be added some twenty-six million Negroes and mulattoes. This would leave only about thirty-four million whites in a total population of almost 110 million. In other words, the pure whites of European descent were in the minority in Latin America as a whole, constituting less than thirty-five per cent of the population. They formed the majority only in Argentina, Uruguay, Chile, and possibly Cuba, Costa Rica, and Brazil. The primitive and mixed races were far in the majority in such countries as Mexico, Paraguay, Bolivia, Peru, Ecuador, Nicaragua, Guatemala, Venezuela, Honduras, and Panama, and whites were very rare indeed in Haiti. This factor alone goes far toward explaining the backwardness of the region.

Of course, it is not our purpose to pass judgment on the ultimate capacity of the mixed and primitive races. It is our intention merely to point out a fact with reference to historical development and the situation in 1929. When the Europeans and the primitive races came in contact with each other in Latin America, most of the primitive peoples were hundreds of years behind the Europeans in their slow ascent toward what we are pleased to call civilization. In viewing their subsequent progress, the time element must be taken into consideration. Moreover, many have contended that the mixture of such diverse races caused great political and cultural confusion and misunderstanding.

Spanish and Portuguese Heritage.—The Spanish and Portuguese heritage was a third factor in the development of Latin America. It will be recalled that Spain established in America an aristocratic society and a class system: officials, mine owners, higher clergy, and landlords at the top; serfs, slaves, and a poorly paid proletariat at the bottom; and no middle class. Few born in the colonies, even if of Spanish parentage, were permitted to participate in the government except in the municipalities. The established church consisted of a powerful Catholic hierarchy and wealthy religious orders—Dominicans, Franciscans, and the rest. The clergy were wealthy, privileged, intolerant, and often corrupt. Furthermore, it will be remembered that Spain's economic policy was characterized by rigid restrictions and exploitation in the interest of the mother country: government monopolies of salt, gunpowder, quicksilver, liquor, playing cards, and tobacco. The cultivation of the olive, mulberry, hemp, flax, and the vine was forbidden. The law did not permit any trade with foreigners: for three centuries trade even with the mother country was restricted to a few designated ports; and commerce was heavily taxed. Such severe and burdensome laws led to disrespect for law and encouraged contraband and graft. The character of the official class was subjected to a strain which it could not withstand. It broke down and had not fully recovered after a century of national existence. Lastly, the Spanish system involved severe intellectual repression. Few printing presses were introduced; books were subjected to rigid censorship (in 1800 five thousand were on the forbidden list); and heretics faced the horrors of the Inquisition. Men were not allowed to think for themselves, and the development of science was consequently greatly handicapped.

If the goal of the Western Hemisphere is democracy and the conquest of the human environment by the application of science, then Spanish America received a poor heritage from the mother country: a class system, little experience in self-government, a wealthy, powerful, and intolerant established church, intellectual repression, and a poor, illiterate, and superstitious population. The dawn of the great era of science, technology, and democracy in Western Europe and the United States found Spanish America in many respects still in the Medieval Age.

The heritage of Brazil differed little from that of Spanish America. There was somewhat more tolerance and a little less repression; but the heritage was essentially the same.

Brazil, however, was not influenced by another factor which was important in the development of Latin America. It escaped the long and bloody struggle for independence and made the transition to the democratic régime by a slow and gradual process rather than by a cataclysm.

Wars of Independence.—Some of the effects of the Wars of Independence in Spanish America were hard to overcome. The revolt of the Thirteen English colonies lasted only six years; that of Spanish America lasted fourteen. While thousands died in our struggle, tens of thousands died in theirs. In order to finance our revolt it was necessary to borrow less than fifty million dollars; in order to conduct theirs they borrowed at least a hundred million and resorted to widespread confiscation. When their long struggle came to an end, the Spanish Americans found themselves deeply in debt, exhausted physically and economically, without experience in practical affairs, and without civic leadership. The American-born Spaniards, who owned most of the potential resources of the region, and who alone possessed the ability to read, numbered under three million and were inexperienced in government and without skill in industry. Yet there were millions of primitive and mixed races, ignorant and fanatical, to mold into national unities. Too often a proper disposition was lacking as well as adequate knowledge, and it was only natural that in most cases tyranny or chaos resulted.

Such were the difficulties which confronted the Latin-American nations during their first century of independence. Few observers who considered their development in the light of such difficulties were inclined to despair of their future. Everywhere they had achieved or seemed to be on the point of achieving religious toleration. Almost everywhere evidences of a deeper sense of obligation on the part of the leaders for the improvement of the masses were appearing: peonage had almost disappeared; the rights of labor were receiving fuller recognition; the state was assuming more responsibility for the health and education of the people; agencies were being set up to look after the welfare of the Indians and other underprivileged groups; land was being distributed to the landless in Mexico, and other countries appeared to be on the point of following Mexico's example; tax systems were being slowly reformed with the view of shifting some of the burden of taxation from the poorer classes; living standards and productive capacity were gradually improving; and leaders in the fields of economics and politics seemed to be slowly forming the concept of the general welfare as the goal of political and economic activity. Unfortunately, however, world forces over which the Latin Americans had little control were on the point of launching them into a period of distress and disorder.

CHAPTER XV

THE GREAT DEPRESSION AND AFTER

LATIN AMERICA's era of progress and reform was followed by a period of depression and revolt. Closely locked in the world's economy, as most of it was by 1929, the region could not be expected to escape the world economic depression. In fact, for several reasons to be noted later, most of the Latin-American nations were peculiarly sensitive to economic conditions abroad. The revolts, which were quite general, were due in part to the economic slump and in part to other factors.

THE DEPRESSION

The Hispanic nations of America were among the first to suffer from the economic difficulties which began to trouble the world in the latter part of the year 1929. The deflation was especially severe in respect to primary materials, and their production consisted mainly in such materials. Their position was rendered even more vulnerable (1) because of their dependence upon two or three basic commodities to meet debt charges and pay for purchases abroad; (2) because the burden of their contractual obligations was greatly increased by the decline in the price of their products; (3) because many of them had borrowed to excess and failed to expend the money wisely, and (4) because their budgetary receipts were largely dependent upon import and export duties, which necessarily declined rapidly with the speedy decrease in their foreign trade. The result was the curtailment of expenditures on education, sanitation, and internal improvements of all kinds, widespread unemployment, labor unrest, revolt, and, in most cases, failure to meet payments due on foreign loans.

A detailed discussion of the course and phases of the depression in all of the republics of Latin America would grow monotonous. A brief summary must suffice.

Bolivia.—Bolivia suffered severely from the drastic deflation of commodity prices. The decline in the value of tin, the principal export of the country, seriously disturbed the trade balance, reduced the government's revenues—which came mainly from an export duty on tin—and led to labor troubles and political unrest through the closing of the mines and the dismissal of public employees. Moreover, the difficulties were accentuated by excessive borrowing, which had brought the national debt to a total of sixty-nine million dollars. In January, 1931, the government announced that it was unable to maintain the service on its foreign loans.

Peru.—Although Peru's industries were more diversified than those of Bolivia, some eighty-four per cent of its exports in 1929 consisted of four commodities—petroleum, copper, cotton, and sugar. Moreover, as in Bolivia, the effects of the depression were intensified by years of extravagant borrowing which had increased the national debt from ten million dollars in 1921 to 107 million in 1930. Accordingly, the prosperity of previous years gave way: mining activities were curtailed, public works were suspended, unemployment became a serious problem, revolutions broke out, and on April 1, 1931, Peru joined Bolivia as a defaulter on its foreign obligations.

Argentina.—Unlike Peru and Bolivia, Argentina is largely an agricultural and pastoral country; but since it lies mainly in the temperate zone, most of its products compete with those of Australia, Canada, and the United States, and their sale in foreign markets was hampered by tariff walls. Moreover, there occurred a sharp decline in the prices of wheat, flaxseed, meat, hides, and wool, which were Argentina's chief exports. Hence, business and agriculture suffered, unemployment was extensive, strikes were frequent, politics unsettled, and the service on the foreign debt difficult to maintain.

Brazil.—The depression was heralded in Brazil by a sharp break in the coffee market and an abrupt drop in exchange. The decline in the value of coffee and the milreis was quickly followed by a slump in the price of sugar, cotton, rubber, and other Brazilian commodities. The depression then took its usual fatal course: curtailment of public works, bankruptcies, unemployment, stagnation in business, agriculture, and industry, revolution, and a very embarrassing decline in public revenues. The break in the coffee market was, however, the most important factor. Not only was the prosperity of the country largely determined by the price of this commodity, but the government had already strained its resources over a period of years in an attempt to maintain the price at too high a level. The failure of its valorization plan tended to aggravate the economic conditions it was supposed to relieve. In September, 1931, Brazil joined the ranks of the countries in default on their foreign loans.

Chile.—The economic depression was severe in Chile because of overproduction and low prices in copper and nitrates, which were its chief products. All efforts to stabilize the prices of these commodities were unavailing. The prosperity of previous decades ceased. Mining operations were sharply curtailed, agriculturists confronted low prices, large manufacturers reduced production, small merchants were compelled to close their stores, government income shrank, construction activity slowed down, revolts occurred, and it became necessary to declare (July, 1931) a moratorium on the foreign debt service.

Colombia.—Mainly because of falling coffee prices and extravagant borrowing from 1925 to 1929, Colombian revenues declined sharply, business failures were frequent, public works were suspended, unemployment was widespread, and, before the end of 1933, defaults had occurred on all the bonds of the foreign debt. But Colombia had no revolt. The hotly contested but orderly election in February, 1930, of Enrique Olaya Herrera, a moderate Liberal, to the presidency gave rise to optimism for the political future. The Conservatives, who had dominated the country for years, permitted the peaceful inauguration of Olaya Herrera. He was followed by Alfonso López in 1934 and Eduardo Santos in 1938, both Liberals. Under López the constitution was revised, limiting the power of the Catholic Church, and plans were made for a wider distribution of land and education.

Ecuador.—Ecuador's commodities are more diversified than those of many tropical countries of Latin America. Yet six products— cacao beans, petroleum, coffee, cyanides, Panama hats, and ivory nuts—constituted some seventy per cent of its exports in 1929, and the first three of these amounted to nearly sixty per cent of its exports. In fact, in normal years, and before the exploitation of petroleum was begun, cacao alone constituted from fifty to sixty per cent of Ecuador's total exports. The economic depression began to be felt in 1926, when an insidious disease attacked the cacao crop, but the situation did not become serious until 1930, when the sharp decline in the prices of raw materials occurred. Thereafter the depression followed its familiar way: a business slump, unemployment, decreased government revenues, salary cuts for government employees, political unrest, defaults on foreign loans, exchange controls, revolution. Few Latin-American countries suffered more from the economic crisis.

Uruguay, Venezuela, and Paraguay.—Uruguay, Venezuela, and Paraguay suffered less during the first eighteen months of the world depression than any of the other countries of Hispanic America. In Uruguay public accounts were slightly "in the red" by the end of 1931, and there was some agitation because of alleged electoral frauds; [1] but major defaults on public debts were delayed until 1933 and 1934. The finances of Venezuela were in good shape, and there was comparatively little unemployment; but foreign trade considerably declined. Moreover, the political situation was rather tense. In Paraguay, where national production was quite diversified, economic gains and losses were approximately balanced. The value of the monetary unit and of foreign trade slightly declined, but national finances maintained their soundness and the public debt was reduced before the Chaco war was resumed in 1932.

Central America.—In Central America, where public debts were fairly large in comparison with national wealth, and where national enterprise was concentrated on the production of sugar, coffee, and tropical fruits, the depression was keenly felt. Labor and political disturbances were almost universal, and in 1932–1933 there were numerous defaults on government or government-guaranteed bonds.

The Island Republics.—In the island republics, where monoculture likewise prevailed, the economic depression was accentuated. In the Dominican Republic the slump was severe because of the decline in prices of sugar and cacao, which make up about four-fifths of the exports of the country. Haiti felt most keenly the deflation in coffee, which constituted ordinarily more than eighty per cent of its exports. Cuba suffered the tragic consequences of the break in the prices of sugar and tobacco, which composed from eighty to ninety per cent

---

[1] Gabriel Terra, the successful candidate in the election of November, 1930, became president on March 1, 1931.

of its shipments abroad. It also felt the effects of the increase in the United States tariff on sugar and the decline in the tourist trade. An international effort to stabilize the price of sugar—the Chadbourne plan (signed at Brussels on May 9, 1931), by which an attempt was to be made to limit the production of sugar in the leading sugar countries for a period of five years—brought only partial relief. Political disturbances occurred in all of these countries and all of them had difficulty in meeting interest payments on their public debts.

Mexico.—Mexico, which was still largely a machineless country and was not handicapped by monoculture, nevertheless felt the effects of the depression—mainly through the slump in the price of silver, through the decline in petroleum production, and from the fact that the country had not yet repaired the losses occasioned by the revolutions of 1911–1920 and the serious outbreak of the spring of 1929. Although no revolution occurred between the latter date and the spring of 1940, political conditions continued to be disturbed by the church issue and the socialization program, and the government did not find it possible to resume payments on the foreign loans.

SUMMARY OF POLITICAL DISTURBANCES

During 1930 and 1931 revolutions occurred in eleven of the twenty Latin-American republics. Beginning in the Dominican Republic in February, 1930, revolts broke out in Bolivia in June, in Peru in August, in Argentina in September, in Brazil in October, and in Guatemala in December; and only pressure and counsel from the United States prevented a revolution in Haiti during the early part of the year. In 1931 uprisings occurred in Panama in January, in Honduras in April, in Chile in July, in Cuba in August, and in El Salvador in December. Other evidences of political discontent in 1931 were revealed in the resignations of the president of Venezuela in June, the president of Ecuador in August, and the president of Paraguay in October.

For this epidemic of revolutions and sudden changes in government, many explanations have been offered: economic depression and the dismissal of government employees in order to balance budgets; the corruption or inefficiency of the executives; social injustice; the oppression and tyranny of dictators; excessive political intolerance; the explosiveness of Latin-American character; the attempts of dictators to control elections and maintain themselves or their favorites in power; popular resentment of a too liberal official policy toward foreign capitalists; and, finally, the desire of the "outs" to possess the government and the contents of the treasury, actual or potential. It is probable that several of these factors were influential in most cases, although the causes for revolt differed somewhat in the different states concerned.

In a sense, the revolts represented a widespread movement toward liberalism in government, for in many of the countries where revolts occurred the executives were illiberal and even despotic. Yet, since autocracy was not new in most of Latin America, a further motive was required to arouse energetic resistance. It was probably "bad business" that eventually "made bad governments seem acutely intolerable." At any rate, most of the revolutions were popular uprisings and not merely contests between rival political chieftains. Moreover, a "notable feature" of these insurrections "was the part played in them by the students, who displayed an interest in self-government and in political betterment and a readiness for self-sacrifice which were unprecedented."

It has been correctly suggested that the "most striking thing about them was their almost uniform success." The revolts in Honduras and Cuba were the only ones which failed to effect a change of government, and the uprising in Cuba at least exacted promises of reform. Lastly, it is worth noting that most of the insurrections were almost bloodless.

REVOLUTIONS IN CENTRAL AMERICA AND THE ISLAND REPUBLICS

Haiti.—The economic depression had little or nothing to do with the threat of revolt in Haiti, which might have initiated the series but for the influence of the United States. Political discontent there was due almost entirely to resentment against President Louis Borno who, with the support of the United States, had ruled the country for two terms without assembling the legislative body, and who

was thought to be planning either to remain a third term or else
to dictate his successor. Student strikes occurred in October and
November, 1929, and mob violence in December. A revolution would
undoubtedly have taken place early the following year if the United
States had not increased its marine force and sent a commission
which managed to mediate an agreement eliminating Borno and
setting up a provisional president (Eugene Roy) who had charge of
the government while elections for members of the legislature and
the presidency were held. On November 18, 1930, Stenio Vincent
was chosen chief executive by the Haitian Congress. He took charge
of the government at once and soon became a dictator. In 1940, however, he surrendered his power to Élie Lescot, the candidate "elected"
to succeed him.

Dominican Republic.—Political disaffection in the Dominican Republic also grew out of the irregular procedure of the chief executive. The term of President Horacio Vásquez should have ended
in July, 1928, but shortly before that date he postponed the national
elections for two years. Then, early in 1930, it became evident that
he was going to seek another term and dominate the election. On
February 23 a revolution began with dramatic suddenness and five
days later Vásquez was overthrown. Only small skirmishes occurred
and there was comparatively little bloodshed. General Rafael E.
Ureña, the principal leader of the uprising, became provisional president. In the regular presidential election of May 16, 1930, the
government candidate, General Rafael L. Trujillo, was successful.
Opposing candidates withdrew shortly before the election and soon
fled to Puerto Rico. Trujillo took charge of his office on August 16 and
still dominates the country (1945).

Cuba.—Discontent in Cuba was no doubt due in part to the economic depression. At the beginning of 1930 emergency taxes were
imposed on all kinds of business, and subsequently the salaries of
civil employees were cut twice. In May, 1931, further reductions were
proposed. There is little doubt, however, that the main cause of the
revolt which broke out in August, 1931, was the dictatorial policy of
President Machado. Sometime before the end of his term (May,
1929) he secured from a pliant Congress a two-year extension. Then,
in April, 1928, a constitutional convention changed the term of the

president from four to six years, and in the following November Machado was reëlected for a period ending in 1935, commencing his new administration on May 20, 1929.

Many Cubans considered this procedure illegal and feared that a dictatorship would be made possible by the president's control of the army and his arbitrary suppression of meetings of opposition parties. In August, 1930, several Radicals accused of plotting against the government were arrested and some of them deported. On the last day of September students of the University of Havana rioted and demanded that Machado be deposed. An obedient Congress thereupon gave the president the right to suspend freedom of speech, press, and assembly, and in December Machado removed professors from the university and closed a large number of schools. The situation became even more tense in May, 1931, when the Supreme Court declared all laws, decrees, and elections since 1928 unconstitutional and therefore null and void. On August 9 a serious revolution under the leadership of former President Mario G. Menocal broke out. The Machado government appeared to be in danger, but the uprising was suppressed. Machado then became a bloody despot, but in August, 1933, he was overthrown. Fulgencio Batista, an army officer, soon became dictator, although he left the presidency for others, except for the period 1940-1944.

Panama.—The Panama revolt of January 2, 1931, may have been influenced by salary cuts and unemployment caused by the economic slump, which began to be keenly felt late in 1930, but it was due mainly to political discontent. In August, 1928, the members of the *Porrista* party, alleging that President Chiari was trying to impose his candidate, Florencio H. Arosemena, upon the nation, had asked the United States to supervise the elections. Secretary Kellogg refused to grant the request but issued a warning against revolution. Fearing that the election would be unfair, the opposition groups abstained from voting and Arosemena won by default. He was inaugurated, as already noted, on October 1. In September, 1930, his opponents forced him to reorganize his cabinet. The political atmosphere then became calm until the early morning of January 2, when two small groups of insurgents representing the *Acción Comunal*—an organization which for three years had been urging electoral reform and honesty in government—stormed the headquarters of the national police, seized the National Palace, and compelled Arosemena to resign, but no further political upsets occurred until 1941, when Arnulfo Arias was deposed by a bloodless coup because of his despotism and Fascist leanings.

Honduras.—The political disturbance in Honduras was occasioned by General Gregorio Ferrara, who had been causing trouble since 1924. In April, 1931, he began his third revolt. The Colindres government at length defeated the insurgents, Ferrara being killed in a skirmish. Tiburcio Carías Andino became president on February 1, 1933, and dictator soon after. In 1945 he was still in power.

Guatemala.—The revolution which occurred in Guatemala in December, 1930, seems to have been merely a political contest between rival chieftains. President Chacón, who had been inaugurated on December 5, 1926, managed to maintain himself in power until he was stricken by a cerebral hemorrhage, four years later. On December 12 the Council of Ministers requested Baudillo Palma, the second designate, to assume authority as acting president, and the Assembly approved the appointment. General Manuel Orellana and other army officers objected, however, and after a brief skirmish in which about fifty persons were killed forced Palma to resign (December 17). The Assembly then entrusted the presidency to Orellana, but the United States immediately notified him that he would not be recognized, and on December 31 José María Reyna Andrada became acting president. Under his auspices an election was held during the following February. General Jorge Ubico, the opponent of Chacón in the 1926 election, was chosen chief executive for a term of six years. Ubico speedily became a dictator and continued in power until he was deposed in 1944.

El Salvador.—El Salvador's revolution, which began on December 3, 1931, was caused mainly by economic depression and a militaristic spirit which was quite unexpected in a little republic where no violent alteration of the constitutional order had occurred in thirty-three years. Chosen chief executive in January, 1931, and inaugurated three months later, Arturo Araujo assumed office in the midst of a severe economic crisis; but his election had been remarkably free from official pressure, and he possessed an enviable record for public spirit and interest in the common people of his country. Although he had had some difficulty with the students and had been accused by certain individuals of inefficiency, corruption, and favoritism in making appointments to the civil service, the uprising of December 3 came as a complete surprise. It was led by a group of young army officers who were dissatisfied because Araujo was deemed unappreciative of the military organization, and because they had failed to receive their pay. There were also suspicions that the movement had been encouraged by certain bankers and by Vice President Maximiliano H. Martínez. After less than a day of sharp fighting in the capital, Araujo was overthrown. The military junta which was set up immediately gave him only twenty-four hours to leave the country. He fled to Guatemala.

A few days later Martínez, who had not been on good terms with Araujo for some time, was made president with the approval both of the military junta and of the Congress. He set up a dictatorship and dominated the country until he was overthrown by revolt in 1944.

POLITICAL UNREST IN SOUTH AMERICA

Bolivia.—The economic depression and unsatisfactory political conditions shared about equally in causing the revolt in Bolivia in June, 1930. The decline in the price of tin, the closing of the mines, and the resulting slump in trade led to labor agitation and threats of a general strike. President Siles "resorted to the necessary but unpopular measure of reducing government salaries and increasing taxes. . . . The government bore most of the blame for the impoverishment of the country, and the people were ready to welcome with enthusiasm new rulers who promised improved conditions and an easier standard of living." Even before the economic depression became serious, however, Siles had displayed tyrannical tendencies, suppressing newspapers, forcibly quelling demonstrations against his government, imprisoning or deporting political rivals. Strained relations with Paraguay (1928 ff.) served as an excuse for even greater tyranny. He called General Hans Kundt, whose name was already somewhat odious because of his connection with the hated Saavedra régime, back to La Paz and made him chief of staff and announced in April, 1930, that the presidential election, due the following month, would be postponed "for reasons of national welfare." These two moves aroused the resentment of the army officers and the National Defense League, a group which had been "organized during the Chaco war scare to arouse patriotic sentiment and obtain subscriptions for the purchase of armaments." President Siles's resignation on May 28, after having appointed a new government with instructions to call an election for a national constitutional convention, caused even greater bitterness, for it was interpreted as a part of the president's plan to perpetuate his rule. The exiled vice president, Abdón Saavedra, issued a manifesto against the convention from Buenos Aires and announced his intention of returning to take charge of the government. Riots of students and workmen soon occurred in La Paz; General Blanco Galindo organized a revolt in the important railroad and mining center of Oruro, and other towns declared themselves in favor of revolution. On June 28 the capital fell into the hands of Galindo and the insurgents. Siles and Kundt took refuge in the foreign legations, and on June 29 a military junta headed by Blanco Galindo took charge of the national government.

The military government promised free elections, the autonomy of the municipalities, an independent judiciary, and a speedy return to the civil régime. A Supreme Council of National Economy was immediately appointed to study foreign trade, exchange, unemployment, and the public debt, and to supervise government transactions in order to guard against fraudulent contracts; the use of the state of siege was restricted and civil rights safeguarded; and in keeping with its promise the military junta permitted the elections to be held in January, 1931. Daniel Salamanca, founder and leader of the Republican party until he was cast aside by Bautista Saavedra in 1921, was elected president, and the junta retired in his favor.[2] But democratic hopes were blasted by the war with Paraguay. In 1934 an army junta seized the government. Chief executives were ephemeral. On April 15, 1940, General Enrique Peñaranda became "Constitutional" president, but he was overthrown three years later.

Peru.—Two months after the overthrow of Siles a successful revolt occurred in Peru. The motives of the insurrection were both economic and political. On the economic side it was alleged that President Leguía was guilty of extravagance and graft, that accomplishments were not in proportion to expenditures, and that the

[2] Ernest Galarza, in *Foreign Policy Reports,* May 13, 1931, p. 110.

tax burden was becoming unbearable. The economic depression increased the irritation against Leguía, since all the economic ills of the country were attributed to his government. On the political side exasperation was intense. A large part of Leguía's constitutional program was never put into effect and the constitution was amended so that he could succeed himself indefinitely. All but three of the political parties—the Constitutional, the Democratic, and the Democratic Reform—were suppressed, and these three were made the tools of the dictator; opposition leaders were jailed or exiled; the schools of the workers were closed, and their organizer forced to flee the country; freedom of the press was denied; local autonomy was not granted, for the three regional legislatures provided by the new constitution were gradually reduced to mere debating societies and the committees which had been in control of departmental finances since 1873 were abolished; several strikes were sternly suppressed; and the Indians not only continued to be deprived of their lands but were subjected to compulsory service on the highways. "As there was no secret ballot, and chairmen of the local electoral boards were appointed by the [national] government, Congress became merely the rubber stamp of the President's wishes. He created a special mounted constabulary trained by Spanish officers—a sort of prætorian guard—which was dissociated from the army and the police." [3] This procedure naturally offended many of the staff officers. Intellectuals who opposed the president were given summary treatment, and the University of San Marcos, by order of Leguía, remained in a "state of reorganization" for seven years. Added to all this, was the dictator's undisguised friendliness toward the United States, an attitude which led ardent nationalists to accuse him of truckling to Washington and selling the country out to Yankee capitalists. Lastly, Leguía had reached his sixty-seventh year and was suffering from physical ailments.

In August, 1930, a military revolt in Arequipa, the menacing proletarian and student mobs in Lima, and the waning loyalty of the officers of the military staff, forced him to resign. He attempted to flee to England, but was overtaken and brought back for trial. Most of his property was subsequently confiscated, and he died in prison on February 6, 1932. The leader of the military revolt,

[3] C. H. Haring, in *Foreign Affairs*, Jan., 1931, p. 287.

Colonel Luis M. Sánchez Cerro, assumed control as provisional president on August 28, 1930, but on March 1, 1931, he was forced to resign his power to a junta of civilians. A week later, after this junta was ousted, David Samanez Ocampo became provisional president. In national elections on October 11, 1931, Sánchez Cerro was chosen president. Assassinated in 1933, he was followed by a military dictator named Oscar R. Benavides, who imposed Manuel Prado as his successor in 1939. In 1945, however, an apparently free and fair election was permitted, and the opposition candidate for the presidency won. Peru seemed to be moving toward a more democratic régime.

Argentina.—Within less than two weeks after the overthrow of Leguía the world was surprised by a revolution in Argentina. The uprising in this republic was caused by business depression and the stubbornness of a dictatorial president. Nothing could have been more unfortunate for Irigoyen's reputation than his reëlection in 1928. He was now seventy-five years old and more strong-willed than ever. Distrustful of his subordinates, he concentrated in his own hands almost all political and administrative decisions. He reduced his cabinet officers to mere figureheads or bureau chiefs, dissolved Congress by having his supporters—the *Personalistas*—absent themselves from its sessions, absorbed the legislative functions of government, and intervened in five of the provinces. Because of the pressure of routine, judgeships and other important posts remained vacant, government bills unpaid, and local bosses without anticipated rewards. In brief, "a slow paralysis crept through all the Argentine national administration." And this occurred at the very time when the world business depression began to be seriously felt in the country. The situation soon became intolerable, and the nation's woes were charged against a president who by setting himself up as a court of last resort for conflicting interests had incurred the "hostility of railway employers, railway workers, dock-laborers, shippers, growers, exporters, small business men, and industrialists." As early as March, 1930, there were signs that his power was beginning to weaken, and after news of the revolutionary movements of Bolivia and Peru reached the country, Irigoyen's overthrow was inevitable.

"On Thursday evening, September 4, there was a demonstration of university students against the Casa Rosada (Government House)

. . . , in which one student was killed and several were wounded by the police. Public sentiment was deeply shocked, and the next morning thousands of students marched in solemn, funereal procession through the streets carrying white flags stained with the blood of the victims. Feeling was so tense that at six in the evening the President was prevailed upon to delegate his power to Vice President Martínez. But the public expected resignation; Martínez was but a screen behind which remained the dominating figure of Irigoyen. Friday morning prominent civilians went outside the city to persuade the armed forces and the military school to join them. The navy concentrated in the harbor refused to defend the government. On Saturday morning General José Uriburu [who had decided to support the revolution as early as August 16] delivered an ultimatum demanding the President's retirement. Troops from the suburban barracks started toward the center; cadets from the military academy were joined . . . by students of the university; with the rectors and professors at its head, the gigantic demonstration moved through the principal avenues down to the central Plaza, and the government unfurled the white flag of surrender. A few casualties occurred at the Plaza del Congreso and before the offices of a semi-official newspaper where the crowd was fired upon. But it was virtually a bloodless revolution, and in every sense a popular and democratic one. It was no barrack uprising, but a spontaneous movement by the people at large" [4] at least by the people of the capital, which contains almost one-fifth of the population of the country.

For more than a year after the downfall of Irigoyen, Argentina was under the practical dictatorship of General Uriburu, an influential figure in the army and the son of a former Conservative president. Supported by a coalition of Anti-Personalists, moderate Socialists, and members of the old Conservative party, his government was "composed almost exclusively of persons whose names carry aristocratic connotations." Opposed to him were many of the Irigoyen faction of the Radicals. Uriburu's appointment of federal "interventors" in twelve of the fourteen provinces and his postponement of the national elections caused considerable resentment, as did likewise his persecution of the Personalists. At last, on November 8, 1931, the presidential election was held and General Augustín P.

---

[4] Haring, in *Foreign Affairs*, January, 1931, pp. 291–292.

Justo, the candidate of the National Democratic party—a group composed largely of Conservatives and anti-Irigoyen Radicals— came out victorious after a strenuous contest with the candidate of a coalition of the Democratic Progressive party and the Socialists. Thereafter Argentina drifted from military dictatorship toward Fascism, especially after a revolution in June, 1943, which led to the dominance of Juan Perón, a young army officer of the Franco type.

Brazil.—The revolution in Argentina was followed less than six weeks later by a widespread insurrection in Brazil. In this vast republic there existed many causes for political unrest, but the outbreak was precipitated by the "coffee defense" scheme and its collapse in January, 1930.

The effective and progressive functioning of national government in Brazil was rendered difficult by lack of adequate communications, illiteracy, political intolerance, state and sectional rivalry, the absence of thoroughly organized parties, and a tendency toward militarism. Although larger than the United States, Brazil had less than twenty thousand miles of railway and comparatively few motor roads. The military strategy of the country was based largely upon the principle of keeping open the water communications: the sea, the Amazon, and the other rivers. Vast distances, divergences in climate, racial elements, and economic pursuits, and political decentralization made sectionalism a difficult problem. From Minas Geraes southward is a region of minerals, coffee, and cattle, while to the north is a country of large plantations. The south is predominantly white; the center and the north are inhabited by mixed races, with the Negro and the Indian strains predominating. The local divisions of the country— the captaincies and the "State of Maranhão and Grão Pará" in the colonial period, the provinces under the empire, and twenty states under the republic—were always jealous of their autonomy. After 1890 some of the ambitious states of the south sought to rule the country. Between 1894 and 1930, with one exception (Epitacio Pessoa of Parahyba, 1919–1922), they succeeded in doing so. Since the establishment of the republic national parties have scarcely existed, although down to 1930 all of the presidents belonged to the so-called Republican party. The place of parties was "occupied by the rivalries of various state organizations," which were usually controlled by "an aristocracy of wealth or a political oligarchy." Candidates for the presidency were chosen in a caucus or convention composed largely of members of the national Congress, who were in turn the supporters and creatures of the state administrations. Nominations were thus determined by the controlling political forces of the more important states. The group in power often interfered with electoral freedom, the prevailing open ballot making such interference easy. Partisan feeling was intense and often led to the persecution of defeated opponents. Lastly, militarism was a serious problem after 1889. The first two chief executives were militarists; Hermes da Fonseca, who served as president from 1910 to 1914, was a militarist; and on several subsequent occasions this group tried to return to power.

In the presidential campaign of March, 1930, Julio Prestes of São Paulo was the official candidate (Republican). He was opposed by Getulio Vargas of the populous southern state of Rio Grande do Sul, with João Pessoa, governor of the state of Parahyba, as his running mate. In the natural order of things, the successor of Washington Luis should have been from Minas Geraes, but the president and the leaders of his native state allowed themselves to be swept away by ambition. The election was bitterly contested but, as was natural, the official candidate won. The opposition charged that Washington Luis had employed military force in Minas Geraes and Parahyba in order to secure the election of his candidate, and that Congress, which was under the control of the president, had fraudulently deprived these states of their legally elected representatives in this body. In July a dramatic turn was given to these and other political events by the assassination of João Pessoa. During the summer of 1930 the political situation was grave, and threats of revolution were heard.

At last, early in October, Vargas, doubtless encouraged by successful uprisings in Bolivia, Peru, and Argentina, began a revolt for the purpose of eliminating the president-elect and dissolving Congress. Minas Geraes and Pernambuco came immediately to his support, while the Luis government was backed mainly by São Paulo and the state and federal district of Rio de Janeiro. The struggle threatened to become one of vast magnitude, for nearly three hundred thousand men were soon under arms; however, after a few battles and skirmishes, in which considerable bloodshed occurred, the president's army deserted him, and he was forced to abdicate (October 24, 1930).

A military junta then took charge of the government pending the arrival of Vargas, who reached the capital a few days later and (November 3) assumed the office of national executive "as chief of the victorious revolution." In accordance with the program of his party—the *Alliança Liberal*—and the promises made during the course of the insurrection, the new ruler announced his intention to carry out far-reaching reforms. Special commissions of investigation were to be set up in order to determine the extent of graft in preceding administrations and to bring the guilty parties to trial; a department of labor was to be created; electoral laws were to be modified so as to insure an effective ballot, after which a constituent assembly would be chosen for the purpose of revising the federal constitution in such a manner as to afford greater protection of individual liberties and guarantee the state against interference by the central government; the gradual extinction of large estates was to be sought; and a sincere effort was to be made to effect greater economy in government expenditures.

A good many of these reforms had been carried out by the end of March, 1932; but since one of the aims of the revolution was the dissolution of what was considered to be an illegal Congress, the work had been done by the executive and his appointees: the cabinet, the federal agents (interventors) at the head of each state, and the prefects at the head of each municipality. This concentration of all administrative and legislative functions in the hands of Vargas and his appointees, together with his delay in calling elections for the proposed constitutional convention, aroused criticism and led to revolts, but Vargas managed to retain his position. He promulgated two centralistic constitutions, the last of them (1937) providing for a sort of corporative state. His rule is a dictatorship but hardly one of the totalitarian variety. He seems to be improving the lot of the masses.

Venezuela.—For the year 1931 the epidemic of revolutions and sudden changes of government in South America began in Venezuela. Either because of the economic depression and revolts and rumors of revolt which occurred in the late spring, or merely because Juan Vicente Gómez demanded such a step, Congress called upon Presi-

dent Juan Bautista Pérez to surrender his office. Although Pérez had
not completed a third of his term, he promptly obeyed (June 13).
Six days later a subservient legislature unanimously elected Gómez
El Benemérito as national executive. He continued in power until his
death in December, 1935, when he was succeeded by General Eleazar
López Contreras, who governed in harmony with democratic principles. In 1941 Isaías Medina Angarita became president.

Chile.—The revolution which resulted in the repudiation of President Carlos Ibáñez of Chile in July was in two respects a remarkable
one. "It was a purely civilian movement, the military having no part
in it except to protect the Government House from mob violence,
and it brought to an abrupt close an administration which many regarded as the most enlightened and stable in South America." It was
a protest against tyranny, a search for equilibrium between the presidential and the parliamentary systems, and the exasperated effort of
a people to find escape from a dreadful economic crisis.

As previously noted, the rise of Ibáñez to power was due to the
"moral and political bankruptcy of the former parliamentary régime
and of the parties which flourish under it." Shortly before his inauguration in 1927 he had been hailed by a son of Balmaceda as the
vindicator of his father's lofty designs. He had set up a strong government and carried out many enlightened reforms. But he had made
two serious mistakes: he had suppressed with too much vigor those
who dared oppose his measures, and he had borrowed too much "easy
money" in the boom days before the autumn of 1929. When the depression came in full force he was unable to cope with it. In fact, he
appeared not to realize its meaning until more than a year after it
began. At any rate, he continued his rather lavish expenditures until
the opening of the year 1931. Then a pliant Congress gave him dictatorial powers for four months to deal with the situation. But not even
a dictator could withstand the pressure of the crisis. He was unable
to prevent a sharp break in the prices of nitrate and copper with all
the consequences that such a break entailed. Early in July he formed
a cabinet of civilian experts, but when it demanded a free hand in
the restoration of constitutional guaranties and in effecting radical
economies, he refused to assent.

The nation was in despair, and discontent with the dictatorship
could no longer be restrained. On July 22 "students in the two uni-

versities declared a four-day strike of protest and took possession of the university buildings." Although the students were ejected by force two days later, it was evident that they had aroused widespread sympathy. "A meeting of prominent citizens called by the President was unattended. Strikes of school teachers, engineers, clerks, and other workers inaugurated a policy of passive resistance to the government, and a general strike was considered." [5] Thus the "student agitation soon developed into a national movement for the elimination of dictatorship and the restoration of constitutional government. On July 26, after three days of street demonstrations and clashes between the populace and the mounted police, President Ibáñez resigned." [6] After a brief interregnum Premier Juan E. Montero became acting president. Ibáñez fled to Argentina.

On October 4, 1931, presidential elections were held. Although there were five candidates, the main contest was between ex-President Alessandri, who appealed to the radical and labor elements, and Montero, who had the support of professional and business classes. Montero won the election and was inaugurated in December, but was overthrown six months later. After more disorders, Alessandri was chosen for a six-year term. Inaugurated in December, 1932, he was followed six years later by Pedro Aguirre Cerda, elected by a Popular Front Coalition. Juan Antonio Ríos became president in 1942.

Ecuador.—The forced resignation of Isidro Ayora, the progressive and enlightened president of Ecuador, on August 24, 1931, may be attributed mainly to the economic crisis. Repeated reduction in expenditures in order to achieve a balanced budget aroused protests from government employees and contractors. The match monopoly granted to the Swedish Match Company in return for a loan in 1928 caused further disaffection. Students who were dissatisfied with conditions in the University of Guayaquil became rebellious, but a barrack revolt was mainly responsible for precipitating the retirement of the president, who had "been convicted by army opinion of being guilty of the world depression." His action probably forestalled more serious disorders. Ayora was succeeded by Luis Larrea Alba, who surrendered his office on October 15, after several military units had attempted to declare him dictator. A period of turbulence followed, and the

[5] Henry Grattan Doyle, in *Current History*, Sept., 1931, p. 921.
[6] Haring, in *Foreign Affairs*, Jan., 1932, p. 330.

country was dominated by a junta of army officers at least until the end of 1938, when Dr. Aurelio Mosquera Narváez became constitutional president. In November, 1939, Mosquera Narváez died, whereupon the executive power was assumed by Dr. Carlos Arroyo del Río, who won the popular election for the presidency soon afterward. In 1944 he was overthrown by José María Velasco Ibarra.

Paraguay.—In Paraguay student rioting, so frequently the forerunner of sudden political change in Latin America, brought about a crisis that resulted in the resignation of President José P. Guggiari on October 26, 1931. The university students, exasperated by Guggiari's moderate policy in the dispute with Bolivia over the Chaco region, were aided and abetted by the Radical opposition. In the course of their demonstration they stoned the president's house and five of them were killed. Bowing to popular demand, Guggiari handed in his resignation and submitted to trial. Absolved at length from all blame for the tragedy, he resumed his duties as chief executive on January 28, 1932. He was succeeded at the end of his term (August 15, 1932) by Eusebio Ayala, the official candidate, but on February 17, 1936, Ayala was overthrown by the partisans of General Rafael Franco, one of the heroes of the Chaco War. On August 15, 1937, Franco was ousted in turn by a coterie of army officers who set up as puppet president a lawyer named Félix Paiva. Two years later Paiva was succeeded by José F. Estigarribia, who was succeeded, after a fatal airplane accident, by a young army officer named Higenio Morínigo.

Uruguay.—Even Uruguay, where at first the depression was not serious, finally suffered from political disorders. Gabriel Terra, who was inaugurated president on March 1, 1931, assumed dictatorial powers on April 1, 1933, after dissolving Congress and the National Council of Administration. Thus South America's model democracy became a dictatorship, the alleged justification for the change being the depression, Communistic and other radical agitators, and administrative paralysis caused by the elaborate checks and balances introduced by Batlle and the reformers of previous decades. Terra promulgated a new constitution in 1934, which nullified the system of Batlle, and continued to rule as despot until June 19, 1938, when he was succeeded by General Alfredo Baldomir, Terra's brother-in-law. It is probable that Baldomir owed his election largely to the support of Terra and hence was likely to be dominated by the former dictator. The new

executive announced, however, that he was resolved to return to democratic procedures, and he appears to have done so in considerable
measure. Juan J. Amézaga became chief executive in 1943.

Such was the panorama of revolts and political upsets that followed
the depression in Latin America. In 1933 signs of recovery from the
economic crisis began to appear, and at the same time political conditions became more stable except in Bolivia, Paraguay, and Ecuador,
where special circumstances aggravated the situation, and in Nicaragua, which was the scene of a *coup d'état* in June, 1936, when General
Anastacio Somoza drove President Juan B. Sacasa into exile. But, as
suggested already, further revolts took place in the 1940's, governments being overturned in Argentina and Bolivia in 1943 and in
Ecuador, El Salvador, and Guatemala in 1944.

Characteristics of the Period.—The years following 1930 plainly
witnessed a resurgence of dictatorships in Latin America. In 1940
more than half of the twenty nations were under the rule of dictators
and near dictators. Those who had felt that the Age of the Caudillos
was rapidly passing were troubled by doubts. Yet comparatively few
of the dictators were of the totalitarian type. Nor were all of them
reactionary. Some were reformers in a hurry or champions of gradual
change, seeking to restrain the masses while forcing greater concessions from the privileged groups. In the countries ruled by the autocrats, as in the more democratic countries, budgets for the public
services were relatively large and wages and working conditions were
decidedly improved. In Mexico, under Lázaro Cárdenas (1935–1940),
a vast program of land distribution went forward; elsewhere, land
reforms were inaugurated, but on a much smaller scale.

The period was marked also by great strides in manufacturing and
by a decided trend toward economic nationalism. A number of new
factories sprang up in most of the nations and industrial progress was
little short of remarkable in Argentina, Brazil, Chile, Mexico, and
Colombia. Economic enterprises of aliens were controlled more rigidly, higher tariffs were levied, foreign exchange was regulated, and
economic diversification and socialization were emphasized. Chile
taxed foreign mining companies more heavily, and Bolivia and
Mexico seized the properties of foreign oil companies.

CHAPTER XVI

THE WESTERN POWERS AND THE INDEPENDENCE MOVEMENT

COLONIAL BACKGROUND

IN the course of the first part of this narrative it was frequently noted that Hispanic America constituted a field of intense rivalry among the leading powers of Europe. The New World was in fact the first non-European area to be seized and Europeanized, the first great battle ground whereon the European nations fought for the privilege of securing metals and other raw materials and of civilizing, Christianizing, exploiting, and sometimes exterminating the native races.

By papal bulls (1493 and 1506) and the Treaty of Tordesillas (1494) the Americas were divided up between Spain and Portugal; but neither nation was content with its portion, and the line of demarcation was never run. Before the middle of the sixteenth century the nationals of the two countries began a struggle in South America which was to last almost three centuries and lead to no definite settlement. Along most of the tributaries of the Amazon and all the eastern tributaries of the Plata, in the very heart of the South American jungle, Spanish soldiers, padres, and converted Indians engaged Portuguese miners, prospectors, and slave hunters in an unending bloody combat; and the independent nations of Latin America inherited the dispute. In general, the Portuguese were victorious, but their successes were not supported by firm legal agreements and the establishment of boundary monuments. Unsettled boundaries and the tradition of rivalry were left to complicate the relations between Brazil and its Spanish-American neighbors for a century.

While the Iberian nations were thus disputing over the partition of South America, they attempted, as we have seen, to shut out all other powers from the New World. The monopoly to which they aspired was threefold: navigation of the seas, trade with the natives, and occupation of the land.

According to their view, only the North Atlantic was open to the explorers, merchants, conquerors, and colonizers of the remainder of Europe. That this pretension could be enforced indefinitely, was hardly to be expected; that it was effectively upheld for many decades, was due to the terrors of unfamiliar seas, the lingering influence of the pope, and the prestige of the Iberian nations, particularly Spain. The monopoly was eventually broken by the combined assaults of France, England, and the Netherlands. Sometimes the blows were delivered by private enterprise acting either independently or in secret coöperation with the governments of these states; sometimes the attacks came directly from the governments themselves. To complete the breakdown in all of its phases almost two centuries were required. Finally, however, the navigation, the trade, and the territorial monopolies of Spain and Portugal were wrested from them. Between 1689 and 1763 a bitter struggle for commerce and empire occurred in America.

At the end of this period the New World was left mainly in the hands of England, Spain, and Portugal. Except for certain fishing rights on the Newfoundland banks, two islands off the northeastern coast, the western portion of Española, a few small islands of the West India group, and a part of Guiana, France was expelled from the Americas. England, now triumphant, confronted Spain along the Mississippi River from mouth to source (except for the Isle of Orleans); beyond the Great Lakes she reigned supreme, hardy pioneers were advancing the British flag toward the Pacific, and British merchants held an enviable position in American commerce.

France and Spain were deeply grieved and were to present ample evidence of their dissatisfaction in the near future. The successful issue of the revolt of the Thirteen English colonies, as is well known, was determined largely by the assistance of these two European powers—granted mainly because of the fears and ancient grudges which they held with reference to England. Nor was this the extent of the service rendered to the United States by the rivalries of the European powers, for these rivalries soon led France to sell Louisiana, recently obtained from Spain, to the new republic in America

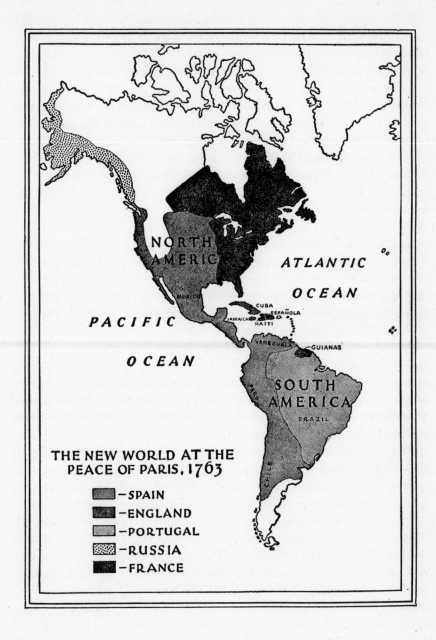

NORTH AMERICA

ATLANTIC

OCEAN

PACIFIC

OCEAN

MEXICO

CUBA
ESPAÑOLA
JAMAICA
HAITI

VENEZUELA
GUIANAS

SOUTH AMERICA

PERU

BRAZIL

CHILE

THE NEW WORLD AT THE PEACE OF PARIS, 1763

■ —SPAIN
■ —ENGLAND
■ —PORTUGAL
▨ —RUSSIA
■ —FRANCE

(1803), and so weakened and preoccupied the nations of Europe that they were unable to prevent the United States from acquiring the Floridas and other territories and thus rounding out a domain which elevated the young nation to the status of a first-rate power.

Indeed the United States speedily became an effective rival of the European nations in America, and especially in Hispanic America. It not only participated in the contest there, but gradually dominated the field to such an extent that the story of Latin America's foreign relations centers largely around the American policy of the United States.

Latin-American Policies of the United States and Europe

Viewed historically, the policies of the United States may be summarized as follows: (1) the extension of its boundaries; (2) the enlistment of the support of Latin America in the struggle for the "rights" of neutrals; (3) trade expansion; (4) the reduction of points of territorial and political contact between Europe and America; and (5) the protection of the life, property, and dividends of its nationals in Latin America. The Gulf and Caribbean areas were particularly emphasized. In this region a strategic motive was uppermost, for the government of the United States felt that the occupation of any portion of land in these areas by a strong power would be a threat to our national security. In consequence, it pursued the policy of dominating the Gulf and the Caribbean to the extent deemed necessary in order to prevent the control of these areas by any other first-rate power.

The relations of the United States with Latin America and with the European nations in respect to Latin America make a long story which can only be summarized in this volume. If, however, these cardinal policies are kept in mind, the chapters which follow may be sufficiently suggestive.

Since 1808, when the independence movement began in Spanish America, the European powers have not often seriously considered the acquisition of territory or protectorates in Latin America. They have been interested mainly in trade and investment opportunities, in the protection of the interests of their nationals, and in checking the political influence of the United States as well as its territorial and economic expansion. That they have not more frequently pursued territorial or political objectives has been due to the Monroe Doctrine, rivalries among themselves, and preoccupations elsewhere. As in the case of the United States, the story of their relations with Latin America can be narrated only briefly.

Some attention must be given also to the conduct and attitude of the Latin-American states. In summary, it may be observed that their main concern was to become the beneficiaries and not the victims of the rivalry between the great capitalistic and industrial Powers. They wished to profit from the contest: to obtain what they needed without jeopardizing their sovereignty. They attempted to set up defensive devices and rewrite international law in their favor. They engaged in multilateral diplomacy within the Western Hemisphere. But until 1907 they were not active participants in world politics.

Early Schemes

Several years before France and Spain sought to humble England by supporting a revolt in its American colonies, the idea of revolutionizing Spanish America had been suggested to the governments of Britain and France, Spain's chief rivals after the decline of the Netherlands. And the insurgent movement which began south of the Río Grande in 1808 was due in some measure to British and French intrigue and propaganda, official and unofficial.

The motives which led to this support of insurgency were mixed. A leaning toward liberalism was doubtless influential with some leaders in both nations; but it is equally certain that rivalries and jealousies played their part. Both England and France perceived the growing impotency of Spain, and each feared that the other might gain some advantage therefrom. Each preferred the achievement of independence by the Spanish colonies to their falling into the hands of its rival, and each expected the successful revolt of these colonies to be attended with some advantage to itself, whether in the form of commerce, territory, new domain for an allied royal house, or a modification of the balance of power. The Portuguese colony of Brazil caused less concern.

One of the earliest to suggest instigating and supporting a revolution in Spanish America was Stephen Deveros in 1741. In a memorial of that year this British subject, who had spent years in the West Indies, deprecated the fact that many Britons favored the conquest of Spanish America. He declared that the retention of this vast region, once the initial conquest had been made, would prove very expensive and troublesome, for the envy of the older powers would be aroused and a formidable coalition would be provoked against England. He therefore contended that the wisest policy would be for Great Britain to form an alliance with the Spanish Americans "as with free people" and help them to throw off the Spanish yoke.[1]

In December, 1776, an actual plan for annihilating "universally the Spanish dominions in America" was laid before the British government. This plan, which had been drawn up by a certain Captain Kaye, suggested that the attack should start from the Mosquito Coast, and that England should furnish some fifteen thousand troops and a fleet. The government of the Incas of Peru was to be restored and the inhabitants of other sections were to be permitted to set up governments of their choice. This project was to be undertaken, apparently, only in case of war with Spain. In carrying it out the ready coöperation of the natives was expected. "What of all things most merits attention," wrote Kaye, "is a predilection which the Natives of Spanish America have in favor of this Expedition, arising from a Prophecy of Old Date, Universally believed and carefully handed down from one Generation to Another: 'That a far distant Nation, Commanding the Sea, Shall Come in Ships to their deliverance, and, freeing them from the Yoke and Oppression of the Spaniards, shall Restore them to the possession of their Liberty and Country.'"[2] Kaye had served on the coasts of Spanish America and must have known something of the inner thoughts and ambitions of the people.

It was only natural that these schemes for detaching the Spanish colonies from the mother country should have multiplied during and after the revolt of the English colonies. Between 1779, when Spain entered the war on the side of the United States, and the close of the Revolution, numerous projects were presented, some of which appear to have been examined by the British government.

[1] Robertson, *Francisco de Miranda* (1907), pp. 197–198.
[2] As quoted in *ibid.*, p. 199.

Moreover, by 1783 the Spanish Americans had become accustomed to looking to Britain for support in their plans for the achievement of independence.

These early proposals are important merely as indicating the trend of the times. Their more serious consideration had to await the turmoil of the Revolutionary and Napoleonic era in Europe. Meanwhile, the soil was being prepared in Spanish America by French radical philosophy and by both the political ideas and the example of the United States.

The Influence of French Radical Philosophy

"In defiance of the Inquisition the works of Montesquieu, Voltaire, and Rousseau had been smuggled into Spanish America and had found thousands of readers. The famous *Encyclopédie,* of which Diderot was the chief editor, was a veritable arsenal from which the Creoles drew their weapons in their attacks on Spain's system of government." [3] A French traveler who visited Venezuela in 1783 relates that a physician of that country led him to a secluded part of his house where he showed him "with infinite satisfaction the works of J. J. Rousseau and Raynal, which he kept concealed as his most precious treasure in a beam scooped out for that purpose." [4] In 1794 Antonio Nariño, of New Granada, printed a Spanish version of the Declaration of the Rights of Man at Bogotá and began its clandestine circulation in northern South America. At about the same time Mariano Moreno edited a translation of the *Social Contract* in the viceroyalty of La Plata. The close of the eighteenth century found the students and faculty at the University of Chuquisaca (Bolivia) discussing the "ideas of Rousseau and Montesquieu and of the French thinkers in general." [5] French revolutionary documents were found among the papers of the insurgent leader Manuel Gual of Venezuela, in 1797; Miranda was steeped in French philosophy; Bolívar often perused the *Social Contract* and the *Spirit of Laws;* and one charge brought by the Inquisition against the Mexican revolutionist Miguel Hidalgo y Costilla was that of reading French

[3] James and Martin, *The Republics of Latin America* (1925), pp. 81–82.
[4] Robertson, *op. cit.,* p. 223, quoting from Ségur.
[5] Raul Orgaz, "A Synopsis of the History of Argentine Social Ideas," in *Inter-America,* VI (1921), 231.

books. The Spanish authorities soon became alarmed at the spread of these radical ideas and placed the works of the French revolutionary writers on the prohibited list.

The Influence of the Political Ideas and Example of the United States

Officially the United States had little to do with the origin of the revolutionary movement in Hispanic America. There was no official propaganda worthy of mention, and the government seldom departed from the path of strict neutrality. And yet the influence of the United States was powerful. Without substantial grounds for such a hope, the Spanish Americans fully expected aid from their North American compatriots, and the character and liberal ideas of the Founding Fathers were ever a potent factor.

While indulging in reminiscence in 1809 Miranda recalled that he had conceived the idea of freeing his fatherland at the time when he was participating in the North American revolution. In 1783–1784 he visited the United States and met such prominent leaders as Alexander Hamilton, Henry Knox, Samuel Adams, Benjamin Franklin, Thomas Paine, and General Washington himself. For many years afterwards he appears to have expected the assistance of some of these leaders in his ambitious enterprise.

In 1794, when Antonio Nariño of New Granada was tried for seditious practices, one of the charges brought against him was that of working in accordance with the Philadelphia Constitution. During his trial he revealed familiarity with the state documents of the United States and expressed great admiration for Franklin, Washington, and Adams.

In 1798 a certain agitator named Juan Picornell was accused of printing the constitution of the United States for distribution in the Spanish colonies. During the same year an exiled Jesuit Father who died in London left with the United States minister at the Court of St. James's a memorial urging the independence of Spanish America. Presumably through his correspondence, he was in close touch with conditions in the Spanish colonies. With respect to his compatriots he remarked, in this memorial, that "the recent acquisition of independence by their neighbors in North America has made the deepest impression on them." That he was not entirely in error is perhaps indicated by the fact that as early as 1791 medals alluding to the achievement of the Thirteen colonies had been struck off and circulated in South America.

The ill-fated expedition launched by Miranda against Venezuela in 1806 must have increased the influence of the United States in insurgent circles of Spanish America. It had been planned in the United States, and it numbered some two hundred Anglo-American enlistments, several of whom shared with the Spanish-American insurgents the pestilential dungeons of Venezuela.

Nor should it be forgotten that Simón Bolívar visited the United States in 1806, at the impressionable age of twenty-three. His itinerary included Boston, Lexington, Concord, New York, and Washington, and he met several of the celebrities of the country. Such an experience must have exerted influence upon his later career.

Another manner in which Anglo-American ideas may have been conveyed to the Spanish Americans was through commercial contacts. These began on the Caribbean and Atlantic coasts at a very early date and extended to the Pacific long before 1800. Pitkin, in his *Statistical View,* estimated the value of the trade between the United States and the Spanish colonies at more than three million dollars in 1795, and at more than twenty-one million in 1801. One does not find it difficult to believe that the merchants introduced liberal ideas along with their commodities.

A loyalist ecclesiastic of Chile, Melchior Martínez, in a denunciation which may probably be taken as typical, makes the following charges: "The Boston republic [the United States] . . . is making its greatest efforts to enlarge its boundaries and to extend its system, as the only method of providing for its stability and maintenance. To this end it puts into action all imaginable means, without hesitating at the most iniquitous and immoral, in order to attract the Spanish colonists to its depraved designs. Freedom of conscience and the freedom of the press assist it in publishing and spreading subversive and seditious principles and maxims, which always find reception with the majority of men, ruled by ignorance and malice. The clandestine trade and the permission to fish for whales introduce traders and adventurers from the United States into all the coast, ports, islands, and other Spanish possessions, giving them op-

portunity to persuade the Spanish colonists of the flourishing state
and advantageous situation of their country, decrying the Spanish
colonial government and subjection to the mother country in Europe as ignominious slavery. They magnify the riches and extent of
these provinces; proclaim the injustice and tyranny with which the
wealth is carried off to enrich Europe; describe the state of obscurity,
abandonment, and civil nullity in which the colonists live; and offer
with impudence all the aid of their great power to the people who
may wish to shake off the yoke of legitimate and just government." [6]

These charges doubtless contained an element of truth. At any
rate, two incidents will serve to indicate the influence attributed to
the ideas and example of the United States at the opening of the insurgent movement in Latin America: (1) The agents whom Napoleon sent to Spanish America were instructed to hold up the United
States as a model and to promise the natives of the country freedom
and independence. (2) The state papers and other writings of the
North American leaders were known and used as propaganda in
most of the early revolutionary centers of Spanish America.

LATER SCHEMES

The year 1790 marks the beginning of serious discussion in European governing circles of the advisability of revolutionizing Hispanic America. It was at this time that the great English prime minister, William Pitt, apprehending a possible general war over the
Nootka Sound dispute, examined attentively the plans of Francisco
Miranda. Miranda's design was to form, with the assistance of Great
Britain, a vast, independent, constitutional empire out of the American domains of Spain.

Pitt was evidently impressed with Miranda's project and more
than once promised to take it up in the event of war. The outbreak
of hostilities at this time would perhaps have given the signal for
the dispatch of three British expeditions to Spanish America, two to
the Atlantic and Gulf coasts, and one (from India) to the Pacific
coast. New Orleans would doubtless have been attacked as a preliminary step in the overland march to Mexico. An attempt would

[6] Quoted by Bernard Moses in *The Intellectual Background of the Revolution in South
America*, pp. 39–41.

also have been made to secure the coöperation of the United States.[7] But a general war was averted by opportune concessions on the part of the Spanish government, which found that revolutionary France was not disposed to stand by the family compact, and feared the consequences of a break with England.

Indeed, the French leaders were so far from accepting this Bourbon alliance that they actually contemplated an attack on the Spanish colonies. Early in 1792 the French minister of foreign affairs began to talk of a coalition between England, France, and the United States for the purpose of opening up the commerce of Spanish America and expelling Spain from the New World. With this idea in mind, Admiral Kersaint placed before the minister an elaborate plan of attack. A quadruple alliance consisting of France, England, the United States, and Holland was to be formed. "England would be attracted to the plan by the immense commercial possibilities involved. In addition, she was to be promised the possession of Cuba. France was to get the Spanish part of Santo Domingo. Porto Rico was to be given to the United States. Trinidad and other small islands along the coasts of Caracas and Louisiana were to be the reward of Holland. There were to be four main attacks north of the equator and three south of that line. The attack on Louisiana was to be confided to the United States, aided by France. The attack on the kingdom of New Granada or the provinces of Caracas and Santa Marta was to be carried on by the Dutch, aided by the Prussians (provided they cared to join the alliance). Cuba and Yucatán were to be attacked by the English and the French. The French, assisted by the English, were to operate against Santo Domingo and Mexico. It was also proposed that the English, reinforced by the French and the Dutch, should proceed against Peru, Chile, and the Philippines. If Portugal would not remain neutral, her colonies were also to be attacked and to be declared independent." [8] Presumably independence was to be given to all of Spanish America except those portions which were considered appropriate spoils for the conquering powers.

The French government even went so far as to approach London with the view of carrying out this grandiose project, but Britain was

[7] Robertson, *Francisco de Miranda*, pp. 266–287.
[8] *Ibid.*, pp. 289–290.

discovered to be inevitably drifting into a coalition against France. The British government was too alarmed at the extravagances of the revolutionary leaders and the downfall of the French monarchy to enter into such a scheme. Until 1795 it remained loyal to the alliance with Spain.

Frenchmen nevertheless continued to consider various projects for revolutionizing Spanish America. One of the most important of these, though less extensive than that of Kersaint, involved the possible coöperation of the United States and probably contemplated the use of Miranda. Writing of the scheme on November 28, 1792, M. Brissot, who virtually dominated the foreign policies of France at the time, suggested that the Precursor be placed in charge of the French West Indies. "Miranda will soon quiet the miserable quarrels of the colonies," said Brissot; "he will soon bring to reason the whites who are so troublesome, and he will become the idol of the people of colour. And then with what ease will he not be able to revolutionize either the islands of the Spaniards or the American continent which they possess? . . . The name of Miranda will be worth an army and his talents, his courage, his genius all promise success. . . ." Professor Robertson thinks "the plans of the French were so all-embracing that at one time they contemplated sending Genêt to the United States and Miranda to Santo Domingo for the purpose of directing simultaneous operations against both the northern and the more southern part of Spanish America." The ill-starred rôle played by Genêt in this vast scheme is well known. As for Miranda, he was not even given an opportunity to display his ability; falling into disfavor, he was cast into a French prison in July, 1793.

The detachment of Spain from the anti-French coalition two years later exerted a profound influence upon British policy toward the Spanish-American colonies. For the next thirteen years, while Spain remained under the domination of Revolutionary and Napoleonic France, the instigation of a Spanish-American revolt became a topic of frequent meditation among British statesmen; for a good part of the time Miranda was pensioned and kept at the British government's right hand, and on several occasions preparations were made for launching English expeditions to carry out some such project. But the statesmen who controlled British policy usually maintained that this step should be taken only in case it should prove necessary in order to prevent both Spain and her colonies from falling into the hands of France. As affairs never actually came to this pass, England did not intervene, and after the Spaniards began a spirited resistance to Napoleonic domination (1808) these plans were abandoned.

Nevertheless British agents, acting during this period under instructions and sometimes contravening instructions, took steps which brought the day for a general revolt in the Spanish-American colonies appreciably nearer.

The propaganda of Thomas Picton from Trinidad furnishes a case in point. When this island was seized by a British fleet early in 1797, Picton was appointed military governor. He was directed to declare the port of Trinidad free, to urge the Spanish Americans to continue their commercial and other communications with the island, and to assure them that if they cared to revolt they could depend upon British assistance. In June, 1797, Picton issued these various declarations (in the form of a proclamation in the Spanish language) which received a wide circulation in northern South America and did much to foster the revolutionary spirit. This favorable beginning was followed by several years of persistent effort which apparently continued to be not without influence. At all events, Picton was optimistic. In September, 1797, he felt that a revolution might be easily brought about by "generally arming the People." In 1798 he declared that if the British government would send an army to the coast of Venezuela and declare its intention of giving the South Americans independence and free trade, they would at once rise up against their corrupt oppressors. In 1804, after he had given up his command in Trinidad, he reported to his government that the outbreak of hostilities with Spain would furnish "a fair opportunity" to "deprive her of all her Continental Colonies." "She holds them by so precarious a Tenure and the Principles of Combustion are so thickly and widely scattered," said Picton, "that a single Spark would communicate the Explosion throughout the whole of the immense Continent." [9]

Doubtless Picton's propaganda was exerting widespread influence, but he exaggerated the spirit of insurgency among the Spanish colonies at this time. This is clearly shown by the unfavorable reception

[9] Robertson, *Francisco de Miranda*, pp. 313–315, 331, 342, note 355, *passim*.

of the Miranda expedition against Venezuela and the spirited resistance to British attacks upon the Viceroyalty of Río de la Plata.

The British expeditions against the Plata region were important both as a revelation of British policy and as an illustration of British influence upon the early revolutionary movement in Spanish America. In the summer of 1806 Sir Home Popham, without explicit instructions, led an expedition from the Cape of Good Hope, where the English had won a recent victory, against Buenos Aires, and succeeded in capturing the city. Popham was recalled and reprimanded for having left the Cape in a defenseless state and seized Buenos Aires without instructions, but the British government nevertheless praised the subordinate officials and the army for the brilliant exploit and prepared to take advantage of the conquest. At the same time, plans were made to conquer Chile. But the militia of Buenos Aires, commanded by Jacques Liniers, an able French officer commissioned by Napoleon, made a brilliant counter-attack and forced the British commander, General Beresford, who had charge of the land forces, to capitulate. British reinforcements arrived too late to save Beresford, but succeeded in taking Montevideo, Maldonado, and Colonia Sacramento. A second assault was then made upon Buenos Aires, but it was heroically repelled by the inhabitants; and the English were soon compelled to evacuate the entire region. Evidently the South Americans were not yet ready to receive the British with open arms.

These attacks nevertheless had an important bearing upon the inception of the revolution in southern South America. As has been noted elsewhere, the viceroy, Rafael Sobremante, proved cravenly inefficient and was removed by the local leaders; the citizens of the province learned to appreciate their prowess; and lastly, the British had given them a taste of the benefits of a more liberal commercial policy, for large quantities of English goods had been introduced and virtual free trade promised.

The attitude of the British government toward these operations in the Plata region reveals that in 1806 and 1807 it entertained ambitions of conquest in Spanish America. In the latter part of 1807 and during the early months of the following year, however, emphasis shifted to the notion of revolutionizing the region. Castlereagh, who had become secretary for war and the colonies in March, 1807, soon drew up a memorandum in which he contended that the British could not afford to undertake "the hopeless task of conquering this extensive country." He urged that they should not allow themselves to appear "in any other light than as auxiliaries and protectors." "In order to prove our sincerity in this respect," continued Castlereagh, "we should be prepared to pursue our object by a native force, to be created under our countenance, and the particular interest which we should be understood alone to propose to ourselves should be the depriving of our enemy of one of his chief resources, and the opening to our manufactures of the markets of that great continent." Sir Arthur Wellesley held a similar view. Were the Spanish Americans ripe for revolt? This question should have given the British statesmen pause; but they nevertheless proceeded with extensive preparations in the spring of 1808, and the effort would doubtless have been made had it not been for the opportune revolt of the Spanish nation against Napoleon, who had recently placed his brother upon the Spanish throne. When news of the revolt reached England, it was decided to send the troops which had been collected for America to the Spanish Peninsula.

But the revolution of Spain's colonies was not long delayed. The task of driving the French troops across the Pyrenees was not quickly performed and, meanwhile, the Corsican was laying plans for the domination of Spanish America. He coveted this area along with Spain as a part of a vast projected empire to be held under his despotic sway; and, as already noted, it was his attempt to realize these ambitions that precipitated the Spanish-American outbreak which European statesmen had long been discussing. The appearance of agents sent by Bonaparte to America furnished the signal for uprisings which began by the formation of juntas to defend the rights of the deposed Ferdinand and ended in the movement for independence from Spain.

THE REVOLT OF BRAZIL

It will be recalled that Napoleon's large schemes also set in motion a train of events which finally resulted in the independence of Brazil. In 1807, when he attempted to seize Portugal and depose the Braganza dynasty, the Portuguese prince regent, with the royal family and the court, made a hasty departure for Brazil on board a British vessel and under cover of the English fleet. Arriving at Rio, this first Old World ruler to visit the New was received with no little enthusiasm. Largely under British influence, he threw open the ports of Brazil, removed many of the restrictions from her industries, and inaugurated several other liberal reforms. Soon after Waterloo, however, conditions in Portugal began urgently to demand the return of the regent (after March, 1816, the king) of the Portuguese dominions. Departing for Lisbon in 1821, he left his son Pedro in charge of Brazil. The king's arrival at the former Portuguese capital was soon followed by an effort to reduce Brazil to its former status of a colonial dependency. This aroused profound resentment among the Brazilians, and at last, on September 7, 1822, Dom Pedro was persuaded to declare for independence.

Thus the movement for independence in Hispanic America was begun under the instigation and encouragement of the European powers. In Brazil, as already noted, it was of short duration and independence was achieved almost without bloodshed. In Spanish America, as we have observed elsewhere, it proved much more complicated and expensive. Would Spanish Americans receive the support of the powers which had urged them to revolt? This only the exigencies of European politics could determine. The omens were far from favorable in 1809.

Treading the Wine Press Alone

There is much pathos in the vain search of the Spanish Americans for outside assistance in their movement for liberation. The British government had long encouraged them, but for more than a decade after July, 1808, its efforts were turned "steadily toward the preservation of the integrity of the Spanish dominions in both hemispheres." At one time it even went so far as to urge Miranda to endeavor to reconcile his compatriots to Spanish rule. Individual Britons joined the ranks of the insurgents in hundreds and even thousands, suffering with them tropical plague and mountain chill, and, above all, contributing their unexcelled knowledge in naval matters; but, except for insisting upon the right to trade with the colonies—a policy which brought them revenues in the form of duties on commerce—

direct official aid was lacking until 1823. Britain was bound by the Spanish alliance and the conservatives were in power.

It was futile to expect assistance from the Continent. French liberalism, to which the revolutionists might have looked for support, was under the smothering despotism first of Napoleon and then of the Metternich system. On one or two occasions the Spanish-American patriots solicited aid from the Corsican, but in vain. Nor could any who aspired to independence under native governments expect anything from the reactionary, legitimist Neo-Holy Alliance.

The Spanish Americans turned with pathetic confidence to the United States, whose political ideas and example had inspired an enthusiastic hope, but considerations of self-interest and security prevented aid from this source. Only a few individuals joined the Mexican patriots or followed in wake of the immortals who sailed with Miranda in 1806. In 1808, while harassed by both England and France and fearing that one of these powers might establish itself in Cuba, Florida, Louisiana, or Mexico, Jefferson's cabinet had found itself "unanimously agreed in the sentiments which should be unauthoritatively expressed by our agents to influential persons in Cuba and Mexico, to wit: 'If you remain under the dominion of the kingdom and family of Spain, we are contented; but we should be extremely unwilling to see you pass under the dominion or ascendency of France or England. . . . Should you choose to declare independence, we cannot now commit ourselves by saying we would make common cause with you, but must reserve ourselves to act according to the then existing circumstances; but in our proceedings we shall be influenced by friendship to you, by a firm feeling that our interests are intimately connected, and by the strongest repugnance to see you under subordination to either France or England, either politically or commercially." [10]

Agents had accordingly been chosen in order to convey these sentiments to Cuba, to Florida, and to the Mexican frontier. To one of these intermediaries Jefferson remarked: "We consider their interests and ours as the same, and that the object of both must be to exclude all European influence from this hemisphere." The agent was authorized to express this sentiment to the Spanish Americans and to inform them that the American government had "nothing

[10] Quoted by Henry Adams in *History of the United States,* IV, 340.

more at heart than their friendship." In conversing with the colonials in these regions the agents may have used even stronger language. But the proceedings of this winter of 1808–1809 and President Madison's later ephemeral schemes regarding the Floridas (1811–1813) mark the nearest official approach on the part of the United States to any action which might be considered as offering encouragement to revolution in the Spanish colonies.

Spanish-American envoys who hurried to the United States upon the outbreak of the wars of independence were unofficially listened to and occasionally supplied with funds for transportation and temporary entertainment, but aside from these polite considerations, which became more and more rare after the negotiations with Spain regarding the Floridas got well under way, there was little departure from the narrow path of formal neutrality. For more than a decade after the Spanish Americans initiated their independence movement they were left to tread the wine press alone.

THE EARLY POLICY OF BRITAIN

In examining the policy of the great powers toward these wars of liberation the course of Great Britain may be taken as the central theme. One of the earliest expressions of the attitude of the British government toward the revolutionary movement in the Spanish colonies is found in the instructions of Lord Liverpool, secretary for war and the colonies, to British officials in the West Indies. Here Liverpool remarked:

"The great object which His Majesty has had in view from the first moment when intelligence was received in this Country of the glorious resistance of the Spanish nation against the Tyranny and Usurpation of France, was to assist by every means in His Power this great effort of a brave, loyal, and high spirited People, and to secure if possible the Independence of the Spanish Monarchy in all Parts of the World. As long as the Spanish Nation persevere in their resistance to their invaders, and as long as any reasonable Hope can be entertained of ultimate Success to their Cause in Spain, His Majesty feels it to be his Duty according to every obligation of Justice and good Faith, to discourage any proceeding which may have the effect of separating the Spanish Provinces in America from the Parent

State in Europe;—the Integrity of the Spanish Monarchy upon principles of Justice and true Policy, being not less the object of His Majesty than of all loyal and patriotick Spaniards." [11]

These instructions were penned on June 29, 1810, and when agents of the Venezuelan insurgents arrived in England less than two weeks later and asked for a conference with Marquis Wellesley, the secretary of state for foreign affairs, an interview was refused on the ground that England was bound to Spain by the alliance of 1808. These agents then declared their loyalty to Ferdinand VII, whereupon audiences were granted. Wellesley urged the Venezuelans to forget their grievances, accept a reconciliation with Spain, and support the mother country in its magnificent struggle against Napoleon. He refused to accept their view that Venezuela could render Spain more efficient aid under an independent government than by reunion with the authorities sent over by the provisional government of the Peninsula, but he eventually promised to use his good offices to promote "an amicable adjustment" between the Venezuelans and the metropolis as well as to protect them from France so long as they refrained from a break with Spain.

Thus, by the summer of 1810 British policy toward the revolting colonies had been clearly formulated. It can be summed up in a few words: moral opposition, a hint of mediation, and protection from France. During the next few years, however, a modification occurred. English policy moved to a position of neutrality and a willingness to mediate upon a liberal basis.

The British ministry made honest and persistent efforts to preserve neutrality. In 1814 a treaty was negotiated with Spain binding Great Britain to prevent its subjects from furnishing "arms, ammunition, or any other warlike article to the revolted in South America." In the fall of 1817 the prince regent of England issued a proclamation warning his subjects not to participate in the war between Spain and her colonies and threatening all offenders with the penalties of felony prescribed by the old statutes of George II. In the summer of the following year other proclamations were issued; and in 1819 a Foreign Enlistment Act was passed making it an offense to enlist in England for foreign service or even to enter the foreign

[11] Quoted by Robertson, "The Beginnings of Spanish-American Diplomacy," in Turner, *Essays in American History,* p. 240.

service at all. By this latter step it will be observed that the British ministry established the principle that "neutrality demands more than an observance of existing laws; it demands that adequate laws shall exist."

Yet, in spite of all these measures, many British subjects joined the ranks of the Spanish-American insurgents. English public sentiment rendered the British judicial system ineffective. When a filibuster's arrest and trial is placed in the hands of his peers he always benefits by every sentiment of sympathy toward the cause he is attempting to serve.

CASTLEREAGH AND THE SPANISH COLONIES

The British government made conscientious efforts to mediate between Spain and her revolting subjects. "One of Castlereagh's first duties at the Foreign Office (1812) had been to define the British position. The Cortes had tried to win British assistance by the offer of special privileges for her commerce. The reply had been definite. The offer of mediation had been accepted, but certain conditions had been laid down as an indispensable preliminary to negotiation. All secret advantages were rejected; the mediation was to apply to all the colonies; and (most important of all) force was not to be used." [12] Spain declined to accept mediation on these terms, and England steadfastly refused to undertake it on any other.

While Madrid continued to importune the London government in the hope that it might relent, Spanish agents sought mediation elsewhere and on a basis more favorable to Spain. When, in the summer of 1817, it appeared that Russia and possibly France might undertake the task, even going so far as to employ armed force, Castlereagh was considerably perturbed. Accordingly, on August 28 he made the first announcement of his policy to the European powers.

He said: "H. R. H. cannot consent that His mediation shall under any circumstances assume an armed character . . . ; nor can H. R. H. become the guarantee [sic] of any settlements that may be effectuated, to the extent of undertaking the obligation of enforcing its [sic] observance by acts of hostility against either of the parties. His intervention must throughout be understood to be confirmed

[12] So writes Webster, "Castlereagh and the Spanish Colonies," in *English Historical Review*, XXVII (1912), 79; but early British policy requires further investigation.

within the bounds of good offices, and the employment of that just influence which must belong to any great power when laboring only to promote the welfare of an allied sovereign and his people . . ." [13]

Thus, as early as August, 1817, Great Britain in effect announced that she "would allow no European interference except on such terms as she chose to dictate." Castlereagh had dared take this bold step in part at least because he and Metternich had virtually become diplomatic allies. Russia, unwilling to oppose England under these circumstances, ceased for a time to insist upon her projects of forced mediation.

A year later, at the Congress of Aix-la-Chapelle, Castlereagh actually secured the acceptance of his basic principles regarding mediation between Spain and the colonies, and Russia went so far as to try to persuade Spain to accept them. But the Spanish government persisted in its obstinacy and nothing was accomplished.

Soon afterwards the British cabinet found cause for alarm in the intrigues of France and the attitude of the United States. First came disquieting rumors of a plot to place Bourbons under French auspices over quasi-independent kingdoms in Spanish America. Next occurred the liberal revolution in Spain, followed by the prospect of European interference, with France as a possible agent. While these important events were taking place in Europe it appeared evident that the United States was moving gradually toward recognition of the new states in Spanish America. The administration was being urged to take this step by liberal public opinion, by commercial interests, and by the factional opposition of Henry Clay. As early as 1810 the United States had begun to send commercial agents to the revolting colonies. Later, in 1817, preparations were begun for dispatching a committee of investigation, and the envoys of the United States in Europe were instructed to drop hints to the effect that the United States was preparing to recognize the insurgent states. At the same time, Henry Clay began to deliver his Pan-American orations in Congress. The government was now held in restraint only by the Florida negotiations and uncertainty regarding the intentions of Europe. Early in 1819 it went so far as to invite an understanding with Great Britain on the question of recognition. Castlereagh's op-

[13] Quoted by Webster, op. cit., pp. 86–87.

position to the employment of forced mediation and the rift in European diplomacy had become known at Washington. But Castlereagh refused to coöperate with the United States on recognition. Then came news that Clay had put through the House (May, 1820, and February, 1821) resolutions in favor of sending diplomatic representatives to the Spanish-American states. This was followed by a copy of Monroe's message of March, 1822, announcing that recognition would soon be granted. The policy of the United States set the British commercial world about Castlereagh's ears. Some action must be taken, they urged, else British trade would be driven from Spanish-American markets by the United States.

Confronted thus by the schemes of France and by the ambitious haste of the United States, what was Castlereagh to do? By the close of 1821 he apparently came to the conclusion that the difficulties between Spain and her colonies could be settled only on the basis of the colonies' independence. He did not seriously object to the recognition of the independence of Spain's former dependencies. What he did oppose, however, was the *recognition of republics* in the New World or the establishment there of monarchies *under the patronage of France*. He had formerly sought to hold the United States in check by the declaration that successful European mediation was imminent and by assurances that force would not be used nor United States commerce subjected to discrimination. When this device at last lost its virtue, he actually turned to France with a proposal of coöperation in the establishment of New World monarchies. But France rejected the overture. Castlereagh then announced (May, 1822) his intention of modifying the English navigation laws and establishing official commercial relations with the insurgent governments. He also instructed himself, in view of the approaching Congress of Verona, to which he was to be a delegate, to fight to the finish any project for combined armed intervention by the European powers in the affairs of Spanish America. He then committed suicide and left posterity to conjecture whether, if he had attended this congress of the powers, he would have promoted the establishment of independent monarchies in the Spanish colonies and secured a concerted announcement of intention to recognize monarchial governments in Latin America and no other.

THE POLICY OF CANNING

Castlereagh's mantle fell upon George Canning, who, though somewhat less conservative than Castlereagh, was by no means eager to change the Spanish-American policy of his predecessor. Commercial recognition had already been granted (June, 1822). Canning thought that political recognition could await further developments, and he hoped that these developments would lead to the establishment of independent monarchies in the New World, although he did not object to a few republics as a counterbalance to European despotisms.

But the attitude both of the United States and of British merchants, as well as the procedure of France, rendered delay somewhat hazardous. The British merchants were determined not to allow their trade to be reduced either by Spanish restrictions or by Yankee competition. France's resolution to suppress the liberal uprising in Spain could not be shaken by the Duke of Wellington, Canning's diplomatic agent at the congress which met at Verona late in 1822. The summer of 1823 witnessed the triumphal march of the French army across Spain. Were Frenchmen returning to the Iberian ambitions of Napoleon?

Already, during the closing weeks of 1822, certain French diplomats had talked ominously of placing the French fleet at the disposition of the Spanish government for the purpose of conveying Spanish troops and a Spanish prince to America. On December 13 the *Journal des Débats* announced that French naval support had been promised for the purpose of establishing Bourbon monarchs in Mexico and Peru. During the following spring and summer discussion of the project continued, and France appeared to be considering the use of force in order to carry it out. In September, 1823, Canning apparently became convinced that France had "all along meditated a direct interference in Spanish America."

Would the resolution not to recognize the insurgent states of America until they had set up monarchies have to be abandoned? Aware of the alarm of the United States with reference to the designs of Russia and the Neo-Holy Alliance, Canning turned to Richard Rush, minister of the United States in London.

"Is not the moment come when our governments might understand each other as to the Spanish-American Colonies?" Canning inquired. "And," he continued, "if we can arrive at such an understanding, would it not be expedient for ourselves and beneficial for all the world that the principles of it be clearly settled and plainly avowed?

"For ourselves we have no disguise.

"1. We conceive the recovery of the Colonies by Spain to be hopeless.

"2. We conceive the question of the recognition of them as independent states to be one of time and circumstances.

"3. We are, however, by no means disposed to throw any impediment in the way of an arrangement between them and the mother country by amicable negotiation.

"4. We aim not at the possession of any portion of them ourselves.

"5. We could not see any portion of them transferred to any other Power with indifference.

"If these opinions and feelings are, as I firmly believe them to be, common to your government and ours, why should we hesitate mutually to confide them to each other, and to declare them in the face of the world?"

While Rush sought advice from Washington, Canning sent out consuls as well as commissioners to America. He also summoned Polignac, French ambassador in London, and demanded explanations with reference to French intentions. During an interview which occurred on October 9, 1823, Canning made three important declarations: (1) "England would recognize the Spanish Colonies if any attempt was made to restrict her existing trade with them." (2) England would consider any foreign interference in the contest between Spain and her colonies "as a motive for recognizing" them "without delay." (3) England, on account of the importance of her Spanish-American interests, was not inclined to enter upon a joint deliberation on "an equal footing" with the other European powers, and would not do so unless the United States were invited to participate.

THE MONROE DOCTRINE—ITS EARLY INFLUENCE

With a fairly definite idea of British attitude but without knowledge of the Polignac interview, Monroe and his cabinet proceeded to discuss and formulate the policy of the United States. The result of their deliberations was the Monroe Doctrine. It differed from Canning's proposals to Rush in several important respects: It was not a joint declaration; it contained no self-denying clause; it interdicted European colonization as well as European political interference in the Western Hemisphere; and it announced a sort of doctrine of two hemispheres. Several motives led these statesmen to prefer independent action: It was necessary to issue a warning to Russia regarding the Pacific coast. It was feared that a joint statement might tend to make the United States, in appearance if not in reality, a mere tail to the British kite, to the great diminution of the country's prestige both in Europe and in America. And lastly, Adams was indisposed to bind the United States never to acquire Spanish-American territory.

This independent course did not involve great risk to the United States, for the Neo-Holy Alliance probably did not seriously contemplate the use of force in Spanish America. Its members could not have agreed among themselves and with Spain as to the specific manner in which and purposes to which force would have been directed even if they had determined to use it, and Britain would have offered vigorous opposition to any drastic measures which might have been undertaken. As for Russian designs on the Pacific coast, they seem to have been of no importance at this time. Russian territorial ambitions were directed mainly toward the Balkans. Even as early as December, 1822, the Russian government had evinced a willingness to come to terms with the United States on the Alaskan boundary issue. The distinguished English specialist on Canning's foreign policy concludes that the evidence is inadequate to support the contention that the European alliance or any member of the alliance seriously considered armed intervention in Spanish America between 1818 and 1824, but he is inclined to believe they did consider it. Carlos A. Villanueva and Dexter Perkins, on the other hand, are positive that the use of force in the Spanish colonies was never seriously contemplated by the Neo-Holy Alliance, or by any government within it.[14]

Moreover, it appears that Adams, who was mainly responsible for

[14] Perkins, "Europe, Spanish America, and the Monroe Doctrine" in *American Historical Review*, XXVII (1922), 207 ff.; Carlos A. Villanueva, *La Monarquía en América*.

the Doctrine, felt at the time that he was not assuming a great risk. Unlike Calhoun, Monroe, Madison, and Jefferson, he did not believe that war was imminent. His manifesto, as a matter of fact, was aimed mainly at Russia, whose subjects appeared to be casting covetous eyes upon the Pacific Northwest, and whose minister had just given him a lecture upon the sacredness of absolutist principles. Adams did not believe Russia or the alliance would fight. If they should really do so, there was the British navy; and, after all, the message of Monroe was so framed as not to commit the United States irrevocably to hostilities. He "could safely blow a blast on the republican trumpet, while sheltered behind the shield of England." [15]

Between 1822 and 1825 the United States completed the process of extending recognition to Colombia, Mexico, Central America, Peru, Chile, and the United Provinces of Río de la Plata. The recognition of Paraguay, Bolivia, Uruguay, and the rest came later. In 1825 some of the nations either had not won independence from Spain or were a part of larger entities. Haiti was not recognized until during the Civil War in the United States.

[15] Temperley, *The Foreign Policy of Canning*, p. 127.

CHAPTER XVII

EARLY RIVALRIES OF THE UNITED STATES AND BRITAIN

FOR almost thirty-five years subsequent to the promulgation of the Monroe Doctrine, and particularly between 1823 and 1827, the United States and Great Britain were energetic rivals in Hispanic America, and the relations of this region with the outside world centered largely around their rivalries. In order to defeat the projects of the Neo-Holy Alliance, Canning had invited the coöperation of the United States; but this did not mean that the two branches of the Anglo-Saxon family were in complete accord. The British foreign secretary was more provoked than pleased by the Monroe Doctrine. Its protest against the armed intervention of the Continental powers tended to support Canning's policy, but this protest was accompanied by two other ideas which gave him no little concern. The message forbade future colonization in America by European powers, and it expressed the view that America and Europe were separate worlds. These notions were acceptable to Canning neither in their commercial nor in their political implications, and during the remainder of his life (1823–1827) his vigorous effort to counteract them increased distrust of England in the United States.

EARLY EVIDENCES OF BRITISH JEALOUSY

Hispanic America had long been considered an important potential market for British goods. Certain profound economic changes which occurred during the first two decades of the nineteenth century made it even more desirable that Englishmen should dominate this market. During the previous century British industries had undergone a marvelous development. British exports had mounted from an annual value of £1,505,285 in 1701 to £41,717,000 in 1801, and British industries had reached a very efficient stage, compared with those of the rest of Europe. But, while the opening decades of the nineteenth century saw no decline in efficiency, they witnessed a decline in the total of British exports, to less than £37,000,000 in 1822. The decrease was due largely to the impoverishment of Europe by the Napoleonic Wars and to an increasing tendency both in Europe and in the United States to encourage home industries by erecting tariff walls. The effect of the tariff was particularly evident in the sum total of British exports to the United States, where the duties levied by the law of 1816 were perhaps responsible for a decline in the importation of English goods from a little less than £12,000,000 in 1815 to less than £4,000,000 in 1820. These circumstances enhanced the value of Spanish-American markets, and British trade with these countries tended to increase rapidly, reaching a total value of a little more than £5,500,000 in 1822 and more than £7,500,000 in 1823. The United States, with a Hispanic-American trade amounting to more than $26,500,000 in 1822 and almost $31,000,000 in the following year, was becoming Britain's most formidable commercial rival.

English capitalists were likewise interested in Hispanic America. Save for occasional French investors, however, these capitalists met few competitors south of the Rio Grande during the first half of the nineteenth century. Most of the new governments of Latin America immediately negotiated loans with British banking houses, and English investors became deeply involved in the mining industry and other enterprises of Hispanic America. By 1830 British investments in the region amounted to almost $200,000,000.

Trade and investments may be profoundly influenced by government policy and hence are closely bound up with politics. Their interrelation in Great Britain is clearly revealed in the contemporary discussions of the British press and of British statesmen. An examination of these will likewise show a lively apprehension of the United States and render evident the motives underlying later British procedure in the Western Hemisphere.

When the agent of the Colombian insurgents in Europe suggested (1823) that the Spanish-American states might accord commercial priority to foreign states in the order in which they extended recognition, the London *Times* accused the United States of catching "at the promised good, by hastening her formal act of recognition." At the same time, it contended that the United States would "thus . . . forestall the merchants of Great Britain in the trade with South America." Coming to the assistance of the *Times,* the *Examiner* inquired whether anything could be "more disgraceful in the British Ministers than to let the North Americans, with nothing like our motives, and some natural feeling to the contrary, get the start of us in establishing a profitable connection with the immense, fertile, and improving States of Southern America."

Similar sentiments were expressed by the petitions of British merchants and by the friends of these merchants in Parliament. As early as 1819 a member of the House of Commons sought to modify British policy by describing the possible action of the United States. Revealing something of jealous contempt on his own part, he said: "Although a sop has, for the present, been given to Cerberus, by the cession of the Floridas to the United States, the policy of the government [at Washington] will not long be able to restrain the wishes of the people, but will be compelled to join this popular and patriotic cause; an event which will at once consummate the independence of South America." In September, 1822, a memorial signed by a group of London merchants prayed for government support on the ground that American citizens threatened to drive British trade from Spanish-American markets.

Still more convincing evidence of British jealousy may be found in the memorials penned by George Canning in his attempt to convince the British Ministry of the advisability of extending recognition to the revolting colonies. Here he gives as one reason for this step the large investments of English subjects in Spanish America. He then continues: "The other and perhaps still more powerful motive is my apprehension of the ambition and ascendancy of the U[nited] S[tates] of Am[erica]: It is obviously the policy of that Gov[ernmen]t to connect itself with all the powers of America in a general Transatlantic League, of which it would have the sole direction. I need only say how inconvenient such an ascendancy may be in time of peace, and how formidable in case of war." After he had at last forced his recognition policy through the cabinet, he wrote to Granville: "The deed is done, the nail is driven. Spanish America is free; and if we do not mismanage our affairs sadly, *she is English.*"

INDICATIONS OF JEALOUSY IN THE UNITED STATES

Thus it will be observed that in England the United States was looked upon as a dangerous rival from the political as well as from the commercial point of view. Although apprehension of England was not so keenly felt in the United States, there are indications of its existence. In his observations on Mexico published in 1824 Poinsett pointed out the alarming extent to which the British were taking possession of the commerce and the economic resources of the country. A year later, on the eve of his departure for Mexico City, where he was to serve as minister, one of his friends, doubtless adapting himself to Poinsett's mood, playfully remarked: "Make a good commercial treaty for us and take care that John Bull gets no advantage of you—if anything get the weather gauge of him. . . ." Henry Clay, when making a desperate bid for political advantage by advocating the recognition of the Spanish-American insurgents, taunted John Quincy Adams with his dependence upon England. "If Lord Castlereagh says we may recognize, we do; if not, we do not," said Clay, and he evidently hoped to profit by the popular dislike for England. The jealousy felt by the mercantile interests of the United States was revealed by the following remark of the New York *Commercial Advertiser:* "A few days since we took the liberty, in a short paragraph, to call the attention of the American merchants to the vast markets about to be opened to the enterprise of the world, in the late American colonies of Spain; and we now beg leave again to direct their attention to the same subject, as we all are apprehensive notwithstanding our propinquity to them, that the vigilant and indefatigable John Bull will get the start of us." The influence of suspicion of British motives in preventing Monroe's administration from accepting Canning's proposal of a joint declaration against the intervention of the Continental powers in Spanish America has already been referred to. Adams, who felt this suspicion most keenly, remarked: "The object of Canning appears to have been to obtain some public pledge from the government of the United States, . . . against the acquisition to the United States themselves of any part of the Spanish-American possessions." He also feared that, by such a joint declaration, the United States would diminish its prestige and fall too much under the influences of Great Britain.

During the four years following the promulgation of the Monroe Doctrine this mutual suspicion and rivalry between the two branches of the Anglo-Saxon family revealed itself on numerous occasions. In the contest for trade and a dominant political influence in Hispanic America, Great Britain, under the leadership of George Canning, was the more aggressive rival; but the United States, once the combat had been joined, frequently managed to return blow for blow. The struggle is illustrated in the attempts at mediation between Argentina and Brazil, in the discussions regarding the status of Cuba, in the attitude of the two governments toward the Panama Congress, and, clearest of all, in the procedure of the agents of the rivals in Mexico.

In the contest Britain had almost every advantage: the prestige of a great and victorious nation; better trained diplomats; the good will of Spanish Americans won by the aid of hundreds of British subjects in the Wars of Independence; her great ability to supply the markets of the New World; capital to lend the struggling new republics. The United States, on the other hand, had only the advantages of being a republic and of having granted prior recognition—and the former even constituted a disadvantage in certain regions where the leaders were strongly monarchical in sympathy.

RIVALRY IN THE PLATA AREA

The war between Argentina and Brazil over the lower eastern bank of the Río de la Plata—a heritage of the old Spanish-Portuguese dispute—gave Canning an opportunity to counteract the notion of nonintercourse between Europe and America. He took advantage of the occasion to teach these states to lean upon England. Both belligerents had appealed to the United States for aid under certain contingencies; but its policy of nonentanglement had led the Washington government to refrain from action and maintain neutrality. The efforts of the United States minister in Brazil to carry out this policy offended the Brazilian government and apparently placed the United States in a position where it could not have served as mediator had it desired to do so. Canning, on the other hand, was diligent in his attempts to mediate the dispute; and although he did not live to see it brought to a successful conclusion, his efforts laid the basis for a satisfactory settlement under British auspices in 1828.

Canning was particularly anxious regarding the outcome of the struggle because he feared that the Spanish-American states might organize a republican league and overthrow the Brazilian monarchy. In this event, he believed, England would lose an important point of contact with the New World, and since Emperor Iturbide (of Mexico) had already fallen, there would be no monarchy left in America to cure the "evil of universal democracy." Almost from the beginning Canning feared that his plan of mediation was likely to be interfered with by his American rival, for he remarked that "jealousy" of Great Britain had been "openly inculcated by the publick press of the United States . . . , and no doubt secretly by their diplomatic agents."

Mutual Suspicions Regarding Cuba

Canning and the American cabinet suspected each other's designs upon Cuba from the time when he took charge of the British Foreign Office until death ended his career. On October 11, 1822, Canning wrote to the British minister at Washington of various indications that the United States desired to seize Cuba, but cautioned him against imputing such a design to the administration lest the charge suggest the very evil "which it deprecates." In 1825 he suspected that the United States was searching for an excuse to occupy the island; for at this time he remarked, "The Yankees may be just the rogues that we have always taken them to be, but which I was willing to hope they might have resolved to be no longer." In 1826, still uneasy with respect to the ambitions of the United States, Canning instructed the special representative of the British government in Panama to warn the Spanish-American states that a concerted attempt on their part to drive the Spaniards out of Cuba might end in the occupation of the island by their North American neighbor.

There is just as convincing evidence of suspicion of the Cuban designs of Great Britain among American statesmen. In the autumn of 1822 Monroe's cabinet was alarmed at the prospect of the seizure of Cuba by England. On December 17, John Forsyth, American minister at Madrid, was directed to investigate the rumor that Britain was treating with Spain for the island and, in case he found it true, to declare that the United States desired Cuba to continue in Spanish hands. In June, 1823, Jefferson declared in a letter to Monroe that Cuba's "possession by England would be a calamity," and suggested that she might be persuaded to join the United States in a guaranty of the island to Spain. With respect to Canning's proposal to Rush in August, 1823, Madison suspiciously inquired: "What is the extent of Mr. Canning's disclaimer as to 'the remaining possessions of Spain in America'? Does it exclude further views of acquiring Puerto Rico, etc., as well as Cuba?" And so the apprehension continued. Just as the great English statesman passed away, the United States minister at Madrid wrote that, in case of war with Spain, England was planning to revolutionize Cuba and the Canary Islands in order "to establish British influence" there and "in the end, probably, to obtain territorial possession of them." If indeed such a project was entertained, it was perhaps in line with plans previously suggested by Canning, for on October 6, 1826, he had written to Liverpool: "One single word I must add in the deepest secrecy. God forbid war; but if Spain will have it, ought not we to think of the Havannah? Where else can we strike a blow? And what other blow would be so effectual? It would settle all better than half a dozen Peninsular campaigns."

The anxiety of both Great Britain and the United States was increased by the mysterious procedure of France in the West Indies and by the more or less open schemes of Colombia and Mexico to deliver Cuba from the Spanish yoke. Each branch of the Anglo-Saxon family sought to restrain the other by disavowing any designs upon Cuba, expressing a desire that the island should remain in the possession of the mother country, and declaring that it could not permit the island to fall into the clutches of any other power. England tried to commit the United States and France to a triple guaranty of Cuba to Spain; and the United States, unwilling to enter into this covenant with Britain, attempted to enlist the European powers in a concerted endeavor to secure the recognition of the insurgent states by Madrid, and thus circumvent the plans of Mexico and Colombia and place at rest all anxieties over the fate of Cuba. In this latter project the European states manifested a real interest, but they found Spain as indisposed as ever to agree to any compromise that the revolting colonies would accept. Nevertheless, these very rivalries of the powers saved Cuba to Spain, for, as the London *Courier* remarked, Cuba had during these early years become the "Turkey of trans-Atlantic politics, tottering to her fall, and kept from falling by those who contend[ed] for the right of catching her in her descent." Colombia and Mexico might have precipitated a crisis by invading the "pearl of the Antilles," but they were first dissuaded by England and the United States and afterwards rendered impotent by domestic discords. During the diplomatic contest Britain scored at least one point over the United States. At the Panama Congress which assembled in June, 1826, she was able to present herself as far less meddlesome and selfish in her Cuban policy than the United States had been.

THE PANAMA CONGRESS

Indeed, the rivalries of the two powers in Hispanic America never appeared more clearly than in connection with this congress. Edward J. Dawkins, whom the British government in response to the invitation of Colombia sent as representative to Panama, was instructed, among other things, to urge the new states to adopt British principles of maritime law, and to do so with vigor. Canning remarked that England would not object to the perfection of a Spanish-American alliance, but that "any project for putting the U. S. of North America at the head of an American Confederacy would be highly displeasing" to her. Thus it was to be Dawkins's duty to advance Britain's maritime interests, to detach the United States from a position of leadership, and to teach these young states to lean upon the experienced arm of Britain.

In one respect Canning misinterpreted American psychology and overestimated the ambitions of the United States in the Western Hemisphere. The majority of Americans were too completely converted to the notion of no entangling alliances to accept even the dignified position of head of a Pan-American league, nor were they desirous of effecting discriminations against the European powers in the markets of Hispanic America. But the interests of mother and daughter nevertheless conflicted at numerous points, as will clearly appear from an examination of the instructions of the delegates of the United States to the Panama Congress. They were directed, for instance, to insist upon the most-favored-nation principle, a broad definition of the rights of neutrals in time of war, and a restriction of the power of blockade. They were also instructed to urge that "whatever may be imported from any foreign country into any one American nation or exported from it in its own vessels may, in like manner, be imported into or exported from the same nation" in vessels of other nations. Lastly, they were directed to encourage these new states to resist European interference or encroachments and to strengthen their faith in republican institutions.

That the commercial phase of these instructions was aimed at Great Britain, there is no doubt. This fact is supported by the numerous references to the experience of the United States during the recent war (1812). It appears just as clearly in the following comments taken from the body of these instructions:

"At all times there has existed more inequality in the distribution among nations of maritime than of territorial power. In almost every age, some one has had the complete mastery of the ocean, and this superiority has been occasionally so great as to more than counterbalance the combined maritime force of all other nations, if such a combination were practicable. But when a single nation finds itself possessed of a power anywhere which no one, nor all other nations, can successfully check or countervail, the consequences are too sadly unfolded in the pages of history." [1]

Nor did the British fail to grasp the significance of these instructions. After they had been made public, in 1829, the London *Times* remarked: "There is an obvious anxiety throughout these long documents to assume . . . that all 'American' states are to constitute a system and a community of their own, recognizing interests and establishing maxims for their regulation as affects each other, and for their separate, exclusive, nay, repulsive use, as regards the other nations of the world. The first obvious consequence of such a scheme, if adopted by Mexico and the states of South America, would be to place the United States at the *head* of the new federation, in vir-

---

[1] For the entire instructions, see *International American Conference*, IV, 113 ff.

tue of superior strength, maturity, safety, commercial and political resources." [2]

A pamphlet published in England at about the same time presented a similar view. Its author declared that the United States had urged "infant states without maritime force, without the possibility of becoming maritime states for many generations, if at all," to adopt in their relations with Europe the "highest pretensions, which, in the maturity of her naval strength, the United States herself ever ventured to urge—and even then without the remotest hope of success." Instead of advising these budding nations to cultivate the most friendly intercourse with Europe and to avoid meddling where their interests were not concerned, the United States had said: "Take the highest ground in your negotiations with Europe, that an old-established, powerful state would propose. Insist that free ships shall make free goods. Demand also a definition of blockade." Nor was this all. "Having recommended to the new states that they should call upon us, to renounce in their favor, a belligerent right which we have never yet conceded to any other power, the elder branch of the American family further suggests to them the experiment of prevailing upon us to make a slight inroad into our navigation act. One of the principles of this code is, that we admit from other nations their own produce, in their own shipping, or in our own; but in no other, unless such produce be again exported from this country. Thus, a ship of the United States brings us cotton or tobacco from New York; but she cannot do so from Colombia; it must come from the latter country either in a Colombian or a British ship. Now, the government of the United States says to these young republics, 'America is one continent—insist in your treaties with Europe that it is one nation—and that it shall be so considered for all commercial purposes—that we, your elder brethren, may come to your ports, and be the carriers of your produce.'" [3]

What did the two rivals achieve at Panama? So far as the United States was concerned, the achievement may be summed up in a word: nothing. The delegates appointed by the Washington govern-

[2] Issue of May 18, 1829, quoted by Lockey in *Pan Americanism: Its Beginnings,* p. 420.
[3] Quoted by Lockey, *op. cit.,* pp. 420–421.

ment never put in their appearance at Panama. One died on the way; the other had not set out before news came of the adjournment of the congress to meet again at Tacubaya (Mexico). In view of the conflicting ideas and interests of the United States and the young Spanish-American nations, it was perhaps well that these representatives did not arrive. The British agent was present at Panama from beginning to end. Although he did not attend the deliberations of the congress, he appears to have held frequent informal conferences with the delegates. His presence supported British prestige and tended to diminish the influence of the United States.

Mexico the Buffer

Canning considered cordial and intimate relations with Mexico as the key to his "later American policy." In one of his memoranda urging British recognition of the Spanish-American states Canning said: "I believe we now have the opportunity (but it may not last long) of opposing a powerful barrier to the influence of the U[nited] S[tates] by an amicable connection with Mexico, which from its position must be either subservient to or jealous of the U[nited] S[tates]. In point of population and resources it is at least equal to all the rest of the Spanish colonies; and may naturally expect to take the lead in its connections with the powers of Europe. . . ." After he had converted the British cabinet to his viewpoint he wrote to his friend John Hookham Frere: "The thing is done. . . . The Yankees will shout in triumph; but it is they who lose most by our decision. The great danger of the time—a danger which the policy of the European System would have fostered, was a division of the World into European and American, Republican and Monarchical; a league of worn-out Govts., on the one hand, and of youthful and stirring Nations, with the United States at their head, on the other. *We* slip in between; and plant ourselves in Mexico. The United States have gotten the start of us in vain; and we link once more America to Europe. Six months more—and the mischief would have been done." [4]

These statements had been made in 1824 and in January, 1825.

[4] Temperley, "The Later American Policy of George Canning," *American Historical Review*, XI (1906), 781–782.

In December, 1822, two years before the British cabinet came to the recognition decision, Canning had accepted the offer of Patrick Mackie to go to Mexico at his own expense on an informal mission. In July and August, 1823, Guadalupe Victoria, as agent of the provisional government which had followed the overthrow of Iturbide, held four informal conferences with Mackie. Nothing of great importance was accomplished or could have been accomplished, considering the nature of Mackie's mission; but the Mexicans were pleased with British attentions and considered this event as the beginning of diplomatic relations between the two countries.

Just before the end of 1823 other British agents arrived in Mexico. They were Hervey, O'Gorman, and Ward, who had been sent out by Canning: (1) to report on the advisability of recognition; (2) to assure the Mexican government that Great Britain did not desire dominion over any portion of Spain's former colonies in America and would not allow them to fall "under the dominion of any other power"; and (3) tactfully to encourage the establishment of a monarchy in case they found Mexican leaders favorably disposed. This commission was so blinded by enthusiasm for Mexico's cause that it reported a stable government after only three weeks' observation and in spite of the fact that an important revolution was then in progress. A few days later Hervey actually guaranteed a loan to support the government in the crisis. For this act he was recalled, and Morier was sent out in his place.

Finally, on January 3, 1825, Canning announced his intention of recognizing the new states of Spanish America. On the same day, he prepared instructions to guide his Mexican commission in the negotiation of a commercial treaty. By April 6 these agents had negotiated an agreement which aroused great enthusiasm among the Mexican leaders. Indeed, it was so favorable to Mexico and so at variance with British policy that Canning refused to accept it.

But the fact that these British agents had, in their friendly fervor for Mexico, allowed themselves to exceed their instructions, did not immediately become known in Mexico City. Throughout the year 1824 and a good portion of the year 1825 the Mexican leaders repeatedly revealed sentiments of gratitude and cordiality toward England. In April, 1824, a public celebration of the birthday of the king of England was seriously considered. Early in the following January Lucas Alamán, Mexican minister of foreign relations, evinced in his report to Congress great partiality for Great Britain, giving her the chief credit for checking the designs of Continental Europe and mentioning the United States only incidentally. On the last day of May, Henry George Ward, a member of the British commission, was granted an enthusiastic reception as *chargé d'affaires* of the British government in Mexico. In a brief speech on this occasion President Victoria expressed profound gratitude for the services of Britain, referring to her as the great nation which was accustomed to sustain the liberties of the world. British popularity in Mexico was rising.

On the other hand, the influence of the United States was on the wane. The struggle for independence in Mexico, as in the remainder of Spanish America, had awakened interest and sympathy among the people of the United States. The government itself adopted a neutral policy, but soon announced the determination to extend recognition and oppose European designs of reconquest. Iturbide, head of the first independent government in Mexico, had expressed admiration for Clay and gratitude for his services in Mexico's behalf in the United States Congress. He had likewise predicted intimate relations between the United States and Mexico for the future. The provisional government which followed Iturbide's brief reign had evinced an equally friendly attitude, and Mexico's first republican constitution had been closely modeled after that of the United States. But these early promises of cordiality were not entirely fulfilled, for the Mexican leaders soon found grounds to suspect the aggressiveness of the United States. Don Luis de Onís, agent of the Spanish government in the United States since 1809, had filled the Mexican archives with alarming accounts of the purposes and ambitions of the Americans of the North, and had even published in 1820 a memorial representing both the government and citizens of the United States as entertaining the desire to expand southward immediately to Panama and ultimately to all the regions of the New World. These reports must have been sufficient to arouse distrust among the Mexican leaders. The menacing attitude of North American frontiersmen and utterances of dissatisfaction with the Louisiana boundary which came from the press and platform of the United States deepened this distrust into anxiety; and before the first minister of the United States arrived in Mexico the Mexican envoy at Washington had been directed to ascertain the attitude of the Adams administration respecting the question of limits between the two countries.

Joel R. Poinsett, who reached Mexico early in May, 1825, in the capacity of envoy extraordinary and minister plenipotentiary of the United States, was not slow to grasp the situation. From Vera Cruz, on May 5, he wrote: "The British government has anticipated us. . . . Their treaty is made, and . . . has been ratified by the lower house. . . . It is now before the Senate . . . no doubt appears to be entertained of the result." As soon as he reached Mexico City he managed to obtain a copy of the British treaty. President Victoria's response to Ward's presentation speech filled Poinsett with envious apprehension. It convinced the American envoy that the time had come to place the attitude of the United States toward Spanish America "in its true light." Accordingly, he took advantage of his public reception, on June 1, to congratulate the Mexican leaders upon the adoption of a republican form of government, to remind the audience of the sympathetic interest with which the people of the United States had viewed the struggle of their neighbors for independence, and to point out that England, in her official procedure toward Mexico, had merely followed the example set by the United States. Three days later he remarked in a letter to Clay that the British had evidently "made good use of their time and opportunities." He then went on to explain that the Mexican president and three members of his cabinet were pro-British, but he also noted, hopefully, that "we have a respectable party in both houses of Congress," and that a "vast majority of the people" were friendly toward the United States and suspicious of Great Britain.

That the American envoy's summary of the situation was essentially correct, is borne out by the testimony of the British chargé himself. The two agents agreed respecting the sentiments of the executive and his cabinet and disagreed only with reference to the uncertain attitude of the people.

Poinsett's instructions had directed him, among other things, to negotiate treaties of commerce and limits, respectively, and to encourage republicanism in Mexico. He soon concluded that he could not accomplish any of these things until a transformation had been effected in the Mexican cabinet. He therefore appears to have associated himself with the opposition with the view of influencing both the Mexican executive and the Mexican congress. He encouraged the formation of lodges of York Rite Masons, which were soon made to constitute the chief political machinery of the opposition party. By the latter part of September, 1825, a cabinet change somewhat favorable to the interests and ideals of the United States had been accomplished.

Soon afterwards Canning returned the British-Mexican treaty of April 6, 1825, unratified. It was now Ward's turn to become alarmed.

The British chargé immediately began to send to his chief accounts of American designs and ambitions which corresponded exactly with the apprehensions which Canning had expressed at the time he was pressing his recognition policy through the British cabinet. "It is the great object of the United States," Ward had written a few days before the Mexican cabinet reorganization took place, "to convince the natives of Spanish America, that there exists between them and their brethren of the North, a community of interests, in which no European power can share." "I think it highly probable," he added, "that they will take the earliest possible opportunity, of cultivating any disposition . . . which might be turned to account, in event of a rupture, at any future period, with Great Britain." After Ward had obtained a more complete revelation of Poinsett's views and influence, he reported: "The formation of a general American federation, from which all European Powers, but more particularly Great Britain, shall be excluded, is the great object of Mr. Poinsett's exertions." And he admitted that "many members of both chambers" had been induced to favor the project and were desirous of sanctioning it by a treaty. Ward viewed with no little anxiety the plans for the proposed Panama Congress, which he expected to furnish a possible occasion for perfecting these Pan-American ambitions.

CONTESTS OF WARD AND POINSETT

Under any circumstances it would have been Ward's duty to counteract the influence of the United States in Mexico. With reference to Mexico and indeed to all Spanish America, as has already

been noted, the interests and ambitions of the two branches of
the Anglo-Saxon family appeared to be widely divergent. Now that
Ward perceived the purposes and the power of Poinsett he was
spurred to even greater exertions. Convinced that the United States
had three objects in view—namely, to stultify European plans
and influence in America, to secure Mexican territory, and to negotiate a commercial treaty which would embody the maritime principles of the United States and grant important privileges to its merchants—and that all of them were opposed to British interests, the
British chargé endeavored to checkmate every move of the American
envoy.

The next two years accordingly witnessed a continuation of the
spirited contest between Ward and Poinsett. Neither employed
methods entirely above reproach, and both professed an unwillingness to enter the fray; but Ward appears to have been more aggressive and uncompromising. "I cannot but regret that the Agent
of the British government should imagine that whatever influence
I may acquire here must of necessity be averse to the interests of
the nation he represents." "I never have and never will oppose the
establishment of friendly relations between the new American States
and Great Britain on such principles as are not hostile to the United
States." This was the spirit of Poinsett. At the same time, Ward declared: "Nothing could have been further from my wishes, on Mr.
Poinsett's first arrival, than to enter into any contest of this description." But once the diplomatic struggle had begun, the British
agent pursued his supposed foe relentlessly. If Poinsett sought to
put through his negotiations by a sort of alliance with the *Yorkinos,*
it appears that the British chargé, with more caution and greater
finesse, associated himself with the opposing party. Ward charged
that Poinsett resorted to intrigue and slander in order to mar the
domestic felicity and destroy the influence of a fair favorite of
President Victoria, but he admitted having made use of this favorite in order to carry out his purposes with the Mexican government.
If Ward accused the American envoy of encouraging the publication
of propaganda calculated to foment suspicion against Great Britain
and advance the commercial and political ideals of the United
States, Poinsett alleged that Ward had published literature designed to prevent the negotiation of a satisfactory commercial treaty,

for Ward's own correspondence shows that he expended funds in preparing a map of Texas and in reprinting the abusive Onís memorial —and did this solely with the view of adding fuel to the flame of Mexican suspicion toward the United States. Each diplomat gave banquets and omitted to invite his rival in order that the occasion might be used to disparage and destroy the influence of the nation whose minister was conspicuous for his absence. Ward eagerly seized upon every opportunity to discredit Poinsett, carrying to the Mexican president numerous reports of the American envoy's utterances and making frequent appeals to the personal prejudices of this chief executive. Recalled early in 1827, the British chargé reported with evident exultation that Poinsett had not been invited to the farewell reception given in his honor.

The Texas question seems to have caused Ward anxiety both in 1825 and during the early days of February, 1827, when he received news of the Fredonian Revolt, an uprising of a few discontented American settlers in eastern Texas. He predicted that the declaration of independence which, according to reports, the Fredonians had made was but the first act in a drama which would end in the incorporation of the region between the Sabine and the Rio Grande into the American Union. He declared that this had been the "great object of Poinsett's mission. "I urged the President strongly," said Ward, "not to underestimate the importance of the contest, nor to imagine that in these adventurers, because they were adventurers, he would find a contemptible enemy:—I told him that they were Men reckless of danger,—excellent Marksmen, and so perfectly acquainted with the Country, that they would be able to meet upon their own ground more than double their number of Regular Troops;—In Short, that too much caution could not be displayed, until a Force was assembled, sufficient to bear down all opposition." [5]

THE AFTERMATH

Ward's Mexican mission ended in 1827, but the currents which he set in motion during his residence were to continue and to have far-reaching results. He had spared no effort in stimulating Mexican apprehensions with respect to the ambitions of the United States

[5] Ward to Canning, No. 34, *Confidential*, Feb. 21, 1827, F.O. 50 (31*), Mexico.

and the menace of the American "backwoodsmen" in Texas. He had expressed his conviction "both publicly and privately, that the Great End of Mr. Poinsett's Mission" was to "embroil Mexico in a Civil War, and to facilitate, by doing so, the Acquisition of the Provinces to the North of the Rio Bravo, by the United States." He had been instrumental in causing the Victoria administration to send to Texas a commission headed by Mier y Terán, of whose unfriendly attitude toward the American settlers he was well aware. He had spread propaganda tending to convince the Mexican reading public of the greed and perfidy of their neighbor. The effect of these acts was irrevocable.

The sequel of Ward's machinations may be observed to some extent in Mexican attacks upon Poinsett. It certainly may be read in the reports of Terán and in the Mexican regulations based upon them. Soon after arriving in Texas this commissioner began to compose alarming accounts of conditions in the province. In a private letter to President Victoria, written from Nacogdoches on June 30, 1828, he remarked: "The whole population here is a mixture of strange and incoherent parts without parallel in our federation: numerous tribes of Indians, now at peace, but armed and at any moment ready for war . . . ; colonists of another people, more progressive and better informed than the Mexican inhabitants, but also more shrewd and unruly; among these foreigners are fugitives from justice, honest laborers, vagabonds and criminals, but honorable and dishonorable alike travel with their political constitutions in their pockets, demanding the privileges, authority and offices which such a constitution guarantees. The most of them have slaves, and these slaves are beginning to learn the favorable intent of the Mexican law toward their unfortunate condition and are becoming restless under their yoke, and the masters, in the effort to retain them, are making their yoke even heavier; they extract their teeth, set on the dogs to tear them in pieces, the most lenient being he who but flogs his slaves until they are flayed. . . ."

Terán then went on to give the following warning: "It would cause you the same chagrin that it has caused me to see the opinion that is held of our nation by these foreign colonists, since, with the exception of some few who have journeyed to our capital, they know no other Mexicans than the inhabitants about here, and excepting the authorities necessary to any form of society, the said inhabitants are the most ignorant of negroes and Indians, among whom I pass for a man of culture. Thus, I tell myself that it could not be otherwise than that from such a state of affairs should arise an antagonism between the Mexicans and foreigners, which is not the least of the smoldering fires . . . I have discovered. Therefore, I am warning you to take timely measures. Texas could throw the whole nation into revolution." [6]

A subsequent letter written under Terán's direction to the Mexican minister of war early in January, 1830, reveals an even more decided distrust of the United States and of the loyalty of the American colonists in Texas. In fact, he went so far as to charge the United States government of collusion in the Fredonian Revolt of 1826–1827 in the eastern part of that state. He also outlined in this letter a plan for checkmating the influence of American settlers in Texas and binding the region more closely to the central government. The encouragement of European and Mexican settlers and the increase of the army were the most important recommendations.

The man under whose eager scrutiny these reports ultimately fell was none other than Lucas Alamán, of whose pro-British sentiments Poinsett had often complained. Several upheavals in Mexican politics had brought him for the third time to the Foreign Office. On January 14, 1830, he sent to the chief executive a preliminary statement based upon the document last analyzed. He had nothing new to offer save a suggestion that Great Britain be invited to make a declaration against any design of the United States upon Texas. On February 8 he transmitted his report to Congress. Except for three recommendations, Alamán simply reiterated the charges and suggestions of Terán. On April 6 Congress accepted his report virtually as presented. At last the Texans were to be taken in hand, and this at the very time when their seven-year tariff exemption had expired and when colonists for the most part with a free-trade philosophy were beginning to feel the weight of a revenue system compared with which the "abominable" duties of the United States Act of 1828 were mild indeed. Moreover, the official who was designated to enforce and carry out all these measures was the same

[6] Quoted by Alleine Howren, "Causes and Origin of the Decree of Apr. 6, 1830," *Southwestern Historical Quarterly*, XVI (1913), 395–398.

Mier y Terán who owed his connection with Texas affairs to Henry George Ward! Events now moved with all the inexorableness of fate toward the Texas revolution. For precipitating this event it is fair to assume that the British chargé was partially responsible.

Britain's Official Responsibility

Were Ward's activities in Mexico duly authorized by the British government? The evidence is somewhat indefinite, but rather conclusive. Canning's American policy, which had as its keynote the checkmating of the influence of the United States by the establishment of British predominance in Mexico, surely must have been known to Ward. This fact being granted, Canning probably thought detailed instructions not only unnecessary but even, under certain possible conditions, inconvenient. Certainly it would be safer to allow Ward, with his general knowledge of the views of his chief, to rely upon his own discretion. If the chargé got his chief into trouble, the chargé could be disowned; if he carried out measures which without undue risk would advance the interests of Great Britain, these might be turned to advantage. The information now available indicates that this was Canning's general attitude.

Moreover, there is no indication that Canning ever reprimanded Ward for publishing and circulating a map of Texas and the Onís memorial with a view to arousing suspicion of the designs of the United States and its citizens; and a few years after the death of the great English statesman one of his devoted followers, who had special knowledge of his American policy, said in the House of Commons: "If the United States have declared that they cannot allow the island of Cuba to belong to any maritime power in Europe, Spain, excepted, neither can England, as the first of those maritime powers—I say it fearlessly, because I feel it strongly—suffer the United States to bring under their dominion a greater portion of the shores of the Gulf of Mexico than that which they now possess." [7]

Great Britain's Early Victory

So in the years immediately following Monroe's trumpet blast the two Anglo-Saxon nations engaged in spirited rivalry at various

[7] William Huskisson, *Speeches* (ed. 1831), pp. 579–580. Speech of May 20, 1830.

points in the New World. In general, it must be admitted that Great Britain was the victor both politically and commercially. Her success in Mexico, the Plata region, and Panama has already been pointed out, and her superior political position finds further illustration in the contemporary journals and state papers of Hispanic America. When publicists and statesmen expressed gratitude for services in the past or hopes for support in the future, England usually came in for first mention. England probably held first place in their esteem in 1827.

In fact, the interpretation which the United States placed upon the Monroe Doctrine during the first months after its promulgation was in some sense a disappointment to the leaders of Hispanic America. The statesmen south of the Rio Grande naturally revealed curiosity as to the exact meaning of the pronouncement as well as an eagerness to give it an application favorable to their interests. The Colombian government, having been alarmed by French activities, called for assistance in July, 1824. Secretary of State Adams replied that the president did not believe an intervention of the European powers now threatened. Whenever he decided that such danger was imminent he would lay the matter before Congress. In any event, the United States "could not undertake resistance to them by force of Arms, without a previous understanding with those European Powers whose Interests and whose principles would secure from them an active and efficient coöperation in the cause. . . ." "The employment of a Spanish force in America, while Spain is occupied by a French army and . . . under the influence of France and her allies, does not constitute a case upon which the United States would feel themselves justified in departing from . . . neutrality. . . ." Somewhat later the Brazilian government, no doubt encouraged by Monroe's message, appealed to President Adams. It asked him to sign a convention to preserve the Brazilian nation against any attempt at reconquest by Portugal or any other European power. It also suggested that the United States and the states of Spanish America unite in a league of defense against the Neo-Holy Alliance. Secretary Clay replied that the Monroe Doctrine would not be involved in the attempt of a mother country to reconquer her colony and ignored the reference to other European powers. A short time previously, Poinsett had explained to Mexico that the Monroe Doctrine was merely a pledge binding on the chief executive but not on the nation unless sanctioned by Congress. The president of Mexico understood this to mean that "the Memorable promise of President Monroe" was "disclaimed." "We have no longer any sort of Guarantee or Promise, on the part of that Government, to take part in the Contest, if a Third Power should become an Auxiliary of Spain," remarked the Mexican executive. Lastly, in response to a plea for assistance in possible contingencies, Henry Clay informed the government of the United Provinces of La Plata that the Congress of the United States alone could decide whether the Monroe Doctrine would be enforced, and that the Doctrine did not constitute a pledge which foreign nations might call upon the United States to fulfill.

Such were the early interpretations of Monroe's manifesto. In them is found little of the purple glow of republican enthusiasm. They certainly could not have added to the prestige of the United States in Latin America. It is no reflection upon the intelligence of statesmen to the south of the United States that they looked upon England as a better friend and champion.

Canning likewise obtained a degree of commercial hegemony. Before his death he had negotiated satisfactory commercial treaties with Buenos Aires, Colombia, Mexico, and Brazil. As late as 1829 the United States had secured only three—namely, agreements with Brazil, Colombia, and Central America. In 1827 British trade with Latin America was nearly three times that of the United States.

Britain's early opposition to the commercial expansion and the political influence of the United States in Latin America had been in no small degree a success. It was to be a long time, however, before that term could be applied again without qualification to the attempts of British statesmen to oppose the policy of the United States in this region.

CHAPTER XVIII

SUBSEQUENT RELATIONS BETWEEN THE UNITED STATES AND ENGLAND WITH REFERENCE TO HISPANIC AMERICA

THE European nations most deeply concerned in the Latin-American policy of the United States between 1830 and 1856, as in the period of 1808–1830, were Great Britain, France, and Spain. The vast territorial acquisitions of the young American republic since it had obtained its independence served to increase their apprehension. England continued to play the leading rôle, and Mexico continued to be an important field of rivalry; but Central America gradually increased in prominence, and occasionally there was a shift to Cuba, the Dominican Republic, and even to some of the states of South America.[1] After 1856 the relations of the two Anglo-Saxon nations with reference to Latin America became more cordial; but the United States then confronted more active opposition on the part of France and Spain, and at one period (1898–1917) suffered considerable uneasiness with reference to the policy of Germany.

The continuance of Canning's devoted followers in politics kept his Mexican policy before the English public. On May 20, 1830, William Huskisson told the House of Commons, as already noted in another connection, that England could never "suffer the United States to bring under their dominion a greater portion of the shores of the Gulf of Mexico than that which they now possess." He remarked that the United States had its eyes upon both Texas and the eastern coast of Mexico and urged his government to renewed effort in behalf of Spanish recognition of that republic. "Let Mexico be at ease in respect to attacks from Spain," he said, "and she will soon become a valuable ally of this country [Great Britain], with

---

[1] Rivalries in the Dominican Republic and South America were of minor importance. When England annexed the Falkland Islands in 1833, the United States made no protest, nor did the Washington government evince great concern with reference to Anglo-French procedure in the Plata region in 1845–1850.

all her interests bound up and identified with the best interests of Great Britain in the New World. On the other hand, let her remain much longer in her present harassed and exhausting condition, and the poverty of her treasury,—the necessity of making head against those attacks, may throw her into the arms of the United States, and force her to sacrifices which would inevitably bring on a maritime war, unless this country be prepared to abandon her colonial empire, her commercial pretensions, and, with them, her maritime ascendency in the New World." [2]

Britain and the Texas Issue

When news of the Texas revolution reached England the supporters of the Canning tradition immediately brought up the matter in the House of Commons. On August 5, 1836, Barlow Hoy moved "that an humble Address be presented to his Majesty, praying him to direct, that such measures may be taken as may seem proper to secure the fulfillment of the existing treaty between this country and Mexico; and to prevent the establishment of slavery and traffic in slaves in the province of Texas, in the Mexican territory." Hoy's speech in defense of his motion constituted an appeal to merchants, capitalists, and humanitarians. British merchants had "embarked 70,000,000 dollars in the Mexican dominions. . . . Neither ought the importance of the possession of the mining districts by America be lost sight of by this country. The mines of Texas were of immense value. . . . Unless Mexico was assisted, as she ought to be by this country, she would be so weakened as soon to become an easy victim to the ambition of the United States. . . ." Again, "There could be no doubt, that if Texas were added to the Union, the basis of the connexion would be to establish slavery, and the slave-trade, permanently, in that province." Would Great Britain, which was now spending more than a million pounds sterling per annum in suppressing and abolishing slavery, render that whole expenditure useless by a refusal to interfere in Texas? Moreover, if the United States should acquire this fertile region, it would thereby be "brought within six weeks sail of China"; and, besides, "would not Cuba and the other Spanish possessions in the Gulf of Mexico then soon fall a prey to the United States?" He therefore contended that England

---

[2] Huskisson, *Speeches* (1831), III, 585–586.

"ought to afford every species of assistance to Mexico, not only by remonstrating in an amicable manner with the United States, but by sending out a naval force to assist Mexico against Texas, and to prevent aggression by the United States."

Hoy's motion was seconded by none other than Henry George Ward, now the representative for St. Albans in the House of Commons! Ten years had not dimmed his memory regarding his Mexican experiences, nor modified his views respecting the purposes and methods of the United States. He was sure that American political leaders were operating in collusion with American frontiersmen to deprive Mexico of the fertile lands of Texas. "There were two considerations which ought to weigh with" British statesmen in regard to the Texas issue. "The first was the question of general policy—whether it were advisable to allow the United States to pursue a system of aggrandisement without any endeavour on our part to check them, and to allow the extension of their territory to the Rio Bravo . . . in such manner as to obtain for them the absolute command of the Gulf; for certainly the acquisition of Texas would give them that command, and would enable them with half a dozen privateers to shut us out entirely from our present trade with Mexico, leaving us no route whatsoever by which to maintain a commercial intercourse with that country save that leading around Cape Horn to its western coast. . . ." The other consideration was that of "moral feeling which must influence every Gentleman acquainted with the condition of Society in the Western States of the Union, and every Gentleman aware of the incalculable misery which the system of slavery, there prevailing, inflicted upon so many millions of human beings."

The reply of Viscount Palmerston, head of the British Foreign Office, indicated that he refused to take the danger seriously. He declared that an address to the Crown at that time would be "in some respects unnecessary, and in other respects premature." "With regard to the political branch of the subject, undoubtedly the probability of the province of Texas being added to the United States . . . would be a subject which ought seriously to engage the attention of the House and of the British public. But with regard to that question he did not think that the events which had so far occurred, afforded any ground to think that there was at present any such probability" as to call for the motion under consideration. "He had too high an opinion of the honour and good faith of the government of the United States not to believe that it would act up to the declarations it had made upon the subject." He ignored the matter of slavery in Texas and expressed doubt as to the existence of any important slave-trade with the province. Nor did he answer the inquiry which Hoy had made with reference to the question whether Mexico had sought the good offices of England in order to prevent the acquisition of Texas by the United States.[3]

Thus it will be observed that in 1836 the followers of Canning, and even Palmerston himself, looked with disfavor upon the southward expansion of the United States. They disagreed only with respect to the immediate probability of such expansion. It will likewise be observed that British support of the Mexican government had become almost traditional in the Foreign Office. During the next decade, however, Texas gradually took the place of Mexico in the American policy of Great Britain.

There were many good reasons for English interest in this new state. It might in the future serve both as a barrier between the United States and Spanish America and as a producer of raw cotton which would relieve British manufacturers of their embarrassing dependence upon the southern states of the American Union; and, if it could be induced to adopt free labor and free trade, it might be a means at one and the same time of advancing British commerce, legitimate and illegitimate,[4] and of striking a blow at the slavery interests of the United States.

Thus, although at first the government of Great Britain appeared to be desirous of seeing Mexico reconquer Texas, by the close of 1838 it decided that reconquest would be extremely difficult, if not impossible. Thereafter it held that further continuation of hostilities between Texas and Mexico would result in injury to British interests, which had now come to be important in both countries. Accordingly, the Foreign Office undertook to mediate between the combatants and to persuade Mexico to recognize her revolting province, although England herself delayed recognition until 1842 in the

---

[3] Hansard, *Parliamentary Debates,* 3rd Series, XXXV, 928–942.

[4] It was felt that Texas might be made the base for extensive smuggling into the United States.

vain hope that the abolition of slavery in Texas might be exacted as a price for this favor. Meanwhile, the United States and France had extended recognition, but Mexico had remained obdurate and was still brandishing threats and wasting money on the Texas question. In all this there was cause for regret and irritation to Great Britain, but the ministry, lulled into a sense of security by the refusal of the United States to annex Texas in 1837 and by what it supposed was a growing sentiment among the Texans themselves against incorporation into the American Union, felt that there was no real cause for alarm. Toward the close of 1843 it was rudely shaken from this false assumption of security.

The shock was occasioned by reports from British diplomatic agents in the United States and Texas that the government at Washington had informally but earnestly suggested that the struggling young republic join the Union, and that President Tyler's annual message hinted at annexation. London immediately sounded out Paris, and an agreement for a joint protest was attempted. Early in May, 1844, the British government was further perturbed by the notice that the United States and Texas had signed an annexation treaty. Just before the close of the month the British secretary of state for foreign affairs had a very earnest interview with Patrick Murphy, the Mexican representative at London. The report of this interview, drawn up by Murphy and corrected by the head of the British Foreign Office runs as follows:

"Lord Aberdeen [the British foreign secretary] expressed a wish to see Mexico acknowledge the independence of Texas. 'If Mexico,' he said, 'will concede this point, England (and I have reason to believe that France will join her in this determination) will oppose the annexation of Texas and moreover *he would endeavor that* France and England will unite in guaranteeing not only the independence of Texas, but also the boundary of Mexico. On the other hand should Mexico persist in declining to recognize Texas, the intentions of England to prevent the annexation of that country might not be put into execution.' Upon my remarking that it was not at all probable [that] the American Government would be willing to drop the annexation affair, even should the American Senate reject the Treaty for the present, Lord Aberdeen replied that *provided that*

England and France were perfectly agreed, 'it would matter little to England whether the American Government should be willing to drop this question or not, and that, should it be necessary, she would go to the last extremity in support of her opposition to annexation; but that for this purpose it was essential that Mexico be disposed to acknowledge the independence of Texas.' "

A few weeks later Aberdeen announced to the Texas diplomatic agent in London that England and France would be willing to unite with Texas, the United States, and Mexico in a diplomatic act designed to secure Texas independence, prevent annexation, and guarantee the Texas-Mexican boundary. Smith, the Texas diplomatic agent, inferred from the interview that England and France were prepared to use force to compel Mexican acquiescence, and that the United States was not expected to come into the plan.

But England's scheme depended upon the attitude of France, Mexico, and Texas. In the summer of 1844 Texas and France appeared to be willing to coöperate, but Mexico refused to comply with the demands made upon her. Soon afterwards Britain decided to await the result of the elections of November, 1844, in the United States. By the time news of the election of Polk on an expansion platform reached Europe, the French government had been forced by popular clamor to decline to support England in further opposition to the United States. Aberdeen then definitely stated to Murphy what had been implied in his position all along; namely, that England alone would not engage in a war with the United States over the Texas issue. Soon afterwards news that the annexation resolutions had passed the United States Congress reached London. Aberdeen thereupon decided to make one more effort to prevail upon Mexico to acknowledge Texas and to persuade Texas to give a pledge not to enter the American Union. This decision was followed by eleventh-hour attempts of British diplomats in Texas and Mexico to accomplish these ends, with results which are well known. All of Aberdeen's instruments had failed him: France had refused to lend aid to the extent of the employment of armed force; Mexico had procrastinated in the matter of recognition; and Texas had at last voted to accept the very destiny which Great Britain had been so eager that this republic should escape.

THE MEXICAN WAR

Nevertheless Mexico had not yet perceived the futility of expecting European aid in her difficulties with the United States. On July 30, 1845, after the annexation of Texas had been consummated, the Mexican government sent identical dispatches to its ministers in Paris and in London. They were instructed to say that Mexico had no recourse left but war with the United States; that she felt she would be unworthy of a place among civilized nations if she failed to prosecute hostilities with vigor; that fourteen thousand troops were now on their march to the frontier and six thousand more were shortly to follow them; and that Mexico had been led by their former interest in Texas to hope that the governments of France and England would lend the cause of the Mexican nation their sympathy and moral support. To Murphy in London was sent another "most secret" instruction stating that the Americans had officially announced a determination to seize the Californias and directing this agent to request Britain's "co-operation to prevent the loss of that important part of her [Mexico's] territory."

Aberdeen and Sir Robert Peel evinced profound interest in preventing California from falling into the hands of the United States. The former consented to sound France once more on the matter of guaranteeing Mexican territorial integrity, and held out a somewhat indefinite promise of alliance with Mexico. On February 1, 1846, Murphy summed up the situation as it appeared to him: "Our position under present circumstances appears to me to be as follows: England will do nothing, either directly or indirectly, to forestall the usurpation of California so long as the Oregon question remains unsettled. If war breaks out, all difficulty on the part of this Cabinet will have ceased, and there is no doubt that one of their first objects will be, in that event, to prevent that usurpation. If on the contrary the dispute over Oregon is amicably settled, England will find herself more free to act in respect to California,—openly and directly in case France continues in the line of policy she has just adopted and lends her aid,—or indirectly by means of some plan of colonization in California."

The reports of the British agents in Europe and the comments of the British and French press appear to have led the Mexican government to anticipate European aid. From what they could learn of the Oregon issue, Mexican statesmen were fully confident that it would end in a trial of arms between the United States and England. Accordingly, when news of the clash with the troops of Taylor in the Rio Grande-Nueces region reached Mexico City it found the Mexicans all the more eager for the combat. They argued somewhat as follows: "Our honor will be vindicated by a brilliant stroke beyond the Rio Grande; European intervention will then occur; the United States will have to pay a round sum for Texas; and we shall obtain a fixed boundary, guaranteed by the leading powers of Europe, that will serve as an everlasting dike against American aggression." [5]

Time of course soon revealed that Mexico had sadly miscalculated. A few days after the outbreak of the war the Oregon dispute was pacifically adjusted, and Great Britain—whether restrained by indisposition to engage in hostilities with the United States or by inability to commit France, it is not now possible to say—flatly refused to lend aid.

On June 1, 1846, Aberdeen directed Bankhead to inform the Mexican government that Great Britain could not depart from the policy of noninterference. "Were Great Britain to interfere in that quarrel, She would involve herself in a war with the United States; and not only that, but She must necessarily play the part, not merely of an auxiliary, but of a principal, in such war; that is, She would find herself engaged in a war with a Nation with which She would have no personal cause of quarrel, in behalf of a Nation and Govt. which she has repeatedly warned in the most friendly and urgent manner of their danger, and which, solely in consequence of their wilful contempt of that warning, have at last plunged headlong down the precipice from which the British Govt. spared no efforts to save them. . . ."

Britain was mainly concerned, after the war had once begun, in a speedy return to peace. During the early months of the struggle she made two vain overtures looking toward mediation, and later, when Nicholas P. Trist, the American peace commissioner, arrived

[5] Smith, *The War with Mexico* (1919), I, 112–116. It should also be remembered that even before the clash took place between American and Mexican troops south of the Nueces, the executive government of the United States had resolved upon war. The motives —alleged and real—were a desire for territory and the settlement of claims.

in Mexico he found British diplomatic agents ready to coöperate with him in securing the acceptance of the olive branch by the unsteady Mexican government. These agents were not authorized, however, to go so far as to guarantee the integrity of the Mexican territory remaining after American demands had been met. Moreover, this suggestion of British guaranty was energetically rejected by Trist. Thus Mexico was left to defend her new boundary without any pledge of assistance from abroad.

BRITAIN AND THE MEXICAN POLICY OF THE UNITED STATES (1848–1856)

Britain's pledge of 1825, that she would not permit the seizure of Spanish-American territory, had been tried and found wanting. England, when the test came, was unwilling to assume the responsibility of a war with the United States in order to save Mexico. This did not mean, however, that all support of the country against the United States was to be withdrawn. The Foreign Office was still resolved to employ all the resources of diplomacy to prevent the domination or absorption of Mexico by its neighbor on the north. The years immediately subsequent to 1848 were to offer ample illustration of this resolution.

The British government was still deeply interested in Mexican commerce and in the investments of its subjects in Mexico. These would be gravely injured, it was thought, if the United States should acquire the mines of northern Mexico, exclusive transit and colonizing privileges on the Isthmus of Tehuantepec, or additional Mexican territory bordering on the Gulf of Mexico. Accordingly, the Foreign Office gave its attention first and foremost to defeating real or apprehended designs of the Yankees in these regions.

With reference to the Isthmus of Tehuantepec, British diplomacy brought pressure to bear upon Mexico in order to prevent too liberal concessions being made to the United States and to persuade the Mexican government to place the region under a joint guaranty of America and Britain. Overtures looking toward the latter arrangement were also made to the United States, but with little success. The Clayton-Bulwer Treaty was considered by Washington as sufficient impediment to the achievement of its isthmian ambitions.

Indeed, Britain once urged that Article VIII of that agreement applied to Tehuantepec. Fortunately for the harmony of the two branches of the Anglo-Saxon family, the persistent improbability that the canal could be completed rendered the contentions over the affair largely theoretical.

In regard to territorial matters, England could only discourage Mexico from projected sales and urge a pacific policy toward the United States in order that the catastrophe of 1848 should not be repeated. These steps were taken time and again between 1848 and 1856, the British agents showing their concern by keeping the closest possible watch over all negotiations between Mexico and the United States regarding territory. On one occasion, indeed, the British and French ministers in Washington, in obedience to instructions, sounded Secretary of State Marcy on certain plans of purchase supposed to be under way. Diplomatic interposition, however, unless supplemented by financial support or material aid in some other form, could be of little service. More than once Mexico sought in vain for British, and indeed French and Spanish, backing, but the Foreign Office constantly refused to grant it. In fact, Great Britain was not even willing to authorize a suspension of the payments on the Mexican bonded debt in order to prevent Santa Anna from selling what has become known as the "Gadsden Purchase." Hence British efforts to prevent the alienation of Mexican territory to the United States were confined to uttering forebodings and arousing suspicions. Such efforts in reality had very little weight. The United States failed to acquire Mexican domain after 1854, not so much because Mexico's political leaders had set their minds firmly against selling it, as because American political leaders could not agree upon the terms of purchase or indeed upon the desirability of purchasing territory at all.

The Cuban Issue

The foregoing discussion of the rivalries of the powers in Mexico renders any extensive treatment of the contest elsewhere in America unnecessary. Indeed the motives and policies were essentially the same whether they referred to Mexico, Cuba, the Dominican Republic, Central America, or other areas.

British interest in Cuba centered mainly around questions of commerce, investments, strategy, and slavery. If Cuba were prosperous,
the revenues of the island might enable Spain to meet her obligations under the heavy British loans outstanding. If the island should
persist in a state of constant insurgency and maladministration, this
prospect would disappear. Similarly, disturbances in the island might
lead the United States to annex it, and this might have essentially
the same result. Moreover, this latter step, like the acquisition of
Mexican territory, would strengthen America's hold on the Gulf and
bolster up the southern slave power. For all these reasons, Britain
set her face firmly against the acquisition of this key to the Gulf by
the United States.

In opposing the expansion of the United States in this direction,
however, the British government appears to have been unwilling to
press matters to the point of an open break. It could insist upon the
suppression of the slave trade with the island without running such
a risk; and this it did. The British government, however, does not
appear to have meddled with the status of slavery itself, although
certain enthusiastic British abolitionists appear to have done so. Nor
was it willing alone at this time to offer Spain what it had been unwilling in the last resort to grant Mexico—a guaranty of territorial
integrity against the encroachments of the United States. It was prepared, however, to use its navy against the American filibusters who
were launching expeditions against Cuba, and it also tried to persuade the United States to sign with England and France a tripartite
guaranty insuring Spain perpetual dominion over the island. Moreover, British diplomats probably encouraged the Spanish government in its resolution not to sell the island, and they certainly urged
Spain to adopt a moderate policy toward Mexico (1857-1858) largely
because they feared that the United States would take advantage of
a Hispano-Mexican war in order to seize Cuba.

But it must be admitted that all of these efforts were somewhat
superfluous. Cuba was indeed retained by Spain during this critical
period, but for this retention British diplomacy deserved little credit.
Public opinion in the United States was divided on the proposed
acquisition of Cuba, and Spain's resolution not to sell the island
needed little tonic. In order to prevent the United States from annexing Cuba, Britain had employed every resource and device of di-

plomacy; but a more profound knowledge of the situation might have saved her the trouble.

THE CONTEST IN CENTRAL AMERICA

The contest of the United States and Britain in Central America was even more energetic than that which took place in Mexico. Mexico's population was much larger, its territory more extensive, and its subsoil resources more valuable; but its location, with respect to world commerce and sea power, was not as favorable as that of Central America. Between 1846 and 1856, in particular, there took place upon the Isthmus a spirited contest between the two branches of the Anglo-Saxon family which gradually became more critical until, near the end of the period, war actually threatened.

British interest in Central America began to develop long before the United States government came into existence. There were three centers of activity—Belize, the islands of Honduras Bay, and the Mosquito Coast—but Britain did not possess sovereignty over any of these regions nor any part of them prior to the proclamation of the Monroe Doctrine. British subjects had dwelt in Belize for the purpose of cutting logwood and collecting other natural products since 1662; they had alternately occupied and abandoned certain of the Bay Islands since 1642; they had maintained fitful settlements on the Mosquito Coast and more or less intimate relations with the natives of the region since the closing decades of the seventeenth century; but by a series of treaties extending from 1786 to 1814 the British government had acknowledged that it had no sovereign rights in these regions, nor were any such claims advanced until long after 1823.

In Central America, as elsewhere, the agents of George Canning expressed uneasiness regarding the designs of the United States; but American statesmen showed little concern regarding British procedure in the area during the Canning era and even down to the time when the acquisition of California became a certainty. Englishmen had only to deal with the weak Central American governments, and these they easily managed by setting state against state and party against party in a somewhat ruthless fashion. Central Americans appealed to Washington in vain; so far as the United States was concerned, Great Britain might work with a free hand.

Between 1830 and 1848 British influence expanded in all three of the regions which had long been the center of attraction in Central America. As early as 1821, in fact, British settlers in Belize had spread out to the south of the Sibun; and in 1838 the British government declared that the southern boundary of this settlement was the Sarstoon. At no time prior to 1848, however, did Britain consent to consider Belize a British colony. In similar manner the Mosquito king had been induced in 1841 to extend his dominion far enough south to take in the mouths of the San Juan and the town of that name; and when Nicaragua contested this claim, the British government supported the native monarch by force of arms, renaming the village Greytown. Lastly, after 1840 the British government came to the support of its subjects which had occupied Roatán, the largest of the Bay Islands. Clearly it was England's intention either to control the canal zone or to prevent the United States from doing so.

At last (1846) American interest in the Isthmus became aroused by these and other British activities, by Central American appeals for succor, and by the prospect of Pacific Coast possessions. While the Mexican War continued, however, the United States government was loath to enter the lists against the British in the Nicaragua region. It sent its agents instead to New Granada, where a treaty relating to Panama was negotiated in 1846. As the war came to a close, however, preparations were made to deal with the rival in Central America proper.

The United States assumed that it was the purpose of Great Britain to acquire territory in Central America and either to dominate the canal route or to obstruct the construction of the canal, and immediately set about to defeat these plans. This end might be accomplished by negotiations in Central America or in England, or in both. Effort was exerted first upon the Isthmus. Elijah Hise and then E. G. Squier were sent to advance the interests of the United States by the negotiation of canal treaties. But first the former agent and then the latter found his exertions fully matched by the work of Frederick Chatfield, the British consul-general. Canal treaties were obtained, but on terms which the United States was not prepared to ratify. Meanwhile (1849), negotiations were opened in England, and not without promise of achievement. William C. Rives, recently appointed minister to France, stopped in London on his way to the

French court and had a frank interview with Palmerston, British foreign secretary. In the course of the interview Palmerston was convinced that the United States, aggressive as its recent career had been, was not really resolved upon the exclusive control of the canal route. At the same time, Rives was given the impression that the main concern of the British had been not so much to monopolize the route as to prevent the United States from doing so. The way therefore seemed clear for mutual concessions and compromises, and negotiations were speedily begun.

They soon led to the Clayton-Bulwer Treaty, signed at Washington on April 18, 1850. That document was the result of a vigorous diplomatic encounter and, as was soon revealed, meant one thing to Clayton and an entirely different thing to Bulwer. Clayton's first purpose in the encounter had been to clear the way for the construction of a canal by an American company which had already obtained a concession from Nicaragua; but public opinion in the United States had forced him later to undertake to obtain from Britain an agreement to withdraw from Central America altogether. The prime concern of Bulwer, who was less interested in the immediate construction of a canal, was to exact from the United States a pledge not to expand into Central America and to do this without giving a reciprocal pledge that England would immediately withdraw. Both diplomats thought, or pretended to think, that they had accomplished their purpose, but it soon became evident that neither had accomplished anything of great importance. The United States government adopted the view of Clayton and demanded that Britain clear out of Central America immediately. The British government accepted the view of Bulwer and made no move to get out at all.[6]

In the meantime, the nationals and agents of the two governments in the contested area committed acts which increased the tension. British settlers and naval officers at Greytown interfered with American trade and transit, and American immigrants on their way to California often became involved in altercations with the British and their allies in Mosquitia. The agitation was heightened in 1852 by Britain's seizure of the Bay Islands and their organization into

[6] The treaty placed the potential canal route under the joint control of the United States and Great Britain and pledged both of these powers not to acquire territory in the region.

an English colony. Matters developed from bad to worse until on
July 13, 1854, the village of Greytown was bombarded by an American man-of-war and then burned to the ground. The act was plainly
a defiance of the British protectorate over the Mosquito Kingdom
which claimed jurisdiction in Greytown, and the London government might have resented it in a forceful manner had it not been
engaged in the Crimean War. As it was, the United States defended
the act of the naval officer, and Britain could do nothing except
remain firm in her Central American claims.

The climax came in the spring of 1856. Irritation in the United
States was still further increased in the latter part of 1855 by John
Crampton's violation of neutrality in soliciting recruits for the Crimean War while serving as minister in the United States. The United
States demanded his recall, but the British ministry refused to take
action. At the same time, there came evidence of Britain's active opposition to William Walker and his filibusters who were undertaking the conquest of Central America and meeting with no little
success because the United States winked at the defiance of its laws
forbidding such piratical operations. The United States at once
recognized the Walker government and broke off diplomatic relations with England. The politicians and the press congratulated
President Pierce, and a demand for war was heard in several quarters.
The situation was most critical, especially since the war in the
Crimea had just ended and left the British government free to act
if it chose.

BRITAIN BEGINS TO RECEDE (1856–1860)

But the crisis in Anglo-Saxon relations was destined to pass without hostilities. In the latter part of 1856 British opposition to the
southward expansion of the United States began to relax, and the
task of circumscribing the Yankees was left to others. After more
than thirty years of almost futile effort Britain slowly weakened,
abandoning one by one many of the positions which she formerly
maintained. It was perhaps this recession alone that prevented war.

Unmistakable indications of a change in the British attitude first
appeared in June. On June 14 the London *Economist* remarked:
"We could not hinder the ultimate absorption by the Anglo-

Saxon republicans of the whole of Central America if we would. . . . We can have no interest in upholding the present wretched and feeble governments of Spanish America. Our interest lies all the other way. We wish ourselves for no extension of territory on that continent. We are half inclined to regret that we hold any possession at all there south of the Union. Desiring no territory, we desire only prosperous, industrious, civilized, and wealthy customers.

". . . Central America peopled and *exploited* by Anglo-Saxons will be worth to us tenfold its present value. We have no fear that our countrymen will be excluded from the commerce of those provinces. We have no fear that our ships will be prohibited from crossing that isthmus when the two seas shall be joined by a canal." [7]

During the same month a writer in *Blackwood's Magazine* expressed similar sentiments. "Great Britain has no great interest in Central America," the writer declared. "She cannot consent to be bullied out of her rights there," he said, "but otherwise she has not the least desire to check the progress of American influence in that region. . . . The paths of Britain and America do not cross. The Isthmus of the New World is the goal of Transatlantic ambition. . . . The Isthmus of the Old World is the cynosure of British policy. . . ." [8]

Before the close of the year the London *Times* fell in line. "In the eye and forecast of the States," said the editor of this journal, "all North America is theirs excepting only those portions already belonging to European Powers, or . . . under a recognized European protection." "For our own part," he continued, "we see no reason why we should resist the process, except where a British community is established and demands our aid, or where some real interest can be shown to be at stake. . . . It must be for our interest to see North America under strong, civilized, uniform, and prosperous government. . . . It does not become us to play the dog in the manger with our fast-growing progeny across the Atlantic. They have too many good reasons, as well as too many bad ones, against allowing us to stand in their way for the mere sake of mischief or pride. . . ."

At the same time, British statesmen and diplomats began to ex-

[7] Quoted in *Littell's Living Age,* 2nd Series, XIV, 312.
[8] XXIX, 742.

press views of a similar nature. On June 16, 1856, Disraeli rose in the House of Commons to speak on the relations of the United States and Britain in America. He thought it would "be wise in England not to regard with the extreme jealousy with which she has hitherto looked upon it any extension of the territory of the United States beyond the bounds which were originally fixed." It was not sound policy to continue to oppose the "so-called 'aggressive spirit' of the United States." Such opposition would not prevent Yankee expansion; but it would involve England in struggles which might prove disastrous. And besides, might not the expansion of the United States in America prove advantageous to England? He recalled that the annexation of California by the United States had been looked upon in the House of Commons as a calamity, but he now asked his colleagues whether that conquest had disturbed the "balance of power" and, indeed, whether any event since the discovery of America had "contributed more to the wealth, and through the wealth, to the power of this country, than the development of the rich resources of California by . . . the United States." Disraeli then proposed a sort of reciprocity plan whereby Britain, by recognizing the necessity for Yankee expansion in the New World, might persuade the United States to abandon the two spheres conception embodied in the Monroe Doctrine as obsolete in an age of steam and expanding trade.[9]

Economic considerations were exerting a strong influence upon British thought. The southward extension of the United States might bring order and higher standards of living, thereby enlarging the market for British goods; and, besides, a war with the United States over the issue of expansion would be attended by economic consequences which could not lightly be passed over. The total value of the trade between Britain and the United States amounted to more than fifty million pounds sterling, and Yankee privateers were dreaded. The editors did not fail to note these facts,[10] and the statesmen soon decided to alter their course.

The Foreign Office considered the cotton trade of the United States as of greater importance than the British stake in Mexico and Central America, and diplomats began to act accordingly. Before the

[9] Hansard, *Parliamentary Debates,* 3rd Series, CXLII, 1511–1512.
[10] See excerpts in *Littell's Living Age,* 2nd Series, XIV, 119, 244.

close of the year attempts were made to harmonize English and American interests in Mexico. British holders of Mexican bonds began work on a scheme designed to divert into their coffers a portion of any cash which the United States might pay Mexico for territory. They strongly urged their plan both upon the Mexican government and upon the minister of the United States at Mexico City; and in the summer of 1856 Martínez del Rio, Mexican agent of the bondholders, visited Washington for the purpose of sounding certain senatorial leaders. Partly as a result of these machinations, perhaps, United States Minister John Forsyth signed a treaty (February 10, 1857) providing for a loan of fifteen million dollars to the Mexican government, four millions of which were to be applied on the British convention debt. Forsyth's procedure was unauthorized, and the loan agreement was not accepted either by President Pierce or by President Buchanan; but the idea made a deep impression on British diplomatic circles. After May 4, 1857, the English ministers in Mexico had standing instructions to the effect that the Mexican government would be expected to pay a portion of any sums received from the United States to British creditors and claimants.

Moreover, W. G. Lettsom, who took charge of the British legation in the summer of 1856, held views not essentially different from those expressed by Disraeli and the British journalists. In July, 1857, he remarked: "I conceive that the absorption of *half* of the Territory of Mexico by the United States would inflict greater injury on British Interests than if the whole Territory were annexed to that Country." He then went on to explain the meaning of this statement:

"If half the territory of Mexico is so absorbed, Mexico, as before, will be burthened with all her present liabilities, while the resources remaining at her disposal to cover them will be diminished by one half, and in this case I need hardly remark that it will be useless to expect she will fulfil her engagements. The manner in which the revenue of Mexico is always frittered away prevents the development of the resources of the Country, while the tariff is constantly such that consumption is impeded as much as possible.

"Were the whole of the Territory of this Republic annexed to the United States the latter Country would have to assume the liabilities of Mexico, the position of the numerous British claimants . . . would be at once ameliorated, while with the general activity then pervading this Country, with the development of its resources, and with the increase of its population, new wants would arise, and these British commerce would be called upon mainly to provide for." [11]

Furthermore, in July, 1858, Lord Malmesbury, British secretary of state for foreign affairs, remarked to George M. Dallas, minister of the United States at London, "that he [Malmesbury] was one of that class of statesmen who believed that all the southern part of North America must ultimately come under the government of the United States: that he had no objection to what seemed the inevitable course of things: that, on the contrary, he thought it would be beneficial as well to the population occupying the countries referred to as to the United States, and the rest of the world." [12] On January 7, following, in response to the sensational dispatches of Otway, the Foreign Office notified its minister that Great Britain would not join France in a dual intervention in Mexico, but that she would be willing to take part in a quadruple action embracing Spain and the United States as well as England and France.

For more than a year and a half this continued to be the policy of Great Britain. When the United States broke relations with the reactionary government in Mexico City and soon afterwards proceeded to recognize the liberal organization of Benito Juárez at Vera Cruz, the minister of the reactionaries at the Court of St. James's urged Britain to protest and use her influence to persuade the United States to withdraw its recognition; but the British secretary of foreign affairs declined to act. Finally, however, on June 28, 1860, the English minister in Mexico was informed of the decision of England, France, and Spain to intervene in Mexican affairs. He was also notified that Great Britain would be glad if the United States would coöperate. In July, following, Lord Lyons, the minister of Great Britain at Washington, actually invited the United States to join the European powers in addressing identical notes to the two governments of Mexico, advising them to find some method for a speedy arrangement of their difficulties. The United States replied that it was opposed to the interference of other powers in the domestic affairs of the independent nations of the New World, and especially

[11] Lettsom to Clarendon, No. 163, July 22, 1857, F.O. 50 (310), Mexico.
[12] Dallas to Cass, No. 99, Mex. Desp., Vol. 71.

of Mexico, and communicated the substance of this reply to Vera Cruz. Without specific directions for such action the legation of the United States in Mexico issued, in December, 1860, a sort of manifesto setting forth the attitude of Washington toward the projected intervention of the European powers. "The government of the United States," read the manifesto, "does not deny to the European powers the right to wage honorable warfare for a sufficient cause, anywhere, or against any nation; nor does it deny their right to demand redress for injuries inflicted on their respective subjects . . . , but it does deny them the right to interfere, *directly,* or *indirectly,* with the political independence of the republic of Mexico, and it will to the extent of its power, defend the nationality and independence of said republic." [13] Commenting upon this document, George W. Mathew, British minister in Mexico, remarked: "If the position of the United States . . . is authorised and maintained, I cannot but view it as binding that country to assume the moral obligation toward other nations, of restoring peace and order in Mexico, and of preventing the recurrence of scenes which disgrace humanity and neutralise . . . the international rights and natural commercial relations of civilized nations." [14]

But the United States had already reached a condition which rendered the fulfillment of this "moral obligation" impossible. Secession and the Civil War concentrated attention upon domestic affairs. The United States found itself in no position to establish a protectorate over Mexico or even to prevent European intervention. Britain's participation in the joint move against Mexico appears, however, to have been in no way influenced by the old motive of circumscribing the United States. Her purpose seems to have been confined to the redressing of injuries and the satisfaction of claims.

The same softening of the British official attitude likewise became evident in Central American affairs. Lord Malmesbury's statement to Dallas in July, 1858, applied to Central America as well as to Mexico. Even before this, Lord Clarendon had expressed similar views. As early as March 13 of the previous year he had written to President Buchanan: ". . . Pray bear in mind that beyond the point of honor respecting the Mosquito Indians we possess no interest in

[13] *House Ex. Doc.* No. 100, 37 Cong., 2 Sess. (Ser. 1136), p. 18.
[14] No. 85, Dec. 29, 1860, to Lord Russell, F.O. 50 (344), Mexico.

Central America, & that, so far from wishing to create one, we would not accept such a 'damnosa possessio' as Central America if it could be offered to England as a gift." [15]

It was therefore largely a question of honor and, Clarendon might have added, of pride. British pride could not tolerate the idea of being "bullied out of rights" in Central America by the Yankees, and British honor could not find satisfaction in the abandonment of the Mosquitoes, who had looked upon England for centuries as their great and good friend, to the tender mercies of Honduras, Nicaragua, and the United States. But the crisis was compelling, and Britain found a way out by direct negotiation with the Central American states.

On November 28, 1859, a treaty was signed with Honduras acknowledging the Bay Islands as the possession of that republic and recognizing its sovereign rights over the portion of the Mosquito territory which lay within its frontiers. Two months later negotiations with Nicaragua resulted in an agreement to recognize the sovereignty of that little state over the part of Mosquitia which lay within its boundaries. The British protectorate over the natives was to cease within three months, and they were to be granted a sort of home rule until they should agree to incorporate themselves into the Nicaraguan republic. Upon ratification, these treaties were forthwith transmitted to the United States, and Britain expressed the hope that they would "finally set at rest the questions respecting the interpretation of the Clayton-Bulwer Treaty which have been the subject of so much controversy between this country and the United States."

It was a clever stroke, and notwithstanding the fact that England still retained Belize with boundaries extending as far south as the Sarstoon, President Buchanan expressed entire satisfaction with the statement. In a message of December, 1860, he took occasion to remark: "The discordant constructions of the Clayton and Bulwer treaty . . . , which at different periods of the discussion bore a threatening aspect, have resulted in a final settlement entirely satisfactory to this government." This was probably the most cordial mention of Great Britain that had appeared in any presidential message up to that time.

[15] J. B. Moore, *The Works of James Buchanan* (1910), X, 115.

One should pause, however, to examine just what concessions Britain had granted, and upon what assumptions they had been based. It will be noted that in reality only one concession had been made. The British government had decided no longer to oppose the southward expansion of the United States, and this decision had been reached upon the presupposition that the United States would not attempt to shut off British merchants from the growing markets of the regions annexed and in the hope, moreover, that the United States might eventually abandon the Monroe Doctrine. This doctrine had not been accepted, nor had joint control over interoceanic communication by way of the Isthmus been relinquished.

A Significant Domestic Change in England

Although England soon withdrew from Mexico, it appeared for a time that the outbreak of the Civil War would furnish occasion for a reversal of British policy. In 1862 the London government organized the Belize settlements into a full-fledged British colony, and near the end of the same year it approached the verge of interference in the struggle between North and South in the United States. The former step, though in line with British procedure in Central America for three decades prior to 1856, was nevertheless out of harmony with the self-denying pledge of Canning and the provisions of the Clayton-Bulwer Treaty, and likewise with the assurances given to Buchanan in 1857 and 1858. The latter procedure would have been inspired in part by the feeling that the unity and continuing prosperity of the American nation would not serve the best interests of Britain, by a complex mixture of economic and political motives, among which not the least would have been the conviction in conservative circles that the failure of American democracy would help to perpetuate the privileges of Britain's aristocracy.

For reasons which need not be related here, the British government did not interfere by armed force in the Civil War. Union and Democracy triumphed; almost at the same time the merchant marine of the United States began to decline; and the great reforms which took place in England "changed Great Britain from a government by aristocracy to one by democracy." Thereafter the clash of political views, and, for a considerable time, maritime rivalry, ceased to be an element of discord between the Anglo-Saxon nations. Purely economic rivalries might continue; Irish and other hostile elements in the United States might try to stir up trouble; boundary and fishery disputes might irritate; even saner Americans, blinded by "bitter and exaggerated memories," might fail to see in the British nation a sister democracy holding out friendly hands to the United States; but the sister democracy was there with extended friendly hands, and this was bound sooner or later to make a difference. Moreover, after 1895 conditions in Europe and Asia were such as to impel the British to seek cordial relations with their Anglo-Saxon kinsmen. Great Britain was confronted by powerful rivals, and the support and coöperation of the United States were greatly needed. The two nations were destined to move toward an era of harmony.

So far as Latin America was concerned, few causes of friction arose during the next half-century. British merchants continued to enjoy a large share of Latin-American trade and to invest large sums of money in these regions. Except in Cuba and Mexico, and to a lesser extent in Central America, Peru, and Chile, the merchants and capitalists of the two nations were not brought into sharp rivalry; and, even in these areas, no more than mild friction occurred. The governments themselves do not appear to have been seriously concerned, although James G. Blaine suffered some uneasiness in regard to Chile and Peru.[16] Only with reference to the control of projected lines of communication between the Atlantic and the Pacific, and the interpretation of the Monroe Doctrine, did a clash between the two governments seem possible.

GROWING OPPOSITION IN THE UNITED STATES TO THE CLAYTON-BULWER TREATY

The question of the abrogation of the Clayton-Bulwer Treaty, though not settled until 1901, was the first to occasion earnest diplomatic discussion. Soon after the close of the Civil War the United States began to act as if this treaty were not applicable to the Panama

---

[16] Blaine declared his conviction that Great Britain instigated the war between Chile and Peru (1879–1883) in the hope that Chile's conquest of the nitrate area would furnish British nationals in Chile an opportunity to exploit this commodity. Some of the diplomatic agents of the United States appear to have held the same view.

route. Recovery from the Civil War and alarm at the prospect of the Panama Canal's being constructed by a French company headed by De Lesseps soon led, in fact, to an open demand for an American canal controlled by the United States. As early as 1881 negotiations were entered upon with Great Britain having this aim in view. The British government was asked to modify or grant the United States release from the Clayton-Bulwer pact. Britain resisted the attempt with irrefragable arguments. Soon afterwards De Lesseps's undertaking showed indications of immediate and certain failure. Interest in the United States then shifted to the Nicaragua route as the most promising one across the isthmus of Central America. Here it was found that Britain was still maintaining intimate relations with the Mosquito Indians, whose reserve was in close proximity to the interoceanic route. Systematic opposition to British policy was at once begun, and before the close of the year 1894 the incorporation of these Indians into the state of Nicaragua had been effected in a manner which appeared for the moment satisfactory both to the United States and to England.

Meanwhile, utterances of the American press and debates in the Senate continued to reveal a growing hostility toward the Clayton-Bulwer Treaty and an increasing demand for an American-built, American-controlled canal. But the policy of the British government was one of firmness tempered with moderation. When questioned about the matter in the House of Commons, Sir Edward Grey, undersecretary of state for foreign affairs, replied that there was no reason to suppose that the United States did not intend to abide by its treaty obligations. And his confidence was justified, temporarily at least, by the stand which Secretary Olney took a short time afterwards, when he condemned ingenious arguments designed to prove the treaty obsolete and declared in favor of "a direct and straightforward application to Great Britain for a reconsideration of the whole matter." Before direct negotiations were begun, however, the first Venezuelan crisis arose and severely tested the friendly relations of the two governments.

THE VENEZUELA DIFFICULTY OF 1895–1896

The immediate occasion of the difficulty was a dispute between the governments of Venezuela and Great Britain over the boundary between British Guiana and its Spanish-American neighbor; [17] but the issues were more far-reaching, and the final settlement of the affair was determined by factors much broader in scope. In the United States there were currents of sentiment which prompted flamboyant jingoism, but there were also saner emotions which demanded sober second thought. In England there was a resurgence of imperialism tempered by a feeling of kinship and a realization of the dangers confronted in Asia, Africa, and Europe. In Venezuela there was evinced a disposition to seek the aid of the United States against England.

Thomas F. Bayard, American ambassador at the Court of St. James's, urged shortly after he reached London (1893) that the time was opportune for the settlement of the dispute: "Great Britain has just now her hands very full in other quarters of the globe. The United States is the last nation on earth with whom the British people or their rulers desire to quarrel, and of this I have new proofs every day. . . . The . . . European nations are watching each other like pugilists in a ring." [18]

In 1894 Scruggs published his *British Aggressions in Venzeuela; or the Monroe Doctrine on Trial;* and the American public was ready for a second edition by 1895. Men celebrated the Fourth of July, 1895, by discussing such questions as the advisability of annexing Canada, Newfoundland, Cuba, and Hawaii, and "Will Uncle Sam eventually rule the American continent?" They also had much to say about the enforcement of the Monroe Doctrine. Henry Cabot Lodge declared in the July number of the *North American Review* that the time for "decisive action" had come. The United States must control the Nicaragua canal and defend the Monroe manifesto. "The supremacy of the Monroe Doctrine should be established and at once—peaceably if we can, forcibly if we must." Albert Shaw, editor of the *American Review of Reviews* (a journal which had been founded in order to promote Anglo-Saxon harmony), was about as aggressive as any of the rest.

On July 20, 1895, Secretary of State Richard Olney sent off his

---

[17] The territory in dispute extended between the Essequibo on the east and the Amacura and the basin of the Cuyuni on the west.

[18] Robert McElroy, *Grover Cleveland* (1923), II, 178.

now famous dispatch. He declared that the Monroe Doctrine was applicable to the boundary dispute which had arisen between Venezuela and British Guiana, and made several other important statements besides. He remarked, for instance, that "distance, and 3,000 miles of intervening ocean, make any permanent political union between any European and any American State unnatural and inexpedient." He also assumed the rôle of champion of the republican system in America and declared: "To-day the United States is practically sovereign on this continent, and its fiat is law upon the subjects to which it confines its interposition." [19]

Such language could but ruffle the disposition of the head of the British Foreign Office. Lord Salisbury took plenty of time to answer Olney's contentions. His reply was set down in two dispatches dated November 26. He not only refused to arbitrate the Venezuelan boundary dispute, except in reference to certain limited phases,[20] but denied the applicability of the Monroe Doctrine to the question and pointedly refused to accept that doctrine. He also took exception to the statement referring to European possessions in the Americas, declaring that "the union between Great Britain and her territories in the Western Hemisphere is [was] both natural and expedient."

After conferring at length on the matter, Cleveland and Olney decided that it was time to lay the question before Congress, and on December 17 the President sent in his message. He invoked the Monroe Doctrine, asked for a committee to investigate and report on the boundary, and declared further: "The dispute has reached such a stage as to make it now incumbent on the United States to take measures to determine . . . the true division line between the Republic of Venezuela and British Guiana. . . . When such report is made . . . it will be the duty of the United States to resist by every means in its power . . . the appropriation by Great Britain of any lands . . . which after investigation we have determined of right belong to Venezuela."

The message and the diplomatic correspondence were at once handed to the press. They were greeted by a jingoist outburst of

[19] U. S. *Foreign Relations* (1895), I, 558 ff.
[20] He refused to arbitrate within a certain line, usually denominated the "modified Schomburgh line."

patriotism more extreme than ever. Outside of a few eastern cities, like New York and Boston, where business interests opposed Cleveland's bellicose policy, the Monroe Doctrine was glorified and the administration upheld. Even the former critics of the president now supported him, and the churches, excepting a few in the cities of the eastern seaboard, approved the American position while praying for peace and arbitration.

Congress was already in a pugnacious mood before Cleveland's message was transmitted. The House of Representatives had been opened on December 3 with the prayer: "Heavenly Father, let peace reign throughout our borders. Yet may we be quick to resent anything like an insult to our nation." [21] A resolution in support of the Monroe Doctrine, introduced on the same day by Senator Lodge, furnished occasion for discussions which revealed at once hostility toward British policy in America and a determination to control interoceanic communications across Central America. Before Senators had finished their speeches, the Cleveland message of December 17 was read. It was received with applause amounting to a demonstration. The House of Representatives, without a dissenting voice, adopted a resolution embodying the president's suggestions. The Senate debated the measure for three days and then unanimously concurred in the action of the House.

During the closing days of the year 1895 the British nation was equally firm in supporting the stand taken by Salisbury. Parliament was not in session, but the press, though it had little knowledge of the issue and its merits, considered it preposterous that an American commission should alone decide a British boundary dispute, and that the president of the United States should propose to support its decision by resort to force. The newspapers of both parties expressed indignation. The London *Chronicle,* the great mouthpiece of the Liberals, was firm but a bit more moderate than the rest. "There is one answer to President Cleveland and America," it declared. "If an enlarged application of a neglected doctrine is to be enforced with all the might of the United States, at least let us be assured that the United States will make itself responsible for the foreign policy of all the petty, impetuous little states on the two continents. There is no international right without a corresponding duty. . . . Unless the

[21] *Cong. Record,* 53 Cong., 2 Sess., Vol. XXVIII, Part I, p. 26.

United States formally proclaims a protectorate over all of the South American Republics we are bound to protect our citizens." [22]

Meanwhile, George W. Smalley, the American correspondent of the London *Times,* was exerting his influence in favor of moderation, and the London *Chronicle* sent Henry Norman, of its editorial staff, to Washington for the purpose of investigating the state of feeling on the Venezuelan matter. His first reports were published on January 2. Through him came the news that the intention of Cleveland's message was amicable; that many who approved the president's policy did not understand it to mean war; that the churches were pleading for peace; but that a national sentiment had sprung up in support of the course outlined by Cleveland and Olney which it would be madness for England to disregard or underestimate. Moreover, Norman reported the information, which he had gained from access to documents in the State Department, that Salisbury's stand was far more uncompromising and dogmatic than had been that of his predecessors in the Foreign Office.

While Norman was giving the British public a correct view of American sentiment and Salisbury's policy, an important event occurred in another part of the world which was destined to exert no little influence on the outcome of the dispute regarding boundaries in South America. On December 29 Dr. Leander Starr Jameson led a small company of Rhodesians against the Boers in the Transvaal. The hostile expedition proved a fiasco, and the invaders were captured on January 2, 1896. German animosity toward England immediately showed itself. German public opinion was greatly excited, the Berlin Foreign Office issued harsh warnings, and on January 3 the Kaiser sent a telegram to President Paul Krüger of the Transvaal congratulating him upon the successful suppression of the raid. The situation was serious. Japan's defeat of China in 1895 had already disturbed the Anglo-Russian balance in the Far East and Turkish massacres in Armenia had brought about a strained condition in the Near East. Clearly it was no time to risk a war with the United States, and British statesmen began to search for a pacific settlement.

On January 12 the Foreign Office sent Lord Playfair on a confidential mission to the residence of the American ambassador, with au-

[22] As quoted in the New York *Tribune,* Dec. 19, 1895, and in *Cong. Record,* 53 Cong., 2 Sess., Vol. XXVIII, Part I, p. 111.

thority to make two important proposals: (1) that the United States should call a conference of all the European powers which then had colonies in America—namely, Great Britain, France, Spain, and Holland—for the purpose of inducing them to proclaim their acceptance of the Monroe Doctrine. Britain would agree to accept it and presumably to persuade the other powers to do so, thus giving the Doctrine the force of international law and removing all danger of the extension of European "influence in that Hemisphere"; (2) that England would agree to arbitrate the entire region in dispute, provided only that areas already occupied should be adjudged to the government whose nationals were in undisputed possession. Bayard telegraphed these proposals to Washington with no little enthusiasm.

In the meantime, the public in both England and the United States had become much calmer. English journalists criticized Salisbury for his translucent dispatches, and American newspapers sympathized with Britain in her South African and European troubles.

When Parliament convened in February, the Lords and Commons were likewise in a conciliatory mood. They declared that the appointment of an American commission to investigate the Venezuela-Guiana boundary was not an insult to Britain and that the Foreign Office could afford to coöperate with them in their investigations. They said that the Monroe Doctrine was not unusual or obnoxious, but merely the limited assertion of the principle that a state may intervene when its interests are menaced. "What other States claim to exercise everywhere the Monroe Doctrine has limited to the American continent." Even Lord Salisbury stated in the House of Lords that the interest of the United States in the dispute, in view of Venezuela's position in the Caribbean, was "no more unnatural . . . than that we should feel an interest in Belgium and Holland." Indeed, he felt that the intervention of the United States would turn out to be an advantage, for the simple reason that the United States would be likely to force Venezuela to abide by any peaceful settlement which might be reached.

Moreover, the closing weeks of January found congressmen and senators in the United States in a saner mood, although a few jingoists continued their efforts to disturb the calm that was settling upon the country. The Senate favored neither a resolution opposing a direct settlement between England and Venezuela nor one proposing to congratulate the South African Republic. The way was clear for a peaceful exit from the tangle, if only Cleveland and Olney would be reasonable.

These statesmen were far more conciliatory than their public utterances had indicated. Neither they nor their supporters had expected the difficulty to eventuate in war. They were not in favor of a congress of European powers to pass upon the Monroe Doctrine, but they did not long oppose a settlement with Venezuela upon the basis proposed by Salisbury through Playfair on January 12. By July the crisis had entirely passed; by February, 1897, all arrangements for arbitration had been made. The entire boundary was to be submitted to an arbitral tribunal, but "adverse holding or prescription during a period of fifty years" was to constitute a good title. On October 3, 1899, the arbitrators announced their decision. On the whole it was more favorable to the claims of Great Britain than to those of Venezuela.

BRITISH ATTITUDE DURING THE SPANISH-AMERICAN WAR

The first Venezuelan crisis had scarcely passed when the prospect of a war between the United States and Spain over Cuban difficulties began to loom in the distance. Cubans had appealed to the United States for assistance, and both our sympathies and our economic interests urged the championship of the Cuban insurgents against Spanish rule. When the war between the United States and Spain began in April, 1898, it found the British public sympathetic toward the United States. Opposition to American expansion into the Caribbean had long since been abandoned; the anti-British attitude of the Kaiser was driving England into the arms of the United States; the coöperation of the United States was needed in the Far East; and, moreover, John Hay, who became ambassador at London in 1898, was an Anglophile statesman not without great influence in the English capital.

Leaving the official attitude of England for more detailed treatment in another connection, we may here note briefly the sentiment of the press. Its position in April, 1898, was summed up by the *Literary Digest* in the statement that the general tenor of the British journals was "in our favor." The hostile *Saturday Review* noted this attitude and scolded its colleagues: "When we find the bulk of the English newspapers calling on us to admire . . . the United States and to accord our moral support . . . , it is time to protest." Henry Norman, speaking of a possible European combination against the United States, declared that Britons would "never stand idly by and see a hundred millions of people who speak English trampled on by people who speak Russian or French or Spanish." Even the London *Times,* always scrupulous in matters of diplomatic decorum, did not fail to let its sympathies be known. And when the close of the war left the Philippines in American hands this strengthening of the position of the United States in the Far East was greeted with almost unanimous approval.

ANOTHER IMPORTANT CONCESSION

The way was now practically cleared for a renewal of the canal negotiations, and the diplomats of the two nations returned to the question without delay. The Spanish-American War was attended by a growing aggressiveness on the part of the United States and the spectacular thirteen-thousand-mile voyage of the *Oregon* around South America emphasized the importance of a channel across the isthmus. Besides, the United States now had very large Pacific interests to guard. The British clearly realized this changed situation. The *Spectator* urged, as early as December 3, that Britain face the facts and abrogate the treaty before the United States had time to demand the step. A few weeks later Sir Charles Dilke expressed a somewhat similar view in Parliament. But neither the *Spectator* nor Sir Charles was ahead of Lord Salisbury. Before the close of December he had told Henry White, who had paid him a visit at Hatfield, that he was willing to agree in principle to the American contention regarding the canal, provided the United States would agree that there should be no discrimination in the matter of tolls when it had been completed. The matter might have been settled at once had it not been complicated by the Alaskan boundary dispute and the insistence of the United States upon the right to police the canal and to stand as the sole guarantor of its neutrality. As it was, the treaty was not signed until the close of the year 1901. Britain then conceded virtually every demand of the United States; the

Washington government obtained a canal concession by supporting the insurgents in Panama, and the United States became practically dominant in the Caribbean.

But the student should take note of an important assumption, an assumption which amounted almost to an understanding—and in one instance, at least, was really an understanding—that underlay all the concessions which Britain had made since 1895. In the case of the Venezuela boundary dispute the editor of the London *Chronicle* had seized the idea when he remarked that Great Britain should not admit the contention of Olney and Cleveland unless the United States was willing to "make itself responsible for the foreign policy of all the petty, impetuous little states on the two continents." Lord Salisbury had the same idea in mind when he remarked that the intervention of the United States government would be an advantage if it should force Venezuela to abide by any peaceful settlement which might be reached. Britain's friendly position during the Spanish-American War had doubtless been based upon the hope that the American acquisition of Cuba, Puerto Rico, and the Philippines would not result in injury to British economic interests but, on the contrary, would support these interests. So it was, likewise, in the case of the Hay-Pauncefote Treaty. Article III of that treaty provided that the canal should be "free and open to the vessels of commerce and of war of all nations . . . , on terms of entire equality." Britain had given way with the understanding that nothing was to be done officially to injure her trade in Hispanic America.

Of course the Monroe Doctrine had not yet formally been accepted: it had in fact been left by Cleveland and Olney "like a volcano suddenly thrust up in mid-ocean"; but the London government had shown some disposition to discuss a plan whereby it might be lifted to the realm of accepted international law. Unless the United States should attempt to give the Doctrine an economic application so as to secure exclusive advantages for itself, it would not be likely to cause trouble.

LATER ISSUES

During the next two decades only two issues arose to interrupt the harmony of the Anglo-Saxon nations in respect to Spanish-

American relations. The Venezuelan difficulty of 1901–1903 was not one of these. The official conduct of England gave little offense, and British diplomats were severely criticized by the British press for joining Germany in the attempt to coerce Venezuela. Moreover, it served as the occasion for further revelation of the assumption underlying British concessions to the United States and of the readiness of British statesmen to accept the Monroe Doctrine. Lord Avebury remarked that "the Monroe claim involves a certain responsibility on the part of the United States to see that the nations of Latin America conduct themselves properly." Arthur J. Balfour, assistant foreign secretary, said: "The Monroe Doctrine has no enemies in this country that I know of. We welcome any increase of the influence of the United States of America upon the Western Hemisphere." The Duke of Devonshire declared that Englishmen accepted "fully and unreservedly the Monroe Doctrine." The Marquis of Lansdowne said that British statesmen did not "have any desire to impugn" that doctrine. Joseph Chamberlain, "with bland indifference to the expressed opinion of his nominal chief" (Lord Salisbury), declared that England recognized the existence of the Monroe Doctrine and had "never thought of impugning it." In like manner, the procedure of the United States in the Panama revolt and the acquisition of the Canal Zone did not call forth severe criticism from British publicists, and the government hastened to recognize the new republic of Panama. The informal protectorate over Mosquitia was finally abandoned in 1906, and the Monroe Doctrine, as defined and delimited, was formally accepted by being incorporated into the League Covenant.[23]

The two issues which caused friction arose almost simultaneously, and both of them related to economic matters. On August 24, 1912, the United States Congress authorized the president "to prescribe and from time to time change the tolls" levied upon the shipping which should pass through the Panama Canal. The act also provided that "no tolls" should be "levied upon vessels engaged in the coastwise trade of the United States." Against this exemption Great Britain protested on the grounds: (1) that it was contrary to the

---

[23] At a Pilgrims Day Dinner in June, 1911, Sir Edward Grey, then British secretary for foreign affairs, virtually announced his acceptance of the Doctrine (*Literary Digest*, June 24, 1911, p. 1234).

Hay-Pauncefote Treaty; (2) that it would increase the toll burden of the other ships using the Canal; and (3) that foreign shippers would be tempted to evade the tolls by landing their cargoes at the nearest United States port and sending them the rest of the journey by the favored coastwise shipping. The protest was without effect upon the Taft administration, however, and was left over to Woodrow Wilson for solution. Meanwhile, another difficulty arose to prevent the frank coöperation of the two powers. It was connected with Wilson's opposition to official economic imperialism in Latin America and his refusal to recognize the government of Victoriano Huerta in Mexico. In both instances the American president was running counter to the economic interests of British citizens, and particularly those of the great oil magnate, Lord Cowdray. After considerable parleying a settlement which represented mutual concession was reached. Wilson persuaded Congress to repeal the obnoxious tolls-exemption clause; Britain allowed him to have his way with Huerta, even going so far as to transfer the British ambassador from Mexico City at Wilson's request. Cowdray withdrew from the oil fields of Colombia and probably suffered losses in Mexico as a result of Huerta's downfall. Both difficulties were settled without serious friction, but they should perhaps serve as danger signals for the future. The idea of an economic Open Door has underlain every concession which Great Britain has made to the United States in Latin America.

In spite of the World War and its aftermath, the British nation managed in large measure to maintain its economic position in Latin America. Its investments were nearly a billion pounds sterling in 1913 and £1,139,659,470 in 1925. It purchased almost twenty-one per cent of Latin America's exports in 1913 and about eighteen per cent in 1925, while it furnished nearly twenty-four per cent of Latin America's imports in the former year and a little less than eighteen per cent in the latter. Britain's Latin-American trade was valued at $897,000,000 in 1924 and $933,000,000 in 1925, as compared with $1,937,000,000 and $2,110,951,000 for the United States and $409,-000,000, and $440,000,000 for Germany. In 1929 and after the British made a vigorous effort to augment their trade with South America. Yet, between 1934 and 1939, they were definitely losing ground to the United States and Germany.

CHAPTER XIX

THE POLICY AND ATTITUDE OF FRANCE

SHORTLY before the British government decided to relax its opposition to the expanding influence of the United States in the Western Hemisphere, France began to reveal a more aggressive disposition. For some time subsequent to 1825 the energies of the French government were largely absorbed elsewhere. French trade with Hispanic America gradually increased until it reached the value of thirty million dollars in 1848, but the attention of French officials was not often directed to this region. True, they had bombarded Vera Cruz in 1838, intervened in Argentina during the years 1838–1840, and joined England in a collective action against the River Plate republics in 1845–1850; but the French government had refused to commit itself to England either on the Texas issue or on the question of interference in the Mexican War.

MAXIMILIAN AND MEXICO

The growing aggressiveness of France in the New World synchronized with the rise of Louis Napoleon to power. In 1851 the navies of France and England were instructed to prevent filibustering operations from the United States against Cuba, and in the following year the ministers of France and England in the United States proposed a tripartite pledge to preserve that island to Spain. In 1854 the British government admitted that it had entered into an agreement with France with reference to the navigation of the leading rivers of South America and the republics bordering upon them. Near the close of the same year the commercial representatives of the United States in the island of Santo Domingo reported Anglo-French interference to prevent the United States from acquiring trade or territorial concessions from the Dominican Republic. Early in 1855 reports reached Washington of similar interference in Ecua-

dor. The French chargé had been particularly obtrusive and menacing. He had tried to dissuade the Ecuador government from
granting guano concessions to the United States and had brandished
the threat that the Emperor Napoleon would turn his attention
toward the New World as soon as the Crimean War was concluded.

All this activity serves as a proper background for French intervention in Mexico. How long before 1861 this enterprise had been
under consideration is not definitely known, but the suspicion of the
United States was aroused as early as 1852, and by 1857 the French
minister in Mexico was causing constant apprehension. At this time
the French and Spanish envoys discussed plans for checking the "expanding and unrestrainable people who occupy the north of the
new hemisphere." Such discussions accurately revealed the true intent of the French project which began to be acted upon in 1861.

It was in October, 1861, that the long apprehended European intervention took place. The reason announced by England, France,
and Spain was a desire to avenge the outrages suffered by their nationals and to force Mexico to live up to its financial obligations. It
soon became evident, however, that France had ulterior designs.
These were revealed in Louis Napoleon's now famous letter to General Forey which deserves to be quoted at some length:

"In the present state of the world's çivilization," said the emperor,
"the prosperity of America is not a matter of indifference to Europe,
because it nourishes our industries and stimulates our commerce.
We have an interest in seeing the Republic of the United States become powerful and prosperous; but we have no interest in seeing it
seize all of the Gulf of Mexico, dominate from there the Antilles
and South America, and become the sole dispenser of the products
of the New World. If the United States should become master of
Mexico and consequently of Central America and the pass between
the two oceans, there would indeed be no other power in America.

"If on the contrary Mexico shall achieve its independence and
maintain the integrity of its territory; if a stable government is set
up by means of French arms, we shall have opposed an impenetrable
dike to the overflow of the United States; we shall have upheld the
independence of our colonies and those of ungrateful Spain; we
shall have established our benevolent influence in the center of
America, and this influence shall radiate to the North as well as to

the South, create immense markets for our commerce, and procure materials indispensable for our industry. . . .

"Thus . . . are now involved our military honor, the exigencies of our policy, the interests of our industry and our commerce; all of which oblige us to advance upon Mexico, resolutely place our flag there, and establish a monarchy—if it is not incompatible with the national sentiment of the country—or at least a government which promises something of stability." [1]

Into the details of Napoleon's Mexican undertaking it is unnecessary to go. Owing to the hostility of the United States, whose assistance against France was eagerly sought by Mexicans and other Latin Americans, owing to the menacing attitude of Prussia, opposition in the French Parliament, and the dogged persistence of the soldiers fighting under the Mexican patriot Benito Juárez, the French troops were finally withdrawn in 1867, leaving Napoleon's puppet Maximilian to the tragic fate which soon overtook him. Louis Napoleon thus suffered a blow to his prestige, and resentment toward the United States was felt in certain circles of France.

Indeed, for many years after the close of the Maximilian period Frenchmen were most persistent and bitter critics of our Latin-American policies. A survey of the French press of the period will reveal several other motives for this attitude than the unpleasant memory of the Mexican fiasco.

Motives for French Criticism

Envy of Success of the United States.—First may be noted a melancholy envy produced by the fact that the United States was achieving success where France had failed. The Mississippi valley, the great treasure house of the United States, once had belonged to France, and, moreover, the products of this enormously fertile region were appearing all over the world in competition with French commodities. This envy comes out clearly in an essay written by Comte d'Haussonville in 1905. As a descendant of Rochambeau, he had been the honored guest of the United States in 1881 at a festival commemorating the centenary of the surrender of Cornwallis at

---

[1] Translated from a copy of the original found in the archives of Marshal Bazaine. (See Genaro García, *Documentos inéditos* . . . , XIV, 13–15.)

Yorktown. While in America he had taken a flying trip across the continent from New York to San Francisco. After the lapse of twenty-four years he still cherished fond memories of the delightful journey, but his pleasure at the time as well as in retrospect was somewhat marred by emotions which forced themselves upon him as he sped over the immense country. "I remember," wrote the Count, "that with the happy feelings of satisfied curiosity there was mingled a certain degree of melancholy when I read on the railway charts and heard pronounced by foreign lips names of cities and stations, great and small, which recalled their French origin: La Nouvelle Orléans, Saint Louis, Vincennes, Saint Geneviève, Versailles; for said I to myself: It is the French who baptized these places, but where is France?" "I experienced other feelings also," continued the Count. "While traveling across immense plains where the steam plow was at work . . . with a view to the approaching seed-time; . . . when crossing large rivers by which I knew wheat, cattle, and fruit were carried to the sea for export to Europe; or when I saw the glare of mighty furnaces and the accumulation of the depots of great vats of petroleum, I became conscious that a powerful rival was preparing himself to deal terrible blows to our agriculture and our industries, and that it would be necessary to defend ourselves against the invasion of his products." [2]

Sentimental Racial Consciousness.—In the second place, there is something of the sentimental, the racial and cultural, behind this French criticism of the procedure of the United States in the Western Hemisphere. Filled with pride because of the fact that they had been the intellectual and cultural leaders of the Hispanic-American peoples, the French were anxious to maintain this leadership unimpaired. And to this cultural sentiment was added a feeling of kinship based upon the Latin element common to the two peoples. As the Anglo-Saxons of the United States gradually encroached upon the Latins to the south, Frenchmen were impelled by racial consciousness to protest against the threatened absorption.

This racial and cultural sentiment, this Pan-Latinism, was one of the motives which influenced Louis Napoleon to undertake his quixotic Mexican expedition. Indeed, it is one of the most persistent factors in shaping French attitude. M. Reclus, writing in the *Revue*

[2] Barral-Montferrat, *De Monroe à Roosevelt* (1907), Introduction.

des Deux Mondes in 1868, urged Frenchmen to cultivate the Hispanic Americans. He sought to console Frenchmen with respect to the Napoleonic fiasco in Mexico by recalling that, "fortunately for France, the affinity of languages assures for her literary and scientific works a decisive influence among the Hispanic Americans, and the grand memories of the Revolution will render them only too indulgent toward our contemporary history." "They recognize with a a sort of filial piety," added Reclus, "that they owe their emancipation to the ideas proclaimed by the men of '89; in spite of all our political blunders we inherit a part of the spirit of gratitude dedicated to our ancestors." In similar vein another writer in the *Revue des Deux Mondes* (1893) pointed out that French political, scientific, and cultural ideas were in the ascendant in Mexico. Díaz's administrative system was modeled after that of the French, the Mexican civil code was almost a literal reproduction of the Napoleonic code, and cultured Mexicans not only read more French than Spanish books, but actually sent their children to Paris to complete their education. These considerations filled the writer with pride, and he expressed the hope that Frenchmen and the French government would assist the Latin nationalities to defend themselves. At the same time, he warned the inhabitants of Spanish America, and particularly the Indian element, that too close relations with the Anglo-Saxons would mean extermination. Again, near the close of the year 1902, several French journals called upon Latin Europe to rescue its American kinsmen from the greedy maw of the United States. One of them remarked: "The nations of Central and South America must be ranked among the Latin people. A positive alliance with these people would be difficult perhaps, because it would arouse the suspicions of the United States. But, at any rate, a cordial understanding is needed, a growing intimacy of relations between the Latin peoples of Europe and those of America." [3] Still another French writer predicted in 1909 that his generation would live to see the greater portion of Hispanic America under the control of the United States. Then, he remarked regretfully, the inhabitants of this vast region would be taught English and sent to the United States to complete their studies; then Rome would be transferred to the New World and Paris would become "no more than another Athens

[3] *Literary Digest*, XXV (Oct. 25, 1902), 530.

which would begin to enter the melancholy shades of the past." [4] This motive comes out again, along with others, in Poincaré's preface to García Calderón's book on Latin America. Here Poincaré says: "May South America while cultivating herself . . . grow ever more and more hospitable to the literature, the arts, the commerce, and the capital of France. Thereby only can the great Latin family gain in material prosperity and moral authority." And lastly, it was expressed in 1912 in the following language: "The future of the Latin race is linked up with South America. . . . We have interests of the first order in the independence of the South American republics because . . . we exercise in those countries a veritable intellectual and moral preponderance, because we are their spiritual guide on the highway to progress. . . ." [5]

Menace of the Expansion of the United States.—There is also an element of self-defense in the French attitude. The importance of the Latin Americans as allies or friendly neutrals in a general war is at once evident. But at this point we refer particularly to the American phase of the question. The French people were uneasy lest the rising tide of Yankee imperialism should result in the loss of French Guiana and the French Antilles. These possessions were (and are), to be sure, of no great importance intrinsically; but they were remnants of empire which reminded Frenchmen of a more glorious past, and there was a strong indisposition to lowering the French flag where it once had floated so magnificently.

A few illustrations of this point will suffice. It will be recalled that Louis Napoleon had this sentiment in mind. The apprehension arose again in 1890, in the discussions occasioned by Blaine's Pan-Americanism. At this time it was asserted that the United States had resolved to expel the Europeans from all their American possessions. The attempt of the United States to force England to arbitrate the Anglo-Venezuelan boundary dispute aroused even more apprehension. It was generally agreed among French journalists that the United States was taking but another step in its general policy of shutting Europe out of the Western Hemisphere. One writer, accepting this view of the matter, warned that the Yankees would find themselves in "conflict with all Europe" if they undertook a

---

[4] Waleffe, *Les Paradis de l'Amérique centrale* (1909), pp. 303-304.
[5] Angel Marvaud, in *Revue politique et parlementaire*, LXIX, 437 ff.

general application of "the pretension of Mr. Cleveland." He furthermore served notice that a concession on England's part in this instance would not obligate other European powers or render them more disposed to submit to "such odious interference." [6] Another journalist, coming nearer the real motive of French apprehensiveness, remarked that, in the dispute regarding the boundary between Brazil and French Guiana, the government of the United States would be likely to assume the same attitude toward Republican France as it had assumed toward monarchial England. He further alleged that, of course, the United States intended at an opportune time to seize all of Europe's colonies in America—perhaps, indeed, the nations of Europe, adopting Russia's policy, should sell them to the United States before it should be too late—but that he did not believe the Yankees were foolish enough to consider the year 1896 a fit occasion for this robbery. On the other hand, he felt quite sure that if France should be "forced to make a naval demonstration in the waters of Rio de Janeiro for the purpose of establishing" her "rights in the contested territories of French Guiana, the admiral commanding the American fleet would do us the honor of coming aboard the French admiral's vessel to dance." Surely the American officer would rather dance on a French man-of-war than dance over a volcano! It would be more cheerful and less dangerous! [7] Indeed the anxiety of the French for the security of the remnant of their American colonies became so evident by 1898 that the German emperor thought France might be persuaded to join in a concerted action against the United States mainly on this basis.

The expansion of the United States into the Pacific and its increasing participation in non-American affairs furnished the French a further motive for criticizing the Latin-American policy of the Yankees. Frenchmen complained that the Yankees, at the very time when they were asserting most loudly their pretensions to a paramount interest which tended to render the Western Hemisphere an exclusive field for their exploitation, were aggressively demanding equal rights with other nations all around the world. They alleged that the United States, starting out with the modest slogan of

[6] A. Merignac, in *Revue du droit public*, V (1896), 202 ff.

[7] Gabriel Couillault, in *Le Monde économique* (Jan., 1896), pp. 7–8. This boundary dispute was settled by arbitration in 1899–1900.

"America for the Americans," had first expanded it into America for the North Americans and later (since 1898) into a maxim which meant no less than "America and the World for the Yankees." They declared that the European powers, while they were asking themselves where the Yankee choice would fall when that nation should be confronted by the dilemma of choosing between the Monroe Doctrine and the world empire, were astounded to behold that the Yankees, after a brief delay, overlooked the dilemma and chose both! Old Count d'Haussonville remarked in 1905 that he had become much wiser regarding the Yankee menace than he had been in 1881. "The idea did not then cross my mind," said the Count, "that a day would come when we should have to occupy ourselves with still another invasion, that of the United States into the politics of Europe and the world." And he was merely voicing a remonstrance that was generally felt in France until the outbreak of the World War.

The Economic Motive.—By far the most important motive for French attacks upon the American policy of the United States, however, was the economic motive. The desire to share the trade and investment opportunities of Latin America was very persistent and very strong. Trade influenced the Hispanic-American policy of France as early as 1823, and it had been largely responsible for French recognition of the new states before the mother country had taken the step. It furnished one of Louis Napoleon's justifications for his Mexican schemes as revealed in his famous letter to General Forey. Nor had France's desire to avail herself of Hispanic-American markets remained unrealized. Her trade with these countries had risen from less than three million dollars in 1825 to thirty million in 1848, to more than eighty million in 1855, and to more than one hundred and twenty-three million in 1860. But during the Civil War the United States underwent a marvelous industrial transformation, the effects of which France was destined to feel, before many years, in the markets and industrial enterprises of Hispanic America. The Hispanic-American trade of France was valued at only a little over one hundred and forty-four million dollars in 1896, even less than this in 1900, only one hundred and fifty-eight million in 1905, and hardly one hundred and eighty-seven million in 1909. The total of French investments is uncertain, but they amounted to hundreds of

millions (perhaps a billion) of dollars in 1914. Of course the United
States was not France's sole competitor in commerce and investments in the Latin-American field (England and Germany were
also very important), but Yankee shrewdness and aggressiveness
were greatly feared. Their competition was always more formidable
in prospect than in reality. Hence the French press was often filled
with exaggerated statements of Yankee commercial designs in the
New World. The Pan-American movement was decried as a Yankee
scheme to erect a Chinese wall between Europe and the three Americas, and the Monroe Doctrine was generally alleged to have a decided commercial aspect.

For instance, it was said in 1890 that Blaine was preparing to prevent the economic as well as the political intercourse of Europe with
America; that the Republican party had resolved "to prohibit all
importation from Europe into the New World." Again, in 1893, a
French writer declared that the Monroe Doctrine signified the economic hegemony of the United States in the Americas, for "in our
day . . . economic interests tend always to dominate political."
Thereafter, this design on the part of the United States appears to
have been taken for granted by French journalists.

The Policy of the French Government

Thus it will be observed that the attitude of the French press
toward the American policy of the United States was generally
unfriendly subsequent to 1867. But what was the official attitude of
France? The documents necessary to answer this question still lie
concealed in the French archives. Since the French government during most of this period was republican in form, it is not unlikely that
it was influenced by the view of the journalists. But whatever the
official attitude, French procedure apropos of the Yankee menace
was necessarily influenced by the prospect of a war with the United
States which an attempt to interfere in America would be likely to
occasion; and still more was it affected by the international situation
in Europe. The fiasco of Louis Napoleon constituted an impressive
lesson in these respects. Confronted by a divided public opinion at
home, by a hostile American army on the Rio Grande, and by a
threatening Prussia across the Rhine, the French emperor had been

compelled to abandon his Mexican undertaking, and France had to reckon with an unpleasant loss on the balance sheet of commerce and prestige. Frenchmen might well hesitate to repeat the project. It seemed more prudent for the government to limit its action to the promotion of trade and the support of the claims of its nationals. And by the time the Yankees had reached the most aggressive stage of their American policy France found that England and Germany were beginning to vie with each other for the friendship of the United States, and that Russia, France's most important reliance in case of a threat from Germany or England, was indisposed to offend the leading nation in the New World.[8] In brief, international complications in Europe placed France in the position of a giantess with hands tied, but with tongue unloosed and wits sharpened because of the very manacles which bound her hands.

All that could be done by criticism, denunciation, and propaganda, Frenchmen did; and they proved themselves the more able in these lines of effort because there was little else they could do. Pan-Americanism and the Monroe Doctrine were held up before the world in general, and before Latin America in particular, as cloaks alternately worn to cover Yankee absorption, monopoly, haughty domination, or imperialism. The Latin Americans were warned to keep up their economic connections with Europe, to cease fighting among themselves and unite, and to lend a willing ear to Pan-Hispanism and Pan-Latinism. "Washington aspires to become the capital of an enormous empire comprising, with the exception of Canada, the whole of the New World," stated Waleffe. "The United States is destined to subject to its imperial sway all the Latin-American states which might conceivably affect the control of the Yankees over the Panama Canal, and the Big Stick and Dollar Diplomacy are its weapons," declared Angel Marvaud. The United States aspires to dominate the New World from "the icy shores of the Arctic Ocean to Cape Horn," wrote Varigny. "Neither Mexico, nor the states of Central America, nor those of South America, have anything to fear from the European powers," assured Leroy-Beaulieu. "It is less certain that the government of Washington will

[8] Apparently the United States experienced uneasiness in regard to French procedure in Panama (1879 ff.), in Venezuela (1881), in the Dominican Republic (1895 and 1903–1904), and in Haiti (1888, 1903, and 1910–1915).

always observe relative to the other states of America a discretion equally absolute," he added. He then urged the Hispanic-American nations not to encourage the application of the Monroe Doctrine. Professor Merignac expressed the hope that the Spanish-American states would seek the assistance of Europe against the pseudo-benevolent and self-appointed intervention of the United States. The *Journal des Débats* remarked ill-humoredly that, "every time a mis-understanding arises between a European power and a country in Central or South America, the United States comes to the front." "She has, however, no right to do so," continued this journal; "she is not the protectress of those republics, and would meet with more than coolness if she attempted to become such. . . ." On another oc-casion the same publication addressed this explicit advice to the Latin Americans: "If you want *rapprochement* . . . look to your mother Spain rather than to the great invading republic of the North." And, to give only one more illustration from the period prior to the World War, the *Economiste français,* returning to the subject again and again, warned the nations of Latin America that they were in grave danger. "The simplest foresight imposes upon Latin America . . . three conditions for the maintenance of inde-pendence," declared the editor of this journal; namely, "order and good government, peace among the various sister republics, and close economic . . . relations with Europe, from which she has nothing to fear."

RECENT COMMENTS

World War I, absorbing, as it did, all of the energies of France and demanding careful cultivation of the United States as a friendly neutral and possible ally, caused a virtual cessation of French criti-cism. But the change was only temporary. The tremendous struggle caused a serious decline in France's Latin-American trade,[9] to say nothing of its injurious effects upon French investments, and the United States was the main power to benefit from French losses. These facts, and the additional fact that the United States sometimes ran counter to French sentiment after the close of the World War, did not dispose Frenchmen more favorably toward the policies of

[9] The decrease in value between 1913 and 1918 was more than fifty-five per cent.

the White House in Latin America. Accordingly, the French nation returned to many of its former attitudes and methods.

Indeed, nothing which happened during the tragic days of 1914–1918 tended to decrease in any marked degree the former deep interest of France in the Latin peoples of America. Even in the dark days when resistance to the German peril demanded every ounce of French energy, Frenchmen found time to consider their relations with these peoples. In the supreme crisis the great resources and friendly disposition of Latin Americans served but to emphasize their importance to France, and French writers surveyed the commerce, investments, cultural influence, and general prestige of their nation in these lands and discussed plans for the future.

The close of World War I found Frenchmen resolved to recoup their losses in Spanish America, and inspired by a Pan-Latin enthusiasm ready to burst out in denunciation of the policies and activities of the United States. "One of the inevitable consequences of the European War will be a most terrible competition in the markets of Latin America. This contest will not be limited to commerce but will extend itself to all of the fields of human activities. There will be a political, financial, industrial, and intellectual contest. It is necessary to prepare for it." Thus wrote one of the journalists just as France entered the era of post-bellum reconstruction. He then went on to speak of the rival powers, sounding the notes of Pan-Latinism and mild resentment toward the United States:

"There are two competitors, Europe and the United States. The United States displays the Monroe Doctrine to exclude, if possible, from the southern markets European capital and production. That political doctrine includes also an economic domination. But the South prefers her liberty to a purely geographical union. Her points of contact with North America are few; neither language nor race nor religion nor customs are included. She will gain little if she enters into the orbit of the United States, but on the contrary will lose much.

"The most active elements in South America today are European emigrants that have maintained close relationships with their fatherland, and the sons and descendants of emigrants who feel and call themselves 'sons of the country,' but who do not wish to deny that they are Latins: Latinity is not a vague and literary phrase, it is a real thing in many economic and political problems. The Latin republics of America feel their affinity of race for the Latins of Europe. We must prepare promptly an army of young men for this new struggle, an army that does not need to be so numerous but well chosen. Only thus shall we be able to conquer the place which the Latins deserve in South America." [10]

It was not long until this resentment deepened into hostility. In 1921 *Le Correspondant* came out with an article which accused the United States of preventing Costa Rica and Nicaragua from joining the Central American Union, and two years later it printed another article which maintained that the Washington government had broken up this Union with the view of dominating the little states which had tried to form it. This last article, indeed, gave a general survey of the recent imperialism of the United States and evinced a severe attitude toward our post-war procedure in Mexico and the Caribbean.

By 1923 French criticism had resumed the hostile tones of 1890–1913. The centenary of the Monroe Doctrine and the Pan-American Congress of Santiago occasioned outbursts similar to those of an earlier period. Pierre Arthuys opened the discussion with a bitter article on Dollar Diplomacy. "In Latin America the United States is trying to reduce her neighbors to economic fiefs, through the agencies of trusts, financial control, loans, and political intervention," wrote Arthuys. This general thesis was then freely developed, and the discussion deserves to be quoted at length:

". . . Europe is financially pauperized and politically insolvent. Latin America cannot maintain itself and make progress without foreign aid. Its needs play directly into the hands of Yankee graspers after power. Wall Street bankers lend money freely because it gives them the key to the door of every one of these countries. The guaranties they exact are most important and often curtail the sovereignty of the borrowing State.

"Your Yankee is a hard-headed, practical man, keenly alive to his own interests. So he insists that customs duties shall be pledged—or city revenues in case of a municipality—as security for what he lends. He likes still better to place a man of his own in charge of the customhouses, or even of a nation's treasury. When he takes a

[10] *Revue Minerva,* as quoted by S. G. Inman, *Problems in Pan-Americanism,* pp. 240–241.

mortgage upon the customs revenues of one of these Republics, he has his hand upon the funds that pay the salaries of presidents, cabinets, and the civil service; for internal taxes are hardly known, and in any case difficult to collect . . .

"Administering the customs, standing guard over the goods that leave the country and the goods that enter it, the Americans are indeed economic masters. They can easily show favor to their own products and discriminate against those of foreign countries. Wherever they get control, they boycott our manufactures, for the United States recognizes no friends when it comes to business. . . .

"All the world knows that the Governments of all the Latin American countries except Argentina, Chile, and a part of Brazil, are unstable. The United States is not unconcerned in the revolutions that afflict them. American money has played a part in many such disturbances and has thereby created excuses for intervention and eventual subjugation. Most Mexican revolutions have been fomented by Yankee intrigues. The Republic of Panama . . . owes its existence to a revolution supported by the Americans. The civil dissensions in Nicaragua, followed by American military occupation, the seizure of Santo Domingo, the practical absorption of Haiti, the dictation to Cuba that makes it a virtual vassal of the United States, all accord with the fundamental policy of a country that represents itself in Europe as a champion of political liberty." [11]

It is needless to present further illustrations. That French criticisms continued may be ascertained by an examination of the comments of the Paris newspapers on the recent trouble between the United States and Nicaragua. An Associated Press dispatch sent out from the French capital on January 7, 1927, stated that condemnation of the United States was universal. The organs of all parties and all classes denounced American imperialism. "For Christ and petroleum," remarked one of the newspapers in describing the motives prompting the landing of American Marines. The Communist *Humanité* declared that American imperialism in 1927 was becoming more dangerous than German imperialism in 1914!

An attempt to determine the amount of truth contained in these assertions—in those of the earlier as well as of the later period—

[11] *La Revue universelle,* Jan. 15, 1923, as quoted by the *Living Age,* Mar. 10, 1923, pp. 571–576.

cannot be made here, and, in fact, would be pointless so far as the main purposes of this chapter are concerned. Their bearing at this place does not depend so much upon their truth or falsity as upon their revelation of French disposition and their possible influence upon the attitude of the Latin Americans toward the United States. It can only be noted for the present that most of this French discussion of the policy of the United States in the Western Hemisphere is in the nature of propaganda and, as such, is characterized by half-truths, exaggerations, and inventions which will not stand the test of careful research. The United States has too often been cast in the rôle of a villain, and its ambitions, great as they may have been and are, have not infrequently been overstated. Frenchmen have been eager to maintain their territorial possessions unimpaired, to retain and even increase their prestige; they have felt a sort of mystical racial and cultural affinity for what they call the Latins of the New World and have been deeply concerned in their welfare; they have looked upon the United States as a possible peril to all of these interests, and have therefore portrayed Yankee policies and ambitions, sometimes unconsciously but more often consciously, in rather sinister outlines.

THE INFLUENCE OF FRENCH OPINION IN LATIN AMERICA

The effectiveness of French effort would be difficult to assess in detail, but there can be little doubt that it has achieved a large measure of success. In spite of all the post-war handicaps, French trade with Latin America had about reached its pre-war proportions by 1923, although French investments probably were still less valuable than in 1914. Nor can one doubt the influence of French writers upon the Latins of America. For many years French books and periodicals have enjoyed a wide circulation south of the Rio Grande, and most of the intellectuals have long looked to France as their guide. The criticisms of the United States contained in the writings of Latin Americans are strikingly similar to those reiterated by the French, and, where citations appear, French authorities are usually referred to. There could be no more striking illustration of French influence than is to be found in two small books published during the second decade of the present century. One of them, written by a Brazilian, represented an effort to counteract anti-Yankee propaganda in Hispanic America. The author occupied himself almost entirely with an analysis of the allegations of various French authors concerning American Imperialism.[12] The other was the work of a Mexican, and one of the most violent indictments of the Latin-American policy of the United States that has ever appeared. It was entitled *The United States versus Liberty*,[13] and the majority of its citations referred the reader to French writings. The attitude of the Latin Americans toward the United States cannot be understood without taking the influence of France into account.

Between 1932 and 1939 French commerce with Latin America suffered a decided decline in comparison with that of France's leading competitors. The influence in Latin America of a fascist France under Nazi domination was a matter for uneasy conjecture in the United States during the early 1940's.

[12] Dunshee de Abranches, *Brazil and the Monroe Doctrine* (Rio de Janeiro: Imprensa Nacional, 1915).

[13] Isidro Fabela, *Los Estados Unidos contra la Libertad* (Barcelona: Talleres Gráficos "Lux" [1920]). The author had recently held a high position in the Mexican diplomatic service.

CHAPTER XX

GERMAN INTERESTS AND ACTIVITIES

To ARRIVE at the beginning of German participation in Latin-American life one would have to go back to the emigration movement of the early nineteenth century and even to the period of the Spanish conquest. For present purposes, however, it is hardly necessary to commence earlier than the year 1896. Prior to that time several thousand Germans had settled mainly in Mexico, Guatemala, Venezuela, Argentina, Brazil, and Chile; considerable capital had been invested; German educators had begun to influence Chile's educational system; a few German officers were beginning to train the armies of some of the Pacific coast states; German vessels were carrying a goodly portion of South American commerce; and the German Empire had negotiated commercial treaties with most of the nations of Latin America. It was at that date, moreover, that many Germans began to clamor for colonies and a navy capable of defending German interests throughout the world. In 1896 there were about 400,000 people of German descent in Latin America, while German investments in the region had reached half a billion dollars, and German trade with these countries amounted to about $146,000,000.

Such was the state of German interests in Latin America at the close of the last century. During the next seventeen years they underwent an increase little short of marvelous. By 1913 German trade reached $470,000,000, German investments $2,000,000,000, and German settlers between 600,000 and 700,000 souls. The growth of German trade was especially noteworthy. The Latin-American commerce of no other nation grew so rapidly. The trade of the United States, Germany's closest competitor, increased 300 per cent while that of the latter increased 325 per cent during the period. Moreover, the Latin-American commerce of the German nation had grown more rapidly than its total commerce, as evidenced by the fact that the latter increased only 265 per cent during the period under consideration. Add to this a large transportation business and the cultural interests which the Germans felt in the people of Latin America as in most of the other peoples of Western Europe and America; note also the immense possibilities for expansion in so undeveloped a region—and it will not be difficult to understand why Germany has frequently turned its attention to Latin-American affairs. A prominent instance of this new orientation occurred in 1898.

THE SPANISH-AMERICAN WAR: MEDIATION OF THE CUBAN DIFFICULTY

Discussion of the attitude of the European nations during the war between the United States and Spain must center mainly around the procedure of Germany. It was generally believed at the time —and the view still persists—that the German government was unfriendly toward the United States, and German diplomats were in fact much interested in the discussions which related to the war and its effects upon world power. Contemporary newspapers of England and the United States conveyed the impression that Germany disapproved of American expansion; that the commander of the German squadron in Manila Bay conducted himself in an offensive manner; that Germany was eager to seize the Philippines; and that the Kaiser even tried to persuade the European powers to interfere in Spain's behalf. Moreover, these journals alleged that Germany and the nations of continental Europe were held in restraint solely by the pro-American attitude of Great Britain.

Documents recently published by the German government afford an opportunity to test these beliefs. The subject quite naturally falls into two divisions: the question of European arbitration and intervention in the Cuban difficulty, and the problem of the disposition of the Philippine and the Caroline Islands. The latter topic does not fall within the scope of this text.

Emperor William II, upon learning that General Woodford, American ambassador in Madrid, had been instructed to protest against Spanish procedure in Cuba and urge Spain to make peace, suggested to the Foreign Office (September 28, 1897) that intervention by the European states in favor of Spain, whose monarchial system would be endangered if she should lose Cuba, might be advisable. The German undersecretary of foreign affairs recommended great caution. He feared that France and England might use Germany's support of Spain to estrange Germany with the United States and secure commercial advantages at Germany's expense. He considered the coöperation of Russia and France an absolute prerequisite. Eulenburg, counselor on the Imperial Staff, thought that Austria, as the most natural advocate of Spain, should be induced to take the lead. The emperor agreed to this plan, remarking that the most expedient method would have to be found; that the end itself, not the means of attaining it, was the important matter. Regarding Eulenburg's apprehensions that the French Republic would not be willing to serve dynastic purposes, the Kaiser remarked that the protection of the colonial possessions of the European powers against transatlantic ambitions might be made the basis of agreement. In like manner he approved of Bernhard von Bülow's recommendation (September 30) that Austria should be urged to take the initiative, with the understanding that England and France would coöperate in the step under consideration.

Accordingly, on October 7, 1897, Bülow authorized Lichnowsky, German chargé in Vienna, to approach Austria. Lichnowsky was instructed to inform the Austrian government—in case the matter of European intervention in the Cuban affair should be brought up again—that, while Germany could not take a definite stand in advance of the other European powers, she would be disposed seriously to consider any proposals received from Paris or London—perhaps upon Austria's suggestion.

After the middle of October the whole affair entered the quiescent stage, only to become more critical than ever in the following February. As the real crisis between Spain and the United States approached, European diplomatic circles buzzed. The Spanish government inquired whether Germany, in order to protect the principle of monarchy, would be inclined to head a European demonstration. Bülow replied that Germany was eager to safeguard that principle, but that France must be persuaded to take the lead in intervention before Germany would be willing to support the move. It soon became evident, however, that neither Austria nor France was willing to take the first step. The Austrian foreign secretary thought that something should be done, but declared that the Austrian government was not strong enough to undertake the initiative. The French ambassador at Vienna revealed anxiety in regard to French colonial possessions in America and admitted that a united European demonstration was necessary. He felt, however, that Russia could not be counted upon, and he "showed an unusual degree of aversion to the Island Kingdom which placed obstacles in the way of necessary French colonial expansion in every quarter of the globe."

Thus matters stood in February. On March 14 the ambassador of Austria-Hungary in Berlin suggested once more that Germany should take the lead against the United States. Again Bülow declined and instructed the German ambassadors in Vienna and Madrid to express his Majesty's regret that he found himself unable to lend any assistance so long as Russia and France failed to give binding promises of active support. In his letter to the German ambassador in Vienna, however, Bülow made the important statement that the emperor, convinced that a separate action of the Triple Alliance was quite out of the question in view of the stand taken by England, France, and Russia, now considered papal arbitration as the only means left to save Spain.

It was, in fact, at the instigation of William II that the pope instructed his nuncio in Madrid to ascertain whether mediation by the Papal See would be agreeable to Spain. Having saved the Spanish monarch from taking the initiative in asking the pope for mediation—a step which the Spanish people might have interpreted as a symptom of royal weakness—the German emperor appears to have considered his mission finished. Thereafter he apparently preferred to leave the matter to the parties concerned. After he learned (April 1) that the Spanish government, contrary to expectations based upon Radowitz's report from Madrid (March 22, 1898), had told the nuncio that Spain could not consider arbitration on the basis of surrendering Cuba, the emperor wrote at the foot of the telegram: "Then there is no help for her! She will lose it anyhow!"

In the meantime, the Madrid representatives of Germany, Austria, France, Russia, Italy, and England were asked (March 26) by the Spanish minister of state to submit the following confidential request to the consideration of their respective governments: "The Powers should advise both Spain and the United States to settle the difficulties to which the questions embodied in Mr. Woodford's [ambassador of the United States in Spain] note of March 23 might give rise by accepting an arbiter, in such a way that peace should not be disturbed." Bülow instructed Radowitz that the emperor still felt Germany should not act before France and Russia had committed themselves. He therefore asked Radowitz to report on the replies given by the other powers.

Soon afterwards (April 4, 1898) Bülow authorized Holleben, German ambassador at Washington, to participate in the diplomatic action suggested by Spain, provided all five of the ambassadors of the great powers should agree to act together. But this concession appears to have been made mainly to oblige Austria. "Since the Vienna Cabinet wishes it," was the remark of Bülow. Germany must not give offense either to the European powers or to the United States, he cautioned Holleben on April 7. On this date the representatives of the great powers handed President McKinley a joint note, dated April 6, urging that peace be preserved.

Thus the German government had participated in this collective action with considerable caution; and, it should be added, without expecting any satisfactory results. On April 5, Bülow had remarked to the Spanish ambassador in Berlin that the powers were too occupied in the Far East to permit of effective measures in Spain's behalf. He personally believed that it would be better for Spain to give the pope *"carte blanche"* to prevent war.

The sequel showed, of course, that Bülow's misgivings regarding the influence of the powers were well founded. Spain was eager for peace and actually directed a suspension of hostilities in Cuba, but on April 11 McKinley sent his message to Congress without any mention of this concession. A few days later the legislative branch of the government authorized McKinley to use force in Cuba. War now appeared to be almost inevitable.

On April 14 Sir Julian Pauncefote, British ambassador in Washington, surprised Holleben by proposing that the diplomatic representatives of the great powers hand the United States another collective note. Pauncefote called the diplomats together, and they decided that this note should express the view that the intervention of the United States in Cuba would not be justifiable under the circumstances. In telegraphing this proposal to the Kaiser, Bülow remarked: "I personally regard such a demonstration somewhat coldly, though I, too, think it desirable that this frivolous attack be branded before the world. A step undertaken here would only decrease the prestige of the Powers, if their representatives have nothing at their command properly to repel an unfriendly answer." At this time—or later, as has been alleged—the emperor commented on Bülow's reaction as follows: "I think it [the demonstration suggested] entirely impracticable, useless and therefore prejudicial! We make ourselves as ridiculous in the eyes of the Americans as we did in those of the Greeks and the Turks, who did not care a straw about our collective notes. . . . I am against this step!"

Nevertheless, Bülow immediately sounded out Russia on the proposed move. The Russian minister of foreign affairs suspected that England had suggested the plan merely to bring discord between monarchial Europe and the United States, and expressed the view that nonintervention would be the best policy. Thereupon Bülow instructed the German ambassador at St. Petersburg to inform the Russian government that his German Majesty was also of the opinion that "Platonic steps with lame protests" would be of no advantage to Spain and would serve only to impair the prestige of the powers. Soon afterwards the matter was dropped.

The negative attitude of Germany and Russia appears to have been decisive, although the position of England may have had considerable weight. On April 16 Bülow remarked in a telegram to the emperor: "This collective action had been suggested by England, which made a Russian rejection appear probable from the beginning. I thought, therefore, that it would be in accordance with your Majesty's highest intentions if I investigated only in Petersburg regarding the reception of the English proposal, so as to avoid taking a rejection exclusively on our own shoulders. The answer of Count Muraviev [Russian minister of foreign affairs] turned out as had been foreseen by your Majesty." Yet Holleben, in a letter to Prince Hohenlohe, imperial chancellor, appears to have agreed with his French colleague when the latter remarked that Pauncefote's plan was not carried out because of the "lukewarm attitude" of England.

At any rate, Great Britain's position must have been puzzling to some of the powers. Holleben wrote to the German Foreign Office that the hesitation of the British government appeared "quite like a riddle," and the Kaiser commented with an "uns auch!" Holleben's comments on this phase of the affair deserve to be quoted at some length. In the letter of April 22, to which reference has already been made, he wrote: "In the beginning of the Cuban conflict England showed toward the United States, probably with special regard to the Far East, a disposition to oblige, which, it is true, was Platonic—at least I still think so—but then she joined the collective action of the powers of the seventh instant without difficulty. Soon after that Sir Julian Pauncefote was even the originator of the further steps which were planned here toward a coöperation of the powers. . . . But nothing further has come of it, as my French colleague tells me, because of England's lukewarm attitude, which, by the way, I do not regret much, as your Majesty knows. Now more recently come the fraternal articles of the two presses, especially of the one here, and the banquet speeches of the American ambassador in London; also there appears here, it is believed on a secret mission, the secretary of the American embassy in London, White; but all this is ridiculed by Sir Julian Pauncefote and as far as manifestations of friendship on the part of America are concerned, he flatly declares them to be hypocritical. From the mouth of Sir Julian that is a good deal regarding America."

This description of Britain's procedure aroused the Kaiser's ire. He suggested that Pauncefote was possibly lying. He then commented on his island rival: "England wants to play the very same game that she played years ago when she admittedly provoked the Graeco-Turkish War. She stirs all the powers to action, pretends to participate until the powers have compromised themselves with the belligerents; then she draws back, pharisaically beats her breast, secretly joins one of the combatants—of course always the stronger —and incites it against the Continental powers. Meanwhile, at their expense, she solicits from it commercial advantages for herself. England positively does not wish to belong to Europe, it won't throw in its lot with the Continental powers [this clause in English], but desires to constitute an independent entity between this continent and America or Asia."

The truth regarding England's position seems to be that Pauncefote either exceeded his instructions in convening the diplomats and planning further joint action, or that the English government underwent a change in sentiment about the time that war broke out between Spain and the United States. The facts in the case cannot be determined until Great Britain and France throw open their archives.

The documents published by Germany appear, however, to make clear the attitude of that government. The Kaiser, though he was the originator of the thought of intervention, can hardly be said to have pursued an aggressive policy with reference to the matter. The German government urged mediation upon the European powers and the pope, but the German Foreign Office pointed out from the beginning that Germany would not lead the movement for intervention. The German government even felt that Spain should give up Cuba in order to avoid war. Throughout the whole affair the Kaiser was primarily interested in the preservation of the "monarchical principle." Possibly he would have joined the powers in the employment of more forceful means to prevent an outbreak of war and the defeat of Spain; but that he undoubtedly would have done so is an inference that is not supported by the documents.

THE VENEZUELAN DIFFICULTY OF 1902–1903

Another demonstration of Germany's growing interest in Latin America occurred in 1902–1903. It had reference to claims of German nationals against Venezuela.

Damage and contract claims have figured largely in the relations of Latin America with the United States and the leading nations of Europe. Political disorders and financial chaos south of the Rio Grande frequently resulted in personal injuries and losses to foreigners. Often their claims were settled by direct negotiations or arbitration, but not infrequently the powers felt it necessary to support their complaining nationals by menace or armed force. It may be doubted whether any other phase of their foreign relations caused the Latin Americans greater anxiety. As early as 1863 Carlos Calvo expressed the view that force should not be used in the collection of damage claims or public debts, and in 1902 Luis Drago advanced the more limited doctrine that armed force should not be employed against a nation merely because of its failure to meet the services on its loans.

Many instances of the employment of force in behalf of claimants might be narrated. It was with the view of exacting indemnity for injuries to its citizens that France bombarded Vera Cruz in 1838 and blockaded the Río de la Plata in 1838–1840. It was with a similar purpose that France, England, and Spain occupied Mexico in 1861, although France had ulterior imperial designs, as we have noted. Injuries to Spanish subjects furnished excuse for a Spanish attack on Peru in 1865. Germany employed force in behalf of her injured subjects in Nicaragua in 1878, and in Haiti in 1898 and 1902. And the claims of United States citizens were partially responsible for the Mexican War (1846–1848). Space, however, does not permit even a summary of this important phase of the foreign relations of Latin America. A rather detailed discussion of the Venezuelan difficulty of 1901–1903, in which Germany played a conspicuous rôle, will suffice to illustrate the nature and significance of the subject.

Political Conditions in Venezuela; Grievances of the Powers.—The opening of the twentieth century found Venezuela in a distressed and bankrupt condition. For several decades the country had been torn and impoverished by civil strife and political corruption. People and resources alike had been the prey of adventurers and rascals. The ruling class, consisting of only about six per cent of the population, not only had exploited the country and wasted its revenues, but had separated into hostile factions which impressed the lower classes into armies that fought for the opportunity of engaging in national plunder. Actuated sometimes by a sincere interest in the material advancement of the nation but more often by mere desire to increase the spoils, these politicians bargained concessions to foreigners who had entered Venezuela in search of trade or of such grants as corrupt officials could offer. These concessions tended to introduce an international factor into the local disorders of the country.

From 1898 to 1902 conditions were worse than usual. Cipriano Castro, a cattleman and bold caudillo of the western mountainous region, was carrying on a bloody civil war in order to secure the government and consolidate his power. Foreigners, who suffered along with Venezuelans, were very loath to submit their complaints to the exclusive jurisdiction of the Venezuelan government. Castro, after seizing the government, soon became a dictator who paid little respect either to the law or to the constitution. In fact, he had not been in power long before he had "a majority of the members of the supreme court arrested, imprisoned, and finally removed from office for intimating that they would not decide a case in the manner desired by the Chief Executive." [1] Instead of appealing to Castro for redress of their grievances, the nationals of several of the European states sought the aid of their home governments. By the closing days of the year 1902, Germany, England, and Italy were ready to undertake joint action for the purpose of obtaining satisfaction for the losses and injuries suffered by their subjects in Venezuela.

The claims whose immediate adjustment these powers were now prepared to demand of Venezuela amounted to less than sixty-two million bolívars, or about twelve million dollars. Like most claims of this nature they fell into two categories; namely, those based upon contractual obligations of the Venezuelan government, and those arising from financial losses and personal injuries suffered during the recent revolution. The most important of the German demands, for instance, related to interest seven years in arrears on Venezuelan bonds, the payment of dividends guaranteed by Venezuela on a German-built railroad, and indemnity for damages, injuries, forced loans, and inconveniences suffered during the civil war of 1898–1900. The claims of England and Italy were of the same general nature and differed only in detail. Moreover, it should be noted that similar claims were asserted by citizens and subjects of the United States, France, Belgium, Mexico, Spain, Sweden and Norway, and the Netherlands.

The imbroglio passed through three phases. The first lasted from December, 1901, when drastic action first began seriously to be considered, until December 17, 1902, when Germany, England, and Italy accepted limited arbitration in principle. The second phase —which was characterized by a long discussion over payment for claims withheld from arbitration, preferred consideration for the claims of the blockading powers, and certain details of procedure —continued from December 18, 1902, to February 14, 1903, when all arrangements for adjudication of the claims were finally effected and the blockade was lifted. The third phase—of minor importance

---

[1] Minister Francis B. Loomis to John Hay, Feb. 22, 1901, in *Sen. Doc.* No. 413, 60 Cong., I Sess. (Ser. 5257), p. 332.

here—related to the final awards of the mixed commissions and The Hague Tribunal. The labor of these bodies was not completed until February, 1904.

The First Phase.—In a survey of the Venezuelan affair two important facts must be kept in mind: (1) Negotiations for an Anglo-German alliance had been in progress since 1899, and although nothing had been accomplished, an understanding may still have been considered remotely possible. (2) Both England and Germany were eager to avoid giving offense to the United States; both thought of the United States as a possible ally, and each was determined not to allow the other to gain any advantage in this rivalry for American friendship.[2]

The first suggestion of a joint Anglo-German action against Venezuela appears to have come from the British Foreign Office on January 2, 1902.[3] Chancellor Bülow looked with favor upon the project, but the Kaiser, suspicious of England, declared that the suggestion was too vague. He also noted that England might take advantage of German proposals of joint action to arouse suspicion against Germany in the United States and thus destroy the effect of the contemplated visit of Prince Henry. "Not until after the expiration of Henry's mission," remarked the Kaiser.[4]

The question of coöperative coercion was accordingly not seriously considered until October, 1902. By the 12th of the following month the two powers had virtually agreed upon a line of procedure,

---

[2] Since Italy's rôle was a minor one, it will receive little attention in this discussion. On Anglo-German relations at this period see *The Cambridge History of British Foreign Policy* (1925), III, 276 ff.

[3] The British correspondence recently published does not confirm this view, but I have been informed by a reliable authority that documents exist in the Foreign Office of the British government which indicate that the suggestion of joint action originated with Lansdowne.

[4] Prince Henry's visit was designed to "win the Americans with manner and appearance, to convince them of the appreciation of his Majesty for the great and rapidly growing American people as well as of the usefulness of good relations between the Germans and the Americans, who are not separated by any political differences but are bound instead by numerous and weighty interests, ancient traditions, and ties of blood." The prince was not to speak on his own initiative of affairs in Central and South America, and especially was he not to speak in detail of German designs in these Latin-American countries. If the Americans revealed anxiety with reference to German influence and possible German acquisitions in this part of the world, Prince Henry was to treat the matter as an absurd phantom, refer to the many problems which Germany must solve elsewhere, and declare that Germany desired "peace throughout the Western Hemisphere and friendly relations with the United States." He was not, however, to make a free and formal explanation.

but on the next day the British government, acting without the knowledge of Germany, handed another ultimatum to Venezuela, the third within six months. Apparently London was hesitating at the last moment to strike a bargain with Berlin. The answer of Venezuela proved unacceptable, however, and it was not long until the arrangement for joint action was completed. Each power was to present Venezuela an ultimatum at the same moment, answer to which would be required in twenty-four hours. In case of an unfavorable reply, Venezuelan gunboats were to be seized, and then, if further action should become necessary, the ports of the country were to be blockaded. There was to be full and frank coöperation between Germany and England, and neither power was to withdraw without the consent of the other.

Affairs now moved rapidly toward a crisis. On December 7 the British and German ultimatums were delivered to the Venezuelan government. Venezuela's response was unsatisfactory and on the following day both legations withdrew from Caracas. On December 9 four Venezuelan gunboats were seized, and three of them sunk. On December 11 Great Britain ordered the blockade of five Venezuelan ports and the mouths of the Orinoco. At about the same time, Italy expressed a desire to participate in the action and offered to furnish two cruisers. The offer was eagerly accepted by the German government, which hoped that England and Italy might move in the foreground and thus divert any hostility which might be aroused in the United States against Germany.[5] Two days later a German and a British cruiser bombarded two forts at Puerto Cabello in retaliation for the seizure of a British steamer and an alleged insult to the British flag. On the same day Venezuela submitted through the United States an arbitration proposal. Soon afterwards the British and the German governments—the former on December 16 and the latter on December 17—agreed to arbitration in principle, reserving certain "first rank" claims. Thus Venezuela had asked for arbitration just four days after the allies began their coercive action, and the allies had accepted a limited arbitration in principle just

[5] The Kaiser commented thus on the dispatch which informed him of Italy's desire to participate: "Approved. Italy may take part and the more ships England sends the better. Just so our action keeps to the rear and theirs comes into the foreground. We shall merely participate in the British programme. . . . We shall let our flag follow the lead of the British."

four days after Venezuela proposed it. So ended the first phase.

Up to this point the United States had taken little part in the affair. The allies had kept Washington informed of their procedure, but formal protest had not been made. The American secretary of state had only remarked that "the United States Government, although they regretted that European powers should use force against Central and South American countries, could not object to their taking steps to obtain redress for injuries suffered by their subjects, provided that no acquisition of territory was contemplated." The United States had merely transmitted the Venezuelan arbitration proposal of December 13 without comment. Only with reference to a "pacific blockade," which Germany desired in order to avoid consulting the Bundesrat, was any objection raised. On this point the United States held the view that under international law there was no such thing as a pacific blockade. The British maritime lawyers agreed with the American contention, and Germany thereupon consented to a regular blockade.

Before the Venezuelan entanglement had passed through this first phase, however, indications that American and British public opinion would have to be taken into consideration were not lacking. As early as December 12 Bülow had pointed out the desirability of avoiding every action which might give support to the impression commonly reported and widely circulated in both the English and the American press, that Germany was the initiator of the movement to coerce Venezuela. He said that most of the adverse criticism of Germany had been called forth by the sinking of the Venezuelan cruisers. He then remarked that this event had called anti-German agitation again to life and respectfully advised that due attention be given to the enlargement of Germany's military force. On the following day Count Metternich, German ambassador in London, also called attention to press criticism, in England and elsewhere, on the gunboat episode and suggested the advisability of a published statement in justification of the act.

During the next few days the tension in diplomatic circles became very decided. Metternich reported that Lord Lansdowne, British foreign secretary, was hesitant and uncertain, that King Edward viewed the joint action against Venezuela with disfavor, and that among political circles in England there was a widespread fear that the movement might lead to "coolness" with the United States. From Holleben, the German ambassador in the United States, came a telegram stating that German-American and English-American financial circles in New York were speaking with anxiety about transactions in Venezuela; that the press, though hitherto reasonably quiet and not unfriendly, was beginning to assume a sharper tone; that some held the view that England, lacking the support of Parliament, might break away from Germany and reach out a hand to the United States behind Germany's back; that certain well informed merchants of Latin America were of the opinion German trade would suffer; that, moreover, it was being urged that after the cannons had spoken and Germany had shown the world her ability and determination to support her just claims, it would be wise and would create a good impression in all America for the Berlin government to accept the principle of arbitration. Holleben urged that this course could be followed without evil consequences, since Germany had already indicated a willingness to submit certain designated claims to mixed commissions. "I believe," concluded Holleben, "that after all this suggestion may deserve some consideration." At the same time, Metternich sent another telegram which reported an interview with Lansdowne. During the interview the British foreign secretary had told Metternich that the cabinet favored arbitration, and that strong opposition to the joint action against Venezuela was developing both in Parliament and in the country at large. He had also called attention to signs that in the United States a storm of opposition was approaching, against which the Washington government would be powerless to proceed. Reflecting upon the situation, Metternich remarked that if the English government were supported by Parliament, the press, and public opinion, Germany might complacently look forward to further developments in the Venezuelan affair and not concern itself with "North American insolence." "But, alas," he continued, "this is not the case." He then concluded his telegram with the advice that the sooner Germany withdrew from the joint affair with England the better, and recommended arbitration. With such information and recommendations before it, the German government had agreed to the principle of limited arbitration in December, 1902. Not official pressure exerted by Washington, but the state of public opinion in the

United States and England, had been responsible for this concession.

The Second Phase.—As matters approached the second stage, the United States revealed a disposition to take a more active part. On the same day that the German government agreed to limited arbitration, but after Germany already had reached this decision, the American ambassadors at London and Berlin, following out Hay's instructions, had repeated the Venezuelan proposal of arbitration "with strong commendation." On the following day, Secretary Hay talked over the situation with Count von Quadt, German chargé in Washington, and assured him that President Roosevelt as well as he himself reposed full trust in Germany so far as the Venezuelan affair was concerned. Moreover, Hay is reported to have declared that the American government was firmly resolved not to interfere in any way. Nevertheless, Hay at the same time expressed the view that because of the excited and nervous state of Congress and the public a speedy solution of the problem was most desirable. A few days later the allied powers, yielding to American opinion, requested Roosevelt to serve as arbiter—a step which was calculated to allay American apprehensions, but which, owing to the president's refusal to accept the offer, failed to bring the difficulties any nearer to a final settlement. It was then decided that the question might be referred to The Hague.

Meanwhile, the three allied powers proceeded to establish a formal blockade of the Venezuelan ports (December 20, 1902). Arrangements for payment of first-rank claims and the adjustment of the details of arbitration promised some difficulty, and the cruisers of the allies might therefore prove useful.

As the year drew to a close, Germany and England presented detailed memoranda of their demands and concessions. First-rank claims—namely, German claims originating in the Venezuelan civil war of 1898–1900 and British claims based upon the imprisonment of British subjects and the seizure of British shipping—were strictly excluded. Venezuela would have to settle directly for these claims, which amounted to about £132,000, and begin payment at once. Even the other claims were to be withheld from a court of arbitration until the Venezuelan government admitted its responsibility in principle.

In declining to serve as arbiter President Roosevelt had suggested that a preliminary diplomatic conference be held in Washington for arranging the details of arbitration. This suggestion the allied powers accepted, although Germany did so with some reluctance. Herbert W. Bowen, minister of the United States in Venezuela, was chosen to represent the Caracas government in the conference. It was not until the latter part of January (1903) that formal preliminary negotiations began at Washington. Many difficulties were confronted and once more the people of the United States became impatient and irritated.

Soon after Bowen arrived in Washington to defend Venezuela's position, news of a ruthless German bombardment of Fort San Carlos was published in the American press. The public immediately lost its temper. "I hear indirectly," cabled Count von Quadt, "that Secretary Hay expressed himself very bitterly concerning our action. . . . At no time since the Venezuelan entanglement has feeling against us been so heated as now." The British public likewise became hostile, and the British government prepared to beat a retreat. On January 23, Britain promised to return to Venezuela the boats (presumably merchant vessels) which she had captured. Germany felt compelled to follow suit. Four days later an agent of the British Foreign Office came to the German minister in London to plead for a curtailment of German demands for cash in payment for first-rank claims. Inasmuch as Britain had decided to be content with £5,500 instead of £66,000, would not Germany agree to a similar reduction? The refusal of Germany to consent to this arrangement would shake the British cabinet, immeasurably increase ill humor toward Germany, and possibly seriously disturb the future relations of the two countries. The next day Germany cabled acceptance of the reduction.

The question as to whether the claims of the blockading powers should have preferential treatment now took the center of the stage. Bowen insisted that all of the powers should be placed on an equal footing. England was hesitant, and Germany appeared to be strongly opposed to such an arrangement. The Venezuelan affair had reached a most critical condition.

On January 28, King Edward had an interview with Count Metternich for the purpose of discussing the difficulty. The king expressed a strong desire to see the matter brought to an immediate conclusion. The count replied that Germany entertained a similar desire but felt that she dare not come out of Venezuela with empty hands. He also complained that British reporters and journalists were largely responsible for the attitude of the American press toward the Venezuelan undertaking.[6]

On the same day Charlemagne Tower, ambassador of the United States at Berlin, reported a conversation of January 27 with the Kaiser, who complained of the recent attacks of the British newspapers. He "declared that the treatment of Germany in regard to the expedition against Venezuela was entirely unfair, because, so far from it being true that Germany had drawn England into this undertaking, the fact is that the expedition was planned in England before Germany knew anything about it. The Emperor said that during his last visit to England Lord Lansdowne had explained to him the difficulties which the British government had met with in attempting to enforce the claims of British subjects in Venezuela, and had told him that . . . the British government believed it to be necessary to adopt stronger measures. Lord Lansdowne thereupon invited the German Emperor to unite with Great Britain in enforcing by joint action the claims of Great Britain and Germany against Venezuela," and the emperor had accepted the invitation.

On January 31 Count Speck von Sternburg, who had just arrived at Washington on a special mission, reported a conference with President Roosevelt, during which the president remarked that the Venezuelan affair had begun highly to irritate public opinion both in America and in Europe, and expressed the ardent hope that it might soon be settled. Three days later Sternburg cabled a nervous report to Berlin. He said nothing of an interview with Roosevelt, but declared that Germany was sacrificing what little sympathy she had left in the United States. He also noted that the Latin-American states were taking offense, and that "Dewey's fleet had received secret orders to hold itself in readiness." He respectfully advised acceptance of Bowen's offer of thirty per cent of the customs receipts of La Guaira and Puerto Cabello for three months in lieu of preferential treatment.

[6] On Jan. 28, White telegraphed from London: "I urge daily great danger of explosion of American opinion if delay in raising blockade is prolonged, which this Government fully realizes and is making every effort to secure Germany's assent to raise it." (State Department MS.)

Meanwhile, the British government had made up its mind to submit the matter of preferential treatment to arbitration. Germany, however, still held out, and Lord Lansdowne, being "a man of honor," was not inclined to break his agreement with Germany. The crisis confronting the British ministry was vividly described in a private dispatch written by Metternich to Bülow on February 4. The king, the queen, and the Prince of Wales were developing a strong aversion to the joint action against Venezuela. They regarded the Germans as mischief-makers, particularly since the bombardment of San Carlos. English public opinion, forgetting that British vessels had bombarded Puerto Cabello not long before, sympathized with Castro. The ministry was beginning to defend its policy in public speeches. If Parliament should convene as scheduled on February 17, and begin to ask questions regarding the originator of the Venezuelan project, the cabinet would be seriously endangered. If President Roosevelt should lose patience, submit to the advice of the yellow press, and demand the lifting of the blockade, the ministry would be overturned in a moment's time.

The Kaiser noted on the margin of this report that the probable successor of the Balfour-Chamberlain-Lansdowne cabinet might be hostile to German interests. Evidently the time had come for Germany to retreat. Accordingly, on February 6, the ambassadors of the three allied powers in Washington agreed to submit the question of preferential treatment to President Roosevelt as arbiter. Germany had apparently consented to this compromise as early as February 4.[7] The question of security for the balance of Germany's "first-rank" claims—namely, those not covered by the cash payment of £5,500 —caused a few more days of argument, but the difficulties were overcome by February 12.

The Third Phase.—The crisis had now passed. Roosevelt was no more willing to serve as arbiter in February than he had been in the previous December, but this was merely a matter of detail. The question of preferential treatment of the blockading powers could be submitted to The Hague. The imbroglio had reached the

---

[7] "Baron Sternburg is instructed to remain squarely in line with Sir Michael Herbert [British chargé in Washington]"—Bülow to Metternich, Feb. 4, 1903. "The English Ambassador has been instructed to submit the question of preferential treatment to the President for arbitration. The Italian Ambassador and I have acceded to his desire."—Sternburg to the German foreign secretary, Feb. 6, 1903.

third phase. All claims except those of "first rank," which had already been arranged, were left to the decision of mixed commissions. It is interesting to note, as bearing upon the justice of the claims, that barely one-fifth of them was allowed by these mixed commissions. On February 22, 1904, a special court of The Hague handed down a unanimous decision in favor of preferential treatment for the blockading powers; and so the Venezuelan episode passed into history.

Roosevelt and the Kaiser.—It remains to inquire what part President Roosevelt played in the settlement and whether Germany entertained ulterior territorial designs. Roosevelt has given his own account of the action which he took in order to hasten the settlement of the Venezuelan imbroglio. He wrote in 1916:

". . . I speedily became convinced that Germany was the leader, and the really formidable party in the transaction; and that England was merely following Germany's lead in rather half-hearted fashion. . . . I also became convinced that Germany intended to seize some Venezuelan harbor and turn it into a strongly fortified place of arms, on the model of Kiauchau, with a view of exercising some degree of control over the future Isthmian Canal, and over South American affairs generally.

"For some time the usual methods of diplomatic intercourse were tried. Germany declined to agree to arbitrate the question at issue between her and Venezuela, and declined to say that she would not take possession of Venezuelan territory, merely saying that such possession would be 'temporary'—which might mean anything. I finally decided that no useful purpose would be served by further delay, and I took action accordingly. I assembled our battle fleet, under Admiral Dewey, near Porto Rico, for 'maneuvers,' with instructions that the fleet should be kept in hand and in fighting trim, and should be ready to sail at an hour's notice. . . . I told John Hay that I would now see the German Ambassador, Herr von Holleben, myself, and that I intended to bring matters to an early conclusion. . . .

"I saw the ambassador, and explained that in view of the presence of the German Squadron on the Venezuelan coast I could not permit longer delay in answering my request for an arbitration, and that I could not acquiesce in any seizure of Venezuelan territory.

The Ambassador responded that his Government could not agree to arbitrate, and that there was no intention to take 'permanent' possession of Venezuelan territory. I answered that Kiauchau was not a 'permanent' possession of Germany's—that I understood that it was merely held by a ninety-nine years' lease; and that I did not intend to have another Kiauchau, held by similar tenure, on the approach to the Isthmian Canal. The Ambassador repeated that his government would not agree to arbitrate. I then asked him to inform his Government that if no notification for arbitration came within a certain specified number of days I should be obliged to order Dewey to take his fleet to the Venezuelan coast and see that the German forces did not take possession of any territory. He expressed very grave concern, and asked me if I realized the serious consequences that would follow such action; consequences so serious to both countries that he dreaded to give them a name. I answered that I had thoroughly counted the cost before I decided on the step, and asked him to look at the map, as a glance would show him that there was no spot in the world where Germany in the event of a conflict with the United States would be at a greater disadvantage than in the Caribbean Sea.

"A few days later the Ambassador came to see me, talked pleasantly on several subjects, and rose to go. I asked him if he had any answer to make from his government to my request, and when he said no, I informed him that in such event it was useless to wait as long as I had intended, and that Dewey would be ordered to sail twenty-four hours in advance of the time I had set. He expressed deep apprehension, and said that his government would not arbitrate. However, less than twenty-four hours before the time I had appointed for cabling the order to Dewey, the Embassy notified me that his Imperial Majesty the German Emperor had directed him to request me to undertake the arbitration myself. I felt, and publicly expressed, great gratification at this outcome, and great appreciation of the course the German Government had finally agreed to take. Later I received the consent of the German Government to have the arbitration undertaken by The Hague Tribunal, and not by me." [8]

That Roosevelt's account of what he did was not mere war-time propaganda or political bombast is strongly supported by a letter

[8] J. B. Bishop, *Life and Times of Theodore Roosevelt* (1920), I, 222–224.

which he wrote to Henry White on August 14, 1906. "At the time of the Venezuela business," he remarked, "I saw the German Ambassador privately myself; told him to tell the Kaiser that I had put Dewey in charge of our fleet to maneuver in West Indian Waters; that the world at large should know this merely as a maneuver and we should strive in every way to appear simply as coöperating with the Germans; but that I regretted to say that the popular feeling was such that I should be obliged to interfere, by force if necessary, if the Germans took any action which looked like the acquisition of territory there or elsewhere along the Caribbean; that this was not in any way intended as a threat, but as the position on the part of the Government which the American people would demand, and that I wanted him to understand it before the two nations drifted into such a position that trouble might come. . . ." [9]

Such are Roosevelt's accounts of his action in the Venezuelan difficulty. It would appear that he did in fact attempt to exert pressure upon Germany, but in his later narratives of his procedure he confused dates and diplomats. He probably did not bring pressure to bear upon Holleben in the middle of December, 1902, but upon Sternburg during the last of January and the first of February, 1903.[10] If he actually took such a step his action may have hastened Germany's agreement to follow England's lead in submitting the question of preferential treatment to arbitration. Two factors appear to have been responsible for this concession: (1) the report of the concentration of Dewey's fleet and the hostility of American public opinion, and (2) news of a cabinet crisis in England. It is impossible to say which was more influential. One thing, however, is certain: Germany was very desirous of avoiding any course which might promote an alliance between the United States and Great Britain. It should also be remembered that Roosevelt had knowledge

[9] Rhodes, *The McKinley and Roosevelt Administrations* (1922), pp. 251–252.

[10] It will be recalled that Germany had agreed to accept arbitration in principle just eight days after the allies began coercive action against Venezuela and only four days after Venezuela asked for arbitration. This period would appear too short for the events described by Roosevelt to transpire. Holleben ceased to function as ambassador about December 17. *Die Grosse Politik* contains only one letter of Holleben's concerning the Venezuelan affair —that of Dec. 16, 1902—and it makes no reference to Roosevelt or the United States government or Admiral Dewey.

of the state of British public opinion, of the anxieties of the British cabinet, and of the fact that the English government was prepared both to give way on the matter of preferential treatment and to urge Germany to grant a similar concession. Under the circumstances he could afford to be bellicose, just as John Quincy Adams and James Monroe had dared "blow a blast on the republican trumpet, while sheltered behind the shield of England."

Germany's Motives.—With reference to German territorial ambitions, Roosevelt was unduly alarmed. Germany's policy of bidding against England for the friendship of the United States would not have permitted the seizure and permanent retention of Venezuelan territory unless England could have been induced to participate in such action and to enter into a general alliance with Germany. With England as a possible enemy, Germany must seek the friendship of the United States or at least avoid any action which would tend to promote Anglo-Saxon rapprochement. No evidence has come to light to indicate that either power entertained ulterior motives hostile to the Monroe Doctrine at any time during the common action against Venezuela.

So far as the immediate Venezuelan problem was concerned, the sole motive of the German government seems to have been a desire to indemnify and protect German subjects and to convince all the states of Latin America of Germany's ability and inclination to defend these subjects wherever they might reside. Bülow argued in September, 1902, for instance, that "a severe policy toward Venezuela would now be desirable for the sake of our reputation in Central and South America and the protection of the large and growing German interests there." Again, on November 3, Bülow urged that if the unjust treatment of Germans in Venezuela remained unavenged, German influence in Central and South America would "necessarily suffer injury." This was evidently Germany's only motive, and it appears to be sufficient to explain German action throughout the Venezuelan difficulty.

Of course this does not mean that Germany under more favorable circumstances would not have been eager to seize Venezuelan territory or domain in other parts of Latin America. It merely indicates that the international stage was not set for such an act in 1902–1903, just as it had not been set for the partition of the Philippines or the occupation of a naval base in the Dominican Republic in 1898.[11]

THE LATIN-AMERICAN POLICY OF GERMANY AFTER THE OUT-BREAK OF WORLD WAR I

The period between 1903 and 1916 brought about no immediate change in the attitude of official Germany. On the contrary, the outbreak of World War I served to emphasize the importance of American friendship. Propaganda in favor of the German cause was at once begun. A special effort was made to cultivate the United States. When German newspapers severely criticized Wilson's Mexican policy, officials of the government counseled moderation, and in September, 1914, the German ambassador in Washington emphatically denied rumors that Germany intended, in the event of victory, "to seek expansion in South America." Bernhard Dernburg, presumably a representative of the Kaiser, publicly stated that if the United States desired assurances on this matter, such assurances would be forthcoming at once. "We have already laid before the Government of the United States an official note stating that Germany would not seek expansion in South America," said Dernburg.

After it became virtually certain that the United States would enter the war on the side of the enemies of the Central Powers and endeavor to bring the Latin-American states into the struggle, the policy of Germany naturally veered from its former course. Thereafter its main purpose was to prevent the Latin-American states from joining the Allies and to divert the energies of the United States by causing trouble in the Western Hemisphere. The position and influence of Germany then became for the first time fairly obvious. The German nation was seen not to be without friends in any part of Latin America. The influence of that procession of military instructors, scientists, bankers, merchants, and professors who had been coming over for years was revealed. Notwithstanding the fact that the combined influence of France, England, Italy, and the United

[11] In this year the Kaiser rejected certain overtures made by the government of the Dominican Republic regarding the cession of a naval base to Germany. He remarked that he would not "fall into such a trap" and expressed an unwillingness to "set himself at variance with the United States."

States was pitted against the Teutons, Brazil was the only important Latin-American nation which entered the lists opposed to Germany, and decidedly pro-German predilections were revealed in several states. Of course this was not a clear test, because other motives entered into the decision; but it did indicate that the Germans were a power to be reckoned with in the lands south of the United States. Sympathy for Germany was perhaps strongest in Venezuela, Colombia, and Mexico, but it probably had more menacing possibilities in Cuba, Haiti, Brazil, and Mexico. German designs are said to have had something to do with the armed intervention of the United States in Haiti in 1916, and it was alleged, but never publicly demonstrated, that Germans instigated a revolt in Cuba in February, 1917. Fear was expressed that emissaries of the Kaiser might endanger the peace and security of Brazil and Uruguay by organizing the German element in southern Brazil, but these Germans proved either too loyal to their adopted country or too indifferent to the fate of the Fatherland.

It was in Mexico that German activities created most excitement. On January 16, 1917, Herr Alfred Zimmermann, German minister of foreign affairs, instructed Eckhardt, the representative of the imperial government in Mexico, as follows:

". . . We intend to begin on the first of February unrestricted submarine warfare. We shall endeavour in spite of this to keep the United States of America neutral. In the event of this not succeeding, we shall offer Mexico a proposal of alliance on the following basis: Make war together, make peace together, generous financial support and an understanding on our part that Mexico is to reconquer the lost territory in Texas, New Mexico, and Arizona. The settlement in detail is left to you. You will inform the President of the above most secretly as soon as the outbreak of the war with the United States of America is certain and add the suggestion that he should, on his own initiative, invite Japan to immediate adherence and at the same time mediate between Japan and ourselves. Please call the President's attention to the fact that the ruthless employment of our submarines now offers the prospect of compelling England in a few months to make peace. . . ." [12]

[12] Quoted in Burton J. Hendrick, *The Life and Letters of Walter Hines Page,* III (1925), 333.

On February 8, Eckhardt was directed immediately to broach the question of alliance to President Carranza and to suggest that Carranza sound Japan. "If the President declines from fear of subsequent revenge," wrote Zimmermann, "you are empowered to offer him a definitive alliance after conclusion of peace, provided Mexico succeeds in drawing Japan into the Alliance." On February 20, Eckhardt had an interview with the Mexican minister of foreign affairs, who "willingly took the matter into consideration, and thereupon had a conversation, which lasted an hour and a half, with [the] Japanese Minister." A few days later the German envoy appears to have begun negotiations with Carranza. The most urgent need of the Mexican president was munitions and arms, and Germany considered plans for partially supplying this need, but suggested that it would be wise for Mexico to look to Japan and South America for these essentials. Evidently progress was being made. On March 1, however, Germany's Mexican project became public information in the United States, and a little more than a month later the United States Congress declared the existence of a state of war with Germany. Shortly afterwards Carranza informed the German minister that he intended to remain neutral. "The alliance . . . had been stultified by its 'premature publication' but would become necessary at a later period." German agents then apparently turned to Francisco Villa to devise plans for setting fire to the Tampico oil wells. Once more, however, their schemes met with failure. With the defeat of Germany all danger passed.

The war and its aftermath inflicted great injury upon German interests in Latin America. For three years German trade was completely wiped out, but it soon began to recover. In 1920 Germany shared a little more than five per cent of Latin America's commerce. By 1928 the value of German trade with Latin America exceeded the total of the pre-war period. The depression years witnessed a decline, but an upturn followed the advent of Adolf Hitler, and by 1937–38 Nazi trade and propaganda drives caused uneasiness regarding Latin-American security. German trade was increased through barter and subsidy, and propaganda was carried on by means of the radio, free news services, the enlargement of the diplomatic and consular staffs, and the exaction of contributions from German residents, some of whom were organized for the purpose of pro-Nazi agitation.

CHAPTER XXI

THE PAN-HISPANIC MOVEMENT

THE latter part of the nineteenth century and the early decades of the twentieth witnessed a gradual drawing together of Spain and her former colonies in the New World. The growing friendship was largely the result of Spanish effort, or, more accurately, of the efforts of a fairly large, intelligent, and enthusiastic group of Spaniards who have labored and are laboring for what they conceive to be the welfare of their country and the interest of the Spanish race. Racial and cultural solidarity has been in fact the keynote of their propaganda. Prior to the opening of the present century they were motivated by the idea of rallying around this slogan the kindred nations oversea with the view of winning allies for a prospective struggle with the United States. More recently, other motives have been prominent.

THE EARLY MOVEMENT

In the fifties of last century, when the remnants of the Spanish empire in the New World as well as the integrity of the newly formed Latin nations, were threatened by the Anglo-American filibusters, Spanish propaganda sought to play upon the note of racial solidarity in order to induce the Hispanic Americans to unite among themselves and with Spain for the purpose of stemming the tide of invasion. Newspapers were established, books were written, and even Spanish diplomats labored to this end.

Early in 1856 the Spanish minister at Washington held conferences with the diplomatic agents of the Hispanic countries resident in the United States for the purpose of discussing plans of union. A project was drawn up which proposed to bind the nations to the south of the Rio Grande not to consent to the abridgment of the independence or the infringement of the territorial integrity of any of the signatory powers, but to treat the offender or invader of any member of the prospective alliance as a common enemy. No provision was inserted, at the time, that would include Spain in the union, but the action of the Spanish minister was approved; and the Spanish secretary of state considered the matter of sufficient importance to communicate it to the captain-general of Cuba.

Yet, while certain Spaniards were urging a rapprochement between Spain and Hispanic America, the Spanish government was slow to put aside the resentment caused by the Wars of Independence. Juan José Flores and the Spanish queen dreamed of reconquering a portion of northwestern South America (1846-1847); vigorous action was taken with reference to obligations and indemnities in Mexico (1856-1862), Venezuela (1860 ff.), and the Pacific States of South America (1865-1866); and recognition of the new republics was long delayed.

In Hispanic America, too, there existed, besides the bitterness which naturally arose from this Spanish stubbornness and these instances of aggression, certain factors which tended to stultify this racial propaganda. In the first place, Cuba and Puerto Rico, still under the Spanish yoke, appealed to the sympathy of their Latin sisters in the New World. On at least two occasions—namely, during the celebrated Panama Congress of 1826, and during the Ten Years' War in Cuba (1868-1878)—the Hispanic-American republics entertained designs of snatching Spain's colonies from her grasp; and there was sympathy for Cuba until the last. In the second place, there continued to exist a deep current of resentment toward Spain as an aftermath of the Wars of Independence, just as Anglophobia held sway in the United States for a century after the achievement of nationality.

These considerations make the absence of friendly relations between Spain and Hispanic America during the greater portion of the last century a fact which will readily be understood. But it would be a mistake to suppose that nothing was accomplished. Beginning with the recognition of Mexico in 1836, Spain very slowly extended this favor to the remaining Hispanic states of the New World, completing the process in the early nineties. At the same time, numerous treaties relating to extradition, postal and telegraphic communications, literary, scientific, and artistic property, and commercial affairs, gave evidence of the abandonment of the policy of aloofness.

It was near the end of this period, also, that the Spaniards who were interested in their kinsmen across the Atlantic founded the Ibero-American Union, and by 1892 old grievances had been so far forgotten that the Hispanic-American states joined the mother country in the celebration of the fourth centenary of the discovery of America.

A Period of More Intense Effort (1895–1915)

This celebration, as was natural, gave considerable impetus to the movement toward intimacy. And feasting and rejoicing had scarcely ended when a renewed revolt in Cuba and war with the United States furnished Spaniards further motive for rapprochement with Hispanic America. The approach of hostilities with the Anglo-American republic caused patriots of the Iberian Peninsula to subject their country to a rigorous inspection and to cast about for possible allies. When the inevitable came, Spain found herself without active friends—unless Germany's demonstration entitled that country to be considered as such—and pathetically unprepared to meet the foe. In a short time all was over, and the last vestige of a once glorious empire in America had passed from Spanish control. The sense of failure and loneliness which came to Spain could scarcely have been more profound. The defeat was followed by a veritable flood of literature dealing with the domestic and foreign problems of the Peninsula, and there was virtual agreement as to what Spain's international policy should be. Pan-Hispanism must be accepted as one of the goals for the future, and in so far as it related to America it was to be forged in part upon the anvil of Yankeephobia.

This anti-Yankee phase of the matter, scarcely to be detected in the more discreet and tactful writers, is clearly seen in such works as those of José F. Gómez and Ricardo Beltrán y Rózpide. The former was inspired by the prospect of war with the United States over Cuba. In his *Latin Solidarity* he advocated a sort of Zollverein as the first step in the formation of a more important union; the pacification of Cuba; and a rapid rapprochement with the peoples of Spanish origin in America. The motives influencing Gómez are very evident in the following passage:

"If we know how to take advantage of the situation, our country may yet become the polar star of a Latin Confederation on this continent against the Saxon preponderance represented by this Anglo-American Colossus which we have opposite us, and we may advance firmly and serenely to a league of race, draw the former possessions to the mother country in the interest of all, and give potency, unity, and fire to the idea of solidarity among the people who pray, make laws, and speak in the beautiful language of Castile."

Beltrán y Rózpide wrote a voluminous history of the Hispano-American peoples in the twentieth century.[1] The work is anti-Yankee from beginning to end. The whole American policy of the United States is painted in blackest terms, and the Yankee peril is constantly held up before the Hispanic Americans with the view of persuading them to enter into a confederation. Rózpide expressed the hope that after such an organization has been formed, Spain and her kinsmen in the New World might enter into a profitable alliance which would give her the position of *"Presidencia de Honor* in the great association . . . of the Hispanic-American people."

Hostility to the United States is even more evident in writings of the journalists. In July, 1898, the *Correo Espanol* (Madrid) remarked: "When Spain has been driven from the continent she created, the possessions of other nations still holding colonies there will soon be disposed of. The dreams of the North American politicians will be realized. Mexico, already mutilated by the amputation of Texas and California, will fall an easy prey. Venezuela will next fall under the talons of the American vulture. Brazil, Chile, Argentina, and the other South American republics would be succulent food. . . . It is not only the Antilles that are threatened; the nations of Central and South America will also disappear before an . . . invasion more terrible than that of the Vandals and the Goths. . . . It is still possible to avoid the danger. The Spanish-Americans must, in union with their mother country, fight for their land, for their religion, and for their race." The *Correo* contended that there was a probability that England would participate in this conquest.[2]

This article was written under the fervor of a war psychosis, but

---

[1] *Los Pueblos Hispanoamericanos en el Siglo XX* (Madrid: Imprenta del Patronato de Huérfanos de Administración Militar, 1907).

[2] Quoted in the *Literary Digest,* XVII (July 23, 1898), 113.

it was little less vigorous than many which followed. Three years
later, for instance, *España Moderna* called upon Europe to "save
us and the virgin South American continent from the barbaric Yankees"; and in 1910 the same journal called attention to the "Yankee
Peril," pointing out that a part of Latin America was in danger of
being "gobbled up," but expressing the hope that some of it might
be saved by an alliance based upon "the traditions of race and the
language of Castile." During the same year Professor Vicente Gay,
of the University of Valladolid, declared that Spain must rescue the
Latin Americans from the intrigues of the United States. "We should
insist upon the common blood of Spain and South America," said
Gay, "and encourage trade and intercourse." "Spain is the Rome of
the West and the fountain of its greatness. In Spain should be recognized the Pantheon of American heroes. . . . It is necessary to bear
this in mind if we would cultivate the Ibero-American spirit which
must prove the salvation of Latin America."

Thanks to the efforts of an able group who, under the name of
"Americanists," rallied around the ideal of Hispano-American friendship, the accelerated movement of the nineties continued. From the
beginning the program set forth by these so-called Americanists
embraced three closely related phases: the racial and cultural, the
economic, and the political. In approving the idea of calling a congress of all the Hispanic peoples at Madrid in November, 1900, the
Spanish minister of state declared that the "social and economic
future" of his country depended to a large extent upon the growth
of "those racial sympathies which Spain has in America," and that
it was an opportune time to cultivate the spiritual affections of the
Hispanic-American peoples and to prepare for the inevitable contest
for their markets. Again, the formal invitation sent to Mexico, which
was probably typical, spoke of racial and cultural bonds, mutual
economic interests, and the advisability of "a common action" which
would result in the well-being of the world. Among the themes to
be discussed at this assembly were: "means for the creation of a
great current of public opinion which would lead the governments
of Spain, Portugal, and the Ibero-American peoples to effect an intimate alliance"; the harmonization of the civil, penal, and administrative laws of these countries; the unification of educational plans;
the modification of commercial agreements; the improvement of

communications; the establishment of international expositions; the creation of banks; and the study of the problem of migration. These ideas, of course, were in harmony with those of the Americanist group who sponsored the congress.

The success of this congress encouraged the calling of others. In 1908 the Hispanic-American states took part in the celebration of the centenary of the Spanish movement for liberation from the Napoleonic yoke; in 1910 a Hispanic-American congress was held in Barcelona; in 1912 the centenary of the meeting of Cortes at Cádiz was celebrated by another Hispano-American Assembly; in 1914 a Hispano-American Historical and Geographical Congress was assembled at Seville in order to commemorate the fourth centenary of the discovery of the Pacific Ocean.

Moreover, statesmen, merchants, and intellectuals founded numerous organizations, which occasionally received subsidies from the government, for the purpose of cementing relations of cordiality with the Hispanic Americans. In fact some forty of these institutions were founded soon after the opening of the century, and many of them were organizations of considerable influence and dignity. Such, for instance, were the *Casa de América* and the center for the cultivation of Hispano-American intimacy in Barcelona; the center of Americanist studies in Seville; the Hispanic-American Royal Academy of Arts and Sciences at Cádiz; and the Hispano-American Royal Academy, the Ibero-American Institute of Law, and the Center of Hispano-American Culture, all three of which are in Madrid. At the same time, some of the most important universities created professorships devoted to the study and teaching of American history, law, and politics; and several journals and publishing houses were established primarily for the purpose of distributing literature and information with reference to Hispanic America.

Such organizations carried their propaganda across the Atlantic. Spanish students were encouraged to pursue their studies in Hispanic America, Hispanic-American students were offered inducements to come to Spain, and professorial interchanges were arranged; some of the leading Spanish Academies, as those of Languages, of Sciences, and of History, established branches, correspondents, and interchanges in and with Hispanic America; the some four million of Spanish immigrants in the Hispanic-American states were organized with solicitous care as one of the best means of fostering friendly relations; and numerous expeditions for the purpose of carrying on propaganda were undertaken.

THE STIMULUS OF WORLD WAR I

The intensified Spanish interest in the Spaniards residing oversea was further stimulated by World War I. That great catastrophe seems to have stirred Spain as profoundly as the defeat of 1898. Spaniards were made to feel the loneliness of their situation, to doubt the efficacy of international law and agreements, and to consider the future of their nation in a world order where force was likely to be dominant for some time. Moreover, the war resulted in the improvement of Spain's commerce and finances and at the same time gave such an impetus to her industries that the importance of Hispanic-American markets was appreciated as never before.

In 1916 considerable discussion of the proposed American policy of Spain was begun in the Spanish Senate. One senator demanded more favorable commercial treaties and careful direction of Spanish emigration to America; another believed that a customs union should be negotiated with the Hispanic-American states in order that Spain might secure the markets which had formerly been supplied by the nations of war-swept Europe; others demanded, in addition to these proposals, numerous reforms connected with steamship, postal, and telegraphic communications; and one of the members went so far as to advocate the establishment of an "Ibero-American Confederation." In response to these discussions the president of the Council of Ministers declared his conviction that the time had come to advance beyond the period of "romantic propaganda" and enter upon the "road of realities."

Once more, too, able writers, for the lack of whom Spain has never suffered, put forth programs and abundant propaganda. Rafael María Labra y Cadrana, who for many years had been vitally interested in America, published numerous pamphlets and made vigorous lecture tours in Spain; Altamira issued his *Spain and the Americanist Program;* Federico Rahola, prominently identified with the Casa de América, formulated his *Americanist Post-War Program;* and Edmundo Gonzáles-Blanco included a discussion of what should be the American policy of Spain in a book dealing with Spain and the World War.[3]

Altamira's proposals differed from those of the earlier publications with which he had been identified in placing somewhat more emphasis upon the political and economic phases of the matter. He advocated such reform of the diplomatic and consular service as would insure a supply of able men for the American field; such a following-up of the emigrant as would insure his preservation as a force making for the perpetuation of Spanish culture and the achievement of Pan-Hispanism; such economic arrangements as would promote the growth of Hispano-American trade; the defense of the Spanish language in all its purity; the fullest and freest intellectual coöperation and interchange. Such a program evinces considerable supplementation of his proposals at the opening of the century, when he took occasion to remark that the policy of the group of which he was a member might be summed up in the phrase "pedagogical politics."

Rahola gave much more emphasis than Altamira to the commercial and political items of the program, although he did not neglect the intellectual and the cultural. He pointed out the commercial significance of the Yankee phrase, "America for the Americans," called attention to the recent marvelous growth of the trade of the United States with Hispanic America, and urged that Spain collect and launch all her commercial forces while the United States was in the midst of the war and its consequent readjustments. He expected the Ibero-American states to be the scene of a titanic commercial struggle in the near future, but in this struggle he believed that Spain would be placed at an advantage because of her geographical position and ethnical affinities. Moreover, if any sort of international concert was to be hoped for, he believed that the mysterious force of racial and spiritual attraction ought to render possible a political union.

Writing in 1917, Gonzáles-Blanco expended a great deal of effort to show that the British and the Yankee peril should be met by Pan-Hispanism. He urged the denunciation and the abrogation of

---

[3] *Iberismo y Germanismo: España ante el Conflicto europeo* (Valencia: Editorial Cervantes, 1917).

the Treaty of Algeciras with the aim of recovering the Strait of Gibraltar, and the consolidation of the Iberian Peninsula by a federation with Portugal, in order to render the holding of that strait by another nation perilous in the future. When the geographical integrity of Spain had thus been restored, the Hispanic-American states might be invited to enter what was destined to be the great "Iberian United States." Would they refuse to accept this invitation? "What oversea peoples whose sons have not lost the ethnical sentiment and the consciousness of that community of customs, of language, and of civilization which perdures between Spain and Latin America, would reject this superb ideal, pledge of great destinies for the future? Who does not see that its realization is the only recourse of which the Ibero-American world can avail itself in order to oppose Yankee imperialism? . . . The immediate subjugation of Central and South America by the syndicates of North America is the future which awaits our brothers of the New Continent if there is not found in union a competent force for resistance." Moreover, when Pan-Iberianism had realized its ideal of unity, it might ally itself with Germany in order that *Iberismo* and *Germanismo* might wrest from the Anglo-Saxons "the palm of victory in the fight for the direction of humanity."

After the outbreak of the World War there were published, also, works of a supposedly scholarly nature which revealed this same Pan-Hispanic aspiration of the Spaniards. Portions of two of these, at least, are of considerable interest in connection with the matter now under consideration. In 1917 Juan Ortega Rubio, an aged professor of the Central University at Madrid, issued the *magnum opus* which had cost him much labor, a three-volume history of America.[4] Two years later a student of a diplomatic and consular institute of Spain published under the auspices of the Royal Academy of Jurisprudence and Legislation an excellent study entitled, *The Geographical Factor in the Politics of South America.*

Some twenty-seven pages of the prologue of Ortega's ambitious work were given to a discussion of the American policy of Spain. Here the author declared that he had been moved to undertake the task while under the weight of age and infirmities, because he felt

---

[4] *Historia de América* (Madrid: Librería de los Sucesores de Hernández, 1917).

that he would thus be rendering a service to Spain and also to her former colonies. He then set forth his viewpoint. He began with the affirmation:

"Our old and beloved Spain does not desire, nor is she able, nor ought she, to think of exercising any hegemony over the Ibero-American peoples. We desire, and we aspire to, only a fraternal communion. . . . Spaniards and Americans of the Iberian race, forgetting old grievances, should in the future think only of living the life of culture and of progress. . . . At the same time that we ask those sons of the republics of our race that they do not forget Spain and that they honor the memory of the discoverers and the colonizers of the Indies, we shall also declare to them that we are admirers of those brave heroes who proclaimed their independence and their liberty. In the accomplishment of such ends we believe that there is fulfilled an historical law that colonies when they reach a certain age, that is, a certain grade of civilization and culture, separate from the metropolis."

The main contentions of the brilliant monograph of Badiá are that there exist in Hispanic America strong supernational aspirations; that these are prevented from being realized by geographical absurdities in the present national boundaries, which furnish the motive for unnecessary squabbles regarding territory; that there are six geographical unities in Hispanic America—the Plata Confederation (embracing the present republics of Argentina, Uruguay, Paraguay, and a portion of southern Bolivia), the Confederation of the Pacific (made up of the central portion of Bolivia, Chile, Peru, and southern Ecuador), the Colombian Confederation (composed of Colombia, most of Venezuela, and the northern part of Ecuador), the Brazilian Confederation (including the present territory of Brazil, the northern portion of Bolivia, the eastern sector of Ecuador, some districts in the south of Venezuela, and the Antilles), and the Mexican Confederation—which, when accepted in the political organization of the republics, would eliminate strife and pave the way to Hispanic-American harmony and solidarity; and that, after their normal life had thus been restored, these American states and Spain would find it natural and easy to form a society of nations, for, aside from the grandeur of such an organization of peoples of the same race and with similar culture and aspirations, the Yankee menace would constitute a powerful force impelling them in this direction.

In view of this array of evidence—and it could be made more formidable if space permitted—there seems to be little room to doubt the existence in Spain of a strong desire for intimacy with Hispanic America.[5] The motives behind such a desire are racial and cultural as well as political and commercial, but the former seem to have been most emphasized. In writing of their aspiration Spaniards sometimes express, and probably more often feel, opposition to the United States, and the Yankee peril is therefore frequently held up before the Spaniards oversea.

Progress of Pan-Hispanism in Hispanic America

What progress has Pan-Hispanism made in Hispanic America since 1895, and what are its prospects for the future?

The revolt in Cuba and the Spanish-American War furnished the people south of the Rio Grande an opportunity to express their sentiments toward the mother country before the enthusiasm aroused by the celebration of the Fourth Centenary of the discovery of America had died away. For instance, in the spring and summer of 1898 some of the leading newspapers of Mexico carried on a spirited discussion regarding what should be Mexico's attitude toward the prospective independence of Cuba. Francisco Bulnes seems to have been one of the important champions of Cuban liberation, but he met with several able opponents, of whom Don Carlos de Olaguibel y Arista, Don Francisco G. Cosmés, and Trinidad Sánchez Santos may be taken as typical. Bulnes attacked Spain's colonial policy severely, defended the Cuban cause as analogous to that of Mexico in 1810, spoke disparagingly of the value of Spanish immigration to Hispanic-American republics, and gave evidence of a friendly disposition toward the United States. His opponents, first and last, defended the Spanish colonial régime and Spanish culture, and declared: that the Cuban separatist movement was similar to the "infamy of Texas" and not to the action of the Spanish colonies at

[5] Other evidences of Spanish interest in a rapprochement with Hispanic America are revealed by the Second Congress of Hispano-American History and Geography, which met in Seville in May, 1921, as well as by the general Hispano-American Congress held in Spain in 1930.

the opening of the nineteenth century; that it would be a mistake for the Hispanic-American states which were trying to preserve the integrity of their national domain under the federalist system to champion the cause of separatism; that in case Cuba achieved its independence from Spain the island would not have the elements and the power to maintain such independence, but would fall, like Texas, into the clutches of the Yankees; and lastly, that Mexico, and the other Hispanic-American states for that matter, could ill afford to place obstacles in the way of the ever-increasing flow of Spanish immigrants who, "identified with us by all those bonds which attach a human group to the spirit and the characteristic tendencies of race," can alone "bring industry, prosperity, order and civilization to the deserts of our domain."

This sympathy for Spain seems to have been somewhat general at the time, in spite of the widespread desire to see Cuba freed from Spanish control. The Chilean writer Alberto del Solar pronounced a terrible tirade against the rudeness, the grossness, and the greed of the United States, and concluded his address with a hymn to Spain; the young Argentinian statesman, Roque Sáenz Peña, expressed the fervent hope that the Spanish forces might be victorious; and numerous others revealed similar sentiment.

The Hispano-American Congress which, at the instance of the *Unión-Iberoamericana,* convened in Madrid two years after the close of the war, gave further evidence of the growing feeling of solidarity between Spain and her erstwhile colonies. This feeling was particularly noticeable during the inaugural session of the congress, when Don Justo Sierra, the distinguished Mexican author and statesman, speaking for the entire Hispanic-American delegation, delivered an address which breathed Pan-Hispanic sentiment from almost every sentence.

The intellectuals of the countries south of the Rio Grande continued to cultivate this attitude. Such important writers as Rubén Darío, José Santos Chocano, Gómez Jaime, Andrade Coello, Rufino Blanco-Fombona, Josá M. Vargas Vila, Eliseo Giberga, J. Francisco V. Silva and José León Suárez are champions of Pan-Hispanism in one form or another. During the first decades of the twentieth century there was, in fact, a considerable group of Hispanic-American idealists who expressed the conviction that the only means of saving their nationalities from deterioration and chaos within, and absorption from without, was a return to the law of their origin, their historical past, their maternal traditions, their primal racial heritage. In the opinion of this group the Hispanic-American nations were threatened with race deterioration, hybridism, spiritual confusion, the disappearance of historical consciousness—in a phrase, denationalization and annihilation—unless they availed themselves of every opportunity to promote a vigorous revival of Hispanism in its fullest and most glorious sense. The significance for Pan-Hispanism of this idea, if it should be generally accepted as a working hypothesis, needs no comment.

As revelations of Pan-Hispanic sentiment in the countries south of the Rio Grande, recent productions of two historians of the Argentine are particularly worthy of note. Late in 1916, or early in 1917, a distinguished professor of the University of Buenos Aires published a booklet [6] on the character of the Hispanic-American revolution, in which he contended, among other things: that it was unjust to blame Spain for not extending liberties to the colonies when despotism held sway in the Peninsula, and for exploiting the riches of the New World when such exploitation accorded with the general colonial concept of the age; that Spain's treatment of the natives was not as cruel as it had been represented; that in Spain many Spaniards who were also seeking larger liberties sympathized with the colonials in their struggle for independence; that the real nature of the revolution can be grasped only when it is considered as a *"crisis fatal* in favor of liberty and of human rights, which was produced as a consequence of the revolutions of the United States and of France at the end of the eighteenth century." All of which seems to be well founded; but the author makes it very clear that he is highly elated at being able to champion such a viewpoint and takes great pains to set forth the significance of his work for the Pan-Hispanic movement. In fact, the author's intense fervor for Spain is evident on almost every page; and, what is more significant, his booklet seems to have aroused widespread interest and met with much commendation in all parts of Spanish America.

Just as this booklet was going through its third edition, another

[6] José León Suárez, *Carácter de la Revolución americana* (Third ed., Buenos Aires: Juan Roldán, 1917).

Argentinian, J. F. V. Silva, published a much more radical work.[7]
Silva went so far as to lament the separation of the Spanish colonies
from the mother country, declaring that Hispanophobia and a
slavish imitation of the United States has been the capital error of
the Latins of the New World. He urged the formation of a vast
empire including Portugal, Brazil, Spain, and the Spanish-American
republics. The capital of this great organization was to be in Spain
and full local autonomy was to be preserved for each of its parts. In
support of his plan of union Silva held up the English, the German,
and the North American perils, but he placed main emphasis upon
the last of these. Nor were his ambitions confined merely to matters
of defense. The new empire would have its *irredenta*. In Europe
there would be a Gibraltar and Morocco; in America, Puerto Rico,
the Falkland Islands, and the Panama Canal must be regained. The
integrity of Mexico must be guaranteed. Yankee influence must be
counteracted in Cuba, Santo Domingo, and Central America. Indeed, the new Hispanic nation should control both the Panama
Canal and the Strait of Magellan, as well as the Caribbean area and
all the islands adjacent to the Central and South American coasts!

This Hispanic friendliness of the intellectuals, and of a large
group of the upper classes in general, has been revealed frequently
by the enthusiastic receptions given to such Spanish scholars as
Altamira and Adolfo Posada, and such statesmen and financiers as
Rahola and Cavestany. The Pan-Hispanic note was particularly prevalent in the numerous addresses given during the extended tour of
Altamira.

More significant perhaps than this evidence of growing friendliness between the intellectuals of Spain and of Hispanic America
were the accumulating indications of increasing intimacy in official
circles. In recent years October 12 has been set apart as a national
holiday in virtually all of the Hispanic-American republics. This,
however, is apparently not to be taken as evidence of a growing
desire to honor the great Italian who, sailing under the Spanish flag,
discovered America. Its significance lies rather in the fact that this
great event is celebrated as *Fiesta de la Raza*—Racial Day—and not

[7] Francisco V. Silva, *Reparto de América Española y Pan-Hispanismo* (Madrid: Francisco Beltrán, 1918).

Columbus Day. The Pan-Hispanic note is universally sounded. Moreover, one who takes the trouble to search through the published correspondence exchanged between Spain and the states of Hispanic America during recent years will discover many documents expressing mutual admiration, confidence and good will.

In his *Informe* from 1910 the Colombian minister of foreign relations took occasion to remark that "Colombia, an American nation which has shown itself most friendly to the mother country, has been especially careful to cultivate with all cordiality and to make day by day more intimate its relations with the noble Spanish people." The minister in charge of the same office remarked in 1919, while lamenting the failure of the Spanish government to participate in the celebration of the centenary of the Battle of Boyacá, that this could in no way break the "bonds which unite us with the mother country or extinguish racial affections."

In 1903 the Venezuelan minister of foreign affairs noted that his government had participated in the celebration of the arrival of Don Alfonso XIII at his majority and expressed gratitude to the queen regent for the generous consideration she had given Venezuela. The dispatch by the government of Spain of a descendant of Don Pablo Morillo, the distinguished general who sought to put down the Venezuelan movement for independence, for the purpose of taking part in the celebration of the hundredth anniversary of the beginning of efforts looking toward emancipation, aroused marked enthusiasm in Venezuela. This act signified forgiveness and the forgetting of past injuries. Venezuela, accepting it in good faith, reciprocated. President Gómez and his government went so far as to lay the corner stones of what were to be two monuments, one to Simón Bolívar and the other to Pablo Morillo, Count of Cartagena. A year later, in receiving the new Spanish minister, the Venezuelan chief executive referred to these events and spoke in fervid language of the love and esteem of his constituency for the mother country. And in 1913, another Spanish minister was received with the cordial assurance that he was coming into the midst of a people "who do not renounce their origin, but who see in Mother Spain the glorious fountain of their life and are delighted with the spectacle of her resurrection under the reign of a great monarch."

Mexico's response to the invitation to attend the Hispano-American Congress of 1900 was one of the most cordial of all those given by the American states. In 1901 the Spanish minister to Mexico was assured that the fraternal sentiments of Spain toward Mexico were fully reciprocated "by the government and people of this Republic. Nor is it possible for less than this mutual and vehement sympathy to exist between two peoples united by tradition, . . . by the blood which courses in their veins," and above all by a similar civilization. The presence of the Spanish representative at the celebration of the centenary of Mexican independence elicited from President Díaz words of rejoicing at this indication of complete reconciliation between mother and daughter. He declared that had Spain been absent a painful void would have been felt, but with Spain present, the occasion possessed all that was necessary to render "unforgettable . . . the annals of a people who do not disdain their origin."

The diplomatic correspondence between Spain and the Argentine Republic indicates that the two countries were on terms of complete and mutual cordiality. The minister sent by the Roca administration (1898–1904) to Spain was reminded that Argentinians "have the duty of maintaining at all costs intimacy with the mother country." During the same administration certain expressions in the Argentinian national hymn which gave offense to Spain were suppressed. A few years later the Argentine minister of war gave an extremely fervent address on the occasion of the departure of the Spanish delegation which had been present at a magnificent horse show. In one of the most eloquent portions of his speech he sounded the Pan-Hispanic note.

Special consideration given by Spain to the Argentine nation in the celebrations connected with its independence met with every token of fullest appreciation. The mother country's proposal to erect a monument to the Argentine nation evoked fervid expressions of friendship in the Plata Congress; the visit of the princess, Doña Isabel de Borbón, in 1910, was greeted with profound and sincere enthusiasm; the raising of the Spanish diplomatic representation in Buenos Aires to the category of an embassy in connection with the celebrations of 1916 was reciprocated by a similar step with reference to the Argentine legation in Madrid, and all was accompanied by frequent and fervent protestations of admiration.

If words and international courtesies had any weight, surely Hispano-American rapprochement had made much progress since the early days of the nineteenth century! In the field of the immediately. practical, however, comparatively little had been achieved. Several arbitration treaties had been signed as well as various pacts relating to commercial and industrial matters, and the tendency to refer disputes between American states to the arbitration of the Spanish government was growing; but the movement of commerce between Spain and the Hispanic American countries did not indicate any solid economic basis for intimacy. Owing largely to the loss of Cuba, Spain's trade with Spanish America and Brazil in 1907 was only half of what it had been in 1897, and no important increase has occurred since 1907. Spain's commerce with the Latins of the New World has not become a matter of any consequence.

The Future of the Movement

Shortly after the close of World War I Spain entered a period of storm and stress. The dictatorship of General Miguel Primo de Rivera, which began in late 1923, was overthrown in 1931 together with the Spanish monarchy, and Spain entered a period of turbulence and reform followed by the outbreak of a destructive civil war, with Italy and Germany supporting the insurgents and France and Soviet Russia to a lesser extent backing the Spanish government. The future of the nation was clouded.

The Hispanic Americans followed developments in Spain with intense interest, but the energies of the mother country were too absorbed in domestic problems to give much attention to kindred nations in America. Latin-American opinion was divided with reference to the forces fighting for mastery in the Iberian Peninsula. In many quarters could be discovered deep sympathy for the insurgent General Francisco Franco and his fascist allies; in others Loyalist sentiment predominated.

In the United States various writers were predicting that a victory for General Franco would promote a fascist drift among Spain's kinsmen overseas. If this triumph should occur—and it did occur at least temporarily in 1939—some type of intimacy, based upon the new ideology as well as upon the old Pan-Hispanic ideals, might rapidly develop.[8] Others had forebodings of the employment of Spaniards as propaganda agents of Italy and Germany in Spanish America to weaken the democratic forces there and stir up animosity against the United States.

These forebodings were not altogether unfounded. Agents of Franco tried to create sympathy for totalitarianism and cause trouble for the more democratic governments in Spanish America. But the growing sentiment for Pan-American solidarity tended to frustrate their efforts, which became more and more futile as the tide of war turned against the Axis Powers. With the defeat of Italy, Germany, and Japan, Franco's prestige declined and the overseas influence of his régime all but vanished. During the second half of the year 1945 his dictatorship appeared to be on the point of collapse and there were indications that the monarchy would be restored in Spain. The future of the Pan-Hispanic movement therefore seemed uncertain. It would depend upon many factors; political trends in Spain and the rest of Europe, the Latin-American policy of the United States, and the intensity of democratic and nationalistic sentiments in Spanish America would be important among them.

[8] It will also be recalled in this connection that Portugal, the mother of Brazil, passed under the control of a dictator of the fascist variety in 1926. Portugal may likewise become an influence in the promotion of fascist ideology in Latin America along with a kind of Pan-Hispanic movement.

CHAPTER XXII

HISPANIC-AMERICAN INTERRELATIONS

The Spanish Americans were one under Spain, but their unity was based on the dependence of each major administrative division upon the mother country rather than on intimate relations among themselves. The struggle for independence brought the colonies closer together: the coöperation of certain extensive regions in the liberation movement will be recalled. But political and geographical factors and the lack of economic interdependence kept the republics apart all through the nineteenth century.

There were four main causes of friction between the new states: (1) unsettled boundaries; (2) disputes over the navigation of international rivers; (3) the military operations of political refugees across international frontiers; and (4) the ambition of certain nations or political leaders to seize territory or rich natural resources belonging to their neighbors, to promote political affiliations across international boundaries, or to create vaster unities by methods of coercion. In view of the numerous motives for disagreement, and in comparison with the intercourse of European nations, their relations have been surprisingly harmonious.

This harmony may be referred to several factors, but the following were probably the most important: (1) the persistence of the will to unity expressed by Miranda, Bolívar, and many other leaders and writers of the early national period; (2) sparsity of population and preoccupation with domestic problems; and (3) the influence of outside pressure or menace. The last of these factors operated in three ways. First, the United States and (less frequently) the European nations intervened to settle disputes between the Spanish-American entities; second, the aggressive policies of these powers constituted a menace which caused the Spanish Americans to search for protection in alliances and multilateral diplomacy; third, the rivalries of the great powers or of their nationals sometimes set the small states of America against each other. Although the Spanish-American desire for unity frequently embraced Brazil, the latter state did not often evince a sentiment for Latin-American solidarity. The Portuguese settlements of America, having maintained a considerable degree of unity under the empire, and later the republic, of Brazil, exhibited an aloofness to projects for a larger unity.

The Six Wars

Disputes between the Latin-American states often led to skirmishes on their frontiers and to somewhat more serious hostilities in South America, in Española, and in Central America, where a single republic dissolved into five small states which were unable to avoid petty armed collisions; but prior to 1940 the states of Latin America had only six real wars among themselves, and of these only four were of any magnitude.

First War.—The first of the wars, that between the United Provinces of Río de la Plata and Brazil, was caused by a dispute over the area that eventually became the republic of Uruguay. The dispute had been inherited from the colonial era, and there had been intermittent fighting since 1814 between the Portuguese in Brazil and their more or less independent Spanish neighbors. Late in 1825, hostilities began in earnest, and Brazil blockaded the ports of the United Provinces. The war continued for almost three years; but, with the mediation of Great Britain, a peace was signed in September, 1828, erecting Uruguay into an independent buffer state.

Second War.—The second international war was caused by the opposition of Argentina and Chile to the formation of the Peru-Bolivian Confederation by Andrés Santa Cruz, the Bolivian dictator. Announced late in 1836, this new entity immediately aroused the opposition of its neighbors to the south. With the aid of Peruvian *émigrés,* Chilean soldiers invaded southern Peru and occupied Arequipa in October, 1837; but in the following month the invaders were compelled to sign a peace. In June, 1838, the Argentine dictator Rosas sent an army into the Bolivian department of Tarija, but this army was likewise defeated. The Chileans, however, soon resumed the struggle, and in January, 1839, General Manuel Bulnes defeated the soldiers of Santa Cruz at the battle of Yungay. The

Confederation was immediately dissolved, and its ambitious champion sailed away to Ecuador.

Third War.—The third war grew out of the situation in southeastern South America. The settlement of 1828, which launched the Oriental Republic of Uruguay, proved unsatisfactory to Manuel Rosas, who, as we have seen, gained control of most of the Plata provinces in 1835. He refused to recognize the independence of either Uruguay or Paraguay. The former, in particular, appeared to be a promising object for his ambition, for this little republic was torn by two bitter parties: the Blancos, led by Manuel Oribe, and the Colorados, headed by Fructuoso Rivera. When the latter raised the red standard of revolt in 1836, Oribe appealed to Rosas for aid, and the Argentine dictator soon sent an army across the Río de la Plata. At the same time, various northern provinces of Argentina supported Rivera and his party, and the French, who were having trouble with Rosas, also backed Rivera and the Colorados. In December, 1839, the armies of the Argentine dictator were driven from Uruguay; but in 1840 the French reached an understanding with Rosas, withdrew from the Plata region, and left the stern dictator free to resume his operations against his little neighbor.

Accordingly, in 1842, Rosas sent his army back across the Río de la Plata. With many Blancos in their ranks and commanded by Oribe himself, the invaders swept rapidly across the plains of Uruguay and in February, 1843, began what proved to be an eight years' siege of Montevideo, which was held by Rivera and the Colorados, supported by three of the northern provinces of Argentina, a legion of foreigners, and the brilliant Giuseppe Garibaldi. Despite further embarrassment of Rosas by the war vessels of England and France (1845–1850), the struggle did not end until 1852. Its bloodiest phase began in 1851 with the formation of an effective alliance against Rosas and the Blancos by Brazil, the Rivera government, and the Argentine provinces of Entre Ríos and Corrientes. In October, 1851, the allies forced Oribe to withdraw. They then invaded Río de la Plata and in February, 1852, routed Rosas and forced him to flee the country. In Uruguay the long struggle is known as *la guerra grande* (the great war).

Fourth War (Paraguayan War).—A little more than a decade later the bloodiest of the five wars, the "Paraguayan War," broke out. It grew out of old enmities between Paraguay and Brazil and Argentina, disputes over boundaries and commercial matters, and mutual suspicions of imperialistic intentions.

After 1851 Brazilian influence became predominant in Uruguay. In that year Brazil took advantage of the helpless condition of the little republic to force a boundary settlement and dictate the terms of a loan guaranteed by Uruguayan revenues. In 1854, at the request of the Colorado President Venancio Flores, Dom Pedro II sent an army of four thousand into the country. After a little more than two years, however, these troops were withdrawn and the Blancos seized the government. In 1864 the empire had trouble with this faction because of alleged ill-treatment of Brazilian subjects residing in Uruguay. Failing to obtain satisfaction, Dom Pedro intervened in behalf of Flores and the Colorados, who were now in revolt.

The Blancos appealed to Francisco López, whose ambition and suspicions of Argentina and Brazil had already caused him to organize and maintain a large army. López called upon these two countries to explain their attitude toward the Blanco government of Anastasio Aguirre in Montevideo. Receiving no response, he protested against the sending of Brazilian troops into Uruguay on the ground that such action tended to disturb the balance of power in the Río de la Plata region. Being ignored a second time, the Paraguayan dictator opened hostilities against Brazil late in 1864 and occupied the state of Matto Grosso. With the view of following this movement up by invading the southern part of the Brazilian empire, López asked Argentina for permission to send his troops across Corrientes. President Mitre refused, and the result was a declaration of war against Argentina (March 18, 1865).

By this time Flores had secured control of the Uruguayan government, and on May 1 Brazil, Argentina, and Uruguay formed a secret alliance against López with the design of driving him from power and annexing considerable portions of adjacent Paraguayan territory. The war now began in earnest.

The struggle lasted for five years and ended, as noted elsewhere, with the defeat and death of López. The cost in blood and finances was enormous. Armies of ten, twenty, and even thirty thousand confronted each other. Paraguay, of course, suffered most. "How frightful the war was for the Paraguayans may be judged from the fact that in 1863 the population was 1,337,489. In 1871 the returns showed only 221,079 persons resident in the Republic. This . . . population comprised 28,746 men, 106,254 women, and 86,079 children. The adult males were those who from infirmity or weight of years had been incapable of bearing arms. . . . In the latter part of the struggle women had been utilized as beasts of burthen. . . ." [1]

War of the Pacific.—The fifth of these wars was that between Chile, Peru, and Bolivia, known as the "War of the Pacific." It had its background in an ill-defined boundary, and its immediate occasion was a dispute over the exploitation of the nitrate (guano and saltpeter) deposits of the Pacific coast region between the nineteenth and the twenty-fifth parallels. Moreover, a significant geographical factor was influential in the negotiations which took place both before and after the catastrophe. Arica, considerably to the north of the rich deposits, is located at the terminus of the best route over the mountains from the Bolivian plateau and, hence, is Bolivia's natural outlet to the Pacific.

At the beginning of the national period Chile certainly did not extend north of the twenty-fifth parallel; but in the course of a few years the importance of nitrates began to be recognized, and the Santiago government laid claim to the region as far north as the twenty-third parallel. Chile's claim was at once disputed by Bolivia, and in 1866 the governments of the two countries agreed, (1) to recognize the twenty-fourth parallel as the boundary, (2) to divide the revenues equally in the area between the twenty-third and the twenty-fifth parallels, and (3) to permit the nationals of either state to work the nitrate beds.

This agreement proved unsatisfactory. Bolivians felt that their government had conceded too much; the nationals of Chile worked the region much more industriously; disputes arose over the nitrate revenues; and Bolivia levied special taxes on the Chilean nitrate exploiters. At length, in 1874, another treaty was signed. By its terms the boundary of 1866 was recognized as permanent, Bolivia bound itself for twenty-five years not to increase the tax laid upon the product of Chileans working on Bolivian territory, and Chile agreed

---

[1] Akers, *A History of South America*, p. 195.

to give up all claims to revenues collected to the north of the boundary.

Meanwhile, Peru had become involved in the question. During the negotiations which culminated in the treaty of 1866, Chile had offered to aid Bolivia in conquering the Peruvian provinces of Tarapacá, Tacna, and Arica, provided Bolivia would cede to Chile all of the former's littoral to the south. Bolivia rejected this proposal, but the secret soon got out. At the same time, the Peruvian government, influenced by certain foreign speculators, conceived the project of buying out the private nitrate companies operating in Tarapacá, monopolizing the rich nitrate beds in that province, and effecting an agreement with Bolivia so as to control the price of the world's supply of guano and saltpeter. Fear of the aggressive policy of Chile caused Bolivian officials to consider offers from its neighbor to the north. In 1873 a secret treaty of alliance was signed between Peru and Bolivia; in 1875 the Bolivian government, evidently at the behest of Peru, undertook to increase export taxes, but desisted because of Chile's protest under the treaty of 1874; in 1878, when Chile was involved in difficulties with Argentina, a tax of ten centavos per hundredweight was actually placed upon all nitrates exported by the Chilean Nitrate Company of Antofagasta—the most important nitrate enterprise operating in Bolivian territory. The company protested vigorously and refused to pay the impost; the Bolivian authorities seized its property with the view of selling it for taxes; the Chilean government protested, and Chilean troops seized Antofagasta on the date set for the sale of the company's property (February 14, 1879); Peru came speedily to the support of her ally; and the "War of the Pacific" began.

The struggle lasted for more than four years and terminated disastrously for Peru and Bolivia. With greater internal stability and superior military forces, and with the encouragement and support of disgruntled nitrate exploiters and resentful holders of old issues of Peruvian bonds,[2] Chile occupied not only the entire nitrate area, but Tacna, Arica, and Lima as well. Thus victorious, the Chilean

---

[2] Some of the private nitrate companies objected to monopolization of the nitrate exploitation in Tarapacá by the Peruvian government. Holders of former issues of Peruvian government bonds were offended because of Peruvian expenditures on the government nitrate business and the construction of railways. Both groups had representatives either in Chile or in contact with Chilean diplomats elsewhere.

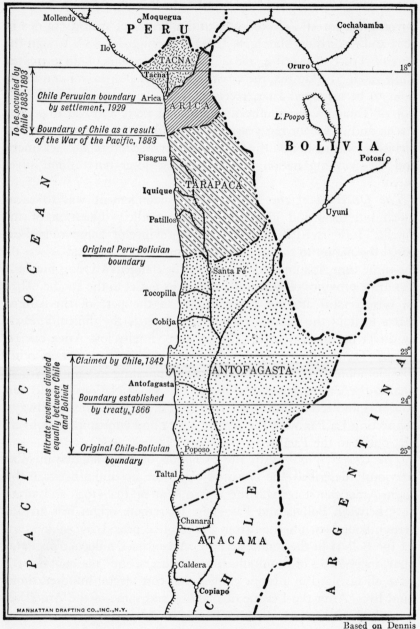

Mollendo   Moquegua
      P E R U   Cochabamba
  Ilo
              TACNA
        Tacna   Oruro   18°
To be occupied by
Chile 1883-1893
    Chile Peruvian boundary   Arica
      by settlement, 1929
             ARICA   L. Poopo
    Boundary of Chile as a result   B O L I V I A
    of the War of the Pacific, 1883
        Pisagua   Potosí

             TARAPACÁ
    Iquique
                          Uyuni
      Patillos
    Original Peru-Bolivian
        boundary
              Santa Fé
    Tocopilla

      Cobija
                                  23°
    Claimed by Chile,1842   ANTOFAGASTA
                                  24°
      Antofagasta
    Boundary established
        by treaty, 1866
                                  25°
    Original Chile-Bolivian   Poposo
        boundary
      Taltal

      Chanaral
             ATACAMA
      Caldera
      Copiapó

MANHATTAN DRAFTING CO.,INC.,N.Y.

Based on Dennis

THE EXPANSION OF CHILE

government forced Peru to agree to the Treaty of Ancón (signed in 1883 and ratified on March 28, 1884) and obliged Bolivia to sign the Pact of Truce of April 4, 1884. "By the provisions of these treaties Chile retained Atacama, the coast province of Bolivia, for considerations to be arranged later, received from Peru the permanent cession of Tarapacá, the southern province of Peru, and was to occupy Tacna and Arica for ten years. At the end of the ten-year period a plebiscite was to decide the permanent ownership of the provinces, and the winning nation was to pay the loser ten million silver pesos." [3]

The Question of the Pacific.—This arrangement was to cause much bitterness and give rise to the so-called "Question of the Pacific." It deprived Peru of its nitrate province of Tarapacá and exposed the nation to the loss of its provinces of Tacna and Arica. At the same time, it subjected Bolivia to the danger of losing not only its nitrate province of Atacama but also its outlet to the Pacific. After an unsuccessful attempt (1925–1926) on the part of the United States to hold the delayed plebiscite and settle the difficulty, Peru, by direct negotiation with Chile in 1929, finally lost Arica but regained Tacna and received six million dollars and certain other considerations from Chile. Bolivia, after appealing in vain to Argentina, to the United States, and to the League of Nations, finally lost Atacama and received only the right to use a Chilean-built railway [4] connecting La Paz with the port of Arica and constituting Bolivia's best outlet to the Pacific.

The Chaco War.—With the exception of the Paraguayan War previously described, the bloodiest of all the hostilities between the Latin-American states was the Chaco War of 1928–1929 and 1932–1935 between Bolivia and Paraguay. Its remote origin was an uncertain boundary inherited from the colonial period, but oil, an outlet for Bolivia to the south Atlantic, Argentina's influence on Paraguay, incitements of munitions manufacturers, and "national honor" were all involved in a tragic contest that cost several hundred thousand lives. After the League of Nations and some of the American states had tried for months to mediate, the United States in collabo-

---

[3] Dennis, *Tacna and Arica,* p. xi.

[4] This railroad was completed in 1912, and the portion lying within Bolivian territory was given outright to Bolivia.

ration with some of the countries adjacent to the belligerents finally stopped the war in 1935, but a definite delimitation of the boundary was not effected until the end of 1938.

THE PACIFIC SETTLEMENT OF DISPUTES

That the small nations of Latin America should favor the pacific settlement of disputes with the United States and the powers of Europe, is not surprising, for they had little hope of victory in armed contests with strong nations. That they frequently adjusted disputes among themselves by means of arbitration, conciliation, or direct negotiation, is in part a tribute to their peaceful disposition and sentiment of solidarity and in part the result of pressure from the United States and the European nations, which did not wish to have their Latin-American relations interrupted by armed conflicts.

Prior to 1940 outside mediation had been proffered in almost every dispute between the Latin-American nations, and had been accepted more often than declined. The United States, England, France, and Spain were most active in mediation.

Moreover, such interposition in disputes between the Latin-American states probably exerted some influence upon European policy with reference to these states, for if European statesmen were to urge pacific settlements with good grace, they must themselves be willing to accept their gospel in disputes with Latin America.[5] Outstanding instances of the use of force by European states in effecting settlements with the Latin-American countries have been discussed elsewhere. At this point it is well to note that between 1823 and 1910 the European powers settled at least fifty-six differences with Latin America by means of arbitration, and that the leading nations of Europe signed arbitration agreements with nearly all of the states of Hispanic America by 1919.

The number of Latin-American difficulties settled by pacific means is more impressive than their wars. Every one of these nations except Cuba inherited boundary disputes, but only a few of these remained unsettled at the end of 1940,[6] twenty having been ad-

[5] The same argument applies to the United States, which arbitrated a good many of its disputes with Latin America while urging the European nations to arbitrate their disputes with the region and exerting its influence in favor of arbitration among the Latin-American states.

[6] Among the unsettled boundary disputes are those between Peru and Ecuador, Nicaragua and Honduras, and Guatemala and Honduras.

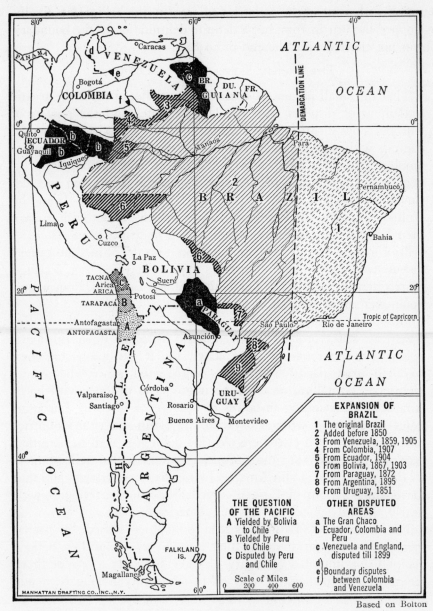

Based on Bolton

AREA OF FRICTION IN SOUTH AMERICA (NINETEENTH AND TWENTIETH CENTURIES)

justed by arbitration and twelve others in whole or in part by direct negotiation. Moreover, there were no longer any disputes regarding the navigation of international rivers; numerous pecuniary claims had been settled by arbitration; and most of the Latin-American nations were obligated by solemn covenants to settle all such claims in a peaceful manner and not to resort to war as an instrument of national policy.

The Movement for Latin-American Solidarity

An interesting phase of the relations between the Hispanic American nations is a series of forty or more congresses and conferences which were held between 1826 and 1931. As in the case of the tendency to settle disputes by arbitration, a tendency which was in fact promoted by such assemblies, these international meetings were prompted by two factors. They were motivated in part by a feeling of racial and cultural affinity and in still greater measure by a sense of common danger from outside aggression or menace.

In an epoch characterized by intense international rivalry and often by the rule of force, the policy of the comparatively weak and sometimes turbulent young states of America with reference to the great powers was naturally a defensive one. In the case of the United States, the Monroe Doctrine has been the most significant expression of this policy. On at least fifty occasions prior to 1917 public officials at Washington expressed alarm, alleged or real, lest European nations should proceed in defiance of the principles promulgated in this doctrine. The Latin-American states, on the other hand, had not promulgated such a doctrine for themselves, but they had been greatly concerned with its application and had at times accepted with gratitude the aid of the United States against European nations.

The Latin Americans did not look upon the Monroe Doctrine, however, as a sufficient guaranty of their territorial integrity and political independence. And they had three reasons for their attitude. In the first place, the doctrine contained no guaranty of security against the United States; in the second place, there was no assurance that the United States would always be willing and able to protect them against the aggressions of non-American Powers; and in the third place, the doctrine tended to place the Latin-American states under the tutelage of the government of the United States, which often insisted on regulating their conduct toward Europe and thus limited their freedom of action. Accordingly, they were compelled to seek security against the United States as well as against the nations of Europe.

Although most of the Latin-American congresses were concerned with political matters, as may be inferred from the motive back of them, social, scientific, cultural, and juridical questions were not neglected. It ought also to be added that the international movement did not confine itself to official conferences and congresses. It also found expression in diplomatic negotiations which did not lead to such assemblies, as well as in literature and student conferences.

The United States was naturally not often invited to attend these meetings held under Latin-American auspices and motivated by a desire for Latin-American solidarity, either general or regional. In several instances, as already intimated, fear of the United States was partially or wholly responsible for their convocation. When the United States was invited, it was usually with the view of obtaining pledges either of self-restraint or of support in defensive measures against Europe.

Although after 1899 a part of the energies of Latin Americanism was drawn into the larger Pan-American movement sponsored mainly by the United States, more than two-thirds of the Latin-American congresses and conferences under consideration were held after that date. Between 1890 and 1931 Latin Americanism was a sort of rival of Pan Americanism.

Obviously all the Latin-American assemblies of a century cannot be discussed here. Attention must be confined to those of greatest interest or significance.

The First Congress.—The first assembly, held in Panama in 1826, was called for the purpose of obtaining peace and security for Spanish America. The United States was invited to send delegates, apparently against the wishes of Bolívar, at whose instance the assembly was convoked. Mexico was one of the governments which invited the United States, but it appears that the Mexican president repented having extended the invitation. The United States was not thought of as a member of the proposed league of nations, which was to be a Spanish-American organization under the patronage and protection of England. The powers feared at that time were Spain and the Neo-Holy Alliance. The congress was a fiasco. Delegates of the four nations represented (which did not include the United States) signed treaties that were never ratified.

The Congress of Lima, Peru.—The second international American congress was the Congress of Lima, Peru (1847–1848). It was convoked mainly for the purpose of adopting defensive measures against Juan José Flores, the Venezuelan soldier of fortune who was supposed to be acting for the queen of Spain in an attempt to reconquer some of the Pacific coast states of South America. Delegates were present from Bolivia, Chile, Ecuador, Peru, and New Granada, and the United States was not invited to attend.[7] The government of New Granada, having recently (1846) obtained from the Washington government what it considered a reliable guaranty of the possession of the Isthmus of Panama, entertained friendly sentiments toward the United States. Its representative at Lima was instructed to bring about an agreement among the confederated states that each should maintain a diplomatic agent at Washington. But the Mexican War was then in progress and the diplomat from New Granada found the atmosphere at Lima hostile toward the United States. He wrote to his government that, "owing to the general and just suspicion which is harbored against the United States in all the American republics," it would not be wise to make the proposal. He said that the delegates at Lima thought the United States was more to be feared than Europe. The government of New Granada insisted that its agent bring the matter before the congress, and when he did so the idea was rejected. Like its predecessor, the Lima Congress accomplished very little. Three treaties were signed; but the immediate danger soon passed, and they were not ratified.

Later Conferences and Congresses.—In 1856 there occurred two Spanish-American diplomatic conferences which were almost entirely due to fear of the United States. One was held at Santiago, Chile, and the other at Washington. The territorial acquisitions of the United States resulting from the Mexican War, the raids of Yankee filibusters against northern Mexico, Cuba, and Central

[7] New Granada apparently issued an invitation to the United States, but the invitation seems to have been irregular.

America, the vigorous attitude assumed by the United States with reference to a riot which occurred in Panama in April, 1856, and the knowledge that England had almost decided to cease its opposition to the southward expansion of the United States—all combined to arouse general alarm in Latin America. Many writers called for defensive preparations. Carrasco Albano of Chile predicted a race war and urged a Latin-American congress. Bilbao, another Chilean, saw in the United States an imperialistic Russia unrestrained by the balance of power and called frantically for a congress to effect the unity of Latin America. Juan N. de Pereda, the Mexican minister in Guatemala, wrote a long memorial on the subject. He contended: (1) that the Latin race in America was threatened with absorption by the Anglo-Saxons of the United States; (2) that a congress of plenipotentiaries should be called in order to arrange an offensive and defensive alliance; (3) that it might be advisable and even necessary to extend the alliance to other Latin states, particularly Spain. Such were the apprehensions which drove the diplomats of New Granada, Guatemala, El Salvador, Mexico, Peru, Costa Rica, and Venezuela to assemble at Washington and those of Peru, Chile, and Ecuador to gather in conference at Santiago. Both groups drew up and signed treaties of alliance; but the danger from the United States decreased with the approach of the Civil War and the pacts were never ratified.

This great struggle in the United States revealed to the nations of Latin America the true dilemma which they confronted. If a powerful United States constituted a danger, a weakened United States was also to be dreaded, for it could no longer ward off European aggressions from America. France, England, and Spain soon invaded Mexico; Spain reannexed the Dominican Republic and threatened the Pacific coast of South America. The Mexican minister in Washington was the first to observe the dilemma. In 1861 he had rejoiced at the prospect of a dissolved union north of the Rio Grande, thinking that Latin America would have less to fear. By 1862 he had changed his mind. His reason he stated as follows:

"Before the civil war commenced in the United States it appeared that they were the only enemies which Mexico had, because their ideas and usurping policy had deprived us of half of our territory and were a constant menace against the integrity of what we had left. Nothing therefore was more natural than to see with pleasure . . . a division which by a fortunate continuation of circumstances would render almost impotent against us each of the parts which remained. But unfortunately the sedition from which we expected such favorable results had hardly begun when we discovered another danger from which the power of this country had freed us and against which its present unity would be the surest guaranty. . . . We therefore find ourselves in the presence of the hard alternative of sacrificing our territory and our nationality at the hands of this country or our liberty and our independence before the despotic thrones of Europe. The second danger is immediate and more imminent; in evading the first we may count upon the future and the lessons of experience." [8]

Once more the Spanish Americans began to advocate a congress as well as to discuss the advisability of inviting the United States to participate. Most of the diplomats seemed to think that it would be a good thing to have the United States represented, provided it could be persuaded to send delegates, but it soon became clear that the Lincoln government was too deeply absorbed in its own domestic problems. The Costa Rican diplomat could not forget the past nor feel secure against the United States for the future. He remarked that the European powers were not alone to be feared. "There are other dangers against which we must take precautions," he said. "Moderate, just, and upright men like those who form the Lincoln administration will not always rule the destinies of this great republic; there exist parties whose views may be fatal for our badly defended nationalities, and we ought not to forget the lessons of the past, nor that to European intervention, although tardy, Central America owes the termination of the vandal raids of the filibusters in the years 1855 to 1860." He then suggested that an effort be made to persuade the United States to contract the solemn obligation of "respecting and causing to be respected the independence, sovereignty, and territorial integrity of its sister republics of this continent," and pledging itself not to acquire by purchase or any other

[8] *Archivo Histórico Diplomático Mexicano*, num. 19, p. 202. Romero to the Mexican minister of foreign relations, Apr. 4, 1862.

title whatsoever any part of their territory, nor to permit filibuster expeditions, nor to infringe in any manner upon the rights of these communities.

It was finally decided not to issue a formal invitation to the United States to attend the congress, which met at Lima in 1864–1865. Delegates from seven Spanish-American states attended, and another treaty of union and alliance was signed only to meet a fate similar to that of previous Spanish-American agreements of this type.

Passing over the projected Panama congress, which was convoked by Colombia in 1881 for the purpose of dealing with arbitration on the American continent but failed to convene on account of the War of the Pacific, we may examine another proposal made by the Colombian minister in Paris under instructions from his government. The president of Colombia had become apprehensive with reference to the policy of the United States toward the Isthmus of Panama. In April, 1886, he had expressed to a friend the conviction that the United States would one day seize the territory necessary for the construction of the Panama Canal. It was this alarm, together with resentment at the procedure of the stronger powers with reference to the claims and complaints of their nationals against Latin America, that led him to instruct his minister in Paris to sound out his colleagues on the advisability of another Hispanic-American congress.

On October 8, 1886, the minister carried out his instructions. He urged upon his colleagues from Argentina, Uruguay, Bolivia, and Guatemala—the Chilean minister was absent on account of illness —the necessity of a congress for the purpose of bringing about a general union of the nations of Hispanic America which should enable them more effectively to resist "the absorbing tendencies of the United States" and the "unjust claims" of the nationals of the great powers of Europe. The project failed to materialize, but the motive back of it was significant.

In 1895–1896 an unsuccessful attempt was made by the government of Ecuador to assemble a congress of all the independent American states in Mexico City. The movement was inaugurated in the midst of the crisis in the relations of the United States and England over the Venezuelan boundary dispute, and was no doubt largely motivated by this crisis. Although the government of Ecuador intimated that the congress should also consider questions of industry and commerce, the main purpose of the assembly was declared to be the "formation of an American Public Law which will give to the Monroe Doctrine every dimension which it merits and the guaranty necessary to make it respected." "Cohesive force" was to be sought in order to "obtain due consideration from the European nations, which, by abusing their power, not only flout the weak states but attempt to extend their dominions to republican America."

The date set for the opening of the congress was August 10, 1896. By July, however, the Venezuelan crisis had passed, and when the time came for the inauguration of the assembly only the representatives from Ecuador and the five republics of Central America had arrived. In view of the situation, it was decided not to inaugurate a formal congress. The delegates organized themselves into a sort of junta, however, and proceeded to draw up a report. In this document they declared that the application of the Monroe Doctrine ought not to constitute "a simple unilateral act of the United States, but that it demands for its efficacy the consent of all and each one of the other republics." They also suggested a study of the advisability of "abolishing forever" from the American continent the right of intervention and of territorial annexation, and they spoke of obligatory arbitration in glowing terms of approval.

After 1895 there was revealed a tendency to change the nature of the Latin-American congresses in two respects. In the first place, they became largely regional assemblies, Central America forming one region and South America another. In the second place, the congresses of the South American states placed much less emphasis on political matters.

The reasons for these changes appear to be as follows: The Central American states felt that their national independence was gravely menaced by internal discord and the aggressive policy of the United States; the South American nations retained little hope of rescuing the republics of Central America from Yankee domination; and the diplomats of South America, and to a considerable extent those of Central America also, transferred political discussions of an international nature to the Pan-American assemblies, the Hague Conference, and the League of Nations.

Accordingly, between 1890 and 1941, the nations of South America convoked a series of conferences dealing with scientific, social, legal, cultural, and economic matters, and the states of Central America frequently assembled their diplomats in an effort to preserve peace and restore something of the unity of the early national period. In 1907 the five republics of Central America set up a court of justice which continued to function, though somewhat feebly, until 1917. In 1921 they made a vain attempt to establish a federal government.

Thus the movement in behalf of Latin-American unity was in many respects a failure. It made some contribution to peace and harmony in Latin America, but it failed to lead to greater political unity or the formulation of a common policy in dealing with the external world.

It should not be concluded, however, that the sentiment of solidarity had vanished. If aspirations for Latin-American unity had virtually disappeared from the discussions of official congresses, they were still to be found in the writings of the intellectuals and in the minds of the youth. Moreover, the bases for closer relationships were gradually being constructed. Many of the old causes of discord had been removed; improved means of transportation and communication were drawing the nations closer together; and some of them were experiencing a larger exchange of ideas and commodities than ever before. It was possible that in the future Mexico or some of the larger states of South America might inject new life into the Latin-American movement, although there were indications that Brazil, which had never taken much stock in Latin Americanism, would hold aloof or seek even closer contacts with the United States. The future of the movement would depend largely upon the fate of Pan-Americanism and the policies of the European governments, especially those at London and Moscow. In the middle 1940's only Argentina seemed to favor the creation of a Latin-American bloc to counterbalance the influence of the United States, and Argentina's dictatorial régime appeared to have little influence in the neighboring countries, where it was viewed with greater apprehension than approval.

CHAPTER XXIII

THE PAN-AMERICAN MOVEMENT (1889-1930)

In the late eighties of the last century, as noted in the previous chapter, the United States became actively interested in the promotion of more intimate relations between the independent states of the New World. Such an interest had been revealed during the period from 1808 to 1826, when Hispanic America was engaged in the struggle for independence, but it had gradually been submerged by other preoccupations.

The motives prompting the political leaders of the United States to initiate this Pan-American movement were mainly economic—trade and investment opportunities—and such motives continued to dominate their activities in respect to the movement. They entered into the consideration of sanitation with some enthusiasm, but this problem is intimately related to trade, investments, and the prosperity of the Panama Canal. Their willingness to discuss arbitration and conciliation was due in part to an interest in peace, which was necessary to prosperous trade relations, and in part to their desire to limit the action of Europe with reference to damage and contract claims and the arbitration or mediation of disputes among the Latin-American nations. Other topics were admitted largely with the view of placating the Latin Americans and diverting their attention from certain unpleasant subjects connected with the vigorous and often domineering rôle of the United States in the New World. Moreover, the numerous conferences and congresses that characterized the movement furnished Yankee diplomats an opportunity for "reassuring" statements regarding the benign purposes of their government in the Caribbean and elsewhere and for the development of sentiment in support of the political institutions of the New World as well as of the policy of the United States with reference to the rights of neutrals and the participation of European powers in the politics of the New World. Indeed, the diplomats of the United States might have entered more freely into the discussion of political matters had it not been for their desire to avoid limiting their nation's freedom of action and the knowledge that their views on such important topics as the Monroe Doctrine, intervention, and recognition would provoke unpleasant, if not embarrassing, discussions.

Of the more than sixty official assemblies convened mainly under the leadership of the United States before 1931, all but six—the series of so-called "international conferences of American states"—were specific in program, rather than general. For instance, nine dealt with sanitation, three with scientific matters, five with child welfare, three with international law, three with commerce, three with Central American affairs, two each with finance, highways, standardization, the Red Cross, postal communications, education, and journalism, and one each with conciliation and arbitration, trade-marks, customs, eugenics and homoculture, aviation, and electrical communications. The programs of the six general conferences were concerned mainly with economic matters, although considerable attention was given to arbitration, conciliation, and international law, and social and cultural matters were not neglected. Despite the opposition of the United States to the inclusion of political topics in the various programs, the Latin Americans insisted on discussions of such topics, for they desired to secure guaranties against both the United States and non-American powers.

THE CONFERENCES

A detailed discussion of some sixty-three conferences and congresses would transcend the scope of the present text. A rapid survey of the programs and work of the six general "international conferences of American states" and of the Conference on Arbitration and Conciliation in 1929 must suffice.

The First Conference.—The first of the general group met in Washington in 1889–1890. It was called by the United States mainly with the view of enlarging its trade with Latin America, but arbitration and international law were given a place on the program. The only achievements worth noting were the actual presence of delegates from all the American nations except the Dominican Republic, and the creation of a Commercial Bureau of American Republics under the direction of the secretary of state at Washington. Not only did the United States find itself under suspicion; the conference also revealed that the Latin-American states did not completely trust one another. James G. Blaine's proposed customs union reminded some of the delegates from the nations south of the Rio Grande of the German Zollverein of an earlier day and Bismarck's policy of "blood and iron." The delegates could not reach a general agreement even on the question of commercial reciprocity.

Certain proposals and discussions indicated that the Latin Americans were seeking security not only against non-American nations but against American nations as well. For instance, the delegations of Argentina and Brazil submitted the following recommendation:

"In cases of war a victory of arms shall not convey any rights to the territory of the conquered. Acts of conquest, whether the object or the consequence of the war, shall be considered to be in violation of the public law of America."

Agreement could not be reached upon this statement of the matter, but after the delegations from eleven states had signed a recommendation that a treaty on arbitration be negotiated, Blaine introduced a similar formula, which was accepted, although its application depended upon the ratification of an arbitration treaty.[1]

The Latin Americans also evinced anxiety regarding the prospect that the strong powers would exert pressure in behalf of the claims of their nationals. A juristic committee recommended the adoption of a declaration to the effect that "a nation has not, nor recognizes, in favor of foreigners, any other obligations or responsibilities than those which are established in favor of the natives, in like cases, by the constitution and the laws."

In this manner the diplomats of Latin America sought to prevent the powerful nations from elevating their nationals into a privileged position and reducing the natives of the weak states of America to the status of stepchildren or aliens in their native land. All the delegates voted in favor of the resolution except those of the United States, who opposed it, and the delegates of Haiti, who abstained from voting.

[1] Since the proposed arbitration treaty was not negotiated, the formula amounted to nothing.

The Argentine delegation was especially disturbed by what it conceived to be the ambitions of the United States. Soon after the conference adjourned Dr. Vicente G. Quesada visited Mexico on a brief diplomatic mission. His main purpose was to ascertain the plans and ideas of the Mexican government with reference to its powerful neighbor, to give Mexican leaders the assurance of moral support in evading pressure exerted from Washington, and to express appreciation for the singular mission which geography imposed upon Mexico "as a dike against the invading torrent of an excluding and powerful" capitalistic influence.

The Second Conference.—The second of the general conferences was held in Mexico City in 1901–1902. During the previous decade two events had occurred to keep alive in Latin America suspicion and irritation toward the United States: the *Itata* and the *Baltimore* [2] incidents, which primarily concerned Chile, and the Spanish-American War, which aroused general uneasiness throughout Latin America. Moreover, the European powers continued to support the claims of their nationals against the small states of America.

The program of the conference included international arbitration, claims, the reorganization of the Bureau of the American Republics, and numerous items relating to industry and commerce. Delegates from all of the independent republics of America were present; but the Brazilian delegate died during the course of the conference, and the Venezuelans withdrew before it was over. Aware of the sensitiveness of the Latin Americans, Roosevelt cautioned his delegates against assuming a prominent rôle in the conference or taking sides upon issues between various Latin-American states.

During the course of the conference the delegates from Hispanic America once more revealed their interest in security and international peace. While they agreed to several treaties and resolutions relating to social, cultural, and economic matters, it was evident that their main concern was with claims, arbitration, the rights of aliens, and international law. All of the delegations signed a protocol of adhesion to the Hague Convention for the pacific settlement of in-

[2] The United States displayed offensive zeal in the capture of the *Itata,* a vessel which was carrying arms and munitions for Chilean insurgents. By a threat of war the United States exacted (1891) indemnity from Chile for the injuries suffered in Valparaiso by sailors from the United States cruiser *Baltimore.*

ternational disputes and a treaty providing for the arbitration of pecuniary claims, and nine of them attached their signatures to a treaty providing for compulsory arbitration.

Moreover, against the wishes of the United States representatives, who abstained from discussion and voting, a convention dealing with the rights of aliens was signed. Its terms were significant:

"First: Aliens shall enjoy all civil rights pertaining to citizens, and make use thereof . . . under exactly the same terms as the said citizens, except as may be otherwise provided by the Constitution of each country.

"Second: The States do not owe to, nor recognize in favor of, foreigners, any obligations or responsibilities other than those established by their constitutions and laws in favor of their citizens.

"Therefore, the States are not responsible for damages sustained by aliens through acts of rebels or individuals, and in general, for damages originating from fortuitous causes of any kind, considering as such acts of war, whether civil or national; except in the case of failure on the part of the constituted authorities to comply with their duties.

"Third: Whenever an alien shall have claims or complaints of a civil, criminal or administrative order against a State, or its citizens, he shall present his claims to a competent Court of the country, and such claims shall not be made through diplomatic channels, except in cases where there shall have been, on the part of the Court, a manifest denial of justice, or unusual delay, or evident violation of the principles of International Law."

Finally, the conference reorganized the International Bureau, enlarging its functions and making it a sort of permanent secretariat of the "Union of American Republics." It also transferred the administration of the Bureau from the secretary of state at Washington to a governing board, "which shall consist of the Secretary of State of the United States of America, who shall be its chairman, and the diplomatic representatives of all the Governments represented in the bureau and accredited to the Government of the United States of America." The main purpose of the transfer was to make the "management of the Bureau more truly international," and the step was doubtless demanded by the Latin Americans.

The Third Assembly.—The third assembly of the general series met at Rio de Janeiro in 1906 and all of the American republics except Haiti and Venezuela were represented. Of the fourteen topics on the program, seven were concerned with economic, social, or cultural matters; one related to future conferences, and the rest were political or semipolitical in nature.

As usual, the latter tended to absorb the attention of the delegates, particularly those of Latin America. Only recently Roosevelt had "taken" the Panama Canal, announced the intention of exercising a self-appointed "international police power" in the Caribbean, and assumed control of the customs of the Dominican Republic in order to prevent France or some other European power from seizing its customhouses. Less than four years before, the war vessels of England, Germany, and Italy had attempted to coerce Venezuela into paying the claims of their nationals and Luis M. Drago had announced the doctrine that force should not be employed in the collection of public debts. The Spanish-American states were apprehensive with reference both to Europe and to the United States.

Aware of their attitude, Elihu Root, then secretary of state, went to Rio in order to be present at the opening of the conference. He also began negotiations with Colombia regarding the Canal question, mainly—it may be presumed—with the view of conciliating its statesmen and preventing its delegates from raising unpleasant issues at Rio. It was on this occasion that Root uttered an eloquent paragraph which evoked general applause and has since often been quoted. Speaking of the United States, he said:

"We wish for no victories but those of peace; for no territory except our own; for no sovereignty except the sovereignty over ourselves. We deem the independence and equal rights of the smallest and weakest member of the family of nations entitled to as much respect as those of the greatest empire, and we deem the observance of that respect the chief guaranty of the weak against the strong. We neither claim nor desire any rights, or privileges, or powers that we do not freely concede to every American Republic. . . ."

This conciliatory statement, the opening of negotiations with Colombia, and the further circumstance that the United States had just increased the prestige of the Latin-American nations by securing for them an invitation to be represented at the peace conference scheduled to meet at The Hague in 1907, placed the delegates from these countries in a more cordial mood toward their big neighbor. Moreover, the program was carefully planned with the view of avoiding topics which would cause disagreement. For all these reasons, the conference was more harmonious than the previous assemblies.

The conference signed one convention and passed numerous resolutions dealing with economic, social, and cultural matters. It also expanded the functions of the Union and made provisions for the construction of a building to house it in Washington. But its most significant work was in the field of world politics.

The delegates signed a resolution of adherence to the principle of arbitration. They also agreed to urge the nations represented at the conference to send delegates to The Hague with instructions to work for a general arbitration convention of world-wide character.

They likewise signed a resolution providing for the creation of a committee of jurists to draft codes of international law. The attitude of the majority of the political leaders of Latin America was probably expressed by the Guatemalan delegates who proposed that the main task of the commission should be: "Clearly to define the status, rights, and duties of aliens and to determine the requirements that their claims must meet in order to be admissible; to establish the cases, mode, and form in which diplomatic intervention and the tender of good offices are to take place; precisely to state under what circumstances and to what extent agents or employees of a government may by their acts engage the responsibility of that government; to determine the value and effectiveness of the ('Calvo') clause which is ordinarily embodied in contracts with aliens and by which they promise to forgo diplomatic action."

With reference to pecuniary claims two important actions were taken. The treaty signed at the previous conference was continued in force until December 31, 1912, and the delegates resolved to recommend to their governments that they "consider the point of inviting the Second Peace Conference at The Hague to consider the question of the compulsory collection of public debts, and, in general, means tending to diminish between nations conflicts having an exclusively pecuniary origin." "A large majority" of the committee which considered the question of continuing in force the treaty providing for the arbitration of pecuniary claims desired to add a section which stated that "arbitration should only take place after the resources afforded by the courts of a signatory country had been exhausted," but an active minority led by W. I. Buchanan of the United States managed to prevent this. The question of the "extent to which force is admissible for the collection of public debts" was said to have "overshadowed in interest all other topics before the Conference." There was evidently great anxiety to ward off "the calamities of conquest disguised under the mask of financial interventions."

The Fourth International American Conference.—The fourth of the group of "International American Conferences" convened in Buenos Aires in 1910, with delegates present from all the republics of the New World except Bolivia. The spirit of harmony which prevailed was so impressive that it was commented upon in the report of the delegation of the United States. The program had been carefully prepared—largely under the influence of the United States, it would appear—and only one topic of a political nature was placed upon the agenda.

A significant development was the examination of the action of the states concerned with reference to the conventions, resolutions, and recommendations of the previous conference. The result was such as to lead many critics to pronounce the movement a failure. Although relatively few of the themes discussed assumed the form of treaties or conventions, even these few were not ratified by many of the states; and the various recommendations often fell upon barren ground.

Most of the work of the fourth conference related to economic and cultural matters: patents, copyrights, trade-marks, customs, communications, statistics, science, sanitation, the interchange of professors and students. Many of its acts took the form of polite gestures relative to celebrations and prominent individuals.

However, a convention for the arbitration of pecuniary claims was signed—a convention which was to endure indefinitely—and not only was the administration of the Bureau modified, but its name was changed to the "Pan-American Union." That organization now had its headquarters in a million-dollar palace constructed on a spacious lot in Washington with funds furnished by Andrew Carnegie and the American republics.

An attempt was made to write into the claims convention a provision to the effect that pecuniary claims were to be submitted to arbitration only when it was evident that there had been a denial of justice in the courts of the state from which indemnity was demanded. But the attempt was defeated largely through the efforts of the delegation from Washington.

In connection with the administration of the Pan-American Union, the Latin Americans raised the objection that an American government not recognized by the United States could not have a representative on the governing board. This unsatisfactory feature was partially remedied by the provision that "any Republic having no representative accredited before the Government of the United States of America may designate a member of the Governing Board to represent it in the Union of American Republics and in this case said representative will have a vote for each representation."

Moreover, the idea occurred to "the delegates of some countries that it would be more in accordance with the equal dignity of all of the members in the union if the chairmanship of the board were made elective, but it was pointed out that by the common practice of international unions a position of similar dignity is usually accorded the minister of foreign affairs of the country in which the union has its seat; and also that the presidency of the Secretary of State would powerfully assist the union and help to increase its dignity and efficiency." The delegation of the United States reported that the "importance of these considerations was universally admitted." If so, the Latin Americans were later to change their minds, as we shall see. At any rate, "the dignity of the presidential office was again conferred upon the Secretary of State of the United States, as an honor freely [??] bestowed by the American nations."

An interesting occurrence during the fourth conference was the attempt made by the Brazilian delegation to bring the Monroe Doctrine before the assembly and secure a general acknowledgment of its benefits for Latin America. Discussion of the proposal carried on privately between various delegations revealed the fact, however, that while the Latin Americans approved the original doctrine, they entertained misgivings regarding some of its more recent implications. Before approving the manifesto they desired to have it defined so that it would "not be understood as an impairment of the Sovereignty of the Latin-American States." They feared that "they might sanction along with it many acts of hegemony committed by the United States by which more than one country had felt its sovereign dignity to have been wounded." This complicated the situation. The delegates of the United States, who were finally consulted, expressed the preference that if the subject was likely to cause dissension in the conference it should not be presented. The Brazilians decided not to push their project, and the matter was dropped.

The Fifth International American Conference.—The fifth of the general conferences had been scheduled to meet in Santiago in 1914, but the World War compelled its postponement until 1923. In the meantime, many things occurred which profoundly influenced the psychology of the independent nations of the New World. Among the changes in attitude none was more important than their increased preoccupation with world politics. Brutal and savage impulses had been unleashed in Europe; the predominance of the United States in America was becoming more pronounced; and the weaker nations of the Western Hemisphere were anxious regarding their sovereignty and security.

Moreover, on March 4, 1913, a political idealist entered the White House. He was more concerned with democracy, liberty, justice, and international peace than with the economic prosperity of his compatriots engaged in big business. He was not afraid of political coöperation or entangling alliances. His Pan-Americanism would not place so much emphasis on purely economic matters. He knew little of the history or the sociology of Latin America, and his spirit of a reformer sometimes overshadowed his tolerance and patience, but he soon sensed both the suspicion of the Latin Americans and its causes, and his lofty idealism profoundly impressed them.

No words could have pleased the Latin Americans more than the following in President Wilson's Mobile Address (October 27, 1913):

". . . The dignity, the courage, the self-possession, the self-respect of the Latin-America States, their achievements in the face of . . . adverse circumstances, deserve nothing but the admiration and the applause of the world. They have had harder bargains driven with them in the matter of loans than any other peoples in the world. Interest has been exacted of them that was not exacted of anybody else, because the risk was said to be greater; and then securities were taken that destroyed the risk. . . . I rejoice in nothing so much as the prospect that they will now be emancipated from these conditions; and we ought to be the first to take part in assisting in that emancipation.

". . . I want to take this occasion to say that the United States will never again seek an additional foot of territory by conquest. She will devote herself to showing that she knows how to make honorable and fruitful use of the territory she has, and she must regard it as one of the duties of friendship to see that from no quarter are material interests made superior to human liberty and national opportunity."

Speaking before a Pan-American Scientific Congress two years later, Wilson correctly stated the main cause of Latin-American suspicion of the United States and expressed a desire to remove it. He said (January 7, 1916):

"The Monroe Doctrine was proclaimed by the United States on her own authority. . . . But the Monroe Doctrine demanded merely that European Governments should not attempt to extend their political systems to this side of the Atlantic. It was a hand held up in warning, but there was no promise in it of what America was going to do with the implied and partial protectorate which she apparently was trying to set up on this side of the water; and I believe . . . that it has been fears and suspicions on this score which have hitherto prevented the greater intimacy and confidence and trust between the Americas. The States of America have not been certain what the United States would do with her power. That doubt must be removed. . . ."

In fact, Wilson had already begun to put his "New Pan-Americanism" into practice. The Latin-American diplomats were being received in Washington as the equals of the European diplomats; some of them had been called into council in dealing with the Mexican problem; and as early as the summer of 1914 Wilson had proposed a Pan-American pact providing, among other things, for the investigation and arbitration of American disputes and a mutual and reciprocal guaranty of territorial integrity and political independence.

The Latin-Americans were highly pleased with the treatment accorded them. They called Wilson's new policy "practical" Pan-Americanism, and by practical they meant political. But Chile opposed the Pan-American pact because of ardent nationalism and ambitions with reference to Tacna and Arica, and by the close of 1916 Wilson had begun to look beyond an American league to a world league of nations. Granted that he could have secured the ratification of such a pact by the Senate—and this might have been possible in 1914 or 1915—the leaders of Hispanic America had lost a great opportunity, an opportunity which some of them had been contemplating since 1862.

The pronouncements of Wilson with reference to the Great War and a world league of nations were heard with enthusiasm in most of Latin America, but a reaction set in soon after the close of the tragic struggle. The Senate of the United States insisted on writing the Monroe Doctrine into the League Covenant and then refused to join the League. This alarmed the leaders of Latin America. Article 10 of this covenant guaranteed the territorial integrity and the national independence of the signatory powers, and these leaders maintained that such a guaranty was also the very essence of the Monroe Doctrine rightly interpreted. The League of Nations would merely seek to extend this principle to the whole world. Then why did the Senate demand express mention of Monroe's manifesto in the League constitution? Latin Americans feared that it was because the interest of the United States in them did not end with this guaranty against Europe. Perhaps the Monroe Doctrine was designed to protect them from Europe in order that in due time they might be dominated and exploited by the United States. The failure of the United States to join the League tended to confirm this view, as likewise did the continued occupation of Haiti, Nicaragua, and the Dominican Republic.

The results of the conference of 1923 were embodied in one treaty, three conventions, and sixty-seven resolutions. The vast majority of these related to economic, humanitarian, and cultural matters. To Latin Americans deeply concerned with political questions they were of secondary importance. The Latin-American delegates had come to Santiago to discover the disposition and purposes of their Yankee neighbors. Would the government of the United States object to a modification or definition of the Monroe Doctrine, a pledge not to encroach upon the rights of Latin America, and such a reorganization of the Pan-American Union as would prevent it from resembling the British Colonial Office? The attempt to secure commitments on these issues was the leading feature of the assembly, and the result was a disappointment to the Iberians of America. Minor changes in the administration of the Union were agreed upon, but the Washington delegates refused either to define or Pan-Americanize the Monroe Doctrine and opposed the Uruguayan proposal to establish an American League based upon national equality and containing a pledge of territorial integrity and national independence for every American state. Truly Wilson had been but a voice crying in the wilderness.

The treaty for the pacific settlement of disputes between American states, signed by sixteen delegations—those of Costa Rica and Salvador abstaining and those of Mexico, Bolivia, and Peru being absent from the conference—was the most substantial political contribution of the assembly; and even this agreement was very limited in scope. It provided for the creation of a commission of inquiry in case of a dispute between any of the American nations, but the findings of the commission were not to have the value or force of judicial decisions or arbitral awards. By 1931 the treaty had been ratified by at least seventeen states.

With reference to the Pan-American Union, the resolution passed by the Santiago conference contained the provision that the chairmanship of the governing board should be elective, and that in the absence of a diplomatic representative a state could appoint a special representative to serve on this board. "It is understood that, following this decision, the Governing Board attempted to elect a chairman, but that rivalry became so keen, it was decided automatically to elect the Secretary of State of the United States as chairman and to rotate the position of vice-chairman between the other members in accordance with the time of their residence in Washington."

The Sixth General Conference.—The sixth general conference met at Havana early in 1928, with intervention in Haiti and Nicaragua and unsettled issues between the United States and Mexico in the background and threatening to disturb the assembly. Delegates were present from all the twenty-one republics of America. Purely political problems had been carefully omitted from the program, although there were two themes likely to carry the conference into the realm of politics; namely, the reorganization of the Pan-American

Union and matters of an inter-American juridical nature. Aside from these topics, there were others dealing with communications, intellectual coöperation, economic problems, and social problems; but it was evident even before the conference convened that political questions were, as usual, to be the chief concern of the Latin-American delegates. The League of Nations and the prostrate condition of Europe continued to furnish them relief from anxiety with reference to European aggression or pressure, so that their attention could now be concentrated, as in 1923, upon their powerful neighbor in America.

The conference adopted eleven conventions, eight motions, three "agreements," and sixty resolutions relating mainly to economic, cultural, and social matters of almost every description, but it was obvious that the delegates from the nations to the south were eager to secure unanimous condemnation of the policy of the United States in the Caribbean and to limit its freedom of action in the Western Hemisphere. And the result was a clear demonstration of the difficulty of the task. The wealth and influence of the United States were so preponderant that the delegates from several of the small states lacked either the disposition or the courage to condemn or decidedly oppose its policies. They represented either governments which depended upon the United States for their stability (such as those of Haiti, Cuba, the Dominican Republic, Nicaragua, and perhaps some of the other states of Central America) or governments which could not afford to offend the United States because of boundary disputes (Peru, Bolivia, and Chile) and financial considerations (Colombia, Cuba, and Mexico). Moreover, Brazil seemed more disposed to follow the United States than to coöperate with her sisters of Spanish origin. Because of this situation only very limited success could be achieved. The Latin Americans failed to obtain universal condemnation of the intervention of the United States in the Caribbean and succeeded only in securing a reorganization of the Pan-American Union somewhat more favorable to their desires, a declaration against aggression, and a resolution providing for an arbitration conference to be held in Washington in 1929. All other political issues were postponed for at least five years.

Two concessions to Latin America were embodied in the resolution reorganizing the Pan-American Union. First, the governments of Pan America were to be permitted to appoint as members of the governing board individuals other than their diplomatic representatives at Washington. Second, the director general was instructed to distribute positions on his staff among the nationals of the countries belonging to the Union.

The resolution against aggression declared that "war of aggression constitutes an international crime against the human species" and then proceeded to resolve as follows:

"1. All aggression is considered illicit and as such is declared prohibited.

"2. The Americans will employ all pacific means to settle conflicts which may arise between them."

The extent to which this resolution will limit the action of the United States will of course depend largely upon the definition of aggression.

The Pan-American Conference on Conciliation and Arbitration, which met in Washington in 1928–1929, signed two treaties and a protocol. According to the first article of the convention on conciliation, the "High Contracting Parties agree to submit to the procedure of conciliation . . . all controversies of any kind which have arisen or may arise between them for any reason and which it may not have been possible to settle through diplomatic channels." The fourth article granted the Conciliation Commission at least six months to exercise its conciliatory functions, and the parties to the controversy might extend the time. Article IX contained this provision, however: "The report and the recommendations of the Commission, in so far as it may be acting as an organ of conciliation, shall not have the character of a decision nor an arbitral award, and shall not be binding on the parties either as regards the exposition or interpretation of the facts or as regards questions of law."

In other words, the findings of the Conciliation Commission were not to be compulsory. Its influence was to consist in the giving of time for passions to cool and in the pressure of public opinion based upon its presumably impartial findings and recommendations.

The General Treaty of Inter-American Arbitration was confined to disputes of a juridical nature which could not be adjusted by diplomacy, such as: the interpretation of a treaty; any question of international law; the existence of any fact which, if established, would constitute a breach of an international obligation; or the nature and extent of the reparation to be made for the breach of an international obligation. The treaty does not apply to controversies which are domestic or nonjuridical in nature, nor to those affecting the interest or referring to the action of a state not a party to the treaty. "The award, duly pronounced and notified to the parties, settles the dispute definitively and without appeal."

This treaty, signed by twenty American states, was the most inclusive and potentially the most effective arbitral agreement ever signed by the independent nations of the New World; but Charles Evans Hughes, one of its negotiators, later declared that questions involving the Monroe Doctrine would not come within its scope. According to his view, matters affecting the interest or referring to the action of non-American states "fall within the exception of the treaty relating to third parties." If this should prove true, it may be doubted whether Latin America will find in the pact security against the "many acts of hegemony committed by the United States" in the name of the Doctrine.

The Washington Conference on Conciliation and Arbitration also signed a protocol of Progressive Arbitration which made provision for the abandonment "in whole or in part" of the "exceptions from arbitration stipulated in the said [arbitration] treaty or the reservation or reservations attached . . . thereto." Presumably this protocol, like the arbitration treaty, would become effective between any number of states which might ratify it.

Such, in brief, was the work of the six "International American Conferences" which assembled between 1889 and 1928 and of the Washington conference which immediately followed the last of them. It is hardly necessary to repeat that despite the persistent recurrence of political discussions, the programs emphasized nonpolitical topics. If space permitted the discussion of the numerous specific conferences convened under the leadership of the United States and dealing with every variety of economic, humanitarian, and cultural subjects, the nonpolitical emphasis of the movement under its auspices would stand more clearly revealed.

Meager Achievement and Conflicting Purposes

What were the achievements of Pan Americanism by 1930? They cannot be measured with any degree of accuracy. The American states had not confined their diplomatic efforts since 1890 to congresses and conferences. They had employed bilateral as well as multilateral diplomacy. Nor had their relations been determined solely or even in major part by diplomacy. The World War, conditions in Europe, and many American factors of a nondiplomatic nature had been operating.

Measured by the number of treaties and conventions drawn up and ratified by the assemblies under Yankee leadership, the achievements are not impressive. The first of the so-called "international American conferences" did not sign treaties or conventions, nor did many of the special conferences; but the other five conferences with programs of a general nature, the Washington Conference on Conciliation and Arbitration, and some of the recent conferences with specific programs, signed a total of forty-four such agreements. Not one of these had been ratified (March 10, 1931) by more than eighteen of the twenty-one states. Some of them were ratified only by two or three states and the average for the entire list of treaties and conventions was only nine. Few of these treaties dealt with political matters; most of them related to social and economic questions.

Some of the nations were more active than others, however. Guatemala led with thirty-two ratifications, followed by the United States and Panama with twenty-seven each; Nicaragua with twenty-six; Costa Rica and Brazil with twenty-five each; and six other states with more than twenty each. Argentina and Venezuela had lagged behind, each having only five ratifications to its credit. All the rest fell between Bolivia and Chile, which had ten and nineteen respectively.

And yet, despite this unimpressive record, it cannot be truthfully asserted that there was not a considerable measure of harmony and coöperation in America. In a century there occurred, as we have seen, only six or seven wars between the independent states of the New World, and only five of these were of any magnitude. In seeking the explanation for this pacific record the ideal of peace nurtured by the Latin-American movement and Pan-Americanism cannot be entirely ignored, although adequate machinery for dealing with the international problems of America was still lacking. The relations of the New World republics during the period became numerous and intimate. An enormous inter-American trade was built up, particularly between the United States and its neighbors to the south; billions of dollars flowed from the United States into needy fields in Latin America; financial experts from the United States gave fourteen Latin-American governments advice which was accepted; and its engineers, physicians, educators, and specialists of every type found profitable employment in these undeveloped nations. The Pan-American movement doubtless played some part in this development; and it is certain that these numerous conferences and congresses enabled the leaders of Pan America to secure more accurate conceptions of one another's needs, anxieties, character, and policies. Of considerable importance also were the more or less permanent international organizations which had been set up, such as the Pan-American Union, the Inter-American High Commission, the Pan-American Bureau of Sanitation, the Inter-American Aviation Commission, the Bibliographical Commission, and the Pan-American Institute of Geography and History.

There was one respect in which the movement had proved disappointing to Latin America. Its leaders had not obtained from the United States the pledges of security which they desired. No general arbitration treaty,[3] no pacts of self-restraint, no definition of the Monroe Doctrine had been granted them. In these assemblies Yankee diplomats had done little more than state their views. They had made few concessions. In 1930 the Latin Americans were still largely at the mercy of our preponderant wealth and power, still virtually unprotected except by public opinion in the United States.

And this was one of the difficulties confronting the Pan-American movement. The motives of the two Americas in supporting this internationalism were obviously in decided contrast. In the main, the Hispanic Americans sought security—security against the United States as well as Europe; territorial security; security against the

---

[3] In the spring of 1932 the United States had not ratified the arbitration treaty of 1929. By March 10, 1931, it had been ratified by only seven states: Cuba, Chile, El Salvador, Guatemala, Mexico, Peru, and the Dominican Republic.

employment of force to collect damage claims and public debts, and against foreign domination of any sort. The United States, on the other hand, sought expansion—expansion of its trade, its investments, its political influence. If it sought security, it was the security of its expanded and expanding interests. If it promoted peace, it was not so much a defensive peace as a peace which would render the field of its economic operations more profitable. In brief, Latin Americans employed the new diplomacy largely for political purposes and the United States used it mainly for economic ends.

Between 1930 and 1945, however, a rapid transformation occurred in the policy of the government at Washington. This significant and opportune transformation will be discussed in the concluding chapter of this volume.

CHAPTER XXIV

PARTICIPATION OF THE LATIN-AMERICAN NATIONS IN WORLD AFFAIRS

In general, it may be said, as already maintained, that the nations of Latin America have agreed with the United States in the policy of opposing European interference in the political affairs of the New World. There have been exceptions, notably during the early national period and in the case of the Dominican Republic and Mexico, but in these instances the invitations to intervene were extended to the European powers by a small minority in defiance of the national will. The Latin-American states have requested the mediation of European governments in their boundary disputes and revealed eagerness for European capital, trade, and cultural contacts, but they have rarely desired political connections.

It is a fact, however, that the governments of Latin America have been less hesitant than the United States in participating in European affairs. It is true that until recently they did not take part in Old World politics, but this cannot be explained entirely by isolation sentiment. They were busy with their own problems, and the great powers had not invited their participation in matters outside of America. Having recognized their independence at the opening of the last century, the European nations had been content to let the new states of Latin America linger "on the margin of international life." Once invited to participate in the affairs of a larger realm, the Latin-American diplomats responded with some eagerness and revealed both industry and talent.

LATIN AMERICA AT THE HAGUE (1907)

With the exception of Mexico and possibly Brazil (which failed to send delegates), these states received no invitation to attend the first peace conference at The Hague. Thanks largely to the influence of the United States, they were asked, however, to send representatives to the assembly of 1907. They responded without hesitation,[1] and their delegates revealed capacities as superior as they were unexpected. Lacking material force to protect themselves, they had the appreciation of all weak states for the legal bulwarks which such a conference might erect.

On the whole, the attitude of the Latin-American delegations at this great assembly accorded with the progressive ideas of the time. They voted unanimously for applying the Red Cross rules to warfare upon the sea and for the prohibition of the bombardment of undefended towns, villages, or buildings, as well as for giving merchant vessels "due warning and fair play at the opening of hostilities." With the exception of the representatives of the Dominican Republic, the delegates unanimously favored "prohibiting the use of unanchored, automatic submarine mines, unless constructed in such a manner as to become harmless within one hour after their control had been lost," and they were unanimous in support of certain other limitations upon the employment of mines and torpedoes. All except the Panama delegation, which abstained from voting, adhered to the proposal to exempt from capture contraband of war found on neutral vessels, and all except the representatives of Panama voted for more humane treatment of prisoners of war. The majority of these delegates also joined in a declaration against warfare in the air and the use of "dum-dum" bullets, but they were not in favor of the proposal to abolish the capture of private property in warfare upon the sea.

In the matter of arbitration they took a stand which subsequent developments rendered most interesting. All but one of the delegations (that of Haiti) supported a resolution accepting obligatory arbitration in "principle," and they unanimously approved a proposal, introduced by Peru, for voluntary arbitration; but a majority of them favored a prize court and a court of arbitral justice only on condition that the judges should be chosen on the basis of the substantial equality of states. If this fact is remembered, the later attitude of Brazil and Argentina toward the League of Nations will more readily be understood.

The main interest of the Latin Americans at The Hague, and an

[1] Costa Rica did not send representatives and those of Honduras arrived too late to take part in the work of the conference.

important motive leading the United States to insist that they be invited to attend, related, however, to the limitation of the employment of force in the collection of damage claims and contract debts. The Venezuelan Imbroglio of 1902–1903 [2] had focused attention upon this important topic and aroused apprehension both in the United States and in Latin America. The United States had insisted that the question be included among those to be discussed at the conference, and it was given a place along with the subject of arbitration.

During the meetings of the First Commission of the conference (namely, the one dealing with arbitration), General Horace Porter, one of the delegates from the United States, introduced several drafts relative to the matter. In the discussions which followed, the Latin-American delegates, particularly Luis M. Drago of Argentina, Ruy Barbosa of Brazil, and Santiago Pérez Triana of Colombia, took a conspicuous part. On July 27 this commission accepted the Porter proposition by a vote of thirty-six, there being none against it and eight abstentions. Among the latter appeared only one Latin-American delegation, that of Venezuela. The proposal was afterwards referred to the Committee of Examination, where the Latin Americans again expressed themselves freely. The final draft was then submitted to the plenary session of the conference, and on October 9 it was adopted by a vote of thirty-nine in favor of the measure, none against, and five abstaining, Venezuela again appearing among the abstaining nations.

The most important provisions of the convention thus adopted were as follows:

"The contracting powers agree not to have recourse to armed force for the recovery of contract debts claimed from the Government of one country by the Government of another country as being due to its nationals.

"This undertaking is, however, not applicable when the debtor State refuses or neglects to reply to an offer of arbitration, or, after having accepted the offer, prevents any *compromis* from being agreed on, or, after the arbitration, fails to submit to the award."

Although the convention would probably not have been accepted

[2] *Cf. ante*, pp. 443–454.

if it had not been for the support of the delegations of Latin America, these delegates were not altogether satisfied with its provisions. In the course of the discussion and votes, they expressed numerous objections; and the majority of them accepted the agreement with reservations.

Naturally, their objections to the convention arose from its failure to go far enough in protecting weak and somewhat disorderly debtor states against the coercion of the stronger powers in behalf of the claims of their nationals. With the exception of the Brazilian representatives, they considered the Porter Convention only a partial victory. Yet there was presented to them a great forum in which to express their views, and their appearance at The Hague marked the beginning of an epoch in their diplomacy. They had passed beyond the margin and entered the great arena of world politics.

LATIN AMERICA AND WORLD WAR I

"Of the twenty Latin-American republics, eight eventually declared war [against Germany and the Central Powers]: Brazil, Cuba, Costa Rica, Guatemala, Haiti, Honduras, Nicaragua, and Panama. Five severed relations with Germany: Peru, Bolivia, Uruguay, Ecuador, and the Dominican Republic. Seven remained neutral: Argentina, Chile, Colombia, Mexico, Salvador, Venezuela, and Paraguay. . . .

"Of the actual belligerents, only two, Brazil and Cuba, may be said to have taken anything like an active part in the war; while Argentina and Chile, both members of the group of the so-called A B C powers, carefully preserved the status of official neutrality. Mexico, the most important state north of the Isthmus, and next-door neighbor to the United States, falls within the same category. In other words, of the four countries of most consequence in the comity of Latin-American powers, three studiously remained aloof from the struggle. It must also be conceded that the military contributions of the Latin-American belligerents to the common cause did little to tip the balance of victory in favor of the Allies. . . . The military and naval aid offered by Brazil and Cuba, owing in part to motives outside their control, was all but negligible. Of much greater weight to be sure, was the material assistance rendered the United States and the Allies. . . ." [3]

To this excellent summary, quoted from the best authority on the attitude of the Latin-American nations toward the World War, only a few comments need be added. It should be noted, for instance, that some of the neutral states, like Mexico and Chile, furnished the Allies commodities most essential to the conduct of the war, such as petroleum and nitrates. It should be noted further that all except one of the belligerent states—namely, Brazil—are situated in the Caribbean area and, hence, were deeply affected by the influence of the United States.

More important, indeed, than the actual participation of these states in the war, were the prestige which the Latin Americans gained and the cross-currents of sentiment that were revealed. Once more they had moved beyond the "margin of international life"; and, moreover, the currents of opinion revealed during the war years served in a measure as a barometer that registered the results of the spirited rivalry outlined in previous chapters. On the side of the Central Powers was the sympathy in some circles for Germany and, to some extent also, for Spain, which was somewhat pro-German. Counterbalancing this were the strong affinity for France and Italy and the economic influence of Great Britain and the United States, to say nothing of the appeal made by the idealism of Woodrow Wilson and perhaps also a certain pressure exerted by Washington in the Caribbean area. Nor should it be forgotten that Mexico's pro-Germanism and Colombia's neutrality were due in part to hostility toward the United States.

LATIN AMERICA AND THE LEAGUE OF NATIONS

Since the close of the Great War the political connections of Latin America with Europe and the League have been somewhat intimate. Thirteen of the Latin-American states were entitled to take part in the Versailles Peace Conference, and eleven of them actually signed the peace treaty, their procedure being subsequently ratified in every instance save one (Ecuador). Thus ten of them became charter members of the League of Nations. By the terms of the annex other

[3] P. A. Martin, *Latin America and the War* (Baltimore, 1925), pp. 1–2.

states were invited to join, and soon afterward all of the nations of Latin America save three—Mexico, which had not been invited; the Dominican Republic, whose national life had suffered a hiatus owing to the intervention of the United States; and Ecuador—voted their adhesion. Moreover, the Dominican Republic became a member in September, 1924, as soon as American military intervention was relaxed, so that all but two of the Latin-American states were listed as members on July 1, 1925, although, as will appear subsequently, the status of some of them was somewhat doubtful.

The motives which impelled these nations to join the League are fairly evident. They were idealism, tradition, and the desire for prestige and protection against possible domination or conquest by some of the great powers. In addition, it must be noted that the Covenant of the League of Nations, which was an outgrowth of the peace settlement, was made an integral part of the peace treaty requiring acceptance along with that treaty, and that some of the states of Latin America had special reasons of their own for joining the League.

President Wilson's addresses describing a new world order in which justice and peace should reign and the weak nations as well as the strong should have their rights respected, made a deep impression upon these naturally idealistic peoples. They hoped that the League might usher in a more enlightened era in which coöperation would take the place of rivalry and law be substituted for force.

Arbitration, multilateral diplomacy, and judicial settlement of disputes had long been their "three watchwords" in international relations. Moreover, Bolívar, their great hero, had advocated an American and perhaps a world league of nations.

The League was also expected to offer them an opportunity to add to their prestige by participating in world affairs and displaying their talents for international law, diplomacy, and forensic discussion. "It was obvious that representation of one of those countries on the Council of the League, or the election of a national as president of the Assembly, would attract the attention of the world. . . . What chance would a delegate from Uruguay or one from Salvador have had to sit in the executive organ of any world institution under the international system outside the American hemisphere prior to 1920? Where had the smaller nations ever been given a forum in which they might voice their grievances? When had the smaller nations ever been given a real voice and responsibility in the problems affecting the peace of the world?" Here indeed was a great opportunity.

Moreover, the League Covenant contained a guaranty of territorial integrity and political independence. It might afford them protection against the great powers of Europe and Asia, and it might also protect them against the United States. The leading authority [4] on the relations of Latin America and the League states: "There is no doubt that those who feared the United States saw in the League a possible protection against encroachments by the North American Republic. The League of Nations afforded to the Latin Americans a hope of a possible counterpoise against the predominant influence of the United States." He also remarks that they "heartily approved the right which each Member has . . . to bring to the attention of the Assembly or the Council any circumstances whatever affecting international relations which threaten to disturb international peace." The delegate from Haiti brings the Union of South Africa to account regarding the treatment of the natives of Southwest Africa. The delegate from Panama rises to call the attention of the Assembly to a dispute with the United States with reference to the sovereignty of the Canal Zone. The Central American representatives ask for a definition of the Monroe Doctrine.

Among the nations of Latin America having special and specific motives for entering the League, only three need be mentioned here. Peru and Bolivia were influenced by the hope that this great organization might be persuaded to take cognizance of the Tacna-Arica question. Chile was spurred on by the news that Argentina had already given adherence and perhaps also in order to be present and defeat the attempt of Peru and Bolivia to induce the League to deal with Tacna and Arica.

Some of the Latin-American nations have taken a fairly prominent part in the proceedings of the League. By 1930 two of their delegates had served as presidents of the Assembly: Agustín Edwards of Chile and Cosme de la Torriente of Cuba; and three of them—Dominio da Gama of Brazil, Alberto Guani of Uruguay, and Francisco José

---

[4] Warren H. Kelchner, *Latin-American Relations with the League of Nations* (Boston, 1930), pp. 12–14.

Urrutia of Colombia—had been presidents of the Council. Two of the eleven judges of the Permanent Court of International Justice in 1930 were from Latin America: Antonio Sánchez de Bustamante of Cuba and Epitacio da Silva Pessoa of Brazil, the latter having succeeded the distinguished Brazilian Ruy Barbosa. In 1932 three of these judges were from Latin America, all three being citizens of Caribbean states. The Latin Americans were likewise represented on some of the standing committees of the League as well as on its staff at Geneva, and the League had set up a Bureau to deal with Latin-American affairs.

Professor Blakeslee has correctly remarked that the "prominent positions to which the Latin-American republics and their citizens have been elected is evidence of the desire of other members to attach them strongly to the League." This doubtless explains the Latin-American Liaison Bureau, the visit of the Secretariat to Latin America in 1927, and the compilation in 1928 of the social legislation of these countries.

On several occasions the Latin-American delegates became conspicuous in discussions relating to the League and its policies. Some of them caused a bit of a stir at the very outset by demanding a definition of the Monroe Doctrine, which, because of the insistence of the United States, was expressly mentioned in Article 21 of the Covenant. A few years later the position of Brazil on the admission of Germany brought the representatives of Portuguese America into the foreground. Between these two events several others reminded the world that a new group of nations was actively participating in its international life.

As soon as the chief of the Honduran delegation, ex-President Policarpo Bonilla, learned of the move to demand the recognition of the Monroe Doctrine in the League constitution, he attempted to secure from the assembled peace conference a definition of the manifesto. In a communication which he presented to that body he stated: "The Monroe Doctrine affects the Latin-American republics directly. As it has never been written into an international document, nor been expressly accepted by the nations of the Old Continent, nor of the New World; and as it has been defined and applied in different manners by presidents and other statesmen of the United States of America, I believe that it is necessary that in the pact about to be subscribed it should be defined with entire clearness, in such a way that it may be incorporated in the written international law."

The Honduran statesman then proposed the following amendment to the League Covenant: "This Doctrine, which the United States of America have maintained since the year 1823, when it was proclaimed by President Monroe, signifies that: All the republics of America have a right to independent existence; that no nation may acquire by conquest any part of the territory of any of these nations, nor interfere with its internal government or administration, nor do any other act to impair its autonomy or to wound its national dignity. It is not to hinder the 'Latin'-American countries from confederating or in any other forms uniting themselves, seeking the best way to realize their destiny."

When the League pact was finally framed, with Article 21 declaring that nothing in the Covenant should be "deemed to affect the validity of international engagements . . . such as the Monroe Doctrine," El Salvador evinced anxiety similar to that revealed by the agent of Honduras. Secretary of State Lansing was called upon to define the Monroe Doctrine.

The secretary took two months to answer the request and then merely stated that the views of the United States could be found in the utterances of President Wilson. Nor was the proposal of Bonilla ever seriously considered by the peace conference. Nevertheless, Honduras and El Salvador joined the League. Their attitude regarding the Monroe Doctrine was merely a straw showing the direction of the wind.

Eight years later the government of Costa Rica expressed a desire "to know the interpretation placed by the League of Nations on the Monroe Doctrine and the scope to be given that Doctrine when it was included in Art. 21 of the Covenant." The president of the League Council felt impelled to make the following answer:

"In declaring that such engagements are not deemed incompatible with any of the provisions of the Covenant, the article refers only to the relations of the Covenant with such engagements; it neither weakens nor limits any of the safeguards provided in the Covenant. . . .

"In regard to the scope of the engagements to which the article relates, it is clear that it cannot have the effect of giving them a sanction or validity which they did not previously possess. It confines itself to referring to these engagements, such as they may exist, without attempting to define them: an attempt at definition being, in fact, liable to have the effect of restricting or enlarging their sphere of application. . . ."

Finally, when Mexico joined the League in 1931, its foreign secretary gave notice that in doing so it was not accepting the Monroe Doctrine as defined in the Covenant.

Soon after the First Assembly of the League began to function, the Argentine delegation caused a disturbance by the submission of three proposals and a spectacular withdrawal when that body failed to consider them. The proposals were: (1) the admission to the League of all sovereign states which should express a desire to join; (2) the adoption of the principle of equality in the election of members of the Council instead of giving the permanent tenure of five places to the great powers; (3) the establishment of a permanent court of international justice and the acceptance of the principle of compulsory arbitration. The influential members of the League were not then ready to accept any of these proposals, and least of all the first, which would have meant the admission of Germany. When a committee of the League reported against the consideration of any amendments to the Covenant at that time, the Argentine delegates withdrew, and Argentina has taken little part in the work of the organization since that date.

Somewhat similar but not precisely analogous was the later attitude of Brazil. In March, 1926, the League Assembly met in a called session to consider the admission of Germany, whose government had made it clear that it would enter the League only on condition that it be given a permanent seat in the Council. It was discovered that the representatives of several nations had been engaging in secret bargaining. Brazil, Spain, and Poland would not vote in favor of admitting the German nation and granting it a permanent seat in the Council unless they also were granted permanent seats. Since Brazil and Spain were then nonpermanent members of the Council and Germany could not be given a permanent seat in that body without their consent, the Assembly was forced to defer the admission of Germany until the following September.

Meanwhile, a commission was appointed to work out a plan for the reconstruction of the Council. Early in June it became clear that this commission would oppose the granting of a permanent Council seat to any other power than Germany, but that it favored increasing the temporary members from six to nine. These were to be elected for a period of three years and were to retire after the expiration of their respective terms, but the Assembly could decide by a two-thirds majority to make exceptions in the case of three of them. This last provision was supposed to be a bait to the three disgruntled candidates—Brazil, Poland, and Spain—but it proved not to be so in the case of Spain and Brazil. The latter, failing to secure the support of the Latin-American delegates in its attempt to secure a permanent place in the Council and confronted with the possibility of losing its temporary seat in September, withdrew both from the Council and from the League (June 11–14, 1926) and never returned. Spain likewise recalled its representatives from Geneva, but sent them back in 1928.[5]

Although the increase in the membership of the Council failed to hold Brazil or to attract Argentina back into the League, it meant an enlarged representation of Spanish America in the Council. Between 1926 and 1932 Latin America was always represented in that body by three states, the delegates of Chile, Salvador, Colombia, Cuba, Venezuela, Peru, Panama, and Guatemala having participated in its deliberations during that period.

Thus it will be observed that some of the delegates of Latin America have at times been conspicuous at Geneva. To the instances already given another might be added. Costa Rica holds the record for having been the first nation to withdraw from the League (announced December 24, 1924; effective January 1, 1927), its withdrawal being due largely to indifference and the feeling that the expense of membership was too great for the service received.

In fact, the League has as yet taken little part in the settlement of difficulties between the nations of Latin America. In 1920 both Peru and Bolivia appealed to it for the revision of the Treaty of Ancón and the settlement of the Tacna-Arica dispute, but the

---

[5] José Carlos de Macedo Soares, *Brazil and the League of Nations,* contends that the main motive for Brazil's withdrawal is to be found in the desire of an unpopular dictator-president of Brazil to find a nationalistic appeal which would strengthen his position.

Chilean delegation, with Señor Agustín Edwards at its head, opposed the consideration of the question by the Assembly and a committee of jurists soon decided that the League had no authority to intervene. For the next eight years the coöperation of Peru and Bolivia was "so intermittent and so casual as to be little more than nominal."

Early in 1921, when news reached Europe that Panama and Costa Rica, both then members of the League, were on the point of war over a boundary dispute, the secretary-general of the League cabled for information. Both states promptly replied; but before the League had time for further action Secretary of State Hughes interfered, and the officials of the League beat "an almost indecorous" retreat.

Although the League played a somewhat more important rôle in the dispute between Bolivia and Paraguay over the Chaco boundary, this dispute was prevented from degenerating into a war largely by the efforts of the Pan-American Conference on Mediation and Arbitration and the conciliatory policy of Argentina and Uruguay. After the threat of hostilities in December, 1928, the League Council repeatedly called the attention of Paraguay and Bolivia to their obligations under the Covenant, but, in appearance at least, it welcomed the news that the American states had taken the matter in hand.

In this connection, M. Briand, president of the Council, said: "The Council, all of whose efforts were directed toward preventing the aggravation of the dispute and facilitating a peaceful settlement by any possible method, cannot but be gratified at the cessation of a conflict between two Members of the League united by common bonds of race and tradition, and at the favorable reception given to the generous initiative of the Pan-American Arbitration Conference. The Council can but trust that the procedure to which the two parties have now agreed will lead to the speediest possible settlement of their dispute and the restoration of a good understanding and of peaceful coöperation between them."

Thanks largely to the efforts of the Pan-American Commission of Inquiry and Conciliation and the persistent mediation of Uruguay, a war between Bolivia and Paraguay was interrupted, and in 1930 the two nations resumed diplomatic relations. What would have happened if the League had insisted upon the exclusive employment of its prerogatives is a matter for speculation. The available evidence seems to indicate that the League revealed no jealousy of the American organization, but modestly coöperated with the American diplomats throughout the crisis. The Chaco War was resumed in 1932 and was terminated in 1935 by the good offices of the Pan-American organization and not by those of the Geneva organization.

Such are the more important phases of the relations of Latin America with the League. Its delegates favored compulsory arbitration and the democratization of the organization, objected to the Monroe Doctrine in the Covenant, and championed the rights of small countries. On the whole, however, they played a minor part in the work of the League; most of the states protested at the expense and were remiss in the making of reports and the ratification of conventions; and some of them failed to pay their quotas promptly. Before 1931, when Mexico joined, the four Latin-American nations not members of the League—Mexico, Ecuador, Costa Rica, and Brazil —plus Argentina, whose relations were uncertain, represented sixty-five per cent of the total area and sixty per cent of the population of Latin America. By 1928 the ardor of Latin-American states for the League had definitely cooled, and, with the rise of aggressive militarism in Europe and Japan and the breakdown of the system of sanctions, the Latin-American states began an exodus from the organization at Geneva. By 1939, when the League virtually ceased to function, most of them had withdrawn.

Latin America and World War II

Despite grave uneasiness in the United States, the alignment of the Latin-American nations during World War II turned out to be far more favorable than during World War I. All of them eventually broke relations with the Axis Powers and most of them actually declared war against the aggressors. Only Chile and Argentina, especially the latter, were reluctant. Mexico and Brazil sent small military forces overseas; and while Argentina's partial failure to suppress totalitarian agents resulted in injury to the cause of the United Nations, it is nevertheless true that every country of Latin America made contributions to the defeat of Italy, Germany, and Japan. Moreover, all were represented at the San Francisco Conference of 1945 and all seemed likely to join the new world organization projected there.

CHAPTER XXV

PREDOMINANCE OF THE UNITED STATES; THE GOOD-NEIGHBOR POLICY AND WORLD WAR II

THE growth of the United States during the last century was so steady and rapid that it soon became politically and economically the predominant power in the New World. The European nations gradually came to recognize its paramount interest and to abandon the disposition to run counter to its will in Latin America. In 1913 its share of Latin-American trade was greater than that of England, and greater than the total Latin-American commerce of France and Germany combined. In 1925 its share was considerably larger than that of all three of these nations, a lead which has since been maintained.

The investments of United States citizens in Latin America, comparatively small until the outbreak of World War I, had risen to a total of nearly six billion dollars by the end of 1929—a sum larger than that of British subjects in 1913 and probably greater than the combined total of German and French nationals in 1929. And, what is more important, the investments of United States citizens were increasing far more rapidly than those of the Europeans. In short, by 1930 the United States and its citizens virtually dominated the economic and political life of many of the republics south of the Río Grande.

There were several reasons for the position of the United States at that time. Its population, with the enormous inflow of immigrants, had increased more rapidly than that of Latin America. Its history had in general been characterized by political stability and growing unity, while the history of Latin America had evinced opposite characteristics. Some of the leaders of Latin America had looked to the United States for financial and technical assistance and political support. And, lastly, the Europeans had been too jealous of one another, too involved in Continental turmoils, and too absorbed elsewhere, to defy the Monroe Doctrine, meet successfully

the economic competition of the United States, or prevent its growing ascendancy.

CARIBBEAN CONTROL

It was in the Caribbean that the expanding political and economic
influence of the United States might be seen most clearly, and only
since 1898 had the most rapid strides been made. The United
States concentrated its attention upon this area mainly because of
its strategic importance. Apprehensions with reference to European
interests and activities caused Washington to be more aggressive.
By 1927 citizens of the United States had two-thirds of the commerce
and the control of a vast majority of the economic resources of the
region. In 1929 the investments of our citizens in the Caribbean, including Colombia and Venezuela, amounted to more than $3,715,-
000,000, while those of British subjects were only $1,530,000. Let
us briefly survey the countries virtually under the domination of
the United States.

Cuba.—For many years the United States had been greatly interested in Cuba. In the early period its main concern was to prevent the island from falling into the hands of a strong European
power, but after 1848 there was considerable sentiment for its acquisition. The value once set upon this "Pearl of the Antilles" may
be judged from the fact that in 1848 the Department of State offered
Spain one hundred million dollars for it—a price in excess of that
paid for all our territorial possessions combined. Between 1901 and
1930 the United States intervened in the island with military force
on four occasions, and it was a protectorate of the United States from
1901 to 1934. In 1895 the value of our trade with the island was a little
less than sixty-six million dollars; in 1923 it amounted to more than
five hundred and thirty-seven million. In 1898 our investments there
amounted to a paltry fifty million; in 1925 they were one billion,
three hundred and sixty million, of which sum one hundred and
ten million represented government loans; in 1929 they were more
than a billion and a half. Our diplomatic representative at Havana
exercises great influence over the political and financial policies of
the country, and its economic life is largely determined "by absentee landlords and bankers living in the United States." The
United States has a navy base on the island, and the Cuban govern-

ment was for many years not allowed to make any loan nor dispose of any territory without Washington's consent.

Panama.—The government and citizens of the United States have been vitally interested in a canal route across Panama since 1846, and in 1903 we acquired this route largely as the result of a military intervention that prevented Colombia, of which Panama was then a part, from suppressing a revolt. From its birth late in 1903 to the year 1936 Panama was virtually dominated by the United States, which prior to 1930 had intervened by armed force on four occasions. Between 1905 and 1925 the value of our trade increased from less than six to more than twenty-two million dollars, and in 1929 the investments of United States citizens were estimated at thirty-six million dollars, of which ten million was in government loans. By the terms of the treaty of 1903 and subsequent agreements, the United States might acquire any Panamanian territory needed for the protection of the Canal, practically dominate the construction of roads, railways, and radio stations, and intervene in the internal affairs of the republic when necessary to restore order. It might also require the disbanding of the Panamanian army—a step which already has been taken—and by insisting upon an exact interpretation of its sovereignty over the zone, it might engage in economic enterprises or permit its citizens residing in the zone to do so in such fashion as greatly to hamper the prosperity of the natives of Panama. In July, 1926, the two countries signed a treaty which required Panama to become our ally in any war which we might undertake against another power; but, owing to the opposition of the Panama Congress, this pact was never ratified.

The Dominican Republic.—The Dominican Republic was a virtual protectorate of the United States from 1905 to 1930, and American Marines occupied the little country almost continually from 1914 to 1924. In 1905 our Dominican trade was worth about six million dollars; in 1927 it exceeded twenty-eight million. By 1929 citizens of the United States had investments there amounting to twenty-three million dollars. Important revenues of the state were in the hands of a general receiver of customs appointed by the president of the United States, and the International Banking Corporation (National City Bank), "with seven branches in the Republic," had "almost complete control over the financial life of the country."

Nicaragua.—The United States government and its citizens have been interested in Nicaragua ever since 1848, when they became rivals of the British for the control of a canal route which crosses its domain. Marines of the United States frequently intervened after 1899 and remained in the country most of the time from 1911, when the republic became almost a protectorate of the United States, until January, 1933. In 1910 our exports and imports were worth three million dollars; in 1927 they were valued at more than eleven million; and they were nearly thirteen million in 1928. Investments of United States citizens in Nicaragua were estimated at three million in 1913 and twenty-four million in 1929. The finances of the country were long in charge of a high commission of three persons— one appointed by the State Department, one by the American bond-holders, and one by Nicaragua—and a Yankee collector-general has been in charge of the customs since 1911. In 1916 a canal option and naval bases were acquired. Late in 1926 several thousand Marines were landed to "protect" American interests and support Adolfo Díaz. Afterwards the United States supervised the national elections.

Haiti.—The United States has been more or less vitally concerned in the fate of Haiti since the opening of the nineteenth century, when Napoleon Bonaparte threatened to make the country the capital of his American empire. Some two thousand Marines were landed there in 1915, and from then until 1934 it was practically a protector-ate of the United States. Although the country was a part of the Spanish empire for two centuries, its people, as previously noted, are mainly African and have been influenced more by French than by Spanish culture. The trade of the United States with Haiti amounted to three million dollars in 1915 and to twelve million in 1927. In 1913 our investments totaled four million; in 1925 they were twenty-three; and in 1929 they were estimated at thirty million. The revenues of the country are under the control of a high commissioner, a general receiver of customs, and a financial adviser, all Yankees appointed by the president of Haiti on the nomination of the president of the United States. In February, 1930, the United States sent a commission to study conditions and make recommenda-tions regarding administrative and political problems. Pledges not to alienate the naval base of Mole St. Nicolas were obtained in 1913-15.

Honduras.—The United States intervened with military force in

Honduras six times between 1907 and 1925. Our trade with the country was worth less than four million dollars in 1910 and more than seventeen million in 1927; our investments rose from three million dollars in 1913 to eight million in 1916, eighteen million in 1920, and forty million in 1925.

Costa Rica.—Diplomatic coercion by the Washington government occurred in Costa Rica in 1917–19. Our trade with the country was valued at six million dollars in 1905, more than nine million in 1923, and fourteen million in 1927. Our investments were worth seven million dollars in 1913, somewhere between twenty and thirty million in 1925, and thirty-five million in 1929.

Mexico.—Military and naval forces of the United States occupied Mexico on numerous occasions between 1846 and 1917, particularly the frontier region, and the Yankees deprived the country, through conquest or purchase, of half of its original territory. The occupation of Vera Cruz in 1914 by the naval forces of the United States, together with Wilson's vigorous opposition to Huerta, was largely responsible for the overthrow of the dictator and the success of the Carranza revolution. Between 1895 and 1929 our Mexican trade increased from less than thirty-one million dollars to more than two hundred and fifty-two million. The United States government has often employed diplomatic pressure in support of our "vested interests"—attempts (1921–1929) to effect a change in the oil and land laws of Mexico being a conspicuous example.

El Salvador and Guatemala.—Here, then, are eight of the republics to the south whose destiny has been greatly influenced by the military, financial, and diplomatic intervention of the United States. But this is not the complete story of our control in the Caribbean. There is El Salvador, whose trade with the United States increased from a little over two million dollars in 1905 to nearly twelve million in 1929; seventeen million dollars' worth of its resources and government loans were owned in the United States in 1925, and its customs were then managed by an American collector appointed by an American corporation with the approval of the Department of State at Washington. There is Guatemala also, where Yankees owned resources and enterprises valued at fifty million dollars in 1925. Its trade with the United States increased from less than six million dollars in 1905 to more than twenty-four million in 1927.

Moreover, it should be added that the political life of the Central American republics has been further influenced by certain treaty agreements signed at the urgent suggestion of the United States. In 1907 the Washington government, assisted by Mexico, induced the five republics to sign a treaty setting up a Central American Court of Justice and pledging their respective executive departments not to recognize any government which might come to power through a military revolt or conspiracy. In 1922 their representatives were invited to Washington, where they were encouraged to sign (early in 1923) a still more rigid agreement forgoing the "right of revolution." The latter treaty, although the United States was not party to it, was advanced as a partial justification for the landing (1923–1931) of Marines in Nicaragua and elsewhere in Central America and for the refusal to recognize presidents in certain states of the region.

The story of our expansion in the Caribbean is still incomplete. The control of the United States government did not extend beyond the Caribbean countries already mentioned, but the economic influence of the United States is very powerful in Venezuela and Colombia, which may in a sense be denominated "Caribbean states."

Venezuela.—Yankee investments in Venezuela mounted from some three million dollars in 1912 or 1913, to seventy-five million in 1925, and more than one hundred and sixty million in 1929 (oil being most conspicuous among the investments), while our trade increased from a little over ten million dollars in 1905 to more than ninety-six million in 1929. It will also be recalled that the United States served as a sort of protector of Venezuela in 1895 and 1902–1903.

Colombia.—The growth of our economic interests in Colombia has been even more rapid. Our investments rose from some four million dollars in 1913 to eighty-seven million in 1925, and two hundred and eighty million in 1930. In 1923 and 1930 commissions of American financial experts reorganized the fiscal system of Colombia and gave the government advice with reference of the expenditure of immense loans as well as of the twenty-five million dollars which the United States paid as compensation for the Canal Zone and in order to prepare the way for valuable oil concessions.

Economic Interests of the United States Beyond the Caribbean

With the exception of the Caribbean area, the United States did not often employ military forces in Latin America. Indeed, they were not employed at all in South America between 1894 and 1942, nor had the official economic intervention of the United States occurred often anywhere in that continent. But even where no form of intervention took place, our commerce and investments experienced a speedy growth. American trade with the five republics of southern South America during the third decade of the twentieth century amounted to about six hundred million dollars annually, while investments of United States citizens in the region amounted to one hundred and thirteen million dollars in 1913, one billion in 1925, and more than a billion and a half in 1929. This meant that our trade with these five countries was considerably more than that of Great Britain, our closest competitor, but that the British had more than twice as much capital invested therein. These countries fall within the sphere marked off by the Monroe Doctrine, but internal stability and distance render the establishment of protectorates, or even of financial receiverships, in most of them very unlikely in the near future.

With respect to Ecuador, Peru, and Bolivia the situation was different. The economic stake of the United States was moving toward a position of such predominance in these nearer and more disorderly nations that intervention was not inconceivable. The trend in these three states may be indicated by reference to a few facts. Our commerce with Ecuador more than doubled between 1913 and 1923; our investments increased from less than nine to twenty-five million between 1913 and 1925; and the Ecuadorian government employed American financial advisers to pave the way for loans. In Peru the investments of United States citizens increased very rapidly during the years following the outbreak of the World War. Amounting to thirty-five million dollars in 1913, they almost reached one hundred and fifty-one million by the end of 1929. Between 1910 and 1927 the trade between the two countries increased from twelve to sixty million. With reference to Bolivia even more rapid strides were made.

Commerce of the United States with this republic increased fivefold between 1913 and 1927, while Yankee investments grew from ten million dollars in 1913 to eighty million in 1925 and more than one hundred and thirty-three million in 1929. Of the total for 1925 about thirty million dollars represented holdings in government loans, most of which had been negotiated by Bolivia's dictator-president upon very onerous terms.[1]

YANKEEPHOBIA IN LATIN AMERICA

Such was our economic and political position in the Western Hemisphere in 1929, and such the rapid movement by which it had been attained. The achievement was often accompanied, however, by irritation and suspicion in Hispanic America. Considerable distrust, fear, and hostility developed along with our hegemony. Yankeephobia had long been a rather prevalent malady south of the Rio Grande. It was confined mainly to literary men and publicists, university students and radicals, but it affected other classes, as already noted in connection with the Latin-American congresses and the Pan-American movement.

Professor J. D. M. Ford states: "In the writings of more recent Spanish-American authors antipathy toward the United States reveals itself in unmistakable terms, and is directed chiefly at what the authors are pleased to term our imperialism, our alleged desire to extend our territorial bounds and absorb the Spanish-American republics."[2] Dr. Isaac Goldberg sums up the attitude of the *literati* of Spanish America in the following language: "At best (always speaking generally) we are in their eyes as yet too engrossed in material ambitions to give attention to spiritual considerations; at worst we are the intriguing nation that despoiled Mexico of Texas and California, and who now, under the shield of the Monroe Doctrine and an alleged Pan-Americanism, cherish imperialistic designs upon the entire southern continent."[3]

---

[1] On Jan. 1, 1932, investments of United States citizens in South America were estimated at $3,078,970,000 and in Central America, Cuba, Haiti, and the Dominican Republic at $3,015,445,000. By that time many of the governments of Latin America had failed to pay interest on their bonds.

[2] *Main Currents in Spanish Literature*, p. 273.

[3] *Studies in Spanish-American Literature*, p. 95.

Yankeephobia, like all sentiments, is subject to ebb and flow. It ran both deep and broad between 1898 and 1929, but the springs of its origin must be sought far back in the mountains of the past. Suspicion and jealousy of the United States showed itself even during the first quarter of the nineteenth century. Fear of the "Colossus" was expressed in Cuba as early as 1811, and by a Mexican diplomat before the close of the year 1822. It would be inaccurate to term the assembly which met at Panama in 1826 a Pan-American congress; for Simón Bolívar, who called the representatives of the American nations together, regretted that the United States had been invited and neither the Mexican president nor Bolívar thought that the Yankee nation should become a member of the American league. Both welcomed English representation as a check upon the United States, and the Mexican delegation sought to hasten the deliberations of the congress so that it might be adjourned before the Washington agents arrived. The annexation of Texas (1845), the Mexican War (1846-1848), the raids of North American filibusters into Mexico, Cuba, and Central America (1850-1857), and the vigorous policy pursued by the United States with reference to a riot in Panama (1856-1857) tended to increase these apprehensions until they were felt by the far-off mountain people of Bolivia.

The danger of European intervention which appeared in so many quarters of America during the sixties of the last century tended to shift the emphasis from the aggressive to the protective phase of Yankee policy, and the preoccupation of the United States with Reconstruction (1865-1876) furnished Latin Americans temporary relief from their anxiety; but Yankeephobia began to develop again during the eighties, and between 1897 and 1912 became more prevalent than ever. The defeat of Spain by the United States in 1898 alarmed many Latin Americans, who "saw in the triumph of 'Yankeeland' . . . the victory of the strong over the weak, of the lusty barbarian over the delicate and exquisite being." Roosevelt's procedure in Panama and his Big Stick policy in the Caribbean, the so-called Dollar Diplomacy of Taft and Knox, Lodge's Magdalena Bay Resolution denying Latin Americans the right to dispose of their territory, and the manner of securing the Nicaragua Canal option, occasioned an epidemic of Yankeephobia throughout Latin America.

Although President Wilson made an earnest attempt to check the malady, his inconsistencies in the Caribbean rendered a complete cure impossible; and, with few exceptions, the world policies as well as the Latin-American policies of subsequent administrations served to aggravate rather than subdue the disease. The Hispanic Americans have seldom been more bitter toward the United States than they were between 1923 and 1928. The procedure of the United States with reference to Mexico (1921–1927) and Nicaragua (1926–1928), particularly the latter, called forth almost unanimous condemnation. The newspapers of the Caribbean expressed antipathy; students, labor organizations, and radicals throughout Latin America were fervent in their denunciations. All this might have been expected, perhaps; but even the great dailies of Argentina, Brazil, and Chile were severe in their comments.

It should not be concluded, however, that this suspicion and hostility was wholly due to the aggressiveness which had characterized the energetic people of the United States. Not our acts alone, but the interpretations of these acts by Frenchmen, Spaniards, Germans, and at times also by Englishmen, together with a traditional attitude south of the Río Grande, were responsible for the apprehension and hostility of the people of Latin America. In order to understand the anti-Yankee sentiment which has been so prevalent in the south, it will be necessary to recall the hostile criticisms of the French and the Spanish—the intellectual leaders of Hispanic America—the propaganda of the Germans, and the severe comments which have sometimes come from the British press. It will also be necessary to keep in mind racial and religious diversities and insurgent nationalism, as well as a certain exclusiveness and intolerance inherited from the Spanish régime.

For Latin America's attitude toward us, then, we were not entirely to blame, but it must be admitted that our course has not been faultless. We have been aggressive and sometimes haughty, we have been impatient and intolerant, we have valued order higher than liberty, and dollars more than democracy. We have shown too scant respect for their sovereignty, and we have acquired most of our territory since 1783 at the expense of Spain and Spanish America. We have wounded their sensibilities, violated their soil, attempted to dictate their domestic policies, and spilled their blood. The fact that all this has at times been done under great provocation and with good intentions has not often been appreciated in Latin America.

The "Good-Neighbor" Policy

Students of international affairs in the United States observed the Yankeephobia malady in Latin America with interest and often with consternation, and some of them attempted to lay the views of our neighbors before the people of this country. At first they brought down upon themselves the odium of our most ardent patriotic societies. Gradually, however, it became evident that the people of the United States at heart did not wish to be imperialistic or to become the object of hatred and denunciation by their neighbors. Previous policies began to be considered by the great majority as unjust or unnecessary, ineffective and unwise. At last the Latin Americans, who had looked about in vain for a bulwark, found one that was adequate to shield them. It was the sentiments of the people of the United States, their democratic idealism and their attitude toward big business and high finance.

Near the end of his administration President Calvin Coolidge became somewhat more conciliatory toward Latin America, and President Herbert Hoover, who made a journey through the countries to the south before taking up the duties of his high office, effected several modifications in Republican policy. (1) The denial of the right of revolution was confined in its application to the five republics of Central America. (2) The lives, property, and dividends of citizens of the United States were protected with somewhat less vigor. And (3) the Roosevelt Corollary of the Monroe Doctrine, which sought to placate European powers by promising to regulate the conduct of certain Latin-American states and had served as the basis for the establishment of the Caribbean protectorates, was quietly renounced while the Marines were withdrawn from Nicaragua and preparations were made for their withdrawal from Haiti.

Such modifications in our Latin-American policy were in many ways a forecast of the good-neighbor policy later proclaimed by Franklin D. Roosevelt. But they were piecemeal and almost surreptitious. They seemed to be made unenthusiastically and reluctantly under the pressure of strong opposition to former aggressiveness—

opposition in the United States and Hispanic America as well. They were reversals of hallowed Republican practices; it would have been embarrassing and impolitic to proclaim them from the housetops.

But Franklin D. Roosevelt's Latin-American policy, in many respects a mere continuation of that of Herbert Hoover, was launched with the enthusiasm of genuine conviction. As early as July, 1928, at a time when the Republican régime had made few modifications in traditional practice and revealed no change of heart, the second Roosevelt published an article in *Foreign Affairs* setting forth his views in detail. He said in effect that the United States should not only renounce territorial conquest but also renounce arbitrary intervention and diplomatic pressure in support of vested interests. His utterances and actions after March 4, 1933, with the possible exception of his policy toward Cuba in 1933–1934, were in harmony with the views expressed nearly five years before his inauguration. He announced the policy of the good neighbor in his inaugural address and frequently elaborated and explained it afterwards, but this good-neighbor policy, in its Latin-American phase, was but the application of the ideas set forth in 1928. And Secretary Cordell Hull was his able collaborator.

The attitude of the delegates of the Roosevelt administration at various Pan-American conferences—Montevideo, 1933; Buenos Aires, 1935 and 1936; Lima, 1938; Panama, 1939—was very conciliatory. The Latin Americans were given the pledges of security which they had long sought at such assemblies. They were permitted to air their grievances freely and were heard with sympathy and a disposition to oblige. Between 1933 and 1939 the following important concessions were made to Latin America: (1) the Platt Amendment was abrogated; (2) a treaty was signed and ratified restoring fuller sovereignty to Panama; (3) the Marines were withdrawn from Haiti; (4) the recognition policy of the United States as applied to the five republics of Central America was reversed, and all attempts ceased to deny the right of revolution to any nation in Latin America; (5) pledges of non-intervention were signed; and (6) a disposition was revealed to transform the Monroe Doctrine from the exclusive instrument of the United States to a Pan-American policy of security. Customs officials or fiscal agents of the United States and American bankers were still in Nicaragua, Haiti, and the Dominican Republic in 1940, but the partnership between the government of the United States and bankers in the making and collection of loans seems to have been dissolved. Despite some evidences of official concern in respect to American properties in Mexico, nationals of the United States with investments in Latin America—including oil companies, whose holdings were seized by Bolivia and Mexico—were left mostly to shift for themselves.

Such were the important changes in the policy of the United States under Hoover and the second Roosevelt. They were welcomed by Latin Americans, who soon began to view the United States with confidence and esteem. The stern policeman and the imperialistic colossus had become the good neighbor. At the end of 1938 the economic position of the United States in Latin America was stronger than ever and it possessed the friendship of most of its neighbors.[4]

World War II

The growing cordiality with Latin America came none too soon. By 1935 dynamic despots were already on the march in Europe. They ridiculed and berated democracy and had no respect for the rights and aspirations of small nations. They based both their domestic and their foreign policies on force, brutal and ruthless. They would soon possess the most terrifying weapons and the most formidable military machines the world had ever known; and Japan, which had invaded Manchuria in 1931 and China proper in 1937, was ready to join them in their aggressions. By the middle of 1940 they had conquered the Baltic states, Albania, Poland, Holland, Belgium, and France, not to mention Austria and Czechoslovakia. When and where their aggressions would stop no one could predict. The Western Hemisphere might soon be in peril. A divided and contentious Europe had long served as a shield for the Americas, but now there was danger that Europe might be subjected and hurled against the New World. Hemispheric defense thus became a paramount problem.

It was not merely a military problem; it was also an economic

[4] The following table gives the percentage distribution of Latin America's trade among the leading competitors in 1913 and 1938:

COUNTRY	EXPORTS TO		IMPORTS FROM	
	1913	1938	1913	1938
United Kingdom	21.2	16.1	24.4	11.8
France	8.0	4.0	8.3	3.4
Germany	12.4	10.3	16.6	16.5
Italy	2.0	1.5	5.1	3.0
United States	30.8	31.3	25.0	34.6

problem. The security of the Americas required speedy armament and prompt military training in every American republic, and it likewise required full economic collaboration among them.

The aggressors might attack directly or indirectly. Hitler and Mussolini might try to seize some of the American colonies of their victims in defiance of the no-transfer principle of the Monroe Doctrine and use these colonies as bases for propaganda, penetration, and eventual assault upon the independent states. Among such colonies, most of which had been acquired in the seventeenth and eighteenth centuries, were Danish Greenland, Dutch Curaçao and Guiana, France's Guiana, Guadeloupe, and Martinique, and a number of well-known English possessions: British Honduras, British Guiana, Trinidad, the Bermudas, the Bahamas, and so on. Hitler and Mussolini might also endanger the peace and security of the Americas by their propaganda, especially among inhabitants of German and Italian descent, and by means of commercial bartering and bullying; and if they won the war in Europe and got control of the eastern Atlantic, they might launch a direct attack by sea and air.

Moreover, the defense problem was complicated by tariffs, by surpluses of raw materials (especially in countries like Argentina and Uruguay), by disagreements with reference to the management, regulation, and yield of investments of United States citizens and other aliens in Latin America, and by possible disagreements in respect to limitations on production and the point of emphasis in the development of new enterprises. Nor would the security of the Americas depend solely upon geography and economic integration; it would also depend upon devotion to liberty, popular sovereignty, and national independence—in short, upon the capacity of the united peoples of the New World to produce the sinews of war and use them effectively in their defense.

Never had the independent nations of the Western Hemisphere confronted a graver peril. But despite the danger of attack from both the east and the west, there was some ground for optimism. The twenty-one independent nations were economically more interdependent than ever before. The United States was determined to put forth its utmost efforts to defend the hemisphere and was prepared to contribute its wealth, energy, and skills to that end. The Latin Americans likewise seemed determined to resist conquest. They were certainly intensely nationalistic; and in spite of many deviations in practice, perhaps the majority of them were also devoted to democracy.

An intensified Pan-Americanism prepared the way for mutual defense. Conference after conference was held as the second world conflict approached and after the beginning of hostilities in 1939. When the Japanese attacked Pearl Harbor on December 7, 1941, the Americas were ready to take up the challenge. Already, by the conference at Lima in 1938, the delegates of the independent American nations had declared that an attack upon any one of them would be considered an attack upon them all. A conference of the representatives of their foreign offices met at Rio de Janeiro in January, 1942, to implement this declaration. When the delegates arrived at the Brazilian capital, twelve of the Hispanic nations already had taken action in support of the United States in its war against Japan, Germany, and Italy. Nine of these had declared war and the other three had broken relations with the Axis Powers. The United States and the twelve nations which had come to its aid hoped now to persuade the other eight to agree at once to sever relations with the Axis. Although only a joint resolution recommending the severance of relations was obtained at Rio, many measures of joint defense were adopted, and by the time the conference was over six more Hispanic-American countries had made the break, thus leaving only Argentina and Chile in a neutral position.

Although this breach in the Pan-American front was disappointing, it was hoped that Argentina and Chile would soon close it. Moreover, it was reassuring to observe that the American front was far more solid than it had been during World War I, when seven of the neighboring nations had remained neutral, four of them—Mexico, El Salvador, Colombia, and Venezuela—located in the Caribbean Danger Zone and three—Argentina, Paraguay, and Chile—in more distant South America. Within a little more than a year after the United States was attacked by Japan and the other Axis allies, and in most cases immediately thereafter, Mexico, the six Central American countries, the three island republics of the Caribbean, and Brazil had joined their Anglo-Saxon neighbor in the war and all the rest of Hispanic America except Chile and Argentina had broken relations with the Axis aggressors. Chile made the break early in 1943, and

Argentina finally severed relations early in 1944, but relations between the United States and Argentina continued to be unsatisfactory because its government was despotic, and apparently in sympathy with the despotisms of Europe even as late as the spring of 1945, when Argentina declared war on the Axis Powers with the obvious desire to gain admission to the United Nations conference at San Francisco.

With the failure of the Nazis to conquer Russia, which they had invaded in June, 1941, the tide of war began to turn against the aggressors. In the summer of 1945, after four years of participation by the majority of the Latin-American countries—either directly in military combat, as in the case of Brazil and Mexico, or indirectly by granting the use of land for air bases or through economic and other forms of collaboration (even reluctant Argentina furnished huge supplies of food)—the totalitarian conquerors were crushed.

Successful in the war, the Pan-American nations now confronted the problems of peace, the apparently eternal problems of security and progress. In February and March, 1945, as the European phase of the war approached its termination, a Pan-American conference, known as the Chapultepec Conference, assembled in Mexico City to consider these problems and promulgate general principles and ideals for the post-war period. The Pan-American nations, for their security, would still depend largely upon the United States, but as the year 1945 drew to a close they appeared to be on the point of joining the new world organization which their delegates had helped to plan at San Francisco. Their prosperity was also closely linked with the United States, which was for most of them the principal market for their exports and the main source of supply for foreign capital and technology; but their prosperity also depended in considerable measure upon the British Empire, which furnished them their second largest market and to which they were still indebted. Although their increased exports to the United States and Great Britain during World War II had enabled them to accumulate large balances in dollars or pounds, they had not by any means paid off their earlier loans. In fact, during the war they had borrowed millions from the government lending agencies of the United States, and while some of the old government bonds held by private investors had been redeemed, investments of capitalists of the United States in various economic enterprises, especially manufacturing establishments, had increased, so that at the end of 1945 the Latin Americans were probably as deeply indebted to the United States as they ever had been, even during the peak year of 1929. In short, among foreign powers, the United States was still predominant in Latin America, the main bulwark of its security and an extremely important factor in its prosperity.

During the immediate post-war years friendly relations with the United States would depend largely upon harmony in the economic realm. The key problem would be the fair distribution of the bene- fits of technological advance, the United States supplying large quan- tities of capital and a number of technicians and the Latin Americans furnishing some of both, as well as the required labor and materials. Cultural relations, which received great stress during the late 1930's and early 1940's, could help to clear away prejudices and resentments, but they could not cloak exploitation, if exploitation and economic imperialism should reappear. Cultural relations might also help to create common ideals, but common ideals would have to be based firmly on common interests.

As the year 1945 approached its end, Argentina continued to be the main rift in the Pan-American front, its dictator, Juan Perón, ready to magnify any disagreements that might arise between the United States and its neighbors. With reference to the forces back of him observers disagreed. Some felt that he merely represented a group of ambitious young militarists; others insisted that he was the agent of the landed aristocracy, who were either opposed to the ex- panding industrialization of Argentina or determined to control it through state intervention. Whatever his backing or his objectives, Perón was hostile to the United States and resentful of its tariff policies and its dominant position in the Pan-American movement. Whether his attitude might be changed by tariff adjustments on meat and other Argentine products and by the progress of democracy among his neighbors and in the rest of the world only the future could reveal. Perhaps he would be forced to resign or mend his ways by the Argentines themselves, with the moral support of the United States and other American countries. Until one or the other of these changes occurred, Argentina would remain an obstacle to the development of full Pan-American harmony.

READING LISTS

I. GUIDES

Samuel Flagg Bemis and Grace Gardner Griffin, *Guide to the Diplomatic History of the United States* (Washington, 1935).

Herbert E. Bolton, *History of the Americas* [*Outlines, bibliography, maps*] (Boston, 1935).

Lewis Hanke, ed., *Handbook of Latin American Studies* (Cambridge, Mass., 1936–). Annual.

Cecil Knight Jones, *Hispanic American Bibliographies* (Baltimore, 1922).

R. Hayward Keniston, *List of Works for the Study of Hispanic-American History* (New York, 1920).

Alan K. Manchester, *Descriptive Bibliography of the Brazilian Section of the Duke University Library* (Durham, N. C., 1933).

Alonso B. Sánchez, *Fuentes de la historia española e hispano-americana* (2 vols., Madrid, 1927).

University of California, *Spain and Spanish America in the Libraries of the University of California* (2 vols., Berkeley, 1928–1930).

A. Curtis Wilgus, *Histories and Historians of Hispanic America* (Washington, 1937).

II. GENERAL HISTORIES AND PERIODICALS

Diego Barros Arana, *Historia de America* (2 vols., Santiago de Chile, 1908).

Raúl Carrancá y Trujillo, *La evolución política de Iberoamérica* (Madrid, 1925).

Charles E. Chapman, *Hispanic America* (2 vols., New York, 1937).

Nels Andrew N. Cleven, *Readings in Hispanic American History* (Boston, 1927).

A. J. Deberle, *The History of Spanish America from Its Discovery to the Present* (London, 1899).

Francisco García Calderón, *Latin America; Its Rise and Progress* (London, 1913).

Samuel Guy Inman, *Latin America* (Chicago, 1937).

H. G. James and Percy A. Martin, *The Republics of Latin America* (New York, 1923).

F. A. Kirkpatrick, *Latin America* (New York, 1938).

David R. Moore, *A History of Latin America* (New York, 1938).

Carlos Navarro y Lamarca, *Compendio de la historia general de América* (2 vols., Buenos Aires, 1910–1913).

Juan Ortega y Rubio, *Historia de America* (3 vols., Madrid, 1917).

Carlos Pereyra, *Historia de la América española* (8 vols., Madrid, 1920–1926). *Breve historia de América* (Madrid, 1930).

William Spence Robertson, *History of the Latin-American Nations* (New York, 1943).

Manuel Serrano y Sanz, *Compendio de la historia de América* (2 vols., Barcelona, 1917).

A. Curtis Wilgus and Raúl d'Eça, *Outline History of Latin America* (New York, 1939).

Mary W. Williams, *The People and Politics of Latin America* (New York, 1938).

American Journal of International Law (New York, 1907–   ).

Boletín de la academia nacional de historia (Caracas, 1912–   ).

Boletín de historia y antigüedades (Bogotá, 1902–   ).

Bulletin of the Pan American Union (Washington, 1893–   ).

Foreign Affairs (New York, 1922–   ).

Foreign Policy Association, *Information Service* and *Foreign Policy Reports* (New York, 1924–   ).

The Hispanic American Historical Review (Baltimore and Durham, 1918–   ).

The Inter-American Quarterly (Cambridge, Mass., 1939–   ).

Mid-America (Chicago, 1918–   ).

Revista argentina de ciencias políticas (Buenos Aires, 1910–   ).

Revista chilena de historia e geografía (Santiago de Chile, 1911).

Revista de historia de America (Mexico, 1938–   ).

Revista do instituto historico e geographico do Brasil (Rio de Janeiro, 1839–   ).

III. THE PHYSICAL ENVIRONMENT

Howard F. Bain and T. T. Read, *Ores and Industry in South America* (New York, 1934).

Isaiah Bowman, *The Andes of Southern Peru* (New York, 1915).

Desert Trails of Atacama (New York, 1924).

South America (New York, 1915).

Fred A. Carlson, *Geography of Latin America* (New York, 1936).

Charles C. Colby, *The Economic Geography of North America* (Chicago, 1921), chaps. XIII and XIV.

Ellsworth Huntington, *Civilization and Climate* (New Haven, 1915).

The Red Man's Continent (New Haven, 1919).

World-Power and Evolution (New Haven, 1919).

Preston E. James, *Latin America* (New York, 1942).

A. H. Keane, *Central and South America* (2 vols., New York, 1909–1910).

Benjamin Miller and J. T. Singewald, *The Mineral Deposits of South America* (New York, 1919).

E. W. Shanahan, *South America, an Economic and Regional Geography* (New York, 1927).

R. H. Whitbeck, *Economic Geography of South America* (New York, 1926).

IV. PRIMITIVE PEOPLES OF AMERICA

Goerge E. Church, *Aborigines of South America* (London, 1912).

Thomas Gann and J. E. Thompson, *The History of the Maya* (New York, 1931).

E. L. Hewett, *Ancient Life in Mexico and Central America* (Indianapolis, 1936).
A. L. Kroeber, *Anthropology* (New York, 1923).
Sir Clements Markham, *The Incas of Peru* (New York, 1912).
The Conquest of New Granada (London, 1912), chaps. I–IV.
Philip A. Means, *Ancient Civilizations of the Andes* (New York, 1931).
Carlos Navarro y Lamarca, *Compendio de la historia general de América*, Vol. I.
Paul Radin, *The Story of the American Indian* (New York, 1934).
Vicente Restrepo, *Los Chibchas* (Bogotá, 1893).
Herbert J. Spinden, *Ancient Civilizations of Mexico and Central America* (New York, 1928).
J. E. Thompson, *Mexico before Cortez* (New York, 1933).
Clark Wissler, *The American Indian* (New York, 1922).

V. OLD WORLD BACKGROUND

R. Altamira y Crevea, *Historia de España* (4 vols., Barcelona, 1909–1914).
J. N. L. Baker, *A History of Geographical Discovery and Exploration* (Boston, 1932).
C. R. Beazley, *Prince Henry the Navigator* (London, 1895).
J. W. Blake, *European Beginnings in West Africa* (New York, 1937).
V. de Bragança Cunha, *Eight Centuries of the Portuguese Monarchy* (New York, 1911).
Charles E. Chapman, *History of Spain* (New York, 1918).
Edward P. Cheyney, *European Background of American History* (New York, 1904).
Ephraim Emerton, *The Beginnings of Modern Europe* (New York, 1917).
J. E. Gillespie, *History of Geographical Discovery* (New York, 1933).
Martin A. S. Hume, *The Spanish People* (New York, 1901).
Spain, Its Greatness and Decay (Cambridge, 1905).
Roger B. Merriman, *Rise of the Spanish Empire* (4 vols., New York, 1918–1934), Vols. I–II.
G. E. Nunn, *The Geographical Conceptions of Columbus* (New York, 1928).
J. P. de Oliveira Martins, *The Golden Age of Prince Henry the Navigator* (New York, 1914).
Historia de Portugal (2 vols., Lisbon, 1901).
A History of Iberian Civilization (New York, 1930).
Edgar Prestage, *The Portuguese Pioneers* (New York, 1934).
H. D. Sedwick, *A Short History of Spain* (Boston, 1925).
H. Morse Stephens, *Portugal* (New York, 1903).
Lynn Thorndike, *History of Medieval Europe* (New York, 1917).
G. Young, *Portugal, Old and Young* (New York, 1917).

VI. THE COLONIAL PERIOD

1. ACHIEVEMENTS OF THE SIXTEENTH CENTURY

Arthur Aiton, *Antonio de Mendoza* (Durham, N. C., 1927).
Hubert H. Bancroft, *History of Central America* (3 vols., San Francisco, 1883), Vol. I.

Frans Blom, *The Conquest of Yucatán* (Boston and New York, 1936).

Herbert E. Bolton, *The Spanish Borderlands* (New Haven, 1921).

Herbert E. Bolton and T. M. Marshall, *The Colonization of North America* (New York, 1920), chaps. II–III.

Edward G. Bourne, *Spain in America* (New York, 1906), chaps. I–XIV.

Charles S. Braden, *Religious Aspects of the Conquest of Mexico* (Durham, N. C., 1930).

R. Fernández Guardia, *Discovery and Conquest of Costa Rica* (New York, 1913).

R. B. C. Graham, *Cartagena and the Banks of the Sinú* (London, 1918).
   The Conquest of New Granada (New York, 1922).
   The Conquest of the River Plate (New York, 1924).
   Pedro de Valdívia (London, 1926).

Earl J. Hamilton, *American Treasure and the Price Revolution in Spain* (Cambridge, Mass., 1934).

Lewis Hanke, *The First Social Experiments in America* (Cambridge, Mass., 1935).

Clarence H. Haring, *Trade and Navigation between Spain and the Indies* (Cambridge, Mass., 1928), chaps. I–II.

Cecil Jane, *Select Documents Illustrating the Voyages of Columbus* (2 vols., London, 1930–1932).

John E. Kelly, *Pedro de Alvarado, Conquistador* (Princeton, 1932).

F. A. Kirkpatrick, *The Spanish Conquistadores* (London, 1934).

J. T. Lanning, *Academic Culture in the Spanish Colonies* (New York, 1940).

Charles F. Lummis, *The Spanish Pioneers* (Chicago, 1925).

F. A. MacNutt, *Fernando Cortés and the Conquest of Mexico* (New York, 1909).

Sir Clements Markham, *The Conquest of New Granada,* chaps. V–XV.

Stella Burke May, *The Conquerors Lady* (New York, 1930).

Theodore Maynard, *De Soto and the Conquistadores* (New York, 1930).

P. A. Means, *The Fall of the Inca Empire* (New York, 1932).
   History of the Spanish Conquest of Yucatán and the Itzas (Cambridge, Mass., 1917).

R. B. Merriman, *The Spanish Empire,* Vol. III.

R. Muller, *History of the Conquest of Quito* (New York, 1929).

F. A. Ober, *Pizarro and the Conquest of Peru* (New York, 1906).

W. H. Prescott, *The Conquest of Mexico* (various editions).
   The Conquest of Peru (various editions).

I. B. Richman, *The Spanish Conquerors* (New Haven, 1919).

H. M. Robinson, *Stout Cortez* (New York, 1931).

William Robertson, *History of America* (4 vols., London, 1800), Vols. I–III.

H. D. Sedgwick, *Cortés the Conqueror* (Indianapolis, 1926).

Leslie B. Simpson, *The Encomienda in New Spain* (Berkeley, 1929).
   The Repartimiento System (Berkeley, 1938).
   Studies in the Administration of the Indians (Berkeley, 1934).

Robert Southey, *History of Brazil* (London, 1810–1819), Vol. I.

J. B. Thacher, *Christopher Columbus* (3 vols., New York, 1903–1904).

J. A. Villacorta, *Cursa de la historia de la América central* (Guatemala, 1928).

R. B. Watson, *Spanish and Portuguese South America during the Colonial* (2 vols., London, 1884), Vol. I.

J. A. Williamson, *The Age of Drake* (New York, 1938).

William Wood, *Elizabethan Sea-Dogs* (New Haven, 1921).

J. A. Zahm, *The Quest of El Dorado* (New York, 1917).

A. F. Zimmerman, *Francisco de Toledo* (Caldwell, Idaho, 1938).

NOTE: See also the various national histories listed below, Section VIII.

2. SPANISH COLONIES, SEVENTEENTH AND EIGHTEENTH CENTURIES

Lucas Ayarragaray, *La iglesia en América y la dominación española* (Buenos Aires, 1920).

H. H. Bancroft, *Central America,* Vol. II.

Herbert E. Bolton, *Outpost of Empire* (New York, 1931).
Rim of Christendom (New York, 1936).
Spanish Borderlands, chaps. VII–X.

Bolton and Marshall, *Colonization of North America,* chaps. XIII–XIV, XVI, XX, XXI.

Charles Chapman, *A History of California: The Spanish Period* (New York, 1921).

Charles A. Cunningham, *The Audiencia in the Spanish Colonies* (Berkeley, 1919).

Lillian E. Fisher, *The Intendant System in Spanish America* (Berkeley, 1929).
Viceregal Administration in the Spanish-American Colonies (Berkeley, 1926).

Thomas Gage, *A New Survey of the West Indies* (New York, 1929).

Clarence H. Haring, *Trade and Navigation,* chaps. III ff.
Buccaneers in the West Indies (New York, 1910).

Alexander Humboldt, *Political Essay on the Kingdom of New Spain* (various editions).
Travels in Equinoctial America (various editions).

Roland D. Hussey, *The Caracas Company* (Cambridge, Mass., 1934).

Jorge Juan y Antonio de Ulloa, *Noticias secretas de América* (London, 1826; Madrid, 1917).
A Voyage to South America (2 vols. London, 1806).

A. G. Keller, *Colonization* (New York, 1908), chaps. IV–IX.

W. H. Koebel, *In Jesuit Land* (London, 1912).

H. C. Lea, *The Inquisition in the Spanish Colonies* (New York, 1922).

I. A. Leonard, *Sigüenza y Góngora* (Berkeley, 1929).
Romances of Chivalry in the Spanish Colonies (Berkeley, 1933).

Leopoldo Lugones, *El imperio jesuítico* (Buenos Aires, 1907).

P. A. Means, *The Spanish Main* (New York, 1935).

Bernard Moses, *South America on the Eve of Emancipation* (New York, 1908).
Spain Overseas (New York, 1929).
Spain's Declining Power in South America (Berkeley, 1919).
Spanish Colonial Literature (New York, 1922).
The Spanish Dependencies in South America (2 vols., New York, 1914).

H. J. Mozans, *Along the Andes and down the Amazon* (London, 1912).
Up the Orinoco and down the Magdalena (New York, 1910).

A. P. Newton, *The European Nations in the West Indies* (New York, 1933).
G. O'Neill, *Golden Years on the Paraguay* (London, 1934).
José María Ots, *Instituciones sociales de la América española en el periodo colonial* (La Plata, Argentina, 1934).
Richard Pares, *War and Trade in the West Indies* (New York, 1936).
Herbert I. Priestley, *The Coming of the White Man* (New York, 1927).
    José de Gálvez (Berkeley, 1916).
F. R. J. de Pons, *Travels in South America* (2 vols., London, 1807).
Agnes Repplier, *Junípero Serra* (New York, 1937).
J. Fred Rippy and J. T. Nelson, *Crusaders of the Jungle* (Chapel Hill, N. C., 1936).
Wilhelm Roscher, *The Spanish Colonial System* (New York, 1904).
Don E. Smith, *The Viceroy of New Spain* (Berkeley, 1916).
F. M. Stanger, "National Origins in Central America," *Hispanic American Historical Review*, XII, 18–45.
A. B. Thomas, *After Coronado* (Norman, Oklahoma, 1935).
J. A. Villacorta, *Historia de América central*, pp. 87–146.
R. G. Watson, *Spanish and Portuguese South American*, Vol. II.
A. Curtis Wilgus, ed., *Colonial Hispanic America* (Washington, 1936).
J. A. Williamson, *English Colonies in Guiana and on the Amazon, 1604–1668* (London, 1923).
Silvio A. Zavala, *La encomienda indiana* (Madrid, 1935).
    NOTE: See also national histories listed below, Section VIII.

3. BRAZIL, 1600–1808

John Armitage, *The History of Brazil* (2 vols., London, 1836), Vol. II, 157 ff.
Da Cunha de Azeredo Coutinho, *An Essay on the Brazils* (London, 1807).
J. Capistrano de Abreu, *Capítulos de historia colonial* (Rio de Janeiro, 1928).
Andrew Grant, *History of Brazil* (London, 1909).
Isaac Goldberg, *Brazilian Literature* (New York, 1922).
Henry Koster, *Travels in Brazil* (2 vols., London, 1817).
Alan K. Manchester, "The Rise of the Brazilian Aristocracy," *The Hispanic American Historical Review*, XI, 145–168.
John Mawe, *Travels in the Interior of Brazil* (London, 1812).
Robert Southey, *History of Brazil*, Vols. II–III.

VII. THE INDEPENDENCE MOVEMENT

Hildegarde Angell, *Simón Bolívar*.
Víctor Andrés Belaunde, *Bolívar and the Political Thought of the Spanish-American Revolution* (Baltimore, 1938).
John Armitage, *The History of Brazil*.
A. S. M. Chisholm, *Independence of Chile* (London, 1911).
Ricardo Fernández Guardia, *La independencia y otros episodios* (San José, Costa Rica, 1928).
Lillian E. Fisher, *The Background of the Revolution of Mexican Independence* (Boston, 1934).
R. B. C. Graham, *José Antonio Páez* (London, 1929).

Margaret Harrison, *Captain of the Andes* (New York, 1942).
Alfred Hasbrouck, *Foreign Legionaries in the Liberation of Spanish South America* (New York, 1928).
Jules Mancini, *Bolívar y la emancipación de las colonias españoles* (Paris, 1923).
Bartolomé Mitre, *The Emancipation of South America* (London, 1893).
   Historia de San Martín (3 vols., Buenos Aires, 1887–1888).
Bernard Moses, *The Intellectual Background of the Revolution in South America* (New York, 1926).
Arthur Howard Noll and A. P. McMahon, *Miguel Hidalgo y Costilla* (Chicago, 1910).
M. de Oliveira Lima, *Dom João VI do Brasil* (2 vols., Rio, 1908).
J. B. Otero, *Historia del Libertador [San Martín]* (4 vols., Buenos Aires, 1932).
F. L. Petre, *Simón Bolívar* (London, 1909).
W. S. Robertson, *Life of Miranda* (2 vols., Chapel Hill, 1929).
   Rise of the Spanish-American Republics (New York, 1918).
John Rydjord, *Foreign Interference in the Independence of New Spain* (Durham, 1925).
G. A. Sherwell, *Antonio José de Sucre* (Washington, 1924).
T. L. Stoddard, *The French Revolution in San Domingo* (New York, 1914).
J. A. Villacorta, *Historia de América central,* pp. 139–152.
R. Walsh, *Notices of Brazil* (2 vols., London, 1830).
   NOTE: See also national histories below, Section VIII.

VIII. THE NATIONAL PERIOD

I. GENERAL OR REGIONAL ACCOUNTS EMPHASIZING THE PERIOD

C. E. Akers, *A History of South America* (New York, 1930).
Hubert H. Bancroft, *History of Central America,* Vol. III.
Carlton Beals, *America South* (Philadelphia and New York, 1937).
James Bryce, *South America: Observations and Impressions* (New York, 1916).
Alfred Coester, *The Literary History of Spanish America* (New York, 1916).
Thomas C. Dawson, *The South American Republics* (2 vols., New York, 1904).
Negley Farson, *Transgressor in the Tropics* (New York, 1938).
Isaac Goldberg, *Studies in Spanish-American Literature* (New York, 1920).
Hubert Herring, *Good Neighbors* (New Haven, 1941).
Chester Lloyd Jones, *Caribbean Backgrounds and Prospects* (New York, 1931).
J. Lloyd Mecham, *Church and State in Latin America* (Chapel Hill, 1932).
Dana G. Munro, *The Five Republics of Central America* (New York, 1918).
Robert Platt, *Latin America* (New York, 1943).
William L. Schurz, *Latin America* (New York, 1942).
George Soule, David Efron, and N. T. Hess, *Latin America in the Future World* (New York, 1945).
Edward Tomlinson, *New Roads to Riches in the Other Americas* (New York, 1939).
A. Curtis Wilgus, ed., *Argentina, Brazil, and Chile since Independence* (Washington, 1937).
   The Caribbean Area (Washington, 1934).

2. Histories of Individual Countries

F. A. Kirkpatrick, *A History of the Argentine Republic* (Cambridge, 1931).

Ricardo Levene, *A History of Argentina* (W. S. Robertson, ed. and trans. Chapel Hill, 1937).

Felix J. Weil, *Argentine Riddle* (New York, 1944).

Alcides Arguedas, *Pueblo enfermo [Bolivia]* (Barcelona, 1910).

W. L. Schurz, *Bolivia: A Commercial and Industrial Handbook* (Washington, 1921).

J. P. Calogeras, *A History of Brazil* (P. A. Martin, ed. and trans. Chapel Hill, 1939).

H. G. James, *Brazil After a Century of Independence* (New York, 1925).
The Constitutional System of Brazil (Washington, 1923).

J. F. Normano, *Brazil, A Study of Economic Types* (Chapel Hill, 1935).

M. de Oliveira Lima, *The Evolution of Brazil* (Stanford Univ., Calif., 1914).

João Ribeiro, *Historia do Brasil* (Rio, 1914).

Agustín Edwards, *My Native Land [Chile]* (London, 1928).

Luis Galdames, *Estudio de la historia de Chile* (various editions).

P. J. Eder, *Colombia* (New York, 1913).

J. M. Henao and G. Arrubla, *History of Colombia* (trans. and ed. by J. Fred Rippy, Chapel Hill, 1938).

C. R. Enock, *Ecuador* (New York, 1914).

E. Unzátegui García, *Historia del Ecuador* (2 vols., Quito, 1929).

Cecilio Báez, *Resumen de la historia del Paraguay* (Paris, 1917).

W. L. Schurz, *Paraguay: A Commercial and Industrial Handbook* (Washington, 1920).

Charles A. Washburn, *History of Paraguay* (2 vols., New York, 1871).

W. E. Dunn, *Peru: A Commercial Handbook* (Washington, 1925).

Clements Markham, *History of Peru* (Chicago, 1892).

Carlos Wiesse, *Historia del Peru* (4 vols., various editions).

Eduardo Acevedo, *Manual de historia uruguayana* (Montevideo, 1935).

Hermano Damasceno (E. Perret), *Ensayo de la historia patria* (Montevideo, 1923).

Simon H. Hanson, *Utopia in Uruguay* (New York, 1938).

P. L. Bell, *Venezuela: A Commercial and Industrial Handbook* (Washington, 1922).

L. V. Dalton, *Venezuela* (New York, 1912).

Erna Fergusson, *Venezuela* (New York, 1939).

J. Gil Fortoul, *Historia constitucional de Venezuela* (3 vols., Caracas, 1930–32).

Ernest Gruening, *Mexico and Its Heritage* (New York, 1928).

Henry B. Parkes, *A History of Mexico* (Boston and New York, 1938).

Luis Pérez Verdia, *Compendio de la historia de Mexico* (Mexico, 1911).

Herbert I. Priestley, *The Mexican Nation* (New York, 1923).

Arthur H. Noll, *A Short History of Mexico* (Chicago, 1890).
From Empire to Republic (Chicago, 1903).

C. E. Chapman, *A History of the Cuban Republic* (New York, 1927).

R. Guerra y Sánchez, *Historia de Cuba* (Havana, 1922).

Hudson Strode, *The Pageant of Cuba* (New York, 1934).

Sumner Welles, *Naboth's Vineyard: The Dominican Republic* (2 vols., New York, 1928).
Chester Lloyd Jones, *Guatemala, Past and Present* (Minneapolis, 1940).
H. P. Davis, *Black Democracy [Haiti]* (New York, 1936).
James G. Leyburn, *The Haitian People* (New Haven, 1941).

3. A SELECTION OF BIOGRAPHIES AND BIOGRAPHICAL SKETCHES

Ramón Azpurúa, *Biografías de hombres notables de Hispano-américa* (Caracas, 1877).
Carlton Beals, *Porfirio Díaz* (Philadelphia, 1932).
I. Bucich Escobar, *Historia de los presidentes argentinos* (Buenos Aires, 1927).
Paul Burgess, *Justo Rufino Barrios* (Philadelphia, 1926).
U. R. Burke, *A Life of Benito Juárez* (London, 1894).
E. C. Corti, *Maximilian and Charlotte of Mexico* (2 vols., New York, 1928).
Camilo Destruge, *Album biográfico ecuatoriano*. Tomo III: *Presidentes de la república* (Quito, 1904).
W. H. Callcott, *Santa Anna* (Norman, Oklahoma, 1936).
R. B. C. Graham, *Portrait of a Dictator: Francisco Solano López* (London, 1933).
David Hannay, *Porfirio Díaz* (London, 1917).
P. A. Martin, "The Career of José Batlle y Ordóñez," *Hispanic American Historical Review*, X, 413–428.
Who's Who in Latin America (Stanford Univ., 1935).
M. de Mendiburu, *Diccionario histórico biográfico del Peru* (8 vols., Lima, 1874–1890).
R. Mesa Ortiz, *Colombianos ilustres* (4 vols., Bogotá, 1916–1922).
W. B. Parker, *Argentines of To-day* (2 vols., New York, 1920).
Bolivians of To-day (New York, 1920).
Chileans of To-day (New York, 1920).
Peruvians of To-day (New York, 1919).
Paraguayans of To-day (New York, 1920).
Uruguayans of To-day (New York, 1921).
Cubans of To-day (New York, 1911).
Ernesto Quesada, *La Época de Rosas* (Buenos Aires, 1923).
J. Fred Rippy, "Dictatorships in Latin America," G. S. Ford, *Dictatorship in the Modern World* (Minneapolis, 1939), pp. 178–214.
Thomas Rourke, *Gómez, Tyrant of the Andes* (New York, 1936).
A. C. Wilgus, ed., *Dictators of South America* (Washington, 1937 [contains numerous bibliographical references]).
Mary W. Williams, *Dom Pedro the Magnanimous* (Chapel Hill, 1937).

IX. INTERNATIONAL RELATIONS

Ephraim D. Adams, *British Interests and Activities in Texas* (Baltimore, 1910).
Alejandro Alvarez, *The Monroe Doctrine* (New York, 1924).
American Academy of Political and Social Science, *The Annals,* July, 1940.
Luis Araquistaín, *La agonía antillana* (Madrid, 1928).
Thomas A. Bailey, *A Diplomatic History of the American People* (New York, 1940).

Camilo Barcía Trelles, *Doctrina de Monroë y cooperación internacional* (Madrid, 1931).

Carlton Beals, *The Coming Struggle for Latin America* (Philadelphia, 1938).

Samuel Flagg Bemis, *The Latin-American Policy of the United States* (New York, 1943).

Pelham H. Box, *Origins of the Paraguayan War* (Urbana, Ill., 1927).

John F. Cady, *Foreign Intervention in the Río de la Plata, 1838–1850* (Philadelphia, 1929).

James M. Callahan, *American Foreign Policy in Mexican Relations* (New York, 1932).

Raúl Cárdenas y Echarte, *La política de los Estados Unidos en el continente americano* (Havana, 1921).

J. Reuben Clark, *Memorandum on the Monroe Doctrine* (Washington, 1930).

Isaac J. Cox, *The United States and Nicaragua* (Boston, 1927).

Council on Foreign Relations, *Survey of American Foreign Relations* (4 vols., New York, 1928–1931).

The United States in World Affairs (New York, 1932–   , annual).

Daniel Dawson, *The Mexican Adventure* [*French Intervention*] (London, 1935).

W. J. Dennis, *Tacna and Arica* (New Haven, 1931).

Harold N. Denny, *Dollars for Bullets: The Story of American Rule in Nicaragua* (New York, 1929).

Miles P. DuVal, Jr., *Cadiz to Cathay: The Story of the Long Struggle for a Waterway Across the American Isthmus* (Stanford Univ., Calif., 1940).

Henry Clay Evans, *Chile and Its Relations with the United States* (Durham, N. C., 1927).

Orestes Ferrera, *The Last Spanish War* [*Diplomacy of the war of 1898*] (New York, 1937).

Russell H. Fitzgibbon, *Cuba and the United States* (Menasha, Wis., 1935).

Charles C. Griffin, *The United States and the Disruption of the Spanish Empire* (New York, 1937).

Charles W. Hackett, *The United States and the Mexican Revolution* (Boston, 1927).

Clarence H. Haring, *South America Looks at the United States* (New York, 1928).

Howard C. Hill, *Roosevelt and the Caribbean* (Chicago, 1927).

Lawrence F. Hill, *The United States and Brazil* (Durham, N. C., 1932).

Roscoe R. Hill, *Fiscal Intervention in Nicaragua* (New York, 1933).

Samuel G. Inman, *Problems in Pan-Americanism* (New York, 1920).

Gordon Ireland, *Boundaries, Possessions, and Conflicts in South America* (Cambridge, Mass., 1938).

Leland H. Jenks, *Our Cuban Colony* (New York, 1928).

Chester Lloyd Jones, *The Caribbean since 1900* (New York, 1936).

W. H. Kelchner, *Latin American Relations with the League of Nations* (Boston, 1930).

Charles D. Kepner and Jay H. Soothill, *The Banana Empire* (New York, 1936).

Melvin M. Knight, *Americans in Santo Domingo* (New York, 1928).

John H. Latané, *The United States and Latin America* (Garden City, 1920).

James B. Lockey, *Pan-Americanism: Its Beginnings* (New York, 1920).

William D. McCain, *The United States and the Republic of Panama* (Durham, N. C., 1937).

Alan K. Manchester, *British Preëminence in Brazil* (Chapel Hill, 1933).

William R. Manning, *Diplomatic Correspondence of the United States Concerning the Independence of the Latin-American Nations* (3 vols., New York, 1925).

Diplomatic Correspondence of the United States: Inter-American Affairs, 1831–1860 (12 vols., Washington, 1932–1939).

Margaret A. Marsh, *The Bankers and Bolivia* (New York, 1928).

Percy A. Martin, *Latin America and the World War* (Baltimore, 1925).

Arthur C. Millspaugh, *Haiti under American Control* (Boston, 1931).

Dwight C. Miner, *The Fight for the Panama Route* (New York, 1940).

Ludwell Lee Montague, *Haiti and the United States* (Durham, N. C., 1940).

Dana G. Munro, *The United States and the Caribbean Area* (Boston, 1934).

Scott Nearing and Joseph Freeman, *Dollar Diplomacy* (New York, 1928).

J. F. Normano, *The Struggle for South America* (New York, 1931).

Paul R. Olson and C. A. Hickman, *Pan American Economics* (New York, 1943).

E. Taylor Parks, *Colombia and the United States* (Durham, N. C., 1934).

Dexter Perkins, *Hands Off: The Monroe Doctrine . . .* (Boston, 1941).

J. Fred Rippy, *America and the Strife of Europe* (Chicago, 1938).

The Capitalists and Colombia (New York, 1931).

The Caribbean Danger Zone (New York, 1940).

Latin America and the Industrial Age (New York, 1944).

Latin America in World Politics (New York, 1938).

Rivalry of the United States and Great Britain over Latin America (Baltimore, 1929).

South America and Hemisphere Defense (Baton Rouge, 1941).

The United States and Mexico (New York, 1931).

William Spence Robertson, *France and Latin-American Independence* (Baltimore, 1939).

Hispanic American Relations of the United States (New York, 1923).

James B. Scott, *The International Conferences of the American States, 1889–1928* (New York, 1931).

William O. Scroggs, *Filibusters and Financiers* (New York, 1916).

Justin H. Smith, *The Annexation of Texas* (New York, 1919).

The War with Mexico (2 vols., New York, 1919).

Graham H. Stuart, *Latin America and the United States* (New York, 1938).

Charles C. Tansill, *The United States and Santo Domingo* (Baltimore, 1938).

Harold V. Temperley, *The Foreign Policy of [George] Canning* (London, 1925).

Manuel Ugarte, *The Destiny of a Continent* (Rippy, ed., New York, 1925).

C. K. Webster, *Britain and the Independence of Latin America* (2 vols., New York, 1938).

Sumner Welles, *Naboth's Vineyard: The Dominican Republic* (2 vols., New York, 1928).

Arthur P. Whitaker, *The Mississippi Question, 1795–1803* (Boston and New York, 1934).

The Spanish-American Frontier, 1783–1795 (Boston and New York, 1929).

John T. Whitaker, *Americans to the South* [*Fascist Penetration*] (New York, 1939).

Mary W. Williams, *Anglo-American Isthmian Diplomacy* (Washington, 1916).

Max Winkler, *Investments of United States Capital in Latin America* (Boston, 1929).

X. LITERATURE

Florence Botsford, *Songs of the Americas* (New York, 1940).

Alfred Coester, *The Literary History of Spanish America* (New York, 1916).

Rex Crawford, *A Century of Latin-American Thought* (Cambridge, 1944).

Isaac Goldberg, *Studies in Spanish-American Literature* (New York, 1920).
Brazilian Literature (New York, 1922).

E. Herman Hespelt and others, *An Outline History of Spanish American Literature,* 2nd ed. (New York, 1942).

Arturo Torres-Ríoseco, *The Epic of Latin-American Literature* (New York, 1942).

INDEX

A B C States, rise of, 239ff.
Aberdeen, Lord, 390–391, **392, 393.**
Aborigines. *See* Indians **and individual** tribes.
Abranches, Dunshee de, cited, **435.**
Acción Comunal, 315.
Acosta García, Julio, 302.
Adams, Henry, quoted, 354.
Adams, John Quincy, 362–363, 367–368, 384, 457.
Adams, Samuel, 345.
Adelantado, in Spain, 40; in Canary Islands, 40; in Spanish colonies, 57, 58.
Agents, British, 375, 390, 392, 394, 397, 399, 451; Texan, 391; American, 398, 399; Mexican, 403.
"Age of the Dictators." *See* dictators.
Agreements: boundary, between Bolivia and Chile and Brazil, 201; between Bolivia and Chile, 483–484; between Chile and Peru, 486.
Agriculture, in Spanish America, in 17th century, 77; in 18th century, 95; in Brazil, 126, 261, 280, 318; in Chile, 247, 310; in Argentina, 253–254, 318; in Uruguay, 284; in Paraguay, 290; in Bolivia, 292; in Mexico, 296, 299; in El Salvador, 301; in Honduras, 304; in Dominican Republic, 320.
Aguilar, Nicolás, 149.
Aguirre, Anastasio, 482.
Aguirre, Lope de, 56.
Agustín I, Emperor of Mexico. *See* Iturbide.
Akers, C. E., quoted, 190, 482–483.
Alamán, Lucas, 375–376, 382.
Albano, Carrasco, 492.
Alberdi, Juan B., quoted, 236.
Alcabala, 69.
Alcaldes mayores, 61, 89, 96, **97.**
Alcaldes ordinarios, 61.
Alcedo, Antonio de, 113.
Alcedo, Dionisio de, 113.
Alcorta, Figuero, 255–256, 255n.
Alegre, Francisco J., 113.
Alem, Leandro, 254, 255.
Alencar, José de, 271.

Alessandri, Arturo, 277–278, 289, 335.
Alfaro, Eloy, 205, 208–209.
Alferez, 61.
Alfonso XIII, king of Spain, 475.
Algeçiras, Treaty of, 469.
Aliens, rights of, 501, 503.
Alliança Liberal, 333.
Alliance, of Peru and Bolivia against Chile, 203, 484; for Latin-American independence considered, 348–349; of Spain and England, 348–349, 354; Neo-Holy, 134, 360, 362, 363, 491; Triple, 439, 460; Anglo-German, 446.
Al Paraná, 113.
Altamira y Crevea, Rafael, 467, 468, **474.**
Alvarado, Pedro de, 52, 53.
Álvarez, Juan, 231.
Alvear, Marcelo T., 279–280.
Amador Guerrero, Manuel, 224.
Amazon River, described, 15–16; use in transportation, 79, 331; explored, 122; missions on, 123.
Ambitions, of United States, 371, 376, 379, 380–381, 394, 500; of Great Britain, 379; of Germany, 457, 541–543.
Ameghino, Florentino, 19.
Americanist Post-War Program, 467.
"Americanists," 465.
American Review of Reviews, 410.
Amézaga, Juan J., 337.
Amunátegui, Miguel L., 269.
Ancón, Treaty of, 486, 526–527.
Andagoya, Pascual de, 49, 65.
Andes, 14–15.
Andrada, José Bonifacio and Martínez Francisco, 161.
Andrade, Victor, 269.
Anglophobia, 462.
Angostura, Congress of, 157.
Antequera, insurgent, 136.
Approaches to America by sea, 18.
Aranda, Count, 138.
Aranha, José P. da Graça, 271.
Araucanians, habitat and culture of, 29; organization and military tactics of, 29; conquest of, 54; work of missionaries

562 INDEX

Guiana, 266; and Dutch Guiana, 266; and Venezuela, 266; Bolivia and Chile, 278, 288, 292; Bolivia and Paraguay, 292–293; Great Britain and Venezuela, 409–415; and United States over Alaska, 416; remaining unsettled in 1930, 487–488, 487n.

Bourbons, Spanish America under the rule of, 94–115; administrative reforms of, 94–101; to be set up in Mexico and Peru, 360.

Bowen, Herbert W., 451.

Boyacá, battle of, 156, 475.

Boyer, Jean, 214.

Brabo, Francisco Javier, cited, 100.

Braz, Wenceslau, 267, 280–281.

Brazil, topography of, 13–14; Indians in, 29–30; discovery and exploration of, 72–73; division of, into captaincies, 73; policy of John III toward, 73–74; settlement of, 73–74; foundation of towns in, 74; French in, 74, 117, 118, 119, 124; Jesuits in, 74, 122, 123; population of and industries in, during 16th century, 74; colonial policy and administration of Portugal, 74–76, 118–120; English in, 116, 119; Dutch in, 117, 119; commerce of, 118–120, 261, 262, 267, 273, 280; taxation of, by Portugal, 119–120; industries of, 120; mining and products of, 120; expansion of, 120–124; boundary agreements regarding, 123–124; political organization of, 124–125; political development of, 125–126; reforms of Pombal in, 125–126; population of, 1776–1823, 127; social classes in, 127–130; colonial culture of, 130–132; church in, 130–131; education in, 130–131; literature of, 131–132; awakening of, 131–132; revolution and independence of, 160–162, 352–353; recognition of, 162; annexes Uruguay, 189; effect of climate on development of, 239–240; Indian elements in, 240; emigration to, 240–241; population of, 241; investments of Europeans and Americans in, 241–242; leadership among peoples of, 242; area of, 257n.; explanation of stability of, 257; political issues in, 257; under rule of Dom Pedro I, 257–260; first constitution of, 258; dissension in, 258–259; war of, with Argentina, 259, 480; Regency for Dom Pedro II, 260–261; progress of, during Regency, 261; under Dom Pedro II, 261–263; era of progress in, 262–263; establishment of republic in, 263; constitution of 1891 in, 264; under Fonseca and Peixoto, 265; under Moraes Barros, Campos Salles,

and Alves, 265–266; under Penna, Peçanha, and Hermes da Fonseca, 266–267; progress of, under republic, 267–268; the arts in, 268; historical writing in, 268; literature in, 268; intellectual life in, 270–271; revolutions in, 1913–1929, 275–276; and prosperity under Braz, 280–281; uprisings in, 1922–1924, 281; under Bernardes, 281–282; under Silva, 282; racial groups in, 314; and depression of 1929, 318–319; political situation in, 1932, 327; revolution of 1930 in, 331–333; reforms in, 333; and the Monroe Doctrine, 384; and World War I, 459, 519, 520; and the Paraguayan War, 482–483; minor wars of, 486; and Pan-American treaties, 513; and the League of Nations, 517, 520–521, 522, 523, 525, 526, 528.

Brazilian Highlands, 13–14.

Briand, M., 527.

Brissot, M., quoted, 349.

Brum, Baltasar, 284.

Bryce, James, quoted, 169–170, 175.

Bucareli, Viceroy of Mexico, 101.

Buchanan, James, 403, 405, 406.

Buchanan, W. I., 504.

Buell, R. L., quoted, 303.

Buenos Aires, made capital, 253; University of, 473.

Bulls, Papal, of 1493, 37, 338; of 1506, 338.

Bulnes, Francisco, 471–472.

Bulnes, Manuel, 244, 480.

Bülow, Bernhard von, 438, 439, 440–441, 446, 448, 453, 457.

Bulwer. See Clayton Bulwer Treaty.

Bureau of American Republics, Commercial, 498–499, 500, 501. See Pan-American Union.

Bureau of Latin-American affairs, 523.

Caballero y Góngora, Antonio, 101.

Cabildos, in Spanish America, 61, 168; in Caracas, 145; in New Granada, 147; in Montevideo, 189.

Cabral, Pedrálvarez, 37.

Cabrillo, Juan R., 49.

Caixa de conversão, 267.

Caldas, Francisco José de, 112.

Calhoun, John C., 363.

California, Indian Culture Area, 23–24; missionary activity in, 104; presidios in, 105; and expansion of United States, 392; immigrants to, 399.

Calleja, Félix, 151.

Calles, Plutarco Elias, 299.